North American Arc

BLACKWELL STUDIES IN GLOBAL ARCHAEOLOGY

Series Editors: Lynn Meskell and Rosemary A. Joyce

Blackwell Studies in Global Archaeology is a series of contemporary texts, each carefully designed to meet the needs of archaeology instructors and students seeking volumes that treat key regional and thematic areas of archaeological study. Each volume in the series, compiled by its own editor, includes 12–15 newly commissioned articles by top scholars within the volume's thematic, regional, or temporal area of focus.

What sets the *Blackwell Studies in Global Archaeology* apart from other available texts is that their approach is accessible, yet does not sacrifice theoretical sophistication. The series editors are committed to the idea that usable teaching texts need not lack ambition. To the contrary, the *Blackwell Studies in Global Archaeology* aim to immerse readers in fundamental archaeological ideas and concepts, but also to illuminate more advanced concepts, thereby exposing readers to some of the most exciting contemporary developments in the field. Inasmuch, these volumes are designed not only as classic texts, but as guides to the vital and exciting nature of archaeology as a discipline.

North American Archaeology

Edited by

Timothy R. Pauketat and
Diana DiPaolo Loren

Blackwell
Publishing

BLACKWELL PUBLISHING
350 Main Street, Malden, MA 02148-5020, USA
108 Cowley Road, Oxford OX4 1JF, UK
550 Swanston Street, Carlton, Victoria 3053, Australia

First published 2005 by Blackwell Publishing Ltd

Library of Congress Cataloging-in-Publication Data

North American archaeology / edited by Timothy R. Pauketat and Diana DiPaolo Loren.
      p. cm. — (Blackwell studies in global archaeology)
   Includes bibliographical references and index
   ISBN 0-631-23183-8 (hardback : alk. paper) — ISBN 0-631-23184-6 (pbk. : alk. paper)
1. United States—Antiquities.   2. North America—Antiquities.   3. Indians of North America—
Antiquities.   4. Excavations (Archaeology)—United States.   5. Excavations (Archaeology)—North
American.   6. Social archaeology—United States.   7. Archaeology—United States.   I. Pauketat,
Timothy R.   II. Loren, Diana DiPaolo.   III. Series.

E159.5.N67 2005
970.01—dc22

                                                                                    2004008957

A catalogue record for this title is available from the British Library.

ISBN 13: 978-0-631-23183-8
ISBN 13: 978-0-631-23184-6

For further information on
Blackwell Publishing, visit our website:
http://www.blackwellpublishing.com

Contents

 # Series Editors' Preface

This series was conceived as a collection of books designed to cover central areas of undergraduate archaeological teaching. Each volume in the series, edited by experts in the area, includes newly commissioned articles written by archaeologists actively engaged in research. By commissioning new articles, the series combines one of the best features of readers, the presentation of multiple approaches to archaeology, with the virtues of a text conceived from the beginning as intended for a specific audience. While the model reader for the series is conceived of as an upper-division undergraduate, the inclusion in the volumes of researchers actively engaged in work today will also make these volumes valuable for more advanced researchers who want a rapid introduction to contemporary issues in specific sub-fields of global archaeology.

Each volume in the series will include an extensive introduction by the volume editor that will set the scene in terms of thematic or geographic focus. Individual volumes, and the series as a whole, exemplify a wide range of approaches in contemporary archaeology. The volumes uniformly engage with issues of contemporary interest, interweaving social, political, and ethical themes. We contend that it is no longer tenable to teach the archaeology of vast swaths of the globe without acknowledging the political implications of working in foreign countries and the responsibilities archaeologists incur by writing and presenting other people's pasts. The volumes in this series will not sacrifice theoretical sophistication for accessibility. We are committed to the idea that usable teaching texts need not lack ambition.

Blackwell Studies in Global Archaeology aims to immerse readers in fundamental archaeological ideas and concepts, but also to illuminate more advanced concepts, exposing readers to some of the most exciting contemporary developments in the field.

Lynn Meskell and Rosemary A. Joyce

# Preface

This book is intended for all students of North American archaeology, for college-level courses that cover the continent, and for people interested in the latest thinking about specific places or time periods. The subject, of course, seems almost unmanageably broad. Today, North American archaeologists include the range of theoretical schools of thought and focus on problems as wide-ranging as the long-term development of hunter-gatherers to the short-term dynamics of religious cults, political change, and cultural clashes. North American archaeologists, including the authors in this volume, are employed by federal and state governments, museums, universities, and private firms. Despite this diversity, all of them study the past, although that past is not always long past, and their purposes in studying that past include desires to understand the present and its varied peoples. That understanding is conveyed in many ways: in classrooms, in museum exhibits, via internet sites, and through the policies of our representatives. What comes through is that there are a vast number of stories about the North American past, some of which are found in popular histories while others are "hidden" histories; alternative stories about the way North Americans have lived their lives.

Given the diversity of archaeologists in North America and the diverse pasts that they investigate, it is no surprise that the chapters in this book were not all woven out of the same theoretical cloth. Two or three contributors favor an "evolutionary" perspective, more common in some regions than in others. These and a couple others celebrate the rich "cultural-historical" approach that characterized most of 20th-century practice. That approach has itself morphed into a newer perspective that pervades this volume and emphasizes theories of practice, landscape, and the human body. Rather than being at cross-purposes, the diverse approaches presented in this volume are intended to give the audience a taste of what North American archaeology has to offer and the directions in which it is currently headed. Each author is a leading figure in her or his respective area, and their take on the problems broached will give the reader fresh new insights into the past, both in North America and beyond.

We do not intend this book to replace all other texts that have sought to synthesize the continent's archaeology. Instead, we believe that our book complements existing works by rethinking what we know in terms of *how* we have come to know it and how we then disseminate that information to students, archaeologists, and the general public. The book does have an agenda: no less than redefining the archaeology of a continent. By including chapters that focus on particular historical moments, cultural practices, or human agents and placing them alongside other essays that summarize the macro-scale patterns of whole regions over hundreds of years, we believe that it will allow the reader to consider anew the relationships between persons, places, and things both past and present in terms of current if untested theories. If there is one story that we want the reader to take home, it is that there are an infinite number of stories that can be told about the past. Some are fantastic, some are imagined, some are put forth by particular political agendas and not everyone agrees on one story. That is, we write about the past in the present, in which we are influenced by present-day worldviews and biases. Our stories about the history of North America change through time as we are presented with new data (archaeological, historical, oral-historical, etc.). These revisions of the past will continue long into the future, as will debates regarding the accuracy or reliability of those past representations.

The book is arranged in chronological and geographical order, and the reader will note that we have not restricted the chapters to either "prehistoric" or "historical" archaeology. In part this is because of our different backgrounds. One of us is a museum archaeologist with a focus in the so-called historic period. The other is an academic archaeologist with research interests in the pre-Columbian past. So, we have been inclusive in our attempt to help bridge the gap between those who study ancient America and those who deal with colonial and post-colonial America. The archaeology of North America, we have decided, is increasingly about studying all people in all times for what they can help us understand about world history and about ourselves.

This is a tall order, but to their credit all of the contributors to this book took it to heart. We lost a couple people along the way, and were not able to cover the entire continent or all of its interesting problems. Then again, at 9 million square miles, total coverage is probably beyond the scope of such a volume. Moreover, this book is intended less as a primer for all of North American archaeology, and more as a series of engaging and thought-provoking explorations of its most interesting and potentially idea-altering parts. We have written this book with the non-specialist reader in mind. As editors, we provided each author with a sense of our mission to bridge history and archaeology, and we provide for you, the reader, the common links between all in the glossary and in our introduction. We are most grateful to the individual authors for tolerating great demands on their time.

We also appreciate the good work of the people at Blackwell Press – Jane Huber especially, who has patiently guided us through this project. Emily Martin, Sarah Coleman, Annie Lenth, and Nathan Brown at Blackwell also proved invaluable aids in wrestling with issues of book format. We would also like to acknowledge Rosemary Joyce and Lynn Meskell for their support of this project. Finally, we owe much to our spouses for tolerating the inordinate amount of time and energy that went into the editing of this book. Lewis provided Diana with an unending and infinitely creative supply of advice, support, and humor throughout the process. Susan balanced Tim's otherwise off-balance days. Thank you!

We dedicate this book to the next generation of North American archaeologists; we expect you to rewrite these pages in the future.

Diana DiPaolo Loren
Timothy R. Pauketat

List of Figures

Notes on Contributors

J. M. Adovasio is Professor of Anthropology and Geology and Executive Director of Mercyhurst Archaeological Institute at Mercyhurst College. A leading scholar in Paleoindian life and material culture analysis, he has carried out fieldwork in North America, western Europe, and the former Soviet Union.

Kenneth M. Ames is Professor of Anthropology at Portland State University. His fieldwork throughout northwestern and western North America contributes to the study of hunters-gatherers and social archaeology.

Elizabeth Chilton is Associate Professor of Anthropology at the University of Massachusetts, Amherst. She has conducted fieldwork throughout northeastern North America. Her research contributes to the study of agriculture, ceramic technology, Native history, and gender.

William S. Dancey is Associate Professor of Anthropology at Ohio State University. His research on the Woodland Period of central Ohio contributes to the study of culture change, issues of scale, and settlement analysis.

Michelle Hegmon is Professor of Anthropology at Arizona State University. Her research is based in the US Southwest and is fundamental to understanding the archaeology of the social realm and archaeological approaches to gender.

Dale R. Henning is Adjunct Research Associate at the Illinois State Museum, Research Associate at the New Mexico Museum of Indian Art and Culture/Laboratory of Anthropology, and Research Associate in the Department of Anthropology at the National Museum of Natural History, Smithsonian Institution. He is recognized as a leading scholar of Oneota culture.

Stephen H. Lekson is Associate Professor at the University of Colorado. His research on the American Southwest, particularly Chaco and Mesa Verde, contributes to study of government, regional patterning, and architecture.

Diana DiPaolo Loren is an Associate Curator at the Peabody Museum of Archaeology and Ethnology, Harvard University. Her research on French and Spanish colonial sites contributes to the study of issues of creolization, race, identity, and the body.

Timothy R. Pauketat is Associate Professor of Anthropology at the University of Illinois. He has conducted research in the American Bottom, particularly Cahokia, and pioneered research in the archaeology of traditions, agency, and political economy. His recent books include *Ancient Cahokia and the Mississippians* (Cambridge University Press, 2004) and *The Archaeology of Traditions* (University Press of Florida, 2001).

David Pedler is editor and graphics specialist at Mercyhurst Archaeological Institute, Mercyhurst College. His research in eastern North America contributes to the study of Paleoindian origins and life.

Dean J. Saitta is Associate Professor of Anthropology at the University of Denver. His fieldwork and research on the American West contributes to the study of labor history, memory, and monumentality.

Kenneth E. Sassaman is Associate Professor of Anthropology at the University of Florida. He has conducted research throughout southeastern North America and his work contributes to the study of agency, practice, and ceramic production during the Archaic period.

Stephen W. Silliman is Assistant Professor of Anthropology at the University of Massachusetts, Boston. He has conducted fieldwork in California and New England, and his research contributes to the study of Native American responses to post-Columbian colonialism.

Theresa A. Singleton is Associate Professor of Anthropology at Syracuse University. She has conducted research in the southern United States and pioneered the archaeological study of African Americans.

Joe Watkins is Associate Professor of Anthropology at University of New Mexico. His work contributes towards developing a more socially appropriate archaeology in relation to indigenous populations and communities throughout the world, and he is known as a leading scholar in the ethics and the practice of anthropology.

1
Alternative Histories and North American Archaeology

Timothy R. Pauketat and
Diana DiPaolo Loren

> North America is one immense outdoor museum, telling a story that covers 9 million
> square miles and 25,000 years (Thomas 2000a:viii)

The chapters in this volume highlight the story of a continent, from the Atlantic to Alaska, from the San Luis mission to Sonora, and from the Kennewick man of nine millennia ago to the Colorado coalfield strikes of nine decades ago (Figure 1.1). Given the considerable span of time and vastness of space, the reader might already be wondering: what holds North American archaeology together? Unlike other portions of the world, it is not the study of the sequential rise and fall of ancient states and empires that unified peoples into *a people* with a single writing system, calendar, or economy. No, North America is, and was, all about *alternative histories*. It is about peoples in the plural.

Peoples did things differently in North America. They made their own histories, sometimes forgotten, subverted, and controversial but never outside the purview of archaeology. Yet, in their plurality, the North Americans of the past show us the commonalities of the human experience. The inimitable ways in which people made history in North America hold profound lessons for understanding the sweep of global history, if not also for comprehending the globalizing world in which we find ourselves today. That is, like all good yarns, there is a moral to this archaeological allegory: what people did do or could do matters significantly in the construction of the collective futures of all people.

In this introduction, we explore the increasingly historical tenor of the archaeology of ancient and not-so-ancient North Americans. We explicate some of the ways that we have come to know the past and recognize some of the biases that were passed off, for a time, as enlightened science. Along the way, we advocate some new ways of knowing the past that bridge science and humanism, dramatized by contrasting long-term developmental trends with key moments of cultural change. The new ways of knowing to which we refer will be unfamiliar to some readers, but are increasingly popular additions to the dig kits of North America's archaeologists.

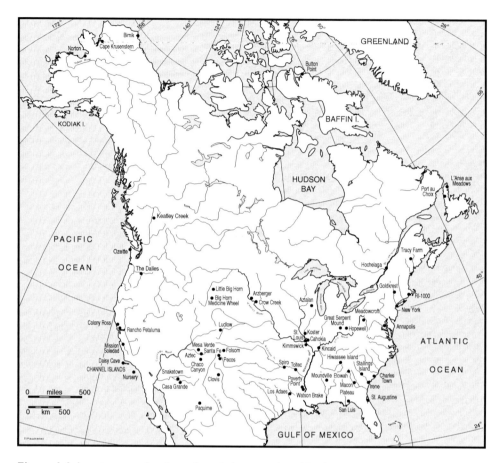

Figure 1.1 Locator map showing selected sites mentioned in the text

North American Cultures-in-the-Making

To some extent, North American archaeologists continue to discover the past just as each encounter between peoples in the past was a discovery of the unknown. In North America, these discoveries marked time, established landmarks, and defined peoples – Columbus and the "Indians," the Vikings and the "Skraelings" (aka Inuit), Cahokians and the Mississippians, the Initial Coalescent peoples and their enemies – all the way back to Clovis, Kennewick, and the first Americans.

Back then, in the Ice Age, North America was a radically different continent, with wandering elephants, herds of giant bison on the Plains, and caribou along the northern ice sheets. Much of the continent, particularly the interior lowlands and coastal plains of the eastern half, was open to the movements of migratory animals and, late in the Pleistocene era, the first Americans. The major physiographic obstacles were the western mountain chains, deserts, the wide Mississippi River, the Great Lakes, and the Appalachians along the eastern seaboard

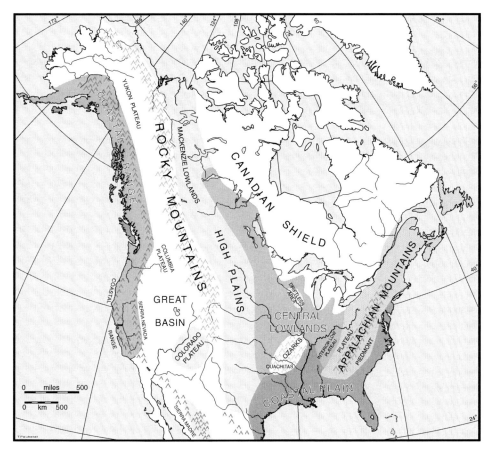

Figure 1.2 Major North American physiographic provinces

(Figure 1.2). Among the best-known European explorers and later Euroamericans are those associated with particular events or places where they passed, or failed to pass, one of these obstacles.

Indeed, as the European and Euroamerican examples attest, legends, sagas, and songs place (literally) persons and historical moments in cultural landscapes that, in turn, define the experiences of peoples. Consider that "Vinland Sagas" record the discovery of what were probably Labrador and Newfoundland around the year A.D. 1000 by the Norseman Eirik the Red and his sons, Leif and Thorvald. Or that the day on which Christopher Columbus set foot on San Salvador on October 12, 1492 is memorialized annually in the United States, a celebration for some and a bone of contention for others. Public parks mark spots where a supposed Viking runestone was found in Oklahoma or where Civil War battles occurred in Virginia.

All such memorials temporalize and spatialize cultural experiences, shaping one's sense of time, space, heritage, and self, and our experiences today take place in these rich landscapes. It was no different in the past. Today, as in the past, cultures are, in effect, peoples' lived experiences and interpretations of the world. They are always being made and remade, told and retold, sung and resung by people through their ongoing encounters with each other and with the sensuous dimensions of social history. They are not, and have never been, timeless, unchanging, bounded things. Cultures are always cultures-in-the-making.

Indigenous populations

It could be ventured that culture-making may be more easily measured in pre-Columbian and colonial North America owing to its modest population densities. North America had nowhere near the population densities of, say, ancient China or Andean South America. Conservative estimates of American Indian populations north of Mexico at the beginning of the 16th century fall around 1 million people, while maximal estimates exceed 10 million (compare Dobyns 1983; Henige 1998; Kroeber 1953). The truth probably lies somewhere in between.

By comparison, the central Mexican Aztec Empire prior to the devastating diseases of the 16th century included at least 6 million people (Brumfiel 2004:241). The most densely populated city in prehispanic Mesoamerica, the Aztec capital (with 200,000 people), sat in the middle of the Basin of Mexico's 1 million or more people (Nichols 2004:271)!

There were concentrations of population in North America, although at a lower order of magnitude than in Mesoamerica. Higher-density populations were situated around the rich salmon fisheries of the Northwest Coast and in the many small territories and language isolates of California (Kroeber 1953). Major southwestern towns had populations of several hundred to 2,000 people each (see Hegmon, this volume; Lekson 1999a; Rice 1998). During the Pueblo II period, up to 2,700 people may have resided permanently in the central cluster of Great Houses at Chaco Canyon (Lekson's "cityscape," this volume). Thousands more would have poured into the canyon to attend the great political-religious festivals there, raising population levels considerably if temporarily.

In eastern North America, densities were higher on average, although individual settlements rarely exceeded 2,000 people. For instance, Jacques Cartier met 1,000 people at the large Iroquoian village of Hochelaga on the St. Lawrence River in 1535 (Pendergast 1998) and other Mohawk and Huron villages in the early 17th century averaged 600–1,700 people (Chilton, this volume; Muller 1997:table 5.6). Likewise, some 1,000 or more people lived at one of the largest Mississippian towns in Alabama (Steponaitis 1998), while an uncounted number of Plains villages, Illinois-valley towns, and St. Francis-type central Mississippian centers had populations of hundreds to perhaps 2,000 people each (e.g., Conrad 1991; Phillips et al. 1951). Large multi-ethnic historic-era towns in the Southeast also had several hundred to 2,000 or so people through the 18th century (Muller 1997:197–198).

Population densities were higher in the greater Cahokia region at about A.D. 1100. This region was probably home to roughly 50,000 people, of whom up to

15,000 resided at the capital of Cahokia itself, disposed in such a way as to meet a generic definition of "city." Whatever it is called, Cahokia was North America's largest settlement until colonial Philadelphia grew larger shortly after A.D. 1800.

Over the millennia, North America's indigenous population did grow through a combination of factors. However, to an important degree, the population concentrations noted above were the results of regional immigrations and multi-ethnic regroupings owing to historical circumstances (e.g., Pauketat 2003). Great social and political happenings in North America seem to have pulled people into them, possibly adding an element of cultural hybridity or pluralism to many population centers or village concentrations. These places may not have been characterized by homogenous cultural "norms" or rules that everyone understood alike. And if North American places pulled populations into them, then perhaps the "culture areas" associated with these historical developments were not stable if even real.

American Indian culture areas

But the early students of the American Indian, in particular Clark Wissler (1926) and Alfred Kroeber (1953), formalized the association of people and environment as "culture areas" to such an extent that it is unavoidable today. They correlated native art styles, languages, and cultural practices with North American deserts, woodlands, plains, and mountains and envisioned at least nine major culture areas (Figure 1.3). Clearly, these divisions encapsulate a certain amount of the trans-continental cultural variation. And there is some validity to analyzing that variability in terms of cultural traditions (see Pauketat 2001). That is, a Kwakiutl design made along the Northwest Coast is easily distinguished from Puebloan decorations owing to the histories of people and the genealogies of their cultural practices in each place.

However, at other scales of analysis, culture areas have fuzzy, indistinct boundaries because traditions are not static things and because analysts decide where lines are drawn depending on whatever traits they feel are significant (Ford 1954). Many contiguous cultures and languages were not necessarily so different. The sharpest boundaries resulted from historical disruptions that separated populations, a process exacerbated by natural obstacles (as in California and the Great Basin) and minimized by unobstructed open land (as in the mid-continent). A map of American Indian languages at around A.D. 1600 betrays millennia-deep histories of interaction and disruption: long-distance trade, political consolidations, pan-regional religious movements, migrations, wars, etc. (Figure 1.4).

Interestingly, culture areas have seldom if ever been used to pigeonhole immigrants or slaves from the Old World, presumably owing to their relatively recent relocation to the New World and the ethnic mixing associated with their new melting-pot homeland. Apparently, Old World diasporas in the New World did not have sufficient time to adapt to their new environments. The processes to which these historic-era people were subjected, then, are commonly assumed to have been unlike those of the "prehistoric" Indians. But was this really the case? No.

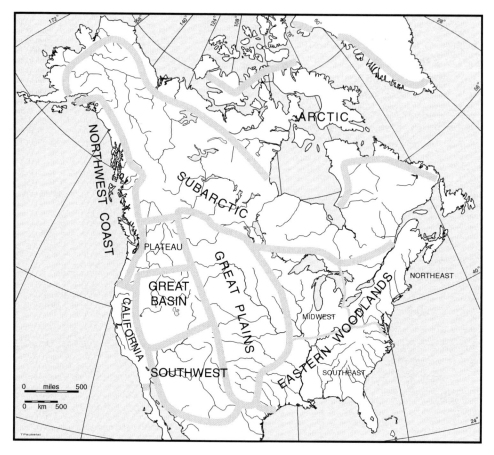

Figure 1.3 Native North American culture areas

Reconceptualizing History and Culture-Making

Conceptualizing American Indians as different from Western people originates in a well-known 18th-century Enlightenment view of American Indians and in the 19th-century "Moundbuilder Myth." In the former case, Indian peoples were seen as uncivilized "noble savages," closer to nature and less morally corrupt than Europeans (Trigger 1989). In the latter case, Indians were thought to be uncivilized and hence incapable of the coordinated labor evident in the ancient earthen mounds that Euroamericans found in the eastern United States. Someone else, a race of lost Moundbuilders, must have built the mounds (see below).

Archaeologists like to think that both views are dead, but they live on in the guise of politically correct stereotypes of North American Indians as more spiritual, ecological, ritual, and traditional than other peoples around the world. They also live on covertly in archaeological models that treat Indians as non-political, prehistoric people who evolved owing to natural forces outside their control.

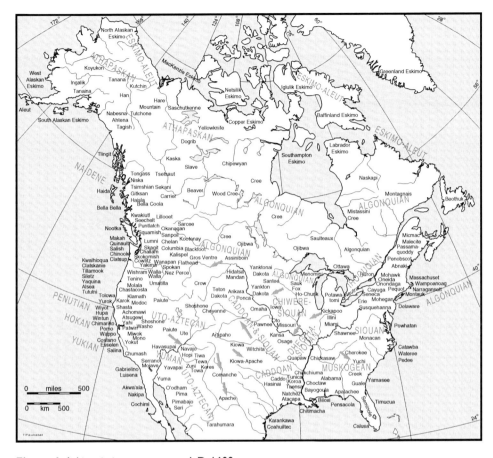

Figure 1.4 Linguistic groups at ca. A.D. 1600

Perhaps using the word "prehistory" to identify a period of time before the written word might seem innocuous enough. After all, the period of European contact in North America was one of incredible change. And of course there was no native North American writing system, strictly defined, until Sequoyah completed the Cherokee syllabary in 1821. But there are two good reasons to avoid the word "prehistory."

First, writing per se was not the great leap forward that some would have it be. Even in ancient societies where writing was invented, only a literate few people (typically, the elite) wrote down supposed facts about the illiterate masses. The problem is, the literati saw things as elitists do, and their histories present only one version of the past – an "official history" – defined and prescribed by peoples who wanted a lasting legacy (Trouillot 1995). At best, official histories only give us part of the story (e.g., Saitta, this volume). At worst, official histories are lies (histories are, after all, written by the victors), a means of controlling the construction of social memories.

Second, the idea of prehistory suggests that American Indians were powerless subjects of the external world, rather than players in history (see Nabokov 2002). The implication is that they had no history that mattered, since their cultural traditions evolved according to the laws of nature and died during the colonial era, as Native Americans were assimilated to European ideas, religions, and material culture.

Native Americans, Americans, and Identity Politics

Now, looking back on this history, we can understand some of the impetus by Native Americans to reclaim their history, heritage, and land, in particular through the Native American Graves Protection and Repatriation Act (NAGPRA) (Watkins, this volume). In recent years, Native Americans have argued their right for a say in the interpretation of history and the ways in which ancestral human and material remains are handled (Echo-Hawk 2000). The recent events surrounding "Kennewick Man" further highlight these issues. Dating to around 7000 B.C., the Kennewick human remains share certain morphological attributes of Eurasian populations unlike contemporary Native Americans, suggesting considerable Paleoindian genetic diversity. Some present-day native tribes argue that Kennewick Man is their ancestor and should be reburied; some archaeologists argue that the scientific study of these human remains should take precedence (Thomas 2000b).

The identity politics of today have a bearing on all of North American archaeology (Echo-Hawk 2000; Schmidt and Patterson 1995). How do peoples in the present define themselves and others and how did they do so in the past? The presumed continuity of cultural traits continues to be a legal criterion for legitimizing identity, thus belying the reality that cultures are always cultures-in-the-making (see Landsman and Ciborski 1992:432; see also Stahl et al. 2004). There is no easy way around this problem, as all peoples around the world are struggling with issues of self-definition and repatriation. Perhaps for our purposes we might consider using the term "American" to get at the host of people and identities that define North America's 9 million square miles and 25,000 years of history.

Archaeological Reflections

Identity politics and alternative histories are not new issues in North American archaeology. From the beginning, some Europeans considered indigenous people to be different from themselves, incapable of rational thought (Loren 2001; Pagden 1982). By the 17th century, various Euroamericans did not believe that the remaining American Indian populations in the eastern United States had ever been capable of the coordinated labor necessary to build the impressive earthworks in the Ohio and Mississippi valleys. Others must have been responsible, they reasoned – perhaps giants, Israelites, Danes, Aztecs, or Toltecs. Perhaps, some thought, the American Indians were a savage race who had eliminated some earlier more industrious race of Moundbuilders, pushing the latter south into Mexico. Thus began the "Myth of the Moundbuilders" (Willey and Sabloff 1993:22–25).

Dis-mything the Moundbuilders

The Moundbuilder Myth was spreading as early as the late 1700s, a time of growing antagonism and unrest between Native Americans and Euroamericans. This myth seems to have reassured the Euroamerican populace that displacement or elimination of the native population was unavoidable and perhaps just, even as the federal government laid claim to Native American lands.[1]

There remained enlightened advocates of American Indian claims to the land in the late 18th and early 19th centuries. George Rogers Clark, hero of the revolutionary war in the west and Virginia neighbor of Thomas Jefferson, argued in print with Noah Webster (of Webster's Dictionary) for the Native American construction of the mounds, based on his own interviews with American Indians near present-day St. Louis (Kelly 1994:4). However, prominent antiquarians and public officials fervently believed in the idea of the Moundbuilders, reflected in the Mexican names given to sites across the continent: Aztalan, Aztec, Montezuma's Castle, Toltec.

After the Civil War ended in 1865, archaeological activities increased markedly. Harvard University's Peabody Museum, founded in 1866 and, by 1874, headed by Frederic Ward Putnam, was an early center of activity. Putnam, an influential advocate of stratigraphic excavation, effectively standardized archaeological practices continent-wide, while the Smithsonian Institution's Bureau of American Ethnology (BAE), founded in 1879, firmly established the continent's American Indian heritage. In the east, Cyrus Thomas had been appointed to resolve the Moundbuilder controversy. He and his field assistants accomplished the task via a 10-year systematic survey, locating many major sites, combined with excavations of more than 2,000 mounds (Thomas 1985[1894]). In the west, there were several BAE expeditions that also combined site survey and excavation to establish the historical linkages between ancient ruins and modern Puebloan peoples (e.g., Mindeleff 1989[1891]).

The culture-historical period

At about this same time, the Southwest began to be populated by Euroamerican ranchers. One of these, Richard Wetherill, was shown a number of sites around Mesa Verde by local Ute Indians. He was startled, and the discovery led him to take up archaeological fieldwork full-time. Wetherill employed stratigraphic techniques and European scientific standards of recording his finds. In 1896 Wetherill turned his attention to Chaco Canyon, excavating 190 rooms in Pueblo Bonito alone by the end of the fourth season and filling the shelves of the American Museum of Natural History back east.

The early part of the 20th century saw the coalescence of a "culture-historical approach" that sought to track the spread of cultures (see Trigger 1989; Willey and Sabloff 1993). There were important stratigraphic excavations everywhere. The "Direct Historical Method" was implemented (i.e., reasoning backwards in time from known Indian practices to ancient ones). "Seriation" became a popular tech-

nique for dating sites based on artifact stylistic change. And the funding of archaeological excavations by various organizations and museums increased.

In 1934 the Society for American Archaeology was founded, with its flagship
journal *American Antiquity*. This professional society, and other regional organizations, were all a part of the increasingly systematized practice of archaeology, which
also saw the refinement of cultural classification systems, the development of dendrochronology, the establishment of the University of Chicago field school (which
trained a generation of eastern archaeologists), and the beginnings of federally
funded excavations under the aegis of Franklin D. Roosevelt's various "New Deal"
programs, especially the Works Progress Administration.

The federally funded excavations, many run by professionals trained at Chicago's
field schools, dug key sites on a year-round basis using out-of-work citizens. Most
of this activity in the 1930s was focused on southeastern sites. Excavations were
extensive, exposing walls, houses, cemeteries, and mound interiors (Figure 1.5).
Importantly, for the first time, archaeology was not simply an elite, academic exercise, but a public endeavor with the full range of citizen participants. WPA crews
included both African American and Euroamerican men and women (e.g., Claasen
1999).

Of course, southwestern archaeological projects, beginning with Richard Wetherill's, had regularly employed Navajo excavators and technicians. And pioneering
female archaeologists such as Ruth Bunzel (1929) and Anna Shepard (1936) moved

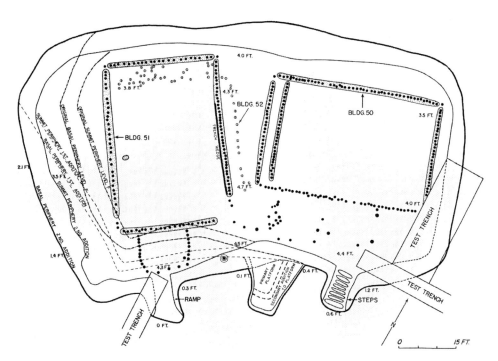

Figure 1.5 A construction stage within the dual platform mound at Hiwassee Island, Tennessee
(Lewis and Kneberg 1946:plate 15; used with permission, University of Tennessee Press)

ceramic studies away from an obsession with chronology-building and toward interpretations of design, meaning, technology, and production. The latter especially
were prescient developments, anticipating today's archaeological theorizing of
agency, the body, and material culture (see below).

To behavior and back again

Prescient also was the beginning in 1940 of what would become the premier "settlement archaeology" study by Philip Phillips, James Ford, and James Griffin
(1951). They used survey, digs, and seriation to reconstruct how whole societies
"functioned" and developed (see Trigger 1989:279–286). Such a functionalist line
of inquiry was the mantra of Walter Taylor, in a book that excoriated prominent
North Americanists in 1948 (Taylor 1983). Around this same time, others began
calling for an ecological approach that emphasized the study of human behavior
and that treated societies as organic systems that adapted to the environment
(Steward and Setzler 1938).

Ideas were changing and the practice of archaeology was also changing owing to
the social, technological, and geopolitical realities of the post-war era: the "GI Bill"
made a university education affordable for returning veterans; radiocarbon dating
revolutionized archaeology everywhere in 1949; and left-wing political overtones
and gendered interpretations were purged owing to conscious and subconscious
fears of America's McCarthyized attitudes in the 1950s (Vincent 1990:238ff).
Cold War presidents, from Truman to Eisenhower to Kennedy, feared invasion,
nuclear war, and the prospect of Russian scientific superiority (heralded in 1959
by Sputnik). And so, federal monies poured into scientific research. Eisenhower,
readying the national transportation system for the potential of nuclear war or
Russian invasion, put into motion the construction of a federal interstate highway
system.

The effect was an overhaul of archaeological theory and practice. Increasingly,
the idea of culture was sidelined, or redefined, as "behavior" emerged in scientific
discourse. In 1959 Joseph Caldwell called for a "New American Archaeology" and,
with his contemporaries, began to construct the new systematics building of settlement archaeology (e.g., "interaction spheres," see Ames, Dancey, this volume).
This incipient development was coopted by Lewis Binford (1962), linked with neoevolutionism, and converted into the "New Archaeology" (aka processual archaeology) of the 1960s and 1970s, a cult-like movement with Binford as its charismatic
spokesperson (see Trigger 1989).

Binford's early students at the University of Chicago spread the new religion
across North America in landmark – if highly criticized – case studies that sought
to demonstrate that "residence patterns" could be determined from statistical analyses of broken village pottery (Binford 1972). Another student, Stuart Struever,
investigated the ecology of Middle Woodland food producers in the Illinois River
valley, converting his research interests into a long-term academic and public
research program. For a time, his deeply stratified Koster-site dig was the most

famous archaeological excavation in the world and, in the person of Stuart Struever, the New Archaeology was promoted and publicized in a way not seen before. Perhaps this was due to the ideology of "logical positivism" prevalent at the time, which seemed to make the unknowable knowable. In any case, the Binfordian movement was a juggernaut that forced archaeologists either to respond or capitulate. New Archaeology's "young turks" created a cause with its own *raison d'être*: the science of human behavior (e.g., Thomas 1979).

The thought was that human behaviors were uniform, adaptive, and rational, and that there were universal laws of behavior out there just waiting to be discovered. The way ancient hunter-gatherers foraged, horticulturalists grew crops, or villagers broke pots could not only be understood by studying analogous behaviors around the world, they might all be explicable with reference to the laws of thermodynamics. By the mid-1970s, the confidence of some young and naive archaeologists in the regularity of human behavior was such that they assumed one need not excavate or analyze much more than 10 percent of any region, site, house, pit, or hearth (Mueller 1975)!

Such sampling strategies drew the ire of the more seasoned veterans, and there was dissent, spurred on by the effective critiques of Michael Schiffer and his band of "Behavioral Archaeology" students and cronies (see Schiffer 1976; Skibo et al. 1995). Schiffer posited that perhaps there were more human and natural factors involved in inferring behaviors than the New Archaeologists realized. To understand them, archaeologists came to realize the critical importance of studying actual human behavior either by conducting "ethnoarchaeology" or through "experimental archaeology."

These were heady times for archaeology, punctuated by near-revolutionary methodological advances in archaeometry, geoarchaeology, taphonomy, and paleoethnobotany. The latter, in particular, benefited hugely from the development of "flotation" technology during Struever's Koster-site excavations. Flotation, a technique where clean water is added to soil samples and the carbonized (and lighter than water) plant bits float to the top, had revolutionary effects on the study of plant-food production and domestication (see Minnis 2003, 2004).

In this same general period, another all-important North American development was occurring: cultural resource management (CRM). Instigated by a series of federal laws in the United States during the 1960s through 1980s, archaeologists under contract with public agencies or private firms (needing to comply with public laws) were required to identify and mitigate any adverse effects to the nation's cultural heritage whenever public monies were expended. It was a boon for North American archaeology, since there were few laws protecting archaeological sites in the early 1960s. This was clearly evident around the Cahokia site, where archaeologists who had learned their trade in the reservoir archaeology of the 1950s in the eastern Plains found themselves up against Eisenhower's interstate highways, which were to slice up major sites in the American Bottom, including Cahokia. The archaeologists, sometimes unsure of how relevant their "salvage archaeology" was to the lofty goals of the New Archaeology, nonetheless tirelessly faced down bulldozers, road graders, and angry union laborers (the latter supported by the Mafia) in what must rank as one of the more colorful and weird episodes of North American archaeology (see Young and Fowler 2000).

However, the archaeologists' hard work built the infrastructure of the largest CRM program with the best track record of publishing its results in the United States – the FAI-270 Highway Mitigation Project and its offshoot, the Illinois Transportation Archaeological Research Program at the University of Illinois (Bareis and Porter 1984; Griffin 1985:16–17; Walthall et al. 1997). Founded in the principles of settlement archaeology, adopting the methodological rigor of the New Archaeology, but avoiding the sampling excesses of the behaviorists, the highway archaeologists insisted on total survey and total excavation, which dovetails nicely with newer historical models of culture change.

In its rigor and publication track record, the FAI-270 project is nearly matched by the Dolores project, near Mesa Verde in Colorado, and the nearby Black Mesa archaeological project. Again, the massive scale of archaeological investigations allowed for a refinement of the regional chronology and an ability to see spatial and temporal variation in horticultural practices that led to the rise of places such as Chaco Canyon to the south, where the National Park Service's Chaco project stands as a CRM runner-up to the list of the biggest and best CRM efforts (see Lekson, this volume; Lipe et al. 1988; Powell and Gummerman 1987).

Today, such upscaled CRM projects are finding a new relevance in what some North Americanists might have initially seen as a non-North American fly in the ointment: Ian Hodder's (1982) "post-processual" archaeology. Although it was slow to penetrate North America (and is still routinely misunderstood), elements of the post-processual movement in archaeology did ring true to a few pre-Columbian archaeologists. More accepting than them, however, were historic archaeologists who regularly encountered diverse colonial and post-colonial ideologies, ethnicities, cultural practices, and power struggles for which traditional cultural-historical or behavioral theory did not work.

Thus, the various sorts of post-processual archaeologies through the 1990s did manage to gain a foothold in North American archaeology (e.g., Duke and Wilson 1995; Loren, this volume; McGuire 1992; Saitta, this volume; Sassaman, this volume). Today, inferences that material culture or landscapes "recursively constructed social realities" or that the body is the "site of cultural production" are not as outrageous to North American archaeologists as they seemed just a few years ago. In fact, there is reason to pick up the positive tone set by the New Archaeologists even as we put considerable distance between their behavioral theories and more recent ones (see Hegmon 2003).

How is the North American Past Knowable?

If history is lived rather than written, then archaeologists can (in fact, must) recover it, although this admittedly demands greater spatial and temporal controls than can typically be recovered from a stratigraphic trench or a 10 percent sample of domestic refuse (see Pauketat 2001). Some think this far-fetched. They think that archaeologists engage in story-telling (i.e., narrative construction or culture-making) and fail to appreciate that archaeology is a long-term self-correcting process involving detection, introspection, and contingent inference construction.[2]

However, many North American archaeologists have the tools and the datasets to understand the past as lived histories with spatial, material, and corporeal dimensions. Minimally, datasets of the scale and temporal resolution available from old WPA collections, settlement pattern studies, and CRM projects allow us to identify and evaluate the historical relationships between the apparent long-term developmental (some would say "evolutionary") trends or "traditions" commonly identified by archaeologists and the real people, places, and moments of cultural construction of the past. Although not all authors in this volume would agree, the former are *patterns* evident at large scales, *not the processes of change themselves*.

These patterns are the beginnings of explanation. They are established through stratigraphy, seriation, horizon markers, the superpositioning of refuse deposits, and absolute dating, and form the basis of current archaeological chronologies in North America (Figure 1.6). Such chronologies typically involve the recognition of long periods of time punctuated by apparent moments of culture change or transition (e.g., climate change, European contact, etc.). Some researchers feel that this is an accurate way of characterizing the past. Certainly, in the absence of written history or large, fine-grained datasets, it is a simpler and less data contingent way. It is, in fact, deceptively simple.

The origins of agriculture, pottery, and the bow and arrow

In thinking about some long periods of time, it is easy to fall into the trap of suggesting that peoples stayed virtually unchanged for thousands of years. People, one might assume, do not alter their ways unless change is forced upon them by some jarring event or persistent external force. Thus, many understand a prolonged warm and dry spell ca. 6000–3000 B.C. – the "Hypsithermal" – to have led to increased population aggregation, sedentism, and, in some places in North America, intensification of food production and domestication. These arguments are based on sound correlations between settlement patterns and climate change. People really did begin concentrating in well-watered locations during this time.

However, correlation is not explanation, and the mere fact of the Hypsithermal is not sufficient to *explain* the various parallel trajectories of increased sedentism, gardening, and domestication leading toward agriculture. Climate change in this case was very definitely a constraint on "human–plant interactions," but the more we know about specific localities in North America (through archaeology), the less we believe that climate directly caused anything. To understand the relationship between climate change and agricultural change, we need to know *how* change was generated in terms of the gendered, meaningful, power-laden cultural histories of food production, storage, religious practice, and political organization (Watson and Kennedy 1991). So, recent discussion has centered on the historically spotty and

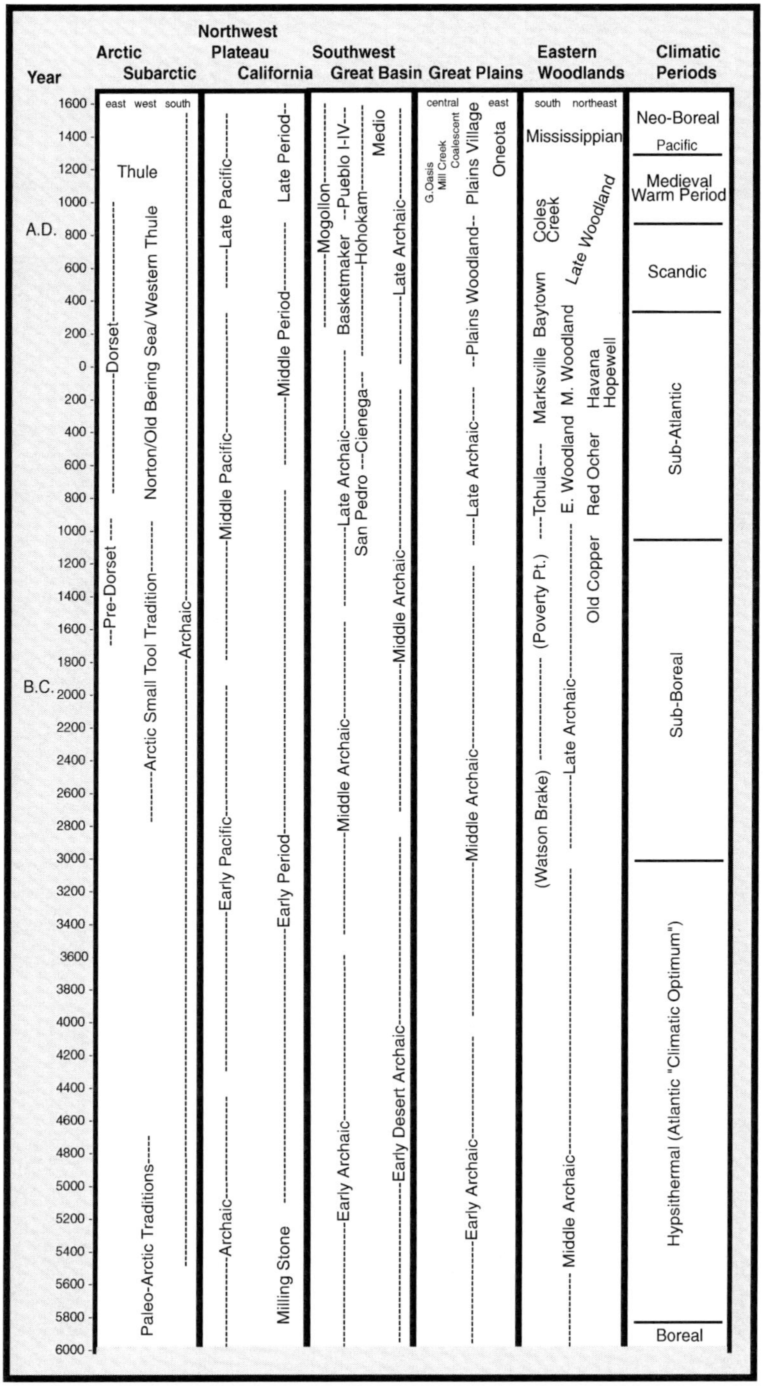
Year
Arctic
Subarctic
Northwest
Plateau
California
Southwest
Great Basin
Great Plains
Eastern
Woodlands
Climatic
Periods
A.D.
B.C.
1600
1400
1200
1000
800
600
400
200
0
200
400
600
800
1000
1200
1400
1600
1800
2000
2200
2400
2600
2800
3000
3200
3400
3600
3800
4000
4200
4400
4600
4800
5000
5200
5400
5600
5800
6000
east
west
south
Thule
Dorset
Pre-Dorset
Norton/Old Bering Sea/ Western Thule
Arctic Small Tool Tradition
Paleo-Arctic Traditions
Archaic
Late Pacific
Middle Pacific
Early Pacific
Archaic
Late Period
Middle Period
Early Period
Milling Stone
Mogollon
Basketmaker
Pueblo I-IV
Hohokam
Medio
Late Archaic
San Pedro
Cienega
Middle Archaic
Early Archaic
Late Archaic
Middle Archaic
Early Desert Archaic
central
east
G.Oasis
Mill Creek
Coalescent
Plains Village
Oneota
Plains Woodland
Late Archaic
Middle Archaic
Early Archaic
south
northeast
Mississippian
Coles Creek
Late Woodland
Baytown
Marksville
Tchula
(Poverty Pt.)
(Watson Brake)
M. Woodland
E. Woodland
Late Archaic
Middle Archaic
Havana
Hopewell
Red Ocher
Old Copper
Neo-Boreal
Pacific
Medieval Warm Period
Scandic
Sub-Atlantic
Sub-Boreal
Hypsithermal (Atlantic "Climatic Optimum")
Boreal

Figure 1.6 Archaeological chronologies for North America (6000 B.C.–A.D. 1600)

discontinuous nature of plant-food production or the avoidance of agriculture or certain crops by some people in some times or places (e.g., Fritz 1990; Hart 1999; Kidder and Fritz 1993). There was no "revolution" or "innovation" of production that rational people readily adopted.

The same seems to apply to the "invention" of pottery, on the one hand, and the adoption of the bow and arrow, on the other. For instance, Ken Sassaman (1995) has argued that social contradictions involving gendered relations, material goods exchanges, and political alliances structured the localized adoption of or resistance to the earliest (Archaic-period) ceramic technology in North America. The evidence is unambiguously in his favor: although first appearing 4,500 years ago on Stallings Island, South Carolina, pottery took a full 1,500 years to be adopted across the Coastal Plain! Thus, Sassaman concludes that there were good reasons why people preferred age-old stone-boiling techniques over clay pots, and he finds those reasons by looking at the variable practices of food preparation and consumption on a site-by-site and region-by-region basis.

Likewise, the bow and arrow at one time was thought a technological improvement, adopted owing to its ability to put more meat on the table. The bow and arrow might have been adopted in certain localities only to be dropped later (Bradley 1997). At A.D. 200, it might have become commonly used in parts of the west, but seems to have spread rapidly around A.D. 600 ± 100, displacing the use of fletched spears (sometimes called darts, thrown with "atlatls" or spear-throwing sticks) across much of continental United States, perhaps owing to social tensions and political developments (Blitz 1988; McElrath et al. 2000; Nassaney and Pyle 1999). Nassaney (2001:160) states that the bow and arrow, used both to hunt and to make war,

> could have simultaneously challenged the relationships it was meant to reinforce. One could make a similar argument for the use of guns by early-nineteenth-century African captives in the American South. Whereas guns were provided to African Americans to allow them to supplement their subsistence base, these same tools were sometimes turned against the slaves' legal owners in rebellion.

Monumentality, cosmology, and catastrophe

How different is the logic of this argument from the case for the relationship of monumentality to culture-making? In the Southwest, Ruth Van Dyke (2003:194) has posited that Chacoan Great Houses, Great Kivas, and even roads were the memorials of later descendants to some idealized ancestral past. However, in so memorializing that past, they changed their present, and "legitimated inequality and consolidated community" in ways radically unlike their predecessors (see Lekson, this volume).

In a similar vein, Pauketat and Alt (2003) have argued that the moundbuilding "traditions" of the mid-continent and Southeast dissolve into a series of commemorative practices that produced the veneer of continuity but that belie a discontinuous history (cf. Sassaman, this volume). The commemoration of someone's ideal in the form of a mound physically altered the landscape of cultural experience and inscribed a new reality into the lives of all people (Pauketat 2000). Similarly, Plains Indian "medicine wheels" are sacred sites, yes, but not static ones (Hall 1996). The circular patterns of stones in the high Plains show evidence of renewal, reconstruction, and revaluation (the latter, for instance, via the gifts of tobacco left behind by specific people for specific reasons). Sacred sites are dynamic sites, and this is increasingly realized to apply to various sorts of so-called ritual places, such as the caves and rock faces inscribed with petroglyphs or pictographs.

Some rock art sites contain actual inscribed narratives of the experiences of people – literally writing on a wall (see Francis and Loendorf 2002; Whitley 2000). Bearing this in mind, how many of the spiral, zoomorphic, and anthropomorphic rock-art panels on the red sandstone cliff faces behind Pueblo Bonito and Chetro Ketl, for instance, are stories of happenings in this innermost sacred and political sanctum of Chacoan space? It has been speculated that at least one pictograph near another Great House in the Canyon records the occurrence of a supernova in A.D. 1054. There are other depictions of this supernova in the Southwest and several around the Cahokia site in Missouri (Diaz-Granados and Duncan 2000:199).

Could there be other such commemorations of astronomical events in North America? At least one researcher, John Kelly (1996:111), has wondered about the shape of a particular icon – the forked-eye motif – that appeared on the earliest Ramey Incised pottery known from Cahokia a few years after Comet Halley appeared in the sky in A.D. 1066. Such associations should be expected. Robert Hall (1989), among others, has noted the many associations, stories, and symbols that connect cosmological and celestial phenomena – stars, sun, moon, etc. – with human or superhuman characters in legend and folklore (e.g., "Red Horn" and the morning star: Pauketat, this volume). Religious leaders, magicians, and politicians – they are not always so different are they? – use the cosmos to explain for themselves and for others the history of people in relation to the supernatural. Some archaeologists suggest, often under their breath, that the mid-11th-century timing of a number of seemingly unrelated big events – Cahokia's "Big Bang," a Chacoan building spree, or even the construction of the anomalous Great Serpent Mound in Ohio (AMS dates of A.D. 1030 ± 70: Fletcher et al. 1994) – could have been related to particular people interpreting the skies with distinct local consequences (Figure 1.7).

Certainly, historical moments encompass natural events that seem outside the control of people. Obviously, such events do occur owing to celestial, geological, and climatological processes, biological agents, or random combinations of the above. Droughts and floods impact or decimate crops. A mudslide buried plankhouses at the small ocean-side village of Ozette along the Northwest Coast, ca. A.D. 1750, perfectly preserving carved wooden planks, nets, fishing kits, clubs, decorated boxes, and in-use household possessions (Samuels 1991). In eastern North America, similar catastrophic artifact assemblages are associated with the floors of thatched-roof Mississippian houses that burned during the occasional 13th- and 14th-century A.D. village conflagration, the results either of natural prairie fires or warfare (e.g., Conrad 1991).

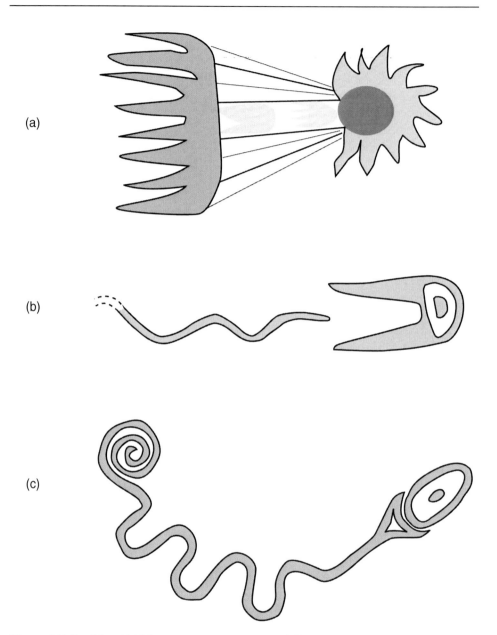

Figure 1.7 Possible mid-11th-century representations of Comet Halley: (a) the Bayeux Tapestry (adapted from Gibbs-Smith 1973); (b) Ramey Incised forked-eye motif (Grossmann site, courtesy Susan Alt); (c) the Great Serpent Mound, Ohio

However, as noted with the Hypsithermal, we should not conclude that the natural event or process actually caused some consequent cultural change. Even in the case of a mudslide or the incineration of a whole village, any attendant cultural changes were caused by the culture-making or "social negotiations" of people in the context of the event, not merely as a result of the event. Different people in other times or places would have understood a similar event differently or reacted in other ways, with divergent consequences. So, the cultural process resides in the experiencing of that particular place with those particular people, not in the catastrophe.

This is perhaps clearer with another climatic shift well known to archaeologists: the Medieval Warm Period. Between A.D. 900 and 1300 or so, the northern hemisphere experienced a prolonged warm, moist period. Perhaps not coincidentally, inequality developed in the west (Ames, this volume); Chaco and the Classic Hohokam arose in the Southwest (Hegmon, Lekson, this volume), maize was intensified and polities or confederacies founded in the east (Chilton, Henning, Pauketat, this volume), and the Thule expansion began in the Arctic.

The Thule, the Vikings, and the Medieval Warm Period (A.D. 900–1300)

By the end of the ninth century A.D., there were two archaeologically distinct groups of peoples, the Dorset descendants of Arctic Small Tool Tradition people in the eastern Arctic and the Canadian archipelago (north to Greenland) and those in the west around Alaska called the Thule (Maxwell 1985). The latter organized themselves in large, gendered, "corporate" residential groups and whaling parties, led by wealthy whaling "captains." The corporate groups included extended families and attached kinfolk who worked together, cooked and ate together, resided together, and identified with one another. Along with other characteristics – the use of large whaling boats, snow sleds, the bow and arrow, a distinctively abstract art style, an elaborate harpoon technology, marked social inequalities, and the potential for outward aggression, etc. – they stand in marked contrast to their Dorset contemporaries in the eastern Arctic (see Maxwell 1985; Park 1993). The latter were seal-hunting foragers who were organized in small groups with shamanistic ritual leaders and less evident potential to generate concentrations of wealth and social inequality.

With the warming up of Arctic waters, the breaking up of ice, and the shifting range of bowhead whales at around A.D. 1000, the Thule people – ancestors of the Inuit – began to migrate eastward from large Alaskan sites like Cape Krusenstern, Birnik, and Norton (see Anderson 1984). Current evidence suggests a contracting Dorset population "in crisis, and probably in severe decline" (Whitridge 1999:65). Earlier Dorset sites, such as Button Point, were abandoned with a retreat as far south as the Port au Choix site in Newfoundland. Whether the Dorset people had vacated the lands they had formerly occupied, were driven out by the immigrant Thule, or overlapped with and were ultimately absorbed into Thule populations (or some other combination of the above) remains uncertain. But the Thule people ended up as far away as Labrador and Newfoundland just a few short years later, where they met Norse colonists sailing in the opposite direction from Iceland and Greenland.

Like the Thule, the Norse exploration of the New World was an outward expression of what being a Viking was all about. As recorded in the Vinland Sagas, there were a number of Norse attempts to explore lands beyond Greenland, which itself had been colonized before A.D. 1000. Apparently, rumors of a wooded land with wild grapes and other natural resources encouraged colonists to sail south, founding at least one small domestic settlement consisting of several sod buildings, cooking pits, boat sheds, cattle corrals, a forge, and a kiln (Ingstad 1985). Known as L'Anse aux Meadows, an unidentified band of Norse families set up a domestic outpost in Newfoundland around A.D. 1000, perhaps abandoning it altogether just after a few years. While exchange of European goods with the Thule peoples continued for a few hundred more years, the Norse colonists in the Arctic were unable to sustain their bases as the Medieval Warm Period drew to a close (McGhee 1984). They retreated to Iceland and Scandinavia with the inhospitable conditions of the Neo-Boreal period, or the "Little Ice Age" (see Fagan 1999).

In both the Thule and Norse cases, the Medieval Warm Period is a necessary part of the explanation of colonization and, ultimately, the abandonment of part or all of the eastern Arctic. But equally obvious is that the social histories of the Dorset, Thule, and Norse predisposed each population to become what they did. Peter Whitridge (1999) notes how being Thule was wrapped up in gendered practices and childhood experiences, such that Arctic colonization was an outward expression of their lived cultures-in-the-making. Climate caused neither the Thule nor the Vikings.

Commensality, inequality, and cultural orders

The locus of Arctic colonizations resided in the practices, production, and experience of people. A similar point can be made for any other case in this book: consider the corporate experience, construction, and commemorations represented by Iroquois or Hopewell houses, culinary practices, and mortuary traditions (see Chilton, Dancey, this volume). Or, consider the Chacoan Great Houses, Great Kivas, and roads, laid out for effect with wall construction mimicking the canyon walls and each Great House sited with respect to the horizon, to an *axis mundi*, to celestial phenomena, and to each other. Merely passing through the canyon, much less experiencing the sights, sounds, and smells of it, was a religious experience (e.g., Farmer 2003; Lekson 1999b). The objects with which people left, or that they associated with Chaco – whether or not utilitarian or ritual – were "pieces" of that place, conveying indelible meanings regardless of where they ended up (Bradley 2000, cited by Hegmon, Pauketat, this volume). In a sense, the effect of Chacoan pieces of place was another kind of Chacoan peace and a new southwestern landscape, *pax Chaco* (Lekson 1999a, 1999b).

The same may apply to southeastern places, such as Poverty Point, where artifacts suggest a close relationship between cooking and craft production (see Sassaman, this volume). Apparently, craft objects were used during on-site public events that, presumably, included large-scale commensal meals or feasts in the large Poverty Point amphitheater (see Gibson 2000). There may be no better illustration of the odd conflation of political and communal or public and private realms than in Poverty Point's seemingly dramatic performances of the mundane.

Likewise, at Cahokia, the mere act of building domiciles, using a particular style of pot, or walking through a public space merged the quotidian with the cosmological (Pauketat, this volume). The gargantuan feasts at that place clearly merged highly sacred acts and objects with the mundane, everyday realm of agrarian life (Pauketat et al. 2002). In this particular case, the politicization of the everyday and the cooptation of the communal produced something of greater magnitude, a subcontinental cultural order – a *pax Cahokiana* – that could also be labeled a "civilization" (see Pauketat 2004).

Embodying North American Archaeology

In contemplating the foundations of such cultural orders, most archaeologists now agree that inequality was an ever-emergent condition of social life (Ames, Sassaman, this volume). Many would also agree that "culture contact" was not a one-time European affair, but in fact characterized many small-scale and large-scale historical encounters of people with each other. What varied widely from people to people was the materiality and spatiality of either the accommodation of, or resistance to, the perceived inequalities or the "other" in culture contact situations (e.g., Alt 2001; Nassaney 2001). We see this historical principle even more clearly in the archaeology of the North America's colonial and antebellum periods.

In the 1970s and 1980s, archaeologists discovered that what they thought they knew about African American slavery, based on written descriptions by literate Euroamerican observers and slave-owners themselves, was not accurate (Singleton, this volume). There was considerable material evidence of daily, covert resistance on the part of the slaves to the sensibilities and ideologies of the dominant Euroamericans – so much so that Southern social history is now understood to have been as much produced on a day-to-day basis by the seemingly powerless and often illiterate slaves as by the elite Southern planters (e.g., Ferguson 1992). Of course, few planters recognized or admitted as much in written texts.

That slaves did this is eye-opening, and allows us to reconsider the history-making processes of all non-literate peoples, lower classes, women, mixed-bloods, Native Americans, and those others "beyond the big house" (see Deagan 1988; Singleton, this volume). Kathleen Deagan's research on Spanish St. Augustine and the 16th-century community of Puerto Real in Haiti focuses on these history-making processes (Deagan 1995). She stresses that the household was the site of "transculturation" – the mutual cultural exchanges between Spanish men and their Indian wives and African slaves. The colonial community was multiethnic; race and status were intertwined and the hybridity of people, architecture, and objects was instrumental in shaping new cultural practices and creolized identities (see Silliman, this volume).

Likewise, Kent Lightfoot's research on the 19th-century community of Fort Ross, California serves as his basis for arguing that "the social environment of most North American colonies was considerably more complex, involving one or more local native populations, European peoples of varied nationalities and backgrounds, and many 'other' peoples of color" (Lightfoot 1995:200). In the case of Fort Ross, the arrangement and use of space, the built environment, trash disposal, and domestic activity constructed new social identities for colonial native Californians, Russians, Alaskans, and mixed-bloods (Lightfoot et al. 1998:202).

Identities and the body

Our understanding of the pluralism of cultural construction and history-making can be taken one step further by reconsidering identity and the body. For years within archaeology, the concept of identity was used to refer to sameness. It was thought that whatever people had in common could be discerned through the identification of "cultural traits" and this, as we have seen, resulted in static conceptualizations of different ethnicities, ideologies, and cultures.[3] But today we recognize the variability and diversity of social identities; identity was a complex negotiation of individuality, community, gender, status, power, personal beliefs, and religious and corporate ideologies (Fisher and Loren 2003). Identity was (and is) about both sameness and difference (Meskell 2002:279–280).

As with culture-making generally, the identities we see at any particular time are always identities-in-the-making. They are fluid, shifting, actively negotiated, and endlessly (re)constructed. So, we are looking at identity processes (rather than identity as product) and multiple identities (rather than just one). I define myself and people define me differently depending on context: what I wear, what language I speak, etc. By doing this, by taking on different personas, individuals cross existing social, racial, and political boundaries to construct new social identities (Loren 2001, 2003, this volume).

Importantly, the relationship between social identity and material culture is not straightforward, but rather ambiguous, as individuals (may have) chosen different kinds of material to express social identity (Upton 1996:5). And, while there is a lingering tendency within archaeology to reduce material culture to essential categories and to assume that only certain groups used certain forms of material culture, material culture is not merely reflective of identity (Upton 1996). Instead, identities formed as people chose or were forced to choose certain forms of material culture in the process of living.[4]

To overcome this lingering conceptual difficulty, North American archaeologists should turn to theories of the body (Joyce 1998; Meskell 2000).[5] Bodily experiences are more than just gendered; they include concerns of race, class, age, status, etc. (Fisher and Loren 2003). There is an experiential aspect to the daily practices of all people in that we experience (or live) the world through our bodies in daily practices that take place in full view, on the landscape.

Conclusion: A Renewed North American Archaeology

The relationship between the landscape, material culture, and the body is active and constitutive: we understand the landscape and other social actors in that landscape by our experience of it (Fisher and Loren 2003:229). This is true of the clothed bodies of multiethnic and creolized French and Spanish colonial sites and the transculturation of landscapes (Loren, this volume). It is true of figurative sculptures and images of bodies, considered as gendered pieces of places (from painted pictographs to Plains Indian children's dolls, Cahokian redstone figures, and Chacoan effigy vessels). It is also true of the dead bodies in Cahokia's Mound 72, in the Crow Creek ditch, or on the Ludlow landscape (Pauketat, Saitta, this volume). In the same way, the body of the Kennewick Man shapes the landscape of American archaeology today.

Such bodies, like cultural objects and architecture in general, were not benign things that merely adapted to external changes. In the same sense, grand monumental expressions in North America were not symbols of raw political power in the hands of self-identified elites. Rather, these were built by individuals whose very bodily movements, during the act of construction, defined their sense of place, personhood, and cosmological order. Objects and houses likewise were pieces of landscapes. The spaces of particular places continued to channel movement and to redefine sensuous experience, cultural practice, and one's own sense of self in North American landscapes. Bodies moved through social spaces and engaged with a world that evoked memories, heightened and solidified notions of self and people, and enveloped the body with history (Bender 2001; Tilley 1994; see also Saitta, this volume).

North America's vast spaces were never neutral playing fields. North American peoples worked in and manipulated the landscape. They built homes and communities over older ones; they traveled on roads to trade and created physical avenues of movement; they migrated across vast and unfamiliar terrains to meet new peoples; and they defended spaces that they called their own. In doing so, and in the many dimensions of being an American, they constructed their futures, and set parameters around ours.

Their alternative histories are sometimes forgotten, occasionally subverted, and often controversial. But they matter in our attempts to understand an expansive and unfolding story of how people make history. Alternative histories are the subject matter of a renewed North American archaeology that, in its own history of practice, its large datasets, and its theoretical directions, is teaching us a lesson that promises to help all peoples understand the sweep of global history and the commonalities of the human experience.

To that end, the chapters in this book open the door to the rich human history on display in North America's immense outdoor museum. We only need look. Turn the page.

NOTES

1 Consider the US legislation governing Native American life, including the Indian Removal Act (1830), the Indian Assimilation Act (1857), the Code of Religious Offenses (1883), and the General Allotment Act of 1887 (see Deloria 1988; Waldman 1985).

2   Consider a couple of well-known North American studies. First, the Tuscon "garbology" project showed how archaeological measures of consumption revealed that some people misrepresent their daily practices (Rathje 1974). Second, the archaeology of the Battle of Little Big Horn undermined the official history of the late 19th century and, instead, verified the account of the Cheyenne and Sioux warriors who were there (Scott and Connor 1999)!

3   In this formula, social complexity and diversity are underestimated and, sadly (and chillingly), such definitions can be used to support nationalist, colonialist, or imperialist claims (Trigger 1989).

4   Once again, we must stop and consider how our identities in the present impact what we have to say about the past (see Meskell 2002:280). For North American archaeologists, this means that we must contend with the legacy of the Moundbuilder Myth, the ties between early archaeology and colonialism, and museum collections obtained by less than ethical means. North American archaeologists no longer operate under the assumption that their subjects are long gone and that they alone have the power to interpret the past (Brumfiel 2003:208; Schmidt and Patterson 1995).

5   Gendered research in archaeology has been around since the 1980s, but the intersections of gender and the body are of more recent origin (see Joyce 1998; Meskell 2002). The body, as it turns out, is the location of identity construction and cultural practice (Butler 1991).

REFERENCES

Alt, Susan M., 2001 Cahokian change and the authority of tradition. In *The Archaeology of Traditions: Agency and History Before and After Columbus*. T. R. Pauketat, ed. Pp. 141–156. Gainesville: University Press of Florida.

Anderson, Douglas D., 1984 Prehistory of north Alaska. In *Handbook of North American Indians, Arctic*. W. C. Sturtevant and D. Damas, eds. Pp. 80–93. Washington, DC: Smithsonian Institution Press.

Bareis, Charles J., and James W. Porter, eds., 1984 *American Bottom Archaeology: A Summary of the FAI-270 Project Contribution to the Culture History of the Mississippi River Valley*. Urbana: University of Illinois Press.

Bender, Barbara, 2001 Landscapes on-the-move. *Journal of Social Archaeology* 1(1), 75–89.

Binford, Lewis R., 1962 Archaeology as anthropology. *American Antiquity* 28, 217–225.

——— 1972 *An Archaeological Perspective*. New York: Seminar Press.

Blitz, John H., 1988 Adoption of the bow in prehistoric North America. *North American Archaeology* 9, 123–145.

Bradley, A. P., 1997 The bow and arrow in the Eastern Woodlands: Evidence for an Archaic origin. *North American Archaeologist* 18, 207–223.

Bradley, Richard, 2000 *An Archaeology of Natural Places*. London: Routledge.

Brumfiel, Elizabeth M., 2003 It's a material world: History, artifacts, and anthropology. *Annual Review of Anthropology* 32, 205–223.

——— 2004 Meaning by design: Ceramics, feasting, and figured worlds in Postclassic Mexico. In *Mesoamerican Archaeology*. J. A. Hendon and R. A. Joyce, eds. Pp. 239–264. Oxford: Blackwell.

Bunzel, Ruth, 1929 *The Pueblo Potter: A Study of Creative Imagination in Primitive Art*. New York: Columbia University Press.

Butler, Judith, 1991 *Gender Trouble: Feminism and the Subversion of Identity*. New York: Routledge.

Caldwell, Joseph R., 1959 The new American archaeology. *Science* 129, 303–307.

Claasen, Cheryl, 1999 Black and white women at Irene Mound. In *Grit-Tempered: Early Women Archaeologists in the Southeastern United States*. N. M. White, L. P. Sullivan, and R. A. Marrinan, eds. Pp. 92–114. Gainesville: University Press of Florida.

Conrad, Lawrence A., 1991 The Middle Mississippian cultures of the central Illinois River valley. In *Cahokia and the Hinterlands: Middle Mississippian Cultures of the Midwest*. T. E. Emerson and R. B. Lewis, eds. Pp. 119–156. Urbana: University of Illinois Press.

Deagan, Kathleen A., 1988 Neither history nor prehistory: The questions that count in historical archaeology. *Historical Archaeology* 22, 7–12.

Deagan, Kathleen A., ed., 1995 *Puerto Real: The Archaeology of a Sixteenth-Century Spanish Town in Hispaniola*. Gainesville: University Press of Florida.

Deloria, Vine, Jr., 1988 *Custer Died For Your Sins: An Indian Manifesto*. Norman: University of Oklahoma Press.

Diaz-Granados, Carol, and James R. Duncan, 2000 *The Petroglyphs and Pictographs of Missouri*. Tuscaloosa: University of Alabama Press.

Dobyns, Henry F., 1983 *Their Numbers Became Thinned: Native American Population Dynamics in Eastern North America*. Knoxville, TN: University of Tennessee Press.

Duke, Philip, and Michael C. Wilson, 1995 *Beyond Subsistence: Plains Archaeology and the Postprocessual Critique*. Tuscaloosa: University of Alabama Press.

Echo-Hawk, Roger C., 2000 Ancient history in the New World: Integration oral traditions and the archaeological record in deep time. *American Antiquity* 65, 267–90.

Fagan, Brian M., 1999 *Floods, Famines, and Emperors: El Niño and the Fate of Civilizations*. New York: Basic Books.

Farmer, James D., 2003 Astronomy and ritual in Chaco Canyon. In *Pueblo Bonito: Center of the Chacoan World*. J. E. Neitzel, ed. Pp. 61–71. Washington, DC: Smithsonian Institution Press.

Ferguson, Leland G., 1992 *Uncommon Ground: Archaeology and Early African America, 1650–1800*. Washington: Smithsonian Institution Press.

Fisher, Genevieve, and Diana DiPaolo Loren, 2003 Embodying identity in archaeology. *Cambridge Archaeological Journal* 13, 225–230.

Fletcher, R. V., T. L. Cameron, B. T. Lepper, D. A. Wymer, and W. Pickard, 1994 *Serpent Mound Project*. Columbus: Ohio Historical Society.

Ford, James A., 1954 On the concept of types. *American Anthropologist* 56, 42–53.

Francis, Julie E., and Lawrence L. Loendorf, 2002 *Ancient Visions: Petroglyphs and Pictographs of the Wind River and Bighorn Country, Wyoming and Montana*. Salt Lake City: University of Utah Press.

Fritz, Gayle J., 1990 Multiple pathways to farming in precontact eastern North America. *Journal of World Prehistory* 4, 387–435.

Gibbs-Smith, Charles H., 1973 *The Bayeux Tapestry*. London: Phaidon Press.

Gibson, Jon L., 2000 *The Ancient Mounds of Poverty Point: Place of Rings*. Gainesville: University Press of Florida.

Griffin, James B., 1985 An individual's participation in American archaeology 1928–1985. *Annual Review of Anthropology* 14, 1–23.

Hall, Robert L., 1989 The cultural background of Mississippian symbolism. In *The Southeastern Ceremonial Complex.* P. Galloway, ed. Pp. 239–278. Lincoln: University of Nebraska Press.

——1996 American Indian worlds, world quarters, world centers, and their shrines. *The Wisconsin Archeologist* 77, 120–127.

Hart, John P., 1999 Maize agriculture evolution in the eastern Woodlands of North America: A Darwinian perspective. *Journal of Archaeological Method and Theory* 6, 137–180.

Hegmon, Michelle, 2003 Setting theoretical egos aside: Issues and theory in North American archaeology. *American Antiquity* 68, 213–243.

Henige, D., 1998 *Numbers from Nowhere: The American Indian Contact Population Debate.* Norman: University of Oklahoma Press.

Hodder, Ian, 1982 Theoretical archaeology: A reactionary view. In *Symbolic and Structural Archaeology.* I. Hodder, ed. Pp. 1–16. Cambridge: Cambridge University Press.

Ingstad, Anne, 1985 *The Norse Discovery of America.* Oslo: Norwegian University Press.

Joyce, Rosemary A., 1998 Performing the body in Prehispanic Central America. *Res* 33, 147–165.

Kelly, John E., 1994 The archaeology of the East St. Louis mound center: Past and present. *Illinois Archaeology* 6, 1–58.

——1996 Redefining Cahokia: Principles and elements of community organization. *The Wisconsin Archeologist* 77, 97–119.

Kidder, Tristram R., and Gayle J. Fritz, 1993 Subsistence and social change in the Lower Mississippi Valley: Excavations at the Reno Brake and Osceola sites, Louisiana. *Journal of Field Archaeology* 20, 281–297.

Kroeber, Alfred L., 1953 *Cultural and Natural Areas of Native North America.* Berkeley: University of California Press.

Landsman, Gail, and Sara Ciborski, 1992 Representation and politics: Contesting histories of the Iroquois. *Cultural Anthropology* 7, 425–447.

Lekson, Stephen H., 1999a Great towns in the Southwest. In *Great Towns and Regional Polities in the Prehistoric American Southwest and Southeast.* J. E. Neitzel, ed. Pp. 3–22. Albuquerque: University of New Mexico Press.

——1999b *The Chaco Meridian: Centers of Political Power in the Ancient Southwest.* Walnut Creek, CA: AltaMira Press.

Lewis, Thomas M. N., and Madeline Kneberg 1946 *Hiwassee Island: An Archaeological Account of Four Tennessee Indian Peoples.* Knoxville: University of Tennessee Press.

Lightfoot, Kent G., 1995 Culture contact studies: Redefining the relationship between prehistoric and historical archaeology. *American Antiquity* 60(2), 199–217.

Lightfoot, Kent G., Antoinette Martinez, and Ann M. Schiff, 1998 Daily practice and material culture in pluralistic social settings: An archaeological study of culture change and persistence from Fort Ross, California. *American Antiquity* 63, 199–222.

Lipe, William D., James N. Morris, and Timothy A. Kohler, 1988 *Dolores Archaeological Program: Anasazi Communities at Dolores, Grass Mesa Village.* Denver: US Department of the Interior, Bureau of Reclamation.

Loren, Diana D., 2001 Social skins: Orthodoxies and practices of dressing in the early colonial Lower Mississippi Valley. *Journal of Social Archaeology* 1, 172–189.

——2003 Refashioning a body politic in colonial Louisiana. *Cambridge Archaeological Journal* 13, 231–237.

Maxwell, Moreau S., 1985 *Prehistory of the Eastern Arctic.* Orlando: Academic Press.

McElrath, Dale L., Thomas E. Emerson, and Andrew C. Fortier, 2000 Social evolution or social response? A fresh look at the "Good Gray Cultures" after four decades of Midwest research. In *Late Woodland Societies: Tradition and Transformation across the Midcontinent*. T. E. Emerson, D. L. McElrath, and A. C. Fortier, eds. Pp. 3–36. Lincoln: University of Nebraska Press.

McGhee, R., 1984 Contact between native North Americans and the Medieval Norse: A review of the evidence. *American Antiquity* 49, 4–26.

McGuire, Randall, 1992 *A Marxist Archaeology*. San Diego: Academic Press.

Meskell, Lynn, 2000 Writing the body in archaeology. In *Reading the Body: Representations and Remains in the Archaeological Record*. A. E. Rautman, ed. Pp. 13–21. Philadelphia: University of Pennsylvania Press.

——2002 The intersections of identity and politics in archaeology. *Annual Review of Anthropology* 31, 279–301.

Mindeleff, Victor, 1989[1891] *A Study of Pueblo Architecture in Tusayan and Cibola*. Washington, DC: Smithsonian Institution Press.

Minnis, Paul E., ed., 2003 *People and Plants in Ancient Eastern North America*. Washington, DC: Smithsonian Institution Press.

——2004 *People and Plants in Ancient Western North America*. Washington, DC: Smithsonian Institution Press.

Mueller, James W., ed., 1975 *Sampling in Archaeology*. Tuscon: University of Arizona Press.

Muller, Jon, 1997 *Mississippian Political Economy*. New York: Plenum Press.

Nabokov, P., 2002 *A Forest of Time: American Indian Ways of History*. Cambridge: Cambridge University Press.

Nassaney, Michael S., 2001 The historical-processual development of Late Woodland societies. In *The Archaeology of Traditions: Agency and History Before and After Columbus*. T. R. Pauketat, ed. Pp. 157–173. Gainesville: University Press of Florida.

Nassaney, Michael S., and Kendra Pyle, 1999 The adoption of the bow and arrow in eastern North America: A view from central Arkansas. *American Antiquity* 64, 243–263.

Nichols, Deborah L., 2004 The rural and urban landscapes of the Aztec state. In *Mesoamerican Archaeology*. J. A. Hendon and R. A. Joyce, eds. Pp. 265–295. Oxford: Blackwell.

Pagden, Anthony, 1982 *The Fall of Natural Man: The American Indian and the Origins of Comparative Ethnology*. Cambridge: Cambridge University Press.

Park, Robert W., 1993 The Dorset-Thule succession in Arctic North America: Assessing claims for culture contact. *American Antiquity* 58, 203–234.

Pauketat, Timothy R., 2000 The tragedy of the commoners. In *Agency in Archaeology*, M.-A. Dobres and J. Robb, eds. Pp. 113–129. London: Routledge.

——2001 Practice and history in archaeology: An emerging paradigm. *Anthropological Theory* 1, 73–98.

——2003 Resettled farmers and the making of a Mississippian polity. *American Antiquity* 68, 39–66.

Pauketat, Timothy R., and Susan M. Alt, 2003 Mounds, memory, and contested Mississippian history. In *Archaeologies of Memory*. R. Van Dyke and S. Alcock, eds. Pp. 151–179. Oxford: Blackwell.

Pauketat, Timothy R., Lucretia S. Kelly, Gayle J. Fritz, Neal H. Lopinot, Scott Elias, and Eve Hargrave, 2002 The residues of feasting and public ritual at early Cahokia. *American Antiquity* 67, 257–279.

Pendergast, James F., 1998 Hochelaga. In *Archaeology of Prehistoric Native America: An Encyclopedia*. G. Gibbon, ed. Pp. 362–363. New York: Garland.

Phillips, Philip, James A. Ford, and James B. Griffin, 1951 *Archaeological Survey in the Lower Mississippi Alluvial Valley, 1940–1947*. Papers of the Peabody Museum of Archaeology and Ethnology, volume 25. Cambridge, MA: Harvard University Press.

Powell, Shirley, and George J. Gumerman, 1987 *People of the Mesa: The Archaeology of Black Mesa, Arizona*. Carbondale: Southern Illinois University Press.

Rathje, William L., 1974 The garbage project: A new way of looking at the problems of archaeology. *Archaeology* 27, 236–241.

Rice, Glen, 1998 War and water: An ecological perspective on Hohokam irrigation. *Kiva* 63, 263–301.

Samuels, Stephen R., ed., 1991 *Ozette Archaeological Project Research Reports*. Department of Anthropology, Washington State University, Pullman, Washington.

Sassaman, Kenneth E., 1995 The social contradictions of traditional and innovative cooking technologies in the prehistoric American Southeast. In *The Emergence of Pottery: Technology and Innovation in Ancient Societies*. W. K. Barnett and J. W. Hoopes, eds. Pp. 223–240. Washington, DC: Smithsonian Institution Press.

Schiffer, Michael B., 1976 *Behavioral Archaeology*. New York: Academic Press.

Schmidt, Peter R., and Thomas C. Patterson, eds., 1995 *Making Alternative Histories: The Practice of Archaeology and History in Non-Western Settings*. Sante Fe, NM: School of American Research Press.

Scott, Douglas D., and Melissa A. Connor, 1999 Post-mortem at the Little Bighorn. In *Lessons from the Past: An Introductory Reader in Archaeology*. K. L. Feder, ed. Pp. 123–129. Mountain View, CA: Mayfield.

Shepard, Anna O., 1936 Technology of Pecos pottery. In *The Pottery of Pecos*, vol. 2. A. V. Kidder and A. O. Shepard, eds. Pp. 389–587. Papers of the Phillips Academy Southwestern Expedition 7. Andover, MA.

Skibo, James M., William H. Walker, and Axel E. Nielsen, eds., 1995 *Expanding Archaeology*. Salt Lake City: University of Utah Press.

Stahl, Ann B., Rob Mann, and Diana DiPaolo Loren, 2004. Writing for Many: Interdisciplinary Communication, Constructionism and the Practices of Writing. *Historical Archaeology* 38(2), 83–102.

Steponaitis, Vincas P., 1998 Population trends at Moundville. In *Archaeology of the Moundville Chiefdom*. V. J. Knight and V. P. Steponaitis, eds. Pp. 26–43. Washington, DC: Smithsonian Institution Press.

Steward, Julian H., and Frank M. Setzler, 1938 Function and configuration in archaeology. *American Antiquity* 4, 4–10.

Taylor, Walter W., 1983 *A Study of Archaeology* (reprint). Carbondale: Southern Illinois University, Center for Archaeological Investigations.

Thomas, Cyrus, 1985[1894] *Report on the Mound Explorations of the Bureau of Ethnology*. Washington, DC: Smithsonian Institution Press.

Thomas, David H., 1979 *Archaeology*. New York: Holt, Rinehart & Winston.

——2000a *Exploring Native North America*. Oxford: Oxford University Press.

——2000b *Skull Wars: Kennewick Man, Archaeology, and the Battle for Native American Identity*. New York: Basic Books.

Tilley, Christopher, 1994 *A Phenomenology of Landscapes: Places, Paths and Monuments*. Oxford: Berg.

Trigger, Bruce G., 1989 *A History of Archaeological Thought*. Cambridge: Cambridge University Press.

Trouillot, Michel-Rolph, 1995 *Silencing the Past: Power and the Production of History*. Boston: Beacon Press.

Upton, Dell, 1996 Ethnicity, authenticity, and invented traditions. *Historical Archaeology* 30(2), 1–7.

Van Dyke, Ruth M., 2003 Memory and the construction of Chacoan society. In *Archaeologies of Memory*. R. M. Van Dyke and S. E. Alcock, eds. Pp. 180–200. Oxford: Blackwell.

Vincent, Joan, 1990 *Anthropology and Politics: Visions, Traditions, and Trends*. Tucson: University of Arizona Press.

Waldman, Carl, 1985 *Atlas of the North American Indian*. New York: Facts on File Publications.

Walthall, John, Kenneth Farnsworth, and Thomas E. Emerson, 1997 Constructing (on) the past. *Common Ground* 2, 26–33.

Watson, Patty J., and Mary C. Kennedy, 1991 The development of horticulture in the Eastern Woodlands of North America: Women's role. In *Engendering Archaeology: Women and Prehistory*. J. M. Gero and M. W. Conkey, eds. Pp. 255–275. Oxford: Blackwell.

Whitley, David S., 2000 *The Art of the Shaman: Rock Art of California*. Salt Lake City: University of Utah Press.

Whitridge, Peter J., 1999 The construction of social difference in a prehistoric Inuit whaling community. Unpublished Ph.D. dissertation, Department of Anthropology. Tempe: Arizona State University.

Willey, Gordon R., and Jeremy A. Sabloff, 1993 *A History of American Archaeology*, 3rd edn. New York: W. H. Freeman.

Wissler, Clark, 1926 *The Relation of Nature to Man in Aboriginal America*. Oxford: Oxford University Press.

Young, Bilone W., and Melvin L. Fowler, 2000 *Cahokia: The Great Native American Metropolis*. Urbana: University of Illinois Press.

2

The Peopling of North America

J. M. Adovasio and David Pedler

The peopling of the New World has fascinated Europeans and their Euroamerican progeny since the late 15th century. Although not amenable to simple answers, the issue has revolved around several relatively simple questions. First, who are the Native Americans – or, in other words, do their origins lie in North America or another continent? Second, if they came to North America from another continent, which one and which specific part of that continent? And third, if the answers to these questions indeed lead to a third one, how did Native Americans make it to North America and at what time in the past?

Despite over 500 years of popular and scientific inquiry, definitive answers to these questions have eluded universal acceptance, and at least the third question has remained at best intractable, leading some researchers to claim that "there is still no definitive evidence that will allow specialists to say when the first Americans initially arrived or who they were" (Bonnichsen and Turnmire 1999:1). This contribution is not intended as a resolution of these issues, but rather as a brief survey of European and Euroamerican attempts to answer the above-listed questions and where current scientific analyses have led the debate.

Who Are the Native Americans?

On October 12, 1492 Christopher Columbus waded ashore on the Caribbean island of San Salvador and soon encountered its aboriginal inhabitants. These Arawak-speaking people, who called themselves Taino, were assumed by Columbus and his exhausted crew to be Asians, perhaps of the same people as those from the semi-mythical Spice Islands in the East Indies. In the kind of deep irony for which only history can be responsible, Columbus was both prescient and dead wrong. Prescient, because he anticipated, by some 450–500 years, the modern scientific view that Native Americans descend from Asian forebears; dead wrong, because this view was derived not from scientific nor even cartographic evidence, but from the mistaken impression that he had met landfall in Asia.

Thus began, with Columbus's "discovery" of America, what Willey and Sabloff (1993:12–37) have termed the Speculative period (1492–1840) of archaeological investigation in the New World. Not recognizable as archaeology in a modern scientific sense, the observations of this period were comprised primarily of incidental accounts offered by explorers, missionaries, and the ever-expanding cadre of functionaries who attend the growth of empires. Many, if not most, of these early accounts focused on physical appearances and ethnography, and their tendency was to describe the Native Americans or "Indians" as a single, discrete people due to an apparent lack of visible differences among them. Hence, Columbus would observe that the natives he encountered on his first voyage were "a well-built people of handsome stature," and that he found "no human monstrosities; on the contrary, among all these people good looks are esteemed; nor are they negroes, as in Guinea, but with flowing hair" (Morison 1955:220). In subsequent early accounts, the assumption continued to hold that the Native Americans who returned to Europe with Columbus and other early explorers were ultimately of Asiatic extraction. An observer of the Caribbean people brought back to Spain from Columbus's second voyage, for example, described them as "dark skinned men with wide faces *like Tartars*, with hair falling to their shoulders, tall and very agile and proud" (Honour 1975:19; emphasis added). Apparently unable to resist embellishment, the same observer also noted that these exotic people "eat human flesh, both children and castrati whom they fatten up like capons and then eat. These men are called 'Canabáli'" (Honour 1975:19).

Accounts like these achieved a long-lived popular currency, despite what is now recognized as the great diversity of cultures and languages among the North American peoples encountered by Europeans in throughout the late 15th and early 16th centuries. Perhaps more importantly, these accounts also had a momentous impact on European commerce and philosophical thought. It should be noted that these early views were not necessarily based entirely on bigotry and unreason, given that whatever differences existed between Native American populations at the time, the degree of difference was then, as it is now, "dwarfed by the distinctions of comparably distant peoples in the Old World" (Brace 2002:53). But, nonetheless, as has been noted extensively in the scholarly literature, these early accounts tell more about the observers than the observed and suggest that much of the ethnographic information obtained via the "discovery" of America was an ethnocentric fiction.

Indeed, the Native Americans at the time of European contact were not even remotely a single people or cultural complex. Presently, for example, it is widely accepted that when Spanish explorers first arrived in the New World there were over 18 million inhabitants, who spoke in excess of 1,000 languages. Extensive trade networks like those associated with the Mississippian and ancestral Puebloan cultures had flourished and were actually on the wane by the early 16th century; the Mayan culture was in its late Postclassic period and the Aztec Empire was at the height of its dominance and wealth (see Lekson, Pauketat, this volume). Moreover, it is probable that the many and varied peoples of the New World held a large variety of customs, values, and beliefs. It is also doubtful that, at the time, these Native Americans considered themselves as anything other than autochthonous – a belief which, in some circles, has persisted into modern times.

The question of Native American origins would remain problematic for quite some time after the initial accounts inspired by Columbus's travels and became even more vexatious when, on September 15, 1513, Vasco Nuñez de Balboa crossed the Isthmus of Panama to observe the Pacific Ocean. Although it probably did not immediately occur to Balboa, this new "discovery" would have profound consequences. Conclusively, it demonstrated that the land mass and offshore islands discovered by Columbus – and subsequently explored by other Spanish, Portuguese, English, and French adventurers – were not part of the Old World, but rather, a new continent and hemisphere bounded by vast oceans on both coasts.

Once European commentators digested this important geographic fact, there emerged a series of florid speculations concerning the identity of the Natives Americans. Some thought they must be the lost tribes of Israel; others the descendants of Danes, Egyptians, Greeks, Norsemen, Phoenicians, or Romans; still others believed them to be surviving remnants of the cataclysm that destroyed mythical Atlantis. Interestingly, though, many of the early European explorers and commentators continued to note the similarity in appearance between Native Americans and Asians. In fact one scholar correctly intuited, at least according to the conclusions of modern scientific thought, the Native Americans' original homeland, and even hazarded a guess as to when and how the first colonists of the New World arrived.

This scholar, Father José de Acosta, was a Spanish Jesuit missionary to Peru who, among his notable credits, was one of the first and most eloquent of the Europeans to speak in defense of the rights and civil liberties of the natives of the New World. This in itself was remarkable, especially given the low opinion most Europeans had of native populations. Honour (1975:20) suggests that heresies like this, in addition to the increasing predations being wrought on Native Americans by European adventurers, were at least partially responsible for the papal bull of 1537 that affirmed or insisted the Indians were in fact "true men."

Perhaps even more remarkably, in terms of the present discussion, Father de Acosta identified the original homeland of the Native Americans as northeastern Asia. In his work entitled *Historia Natural y Moral de las Indias*, which appeared in 1590, de Acosta opined that the ancestors of the Indians arrived in the New World via a slow *pedestrian* migration from northern Asia. He even offered the suggestion that this migration may have occurred as early as 2,000 years before the arrival of the Spaniards, or ca. 2450 B.P. De Acosta's pronouncement is amazing from several perspectives, not the least of which was the fact that during his time Europeans had no notion of the general geography of northeastern Asia, which was called "Tartary" on contemporary maps. Nor would anyone have been even remotely familiar with the intricate local geography of the Bering Strait for centuries, until well after the

Danish explorer Vitus Bering penetrated this remote area in the service of the Russian tsar in 1714.

Despite de Acosta's uncannily accurate answers to the first two questions posed in the introduction to this chapter, his work was not widely read for the next three centuries. Throughout that time, many commentators still preferred more exotic pedigrees and more mysterious homelands for the first colonists of the New World, and those who perhaps otherwise would have been best suited to pursuing the matter were instead swept into attempts to resolve the controversy of the Mound-builders. In fact, it was one of the more prominent investigators of the Mound-builders, Benjamin Smith Barton, who in the late 18th century rejected his own earlier hypothesis that the mounds had been built by Danes and argued for an ulti-mate Asian provenance for the people who had constructed them. Barton's specu-lation found an ally in his contemporary Thomas Jefferson, who claimed an eastern Asian origin for Native Americans, again based on their apparent resemblance to Asians.

Space precludes a detailed discussion of how the question of Native American origins was resolved, but suffice to say it was not until the late 1890s that it became commonly accepted that the ancestors of almost all Native Americans indeed derived from Asia.

Resolution of the question of Native American origins and a gradual shift of the debate from questions of "who" to issues of precisely "from where," "how," and "when" owed to a number of significant developments in contemporary thought and American archaeology throughout the very late 19th and early 20th centuries. Perhaps foremost among these developments was the hastening of a gradual falling away of theological dogma that had either denied or obscured such basic facts as the antiquity of the Earth and humankind. Lyell's *Principles of Geology* and Darwin's *The Origin of Species* exerted a profound influence on conceptions of antiquity, and led to more critical thinking and intellectually rigorous approaches to humankind during the Pleistocene, which in turn had profound implications for American archaeology and the antiquity of humans in the New World.

Where Did the Native Americans Come From?

Despite the now all but unanimous consensus that virtually all Native Americans are ultimately of Asiatic derivation, considerable disagreement has always existed over precisely which part or parts of that continent contributed populations to the initial peopling events. Several kinds of evidence have been employed to address this issue, including anthropometric and osteometric data, dentition, gene fre-quencies and blood groups, linguistics, archaeology, and, most recently, mitochon-drial DNA (mtDNA) and Y-chromosome research. Not surprisingly, while the results of these multiple lines of inquiry have occasionally appeared to be congru-ent or mutually supportive, upon closer examination the fit between the datasets is

frequently ambiguous at best and contradictory at worst. A brief review of some of
the evidence is in order.

Anthropometry and osteometry

As noted above, several early European observers and later commentators noted
the physical resemblance between Native Americans and Asians, some of them
further observing that, compared to Old World populations, the former population
exhibited fewer differences between subgroups than were evident in Europe, Africa,
or Asia. The alleged similarity in Native American phenotypic appearance was
extended quite early to skeletal indices. Indeed, as noted by Meltzer (1993:87–88),
as early as the 1920s, Aleš Hrdlička attempted to distill a series of physical traits
putatively common to *all* Native Americans. Of course, by minimizing osteometric
variation Hrdlička was not-so-subtly promoting his own view of the recency of
human occupation of the western hemisphere by stressing the lack of time depth
for extensive variation to develop. The supposed degree of "sameness" also directly
suggested that all Native Americans descend from parent populations deriving from
a very circumscribed part of the Old World. Again, based on logic and geographical propinquity, the source area for such colonizing populations must be northeastern Asia.

Northeastern Asia is, of course, a huge place. Its geographic boundaries,
however, are well defined and it is also an area which in the recent past has exhibited considerable variation in both anthropometric and osteometric variables
(Alexseev 1979). In addition, there is also considerable variability exhibited from
the coastal east to the western interior. As a result of this heterogeneity, it is probably unwise to attempt to pinpoint on exclusively osteometric or anthropometric
grounds any one area or population that may have supplied the donor groups or
emigration points for the New World's first inhabitants.

The "where" issue becomes further clouded when the alleged "sameness" of
recently living or long-dead populations of Native Americans is critically scruti-
nized, particularly in light of the very small skeletal samples available for the earliest Americans. Despite its methodological flaws, a systematic study of American
Indian skeletal populations by Neumann (1952) resulted in the identification of
eight allegedly distinct morpho-statistical groups or clusters minimally spanning the
entire Holocene. The earliest of these clusters, which Neumann labeled *Otamid*,
was claimed to be similar to the latest skeletal material from the upper cave at Zhou-
kou-dian. Whatever the reality of Neumann's groups or his claims for a north
Chinese connection, such studies served to illustrate that much more osteometric
diversity existed among Native Americans than was allowed by Hrdlička.

Despite the fact that there are only 321 skeletal individuals older than 7000 B.P.
known in all of North America (Doran 2002:34), and that fewer than six of these
individuals are certifiably older than 10,000 B.P., there has been a renewed interest
in attempting to use osteometric data to identify a geographic source area or areas
for the First Americans. Based on exceedingly small and therefore patently

*un*representative samples in statistical terms, several scholars are convinced that most of the earliest Native American skeletal individuals are osteometrically distinct from virtually all living Native Americans (notably Chatters 2001; Doran 2002; Jantz and Owsley 1998; Neves and Blum 2001; Neves et al. 1999; Powell and Neves 1999).

Even if the relevant skeletal sample sizes were larger, the issue of osteometrically determined "relationships" remains contentious. In short, comparisons between scant skeletal assemblages of early Native Americans and contemporary or earlier Asians, or even comparisons between early Native American remains and osteo-metric indices of living Asiatic groups, may well never by themselves conclusively demonstrate relatedness, or answer the "where" question.

Dentition

To partially negate the possible temporal plasticity of osteometric attributes such as craniofacial dimensions and to alleviate the problem of small sample size, several authorities have elected to address the "where" question by examining not bones, but teeth. As long stressed by Turner (1986, 1989) and reiterated by Meltzer (1993:88–91), the study of teeth affords several distinct advantages over osteome-try. First, all anatomically modern humans have 32 teeth which bear the same pro-portions of incisors, canines, premolars, and molars. More importantly, the basic configuration of dental anatomy is inherited but, unlike craniofacial morphology or body proportions, it is not subject to extensive modification by the vicissitudes of environmental change, alterations in use patterns, perturbations in health, or dietary specializations. Perhaps as important, teeth preserve remarkably well even in set-tings where bone decomposes rapidly. Put simply, not only are there far more pre-historic teeth than skeletal parts represented in most parts of the world, they are also resistant to many of the factors that affect the stability of osteometric indices.

Population analyses using teeth have other advantages as well. Despite the fact that all humans share the same basic 32-tooth pattern, they differ in secondary dental attributes such as the presence of lateral winging or "shoveling" of the upper incisors, the number of roots on the first upper premolar and the lower first molar, the presence of an extra cusp (Carabelli's cusp) on the upper first molar, the cusp patterns of the lower first and second molars, the existence of an hypocone on the upper second molar, and the presence of a Y-groove in the second lower molar. These secondary dental characters are differentially distributed among the world's populations and their relative frequencies change through time. Hence, the com-parative study of their characteristics potentially affords the opportunity of defin-ing group relationships, both spatially and temporally.

Systematic studies of human teeth from the perspective of establishing possible genealogical affinities extend back to Hrdlička, but undoubtedly the most extensive research of this genre is attributable to Turner. Turner (1986, 1989) has examined non-metric dental features within a sample of 200,000 teeth deriving from 9,000 prehistoric individuals recovered throughout the western hemisphere. He compared them to one another as well as to tooth "populations" from Siberia, southern Asia,

Africa, and Europe. Based on these comparisons, Turner concluded that it was possible not only to distinguish Asian teeth from African and European teeth, but also to separate the Asian teeth into two separate groups.

One group, called *Sundadont*, is characteristic of teeth from southeastern Asia and is evident in the upper cave hominids from Zhou-kou-dian in China; some of the specimens in this group date as early as ca. 30,000 B.P. A second group, called *Sinodont*, allegedly evolved from this group ca. 20,000 B.P. in northern Asia. The Sinodont pattern putatively characterizes most northern Asians and *all* the populations of the western hemisphere.

Within the Americas, three Sinodont subgroups may be distinguished which differ not only from each other, but also collectively from their presumed northern Asian Sinodont "ancestors." The New World groups were originally assigned either to the Eskimo-Aleut, Greater Northwest Coast, or a third, unnamed, cluster. Penecontemporaneously with the promulgation of Greenberg's (1987) grand linguistic scheme, which is discussed below, the second and third groups were reflagged as *Na-Dene* and *Amerind*, respectively. According to Turner, these groups all descended from the same 20,000-year-old Siberian population whose ultimate "home" was northern China. Turner hypothesized that, once these immigrant Sinodonts made their way into Siberia, they bifurcated and followed different routes to arrive in and sequentially become the three Sinodont populations of the New World. The proto-Amerinds allegedly moved west from their northern Chinese homeland, then north via the Lena drainage, and ultimately crossed into the New World through northern Beringia. The proto-Na-Dene spread east generally, south of the Amerinds and north of the Eskimo-Aleuts. The Eskimo-Aleut, who initially moved east then north, followed the Amur River to its confluence with the Bering Sea. They then moved to Hokkaido, and thence passed up the Sea of Okhotsk to the Aleutian Islands. While this dental roadmap seems to offer a much greater level of geographic specificity than is afforded by the osteometric or anthropometric data, as will be discussed below, the homeland(s) of Native Americans cannot presently be determined by paleodental data alone.

Blood groups and gene frequencies

According to a recent rendition of the Human Genome Project fact sheet, the human genome contains ca. 3,165 *million* chemical nucleotide bases, with the average human gene consisting of 3,000 bases. The total number of human genes is currently estimated at 30,000–35,000, composing nucleotide bases of which 99.9 percent are almost the same in all people. The frequency, patterning, and occurrence of these genes and mutations thereof provide the basis for establishing degrees of affinity or, conversely, for demonstrating genetic distance between populations.

Although recent research suggests that New World populations are ca. 15 percent less diverse than African groups, the genetic diversity evident in Native Americans is nonetheless considerable (Szathmary 1994:17). This variability has been the object of extensive research for more than half a century. While much of this research has focused on the occurrence or frequency of fewer than a hundred genetic attributes, mostly one or another serological marker or enzyme, considerable effort has been directed at multiple genetic markers explicitly from the standpoint of determining degrees of affinity or separation. Until relatively recently, the most extensive and detailed studies on genetic variation in North America were conducted by Spuhler (1979), who examined gene frequencies of red blood cellular antigens among 53 different North American tribes and then transformed these data into indices of genetic distance. Spuhler demonstrated that there was considerable correlation between genetic profiles and specific language groups within particular culture areas. He was quick to point out, however, as have others before and since, that the association of genetic clusters with particular languages is not perfectly consistent even in areas where one would expect it, as among the Eskimo. While among the earliest to demonstrate what a recent researcher calls the "discordant variation" of New World populations (Meltzer 1993), Spuhler did not concern himself with the issues of origins or potential genetic homelands.

Like Spuhler's original research, recent non-mtDNA genetic studies of the "where" question have tended to be restricted to a relatively limited number of genetic systems. Furthermore, like Spuhler's, these studies have been hampered by widely variable datasets; the difficult of quantifying the effects of recent European, or in some cases African, admixture; and, much more basically, indeterminate amounts of inter-population gene flow that are compounded by varying degrees of inbreeding. As a result, the use of so-called classical genetic markers to establish a specific point of origin for Native Americans has often proved to be a frustrating exercise.

Despite the many pitfalls associated with the study of population affinities using classic genetic or serological markers, Szathmary has devoted a career to this enterprise (Szathmary 1994; Szathmary and Ossenberg 1978). Among her most controversial conclusions is the position that available serological data do not support Turner's tripartite model based on teeth and, furthermore, that Eskimo and Na-Dene populations exhibit much more affinity with each other than either does with most other Native American groups. Moreover, though she notes various affinities between one or another Native American and contemporary Siberian group (e.g., Nenets and St. Lawrence Eskimo), it is not presently possible to precisely answer the "where" question using serological data from only ca. 15 genetic systems and a very restricted set of sample populations. At the very least, Szathmary's research suggests multiple peopling events from northeastern Asia and multiple homelands, a theme to which we will return shortly.

Linguistics

When Columbus landed on San Salvador in 1492, Native Americans probably spoke more than 1,000 distinct languages, of which perhaps 60 percent are still spoken today. While there have been numerous schemes to classify and arrange these languages, their interrelationships presently remain controversial. Probably the first serious attempt to order Native American languages was by Gallatin (1848), who concluded that 32 distinct language families existed in aboriginal North America. In 1891 Brinton estimated the number of North American language families at ca. 80, with an equal number in South America. Although his classification was quickly and conclusively supplanted by Powell's (1891), some of the terms coined by Brinton, notably Uto-Aztecan, persisted in all subsequent classifications to this day.

Powell (1891) grouped North American languages into 58 families, a number that was soon reduced to 55 (Boas 1911), and ultimately, to six (Sapir 1921). Sapir's six macrofamilies, or superstocks, had a profound and lasting impact (Campbell and Mithon 1979:30), although his scheme was attacked by those who thought it overly reductionist. At a 1964 conference on the classification of Native American languages (Voeglin and Voeglin 1965), Sapir's six superstocks were renamed phyla and formally subdivided into language families and language isolates.

The refining of the 1964 classification continued into the early 1980s, and in 1987 Greenberg reduced Sapir's six families to three: Eskimo-Aleut, Na-Dene, and a third residual family termed Amerind. Greenberg further opined that Na-Dene and Eskimo-Aleut were both derivatives of some form of Amerind, the language spoken by the first arrivals in the New World. Although it appeared to be congruent with other lines of evidence derived from biological anthropology and archaeology, Greenberg's revolutionary scheme was quickly subjected to spirited counter-attacks, notably by Goddard and Campbell (1994) and Nichols (1995).

With a vehemence normally reserved for archaeology or politics, Goddard and Campbell assailed Greenberg's classificatory methodology – called multilateral comparison – and labeled the results derived from that methodology as "superficial," "specious," and "fundamentally flawed." They further termed his proposed Amerind grouping "a vacuous hypothesis" (Goddard and Campbell 1994:204). Among their many objections to Greenberg's scheme was the charge that tracking languages back beyond six millennia, as Greenberg does, is simply impossible in light of the questionable comparative methodology that was employed.

Interestingly, another of Greenberg's chief critics, Nichols, also purported to be able to generate language relationships in the remote past or at least beyond 6,000 years, but with a methodology and results very different from those of Greenberg. Space precludes a formal explanation of Nichol's position, but suffice to note that, by examining the two dozen or so grammatical regularities within a language (like verb position in a sentence or ergativity [i.e., the use of prefixes or suffixes to modify a verb]) and mapping their distribution, it is possible to establish linguistic relationships both in time and through time. Using this approach, Nichols concluded that there are 51 linguistic stocks and 69 language families in North America, and that multiple migrations were involved in the initial peopling of this hemisphere.

In the present context of attempting to circumscribe the source area(s) for these peopling pulses, it actually matters very little if one sides with Greenberg or Nichols. The reason is simple: despite claims to the contrary – and with the solitary exception of Eskimo, which is spoken by Eskimos on both sides of the Bering Strait – *no* Native American language family has even been linked conclusively to an Asiatic language family anywhere (cf. Szathmary 1994). In short, linguistics provides no more help in refining the "where" answer than any of the other datasets discussed above.

Archaeology

Even if osteometric, anthropometric, or linguistic evidence points to a specific area of eastern or northeastern Asia as the potential area of origin for the first colonists of the New World, confirmation of this postulate must be supported by archaeological data that demonstrate this population movement. Lamentably, such data do not presently exist.

While it is generally conceded that hominid populations are present in the more temperate portions of eastern Asia by no later than 1 million years ago (Klein 1999), the initial peopling of the colder sections of northeastern Asia remains contentious. The initial penetration of the more northerly environs of eastern Asia, however, is the subject of considerable dispute. Claims for a very early human presence at Diring-Iuriakh in the Lena Basin were initially published by Mochanov (1988). An area of ca. 12,000 m^2 was excavated between 1982 and 1984, yielding 3,166 artifacts from 16 putatively "discrete" clusters. All of the putative tools fit conformably into the eastern Asian tool tradition, but the dating of this site is very controversial. Initial claims of an age of 3.2–1.8 million years B.P. were systematically revised upward. While some scholars, notably Mochanov, still believe the site is at least 1 million years old, others (e.g., Derevianko 1998) believe the site is only ca. 270,000 years old. Although many Western scholars dispute even this more recent assessment, it is certainly not impossible that this site may reflect the initial peopling of far northern Asia, as claimed by Derevianko (1998:357). While a few other sites of this putative age exist in northern Asia, their dating is even more controversial but, collectively, there is some suggestion of an ephemeral human foothold in the far north by the late Middle Pleistocene.

To date, and again despite claims to the contrary, no comparably old material has been found within striking distance of the Asian side of the Bering Strait land bridge. Within Yakutia, Mochanov (1977) has defined a D'uktai culture based on the excavation of one closed site, the type locality D'uktai Cave, and a series of open river terrace sites on the middle Aldan and contiguous drainages. Mochanov claims all of these sites are manifestations of the same Upper Paleolithic culture, a claim that has been vigorously disputed (Derevianko 1998). Mochanov also claims an antiquity of ca. 35,000 B.P. for the onset of this complex. Unfortunately, D'uktai Cave is no older than 14,000–12,000 B.P. and almost all of the D'uktai open sites are extensively disturbed and/or their contents have been redeposited. Recent assessments of the age of this entity, whatever it represents, suggest an antiquity no older than 18,000 B.P. (Yi and Clark 1985).

Whatever its age, the artifact assemblages from the D'uktai sites, which include large and small (but not micro-) blades, bifacial projectile points, and an assortment of retouched pieces, do not conclusively demonstrate technological affinities to *any* early North American culture. While elements of D'uktai technology are reminiscent of both Clovis era and pre-Clovis technology (Adovasio 1993; Adovasio et al. 1988; Adovasio et al. 1999), the ties are very general, and the D'uktai artifact suite cannot presently be used to settle the issue of a specific northeastern Asian homeland for the Native Americans.

Molecular biology

Over the past decade, arguably the most productive lines of research for identifying the potential source(s) of New World colonists have derived from molecular biology. Within that academic arena, studies involving two genomes, mtDNA and the Y-chromosome, afford the best lenses through which to view the "where" question (and, as discussed below, perhaps the "how" and "when" issues as well). Following Schurr (2002), from which much of the following is summarized, both of these genomes are uniparentally inherited and non-recombinant, and each possesses a series of different markers that can assist in identifying and defining genetic lineages within human populations. By analyzing the variation in these genomes and establishing their temporal sequencing, considerable insights may be gleaned about the identity and derivation of the First Americans.

As is by now well known, human mtDNA presents a unique vehicle for analysis because of its exclusive transmission through females (male mtDNA is deleted from sperm cells at fertilization), the attendant lack of recombination, and the accumulation of mutations in a linear fashion. As noted by Schurr (2002:62), another benefit is that mtDNA mutations tend to correlate well with specific geographic regions in which the mutations first appear. Because of all these attributes – coupled with the fact that mtDNA profiles can often provide a very accurate record of genetic drift, population movements, and/or population isolation – mtDNA studies provide an unusually acute way to address "where" issues.

Two regions of the mtDNA genome have been extensively studied in human groups. These include the majority portion (94 percent) of the genome, which encompasses all of its coding functions, and the minority portion in which mtDNA replication is controlled. As detailed by Schurr (2002:62–64), two different analytical methods have been employed with mtDNA. One technique, termed restriction fragment length polymorphism (RFLP) analysis, is directed at the coding region of the genome, and the other involves the direct sequencing of a segment (HVR-1) of the control region.

Using RFLP analysis, researchers have defined haplogroups A, B, C, D, and X, which represent, in effect, the surviving genetic lineages of the founding populations represented in living Native American groups. Most Native Americans belong to haplogroups A–D. These haplogroups include almost all aboriginal skeletal populations from which mtDNA has been extracted. The last haplogroup, X, and specific HVR-1 lineages linked with it, are much rarer and, as discussed below, its characteristics and presence in Native American populations have been the subject of no little debate. All four of the major haplogroups occur in populations that presently live in North, Central, and South America. From north to south, haplogroup A decreases in frequency, haplogroups C and D increase, and no cline is discernable for haplogroup B, which is most common in the Greater American Southwest. Haplogroup X is found exclusively in North American groups, especially among Algonquian speakers.

Studies of the Y-chromosome, which is uniparentally transmitted paternally and also accumulates mutations in a linear, time-transgressive fashion (although slower than mtDNA), allow for the delineation of Y-haplotypes or chromosome lineages based on a number of different marker systems. This has resulted in the generation of a series of Y-chromosome lineages far more numerous than those defined by mtDNA. Two of these Y-chromosome paternal lineages, M3 and M45, are widely distributed in the Americas. M3 occurs in high (56 percent) frequencies in most Native American groups and exhibits an increasing north-to-south cline, while M45 is also well represented (29 percent) in North, Central, and South America. The remaining 5 percent of Y-chromosome lineages exhibits a much more restricted distribution.

The distribution of the New World mtDNA haplogroups and Y-chromosome lineages in the Old World probably provides the best answer to the "where" question presently available to students of the peopling of the New World. As Schurr (2002:74) succinctly observes, all of the current molecular biology studies confirm an Asian origin for Native American populations and, hence, directly validate de Acosta's prescient prediction of over 300 years ago. Furthermore, most of these studies indicate that the Native American founding populations derived from a region that extends from central Siberia to the Altai mountains on the west to southeastern Siberia and northern China on the east. The Y-chromosome data specifically suggest a south-central and eastern Siberian contribution, as does a conservative reading of the Old World distribution of the X haplotype, which is apparently trans-Eurasiatic in occurrence. A more extreme view of the source of the X haplotype is discussed below.

How Did the Native Americans Get To North America?

In our view, the question of "how" is composed of two elements: (1) which geographic route or routes did human populations use in entering the New World, and (2) what were the environmental conditions and techno-cultural mechanisms that allowed these routes to be followed? Until very recently, only two basic routes and a combination thereof have been advanced to address the geography of the colonization issue. By far the longest-lived of these alternatives has been the so-called interior route or "Ice-free Corridor" hypothesis, which in its first foreshadowing actually goes back to de Acosta.

In this still enduring scenario, colonizing populations crossed the Bering–Chukchi shelf, also known as the Bering land bridge or Beringia, when the sea level had fallen due to glacial activity. It is interesting to note that, at its narrowest point, the present Bering Strait is only 80 km wide, and that a modest sea-level drop of only 46 m would expose a land connection between Siberia and Alaska via St. Lawrence Island (Hopkins 1967). An additional drop of 50 m would create a second narrow connection north of the first, and a full glacial sea-level depression of 100–150 m or more would expose the entire shelf, which measures almost 1,500 km in width from north to south.

In the classic rendering of the pedestrian traverse land bridge/interior route scenario, migrants to the New World crossed it dry-shod (again as foreshadowed by de Acosta), arrived in the never-glaciated Bering Refugium of interior Alaska, and then perambulated down the MacKenzie River valley in an ice-free corridor between the serpentine Cordilleran ice sheet (which covered the mountain spine of western North America) and the much more massive Laurentide ice sheet (which covered most of Canada and a substantial portion of the eastern United States). A slight variation of this scenario again proposes that populations emigrated across the land bridge and then proceeded south through interior British Columbia, possibly during an interstadial or even an interglacial.

An alternative route initially advanced by Fladmark (1978), long championed by Gruhn (1994), and more recently endorsed by Dixon (1999), suggests that populations migrated into the New World along the coast of Siberia and the south coast of the land bridge (as suggested years earlier by Debets [1951]) and thence down the Pacific Northwest Coast. Though proponents of this scenario envision some pedestrian traverse, most of the journey is presumed to have been by boat. A third alternative envisions the utilization of *both* the interior and coastal routes perhaps (but not necessarily) synchronously and presumably by different populations of colonists.

Integral to the interior scenario is the equally (if not more) persistent notion that early populations arrived in North America, essentially unwittingly, by following great herds of big game animals, like mammoth, upon which their highly focused and specialized hunting lifeway was presumed to be utterly dependent. Moreover, this same set of circumstances was presumed to hold for their aboriginal northeastern Asian homeland *and* the New World territory of their Paleoindian progeny. This specialized big-game-hunter scenario, with its muscular, fur-clad men wielding stone-tipped spears to slay large mammals, is the unfortunate legacy of 150 years of paleoanthropological research conducted largely, until recently, by men (Adovasio and Page 2002). This ultimately simplistic, if not misogynist, worldview is predicated on and facilitated by a disproportionate interpretive emphasis on putative large animal "kill" sites where one or another Pleistocene beast was allegedly dispatched, and on two far more subtle prejudices. Constantly lurking in the background of the interior scenario is: (1) a longstanding bias against boat travel by later Pleistocene populations, and (2) an almost total ignorance of the role of non-durable technologies, especially plant-fiber-derived products, in the adaptive success of hunter-gatherers in all environmental settings, specifically including the far north (Adovasio et al. 2001). That both of those biases should continue to characterize mainstream American, European, and, for that matter, world archaeological thought is enigmatic – and vexatious, in our opinion – especially given the demonstrated antiquity of prehistoric plant fiber manipulation in both the Old and New Worlds (Adovasio et al. 2001; Soffer et al. 2000) and the even greater time depth now known or strongly implied for watercraft.

Basketry and textiles, specifically including clothing and containers, are now well documented for various Upper Paleolithic populations of Europe, and their manufacture and use presently extend back to 27,000–29,000 B.P., and tools suitable for their production are even older (Soffer et al. 2000). In many of the Upper Paleolithic sites yielding basketry/textiles, the presence of cordage and cordage byproducts, especially netting, is also documented. The coexistence of these interrelated industries early in the Upper Paleolithic may well prove to be a critical component in the behavioral repertoire of anatomical moderns and a signature artifact of behavioral modernity (Adovasio et al. 2001; Soffer et al. 2000). The early elaboration of basketry, textiles, cordage, and netting has potentially profound implications because of their multifaceted roles in food procurement, storage, and transportation. Netting, in particular, with its potential applications in the manufacture of bags as well as hunting, fishing, and fowling nets, affords a vehicle for the nonconfrontational, large-scale or mass harvesting of diverse terrestrial, marine, and avian fauna. Moreover, net hunting provides a medium which, based on ethnographic analogs, frequently involves individuals of *both* sexes and *all* ages. Additionally, since the manufacture of most plant-fiber-based technologies is usually associated with female labor, the hitherto ignored role of females in the colonization process is brought into very sharp relief (Adovasio et al. 2001).

The implications of the existence of watercraft and, therefore, of population movement by boat, are equally profound but in a different way. Recent research suggests that open-water boat use is far more ancient than virtually anyone had imagined, with evidence that this was occurring by 880,000–781,000 B.P. in Indonesia (Sondaar et al. 1994; see also Ames, this volume). Given the implied existence of watercraft in the early Middle Pleistocene, it is scarcely surprising that the first peopling of Australia, which was never connected to mainland Southeast Asia, also required watercraft. Indeed, aboriginal travel to Australia necessitates the crossing of 90 km of open, deep water. Since controversial dates place this event as early as 60,000 B.P. and, furthermore, since humans are definitely in Australia by 40,000 B.P., the colonization of this continent demonstrates the pivotal role of watercraft in the later Upper Pleistocene movement of human populations to hitherto unoccupied areas.

If boats were in regular use in open Southeast Asian waters 40,000–60,000 years ago, their availability to the earliest coastal populations in north Asian waters is highly likely. If the use of watercraft extends back more than 10 times that far, then it is a certainty that the first northeastern Asians had access to boats. Needless to add, the accessibility of boats to the first colonists of the New World renders *all* discussion of the timing of the exposure or inundation of the land bridge, or of the opening or closing of the interior corridor, moot.

By stressing the potential roles of fiber artifacts and boats in the colonization process, we are not minimizing the importance of tailored fur clothing, the development of weatherproof housing, the elaboration of food storage and preservation capabilities, or even the invention of atlatls and projectile weaponry in facilitating the successful penetration of the New World. All of these innovations doubtlessly facilitated the movement into and, thereafter, the success of the first arrivals in the New World; moreover, they also help to explain "how" this momentous event occurred. Indeed, successful colonization could not have occurred without these cold weather technological innovations. Significantly, many of these technological activities – notably, the tailoring of clothing – are the normal province of females. If fur-clad, spear-wielding males remain an enduring part of the colonizing saga, the fact that they would be naked without female agency should also be recalled.

As to the archaeological evidence of which route or routes were actually employed for entering the New World, it is all very circumstantial. As is discussed below, none of the earliest known North American sites is located directly proximal to the American side of the Bering land bridge (Hamilton and Goebel 1999) nor within the Bering Refugium. Additionally, despite the recent discovery of submerged sites in coastal British Columbia and the potential for even deeper and older sites in the same area (Dixon 1999; Fedje 2002), none of them is presently old enough to conclusively demonstrate an early use of the coastal route. Similarly, there are no very early sites in the interior corridor (Wilson and Burns 1999; see also Ames, this volume).

In short, the only real evidence that any of the hypothetical routes into the New World were ever used at all is the presence of humans in the New World. Presently, we simply do not know which route or routes were actually followed and, as discussed below, how early or if they were used contemporaneously.

As a final point, but by no means an afterthought, it should be noted that some American scholars (Stanford and Bradley 2000) have recently resurrected and elaborated an old idea (Mason 1962) and are now offering a fourth entry possibility. Stanford and Bradley have suggested a population movement by boat from coastal southwestern Europe – that is, Iberia, not Siberia. This trans-Atlantic route, interestingly, would also have provided another point of entry for haplogroup X populations into the Americas. Suffice to say, however, that acceptable proof for the utilization of this route is presently lacking (cf. Strauss 2000), though, technically, such a voyage was certainly feasible.

When Did Native Americans Arrive in North America?

If the answers to the "where" and "how" and, for a few, even the "who" questions remain unacceptably vague, the answer to the "when" query is presently almost as intractable as it was 500 years ago. As noted above, de Acosta provided the first temporal benchmark for this event or series of events when he speculated that Native Americans had arrived 2,000 years before the Spanish entrada. Since then, the temporal pendulum has swung back and forth between an abbreviated chronology for a human presence in the New World and a very deep antiquity.

Though the early history of this controversy makes for fascinating reading (see Adovasio and Page 2002; Meltzer 1993), space precludes detailed treatment of this remarkably contentious period in American archaeological research. That said, the modern and even more vituperative timing debate begins with the pivotal and truly watershed discoveries near Folsom, New Mexico, in 1926 (see Figure 1.1). There, in a place called Wild Horse Arroyo, artifacts of indisputably human manufacture were found for the first time in direct association with the remains of an extinct form of bison in unimpeachable stratigraphic contexts of Late Pleistocene age. This seminal discovery – or, more accurately, this refinement, elaboration, and confirmation of a discovery that had actually been made 18 years earlier by an observant ranch foreman and former slave, George McJunkin – was the first in a series of events that would gauge a new time of arrival for and create an enduring image of the First Americans. Moreover, this age and lifeway characterization would become the received wisdom concerning Native American origins that would endure for more than half a century.

Folsom was interpreted as a kill site, based on the conclusive evidence that the thin and delicately bilaterally channel-flaked or fluted points, ultimately named after this locality, were clearly used to dispatch late Ice Age bison. A few years later, another discovery at Blackwater Draw in northeastern New Mexico identified both additional Folsom points (again associated with bison) and – from deeper levels – a generally larger and coarser fluted lanceolate point, this time in association with

2 cm

Figure 2.1 A fluted Clovis projectile point

mammoths. This portion of the site, called Blackwater Locality Number 1, would become the type locus for an archaeological manifestation named after a nearby town, Clovis. The signature artifact of this archaeological entity, the Clovis fluted projectile point, was soon documented across wide expanses of North America and even down into Central and, in attenuated form, South America. Although the point type usually occurred as a solitary surface find, its frequent recovery in contexts that included Pleistocene megafauna reinforced the idea that its makers were specialized big-game hunters (Figure 2.1).

With the appearance of radiocarbon dating in 1948 and its subsequent application to both Folsom and Clovis sites, the ages of these sequent and obviously related manifestations was initially fixed at ca. 10,500–10,000 B.P. and 11,500–11,000 B.P., respectively. As discussed below, these dates would subsequently be revised and tightened; however, the "old" initial date for Clovis of 11,500 B.P. became the benchmark for the first peopling of the western hemisphere. For a faithful few, this date remains the benchmark.

Because of the widespread, but by no means universal, North American distribution of the Clovis point type (Haynes 1964), its temporal circumscription to a relatively narrow time period, and its co-occurrence with extinct and often large fauna, the Clovis point became the lithic ensign or symbol of what came to be

1 cm

Figure 2.2 An unfluted Miller Lanceolate projectile point from Meadowcroft Rockshelter

viewed, almost unanimously, as a highly mobile and unitary "culture" that putatively specialized in the systematic predation of Pleistocene megafauna. This culture was formally defined by Haynes, and a series of other durable diagnostics was added to the distinctive point to constitute a diagnostic Clovis artifact suite (Haynes 1964, 1993).

Because of the apparent synchrony of the spread of Clovis and the widespread extinction of Ice Age megafauna, a causal relationship was presumed to exist between that extinction episode and Clovis. In a series of articles, Martin developed and refined the notion of Clovis as the perpetrator of a veritable "blitzkrieg" of megafauna predation which, in the space of less than 500 radiocarbon years, caused the extinction of most of the Pleistocene megafauna and led to the peopling of the entire hemisphere (Martin 1967, 1990).

Despite the fact that the colonization of no other part of the world paralleled the posited rapid spread of Clovis, the Clovis First model, as it is now known, was widely considered to answer the "when" question and has enjoyed a remarkable tenure for several reasons. First, it appeared to be supported both by Greenberg's tripartite language classification (in which the ancestral Amerinds are equated with Clovis) and also by Turner's dental chronology (in which the earliest Sinodonts [the Amerinds] are likewise considered to be Clovis). Secondly, the spread of Clovis seemed to fit paleoenvironmental and paleoclimatic data, which suggested that the Ice-free Corridor was impassable until just before the Clovis efflorescence. Thirdly – and, as far as we are concerned, far more importantly – before 1970, no archaeological site or complex that was definitively older than the Clovis horizon had been identified in North or South America.

The Clovis First model began to unravel in the mid- to late 1970s, however, with the discovery of sites like Meadowcroft Rockshelter in southwestern Pennsylvania (Adovasio et al. 1977, 1984; Adovasio et al. 1988; Adovasio et al. 1990; Adovasio and Page 2002; Adovasio and Pedler 2004; Carlisle and Adovasio 1982). This locality yielded artifacts radically different from Clovis material culture and recovered from radiocarbon-dated contexts at least 1,000–2,500 radiocarbon years earlier than the Clovis First model's presumed crossing of the Bering Strait.

Meadowcroft Rockshelter is a deeply stratified, multicomponent site on the north bank of Cross Creek, a tributary of the Ohio River, southwest of Pittsburgh, Pennsylvania. The 11 strata at Meadowcroft, which represent the longest occupational sequence in the New World, yielded a remarkable corpus of artifactual, floral, and faunal data anchored by 52 stratigraphically consistent radiocarbon dates. Human use of the site minimally extends from ca. 12,500–12,000 B.C. to A.D. 1776. The earliest occupants at Meadowcroft ascribe to the Miller complex (Adovasio 1998), a pioneer population of generalized hunter-gatherers with a sophisticated lithic technology based on the production of blade tools produced from polyhedral blade cores and also characterized by the manufacture of a distinctive unfluted projectile point form called the Miller Lanceolate (Figure 2.2). Significantly, the extant paleoenvironmental data indicate that the site's earliest inhabitants operated in an environment not radically different from that of present times (Adovasio et al. 1984).

In addition to Meadowcroft, other pre-Clovis sites have been discovered at widely separated loci in North America, all of which are demonstrably as old as or significantly older than Clovis, and none appears to be related to that entity. Significantly, the lifeways reflected at several of these sites reflect the same sort of generalized hunting and gathering pattern evinced at Meadowcroft.

Based on data from archaeological sites that are penecontemporaneous with and substantially older than Clovis, it is now clear that the first Paleoindians entered the New World well before Clovis, and despite whatever climatic or environmental barriers putatively existed to hinder this movement. How much earlier this entry occurred remains the intractable part of the "when" question.

Current interpretations of the linguistic (Nichols 1995) and mtDNA/Y-chromosome data (Schurr 2002) suggest a great time depth, perhaps up to 35,000 years for human populations in the New World. To date, however, no site has been conclusively demonstrated to be older than ca. 16,000 B.P. But even if this date is considered to represent the current baseline, the initial crossing of the Bering–Chukchi shelf may well have taken place *before* the last glacial maximum, which is appears to have occurred ca. 20,000 B.P. (Madsen 2004).

Whenever they arrived, these First Americans clearly belonged to several distinct cultural traditions and may well have originated from different parts of northeastern Asia. Additionally, their percolation into the New World appears not to have been a single movement but rather a series of peopling incursions, some of which doubtlessly failed to survive. In addition to the traditional pedestrian route across the interior of the glacially exposed Bering land bridge, a combination of land and sea travel almost certainly occurred on the southern margin of the bridge. Thereafter, movement south could have occurred through the so-called Ice-free Corridor as well as down the Pacific Coast, again via a combination of land and sea travel.

Discussion: The First Americans

The answers to the relatively simple questions posed in the introduction to this chapter, as well as the intellectual and methodological approaches employed in answering those questions, have undergone exhaustive refinement since they were first asked over 500 years ago. From our contemporary perspective, it is now clear that the earliest answers to these questions, as brilliantly prescient and intuitive as some of them may have been, in the final analysis were mere stabs in the dark. At the same time it must be admitted, however, that while multiple lines of modern scientific inquiry have provided better answers – and, in many cases, have generated even more complex questions – truly definitive answers to at least some of these questions have remained elusive.

Perhaps the best-answered questions are: who were the Late Pleistocene colonists of North America, and where were they from? Although some disagreement continues to exist, it is more or less accepted by most archaeologists that the First Americans derived from northern or northeastern Asia. The issue of *precisely where* in that vast portion of the world's largest continent is a great deal more contentious, but anthropometric, osteometric, paleodental, and molecular biological analyses strongly suggest a northeastern Asian derivation. As that region encompasses millions of hectares, however, scholars can hardly lay claim to any precision in this regard, and a concomitantly vast amount of research remains to be done on population movements east of the Bering Strait during the Late Pleistocene.

The questions of how and when the First Americans arrived in the New World have produced more hypotheses than definitive answers, and adequately addressing these questions has been hampered by a lack of acceptable archaeological data. Archaeological evidence supporting the hypothesized route(s) employed by the pioneering population is circumstantial, and there are still no sites known in greater Beringia that even suggest, much less conclusively demonstrate, when the event or events occurred. In short, whatever the precise date of the initial peopling pulse into the New World – and without regard to whether those people walked, paddled, or even sailed – the event is all but invisible archaeologically. This invisibility is understandable, considering that First Americans population densities were undoubtedly thin and, hence, less likely to leave an imprint on the landscape. In fact, it is quite unlikely that the arrival date of the First Americans will ever be known and perhaps even less likely that human remains or artifacts associated with these colonists will be recovered.

What is quite likely if not certain, on the other hand – as Meltzer (1993) and others have noted – is that the Clovis phenomenon was not the beginning of the peopling process but, rather, the beginning of the archaeologically visible portion of that process. Very instructive in this regard are the observations of Housley and his associates regarding the initial penetration of formerly glaciated northern Europe at the end of the Pleistocene (Housley et al. 1997). In an article that is rarely cited by North American scholars, these researchers stress that it took nearly 4,000 years for humans to spread north over a distance of ca. 1,300 km into a region that they *already knew existed* – which was not a condition faced by the First Americans and hardly suggests the kind of blitzkrieg posited by Martin (1967), as briefly discussed above.

More importantly, Housley et al. (1997) also stress the nature of the evidence for the initial penetration of the northern third of the deglaciated European continent, which has a direct bearing on the peopling of North America. The earliest northern European sites are sufficiently few, small, widely dispersed, and invisible that Housley et al. (1997) ascribe the populations that used them to a Pioneer phase of colonization. This condition would persist for several thousand years, as would its archaeological ephemerality, until populations began to increase significantly, sites became larger and more common, and the threshold of visibility had been crossed. At this point, following this scheme, humans would have passed into what Housley et al. (1997) call the Residential phase of colonization, which is widely and more readily detectable on the landscape. (On a visit to Meadowcroft, Clive Gamble, one of Housley's co-authors, suggested that the Clovis horizon was the threshold of visibility in North America and that sites like Meadowcroft, Cactus Hill, and Monte Verde represent the much more rarely observed Pioneer phase.)

The question remains, however: what precisely is the Clovis horizon? Now even more tightly circumscribed to ca. 11,200–11,000 B.P., or slightly later in eastern North America, Clovis continues to be viewed by traditionalists as much more than simply a distinctive technological suite. Even those who are well disposed to a deep human antiquity in this hemisphere (e.g., Frison 1999; Frison and Walker 1990) continue to think of Clovis as a unitary sociopolitical and, presumably, genetic and linguistic entity as well. Also inherent in this view is the perception that Clovis populations were first and foremost big-game hunters who played *the* critical role in North American Pleistocene extinctions.

The evidence, however, does not support this interpretation. As Meltzer (1988, 1993) and Stanford (1978) pointed out long ago, there was not one single specialized Clovis adaptation or culture, there were many. Clovis was not a unitary lifeway but, rather, a brief artifact-signaled moment when many *different* lifeways appear to have coexisted. Like the succeeding Archaic period, which is artificially separated from the time under discussion by only ca. 1,000 years, at least some of the Clovis era lifeways employed broad-spectrum subsistence strategies. Although some of these populations undoubtedly could, and in fact did, kill Pleistocene megafauna, a detailed reanalysis of all of the alleged Clovis era kill sites definitively indicates that the available evidence simply does not support a significant or, indeed, detectable Clovis role in the extinction process (Grayson and Meltzer 2003).

As of this writing, it is not really known what Clovis was or even where or when it crystallized. No early Clovis points have been identified in Alaska (Hamilton and Goebel 1999), the Ice-free Corridor (Wilson and Burns 1999), or along the Pacific Coast. Based on sheer density, some scholars (e.g., Mason 1962) have suggested that the Clovis projectile point form originated in the American Southeast and then spread rapidly to other parts of North America. Indeed, Stanford and Bradley (2000) posit that Clovis's genesis in the Southeast may have been stimulated by the trans-Atlantic movement of Upper Paleolithic Solutrean populations, as discussed above.

Wherever and under whatever circumstances it originated, the reasons for the rapid spread of the Clovis point or its many variants remain enigmatic. The diagnostic fluting of Clovis and later Folsom points conveyed no particular advantage over their unfluted counterparts in the hafting process, nor in facilitating the penetration of tipped shafts into the hides of animals. Often found unused in special caches (cf. Butler 1963; Frison 1991, 1999), Clovis points may have had much more social than technological significance. Indeed, as Meltzer (1993) suggests, these much-debated items may have played a greater role outside the techno-subsistence arena, perhaps as social bonding devices between far-flung groups.

Whatever Clovis was, it was not alone. Penecontemporaneous complexes in North America appear to include Nenana, a possible Clovis ancestor candidate in Alaska (see earlier); Goshen in the northwestern Plains (Frison 1991, 1999); and the so-called stemmed point complexes of the Great Basin, the Columbia and Snake River Plains, and the Pacific Northwest (Bryan and Tuohy 1999). In at least two of these cases – that is, Nenana and many of the stemmed point sites – the classic Clovis point is totally absent. Whatever their relationship to whatever Clovis is, it is clear that Clovis is *not* the ancestor of all of them.

By the end of Clovis times (ca. 11,000 B.P.), all of unglaciated North America was populated, albeit thinly in most places. Interestingly, although many of the excavated Paleoindian sites are large mammal-processing localities (Frison 1999), extensive multi-seasonal campsites attest to the rapid increase of populations in later Paleoindian times.

By ca. 10,750–10,450 B.P., Clovis point-making populations in western North America had been succeeded by makers of Folsom points; those populations were in turn succeeded by makers of a wide array of delicately pressure flaked points collectively called Plano (see Frison [1999] for a detailed discussion of these complexes). These later Paleoindians were, like their predecessors, hunter-gatherers who manifested widely varying degrees of mobility and subsistence strategies, which in many areas included the systematic predation of both extinct (*Bison antiquus*) and modern (*Bison bison*) bison, usually via communal hunting techniques. Despite a focus on bison, these later Paleoindian groups also exploited a wide array of small to medium-sized game as well as plants, waterfowl, and many other non-megafaunal resources. Indeed, many of these groups led broad-spectrum foraging lifeways that were virtually identical to those of the generally later Western Archaic populations that replaced them or into which they evolved ca. 9950–8950 B.P.

In eastern North America, Paleoindians only occasionally, if ever, hunted mastodon (Grayson and Meltzer 2003), and more often focused on a mixed diet of caribou, white-tailed deer, elk, smaller game, fish, and a broad assortment of plants (Carr et al. 2001; Lepper 1999; Meltzer 1988). As in western North America, the Paleoindian period in eastern North America grades almost imperceptibly into the Eastern Archaic, which begins ca. 8950–7950 B.P. (Anderson and Sassaman 1996; Prufer et al. 2001; Raber et al. 1998; Sullivan and Prezzano 2001).

ACKNOWLEDGMENTS

The authors wish to acknowledge J. S. Illingworth, Mercyhurst Archaeological Institute, for providing typing support and other assistance in the preparation of this chapter.

REFERENCES

Adovasio, J. M., 1993 The ones that will not go away: A biased view of pre-Clovis populations in the New World. In *From Kostenki to Clovis: Upper Paleolithic–Paleo-Indian Adaptations*, O. Soffer and N. D. Praslov, eds. Pp. 119–218. New York: Plenum Press.

——1998 Miller complex. In *Archaeology of Prehistoric Native America*. G. Gibbon, ed. Pp. 524–527. New York: Garland.

Adovasio, J. M., A. T. Boldurian, and R. C. Carlisle, 1988 Who are those guys? Some biased thoughts on the initial peopling of the New World. In *Americans Before Columbus: Ice-Age*

Origins. R. C. Carlisle, ed. Pp. 45–61. Ethnology Monographs 12. Pittsburgh: Department of Anthropology, University of Pittsburgh.

Adovasio, J. M., J. Donahue, R. C. Carlisle, K. Cushman, R. Stuckenrath, and P. Wiegman, 1984 Meadowcroft Rockshelter and the Pleistocene/Holocene Transition in Southwestern Pennsylvania. H. H. Genoways and M. R. Dawson, eds. Pp. 347–369. Carnegie Museum of Natural History Special Publication 8. Pittsburgh: Carnegie Museum of Natural History.

Adovasio, J. M., J. Donahue, and R. Stuckenrath, 1990 The Meadowcroft Rockshelter radio-carbon chronology 1975–1990. *American Antiquity* 55(2), 348–354.

Adovasio, J. M., J. D. Gunn, J. Donahue, and R. Stuckenrath, 1977 Meadowcroft Rock-shelter: A 16,000 year chronicle. In *Amerinds and their Paleoenvironments in Northeastern North America*. W. S. Newman and B. Salwen, eds. Pp. 137–159. Annals of the New York Academy of Sciences, vol. 288. New York: New York Academy of Sciences.

Adovasio, J. M., D. C. Hyland, and O. Soffer, 2001 Perishable technology and early human populations in the New World. In *On Being First: Cultural Innovation and Environmental Consequences of First Peopling*. J. Gillespie, S. Tupakka, and C. de Mille, eds. Pp. 201–221. Proceedings of the 31st Annual Chacmool Conference. Calgary: Chacmool, Archaeolog-ical Association of the University of Calgary.

Adovasio, J. M., and J. Page, 2002 *The First Americans: In Pursuit of Archaeology's Greatest Mystery*. New York: Random House.

Adovasio, J. M., and D. R. Pedler, 2004 Pre-Clovis Sites and their implications for human occupation before the last glacial maximum. In *Entering America: Northeast Asia and Beringia before the Last Glacial Maximum*. D. B. Madsen, ed. Salt Lake City: University of Utah Press (in press).

Adovasio, J. M., D. R. Pedler, J. Donahue, and R. Stuckenrath, 1999 No vestige of a begin-ning nor prospect for an end: Two decades of debate on Meadowcroft Rockshelter. In *Ice Age People of North America*. R. Bonnichsen and K. L. Turnmire, eds. Pp. 416–431. Corvallis: Oregon State University Press.

Alexseev, V. P., 1979 Anthropometry of Siberia peoples. In *The First Americans: Origins, Affini-ties, and Adaptations*. W. S. Laughlin and A. B. Harper, eds. Pp. 57–90. New York: Gustav Fischer.

Anderson, D. G., and K. E. Sassaman, eds., 1996 *The Paleoindian and Early Archaic South-east*. Tuscaloosa: University of Alabama Press.

Boas, F., 1911 Introduction. In *Handbook of American Indian Languages*. Pp. 1–83. Bulletin 40. Washington, DC: Government Printing Office.

Bonnichsen, R., and K. Turnmire, 1999 An introduction to the peopling of the Americas. In *Ice Age Peoples of North America: Environments, Origins, and Adaptations of the First Ameri-cans*. R. Bonnichsen and K. L. Turnmire, eds. Pp. 1–26. Corvallis: Oregon State Univer-sity Press.

Brace, C. L., 2002 Background for the peopling of the New World: Old World roots for the New World branches. *Athena Review* 3(2), 53–61, 103–104.

Bryan, A. L., and D. R. Tuohy, 1999 Prehistory of the Great Basin/Snake River Plain to about 8,500 years ago. In *Ice Age Peoples of North America: Environments, Origins, and Adaptations of the First Americans*. R. Bonnichsen and K. L. Turnmire, eds. Pp. 249–263. Corvallis: Oregon State University Press.

Butler, B. R., 1963 An early man site at Big Camas Prairie, south-central Idaho. *Tebiwa* 6, 22–33.

Campbell, L., and M. Mithon, eds., 1979 *The Languages of Native America: Historical and Comparative Assessment*. Austin: University of Texas Press.

Carlisle, R. C., and J. M. Adovasio, eds., 1982 *Meadowcroft: Collected Papers on the Archaeology of Meadowcroft Rockshelter and the Cross Creek Drainage*. Pittsburgh: Department of Anthropology, University of Pittsburgh.

Carr, K. W., J. M. Adovasio, and D. R. Pedler, 2001 Paleoindian populations in trans-Appalachia: The view from Pennsylvania. In *Archaeology of the Appalachian Highlands*. L. P. Sullivan and S. C. Prezzano, eds. Pp. 67–87. Knoxville: University of Tennessee Press.

Chatters, J. C., 2001 *Ancient Encounters, Kennewick Man and the First Americans*. New York: Simon & Schuster.

Debets, G. F., 1951 *Anthropological Investigations in the Kamchatka Region*. Moscow: Trudy IE.

Derevianko, A. P., 1998 The Paleolithic of Siberia: New Discoveries and Interpretations. Urbana: University of Illinois Press.

Dixon, E. J., 1999 *Bones, Boats and Bison: Archeology and the First Colonization of Western North America*. Albuquerque: University of New Mexico Press.

Doran, G. H., ed., 2002 *Windover: Multidisciplinary Investigations of an Early Archaic Florida Cemetery*. Tallahassee: University Press of Florida.

Fedje, D., 2002 The early post-glacial history of the northern Northwest Coast: A view from Haida Gwaii and Hecate Strait. *Athena Review* 3(2), 28–30, 100.

Fladmark, K. R., 1978 The feasibility of the Northwest Coast as a migration route for early man. In *Early Man in America from a Circum-Pacific Perspective*. A. L. Bryan, ed. Pp. 119–128. Occasional Papers 1. Edmonton: University of Alberta.

Frison, G. C., 1991 The Clovis cultural complex: New data from caches of flaked stone and worked bone artifacts. In *Raw Material Economies among Prehistoric Hunter-Gatherers*. A. Montet-White and S. Holen, eds. Pp. 321–334. Lawrence: University of Kentucky Press.

——— 1999 The Late Pleistocene prehistory of the northwestern Plains, the adjacent mountains, and Intermontane Basin. In *Ice Age Peoples of North America: Environments, Origins, and Adaptations of the First Americans*. R. Bonnichsen and K. L. Turnmire, eds. Pp. 264–280. Corvallis: Oregon State University Press.

Frison, G. C., and D. N. Walker, 1990 New World paleoecology at the last glacial maximum and the implications for New World prehistory. In *High Latitudes*, vol. 1 of *The World at 18,000 B.P.* O. Soffer and C. Gamble, eds. Pp. 312–330. London: Unwin Hyman.

Gallatin, A., 1848 Hale's Indians of Northwest American and Vocabularies of North America, with an Introduction. *Transactions of the American Ethnological Society* 2(XXIII–CLXXX), 1–30.

Goddard, I., and L. Campbell, 1994 The history and classification of American Indian languages: What are the implications for the peopling of the Americas? In *Method and Theory for Investigating the Peopling of the Americas*. R. Bonnichsen and D. G. Steele, eds. Pp. 189–208. Corvalis: Center for the Study of the First Americans.

Grayson, D. K., and D. J. Meltzer, 2003 A requiem for North American overkill. *Journal of Archaeological Science* 30, 585–593.

Greenberg, J., 1987 *Language in the Americas*. Palo Alto: Stanford University Press.

Gruhn, R., 1994 The Pacific Coast route of initial entry: An overview. In *Method and Theory for Investigating the Peopling of the Americas*. R. Bonnichsen and D. G. Steele, eds. Pp. 249–256. Corvallis: Center for the Study of the First Americans.

Hamilton, T. D. and T. Goebel, 1999 Late Pleistocene peopling of Alaska. In *Ice Age Peoples of North America: Environments, Origins, and Adaptations of the First Americans*. R. Bonnichsen and K. L. Turnmire, eds. Pp. 156–199. Corvallis: Oregon State University Press.

Haynes, C. V., 1964 Fluted projectile points: Their age and dispersion. *Science* 145(3639), 1408–1413.

—— 1993 Clovis-Folsom geochronology and climate change. In *From Kostneki to Clovis: Upper Paleolithic–Paleo-Indian Adaptations*. O. Soffer and N. D. Praslov, eds. Pp. 219–236. New York: Plenum.

Honour, H., 1975 *The European Vision of America*. Cleveland: Cleveland Museum of Art.

Hopkins, D. M., ed., 1967 *The Bering Land Bridge*. Stanford: Stanford University Press.

Housley, R. A., C. S. Gamble, M. Street, and P. Pettitt, 1997 Radiocarbon evidence for the late glacial human recolonisation of northern Europe. *Proceedings of the Prehistoric Society* 63, 25–54.

Jantz, R. L., and D. W. Owsley, 1998 How many populations of early Americans were there? *American Journal of Physical Anthropology, Supplement* 26, 228.

Klein, R. G., 1999 *The Human Career: Human Biological and Cultural Origins*, 2nd edn. Chicago: University of Chicago Press.

Lepper, B. T., 1999 Pleistocene peoples of midcontinental North America. In *Ice Age Peoples of North America: Environments, Origins, and Adaptations of the First Americans*. R. Bonnichsen and K. L. Turnmire, eds. Pp. 362–394. Corvallis: Oregon State University Press.

Madsen, D. B., ed., 2004 *Entering America: Northeast Asia and Beringia before the Last Glacial Maximum*. Salt Lake City: University of Utah Press (in press).

Martin, P. S., 1967 Pleistocene overkill. *Natural History* 76(10), 32–38.

—— 1990 Who or what destroyed our mammoths? In *Megafauna and Man: Discovery of America's Heartland*. L. D. Agenbroad, J. I. Mead, and L. W. Nelson, eds. Pp. 109–117. Hot Springs, SD: Mammoth Site of Hot Springs.

Mason, R. J., 1962 The Paleo-Indian tradition in eastern North America. *Current Anthropology* 3, 227–283.

Meltzer, D. J., 1988 Late Pleistocene human adaptations in eastern North America. *Journal of World Prehistory* 2(1), 1–52.

—— 1993 *Search for the First Americans*. Washington, DC: Smithsonian Institution Press.

Mochanov, Y. A., 1977 *The Most Ancient Stages of Human Settlement of Northeast Asia*. Novosibursk: Science Press, Siberian Division.

—— 1988 The oldest Paleolithic of Diring and the problem of the nontropical homeland of mankind. *Arkheologiya Yakutii* 15–53.

Morison, S. E., 1955 *Christopher Columbus, Mariner*. Boston: Little, Brown.

Neumann, G. K., 1952 Archeology and race in the American Indian. In *Archeology of Eastern United States*. J. B. Griffin, ed. Pp. 13–34. Chicago: University of Chicago Press.

Neves, W. A., and M. Blum, 2001 "Luzia" is not alone: Further evidence of a non-mongoloid settlement of the New World. *Current Research in the Pleistocene* 18, 73–77.

Neves, W. A., J. F. Powell, and Erik G. Ozolins, 1999 Modern human origins as seen from the peripheries. *Journal of Human Evolution* 37, 129–133.

Nichols, J., 1995 Linguistic diversity and the first settlement of the New World. *Language* 66(3), 475–521.

Powell, J. F., and W. A. Neves, 1999 Craniofacial morphology of the first Americans: Pattern and process in the peopling of the New World. *Yearbook of Physical Anthropology* 42, 153–188.

Powell, J. W., 1891 *Indian Linguistic Families of America North of Mexico*. Seventh Annual Report, Bureau of American Ethnology, 1–142.

Prufer, O. H., S. E. Pedde, and R. S. Meindl, 2001 *Archaic Transitions in Ohio and Kentucky Prehistory*. Kent: Kent State University Press.

Raber, P. A., P. E. Miller, and S. M. Neusius, eds., 1998 *The Archaic Period in Pennsylvania: Hunter-Gatherers of the Early and Middle Holocene Period*. Recent Research in Pennsylvania Archaeology 1. Harrisburg: Pennsylvania Historical and Museum Commission.

Sapir, E., 1921 A bird's-eye view of American languages north of Mexico. *Science* 54, 408.

Schurr, T. G., 2002 A molecular anthropological perspective on the peopling of the Americas. *Athena Review* 3(2), 62–75, 104–108.

Soffer, O., J. M. Adovasio, J. S. Illingworth, H. A. Amirkhanov, N. D. Praslov, and M. Street, 2000 Palaeolithic perishables made permanent. *Antiquity* 74, 812–821.

Sondaar, P. Y., G. D. van den Bergh, B. Mubroto, F. Aziz, J. de Vos, and U. L. Batu, 1994 Middle Pleistocene faunal turnover and the colonization of Flores (Indonesia) by Homo erectus. *Comptes Rendus de l'Académie des Sciences, Paris* 319, 1255–1262.

Spuhler, J. N., 1979 Genetic distances, trees, and maps of North American Indians. In *The First Americans: Origins, Affinities, and Adaptations.* W. S. Laughlin and A. B. Harper, eds. Pp. 135–184. New York: Gustav Fischer.

Stanford, D., 1978 Some Clovis points. Paper presented at the Biennial Meeting of the American Quaternary Association, Edmonton, September 2–4.

Stanford, D., and B. Bradley, 2000 The Solutrean solution. *Discovering Archaeology,* February, 54–55.

Strauss, L. G., 2000 Solutrean settlement of North America? A review of reality. *American Antiquity* 65(2), 219–226.

Sullivan, L. P., and S. C. Prezzano, eds., 2001 *Archaeology of the Appalachian Highlands.* Knoxville: University of Tennessee Press.

Szathmary, E. J. E., 1994 Modelling ancient population relationships from modern population genetics. In *Method and Theory for Investigating the Peopling of the Americas.* R. Bonnichsen and D. G. Steele, eds. Pp. 117–130. Corvallis: Center for the Study of the First Americans.

Szathmary, E. J. E., and N. S. Ossenberg, 1978 Are the biological differences between North American Indians and Eskimos truly profound? *Current Anthropology* 19(4), 673–702.

Turner, C., 1985 1986 The first Americans: The dental evidence. *National Geographic Research* 2, 37–46.

—— 1989 Teeth and prehistory in Asia. *Scientific American* 260(2), 88–96.

Voeglin, C. F., and F. M. Voeglin, 1965 Classification of American Indian languages. *Anthropological Linguistics* 7(7), 121–150.

Willey, G. R. and J. A. Sabloff, 1993 *A History of American Archaeology,* 3rd edn. San Francisco: W. H. Freeman.

Wilson, M. C., and J. A. Burns, 1999 Searching for the earliest Canadians: Wide corridors, narrow doorways, small windows. In *Ice Age Peoples of North America: Environments, Origins, and Adaptations of the First Americans.* R. Bonnichsen and K. L. Turnmire, eds. Pp. 213–248. Corvallis: Oregon State University Press.

Yi, S., and G. Clark, 1985 The "Dyuktai Culture" and New World origins. *Current Anthropology* 26(1), 1–13, 19–20.

3

Tempo and Scale in the Evolution of Social Complexity in Western North America: Four Case Studies

Kenneth M. Ames

The evolution of complex human societies, including permanent social inequality, is a central issue confronting archaeology. Within the last 30 years, considerable effort has focused on the evolution of social complexity among hunter-gatherers. This chapter does not directly attempt to explain the evolution of complex hunter-gatherer societies; it is a preliminary attempt at establishing appropriate temporal and spatial scales for explanation by comparing the evolutionary sequences of four regions in western North America over the last 12,000 years: Kodiak Island, the Northwest Coast, the Intermontane Plateau, and the Southern California Bight (Figure 3.1). These regions were selected because social and economic complexity evolved in all four and they have relatively well-known cultural sequences. This chapter's focus, and the framework for evaluating possible causes, is the tempo and the scale of change: how fast or slowly did changes occur, in what patterns, and at what geographic and temporal scales?

Cultural Evolution: Causes, Preconditions, and Tempo

This chapter is conceptualized within an evolutionary framework. It is beyond its scope to explain or defend this approach beyond a few comments. The interested reader is referred to Boyd and Richerson (1985), Bettinger (1991), Maschner (1996), Barton and Clark (1997), O'Brien and Lyman (2000), and Shennan (2002). Controversy exists among archaeologists over how (and even if) evolutionary theory ought to be employed and the form it should take when applied to socio-cultural change (cf. Pauketat and Loren, this volume). However, certain crucial matters can be fruitfully addressed without resolving the debates.

Evolutionary theory recognizes a two-level hierarchy of causation: ultimate causes and proximate causes. We can identify a third level: necessary conditions that

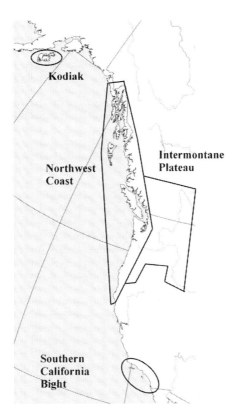

Figure 3.1 Map of western North America showing regions

do not cause change, but which must be present for the change to occur. Ultimate and proximate causes are central to evolutionary accounts to establish the scope and scale of explanation. An example makes the distinction clear (e.g., Mayr 1982). As I type, my eyes read my computer screen. A proximate explanation of that ability describes how light striking the retina is translated into nerve impulses that move into my brain and are turned into visual images. An ultimate explanation specifies the evolutionary mechanisms, including natural selection, that produced my eye. Necessary conditions are "necessary but not sufficient." For example, Testart (1982) argued food storage caused inequality among hunter-gatherers. However, many groups that store foods do not have permanent inequality although many groups with permanent inequality store food. Thus food storage does not inevitably cause inequality, but it often appears to be part of the conditions required for inequality to evolve.

Tempo and scale

Evolution's tempo is its speed. In biological evolution there is significant debate over tempo. Darwin and his successors assumed evolution is gradual, with new traits slowly accumulating through time, although not precluding rapid and abrupt – quantum – changes or a mosaic of tempos (Mayr 1982). The modern debate over tempo was fueled by the theory of punctuated equilibrium that postulates significant evolutionary change occurs very rapidly in isolated populations (Gould 2002). These relatively rare events unpredictably punctuate long periods of stability or stasis during which little change occurs.

This debate also concerns causal connections between levels of evolutionary phenomena. Gradualism maintains macroevolution is the sum of microevolutionary processes, while Gould and others argue macroevolution is processually distinct. Most theories of cultural evolution are microevolutionary (e.g., Boyd and Richerson 1992). An underlying question here concerns the temporal and spatial scales at which such processes must work. Archaeologists are generally little interested in tempo. Richerson and Boyd (2000) suggest tempo is regulated by four broad factors: (1) geography, including population size; (2) climate change; (3) coevolutionary forces; and (4) cultural evolutionary forces. They speculate tempo is potentially faster in large geographic regions with large populations, extensive interaction among groups, and a geography facilitating interactions. Under these conditions innovations are more likely to arise and spread. Conversely, change will be slow in small isolated groups.[1] They see a minor role for climate changes and significant roles for coevolutionary forces, including disease patterns and environmental limitations. They assign greatest importance to cultural evolutionary processes, arguing new technologies and economic and social institutions "evolve with difficulty" and rates of economic and social innovation are the most important for regulating the tempo of cultural evolution. They imply changes will be slow, but accelerate through time.

Other researchers looking at these same factors come to different conclusions. Bettinger (1999) argues subsistence and technological systems are functionally well integrated, and cannot change slowly; they can only change through massive reorganization or replacement, producing sudden rapid change. Many see high levels of subsistence risk accelerating culture change (e.g., Arnold 2001a; Fitzhugh 2001). In contrast, Hayden (2001) theorizes high levels of subsistence risk slow culture change and stable, productive resource bases accelerate it. Arnold (1996, 2001b), Clark and Blake (1994), Hayden (2001), and Maschner (1992), among others, agree the activities of self-interested aggressive individuals – aggrandizers – accelerate culture change, under the right conditions.

What is slow and fast change? The answer depends partly on the length of the evolutionary sequence. In an evolutionary history many millions of years long, a change requiring 200,000 years is rapid, while a change requiring 30,000 years in a history 50,000 years long is slow. In determining evolutionary tempo in North America, it is necessary to examine the full 12,500-year sequence.

It is also important to identify the appropriate evolutionary unit. In cultural evolution, it is generally accepted to be a "cultural tradition" (O'Brien and Lyman 2000; Shennan 2002). There is debate over what a cultural tradition is and how to define it (cf. Pauketat and Loren, this volume). Here, this question is addressed for each case study based on the geographic and social scale of events (Ames 1991a).

The case studies represent different geographic scales: the Northwest Coast and Intermontane Plateau are sub-continental in size while Kodiak Island and the Santa Barbara channel are smaller.

Social Complexity

For present purposes, complexity has two important qualities: the degree to which a society is differentiated (the number of parts) and the interrelationships among the parts (Kauffmann 1993). Complexity also involves power, for which Wolf (1999) identifies four scales: individual, social, tactical, and organizational. People in all societies exercise individual and social power, but tactical and organizational power are financed, entailing the development of a political economy to control labor and sustain the emerging elite (Arnold 1993, 1996; Donald 1997). Currently, the concept "complex societies" includes "middle-range" or "transegalitarian" societies with permanent social inequality and institutionalized leadership, but often lacking class systems and the political, bureaucratic, and power apparatus of states. These include hunter-gatherer societies, which vary greatly from small, egalitarian social groups (with fluid membership, little or no personal property, high mobility, and no food storage) to more complex hunter-gatherers (see Arnold 1996; Rowley-Conwy 2001).

This chapter does not discuss the full array of secondary causes and preconditions scholars advance to explain social complexity. It focuses on those that either are most often proposed, or play the greatest role in explanations of the evolution of complexity in western North America. The expectation is that, as preconditions or secondary causes are present, evolutionary tempo should increase. For example, if maritime or aquatic economies develop, complexity should evolve faster than in terrestrial cases. Likewise, the evolution of logistical mobility patterns should be followed by accelerating culture change. If Hayden is correct, the evolution of inequality will accelerate with greater subsistence stability; if Arnold is correct, permanent inequality will develop rapidly in times of significant stress.

Case Studies

The case studies come from western North America (Figure 3.1) and the sequences are discussed using Early, Middle, and Late subdivisions of the Holocene (Figure 3.2, see also Lightfoot 1993; Moss and Erlandson 1992). The earliest sites among the case studies date to about 12,500 years ago and are located in the Intermontane Plateau. The earliest sites along the coast are somewhat younger, post-dating 9000 B.C.

The Late Pleistocene (LP) and the Early Holocene (EH) were environmentally unstable, although generally the climate became warmer and drier (e.g., Hu et al. 1999). Plant and animal distributions shifted to accommodate climatic fluctuations

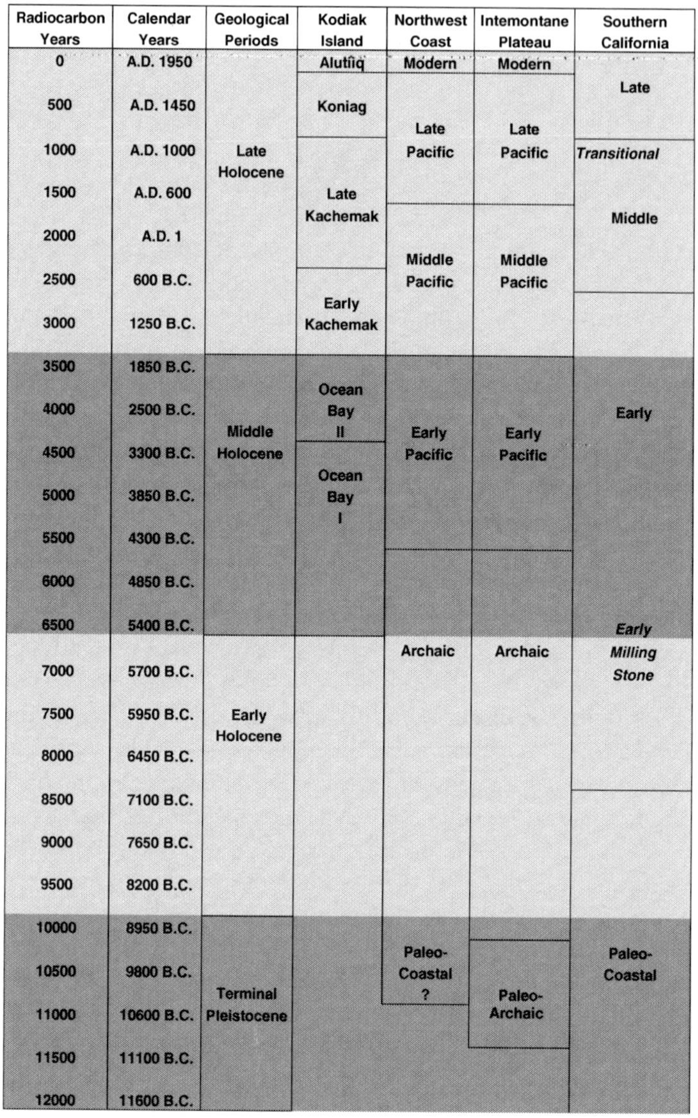

Radiocarbon Years	Calendar Years	Geological Periods	Kodiak Island	Northwest Coast	Intermontane Plateau	Southern California
0	A.D. 1950		Alutiiq	Modern	Modern	
500	A.D. 1450		Koniag			Late
1000	A.D. 1000	Late Holocene		Late Pacific	Late Pacific	Transitional
1500	A.D. 600		Late Kachemak			
2000	A.D. 1					Middle
2500	600 B.C.			Middle Pacific	Middle Pacific	
3000	1250 B.C.		Early Kachemak			
3500	1850 B.C.					
4000	2500 B.C.	Middle Holocene	Ocean Bay II	Early Pacific	Early Pacific	Early
4500	3300 B.C.					
5000	3850 B.C.		Ocean Bay I			
5500	4300 B.C.					
6000	4850 B.C.					
6500	5400 B.C.					Early Milling Stone
7000	5700 B.C.			Archaic	Archaic	
7500	5950 B.C.	Early Holocene				
8000	6450 B.C.					
8500	7100 B.C.					
9000	7650 B.C.					
9500	8200 B.C.					
10000	8950 B.C.					
10500	9800 B.C.			Paleo-Coastal ?		Paleo-Coastal
11000	10600 B.C.	Terminal Pleistocene			Paleo-Archaic	
11500	11100 B.C.					
12000	11600 B.C.					

Figure 3.2 Archaeological sequences in the four case studies

(e.g., Whitlock 1992). Deglaciation after 18,000 years ago was rapid (Clague et al. 2004) and sea levels rose swiftly until about 5000 B.C. (Stanley and Warne 1997). The Middle Holocene (MH) was marked by a change first to a warmer, moister climate and then to a moister, cooler climate (e.g., Ames and Maschner 1999; Glassow 1997a; Kennett and Kennett 2000; Mann et al. 1998; Steig 1999). A major cooling trend, the Neoglacial, began around 2500 B.C., initiating a series of warmer/cooler oscillations. Sea levels rose more slowly, from perhaps −10 m to within −4 m 5,000 years ago (Stanley and Warne 1997).

The Late Holocene (LH) may be climatically more variable. The warmer/drier, cooler/wetter fluctuations continued, including the Medieval Warm Period (A.D. 900–1350) and the Little Ice Age (A.D. 1350–1900) (e.g., Boxt et al. 1999; Mann et al. 1998).

The Kodiak Archipelago

The Kodiak Archipelago lies off Alaska's Pacific Coast. Kodiak Island is its principal island. The islands are the traditional territory of Alutiiq (formerly Koniag) peoples who, at contact, lived in large settlements, had a permanent elite, and held slaves. The archipelago's waters are highly productive and the island's long, extremely complex coastline increased environmental productivity while its terrestrial environments were rather impoverished. The archaeological record contains several seemingly abrupt changes suggesting population replacements to some, but the current view, followed here, is that there has been long-term cultural continuity (e.g., Clark 1998; Fitzhugh 1996).

At present, MH "Ocean Bay" peoples are Kodiak's first archaeologically visible occupation. Probably maritime foragers, they exploited both marine and terrestrial mammals and fish (Clark 1998; Fitzhugh 1996, 2002, 2003). They had no specialized maritime gear, just hooks and lines, and harpoons and lances armed with chipped stone points; however, by the late MH there is some evidence of specialized marine hunting tools. Doubtless, they had seaworthy boats capable of carrying all group members. Their populations and settlements were small and dispersed, but grew during the MH. Residential structures were tents only 2–3 m in diameter, indicating small domestic groups. Small pit houses replaced the tents around 2000 B.C. (Fitzhugh 1996).

The LH contains four cultural periods: the Early Kachemak (1850–500 B.C.), Late Kachemak (500 B.C.–A.D. 1200), Koniag (A.D. 1200 to contact with Europeans) and Alutiiq (Modern). During the first period, mobility patterns shifted from residential (i.e. foragers) to logistical (i.e. collectors). Houses were small (ca. 15 m^2). Some residential sites have multiple houses, suggesting either reoccupation with rebuilding of houses (implying increased investment), or larger community sizes. Technological and subsistence changes indicate increased efficiency in taking marine/littoral resources (toggling harpoons, netweights, ground slate points), bulk harvesting, (nets), and increased efficiency at processing foods (ulus – a distinctive form of chopping/slicing knife) for storage (Clark 1997, 1998; Fitzhugh 1996, 2002, 2003).

Late Kachemak populations were relatively large. Mobility patterns became increasingly logistical as some community sizes increased, with settlements having one to 10 houses. Clay-lined pits and internal storage facilities in some houses indicates storage (Partlow 2000). Households may have been corporate groups with multi-generational control of property (Hayden and Cannon 1982). Mortuary practices were elaborate, and included grave goods and defleshing of individuals (Simon and Steffian 1994). Likewise, the presence of lip labrets suggests increased social differentiation (Keddie 1981; Steffian and Saltenstall 2001).[2] There was increasing craft specialization, particularly labrets and oil lamps, indicating greater labor investment and greater residential stability (Steffian 1992; see also Clark 1998; Fitzhugh 1996). Warfare probably intensified and refuge sites are common after A.D. 800. Dietary stress appears to have been widespread (Steffian and Simon 1994).

Despite technological continuity between the Late Kachemak and the Koniag periods, marked and seemingly rapid changes occurred (Clark 1998). Populations peaked during the Koniag period and house and settlement sizes increased markedly, suggesting social ranking. These new large houses were also architecturally elaborate and the volume of storage features increased sharply. They were pit-dwellings with rectangular central sections and smaller circular features, or "lobes" connected to them by short tunnels. Villages shifted to Kodiak Island's outer coast at this time, perhaps for better access to whales and improved defense (Fitzhugh 1996). There is also evidence of intensified salmon fishing, food production and processing specializations, exchange, and investment in carpentry (wood or perhaps whalebone, since large trees are rare on Kodiak) (Clark 1998; Fitzhugh 2002).

The Northwest Coast

The Northwest Coast extends from southeast Alaska to northern California, and from the Pacific to the Cascade/Coast range crest (Ames 1994, 2003; Ames and Maschner 1999). Its wet, mild climate supported a temperate rainforest that produced crucial raw materials while ecologically productive waters supported a vast array of fish and sea mammals.

The coast was densely populated. Its economy depended on stored foods, particularly salmon. Society was stratified into two classes, including a hereditary elite. There was some production specialization, as well as long-distance trade and intense interaction. Warfare was widespread. The Northwest Coast is treated here as a single cultural tradition, although there were several interacting traditions and population shifts (Cybulski 2001; McMillan 2003; Suttles 1990). Addressing these is unnecessary here.

The earliest known occupations, by mobile foragers, just post-date 10000 B.C. (Ames 2003; Ames and Maschner 1999). Sites are small, suggesting short-term occupations by small communities. A few sites were regularly reused. There is no evidence suggesting differentials in status or for conflict. Mobility was the primary means of coping with unstable, variable environments. Boats facilitated access to distant littoral and terrestrial resources and to small, widely scattered social groups. Technology on the northern coast was dominated by microblades after 9500 B.C. (Fedje 1997), while foliate bifaces and cobble tools were common on the central and southern coasts. Bone tools include barbed points or harpoons, wedges, and fish gorges. There is indirect evidence for fishhooks and lines and probably for nets.

Middle Holocene residential patterns were more stable with some settlements reused regularly over lengthy periods, suggesting tethered foraging (e.g., Cannon 2002). This stability is marked in part by large shell middens. There is no evidence for houses until the end of the MH, when semi-subterranean houses dating to ca. 4000 and 3000 B.C. occur in southern British Columbia (Mason 1994). Terrestrial and aquatic resources were harvested, including marine mammals and fish such as salmon, flat fish, and herring; the herring implying bulk harvesting gear (Ames and Maschner 1999). Human bone chemistry indicates that virtually all dietary protein came from marine sources (Chisholm et al. 1982). The shell middens reflect intensification of intertidal resources. Ubiquitous large harpoon heads and ground slate points indicate increased sea mammal hunting efficiency. There is no evidence for storage. Other technological changes indicate expanded woodworking, probably including dugout canoes.

Burials and perhaps cemeteries are present by 4000 B.C. Cemeteries are clearly present by 2000 B.C. Some cemeteries were used over lengthy periods, suggesting long-lived, stable territorial social groups. Mortuary treatment differs among individuals. Grave goods range from utilitarian items to marine hunting gear, shell bowls, and carved antler spoons. Labrets are present by 4000 B.C. (Ames and Maschner 1999). These differences raise the possibility that inequality was present by 2000 B.C., although probably not permanent ranking.

Limited osteological analysis suggests relatively high levels of physiological stress on the southern coast (Dale 1994). Analysis of larger samples from the entire coast suggests good overall health during the Middle and Late Holocene (Cybulski 1994). Violence levels were high all along the coast.

Regional interaction spheres formed during the MH, if not earlier (Ames and Maschner 1999; Carlson 1994; Moss 1998; Suttles 1990). These spheres were the geographic framework for subsequent LH social and economic developments and the evolution of regional variants of the Northwest Coast art style.

Ames and Maschner (1999) divide the Late Holocene into three periods: Middle Pacific (MP) (1800 B.C.–A.D. 200/500), Late Pacific (A.D. 200/500–A.D. 1770), and the Modern period (A.D. 1770 to the present). MP population levels were higher than in preceding periods (Ames and Maschner 1999). Food production intensified, particularly between 2500 and 1000 B.C. This is indicated by increased numbers of net weights, toggling harpoons, and perhaps fish weirs, evidence for storage boxes, greater labor investment in woodworking, changing site distributions, and indirect evidence for boats hauling processed foods. Marine and terrestrial animals were harvested, although virtually all dietary protein was marine (Chisholm et al. 1982). Mobility was logistical, with residential sites used over long periods. Settlement sizes increased. Linear villages imply community-level social or political organization. Rectangular surface dwellings occur by the middle of the MH, although there is no firm evidence for them on the central coast until the end of the MP (e.g., Grier 2001). Households in some areas were corporate groups. Such households were the core Northwest Coast institution in the Early Modern period. Their development in the MP was probably the result of the labor demands of the changing economy (Ames 2003; Ames and Maschner 1999).

Labor organizational changes extend to craft specialization, including copper-working by 900 B.C. (Ames and Maschner 1999), and probably basket-making after 500 B.C. (Bernick 1998) and specialized food-harvesting within houses by ca. A.D. 500 (Chatters 1989; Grier 2001). The evolution of the Northwest Coast art style also suggests specialization (Ames and Maschner 1999). The introduction of slavery is another possible change in labor organization. It may date to the beginning of the MP (Ames 2001).

Permanent social ranking emerged at the beginning of the MP if not somewhat earlier. Households and communities may have been ranked, at least on the northern coast (Ames 2001). Ranking was not yet expressed in house sizes. Cemeteries and dwellings were used for periods ranging from a few centuries to over a millennium, suggesting long-lived corporate groups (e.g., Ames 1996; Grier 2001).

The regional interaction spheres continued through the MP (Ames and Maschner 1999). The status system developed a regional dimension as labret-wearing became restricted to the northern coast, replaced on the central and southern coasts by cranial deformation. Warfare levels remained high in the north, but declined in the south (Cybulski 1994).

Populations peaked at some point in the Late Pacific period. Intensification of food production continued. Logistical mobility patterns are clearly evident (e.g., Coupland 1998; Townsend 1978). Specialized tackle proliferated, and hunting and fishing gear became more uniform along the coast (Ames and Maschner 1999). Woodworking intensified. Plankhouses and linear villages were present everywhere along the coast. Houses varied markedly in size, reflecting differences in household status (Acheson 1991; Archer 2001; Maschner 1992) and suggesting political inequalities by A.D. 500 (Grier 2001). Mortuary practices changed dramatically. Burial mounds appeared on the southern coast. While many were small and simple, some were large, elaborate, and richly furnished (e.g., Lepofsky et al. 2002). Midden burial virtually ceased by ca. A.D. 1000–1200. The regional interaction spheres remained stable. Warfare intensified along the coast. Fortifications became increasingly common after ca. A.D. 800 (Moss and Erlandson 1992).

The Intermontane Plateau

The Intermontane Plateau lies between the Cascade/Coast ranges on the west and the northern/Canadian Rockies on the east (Ames et al. 1998). The climate is continental, with cold winters and hot summers. It is dry. Principal resources included salmon, a range of herbivores (elk, deer, and antelope) and geophytes.

Contact-era populations were lower than on the coast, settlements smaller, and mobility levels higher. Early ethnographers regarded Plateau societies as egalitarian, but recent work challenges that view (e.g., Hayden and Spafford 1993). While archaeologists generally assume cultural continuity during the Holocene, controversy exists over whether the region's earliest inhabitants were biologically or culturally ancestral to later peoples (e.g., Ames 2000; Chatters 2001; Leonhardy and Rice 1970).

The Plateau's earliest cultural manifestation may be widely and thinly scattered Paleoindian Clovis material (Adovasio and Pedler, this volume; Fiedel 1999). The earliest radiocarbon samples date Paleoarchaic Windust materials, clustering between ca. 11500 and 9600 B.C. (Ames 2000; Beck and Jones 1997). LP/EH economies focused on moist-wet environments, harvesting fauna from rabbits and bison to fish, although primarily targeting large mammals.[3] Periodic food shortages occurred (Green et al. 1998). Windust people were foragers with some logistical movement; population densities were low (Ames 1988, 2000; Ames et al. 1998; Connolly 1999). Technology was geared to high mobility.

Middle Holocene residential patterns are controversial, and the records for houses, mobility patterns, and subsistence and mortuary patterns are rather contradictory. Some scholars suggest very stable tethered foraging patterns in which residential camps were reused over many years without depleting adjacent resources. Others argue long-term residential stability on the Plateau is only possible with logistical mobility and storage. Presently, however, evidence for storage is nil and for logistical mobility weak. The oldest substantial residential structure dates between 5500 and 4300 B.C. (Pettigrew and Hodges 1995). Such dwellings are distributed from central British Columbia to southwestern Idaho (Ames 2000). Although settlements were small, houses were substantial, with internal areas of some 70 m², suggesting six to 10 residents (Ames 1991b). Houses disappear for a time after 2800 B.C.

Elaborate cemeteries dating between ca. 5000 and 2500 B.C. are found in some areas. While cemeteries and houses overlap in time, they only partially overlap in space, particularly in southwestern Idaho, where the cemeteries constitute the "Southwest Idaho Burial Complex" (Pavesic 1985). Individuals were interred flexed, and may have been moved and reburied after exposure and possibly defleshing (Reid and Chatters 1997). Associated grave goods imply differential access to social or spiritual resources but not ranking (Pavesic 1985; Reid and Chatters 1997).

Middle Holocene people harvested elk, deer, and antelope, a range of plant resources, and fish, including salmon. The most visible technological changes are the replacement of lanceolate projectile points by side- and corner-notched points just before the MH, and the widespread presence in early houses of mortars, pestles, and hopper mortar bases. These are often substantial, representing significant investments of time and labor (Ames 2000; Ames et al. 1998). Long-distance interaction was primarily oriented to the south and west, perhaps as far as southern California (Erickson 1990; Galm 1994). There is no evidence bearing on violence and competition until the subsequent Late Holocene period.

The Late Holocene is divided into the Middle Pacific (1850 B.C.–A.D. 200/500), Late Pacific (A.D. 200/500–1720) and the Modern period (Early Modern 1720–1855, Late Modern 1855 to the present). MP populations were larger than in previous periods. Pithouses were again present, but were less substantial than previously (Ames 1991b). Storage was practiced. Subsistence appears focused on salmon, roots, and large mammals. Intensification of fishing is indicated by increasing numbers of net weights and the introduction of toggling harpoons by A.D. 200

(Ames 2000). Logistical mobility patterns were clearly present. However, occupations of residential sites were brief, lasting perhaps a few years. While settlements were small, villages had cemeteries, suggesting long-term social and territorial ties to village locations (Ames 2000). High mobility, coupled with cemeteries, suggests residential sites shifted regularly through a defined territory. Regional interaction, shifting towards the Northwest Coast, increased as territory sizes declined (Connolly 1999; Hess 1997).

Populations peaked during the Late Pacific period. Mobility patterns became increasingly logistical. On the Columbia Plateau, pithouses were gradually replaced by mat-lodges, a flexible house form of poles covered with mats that accommodates rapid alterations in household size (Ames 1991b, 2000; Rice 1985). Settlements varied from quite small to very large, with perhaps several hundred people. Very large settlements with community cemeteries and extensive storage features are a distinctive feature of the LP. Intensification of food production may have led to greater reliance on salmon and roots and a widening of the diet (Ames 1991b). Bison were exploited for the first time since the Early Holocene; the bow and arrow gradually replaced the atlatl over a millennium.

During the LP, there is some evidence of ranking and increasing social inequality (Ames et al. 1998; Schulting 1995). The Keatley Creek site in south-central British Columbia provides an excellent example of a large LP aggregation and of the evidence for increasing inequality. The village formed ca. A.D. 300 and flourished until ca. A.D. 1150 (Prentiss et al. 2003). It contains several score pit-dwellings varying markedly in size, which may reflect differential household prestige and status (Hayden and Schulting 1997). The cause of abandonment is controversial, but all agree the Keatley Creek pattern of large villages was replaced by small settlements in this part of the Plateau (e.g., Hayden and Ryder 1991, 2003; Kuijt 1999; Prentiss et al. 2003). Hayden and Schulting (1997) suggest that a Plateau Interaction sphere formed during the LH, but this happened much earlier, by 1500 B.C. (Ames 2000; Erickson 1990; Galm 1994). The Plateau Interaction sphere involved the movement of a wide range of prestige goods. At the same time, warfare intensified, peaking between ca. A.D. 500 and 1000 (Chatters 1988).

The Southern California Bight

The Southern California Bight includes California's semi-arid coastline from Point Conception to Mexico, the offshore Channel Islands, and the Santa Barbara Channel. Terrestrial environments are topographically variable, ranging from a narrow coastal plain in places to the rugged coast range. Strong ecological contrasts between the Channel Islands and the mainland profoundly affected cultural evolution (Vellanoweth and Grenda 2002). Offshore aquatic environments were productive and ranged from coastal estuaries to deep, pelagic waters, and supported a diverse array of animals and intertidal mollusks. The Channel Islands differ in size and ecology; most importantly, only the largest have year-round fresh water.

The region includes the traditional territories of the Chumash, Gabrieliño, and other groups. The Chumash and Gabrieliño, although speaking unrelated

languages, were culturally similar. The contact-era Chumash and Gabrieliño epitomize hunter-gatherer complexity: large, dense populations, sedentism, and a permanent elite. The Chumash were apparently organized into a series of small polities,
each with one or more chiefs whose power extended beyond the household.

A good sample of sites gives a picture of EH life (Erlandson 1994; Erlandson
and Colton 1991). Mollusks, rather than terrestrial mammals, marine mammals,
or fish, appear to have been the primary protein source (Rick and Erlandson 1999,
2000; Rick et al. 2001). Fish were more important on the Channel Islands, where
seed-bearing plants were uncommon or absent. Seeds were collected and, by 7500
B.C., processed using small milling stones (Jones et al. 2002).

The area's earliest inhabitants were probably foragers, living in small fluid communities. Analysis of human skeletons suggests people were healthy, especially
relative to the LH (Lambert 1994). There were low levels of person-to-person
violence. LP/EH settlements were generally small and short-term (Erlandson
1994). By the end of the EH, residential patterns appear to become more stable
and settlements were reoccupied regularly (Erlandson 1994; Glassow 1995;
Kennett 1998). This stability, as well as the presence of cemeteries, may point to
the evolution of logistical mobility patterns, but it could also reflect tethered
foraging.

The MH spans much of the "Early" period in the regional chronology. The
southern California MH is reminiscent of this period on the Plateau, both areas
sharing elaboration of mortuary practices and ambiguous settlement patterns. Generally, it appears that MH peoples in the region were foragers linked with others
via extensive interaction networks (Erickson 1990; Howard and Raab 1993; Raab
1997). Burials contain a range of grave goods, but most particularly abalone (*Hali-
otis sp.*) shell beads and pendants. Variations in the numbers and the likely value of
grave goods may point to differential access to leadership and wealth, although societies were likely still "egalitarian" (King 1990). Sites are small, lacking evidence for
prolonged occupation, although large, deep sites do occur, suggesting the possibility of tethered foraging and semi-permanent occupation, or some degree of logistical mobility (Erlandson 1997; Glassow 1997a, 1997b; Kennett 1998; Kennett and
Kennett 2000; King 1990). Houses are rare, but the Nursery site on San Clemente
Island is a dramatic exception (Raab 1997). There, a number of pit houses – probably with whalebone superstructures – occur between 3100 and 2100 B.C. (contemporary with the peak of house construction on the Plateau and the earliest
structures in southern British Columbia).

Technological innovations include ground stone mortars and pestles as early as
4700 B.C., earlier than on the Columbia Plateau (Glassow 1996, 1999; Jones et al.
2002). These tools indicate increased investment in food-processing, perhaps for
storage. Increased fishing efficiency is indicated by the apparent development of
compound bone fishhooks and new forms of net weights (Glassow 1999). Shellfish
continued to be important protein sources, as they were during the EH (Glassow
1999).

Populations grew steadily through the Late Holocene, peaking after ca. A.D.
1000. Stress levels and violence increased and overall health declined, reaching a
nadir around ca. A.D. 600–1200 before the population peaked. The stable Middle

Holocene settlement patterns changed by ca. 1000 B.C., if not earlier, becoming clearly logistical. On the Channel Islands, people located residential bases on the coast and exploited the interior logistically. Houses are rare, but large houses of the type built by the Chumash were present by A.D. 1300. Technological innovations include shell fishhooks ("J" hooks), compound barbed bone points, and the tomol, a seaworthy plank canoe made from beached redwood logs (Gamble 2002). The tomol, capable of longer trips, provided access to new marine habitats, and had important freight-hauling capacity, facilitating exchange among the islands and between the islands and the mainland. Changes in settlement patterns and technology (such as net weights) are part of a general intensification of marine resources, including shellfish, fish, and marine mammals from littoral and sublittoral habitats (e.g., Kennett 1998).

The tempo of social, economic, and political changes in the Bight, particularly on the Channel Islands between A.D. 600 and 1300, is the subject of intense debate among archaeologists (e.g., Arnold 2001a, 2001b; Erlandson 2004; Kennett 1998; Raab and Larsen 1997). Some see ranking and control of specialized labor as developing late (Arnold 2001b), while others argue that ranking had greater antiquity (e.g., Arnold and Green 2002; Kennett 1998; King 1990; Gamble et al. 2001, 2002). These developments may be related to the invention of the tomol, its control by emerging elites, and intensification of the production of shell beads on the islands. Shell bead-making, and the manufacture of stone drill bits for bead-making, was intensified particularly around A.D. 900. Arnold (1995) sees specialization in bead- and drill-making by A.D. 1150–1200 as part of a developing political economy. Shell beads were part of social exchanges with the mainland, and functioned as a kind of currency in the Early Modern period.

Settlement patterns shifted at this time, with sites occupied since the MH being abandoned and new residential sites established. There are suggestions that the islands themselves were briefly abandoned, or at least suffered a short period of population decline (e.g., Arnold 2001b; Kennet 1998). These events may be due to environmental stress. Arnold (2001a, 2001b) attributes this sudden development to the impact of a severe El Niño event on the productivity of the marine waters around the Channel Islands. Others argue that the cause was drought. Still others dispute both the chronology of and the evidence for the El Niño event (Erlandson 2004; Gamble et al. 2001; Kennett and Conlee 2004; Kennett and Kennett 2000; Raab and Larson 1997). Be that as it may, there were rapid social, economic, and political developments in the Santa Barbara Bight between ca. A.D. 600 and 1300. While evidence suggests that poor health and violence peaked before A.D. 1000, and some degree of ranking and specialization existed earlier, there was a major sociopolitical reorganization after A.D. 1100.

Discussion

The tempos of developmental patterns summarized above were mosaics: some changes proceeded slowly while others were swift and abrupt. There are two periods of particularly rapid change: one between ca. 1800 and 800–300 B.C. and a second between ca. A.D. 500 and A.D. 1300–1400. The first period is marked by the appearance of logistically oriented collectors in all study areas, widespread intensi- fication of food production, and important technological innovations. The second period is marked by increased warfare and violence in all four areas, significant physiological stress in California, dietary stress on Kodiak Island, the formation of larger settlements in all areas, intensification of specialist production in California, increasing wealth differentials in many areas, significant demographic disruptions toward the end of the period in many areas, and sociopolitical reorganization every- where. In some places, such as the Santa Barbara Bight and Kodiak Island, elites appear to have been present by the end of the period. On the Northwest Coast, household and elite organization changed, but inequality did not disappear.

All regions share "a muddle in the middle" – the Middle Holocene – marked by residential mobility patterns not readily described by the collector/forager dichotomy. These appear to be tethered or stable foraging patterns with enough residential stability to permit the construction of houses, a practice that seems to peak everywhere around 3000–2800 B.C. These mobility patterns are coupled with relatively elaborate mortuary practices, suggesting some forms of territoriality and perhaps social distinctions.

Pinpointing when permanent inequality and ranking first evolved remains con- troversial in most areas. On the Plateau, evidence suggests increasing levels of inequality during the Late Holocene, but not rapid, quantum changes. On the Northwest Coast, permanent status differences may have preceded the economic and social reorganization of the late Middle Holocene, but social ranking seems to have developed as part of that rapid reorganization.

When inequality emerged in California is uncertain. Part of this may reflect an analytical confusion between inequality and political economy, the latter but not the former implying tactical power. The economic reorganizations associated with the development of a political economy and tactical power appear to have happened relatively rapidly on the Northwest Coast at the end of the Middle Holocene and very rapidly in California in the Late Holocene. This suggests that political economies can evolve rapidly once inequality exists.

Late Holocene demographic disruptions, settlement pattern shifts, and major sociopolitical changes appear to have occurred at more or less the same time across western North America, strongly indicating common external causes (cf. Pauketat and Loren, this volume). The timing of these changes, around A.D. 1100–1300, suggests impacts of the end of the Medieval Warm Period and the onset of the Little Ice Age (e.g., Jones et al. 1999; Kennett et al. 1999; Mann et al. 1998; Raab and Larson 1997). The swiftness of the Late Holocene changes could be seen as punc- tuated equilibria. However, many (but not all) of the changes are anticipated by earlier developments; the changes are not unpredictable given what precedes them.

Important differences exist among the case studies. Inequality, significant inten- sification of production, and storage appear to have evolved earliest on the North- west Coast. On the Plateau, the Late Holocene event seems to have produced a reduction in complexity or inequality (which also may have happened to a much lesser degree on the southern Northwest Coast). Why? It is plausible that the apparently more rapid evolution of complexity on the Northwest Coast is the result of its size, environmental diversity, and the relative ease of communication across vast distances using boats (see Ames 2002). These factors also suggest that the tempo of cultural evolution is controlled by difficulties inherent in technological and social changes. As noted above, major social changes do appear to have happened rapidly; however, they did not occur *de novo*.

The development of elites in the California Bight in the Late Holocene is the clearest example of this. The apparent rapid development of an elite and a political economy after A.D. 1100 appears rooted in developments that become archaeologically visible by A.D. 600. The pattern of slow incremental change followed by rapid social/political change could be due to (1) external causes or stresses happening at just the right moment, and (2) the accumulation of small changes (or secondary causes) to the point of criticality so that any additional change causes sudden, rapid, and major organizational change (e.g., Bentley 2003; Kauffmann 1993).

Taken together, these case studies seem to contradict Rowley-Conwy's (2001) claim that there is no general trend in hunter-gatherer social-cultural evolution from simple to complex. There clearly *is* more complexity at the end of the Holocene than at the beginning. However, scale is crucial here. Taken individually, the case studies do support his contention, with the clearest example being the Canadian Plateau, where the large aggregations represented by Keatley Creek disappeared.

Conclusion

It is not possible to discuss all secondary causes and preconditions, but a few conclusions are in order. First, while it has been widely postulated that maritime economies accelerate the evolution of social complexity, these case studies indicate that exploitation of marine resources, by itself, does not produce the rapid development of sedentism, storage, or social inequality. The pace of change along the Santa Barbara Bight, the Intermontane Plateau, and Kodiak Island is similar.

Second, while there is evidence for the intensification of production in all case studies and for the initiation of storage in all but California, nowhere did major social changes follow immediately afterward. On the Northwest Coast, storage appears to have been part of the reorganization of production. On Kodiak Island and the Plateau, significant storage was part of the evolution of logistical mobility at about the same time, but perhaps 2,000 years before the evolution of inequality.

Third, while many argue that collector mobility was a critical precondition to the evolution of hunter-gatherer complexity, in three of the case studies reviewed here 1,500 to 2,000 years separate the appearance of collectors and clear evidence of permanent inequality in the Late Holocene.

Fourth, technological innovations can either have very quick effects or almost no visible effects. On the Northwest Coast, technological changes and innovations (storage boxes, rectangular houses, etc.) were part of the rapid changes between ca. 1850 and 300 B.C. At present, however, it is impossible to establish temporal priority (did the technological changes precede, accompany, or follow the social/ economic changes?). However, none of the major technological innovations such as toggling harpoons and adzes seems to have inevitably sparked immediate or rapid changes that are visible in the archaeological record. The introduction of the bow and arrow, the tomol canoe, and heavy-duty ground stone food-processing equipment are cases in point. The complete replacement of the atlatl by the bow and arrow took at least a millennium on the Intermontane Plateau, as both were used simultaneously. This period (ca. A.D. 1–1000) was associated with high levels of warfare, although high levels of warfare also existed before the bow's introduction in some areas. The invention of the tomol canoe, assuming it was developed by ca. A.D. 700, may have significantly accelerated social and economic changes in the California Bight within the span of two or three centuries. Recently, Fagan (2004) has suggested that the tomol canoe, or canoes with equivalent maritime qualities, may have existed in the California Bight for at least 8,500 years. If so, then the initial, visible social impact of the tomol may have been nil.

Lastly, the rapid, punctuated evolution of social inequality on Kodiak and in the California Bight clearly relates to a sudden, large-scale climatic event or events. The issue becomes not the action of aggrandizers (they are everywhere) but which event or events offered them scope, or which secondary causes were in place to support their activities when their chance arrived. In short, the actions of aggrandizers do not appear to accelerate the tempo of cultural evolution. Explanation shifts away from aggrandizers to circumstances.

ACKNOWLEDGMENTS

I would like to thank Timothy Pauketat and Diana Loren for the invitation to contribute to this volume and their extraordinary patience in waiting for this chapter. Many helped in its preparation, through discussion and providing manuscripts. I thank Michael Glassow, Patricia Lambert, Jon Erlandson, Douglas Kennett, Ben Fitzhugh, John Clague, Herbert Maschner, and William Prentiss. Gretchen Kennedy provided essential help with the bibliography. All errors are mine alone.

NOTES

1   The theory of punctuated equilibrium postulates significant evolutionary change (speciation) occurs in small, isolated populations. If isolation breaks down, the new species can spread, displacing the ancestral species.

2   Labrets are stone or wood lip and cheek plugs. During the Early Modern period, they
    were worn only on the northern Northwest Coast by free women. The size of the labret
    reflected the woman's status.
3   The Kennewick remains are an exception to this. His 13C/12C ratio suggests that over
    half of his diet may have come from marine sources – salmon. However, it could also
    have come from bison, which were hunted on the Plateau during the EH.

REFERENCES

Acheson, Steven. R., 1991 In the wake of the *ya'åats' xaatgáay* ["Iron People"]: A study of
    changing settlement strategies among the Kunghit Haida. Ph.D. dissertation, Oxford
    University.
Ames, Kenneth M., 1988 Early Holocene forager mobility strategies on the southern
    Columbia Plateau. In *Early Human Occupation in Western North America*. J. A. Willig, C.
    M. Aikens, and J. L. Fagan, eds. Pp. 325–360. Anthropological Papers 21. Carson City:
    Nevada State Museum.
——1991a The archaeology of the *longue durée*: Temporal and spatial scale in the evolution
    of social complexity on the southern Northwest Coast. *Antiquity* 65, 935–945.
——1991b Sedentism, a temporal shift or a transitional change in hunter-gatherer mobility
    strategies. In *Between Bands and States: Sedentism, Subsistence, and Interaction in Small Scale
    Societies*. S. Gregg, ed. Pp. 108–133. Carbondale: Southern Illinois University Press.
——1994 The Northwest Coast: Complex hunter-gatherers, ecology, and social evolution.
    Annual Reviews of Anthropology 23, 209–229.
——1996 Life in the Big House: Household labor and dwelling size on the Northwest Coast.
    In *People Who Lived in Big Houses: Archaeological Perspectives on Large Domestic Structures*.
    G. Coupland and E. B. Banning, eds. Pp. 131–150. Monographs in World Prehistory, vol.
    27. Madison: Prehistory Press.
——2000 *Kennewick Man Cultural Affiliation Report Chapter 2: Review of the Archaeological
    Data*. Electronic document. <http://www.cr.nps.gov/aad/kennewick/ames.htm>.
——2001 Slaves, chiefs and labour on the northern Northwest Coast. *World Archaeology*
    33(1), 1–17.
——2002 Going by boat: The forager-collector continuum at sea. In *Beyond Foraging and
    Collecting: Evolutionary Change in Hunter-Gatherer Settlement Systems*. B. Fitzhugh and J.
    Habu, eds. Pp. 19–52. New York: Kluwer Academic/Plenum.
——2003 The Northwest Coast. *Evolutionary Anthropology* 12, 19–33.
Ames, Kenneth M., Don E. Dumond, Jerry R. Galm, and Rick Minor, 1998 Prehistory of
    the Southern Plateau. In *Handbook of North American Indians*, vol. 12: *Plateau*. D. E. Walker,
    ed. Pp. 103–119. Washington, DC: Smithsonian Institution.
Ames, Kenneth M., and Herbert D. G. Maschner, 1999 *Peoples of the Northwest Coast: Their
    Archaeology and Prehistory*. London: Thames & Hudson.
Archer, David J. M., 2001 Village patterns and the emergence of ranked society in the Prince
    Rupert area. In *Perspectives on Northern Northwest Coast Prehistory*. J. S. Cybulski, ed. Pp.
    203–222. Mercury Series Archaeological Survey of Canada Paper 160. Hull: National
    Museum of Civilization.
Arnold, Jeanne E., 1993 Labor and the rise of complex hunter-gatherers. *Journal of
    Anthropological Archaeology* 12, 75–119.

—— 1995 Transportation innovation and social complexity among maritime hunter-gatherer societies. *American Anthropologist* 97(4), 733–747.

—— 1996 The archaeology of complex hunter-gatherers. *Journal of Archaeological Method and Theory* 3(2), 77–126.

—— 2001a The Chumash in world and regional perspective. In *The Origins of a Pacific Coast Chiefdom: The Chumash of the Channel Islands*. J. E. Arnold, ed. Pp. 21–53. Salt Lake City: University of Utah Press.

—— 2001b Social evolution and the political economy in the northern Channel Islands. In *The Origins of a Pacific Coast Chiefdom: The Chumash of the Channel Islands*. J. E. Arnold, ed. Pp. 287–297. Salt Lake City: University of Utah Press.

Arnold, Jeanne E., and Terisa M. Green, 2002 Mortuary ambiguity: The Ventureno Chumash case. *American Antiquity* 67(4), 760–771.

Barton, C. Michael, and Geoffrey A. Clark, eds. 1997 *Rediscovering Darwin: Evolutionary Theory in Archeological Explanation*. Archaeological Papers, vol. 7. Arlington: American Anthropological Association.

Beck, Charlotte, and George T. Jones, 1997 The Terminal Pleistocene/Early Holocene archaeology of the Great Basin. *Journal of World Prehistory* 11(2), 161–236.

Bentley, R. Alexander, 2003 An introduction to complex systems. In *Complex Systems and Archaeology: Empirical and Theoretical Applications*. R. A. Bentley and H. D. G. Maschner, eds. Pp. 9–24. Salt Lake City: University of Utah Press.

Bernick, Kathryn, 1998 Stylistic characteristics of basketry from Coast Salish area wet sites. In *Hidden Dimensions: The Cultural Significance of Wetland Archaeology*. K. Bernick, ed. Pp. 139–156. Vancouver: University of British Columbia Press.

Bettinger, Robert L., 1991 *Hunter-Gatherers: Archaeological and Evolutionary Theory*. New York: Plenum.

—— 1999 From traveler to processor: Regional trajectories of hunter-gatherer sedentism in the Inyo-Mono region, California. In *Settlement Pattern Studies in the Americas: Fifty Years Since Viru*. R. Billman and G. M. Feinman, eds. Pp. 39–55. Washington, DC: Smithsonian Institution Press.

Boxt, Matther A., Mark L. Raab, L., Owen K. Davis, and Kevin O. Pope, 1999 Extreme Late Holocene climate change in coastal southern California. *Pacific Coast Archaeological Society Quarterly* 35(2–3), 25–37.

Boyd, Robert, and Peter J. Richerson, 1985 Culture and the evolutionary process. Chicago: University of Chicago Press.

—— 1992 How microevolutionary processes give rise to history. In *History and Evolution*, M. H. Nitecki and D. V. Nitecki, eds. Pp. 179–210. Albany: State University of New York Press.

Cannon, Aubrey, 2002 Sacred power and seasonal settlement on the central Northwest Coast. In *Beyond Foraging and Collecting: Evolutionary Change in Hunter-Gatherer Settlement Systems*. B. Fitzhugh and J. Habu, eds. Pp. 311–338. New York: Kluwer Academic/Plenum.

Carlson, Roy. L., 1994 Trade and exchange in prehistoric British Columbia. In *Prehistoric Exchange Systems in North America*. T. G. Baugh and J. E. Ericson, eds. Pp. 307–361. New York: Plenum Press.

Chatters, James C., 1988 Pacifism and the organization of conflict on the Plateau of northwestern America. In *Cultures in Conflict: Current Archaeological Perspectives*. D. C. Tkaczuk and B. C. Vivian, eds. Pp. 241–252. Calgary: University of Calgary.

—— 1989 The antiquity of economic differentiation within households in the Puget Sound region, Northwest Coast. In *Households and Communities*, S. MacEachern, D. J. W. Archer, and R. D. Garvin, eds. Pp. 168–178. Calgary: Archaeological Association, University of Calgary.

——2001 *Ancient Encounters: Kennewick Man and the First Americans*. New York: Simon & Schuster.

Chisholm, B. S., D. E. Nelson, and H. P. Schwarcz, 1982 Stable carbon isotope ratios as a measure of marine vs. terrestrial protein in ancient diets. *Science* 216, 1131–1132.

Clague John J., R. W. Mathewes and T. A. Ager, 2004 Environments of northwest North America before the last glacial maximum. In *Entering America: Northeast Asia and Beringia before the Last Glacial Maximum*. D. Madsen, ed. Salt Lake City: University of Utah Press (in press).

Clark, Donald W., 1997 *The Early Kachemak Phase on Kodiak Island at Old Kiavak*. Mercury Series Archaeological Survey of Canada Paper 155. Hull: Canadian Museum of Civilization.

——1998 Kodiak Island: The later cultures. *Arctic Anthropology* 35(1), 172–186.

Clark, John E., and Michael Blake, 1994 The power of prestige: Competitive generosity and the emergence of rank societies in lowland Mesoamerica. In *Factional Competition and Political Development in the New World*. E. Brumfiel and J. W. Fox, eds. Pp. 17–30. Cambridge: Cambridge University Press.

Connolly, Thomas J., 1999 *Newberry Crater: A Ten-Thousand-Year record of Human Occupation and Environmental Change in the Basin-Plateau Borderlands*. Salt Lake City: University of Utah.

Coupland, Gary, 1998 Maritime adaptation and evolution of the developed Northwest Coast pattern on the central Northwest Coast. *Arctic Anthropology* 35(1), 36–56.

Cybulski, Jerome S., 1994 Culture change, demographic history, and health and disease on the Northwest Coast. In *The Wake of Contact: Biological Responses to Conquest*. R. G. Miller and C. S. Larsen, eds. Pp. 75–85. New York: Wiley–Liss.

——2001 Human biological relationships for the northern Northwest Coast. In *Perspectives on Northern Northwest Coast Prehistory*. J. S. Cybulski, ed. Pp. 107–144. Mercury Series Archaeological Survey of Canada Paper 160. Hull: National Museum of Civilization.

Dale, Jacqueline M., 1994 Cribra Orbitalia, Nutrition, and Pathogenic Stress in Prehistoric Skeletal Remains from the Pender Island Canal Sites (DeRt 1, DeRt 2), British Columbia, Canada. Unpublished Masters thesis, Simon Fraser University.

Donald, Leland, 1997 *Aboriginal Slavery on the Northwest Coast of North America*. Berkeley: University of California Press.

Erickson, Kevin, 1990 Marine shell in the Plateau culture area. *Northwest Research Notes* 24(1), 91–44.

Erlandson, J. M., 1994 *Early Hunter-Gatherers of the California Coast*. New York: Plenum Press.

——1997 The Middle Holocene on the western Santa Barbara coast. In *Archaeology of the California Coast during the Middle Holocene*. J. M. Erlandson and M. A. Glassow eds. Vol. 4, pp. 91–110. Los Angeles: Institute of Archaeology, University of California.

——2004 Cultural change, continuity, and variability along the Late Holocene California coast. In *Catalysts to Complexity: Late Holocene Societies of the California Coast*. J. M. Erlandson and T. L. Jones, eds. Los Angeles: Cotsen Institute of Archaeology (in press).

Erlandson, Jon M., and Roger H. Colton, eds., 1991 *Hunter-Gatherers of Early Holocene Coastal California*. Los Angeles, Institute of Archaeology, University of California.

Fagan, Brian, 2004 The House of the Sea: An essay on the antiquity of the planked canoe in southern California. *American Antiquity* 69, 7–16.

Fiedel, Stuart J., 1999 Older than we thought: Implications of corrected dates for Paleoindians. *American Antiquity* 64(1), 95–115.

Fitzhugh, Ben, 1996 The evolution of complex hunter-gatherers in the north Pacific. Unpublished Ph.D. dissertation, University of Michigan, Ann Arbor.

—— 2001 Risk and invention in human technological evolution. *Journal of Anthropological Archaeology* 20, 125–167.

—— 2002 Residential and logistical strategies in the evolution of complex hunter-gatherers on the Kodiak Archipelago. In *Beyond Foraging and Collecting: Evolutionary Change in Hunter-Gatherer Settlement Systems*. B. Fitzhugh and J. Habu, eds. Pp. 257–306. New York: Kluwer Academic/Plenum.

—— 2003 The evolution of complex hunter-gatherers on the Kodiak Archipelago. In *Hunter-Gatherers of the North Pacific Rim*. J. Habu, J. N. Savelle, S. Koyama, and H. Hongo, eds. Pp. 13–48. Senri Ethnological Studies 63. Osaka: National Museum of Ethnology.

Galm, Jerry R., 1994 Prehistoric trade and exchange in the Interior Plateau of northwestern North America. In *Prehistoric Exchange Systems in North America*. T. G. Baugh and J. E. Ericson, eds. Pp. 275–305. New York: Plenum Press.

Gamble, Lynn H., 2002 Archaeological evidence for the origin of the plank canoe in North America. *American Antiquity* 67(2), 301–316.

Gamble, Lynn H., Phillip J. Walker, and G. S. Russell, 2001 An integrative approach to mortuary analysis: Social and symbolic dimensions of Chumash burial practices. *American Antiquity* 66, 185–212.

——————— 2002 Further considerations of the emergence of Chumash chiefdoms. *American Antiquity* 67(4), 772–777.

Glassow, Michael A., 1995 *Purisimeño Chumash Prehistory: Maritime Adaptations Along the Southern California Coast*. New York: Wadsworth.

—— 1996 The significance to California prehistory of the earliest mortars and pestles. *Pacific Coast Archaeological Society Quarterly* 32(2), 14–26.

—— 1997a Middle Holocene cultural development in the central Santa Barbara Channel region. In *Archaeology of the California Coast during the Middle Holocene*. G. Jon M. Erlandson and Michael A. Glassow, eds. Pp. 73–90. Los Angeles: Institute of Archaeology, University of California.

—— 1997b Research issues of importance to coastal California archaeology of the Middle Holocene. In *Archaeology of the California Coast during the Middle Holocene*. Jon M. Erlandson and Michael A. Glassow, eds. Pp. 151–162. Los Angeles: Institute of Archaeology, University of California.

—— 1999 Development of maritime adaptations during the Middle Holocene of the California coast. *Revista de Arqueología Americana* 16, 155–182.

Gould, Steven J., 2002 *The Structure of Evolutionary Theory*. Cambridge, MA: Harvard University Press.

Green, Thomas J., Bruce Cochran, Todd W. Fenton, James C. Woods, Gene L. Titmus, Larry Tieszen, Mary Ann Davis, and Susanne J. Miller, 1998 The Buhl burial: A Paleoindian woman from southern Idaho. *American Antiquity* 63(3), 437–456.

Grier, Colin, 2001 The social economy of a prehistoric Northwest Coast plankhouse. Unpublished Ph.D. dissertation, Arizona State University, Tempe.

Hayden, Brian, 2001 Richman, poorman, beggarman, chief: The dynamics of social inequality. In *Archaeology at the Millennium: A Sourcebook*. G. Feinman and T. D. Price, eds. Pp. 231–272. New York: Kluwer Academic/Plenum.

Hayden, Brian, and Aubrey Cannon, 1982 The corporate group as an archaeological unit. *Journal of Anthropological Archaeology* 1(1), 132–158.

Hayden, Brian, and J. Ryder, 1991 Prehistoric cultural collapse in the Lillooet area. *American Antiquity* 56(1), 50–65.

——————— 2003 Cultural collapses in the Northwest: A reply to Ian Kuijt. *American Antiquity* 68(1), 157–160.

Hayden, Brian, and Rick Schulting, 1997 The Plateau Interaction Sphere and late prehistoric cultural complexity. *American Antiquity* 62(1), 51–85.

Hayden, Brian, and J. Spafford, 1993 The Keatley Creek site and corporate group archaeology. *BC Studies* 99, 106–139.

Hess, Sean C., 1997 Rocks, range and Renfrew: Using distance-decay effects to study late pre-Mazama period obsidian acquisition and mobility in Oregon and Washington. Dissertation, Washington State University.

Howard, William J., and L. Mark Raab, 1993 Olivella grooved rectangular beads as evidence of an Early-Period southern Channel Islands interaction sphere. *Pacific Coast Archaeological Society Quarterly* 29(3), 1–11.

Hu, F. S., D. Slawinski, H. E. Wright Jr., E. Ito, R. G. Johnson, K. R. Kelts, R. F. McEwan, and A. Boedigheimer, 1999 Abrupt changes in North American climate during Early Holocene times. *Nature* 400, 437–439.

Jones, Terry L., Gary M. Brown, L. Mark Raab, Janet L. McVickar, W. Geoffrey Spaulding, Douglas J. Kennett, Andrew York, and Phillip L. Walker, 1999 Environmental imperatives reconsidered: Demographic crises in western North America during the Medieval Climatic Anomaly. *Current Anthropology* 40(2), 137–170.

——2002 The Cross Creek site (CA-SLO-1797) and its implications for New World colonization. *American Antiquity* 67(2), 213–231.

Kauffmann, Stuart A., 1993 *The Origins of Order: Self-Organization and Selection in Evolution.* Oxford: Oxford University Press.

Keddie, Grant R., 1981 The use and distribution of labrets on the North Pacific Rim. *Syesis* 14, 60–80.

Kennett, Douglas J., 1998 Behavioral ecology and the evolution of hunter-gatherer societies on the northern Channel Islands, California. Ph.D. dissertation, University of California.

Kennett, Douglas J., and Christina A. Conlee, 2004 Emergence of Late Holocene sociopolitical complexity on Santa Rosa and San Miguel Islands. In *Catalyst to Complexity: The Holocene Archaeology of the California Coast.* J. M. Erlandson and T. L. Jones, eds. Pp. 1–45. Los Angeles: Institute of Archaeology, UCLA (in press).

Kennett, Douglas J., and James P. Kennett, 2000 Competitive and cooperative responses to climate instability in coastal Southern California. *American Antiquity* 65(2), 379–395.

Kennett Douglas J., Andrew York, and Phillip L. Walker, 1999 Environmental imperatives reconsidered: Demographic crises in western North America during the Medieval Climatic Anomaly. *Current Anthropology* 40, 137–170.

King, Chester D., 1990 *Evolution of Chumash Society: A Comparative Analysis of Artifacts used for Social System Maintenance in the Santa Barbara Channel Region before AD 1804.* New York: Garland.

Kuijt, Ian, 1999 Reconsidering the cause of cultural collapse in the Lillooet Area of British Columbia, Canada. *American Antiquity* 66, 692–703.

Lambert, Patricia M., 1994 War and Peace on the Western Front: A Study of Violent Conflict and its Correlates in Prehistoric Hunter-Gatherer Societies of Coastal Southern California. Unpublished Ph.D. dissertation. Santa Barbara: University of California.

Leonhardy, Frank C., and David G. Rice, 1970 A proposed culture typology for the Lower Snake River region, southeastern Washington. *Northwest Anthropological Research Notes* 4(1), 1–29.

Lepofsky, Dana, Michael Blake, Douglas Brown, Sandra Morrison, Nicole Oakes, and Natasha Lyons, 2002 The archaeology of the Scowlitz site, southwest British Columbia. *Journal of Field Archaeology* 27(4), 1–29.

Lightfoot, Kent G., 1993 Long-term developments in complex hunter-gatherer societies: Recent perspectives from the Pacific Coast of North America. *Journal of Archaeological Research* 1(2), 167–201.

Mann, Daniel H., Aaron Crowell, Thomas D. Hamilton, and Bruce D. Finney, 1998 Holocene geologic and climatic history around the Gulf of Alaska. *Arctic Anthropology* 35(1), 112–131.

Maschner, Herbert D. G., 1992 The origins of hunter-gatherer sedentism and political complexity: A case study from the northern Northwest Coast. Ph.D. dissertation, University of California, Santa Barbara.

Maschner, Herbert D. G., ed., 1996 *Darwinian Archaeologies*. New York: Plenum.

Mason, A. R., 1994 *The Hatzic Rock Site: A Charles Phase Settlement*. Unpublished Masters thesis, University of British Columbia.

Mayr, Ernst, 1982 *The Growth of Biological Thought; Diversity, Evolution and Inheritance*. Cambridge, MA: The Belknap Press of Harvard University Press.

McMillan, Allen D., 2003 Reviewing the Wakashan migration hypothesis. In *Emerging from the Mist: Studies in Northwest Coast Culture History*. R. G. Matson, G. Coupland, and Q. Makie, eds. Pp. 244–259. Vancouver: University of British Columbia Press.

Moss, Madonna L., 1998 Northern Northwest Coast regional overview. *Arctic Anthropology* 35(1), 88–111.

Moss, M. L., and J. M. Erlandson, 1992 Forts, refuge rocks, and defensive sites: The antiquity of warfare along the North Pacific Coast of North America. *Arctic Anthropology* 29, 73–90.

O'Brien, Michael, J., and R. Lee Lyman, 2000 *Applying Evolutionary Archaeology: A Systematic Approach*. New York: Plenum.

Partlow, Megan A., 2000 Salmon intensification and changing household organization in the Kodiak Archipelago. Unpublished Ph.D. dissertation, University of Wisconsin, Madison.

Pavesic, Max G. 1985 Cache blades and turkey tails: Piecing together the western Idaho Archaic Burial Complex. In *Stone Tool Analysis: Essays in Honor of Don E. Crabtree*. M. G. Plew, J. C. Woods, and M. G. Pavesic, eds. Pp. 55–89. Albuquerque: University of New Mexico.

Pettigrew, Richard M., and Charles M. Hodges, 1995 Prehistoric hunter-gatherer land-use systems: Pacific Northwest. In *Synthesis of Findings*. M. Moratto, ed., Archaeological Investigations PGT-PG&E Expansion Project Idaho, Washington, Oregon, and California, vol. 4. Fresno: INFOTEC Research Inc.

Prentiss, William C., Michael Lenert, Thomas A. Foor, Nathan B. Goodale, and Trinity Schlegel, 2003 Calibrated radiocarbon dating at Keatley Creek: The chronology of occupation at a complex hunter-gatherer village. *American Antiquity* 68(4), 719–736.

Raab, L. Mark, 1997 The Southern Channel Islands during the Middle Holocene: Trends in maritime cultural evolution. In *Archaeology of the California Coast during the Middle Holocene*. Jon M. Erlandson and Michael A. Glassow, eds. Vol. 4, pp. 23–34. Los Angeles: Institute of Archaeology, University of California.

Raab, L. Mark, and D. O. Larson, 1997 Medieval climatic anomaly and punctuated cultural evolution in coastal southern California. *American Antiquity* 62(2), 319–336.

Reid, Kenneth C., and James C. Chatters, 1997 *Kirkwood Bar: Passports in Time Excavations at 10IH699 in the Hells Canyon National Recreation Area, Wallowa-Whitman National Forest*. Pullman, WA: National Forest Service.

Rice, Harvey S., 1985 *North American Dwellings and Attendant Structures on the Southern Columbia Plateau*. Cheney: Eastern Washington University, Archaeological and Historical Services.

Richerson, Peter J., and Robert Boyd, 2000 Institutional evolution in the Holocene: The rise of complex societies. In *The Origins of Human Social Institutions.* W. G. Runciman, ed. Pp. 197–204. British Academy/Novartis Foundation.

Rick, Torben C., and Jon M. Erlandson, 1999 *Fishing Practices of Early Holocene Coastal California: Preliminary Evidence From Daisy Cave (CA-SMI-261).* Proceedings of the Society for California Archaeology, Fresno, 1999. Vol. 13, pp. 194–201. Society of California Archaeology.

———— 2000 Early Holocene fishing strategies on the California coast: Evidence from CA-SBA-2057. *Journal of Archaeological Science* 27, 621–633.

Rick, Torben C., Jon M. Erlandson, and Rene L. Vellanoweth, 2001 Paleocoastal marine fishing on the Pacific Coast of the Americas: Perspectives from Daisy Cave, California. *American Antiquity* 66(4), 595–613.

Rowley-Conwy, Peter, 2001 Time, change and the archaeology of hunter-gatherers: How original is the "original affluent society"? In *Hunter-Gatherers: An Interdisciplinary Perspective.* C. Panter-Brick, R. H. Layton, and P. Rowley-Conwy, eds. Pp. 39–72. Cambridge: Cambridge University Press.

Schulting, Rick J., 1995 *Mortuary Variability and Status Differentiation on the Columbia-Fraser Plateau.* Burnaby, BC: Archaeology Press, Simon Fraser University.

Shennan, Stephan, 2002 *Genes, Memes and Human History.* London: Thames & Hudson.

Simon, James J. K., and Amy F. Steffian, 1994 Cannibalism or complex mortuary behavior? An analysis of patterned variability in the treatment of human remains from the Kachemak Tradition of Kodiak Island. In *Reckoning with the Dead: The Larsen Bay Repatriation and the Smithsonian Institution.* T. Bray and T. W. Killion, eds. Pp. 75–101. Washington, DC: Smithsonian Institution Press.

Stanley, Daniel F., and Andrew G. Warne, 1997 Holocene sea-level change and early human utilization of Deltas. *GSA Today* 7(12), 1–6.

Steffian, Amy F., 1992 Archaeological coal in the Gulf of Alaska: A view from Kodiak Island. *Arctic Anthropology* 29(2), 111–129.

Steffian, Amy F., and Patrick G. Saltenstall, 2001 Markers of identity: Labrets and social organization in the Kodiak Archipelago. *Alaska Journal of Anthropology* 1(1), 1–27.

Steffian, Amy F., and James J. K. Simon, 1994 Metabolic stress among prehistoric foragers of the central Alaskan Gulf. *Arctic Anthropology* 31(2), 78–94.

Steig, Eric J., 1999 Mid-Holocene climate change. *Science* 286, 1485–1487.

Suttles, Wayne, 1990 Introduction. In *Handbook of North American Indians*, vol. 7: *The Northwest Coast.* W. Suttles, ed. Pp. 1–15. Washington, DC: Smithsonian Institution.

Testart, Alain, 1982 The significance of food storage among hunter-gatherers: Residence patterns, population densities, and social inequalities. *Current Anthropology* 23(5), 523–538.

Townsend, Gail, 1978 *Prehistoric Settlement Changes in the Southern Northwest Coast: A Functional Approach.* University of Washington Department of Anthropology Reports in Archaeology 5. Seattle.

Vellanoweth, Rene L., and Donn R. Grenda 2002 Paradise or Purgatory, Environments Past and Present. In *Islanders and Mainlanders: Prehistoric Context for the Southern California Bight.* J. H. Altschul and D. R. Grenda, eds. Pp. 67–84. Tucson: SRI Press.

Whitlock, Cathy, 1992 Vegetational and climatic history of the Pacific Northwest during the last 20,000 years: Implications for understanding present-day biodiversity. *Northwest Environmental Journal* 8, 5–28.

Wolf, Eric R., 1999 Envisioning Power, Ideologies of Dominance and Crises. Berkeley, CA: University of California Press.

4

Structure and Practice in the Archaic Southeast

Kenneth E. Sassaman

The Archaic period (10,000–3000 radiocarbon years before present [rcybp, here-after B.P.]) of the American Southeast and the hunter-gatherer societies that existed during this time are being thoroughly redefined by archaeological discoveries that erode orthodoxy. New evidence for complex moundbuilding practices, circular-village plaza compounds, and symbolic action begs critical review of deeply entrenched assumptions about the sociality of small-scale societies. The Archaic period was long ago painted as a transitional stage between the big-game hunters of the Late Pleistocene, and farmers of the Woodland and Mississippian periods of the past two millennia. Archaeologists today acknowledge a great deal of variation among Archaic hunter-gatherers, even beyond the usual tripartite scheme that divides the Archaic into Early (10,000–8000 B.P.), Middle (8000–5000 B.P.) and Late (5000–3000 B.P.) periods. So many of the traits that originally defined and separated each of these periods have proven unreliable for evolutionary models but enormously fruitful for contemporary analyses of historical process. Archaeologists have much new data to digest.

As students of Archaic (pre)history come to grips with new data, several deeply entrenched ontological premises can be profitably abandoned. One is that Archaic societies are best understood as natural, not cultural phenomena. As with hunter-gatherers in general, Archaic societies have long been regarded as small-scale, mobile, and simple formations whose settlement practices, subsistence choices, and ideologies were strongly influenced, if not determined, by the constraints and opportunities of nature. Ancillary to this premise is the logic that social formations were localized and self-contained, homeostatic systems that changed largely in response to imbalances between population and resource potential. A body of new ecological theory foregrounding the cultural and historical construction of nature (i.e., the cognized environment) has superseded the ecofunctionalist doctrine of the last century (Biersak 1999), and, happily, some of this new theorizing has begun to infiltrate Archaic studies.

A more recalcitrant premise is the notion that Archaic societies were constituted primarily on principles of egalitarianism and equality. Several threads of logic lead to this premise. First, from a behavioral ecological perspective, food-sharing and other means of alleviating inequality are beneficial to individuals in small-scale formations when the risk of failure from acting alone (e.g., hoarding) is greater than the costs of sharing with others (Kelly 1995:168–181). This logic establishes a threshold condition whereby a shift to less risky economic situations – be it through innovation (e.g., food production) or environmental change (e.g., stabilization of sea levels) – lifts the constraints on selfish behavior and opens the door to institutionalized social inequality (Hayden 1995). It also reifies egalitarianism as antecedent to complex society, a fundamental tenet of cultural evolutionism.

Throughout the world, societies are assumed to have become more complex through time as they have grown in size and become increasingly linked through institutions of religion, economics, and politics. Being antecedent to the Mississippian chiefdoms and Woodland tribes of the late pre-contact period, Archaic societies are assumed, *a priori*, to be somehow less complex than what followed. Whereas this is true on many levels, our sense of relative complexity is strongly influenced by the program of research in the 20th century that set out to establish the essential qualities of "primitive" societies through the study of modern foragers (Leacock and Lee 1982; Lee and DeVore 1976). The uniformitarian rationale for this effort was sound, but the program generally failed to recognize that the egalitarian structures of modern foragers were historically constituted through interactions with complex societies (Schrire 1984; Wilmsen 1989; Woodburn 1982), and thus could not be assumed to reflect the sociality of hunter-gatherers in a world of hunter-gatherers (i.e., the "primitive" state of humanity).

Following from this is a final problematic premise about the nature of cultural complexity. While most anthropologists today agree that so-called egalitarian societies are rife with inequalities (Flanagan 1989), many continue to distinguish such societies from chiefdoms and states because inequalities among the former were neither institutionalized nor of economic and political consequence. It is on this point that progress in our understanding of new data on the Archaic Southeast will turn. If we allow that relations of inequality, ranking, or even stratification can exist in cosmological or ideational realms without being manifest in structures of political authority or economic control, then the Archaic Southeast and "complex" hunter-gatherers in general have much to teach us about the origins of institutionalized inequality (Sassaman 2004a). Indeed, transformations in economy and politics must be preceded by the cultural logic for differentiation, and I believe we can find this cultural logic deeply rooted in the practices of Archaic life. Transformations leading from Archaic to Woodland culture, and from Woodland to Mississippian culture, are certainly worthwhile research topics, but equally important are the sociohistorical structures that enabled these changes. It is my aim in this chapter to demonstrate that the cultural logic for ranked societies was in place throughout the Archaic period. To the extent they existed at all, egalitarian social formations of the Archaic period were a consequence of, and not a precondition for, sociohistorical structures of ranking or inequality.

The burden of proof for these bold assertions hinges as much on theoretical justification as it does on empirical validation. Indeed, it is not enough to argue that newfound data on Archaic complexity speak for themselves, for they do not. The body of theory known broadly as landscape archaeology provides insight into the myriad ways non-Western societies live *through*, and not simply *in*, environments, and how places, pathways, and resources are imbued with meaning through histories of movement, settlement, collective identities, group fissioning, and subsistence practices. Encoded in the built environments of Archaic mound complexes, for example, is the rationale for cultural identity and difference, inspired perhaps by the metaphors of nature, but constituted recursively by the actions of those engaged in their construction and use. This ongoing process of becoming was not likely a corporate affair in the sense that its participants were like-minded and self-identified as "one people." Rather, these were likely the consequence of collective actions involving people of somewhat different and perhaps contradictory histories, ethnic affiliations, and cultural traditions.

A historical process driven by the contradictions inherent to heterogeneous social formations encourages us to locate cultural difference where we expect none. It is difficult to justify the claim that Archaic societies were self-contained units of collectivism with so much material evidence for interactions among them. Intermarriage between communities that assert different cultural identities, for instance, results in multiethnic households whose internal contradictions in everyday practice were metaphors of (indeed the rationale for) social ranking at the community and regional scales (e.g., Grinker 1994). It follows that cultural differences in Archaic societies were transposed across a number of levels, from regional landscapes of power to local communities of practice. Negotiations of contradictions between these realms of experience – through group fissioning, shifting alliances, migration, and the like – were the forces of cultural change.

I cannot in this chapter provide a thorough exposition of the knowledge claims outlined above, for indeed that would take many more pages and much more data. My intent here is to simply tantalize the reader with some of the region's latest finds and novel ways of interpreting them. Above all, my intent is to show that the Archaic archaeological record needs to be redefined as the organization, reproduction, and transformation of cultural diversity. The unilineal logic of cultural evolutionism and the normative perspective of historical particularism are, for the most part, relicts of a bygone era. In their place have come the rudiments of a social theory that foregrounds cultural identity, meaning, power, and history as core concepts (Pauketat 2001). As we will see, archaeological evidence for these dimensions of human experience is not often accessible, and even then, always cryptic. However, I would assert that much of the recent archaeological evidence of Archaic traditions and practice cannot be fully understood through the shopworn ontologies of cultural ecology and evolutionism. New discoveries require new ways of thinking (arguably, new discoveries *come* from new ways of thinking), and the Archaic Southeast, with its rich new data, is quickly becoming fertile ground for theoretical developments in anthropology at large.

Assertions of Identity

Archaic cultures are typically identified by the stone tools they made, the so-called diagnostic artifacts whose distribution in time and space allow archaeologists to recognize and compare different cultural traditions. Because diagnostic artifacts are generally portable, the geographic displacement of such items from the sources of raw material used to make them is a proxy for the physical and social scale of human activities across the landscape. Hence, the presence of non-local lithic raw materials in archaeological assemblages is an indicator of interactions of personnel between communities.

The practice of long-distance exchange among Archaic societies has roots extending back to the Paleoindian era. Assemblages containing Paleoindian Clovis points, for instance, typically contain bifaces made on materials some 300 km or more from geological sources. However, many archaeologists argue that the geographic dispersal of toolstone signals long-distance movements by residential groups, not exchange between them (Meltzer 1989). The presumption here is that Clovis populations were too sparse and too transient to have experienced the need to assert boundaries amongst themselves and to reproduce those boundaries through alliance and exchange.

By some accounts, Paleoindians even lacked a sense of place, a historical connection to particular locations and landscapes. Kelly and Todd (1988) paint a picture of highly mobile hunters in the changing, unpredictable environments of the Late Pleistocene, relying on a storehouse of knowledge for tracking and dispatching large game. Their structuring principles centered on the behavior of migratory game, herds whose transient relationships with shifting grasslands and a retreating northern glacial front precluded the development of deeply inscribed land use patterns, and thus no ties to particular places. Plus, with open terrain to receive daughter communities as local populations grew and budded off, institutional boundaries among groups were unlikely, perhaps nonexistent. Of course, Kelly and Todd (1998), among others (Anderson 1990; Walthall and Koldehoff 1998), recognize the need for intergroup alliances for purposes of marriage, but the process is generally regarded as open-ended, flexible, and facilitated by seasonal aggregations among adjacent groups. The expansive distribution of Clovis points and the clinal patterns of its metric variances attest to unfettered flows of personnel across the Southeast.

This is a compelling model if Clovis-age people were indeed the first colonists of eastern North America. The growing body of evidence for precursors and contemporaries of Clovis populations throughout the New World suggests otherwise (Adovasio and Pedler, this volume). There is in fact good reason to believe that Clovis is a southeastern US original, and thus necessarily with local antecedents. It follows that Clovis populations in the Southeast had centuries of experience in the region under their collective cultural belt. The incredible number of Clovis points found in places like the middle Tennessee River valley argues convincingly for redundant, even permanent use of preferred locales. Indeed, such locales have been regarded as staging areas (Anderson 1990) for early populations, locations that were home to generations of Paleoindian bands. It follows that non-local raw material in Clovis assemblages of the Southeast could signify alliances between groups with long-term, routinized distributions across the landscape, that is, people of places.

Whereas the Clovis archaeological record remains ambiguous on the issue of intergroup dynamics, that of the succeeding Dalton period (10,500–10,000 B.P.) includes evidence that unequivocally speaks of boundaries and alliances. The rich Dalton archaeological record of the central Mississippi valley includes locations where unusually large and exotic lanceolate blades were cached (Gramly and Funk 1991; Morse 1997:17; Walthall and Koldehoff 1998). These hypertrophic blades measure up to 38 cm in length and exhibit remarkable workmanship on high-quality raw material (Figure 4.1). They have been found in over 30 locations along a 700 km stretch of the central Mississippi valley, from the American Bottom to northeast Arkansas. Most often they are isolated finds, but at least six caches of up to nine large blades each have been recorded in the southern half of this region (Walthall and Koldehoff 1998:260). Among the 146 Dalton points recovered from the Sloan site in northeast Arkansas are over two dozen described by Morse (1997:17–18) as "Large Daltons." All but two were made from non-local materials, and only six show signs of being used, damaged, and/or resharpened. These and other chipped stone artifacts were found distributed among 29 clusters or caches that Morse and colleagues (1997) convincingly argue were locations of human interment.

Burlington chert of the Crescent Quarries of east-central Missouri was a preferred material for making oversized Daltons (Walthall and Koldehoff 1998:263). Most of the isolated occurrences are located within 100 km of the Crescent Quarries, generally at locations along the Mississippi, Missouri, and Illinois rivers. Crescent Quarry chert was preferred for its superior quality, but it also occurs in blocks or boulders of up to 1 m in diameter, is located near the confluence of major rivers, and is thus readily accessible by boat (Walthall and Koldehoff 1998:263). About half of the oversized Daltons from the Sloan site were made from Burlington chert, at least seven from Crescent Quarries more than 300 km to the north (Morse 1997:17).

A similar pattern of hypertrophic biface production and exchange is seen in the Middle Archaic Benton tradition (ca. 5800–5200 B.P.) of the Midsouth (Johnson and Brookes 1989). Over 13 caches from five sites in northeast Mississippi have yielded examples of large, oversized Benton bifaces, Turkey-Tail bifaces, and related cache blades, most made from blue-gray Fort Payne chert of the Tennessee River valley to the north. According to Johnson and Brookes (1989), some of these caches were likely mortuary. Hypertrophic bifaces and other elaborate artifacts are clearly associated with Middle Archaic burials (cremations) in the Duck River valley of central Tennessee (Hofman 1986) and in the Pickwick Basin of the Middle

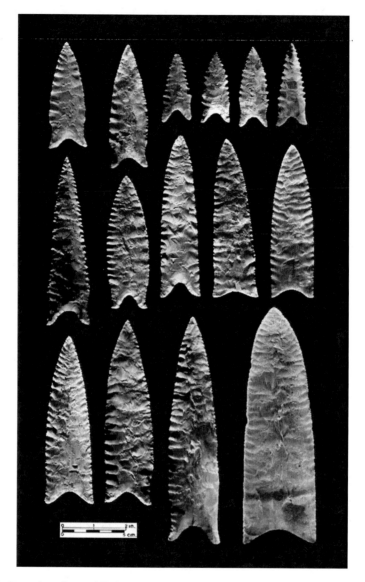

Figure 4.1 Examples of typical Dalton points (upper right) and oversized Dalton and Sloan points from the Sloan site in Arkansas (used with permission of Dan F. Morse)

Tennessee (Webb and DeJarnette 1942). Their use in mortuary ritual, according to Johnson and Brookes (1989), and following Brose (1979), is merely symbolic of secular exchange relationships that acted to buffer economic risk, a form of "subsistence insurance."

A parallel explanation for hypertrophic bifaces is proffered by Walthall and Koldehoff (1998:266) when they refer to oversized Daltons as "primitive valuables." The production and exchange of such valuables among hunter-gatherers is often viewed as a means of integrating groups into regional alliance networks for purposes of marriage, resource management, and information exchange. In this sense, the manipulation of valuables structures social interactions through ritual acts in the context of group aggregations. The inherent "power" of valuables resides in their function to reproduce social alliances (Walthall and Koldehoff 1998). Johnson and Brookes (1989) concur in their interpretation of Benton exchange.

This functionalist perspective on the manufacture and exchange of oversized Daltons and Bentons overlooks the possibility that possession and use of such items was intended to make a statement. The actual messages encoded in such items may never be revealed, but that is secondary to the structuring aspects of such actions, and in the consequences such uses may have to alter structure (to change history). Above all else, these were arguably assertions of identity, and, as such, they were clearly relational actions (i.e., multicultural or multiethnic).

One additional example of hypertrophy in Late Archaic polished stone technology helps to illustrate this point. In several cases regionwide, oversized bannerstones and grooved axes punctuate an otherwise pervasive record of mundane material culture (e.g., Fortier 1984; Hassen and Farnsworth 1987; Roper 1978). Among the better-dated examples are bannerstones of the middle Savannah River (Sassaman 1998; Figure 4.2). Presumed to be weights for spearthrowers, bannerstones are polished stone objects whose large size, elaborate shape, or especially good workmanship transcend the technical requirements or tolerances for delivering spears (darts), and thus, in their elaborateness, likely encoded cultural significance beyond the act of hunting itself. Indeed, bannerstones of the middle Savannah River occasionally have exaggerated dimensions and intricate designs. Many examples of the so-called Notched Southern Ovate are over 20 cm in diameter and feature a deeply recessed spine that is drilled longitudinally, with wings on either side of the spine tapering to but a few millimeters thick, and delicate, tapered ridges along the medial edges of the wings, all highly polished (Knoblock 1939).

The specific timing and context of Notched Southern Ovate bannerstones in the middle Savannah region is linked to sustained contacts between groups of distinctive cultural identity and history. The forms are well dated to the Mill Branch phase of ca. 4200–3800 B.P. (Elliott et al. 1994; Ledbetter 1995). They are preceded by a smaller, related form, the Southern Ovate (Knoblock 1939), dating to the Paris Island phase, ca. 4500–4200 B.P. (Elliott et al. 1994; Wood et al. 1986). Mill Branch culture is clearly derived from Paris Island culture, itself apparently derivative of indigenous roots in the region. In both its exaggerated bannerstones and comparatively large bifaces, Mill Branch culture evokes the image of Paris Island culture blown out of proportion.

Secure evidence links this moment of elaboration to the first sustained presence of interlopers from downriver, members of the early Stallings populations of the Atlantic Coast and lower Coastal Plain. Interactions between early Stallings groups and middle Savannah indigenes throughout the Paris Island phase is evidenced by the movement of soapstone from sources in the lower Piedmont and Fall Zone to the middle Coastal Plain. These existing relations apparently afforded the opportunity for certain early Stallings groups to relocate to the middle Savannah start-

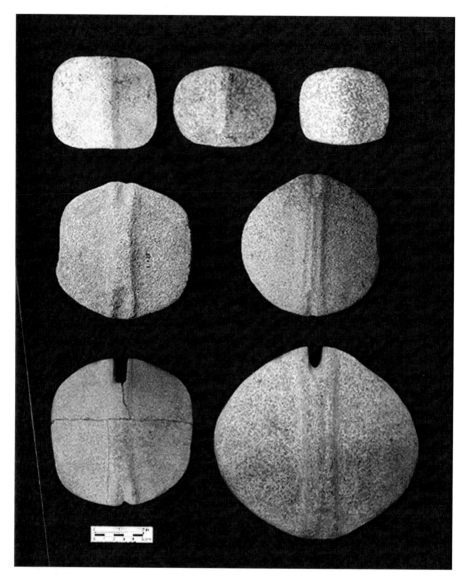

Figure 4.2 Examples of Southern Ovate (upper row) and Notched Southern Ovate bannerstones, including several preforms, the largest from Stallings Island (bottom right) (used with permission of the Peabody Museum, Harvard University)

ing about 4200 B.P., the moment of transformation that led to the exaggerated material expressions of Mill Branch culture.

It is not altogether clear how elaborate bannerstones figured into interactions between indigenous peoples of the middle Savannah and their Coastal Plain neighbors, although there is little to recommend that they simply embodied reciprocal relations among social equals. As a transformation of Paris Island practice and tradition, the emergence of Mill Branch culture coincides with the sustained presence of a "foreign" people in their traditional land. Elaborate bannerstones may have been a medium of interaction between these groups, perhaps a form of wealth for brokering marriages and other alliances. In systems-serving terms, such interactions may have underwritten insurance against failure, a means to alleviate conflict, even divert tendencies for competition into economically inconsequential directions.

More likely, elaborate bannerstones signal efforts on the part of certain individuals or subgroups to assert identity in resistance to assimilation. Evidence for this may be seen in the circumstances surrounding the demise of bannerstones. Between 3800 and 3700 B.P., after a span of five centuries in the middle Savannah, the tradition of bannerstone-making was abandoned altogether. This is the time when Classic Stallings culture appears as a distinct archaeological culture (3800–3500 B.P.). Noted for its elaborate punctated pottery, Classic Stallings culture is likely the ethnogenetic consequence of interactions between Mill Branch and early Stallings groups, that is, the emergence of a new collective identity. On the geographical peripheries of this development we find other assertions of identity and alliance-building, notably the innovation of soapstone vessel technology and its exportation westward (Sassaman 1998). The roots of this development also lie in the ethnogenesis of Classic Stallings culture, but, in this case, as resistance to change by the displaced bearers of Mill Branch tradition (Sassaman 2001a).

I suspect that all cases of hypertrophic material culture discussed above were precipitated by the impingement of one group into another's culturally meaningful space (places). Whether this involves efforts on the part of some to engage interlopers in alliance, or rather, throw up boundaries of resistance to impingements on autonomy, or both, is not at all clear. However, there is ample reason to assert that hypertrophic forms arose as a declaration of identity among individuals resistant to assimilation or other impositions. These were likely acute responses to perceived threats, much in the same way that many Americans trumpeted the symbols of nationalism in the wake of September 11 attacks.

In this sense hypertrophic actions were likely short-lived and perhaps expressive of only a segment of a population. But they were not terribly novel actions, as they drew inspiration from traditional practice. They signify efforts to reach back, through discourse and material symbol, into the past, and across space, to construct an image and sentiment that would shape people's motives and actions. And such actions were not simply the invoking of cultural symbols at the juncture and context of intergroup interaction. Rather, they embody divisions within groups as to how to engage the "other"; it is unlikely that all agreed upon any single stratagem, and thus such bold assertions of identity likely resulted occasionally in group fissioning.

The point of this discussion is that it may be erroneous to conclude that the actions of representation seen in the production and caching of hypertrophic items were corporate actions. Rather, such actions took place in multiethnic or multicultural contexts with claims and counterclaims over privilege, status, and identity. Analysts of the later Mississippian period have begun to consider seriously how the multiethnic composition of communities was to a large extent the fuel of sociopolitical change (e.g., Blitz 1999; Pauketat 2003). Indeed, ethnic divisions were the basis for ranked dual organization of Mississippian chiefdoms, and they formed the cleavage planes along which polities coalesced and divided. This process is evident in the occupational sequences of places on the landscape that were imbued with history and ancestry and thus defined and redefined as places of origin. In their construction of mounds and monuments, as well as in their cemeteries and other vestments in place, societies of the Archaic Southeast inscribed this social logic on the landscape at least 5,000 years before the Mississippian era.

Shell Mound Archaic

A penchant for freshwater mussels and snails resulted in massive accumulations of shell among several distinct cultural traditions of the lower Midwest, the Midsouth, and peninsular Florida, known collectively as the "Shell Mound Archaic" (Figure 4.3). Although the procurement of freshwater shellfish has great antiquity in the East, routine shellfishing and the formation of large middens/mounds along rivers of the Midsouth and lower Midwest began at about 7500 B.P. (Dye 1996) and ceased at about 3000 B.P. Mounds began to accumulate in Florida as early as 6000 B.P. and continued through the St. Johns tradition of the past three millennia. Human interments are common at many shell mounds across the East (Haskins and Herrmann 1996), owing, in part, to the excellent preservation afforded by the chemical composition of shell.

Figure 4.3 Shell Mound Archaic dig (Webb and DeJarnette 1942:plate 162)

Through the 1980s, research on the Shell Mound Archaic centered on three related topics: (1) explaining the economic change of a seemingly expanded diet and intensified land use (e.g., Bender 1985; Brown 1985; Brown and Vierra 1983; Marquardt and Watson 1983); (2) reconstructing the patterns and mechanisms of long-distance exchange (e.g., Goad 1980; Marquardt 1985; Winters 1968); and (3) detecting social differentiation in burial practices (e.g., Rothschild 1979). More recently, Claassen (1991, 1992, 1996) has championed the notion that the Shell Mound Archaic was primarily a mortuary tradition involving the use of shell as a medium for moundbuilding. Earthen mounds featuring ranked interments are a key feature of the Adena and Hopewell traditions of the Woodland period, and Late Archaic burial mounds in the lower Midwest have been interpreted as markers of corporate territories (Charles and Buikstra 1983). Mound construction for mortuary purposes is thus a hallmark feature of several regional traditions.

Nonetheless, Claassen's hypothesis has met with considerable resistance by those pointing out that most of the so-called "mounds" of the Shell Mound Archaic are merely midden deposits (Milner and Jefferies 1998) and that so many shell-bearing sites lack human interments (Hensley 1994).

While debate continues over the mortuary functions of shell-bearing sites in the mid-continent, shell mounds along the St. Johns River of northeast Florida provide unassailable proof that shell was mounded over human interments during the Archaic period. The best example thus far comes from Tick Island on the middle St. Johns River (Aten 1999). Burials salvaged by Bullen from a basal component of a shell-mound complex known as Harris Creek, dated to ca. 5500 B.P., were clearly set in a stratum of white sand beneath shell midden and a second mortuary layer dating to ca. 5300–5000 B.P. Successive layers of shell midden, clean shell, and earth spanning the ceramic Orange period (ca. 4200–3000 B.P.) capped the remnant of the mound. By all accounts, the overlying strata that were mined in the 1960s contained burials of St. Johns II age (post-1250 B.P.).

Ongoing research in Florida is bolstering the evidence from Tick Island for mortuary practices at shell mounds, although many related questions remain unanswered. As in the mid-continent, riverine shell mounds of Florida have yet to provide sufficient data on social structure and regional integration. The configuration and placement of mounds across the landscape is a potentially fruitful source of data in this regard, although perhaps unattainable given the widespread destruction of shell mounds over the past century. Fortunately, two other venues of Archaic moundbuilding in the East, each involving non-mortuary mound-plaza complexes, are providing new insight into social structure at both local and regional scales.

Mound Complexes in the Lower Mississippi Valley

Eleven earthen mound complexes in the lower Mississippi valley have been dated to the Middle Archaic period, and several others are likely that age or older (Russo 1996:table 1). At possibly over 7000 cal. B.P., Monte Sano in southern Louisiana is the oldest (R. Saunders 1994). Three of the better-documented complexes –

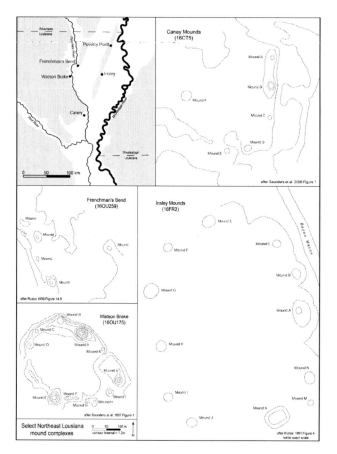

Figure 4.4 Topographic maps of three known Archaic mound complexes and a sketch map of one suspected Archaic mound complex (Insley) in northeast Louisiana, with inset map to upper left showing locations of mound complexes in relation to Poverty Point

Watson Brake (Saunders et al. 1997), Caney (Saunders et al. 2000), and French-man's Bend (Saunders et al. 1994) – are securely dated to 5600–5000 cal. B.P. (Figure 4.4). Four others apparently predate or are coeval with Watson Brake, Caney, and Frenchman's Bend, including the Lower Jackson mound near Poverty Point (Saunders et al. 2001). The latest Middle Archaic mound complex is Hedgepeth, dating to ca. 5200–4500 cal. B.P. Subsequent mound construction in the region leading up to Poverty Point at ca. 3400–2800 cal. B.P. is not well documented, although enough evidence exists to suggest that earth-moving traditions continued unabated through the Late Archaic period. In the words of one specialist, "the Mississippi Valley Archaic mound tradition, extending from the Middle Archaic to Poverty Point traditions, lasted longer than any later southeastern mound-building traditions dependent on horticulture or intensive agricultural production" (Russo 1996:285).

Of the confirmed Middle Archaic mound complexes, two are single mounds, four are paired mounds, and one each has three, five, six, and 11 mounds. All paired mounds include one in the range of 4–6 m in height, the other about 1.5 m. Distance between paired mounds varies from 50 to 200 m. The tallest mounds in complexes of three or more are also in the range of 4–6 m, with the exception of the 7.5 m-high Mound A at Watson Brake. All sites that have been adequately tested show evidence for staged construction in at least one mound. Finally, mounds excavated to date have included some sort of architectural components at their bases.

Below mounds at Monte Sano and Banana Bayou were burned surfaces (pyres?), the former accompanying the remains of a rectangular structure (Russo 1996:270; R. Saunders 1994). Postholes and thermal features were uncovered at the base of Mound A at Frenchmen's Bend (Saunders et al. 1994:141), and a burned post marked the initiation of Mound C construction at Stelly (Russo 1996:278). The significance of these finds lies in the fact that locations of mound erection were preceded by constructions that marked place. Each of the three well-documented complexes mentioned earlier (Watson Brake, Caney, Frenchman's Bend), and a fourth with possible Archaic origins (Insley), exhibits a series of spatial regularities that suggest they were constructed according to a common plan.

The most spectacular of the Archaic mound complexes is Watson Brake, an 11-mound elliptical complex some 370 m in length and 280 m wide, which has been well documented by Saunders et al. (1997). The largest mound (Mound A) is 7.5 m high. Opposite the largest mound, is a 4.5 m-high "backset" mound (Mound E). All the mounds, including nine subordinate mounds, are linked in a meter-high ridge defining an elliptical central plaza area. As is common to all of the complexes with a shared plan, Watson Brake is situated on the edge of an alluvial escarpment, in this case a Pleistocene-age terrace overlooking the Ouachita River.

Caney Mounds is a six-mound complex in an arc nearly 400 m in maximum dimension. First recorded in 1933, Caney has been investigated intermittently ever since (Gibson 1991), most recently by Saunders et al. (2000). Its plan duplicates the relative positions of the major mounds at Watson Brake. The third confirmed site, Frenchman's Bend (Saunders et al. 1994), bears some geometric similarity to Watson Brake and Caney, albeit with fewer mounds. Insley Mounds, located just south of Poverty Point (Kidder 1991), is an elliptical complex of 12 mounds with a plan highly reminiscent of Watson Brake. Although dating is uncertain and later Poverty Point and younger components are apparently present at the site, the overall similarity in plan between Watson Brake and the significantly larger Insley complex suggests initial mound construction dates to the Middle Archaic period.

A replicated plan of mound construction has been inferred from a series of proportional and geometric regularities at each site (Sassaman and Heckenberger 2004a, 2004b). In addition to these site-specific relationships, variations in the orientation of terrace lines and baselines with respect to cardinal directions suggest that individual complexes were part of a regional landscape of monument construction. In terms of scale, individual components were constructed on a ranked proportionality. Watson Brake and Frenchman's Bend are similar in size, but Caney is 20 percent larger and Insley twice the size of the first two.

Clark (2004) has successfully inferred the units of measurement employed to site mounds in each of the complexes, which, apparently, was also used to site complexes over the greater Archaic landscape. Given the apparent engineering behind all this, it stands to reason that mounds were arranged for astronomical or calendrical purposes. However, the varied orientation of mound complexes to cardinal directions precludes such a possibility. Instead, a more complex arrangement across sites is suggested by the regional pattern of cardinality. Georeferencing all sites to the respective largest mounds and orienting each to magnetic north, a pattern of geometric integration is revealed (Sassaman and Heckenber 2004b). This arrangement clearly is not fortuitous. Rather, the integration of all four sites into a regional pattern of alignment suggests that entire landscapes of monumental architecture, and not just individual sites, were planned constructions.

Poverty Point

The relationship of Poverty Point to all of this is uncertain but provocative. Emerging after ca. 3700 B.P. and developing over several ensuing centuries, Poverty Point culture involved unprecedented levels of mound construction and interregional exchange centered on the type site, Poverty Point, a $3\,km^2$ complex of nearly 1 million cubic yards of mounded earth in six nested, elliptical half-rings, two massive bird-shaped effigies, and a few conical and flat-topped mounds (Ford and Webb 1956; Kidder 2002). Other settlements of Poverty Point affiliation were distributed across a 700-square-mile area centered on the type site, with more distant communities participating through exchange with core groups (see papers in Byrd 1991).

Resident population size and sociopolitical complexity are debated aspects of Poverty Point culture. Clearly an earth-moving project of this magnitude and sophistication, no matter how protracted over time, required not only a large pool of labor, but also formal orchestration. Ford and Webb (1956) asserted that Poverty Point was home to thousands of people, whose houses were distributed along each of the six nested ridges. Unfortunately, evidence for domestic architecture along ridges is cryptic at best, although midden accumulation at the site is sufficiently large to support an argument for repeated episodes of large-scale aggregation, if not continuous occupation.

Raw materials imported from as far away as the Great Lakes and the Appalachians, while impressive in volume and diversity, were often used to make mundane items: soapstone for cooking vessels; granite, basalt, and greenstone for celts; hematite and magnetite for plummets; and various cherts for projectiles and cutting tools, to name but a few. Coupled with the ubiquitous baked clay objects, hearths, pits, and midden accumulation, the inventory of subsistence technology strongly suggests that Poverty Point was a place of residence (Gibson 2000:157), but again, direct evidence for permanent residence remains elusive.

The regional integration of Poverty Point culture is likewise uncertain. Obviously, members of local populations were well connected to the outside world through trading partnerships stretching vast distances in virtually all directions. Communities in a 700-square-mile area centered on the type site shared many of

the distinctively Poverty Point traits, yet the degree of similarity is not simply a function of distance from the core locale. This suggests that communities were economically and politically autonomous. Indeed, Gibson (2000) no longer subscribes
to the chiefdom model of regional hierarchy, suggesting instead that Poverty Point
culture was foremost a shared belief system, organized at a corporate level for public
works and ritual, but underwritten by an egalitarian ethos.

The populations that built, occupied, and visited Poverty Point may have consisted of small-scale corporate groups whose internal sociality was based on principles of egalitarianism, but it is hard to defend the position that such constituent
units were not ranked relative to one another. Poverty Point was a place of pil-
grimage, and it drew from a pool of congregants with different histories, experiences, and know-how. People repeatedly traveled to Poverty Point from far-away
places, bringing with them local materials that were left at the site or distributed
locally. And they seem to have returned to their home lands with only ideas, as few
of the material and objects entering the greater Poverty Point area appear to have
left. In a sense, Poverty Point may have been the place of origin for all those who
visited, but it is unlikely that all such persons could claim equal status. As in the
origins myths of hunter-gatherers elsewhere, the sequential creations of different
types of people are the rationale for ranking among the living.

Geometric patterning among Archaic mounds, including those of Poverty Point,
is an archaeological fact whose significance lies not so much in the labor needed
to erect them, but in the ideas needed to conceive of them. Arguably similar in
function to diagrammatic mound centers of Mississippian society (Knight 1998),
Archaic mound complexes may have served as sociograms, locations at which
"public architecture (was) deliberately arranged in such a manner as to evoke and
reinforce key social distinctions" (Knight 1998:60; see also DeBoer 1997). The
central spaces or plazas created by the circular or elliptical arrangement of mounds
may have been especially significant in reproducing hierarchy, as they continue to
do today among Xinguanos of central Brazil (Heckenberger 2004). Archaic shell
rings on the Atlantic Coast may likewise have enabled the reproduction of hierarchical social relationships.

Coastal Shell Rings

Scores of shell deposits generally conforming to circular or semicircular shapes and
ranging from tens to hundreds of meters in diameter have been documented along
the south Atlantic and Gulf coasts (Russo and Heide 2001; Figure 4.5). Although
sites with arcuate shapes of shell-bearing middens formed well into the Woodland
period on the Gulf Coast, sites referred to as shell rings on the south Atlantic Coast
generally date from about 4500 to 3000 B.P., the Late Archaic period. Investigations through the 1980s led researchers to suggest that rings formed from the accumulation of refuse from communities arranged in a circle around an open public
space (plaza). Trinkley's (1985) work at two small shell rings north of Charlestown,
South Carolina, was particularly influential in shaping opinion that shell rings were

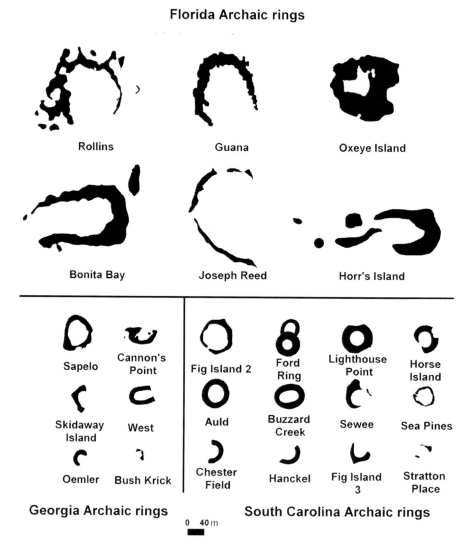

Figure 4.5 Plan drawings of Late Archaic coastal shell rings and related sites in the southeastern United States (used with permission of Michael Russo)

simply accumulations of domestic refuse. Trinkley (1985) also championed the idea that the circular plan of shell rings reflected a community plan whose symmetry reinforced egalitarian relations among co-residents.

Recent fieldwork at shell rings by Michael Russo and Rebecca Saunders calls into question any simplistic claims about ring function and a presumed egalitarian social order. Detailed mapping, soil analysis, and excavation at several sites across the region have revealed much greater complexity in shell ring form and function than ever imagined. There is now abundant evidence that shell was deposited rapidly in large quantities, often over prepared surfaces or low sand mounds (Cable 1993; Russo 1991; Russo and Heide 2002; Saunders 2002). Deposits grew disproportionately across areas receiving shell, resulting in asymmetries in height and width. Russo (2002) and Saunders (2002) agree that large deposits of shell resulted from feasting activities, presumably competitive feasting.

Russo (2002) has focused on this complex geometry as a window into social ranking among shell ring feasters. Few that have been mapped are actually circular in plan; instead, they often assume asymmetrical forms that more than likely mirrored and reproduced social differentiation. Accepting that shell rings accumulated not haphazardly, but rather systematically, if not deliberately, Russo (2004) explores possible sociological implications of asymmetries in ring configuration. Often rings have one of more segments that are taller and broader at the base than other segments, and are rarely perfectly circular in plan.

The Fig Island site on the south Atlantic Coast of South Carolina exemplifies the complexity of shell ring formations (Saunders 2002). The site consists of three "rings" over some 5 hectares in an estuarine biome (Figure 4.6). Fig Island 2 is the closest to an actual ring, at some 77 m in diameter and about 2.5 m above the underlying marsh surface. Fig Island 3 is an arcuate midden about 50 m in maximum

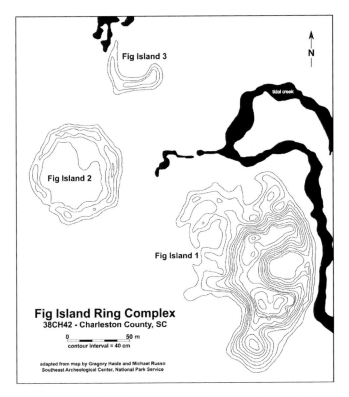

Figure 4.6 Topographic map of the Fig Island shell-ring complex, Charleston County, South Carolina (used with permission of Michael Russo)

dimension that was connected to Fig Island 2 by a shell causeway. The largest feature, Fig Island 1, is a 157 m long, 111 m wide deposit some 5.5 m tall consisting of one large, steep-sided ring enclosing a small plaza and at least two small "ringlets" attached to the arc and enclosing additional small plazas.

The sheer complexity of Fig Island 1 leaves much to the imagination, but even the circular Fig Island 2 is actually structurally asymmetrical. As Russo (2002) notes, the ring is hexagonal in plan, with an opening to the southwest at the midpoint of one of its six sides. Opposite the opening are the widest and tallest segments of the enclosure; behind them is the causeway linking it with Fig Island 3, whose highest and widest aspect lies at one end of the arc. Russo (2002) reviews ethnographic literature of community plans to argue that either of the vertically accentuated features likely supported individuals of privilege or authority.

Fig Island is indeed among the more complex shell rings known, but it, along with others from South Carolina and Georgia, pale in size compared to several of those from Florida. Rings and arcuate structures at least 150 m and as much as 250 m in diameter have been documented at six sites in the state (Russo and Heide 2001; Russo et al. 2002). They typically have peaks at the top of the arcs, and those from south Florida (Horr's Island and Bonita Bay) have elongated U-shaped plans with associated sand/shell mounds.

Circular Village Plaza Complexes

As with Archaic mounds in general, evidence for domestic architecture at coastal shell rings is lacking. Russo (1991) documented an array of postholes in the open space bounded by mounds at Horr's Island in Florida, and Trinkley's (1985) work at Stratton Place revealed an array of features presumed to be associated with domestic space along the ring's outline, but few other data are available. Still, a community pattern of houses arranged in more or less circular fashion around an open space (plaza) can be inferred from the overall plan of most shell rings. Given Russo's (2002) line of argumentation for asymmetries in shell ring form and the general association of circular village plazas with hierarchy (Heckenberger 2004; Lévi-Strauss 1963), it stands to reason that inter-household comparisons, if they were possible, would reflect some measures of social differentiation. It is indeed frustrating that we cannot compare the residues of everyday life across households to see how routine practices reproduced and transformed structures of inequality, or, alternatively, how the routines of everyday life contradicted such structures.

One venue of ongoing research is beginning to produce evidence for small circular village plazas. Direct evidence of a circular village plaza complex has been documented at one middle Savannah site and inferred indirectly from two other, contemporaneous sites of Classic Stallings cultural affiliation (ca. 3800–3500 B.P.). The best example comes from Mims Point, a small shell-bearing site on a ridge nose at the confluence of Stevens Creek and the Savannah River, 1 km north of Stallings Island (Sassaman 1993). Middle Archaic and Late Woodland components interfere only slightly with an otherwise discrete Classic Stallings habitation. Although house floors were compromised by historic-era plowing, clusters of pit features attest to a circular village plaza configuration. Hand excavation of $364\,m^2$ exposed several of these feature clusters. The two best-preserved clusters include one or two deep storage pits, four to five shallow basins, and at least one hearth. Nearly all such features yielded punctated fiber-tempered pottery. The excavated space between major pit clusters was generally devoid of features. Those present in this central, plaza-like area some $16\,m$ in diameter are mostly ephemeral and none contained Classic Stallings pottery. In sum, the evidence points to a circular compound of seven to nine structures, spaced $4–6\,m$ apart, each defined by pit clusters $5–6\,m$ in diameter. Indirect evidence for a circular village plaza complex of equal size has been uncovered at the nearby Ed Marshall site.

The Stallings Culture type site, Stallings Island, also has yielded evidence for a circular village plaza configuration, in this case with an interesting twist (Figure 4.7). Excavations at Stallings Island in 1929 exposed scores of pit features and burials, but no obvious evidence for house floors. Using unpublished field notes on the size, depth, and content of pits, Blessing and Sassaman (2001) were able to infer a pattern of settlement similar to Mims Point and Ed Marshall. Each of the five discernible pit clusters at Stallings Island contained at least one large storage pit, each placed to the right of the aspect (entrance?) facing the interior plaza, with

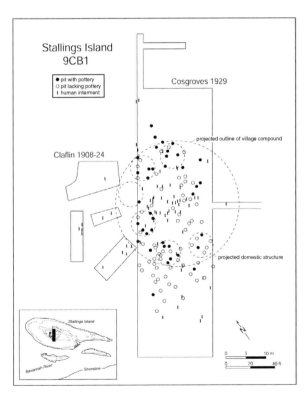

Figure 4.7 Plan schematic of the 1929 block excavation of Stallings Island, showing locations of pit features, burials, and projected domestic structures arrayed in circular fashion around a central plaza

one exception to the left. Frequency distributions of pit types across clusters were similar, lending further support to an inscribed, routinized practice of community layout.

Unlike those at Mims Point and Ed Marshall, the Stallings compound includes a sizeable burial population in the central plaza. The site-wide distribution of burials reveals an unequivocal non-random pattern for location within the projected plaza. Noteworthy in this distribution is the tendency for subadults to be placed on the north side of the central space, and for females to be located in the southeast quadrant. Small sample size notwithstanding, these tendencies give us cautious optimism that the layout of mortuary space was highly structured and thus indicative of social identity, possibly rank.

Stallings Island is the only site in the middle Savannah River valley to contain a large population of burials dating to Classic Stallings times, when circular village plazas were occupied. It is also the only site to produce a large fraction of sherds from carinated vessels (Sassaman 2004b). Using the Mississippian analog for carinated forms (Hally 1986), many of the Stallings Island vessels may have been used for serving in highly social contexts, perhaps mortuary feasting. In this regard Stallings Island was a special place on the landscape, and perhaps something of a center of a local settlement hierarchy. It remains for future work to compare middle Savannah community patterning with that of coastal shell rings to delve further into the symbolic and sociopolitical implications of circular village plazas.

Genesis of the "Powerless"

Lest the reader conclude at this point that the Archaic Southeast consisted exclusively of sedentary, moundbuilding societies structured by principles of hierarchy, allow me to briefly touch upon those unassuming, inconspicuous communities who occupied the interstitial spaces and "quiet" periods of the Archaic past. Indeed, the archaeological record of the Archaic Southeast is replete with evidence for societies whose generalized foraging, frequent mobility, and simple technology mirror the egalitarian formations of the ethnographic present.

The Morrow Mountain tradition of the Georgia-Carolina Piedmont is a case in point (Sassaman 2001a, 2001b). Sites of this tradition are highly redundant, showing little bias for particular locations of the landscape, limited midden accumulation, and nearly exclusive use of local raw materials for tool manufacture. In one sense, these features of the Morrow Mountain record are the expected long-term consequence of adaptation to the relatively homogeneous resource structure of the Piedmont, as Binford's (1980) model of forager settlement organization would predict. However, consideration of the deeper historical and cultural contexts of the Morrow Mountain tradition leads one to a more complicated scenario.

Roots of the Morrow Mountain tradition lie in major river valleys of the Midsouth, where the basal components of shell middens dating to ca. 7500 B.P. contain the tapered stemmed bifaces that is a hallmark of this tradition (Dye 1996). These strata signal the radical change in settlement organization that is the genesis of Shell

Mound Archaic traditions. For the first time in the region, groups began to occupy riverine sites repeatedly, if not permanently, to intensify production to meet increasing economic demand, to inter their dead in shell deposits, and to routinely engage in long-distance exchange and perhaps warfare.

These conditions no doubt spawned scores of ethnogenetic events as groups coalesced and fissioned. The cultural boundaries asserted and redefined through alliances of marriage, exchange, and the like did more than simply demarcate one Shell Mound Archaic group from the next. They likewise excluded certain factions, and simultaneously, spurred some to resist impositions by asserting autonomy and new collective identity by relocating elsewhere.

Bearers of Morrow Mountain material culture appeared in the southern Piedmont shortly after 7500 B.P. and persisted in a virtually unchanging mode of generalized foraging for over 1,500 years. I have argued that, under these specific historical circumstances, the Morrow Mountain tradition had become a culture of resistance, asserting a new identity through practices that were antithetical to those of their immediate ancestors (Sassaman 2001a). By the time bearers of Morrow Mountain culture came to dominate the southern Piedmont landscape, the egalitarian relations they asserted were effectively reproduced for centuries through the routine practices of settlement mobility, food-sharing, generalized foraging, and expedient tool use. Because these practices were so well tuned to the local conditions of the Piedmont, it is easy to lose sight of the fact that the cultural logic underwriting them were historically derived from events and circumstances so distant in time and space.

Discussion and Conclusion

The empirical record of the Archaic Southeast has expanded dramatically in the past two decades to encompass traits hitherto deemed exclusive to food-producing societies of later times. The expanded purview of Archaic archaeology has generated a bit of controversy and skepticism (e.g., Russo 1994). Now that the archaeological community accepts the empirical reality of Archaic mounds, we face the tougher challenge of making sense of these new data. In this regard, a particularly interesting problem lies in the conflicting signals of complex ritual and the underpinnings of hierarchical structures with an archaeological record of everyday practice generally consistent with egalitarian practices. Rather than accept the need to retool conceptually to understand complexity among Archaic societies, the tendency on the part of some skeptics has been to argue that you do not need complex society to build mounds.

No matter what they say about daily practice, Archaic mounds and circular villages reflect and served to reproduce structures of ranking in Archaic cosmologies. The practices of mounding and village construction were institutions that transcended individual experiences and they involved esoteric knowledge that was unlikely to have been shared by all. There is little to suggest that the collectives involved in mound construction were corporations of like-minded people. Rather, mound complexes may have been focal points for the negotiation and reproduction of diversity, and thus constantly in a state of becoming, never fixed or uncontested. For instance, cyclical movement through an integrated landscape of mound complexes, such as those of northeast Louisiana, could have reproduced a set of shifting ranked relationships among constituent parties with claims over origins at specific sites (stages) in the cycle, as in the concepts of sequential hierarchy (Johnson 1982) or heterarchy (Crumley 1987). Contrast this with Poverty Point, where arguably the entire regional landscape was telescoped down to the place of all origins, and where institutions of economic and political control would surely have emerged if only everyone stayed in residence long enough.

I submit that Archaic moundbuilding traditions embodied the root metaphors for hierarchical structures in the moundbuilding traditions of the Woodland and Mississippian traditions. In support of this assertion, I remind the reader of the need to separate the act of moundbuilding from the activities taking place on mounds (e.g., Knight 2001:302). Platform mounds of Mississippian chiefdoms were platforms for buildings of the elite and access to them was limited; they were explicitly about social differentiation. Similar constructions of the Middle Woodland period were locations of feasts and mortuary ritual, actions arguably serving to integrate, rather than to differentiate, social identities (Knight 2001; Lindauer and Blitz 1997). There are as yet few data on the activities taking place at Archaic mound complexes, but, given the absence of platform constructions, they were not likely used as ritual surfaces or residences per se. Thus, each of the major moundbuilding traditions involved different types of activities and most likely different structural relationships among mounds, ritual actions, and routine practice.

As we continue to understand how and why mound uses changed over the course of the pre-Columbian Southeast, we should not lose sight of the threads of continuity (or similarity) among the various moundbuilding traditions in the ways that mounds were conceived, sited, and erected. Mound construction was a staged process among all traditions. In Mississippian cosmology, mounds were earth symbols, and adding a stage was an action of renewing the earth (Knight 1989). This same symbolism can be read into the staged construction of Woodland mounds (Knight 2001), and may very well have parallels in Archaic mounds.

In addition, all mound traditions of the Southeast involve locations with single mounds and contemporaneous locations with multiple mounds. Multi-mound complexes almost always involve mounds of variable size. Moreover, locations of three or more mounds across time were laid out according to replicated plans, with the largest mounds usually occupying prominent positions at the center or at the apex of an array of mounds. Such arrangements have been demonstrated to reflect social ranking or divisions in Woodland and Mississippian societies (DeBoer 1997; Knight 1998). Astronomical alignments have been implicated in many cases. Finally, mound complexes in Archaic, Woodland, and Mississippian traditions include examples with centrally enclosed space, typically regarded as plazas.

Given similarities in structural aspects of Archaic, Woodland, and Mississippian moundbuilding traditions, it is reasonable to expect continuity in the act of moundbuilding itself, even if the practices taking place on mounds changed repeatedly. Here the Archaic record seemingly belies continuity. The gap of over 1,000 years that separates the latest Middle Archaic mounds from Poverty Point is matched by a nearly comparable gap between the latest Poverty Point construction and those of the Woodland period.

However, like the time separating episodes of Woodland and Mississippian moundbuilding, these gaps are more apparent than real. If we expand the scale of observation beyond the Mississippi valley to include the entire eastern Woodlands, moundbuilding appears as a temporally continuous, albeit geographically discontinuous, phenomenon. From 4500 to 3500 B.P., when moundbuilding had slowed or ceased in the lower Mississippi valley, shell rings (mounds) were being built on the Atlantic and Gulf coasts, and the shell mounds of the middle St. Johns of Florida were expanding rapidly. We may likewise include here some sites of the interior Shell Mound Archaic, as well as Stallings circular village plazas, which date to the late centuries of this interval. The point is that once on the greater southeastern landscape, moundbuilding never ceased, and, of course, the mounds themselves became permanent fixtures on the landscape. The specific meanings of mounds indeed changed, as did activities associated with mounds, but the underlying principles of ranking and cyclical processes evident in their configuration and staged construction never disappeared.

Clark (2004) has suggested that the cultural logic for siting and building mounds was carried forward in everyday practice, in, for instance, the way houses were constructed and spaces arranged within, around, and between residences. I fully agree, but would add that potential contradictions between daily practice and ritual practice make it hard to imagine that the quotidian of Archaic life was always consonant with the proscriptions of sacred belief. I have two reasons for asserting this. First, the lack of secure evidence for large-scale, perennial occupations at Archaic mounds, shell rings, and even Poverty Point, means that middens and material assemblages accumulated from intermittent, transient visits by people who spent most of their time away from ritual centers. Poverty Point and sites of the Shell Mound Archaic suggest either that those visiting these locations came from great distances, or that visiting involved the travels of local residents to far-away places, or both. The beliefs these people carried with them as participants of Archaic religion(s) may not have squared with the experiences of living through such varied material circumstances. In other words, beliefs shaped the worlds that Archaic people experienced, but undoubtedly contradictions continuously arose between the ideal and the real in matters as mundane as the edibility of certain foods, the appropriateness of first-cousin marriages, and settlement near a swamp.

A related matter is the reality that Archaic moundbuilding ritual seems to have drawn in and integrated people of different cultural identity (ethnicity). Participants in group ritual no doubt filtered the deep structures of belief through the surface structures of their respective histories, and, in turn, altered deep structures through the routines of their daily lives. Put back into the context of aggregation at ritual centers, these altered structures no doubt fueled factionalization and ultimately the transformation of collective practice (at least in that one location).

Assertions of cultural identity permeated many aspects of social life in the Archaic, as they do in all times and places. These symbolic actions have too often been shrouded in theory aimed at emergent properties of social life (e.g., adaptation, mode of production), or reduced to essentialist dimensions of identity (e.g., an archaeological culture, consisting of methodological individuals). The instances of hypertrophy evident in the Archaic record provide an opportunity to investigate how material culture is manipulated, through tradition, to affect social identities and the links among them. But these instances of "culture blown out of proportion" are not singular in their potential to inform on historical process.

It is imperative that we continue to expand our methods for tracing the histories of population movements, interethnic encounters, and instances of ethnogenesis, for these are common causes of cultural variation and change, and they occurred repeatedly throughout the Archaic. And, in constructing a historical processualism (Pauketat 2001) for the Archaic Southeast, the next generation of researchers must jettison the received wisdom of their forebears who, in canonizing the Archaic as the antecedent to "complex" society, perpetuated the myth that little of interest took place. Clearly that was not the case.

ACKNOWLEDGMENTS

Portions of this chapter were adapted from a paper published in the *Journal of Archaeological Research* (Sassaman 2004a). My thanks to the publisher, Kluwer Academic, for permission to use this material. I am grateful to Mike Russo for permission to use figures from his work on shell rings and for his help in modifying them for use here. Thanks also to go to Dan Morse for permission to use some of his excellent photographs of Dalton and Sloan points from the Sloan site. Permission to use bannerstones from the Willima H. Claflin collection was enabled through the kind assistance of Viva Fisher, Peabody Museum, Harvard University.

REFERENCES

Anderson, David G., 1990 The Paleoindian colonization of eastern North America: A view from the southeastern United States. In *Early Paleoindian Economies of Eastern North America*. K. B. Tankersley and B. L. Isaac, eds. Pp. 163–216. Research in Economic Anthropology, Supplement 5. Greenwich, CT: JAI Press.

Aten, Lawrence, 1999 Middle Archaic ceremonialism at Tick Island, Florida: Ripley P. Bullen's 1961 excavation at the Harris Creek site. *The Florida Anthropologist* 52, 131–200.

Bender, Barbara, 1985 Emergent tribal formations in the American midcontinent. *American Antiquity* 50, 52–62.

Biersak, Aletta, 1999 Introduction: From the "New Ecology" to the new ecologies. *American Anthropologist* 101, 5–18.

Binford, Lewis R., 1980 Willow smoke and dogs' tails: Hunter-gatherer settlement systems and archaeological site formation. *American Antiquity* 45, 4–20.

Blessing, Meggan E., and Kenneth E. Sassaman, 2001 New perspectives on spatial patterning of Stallings communities. Paper presented at the 58th Annual Meeting of the Southeastern Archaeological Conference, Chattanooga.

Blitz, John H., 1999 Mississippian chiefdoms and the fission-fusion process. *American Antiquity* 64, 577–592.

Brose, David S., 1979 A speculative model on the role of exchange in the prehistory of the Eastern Woodlands. In *Hopewell Archaeology: The Chillicothe Conference*, D. S. Brose and N. Greber, eds. Pp. 3–8. Kent, OH: Kent State University Press.

Brown, James A., 1985 Long-term trends to sedentism and the emergence of complexity in the American Midwest. In *Prehistoric Hunter-Gatherers: The Emergence of Cultural Complexity*. T. D. Price and J. A. Brown, eds. Pp. 201–231. New York: Academic Press.

Brown, James A., and Robert Vierra, 1983 What happened in the Middle Archaic? Introduction to an ecological approach to Koster site archaeology. In *Archaic Hunter-Gatherers in the American Midwest*. J. L. Phillips and J. A. Brown, eds. Pp. 165–195. New York: Academic Press.

Byrd, Kathleen M., ed., 1991 *The Poverty Point Culture: Local Manifestations, Subsistence Practices, and Trade Networks*. Geoscience and Man, vol. 29. Baton Rouge: Louisiana State University.

Cable, John R., 1993 Prehistoric chronology and settlement patterns of Edisto Beach State Park. In *Cultural Resources Survey and Archaeological Site Evaluation of the Edisto Beach State Park, Colleton County, South Carolina*. Pp. 158–205. Report on file with South Carolina Department of Parks, Recreation, and Tourism, Columbia, South Carolina. Stone Mountain, GA: New South Associates.

Charles, Douglas, and Jane Buikstra, 1983 Archaic mortuary sites in the central Mississippi drainage: Distribution, structure, and behavioral implications. In *Archaic Hunter-Gatherers in the American Midwest*. J. L. Phillips and J. A. Brown, eds. Pp. 117–145. New York: Academic Press.

Claassen, Cheryl, 1991 New hypotheses for the demise of the Shell Mound Archaic. In *The Archaic Period in the Mid-South*. C. McNutt, ed. Pp. 66–72. Archaeological Report 24. Jackson: Mississippi Department of Archives and History.

—— 1992 Shell mounds as burial mounds: A revision of the Shell Mound Archaic. In *Current Archaeological Research in Kentucky*, vol. 2. D. Pollack and A. G. Henderson, eds. Pp. 1–12. Frankfort: Kentucky Heritage Council.

—— 1996 A consideration of the social organization of the Shell Mound Archaic. In *Archaeology of the Mid-Holocene Southeast*. K. E. Sassaman and D. G. Anderson, eds. Pp. 235–258. Gainesville: University Press of Florida.

Clark, John, 2004 Surrounding the sacred. In *Signs of Power*, J. Gibson and P. Carr, eds. Pp. 162–213. Tuscaloosa: University of Alabama Press.

Crothers, George M., 1999 Prehistoric hunters and gatherers, and the Archaic period Green River shell middens of western Kentucky. Ph.D. dissertation, Department of Anthropology, Washington University, St. Louis.

Crumley, Carole L., 1987 A dialectical critique of hierarchy. In *Power Relations and State Formation*. T. C. Patterson and C. W. Gailey, eds. Pp. 155–159. Washington, DC: American Anthropological Association.

DeBoer, Warren, 1997 Ceremonial centers from the Cayapas (Esmeraldas, Ecuador) to Cillicothe (Ohio, USA). *Cambridge Archaeological Journal* 7(1), 1–15.

Dye, David H., 1996 Riverine adaptation in the Midsouth. In *Of Caves and Shell Mounds*. K. C. Carstens and P. J. Watson, eds., Pp. 140–158. Tuscaloosa: University of Alabama Press.

Elliott, Daniel T., R. Jerald Ledbetter, and Elizabeth A. Gordon, 1994 *Data Recovery at Lovers Lane, Phinizy Swamp and the Old Dike Sites Bobby Jones Expressway Extension Corridor*

Augusta, Georgia. Occasional Papers in Cultural Resource Management 7, Georgia Department of Transportation, Atlanta.

Flanagan, J. G., 1989 Hierarchy in simple "egalitarian" societies. *Annual Review of Anthropology* 18, 245–266.

Ford, James A., and Clarence H. Webb, 1956 *Poverty Point, a Late Archaic Site in Louisiana*. Anthropological Papers, vol. 46, pt. 1. New York: American Museum of Natural History.

Fortier, Andrew C., 1984 *The Go-Kart Site*. American Bottom Archaeology, FAI-270 Site Reports 9. Urbana: University of Illinois Press.

Gibson, Jon L., 1991 Catahoula: An amphibious Poverty Point manifestation in eastern Louisiana. In *The Poverty Point Culture: Local Manifestations, Subsistence Practices, and Trade Networks*. K. M. Byrd, ed. Pp. 61–87. Geoscience and Man, vol. 29. Baton Rouge: Louisiana State University.

—— 2000 *The Ancient Mounds of Poverty Point: Place of the Rings*. Gainesville: University Press of Florida.

Goad, Sharon, 1980 Patterns of Late Archaic exchange. *Tennessee Anthropologist* 5, 1–16.

Gramly, Richard M., and Robert E. Funk, 1991 Olive Branch: A Large Dalton and Pre-Dalton encampment at Thebes Gap, Alexander County, Illinois. In *The Archaic Period in the Mid-South*. C. H. McNutt, ed. Pp. 23–33. Archaeological Report 24. Jackson: Mississippi Department of Archives and History.

Grinker, Richard Roy, 1994 *Houses in the Rainforest: Ethnicity and Inequality among the Farmers and Foragers in Central Africa*. Berkeley: University of California Press.

Hally, David J., 1986 The identification of vessel function: A case study from northwest Georgia. *American Antiquity* 51, 267–295.

Haskins, Valeria A., and Nicholas P. Herrmann, 1996 Shell Mound bioarchaeology. In *Of Caves and Shell Mounds*. K. C. Carstens and P. J. Watson, eds. Pp. 107–118. Tuscaloosa: University of Alabama Press.

Hassen, Harold, and Kenneth B. Farnsworth, 1987 *The Bullseye Site: A Floodplain Archaic Mortuary Site in the Lower Illinois River Valley*. Reports of Investigation 42. Springfield: Illinois State Museum.

Hayden, Brian, 1995 Pathways to power: Principles for creating socioeconomic inequalities. In *Foundations of Social Inequality*. T. D. Price and G. M. Feinman, eds. Pp. 15–86. New York: Plenum Press.

Heckenberger, M. J., 2004 *The Ecology of Power: Archaeology, History, and Memory in the Southern Amazon*. New York: Routledge.

Hensley, Christine, 1994 The Archaic settlement system of the Middle Green River valley. Ph.D. dissertation, Department of Anthropology, Washington University, St. Louis.

Hofman, Jack L., 1986 Hunter-gatherer mortuary variability: Toward an explanatory model. Ph.D. dissertation, Department of Anthropology, University of Tennessee, Knoxville.

Johnson, Gregory, 1982 Organizational structure and scalar stress. In *Theory and Explanation in Archaeology*. C. Renfrew, M. J. Rowlands, and B. Segraves, eds. Pp. 389–342. New York: Academic Press.

Johnson, Jay K., and Samuel O. Brookes, 1989 Benton points, turkey tails, and cache blades: Middle Archaic exchange in the Midsouth. *Southeastern Archaeology* 8, 134–145.

Kelly, Robert L., 1995 *The Foraging Spectrum: Diversity in Hunter-Gatherer Lifeways*. Washington, DC: Smithsonian Institution Press.

Kelly, Robert L., and Lawrence C. Todd, 1988 Coming into the country: Early Paleoindian hunting and mobility. *American Antiquity* 53, 231–244.

Kidder, T. R., 1991 New directions in Poverty Point settlement archaeology: An example from northeast Louisiana. In *The Poverty Point Culture: Local Manifestations, Subsistence Practices, and Trade Networks*. K. M. Byrd, ed. Pp. 27–53. Geoscience and Man, vol. 29. Baton Rouge: Louisiana State University.

——2002 Mapping Poverty Point. *American Antiquity* 67, 89–101.

Knight, Vernon J., Jr., 1989 Symbolism of Mississippian mounds. In *Powhatan's Mantle: Indians in the Colonial Southeast*. P. H. Wood, G. A. Waselkov, and M. T. Hatley, eds. Pp. 279–291. Lincoln: University of Nebraska Press.

——1998 Moundville as a diagrammatic ceremonial center. In *Archaeology of the Moundville Chiefdom*. V. J. Knight, Jr. and V. P. Steponaitis, eds. Pp. 44–62. Washington, DC: Smithsonian Institution Press.

——2001 Feasting and the emergence of platform mound ceremonialism in eastern North America. In *Feasts: Archaeological and Ethnographic Perspectives on Food, Politics, and Power*. M. Dietler and B. Hayden, eds. Pp. 311–333. Washington, DC: Smithsonian Institution Press.

Knoblock, Byron, 1939 *Bannerstones of the North American Indian*. LaGrange, ILL: privately published.

Leacock, Eleanor, and Richard Lee, 1982 Introduction. In *Politics and History in Band Societies*. Eleanor Leacock and Richard B. Lee, eds. Pp. 1–20. Cambridge: Cambridge University Press.

Ledbetter, R. Jerald, 1995 *Archaeological Investigations at Mill Branch Sites 9WR4 and 9WR11, Warren County, Georgia*. Technical Report 3. Atlanta: Interagency Archeological Services Division, National Park Service.

Lee, Richard B., and Irven DeVore, eds., 1976 *Kalahari Hunter-Gatherers: Studies of the !Kung San and their Neighbors*. Cambridge, MA: Harvard University Press.

Lévi-Strauss, Claude, 1963 *Structural Anthropology*. New York: Basic Books.

Lindauer, Owen, and John Blitz, 1997 Higher ground: The archaeology of North American platform mounds. *Journal of Archaeological Research* 5, 169–207.

Marquardt, William H., 1985 Complexity and Scale in the Study of Fisher-Gatherer-Hunters: An example from the eastern United States. In *Prehistoric Hunter-Gatherers: The Emergence of Cultural Complexity*. T. D. Price and J. A. Brown, eds. Pp. 59–97. New York: Academic Press.

Marquardt, William H., and Patty Jo Watson, 1983 The Shell Mound Archaic of western Kentucky. In *Archaic Hunters and Gatherers in the American Midwest*. J. A. Phillips and J. A. Brown, eds. Pp. 323–339. New York: Academic Press.

Meltzer, David, 1989 Was stone exchanged among eastern North American Paleoindians? In *Eastern Paleoindian Lithic Resource Use*. C. J. Ellis and J. C. Lothrop, eds. Pp. 11–39. Boulder: Westview Press.

Milner, George R., and Richard W. Jefferies, 1998 The Read Archaic shell midden in Kentucky. *Southeastern Archaeology* 17(2), 119–132.

Morse, Dan F., 1997 *Sloan: A Paleoindian Dalton Cemetery in Arkansas*. Washington, DC: Smithsonian Institution Press.

Pauketat, Timothy R., 2001 Practice and History in Archaeology: An Emerging Paradigm. *Anthropological Theory* 1(1), 73–98.

——2003 Resettled farmers and the making of a Mississippian polity. *American Antiquity* 68, 39–66.

Roper, Donna C., 1978 *The Airport Site: A Multicomponent Site in the Sangamon Drainage*. Papers in Anthropology 4. Springfield: Illinois State Museum.

Rothschild, Nan, 1979 Mortuary behavior and social organization at Indian Knoll and Dickson Mounds. *American Antiquity* 44, 658–675.

Russo, Michael, 1991 Archaic sedentism on the Florida coast: A case study from Horr's Island. Ph.D. dissertation, Department of Anthropology, University of Florida, Gainesville.

—— 1994 Why we don't believe in Archaic ceremonial mounds and why we should: The case from Florida. *Southeastern Archaeology* 13, 93–108.

—— 1996 Southeastern Archaic mounds. In *Archaeology of the Mid-Holocene Southeast*. K. E. Sassaman and D. G. Anderson, eds. Pp. 259–287. Gainesville: University Press of Florida.

—— 2002 Architectural features at Fig Island. In *The Fig Island Ring Complex (38CH42): Coastal Adaptation and the Question of Ring Function in the Late Archaic*. R. Saunders, ed. Pp. 85–97. Report submitted to South Carolina Department of Archives and History under grant #45-01-16441.

—— 2004 Measuring shell rings for social inequality: Towards an understanding of circular community dynamics. In *Signs of Power*. J. Gibson and P. Carr, eds. Pp. 26–70. Tuscaloosa: University of Alabama Press.

Russo, Michael, and Gregory Heide, 2001 Shell rings of the southeast US. *Antiquity* 75(289), 491–492.

—— 2002 The Joseph Reed shell ring. *The Florida Anthropologist* 55(2), 67–88.

Russo, Michael, Gregory Heide, and Vicki Rolland, 2002 *The Guana Shell Ring*. Report submitted to the Florida Department of State Division of Historical Resources, Historic Preservation Grant F0126.

Sassaman, Kenneth E., 1993 *Mims Point 1992: Archaeological Investigations at a Prehistoric Habitation Site in the Sumter National Forest, South Carolina*. Savannah River Archaeological Research Papers 4. Occasional Papers of the Savannah River Archaeological Research Program, South Carolina Institute of Archaeology and Anthropology. Columbia: University of South Carolina.

—— 1998 Crafting cultural identity in hunter-gatherer economies. In *Craft and Social Identity*. C. L. Costin and R. P. Wright, eds. Pp. 93–107. Archeological Papers of the American Anthropological Association 8. Washington, DC: American Anthropological Association.

—— 2000 Agents of change in hunter-gatherer technology. In *Agency in Archaeology*. M.-A. Dobres and J. Robb, eds. Pp. 148–168. London: Routledge.

—— 2001a Hunter-gatherers and traditions of resistance. In *The Archaeology of Traditions: Agency and History Before and After Columbus*. T. Pauketat, ed. Pp. 218–236. Gainesville: University Press of Florida.

—— 2001b Articulating hidden histories of the mid-Holocene in the southern Appalachians. In *Archaeology of the Appalachian Highlands*. L. P. Sullivan and S. C. Prezzano, eds. Pp. 103–121. Knoxville: University of Tennessee Press.

—— 2004a Complex hunter-gatherers in evolution and history: A North American perspective. *Journal of Archaeological Research* 12, 227–280.

—— 2004b Common origins and divergent histories in the early pottery traditions of the American Southeast. In *Early Pottery in the Lower Southeast*. R. Saunders and C. Hays, eds. Tuscaloosa: University of Alabama Press (in press).

Sassaman, Kenneth E., and Michael J. Heckenberger, 2004a Crossing the Symbolic Rubicon in the Southeast. In *Signs of Power*. J. Gibson and P. Carr, eds. Pp. 214–233. Tuscaloosa: University of Alabama Press.

—— 2004b Roots of the theocratic formative in the American Southeast. In *Hunter-Gatherers in Theory and Archaeology*. G. M. Crothers, ed. Pp. 422–443. Carbondale: Center for Archaeological Investigations, Southern Illinois University.

Saunders, Joe W., Thurman Allen, and Roger T. Saucier, 1994 Four Archaic? Mound complexes in northeast Louisiana. *Southeastern Archaeology* 13, 134–153.

Saunders, Joe, Thurman Allen, Reca Jones, and G. Swoveland, 2000 Caney Mounds (16CT5). *Louisiana Archaeological Society Newsletter* 27(3), 14–21.

Saunders, Joe, Thurman Allen, Dennis LaBatt, Reca Jones, and David Griffing, 2001 An assessment of the antiquity of the Lower Jackson Mound. *Southeastern Archaeology* 20, 67–77.

Saunders, Joe W., Rolfe D. Mandel, Roger T. Saucier, E. Thurman Allen, C. T. Hallmark, Jay K. Johnson, Edwin H. Jackson, C. M. Allen, G. L. Stringer, Douglas S. Frink, James K. Feathers, Stephen Williams, Kristin J. Gremillion, M. F. Vidrine, and Reca Jones, 1997 A mound complex in Louisiana at 5400–5000 years before the present. *Science* 277, 1796–1799.

Saunders, Rebecca, 1994 The case for Archaic mounds in southeastern Louisiana. *Southeastern Archaeology* 13, 118–134.

——— 2002 Summary and conclusions. In *The Fig Island Ring Complex (38CH42): Coastal Adaptation and the Question of Ring Function in the Late Archaic.* R. Saunders, ed. Pp. 4–159. Report submitted to South Carolina Department of Archives and History under grant #45-01-16441.

Schrire, Carmel, 1984 Wild surmises on savage thoughts. In *Past and Present in Hunter-Gatherer Studies.* Carmel Schrire, ed. Pp. 1–25. Orlando: Academic Press.

Trinkley, Michael B., 1985 The form and function of South Carolina's Early Woodland shell rings. In *Structure and Process in Southeastern Archaeology.* Roy S. Dickens, Jr., ed. Pp. 102–118. Tuscaloosa: University of Alabama Press.

Walthall, John, and Brad Koldehoff, 1998 Hunter-gatherer interaction and alliance formation: Dalton and the cult of the long blade. *Plains Anthropologist* 43, 257–273.

Webb, William S., 1974 *Indian Knoll.* Knoxville: University of Tennessee Press.

Webb, William S., and David L. DeJarnette, 1942 *An Archaeological Survey of Pickwick Basin in the Adjacent Portions of the States of Alabama, Mississippi, and Tennessee.* Smithsonian Institution Bureau of American Ethnology, Bulletin 129. Washington, DC.

Wilmsen, Edwin, 1989 *Land Filled with Flies: A Political Economy of the Kalahari.* Chicago: University of Chicago Press.

Winters, Howard D., 1968 Value systems and trade cycles of the Late Archaic in the Midwest. In *New Perspectives in Archaeology.* S. R. Binford and L. R. Binford, eds. Pp. 175–221. Chicago: Aldine.

Wood, W. D., D. T. Elliott, T. P. Rudolph, and D. B. Blanton, 1986 *Prehistory of the Richard B. Russell Reservoir: The Archaic and Woodland Periods of the Upper Savannah River. Russell Papers.* Atlanta: Interagency Archeological Services Division, National Park Service.

Woodburn, James, 1982 Egalitarian societies. *Man* 17, 431–451.

5

The Enigmatic Hopewell of the Eastern Woodlands

William S. Dancey

Soon after European colonists on the east coast of North America began their western expansion across the Appalachian mountain range in the late 1700s, they encountered ancient burial mounds and monumental earthworks. Reports of these discoveries and the artistically fabulous artifacts they contained constitute some of the first publications in American archaeology (Atwater 1820; Squier and Davis 1848). Although more often than not the newcomers were skeptical of the Indian origin of these mounds, earthworks, and artifacts, we know conclusively today that they were the creations of indigenous, North American Indians (Pauketat and Loren, this volume).

By the time archaeology in the Americas was becoming professional in the late 1800s many forces were altering or destroying these ancient monuments. In the early 1890s, Frederick Putnam, a leading figure in transforming American archaeology from an antiquarian to a scientific pursuit, commissioned Warren King Moorehead to acquire artifacts from Ohio for the upcoming 1893 Columbian Exhibition in Chicago (Willey and Sabloff 1993). In 1891, after preliminary work at the Fort Ancient earthwork in southwestern Ohio, Moorehead moved his operation to the Clark's Works in south central Ohio (Figure 5.1). Here he began excavation of the numerous mounds contained within what had been recorded by Squier and Davis (1848) in the 1840s as the largest earthen enclosure in the Ohio River valley (Greber and Ruhl 2000; Moorehead 1922). The site consists of more than 3 km of a continuous earthen and stone embankment enclosing 51 ha of a burial mound district containing at least 40 burial mounds, including Mound 25, the largest earthen burial mound in North America measuring approximately 55 × 152 m at the base and 9 m tall. The artifacts and burials Moorehead unearthed at the site caused a sensation at the exhibition and the site was renamed Hopewell after the current owner, Captain M. C. Hopewell. This site embodies the features that would later be identified as the Hopewell

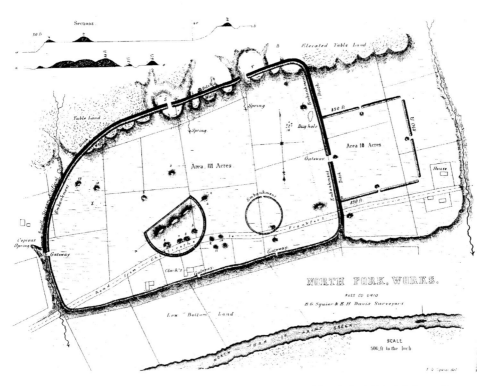

Figure 5.1 The Hopewell Earthwork (aka Clark's Works and North Fork Works), Ross County, Ohio. The three aligned mounds at the mouth of the hemispheric embankment near the center of the figure are known today as Mound 25 (Squier and Davis 1848:plate X)

culture: extravagant burial ceremonialism, diversified craft arts, and inter-regional exchange.

Over the next decade or so, as human remains and artifacts from old and new excavations in southern Ohio were compared, distinctions emerged that led to the crystallization of the Hopewell culture concept. Hopewell was thought to fall in the Middle Woodland period (now dated 200 B.C. to A.D. 400) and in many areas the terms Hopewell and Middle Woodland are still used interchangeably. In a classic paper published in 1967, James B. Griffin synthesized knowledge of eastern North America gained since the turn of the century. Reflecting the perspective of most archaeologists of the time, he identified the most important outside influence as that of the introduction of agriculture from Mesoamerica beginning about 1000 B.C. Also in synch with current thought, he identified two cultural climaxes: the Hopewellian florescence, during the Middle Woodland period, and the Mississippian climax after A.D. 1000. Thus, from the time of its removal from the general class of Moundbuilders at the turn of the 20th century, Hopewell retained its status as a unique cultural type and came to be heralded as one of the major achievements of past Native Americans.

The Middle Woodland Archaeological Record

The present chapter aims to summarize current thought and knowledge of the Hopewell cultural tradition within the Middle Woodland period. Before beginning, however, it is necessary to identify some obstacles in the way of this goal. Ideally, it would be of advantage to have a representative sample of all the kinds of archaeological remains resulting from human activity during our period of interest. This is rarely achieved for any period anywhere in the world, however, and any honest summary of a region's archaeology must acknowledge the ways in which the record falls short of this ideal. In our case, a multitude of interrelated biases contribute to an unrepresentative sample. A few of these will be identified in order to put the present summary in perspective.

One of the most dramatic biases is the preference shown by archaeologists for burial mounds and earthworks over settlements. This lopsided view of the record is nowhere more vivid than in southern Ohio, where until recently only one or two Middle Woodland settlements had been documented (Dancey and Pacheco 1997a). As a result, the social context of the people buried in the mounds and who built the earthworks is poorly known in this area. The situation is better in regions such as the Illinois River valley and the upper Tennessee valley where mound burial was more modest and earthwork construction minor (Seeman 1992). A related bias is the concentration of archaeological activity in areas containing mounds and earthworks and on the periods containing these kinds of remains. The cumulative effect of these biases is a highly uneven time-space documentation of the archaeological record in the east.

Bias appears also in how mounds were selected for excavation, how they were excavated, and the extent to which the work was reported (Figure 5.2). Low mounds with burials containing skeletons unaccompanied by grave goods often were described in only a sentence or two. Even large mounds containing tombs and lavish burial furniture more often than not would be incompletely explored as attention centered on finding the most extravagant interments. Mound fill was seldom examined in detail, nor was the soil around a mound. Furthermore, inter-mound space was rarely examined at multiple mound sites.

Additionally, it must not be forgotten that most of the known Hopewellian artifacts are durable objects that have survived because they were taken out of circulation by being placed in burials. Perishable items survive only through accidents of preservation. Hopewellian fabrics, for example, are preserved in rare cases where they came into contact with copper; the copper salts replaced the structure of the fibers creating a pseudomorph. Fabrics and wooden artifacts are sometimes preserved in anaerobic contexts, as would occur if the context of burial became immediately waterlogged.

The caching of artifacts by ancient people has also led to large assemblages of intact Hopewellian artifacts in a number of cases. Here, in a manner similar to the protection afforded by being in a mound, the artifacts were sealed in time capsules, out of range of modern land use such as plowing. Taken out of these protective contexts, even durable objects would seldom preserve either, because they would enter

(a)

(b)

Figure 5.2 Excavation techniques: (a) early 20th century (Tremper Mound, Scioto County, Ohio; Otto 1984:19); (b) modern (Robert Harness Mound, Liberty Works, Ross County, Ohio; Greber et al. 1983:fig. 1.1); reproduced with permission of the Ohio Historical Society

the archaeological record only if broken or lost, and be subject to further frag-
mentation through trampling or recycling. Not all Hopewellian mortuary practices
safeguarded artifacts, for in many cases they were deliberately broken or inciner-
ated on a cremation pyre.

The East before the Middle Woodland

Despite the biased nature of the data available to him, recent research suggests that
the hard-won reconstruction of James B. Griffin in 1967 is essentially correct for
the Middle Woodland period and the Hopewell culture. During the 600-year period
of time between approximately 200 B.C. and A.D. 400 people in many parts of the
east invested significant amounts of energy in elaborate cultural practices, including mortuary ceremonialism. Although peaking between A.D. 0–200, these complicated practices did not spring up suddenly in most cases, but instead were rooted
in similar, though more modest, practices initiated in many cases thousands of years
earlier. As Griffin and others have pointed out, Hopewell is a cultural climax (Hall
1980). Because of this, it is instructive to look at its foundation, if only briefly, before
opening the door on the Hopewell world any wider. Significantly, current archaeological reporting for the east documents a very early beginning for many Middle
Woodland practices.

Current evidence suggests that the east was populated during the Paleoindian
period between 11,500 and 10,800 years B.C. and that the prevalent foraging
strategy led to slow population expansion over most of the east, except for the
Appalachian mountain chain (Adovasio and Pedler, this volume). Residential stability including sedentism was established soon after (certainly by the Middle
Archaic, ca. 7500 B.P.), and all parts of the landscape became occupied, or were
utilized to some degree. Relationships intensified between regions, often resulting
in pan-regional exchange networks such as represented in the Late Archaic by the
Old Copper, Red Ocher, Green River, and Poverty Point complexes (Sassaman,
this volume). These networks can be seen as precursors to what has been called the
pan-eastern "Hopewell Interaction Sphere" of the Middle Woodland (Caldwell
1964).

Intensified procurement of local flora precipitated the appearance of domesticated native plants in the second millennium B.C. (Smith 1989). By the Early
Woodland period, the list of domesticates had come to include most of the members
of a suite of plants often referred to as the Eastern Agricultural Complex, namely
squash, marshelder, goosefoot, sunflower, erect knotweed, maygrass, and little
barley. Together, these cultigens made full-scale food production possible by the
Late Woodland period. Recently, Gremillion (2002) has pointed out that pre-maize
agriculture developed principally in the Midwest and Midsouth in areas drained by
the Mississippi, Missouri, Ohio, and Tennessee rivers.

An increased carrying capacity induced by the success of plant domestication
probably led to increased populations and higher population densities in some
areas. The frequency of innovation and the dissemination of information, ideas,

materials, and goods would have also increased under these conditions. Given that there are few significant barriers to human movement in the well-populated east, it is not surprising to see that raw materials and artifacts, and probably people as well, circulated over great distances. Exchange networks linked the peoples of the Great Lakes in the north with peoples in the riverine and prairie areas of the mid-continent and the alluvial lowlands of the Deep South. The Atlantic coastal states north of Georgia were not included.

By the Middle Woodland period, then, the people of the eastern Woodlands had discovered and put to use a broad spectrum of resources in their environment, and even domesticated some plant species. Economically, local communities epitomized what Joseph Caldwell (1962) called "Primary Forest Efficiency," meaning that human use of the available resources approached the absolute carrying capacity of the environment. Food production, where it occurred, was seen as extending this efficiency but not freeing communities from mapping on to the distribution of naturally recurring food and material resources. While archaeologists have documented population increases over the millennia, Middle Woodland populations were not large by modern standards. For example, estimates based on human remains and settlements in the lower Illinois River valley are in the range of 1,290 to 4,500 individuals for a 140-mile stretch of river (and a region of 2,800 square miles), a population density of between 0.46 and 1.6 persons per square mile (Asch 1976; Buikstra 1976). A similar estimate has been derived for southern Ohio (Pacheco and Dancey n.d.). Whatever the actual population size, widespread interpersonal contact between people of distant regions is implied by the presence of exotic materials and artifacts far from their sources. There can be little doubt that people along the major travel routes knew quite a bit about the outside world.

If the distribution of mounds and earthworks is any indication, population density was probably highest along the major waterways and the overland trails that probably crisscrossed the east. This pattern is reflected in the map accompanying Griffin's classic 1967 paper that shows a nearly continuous distribution of sites along the Mississippi River and its tributaries. As might be expected, regional traditions developed at intervals along these rivers, undoubtedly reflecting small-scale, ecologically bound interaction spheres. From south to north along the Mississippi there are the Marksville (Louisiana), Miller (Mississippi), Havana (western Illinois), and Trempealeau (Wisconsin) traditions; along the Ohio the Crab Orchard (southern Illinois and Indiana), Scioto (southern Ohio), and Armstrong (West Virginia) traditions; on the middle Tennessee River and in the southern Appalachian area as a whole the Copena and Connestee traditions; and on the Missouri River, the Kansas City tradition. Griffin's (1967) map also shows a Goodall tradition in southwestern Michigan, a Point Peninsula-New York tradition in the eastern Great Lakes, and the Porter and Santa Rosa-Swift Creek traditions centered on the Tombigbee and Savannah rivers, respectively, in the Southeast.

Given this array of traditions, a question posed often by early Hopewellian scholars remains: where exactly did the Hopewell culture originate? The answer used to be that every change in the archaeological record within a region or area was thought to represent a migration or a diffusion of ideas. Even after indigenous origins were accepted by most archaeologists it was not uncommon to read that Hopewell populations originated in western New York and moved south into Ohio where they built upon the local Adena mortuary tradition. Or Hopewell was said to have originated in western Illinois and spread by diffusion – perhaps carried by a religious elite – to southern Ohio (Prufer 1964). Similarly, the Havana Hopewell tradition was thought to have spread up the Illinois River and into southwestern Michigan, spawning Goodall Hopewell. Large-scale movements like this are rarely discussed today, although micro-population movements have been identified. However, if Hopewell is viewed more as a historical process, in the manner alluded to above, we may well have to accept the proposition that Hopewell does not have a single point of origin (Penney 1989).

What is Hopewell?

Artifacts

One of the striking properties of the Hopewellian artifacts found in Middle Woodland burial mounds and associated archaeological deposits is the great variety of artifact classes represented (Figure 5.3; see Braun 1986). A list of the most common kinds includes ceramic vessels, hand-held and stationary smoking pipes, clay human figurines, conch shell dippers, mica mirrors, panpipes, flint bladelets, non-utilitarian celts, awls, and projectile points, modified human remains, body ornaments such as earspools, headplates, finger rings, bracelets, necklaces, pendants, gorgets, and breastplates, fabrics for clothing and wrappings, attachments for clothing such as buttons, beads, cutouts, and tinklers. The variety of materials used is enormous as well and includes nearly everything in the natural world, animal (including human), vegetal, and mineral alike, with special emphasis on things that glitter. The list of minerals includes the metals copper (both mined and float), meteoric iron, galena, hematite, silver, and gold (both rare), along with mica, quartz crystal, chalcedony, hornstone, pipestone, sandstone, steatite, gypsum, and cannel coal. From the animal world come antler, bone, and teeth (especially bear canines, and alligator and shark teeth), marine and freshwater pearls, marine and freshwater shell, feathers, hair, and skin. Human skulls, mandibles, and long bones were also used on occasion. Cloth and cloaks were made from plant fibers, animal hair, and bird feathers, and undoubtedly many artifacts, mostly perishable, were made of wood and skin.

Another striking fact about Hopewellian artifacts is that many of the materials came from sources far from where they were made and used (Figure 5.4). Although recent mineralogical testing has cast doubt on many of the non-local sources once claimed for some artifacts (Hughes et al. 1998), there are some indisputable cases. Obsidian is the most dramatic example for there are no sources of this volcanic rock in the east; known sources have been identified in the Yellowstone Park region of the Rocky Mountains in Wyoming (Hughes 1992). Mica was acquired largely from localized sources in the southern Appalachians of western North Carolina, and

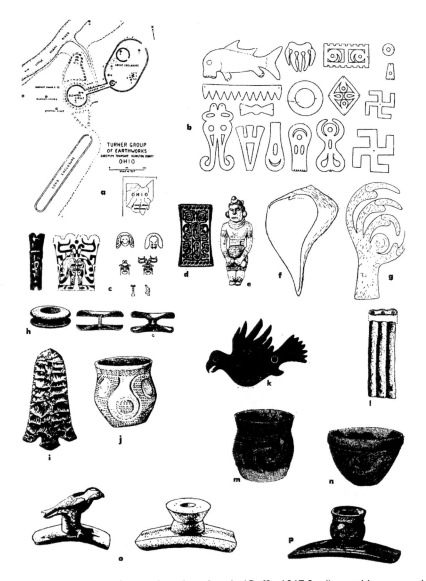

Figure 5.3 Hopewellian artifacts and earthwork style (Griffin 1967:fig. 4); p and l are reproduced with permission of the Ohio Historical Society

while often present in gravels in the glaciated parts of the east, and in several areas in the southeast, most copper appears to have been mined in the Lake Superior area. Conch shells, which together with mica and copper are the most widespread Hopewellian materials, obviously derive from the salt waters of coastal areas, as do fossil sharks' teeth, principally the Gulf of Mexico. With respect to chert for chipped stone artifacts, while this material is found in abundance in most areas of the east, the fine-grained materials preferred for Hopewellian artifacts come from localized sources in Ohio (Flint Ridge, or Vanport), southern Indiana (Hornstone, or

Figure 5.4 Map of areas where the raw materials used to make Hopewell artifacts can be found (Struever and Houart 1972:fig. 5)

Wyandot chert), southern Illinois (Cobden chert), Missouri (Burlington chert), and even as far west as North Dakota (Knife River chalcedony). It would be tedious to go down the entire list of Hopewellian materials and identify their sources; suffice it to say that very few, if any, occur abundantly throughout the east.

As might be expected, one of the defining properties of Hopewell is a high level of mastery of the arts (Brose 1985). The birds and mammals carved on some Hopewellian platform pipes are nearly exact replicas of their subjects, complete with a sense of movement. Conversely, some Hopewell art shows animals and animal parts, including humans, in silhouette fashion in copper and mica cutouts. The cutouts also include plain geometrical shapes or abstract designs. Miniature ceramic vessels were decorated with abstract symbols and stylized representations, usually of birds. Ceramic vessels were thin-walled and small, uniquely decorated with imaginative patterns. Miniature clay human figurines show men and women in everyday poses. Artifacts such as earspools, antler headplates, panpipes, and bear canines represent multi-part constructions in which sections of the same or different materials are joined to form the artifact. In every way, from design to execution, and at various scales, Hopewellian artifacts qualify as a "great art."

Does Hopewellian art represent art for art's sake, or is it a material manifestation of a worldview or cosmology? The realistic nature of much of it might favor the former, yet many archaeologists believe the choice of subjects and the organization of designs suggest otherwise. For example, Greber and Ruhl (2000:216–224) have identified dualities in the pairing of artifacts and raw materials within and between mounds at the Hopewell site (e.g., mica and copper, pipes and projectile points), and in animal symbolism (e.g., deer and bear); they suggest that dualities are found in the selection of mound fill (red and yellow soil) and earthwork design (circles and squares) as well. DeBoer (1997) sees the three-part structure of the Ross County, Ohio, earthworks mirrored in the animal effigies of the platform pipes as liminal interfaces between sky, water, and earth (Figure 5.5; e.g., heron eating a fish, otter with a fish in its mouth). Brown (1997) explores the possibility that the images and artifacts are linked to shamanism.

When burial mounds were the exclusive source of information about Middle Woodland people it was thought that the distinctive Hopewellian artifacts were crafted specifically for mortuary ritual. Investigation of habitation sites in the Illinois River valley quickly dispelled this idea (Griffin 1952), however, many of the kinds of artifacts associated with human remains under the mounds were found also in settlement debris, despite the reduced likelihood of their preservation or discovery, as discussed earlier. This has been found to be true in most other

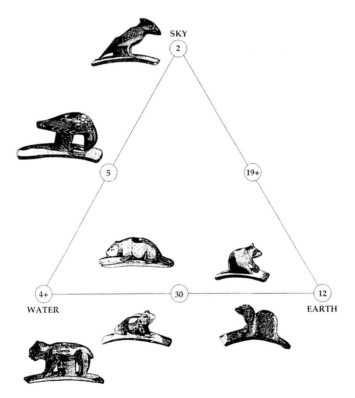

Figure 5.5 An interpretation of the cosmological associations of Hopewell effigy pipes (DeBoer 1997:fig. 9; numbers pertain to effigy pipes assigned to the six polar or liminal positions on the triangle)

Hopewellian areas where Middle Woodland archaeology has included settlements. The obvious implication is that Hopewell artifacts functioned among the living. Some, such as earspools, may have been part of everyday ornamentation, or personal mementos and amulets. Others may have been part of costuming used for ritual, ceremony, or entertainment. Displaying them may have conferred prestige on the person or household possessing them.

Burial and Platform Mounds

Apart from distinctive artifacts, Hopewell is recognized for the practice of heaping dirt over burials to form landscape features. At one time it was thought that this constituted an historical milestone in the progress of culture. Thus, Middle Woodland was said to represent a Burial Mound period during which mound-building was devoted to mortuary events while a subsequent Temple Mound (or Mississippian) period saw the emergence of moundbuilding as a means of elevating public structures above normal ground level (Willey 1966; see also Pauketat, this volume). Today, this simple scheme is found wanting on a number of grounds, not the least of which is the demonstration that a rich moundbuilding tradition occurred in the Deep South during the Late Archaic (Russo 1994; Sassaman, this volume). Mounds at that earlier time were conceived as site architecture more than as burial markers. Also challenging the burial mound to platform mound sequence is the documentation of dozens of platform mounds that were built and used during the Middle Woodland in the Southeast (e.g., Mainfort 1988).

Hopewellian burial, continuing earlier practices, included flexed and extended in-the-flesh inhumation, re-deposited bundle burial, cremation and re-deposited cremation, for single individuals or groups. The remains could be placed on the ground, or on mound fill, but more commonly the interment was in a crypt (i.e., tomb) or an above-ground, roofed charnel house (Figure 5.6; see Brown 1979). Unlike burial ritual in modern industrial states, where the mortuary process may be completed within a few days or weeks, it is clear that for Hopewellians it took place over extended periods of time (months, if not years).

Crypts took various forms, from subfloor to floor-level log tombs consisting of earthen, bark, or stone-lined graves covered with a log lid. Corpses were placed in extended positions within a crypt to deflesh before the cleaned bones were gathered into a bundle for storage in a corner of the crypt or in a pit dug into the earthen ramp surrounding the crypt. It is apparent that a given crypt was used for some time as the dead of a community were cycled through the mortuary program. At an appointed time the process ceased and the crypt was covered with earth. A new crypt was then constructed and the process began over again. Earth-covered crypts, i.e., burial mounds, were normally constructed on high points overlooking settlements. This manner of burial was typical of the Havana Hopewell and Havana-like complexes on the Mississippi and Illinois rivers.

Charnel houses consisted of pole structures often provided with internal partitions constructed specifically for mortuary activities. They were more expensive to build and demanded more maintenance than a crypt, but offered privacy, shelter,

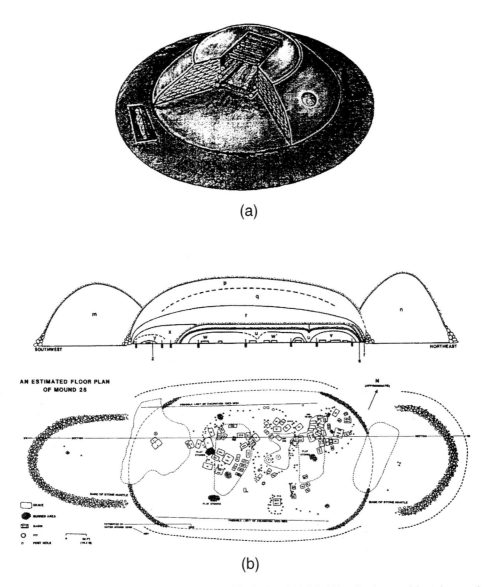

(a)

(b)

Figure 5.6 Crypt and charnel-house burial: (a) idealized Middle Woodland period burial mound in western Illinois illustrating a central log crypt reinforced by layered loads of earth, a bundle burial in the earthen ramp (circular figure on right), and a peripheral burial in mound skirt (rectangular figure on left) (Buikstra and Charles 1999:fig. 9.6); (b) floor plan (lower) and cross-section (upper) of Mound 25 at the Hopewell site in Ohio illustrating charnel-house burial and the growth of the mound in height and area with the successive addition of layers of earth (Greber and Ruhl 1989:fig. 2.14 [upper] and fig. 2.15 [lower])

and ample workspace. Charnel houses often had crematoriums, at least in the Ohio Hopewell tradition where cremation was most commonly practiced. As with crypt burial, the mortuary program appears to have unfolded in stages, with corpses first placed on clay platforms enclosed in allocated space to deflesh before being cremated and then deposited as secondary burials in another part of the structure. The openness and continuous accessibility of a charnel house invited the use of identifying symbols or trophies. When full, a structure was burned and covered with earth, and a new one was started. In some cases these charnel houses were extremely large. For example, the remains of the structure buried under the Edwin Harness Mound (Greber et al. 1983) within the Liberty Works in Ohio measures 13 × 35 m and held more than 175 burials. Charnel-house burial was common in Ohio Hopewell, but rarely turns up in western Illinois or the Southeast.

The closing of a particular facility, whether a crypt or charnel house, and its burial, did not necessarily signal the end of moundbuilding. Successive layers of rock and dirt were often added without additional human burial. The soil usually consisted of deliberately chosen contrasting colors. Presumably this was going on while burials were being added to the new, adjacent facility. At Mound 25 within the Hopewell site (Greber and Ruhl 2000), for example, a gravel layer was spread over the 3.7 m high buried charnel house and at least four more layers of dirt were added to bring the total height of the mound to more than 9 m above ground level. Gravel was then placed around the circumference of the mound, apparently finishing off the process. Almost no burials were encountered above the level of the charnel-house floor. This practice of layering is represented in Havana Hopewell as well, as shown at the Pete Klunk mound group (Perino 1968).

As noted above, archaeologists thought at one time that platform mounds were only Mississippian period monuments (Figure 5.7). Thus, in the Middle Ohio valley, the Marietta Earthworks was said to have a Fort Ancient tradition (A.D. 1000–1500) occupation because two of the mounds in the complex are flat-topped. Today, however, we know that the Marietta platform mound contains Middle Woodland artifacts and undoubtedly is Hopewellian (Pickard 1996). Platform mounds are also found at other Scioto tradition earthworks, such as the Newark Works and Ginther. The Mann site near the mouth of the Wabash River, commonly identified as part of the lower Ohio valley Crab Orchard tradition, also contains platform mounds (Kellar 1979). Better known are the Middle Woodland platform mounds of the Southeast, where they occur in the Marksville, Miller, Copena, and Connestee traditions (Knight 2001). The archaeological assemblages associated with use of platforms suggest the remains of feasting, but there is no compelling evidence of mortuary activity. At many of these sites (e.g., Tunacunhee and Walling) there is also settlement debris and burial mound construction.

Geometric Enclosures

Another distinctive Hopewellian archaeological remain is the geometric earthwork (Morgan 1999). The best-known examples occur in southern Ohio, but a detailed map of these architectural marvels would show that they extend from western New York along the western escarpment of the Appalachian Plateau and into southeastern Indiana. Beyond that linear band isolated examples have been documented in the Crab Orchard (Mann and Twenhafel sites), Havana (Golden Eagle site), and

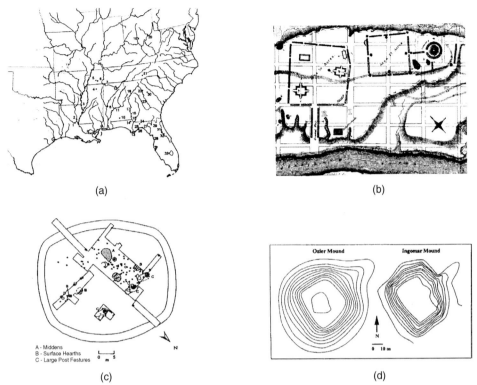

(a)

(b)

(c)

A - Middens
B - Surface Hearths
C - Large Post Features

(d)

Figure 5.7 Middle Woodland period platform mounds: (a) distribution map of major sites (Knight 2001:fig. 11.1); (b) the Marietta site, Ohio (site 20 on the map) (Squier and Davis 1848:plate XXVI); (c) cultural debris and features on the surface of the mound at the Walling site, Alabama (site 12 on the map) (Knight 2001:fig. 11.3); (d) contour maps of platform mounds at the Pinson and Ingomar sites (sites 6 and 4 on the map, respectively) (Rafferty 2002:fig. 10.9)

Marksville (Marksville and Pinson Mounds sites) traditions. Most of them co-occur with burial mounds, but some have no directly associated mounds, as at High Bank in Ross County, Ohio. The independence of burial mounds and earthworks is illustrated at Mound City, also in Ross County, where the embankment enclosing the majority of the mounds was constructed late in the site's history.

Like everything else Hopewell, enclosures were constructed in many ways (Figure 5.8). Some were built with earth excavated from ditches on the inside or outside of the embankment. Others have no adjoining ditch and were made by scraping up adjacent soil, digging it out of nearby borrow pits, or bringing it in from a nearby watercourse or marsh. Some extend continuously over great distances, while others are broken at frequent intervals. Some are constructed on level outwash terraces; others are constructed along the edge of cliffs, and quite a few are built around the pinnacles of prominent hills.

Not many enclosures have been trenched, but those that have invariably produce stratigraphic evidence of multiple constructions. It might be two layers as revealed

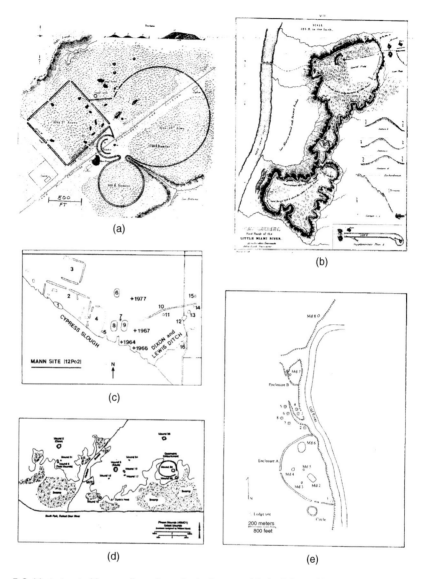

Figure 5.8 Variation in Hopewell earthwork site layouts: (a) the Liberty Works, Ross County, Ohio (Squier and Davis 1848:plate XX); (b) the Fort Ancient Works, Warren County, Ohio (Squier and Davis 1848:plate VII); (c) the Mann site, southern Indiana (Kellar 1979:fig. 14.1); (d) Pinson Mounds, western Tennessee (Thunen 1998:fig. 4.1); (e) the Marksville site, southern Mississippi (McGimsey 2003:fig. 2)

in Ohio at Fort Hill (Prufer 1997) and the Great Circle at Newark. Or it might be multiple levels as revealed in the Pollack Works, also in Ohio, where a succession of walls, some of them stockades, subsequently covered with rock or dirt has been documented (Riordan 1998). Even the complex, three-part (tripartite) geometric earthworks of Ross County, Ohio, composed of similarly shaped, attached elements (square, large circle, small circle) are known to have grown in complexity over many generations (Greber 1997).

Despite the longevity factor, archaeologists have often thought that earthwork designs were planned to some extent. The Ross County tripartite earthworks (Figure 5.8a), five in all, spark such interest because of their similar shapes and from the fact that the outer square, inner large circle, and outer small circle of each of these sites are exactly or approximately the same size: 11, 16, and 4.5 ha, respectively (see DeBoer 1997:233). Although identical in size and shape, the squares are oriented differently and are connected in unique ways to the circles. Whether oriented the same or not, there would seem to be meaning in the linkage of the three elements in which the small circle is attached to the large circle which in turn is attached to the square. Even in a case in which the square is adjacent to the small circle there is no passageway between the two.

According to Robert Connolly (1998), the Fort Ancient Works, in Warren County, Ohio, reflects long-term planning (Figure 5.8b). This earthwork was formed over a 300-year period (200 B.C.–A.D. 400) by constructing a 5.7 km long series of up to 6 m high clay embankment walls segmented by 67 "gateways" along the edge of a steep sided peninsula of land 79 m above the Little Miami River. Connolly argues that the builders began construction with a complementary pair of earthwork segments placed at the terminus of the peninsula and continued to add paired segments over successive generations until both sides of the figure were joined to complete a design created at the beginning of the work. In western Illinois, Buikstra and her colleagues (1998) have found that the floor at Mound House was rebuilt repeatedly using soils of different color and composition; it appears also that screens serving to define the major activity were rebuilt numerous times. It is on this basis that these archaeologists believe Havana tradition society consisted of hierarchically ranked lineages.

Whatever the social relations, and however earthworks were built, the enclosures must have defined space by controlling access and inhibiting visibility. Even though many are called forts, and early reports referred to some as defensive works, it is unlikely that any of them would have been effective militarily. The large size of many is out of proportion to the estimated population available to "man the trenches" and the numerous gaps in most of them offer too many opportunities for an enemy to breach. More credible is the proposition that they prevented outsiders from seeing in. Yet even this is suspect since stratigraphic data indicate that the earthworks increased in height over time; unless fences were erected on them, the early embankments alone may not have restricted visibility. At the very least, however, they blocked out space for human activity. Where there are a number of enclosures, as in Ohio, they are often connected directly or with an enclosed walkway. Several, including the Newark Works, evoke images of ceremonies, games, or rituals channeled through the complicated corridors of this 3 km^2 earthwork district, as described above.

One popular proposition for the shapes of the earthworks is that they were laid out to record astronomical observations, such as the movement of the sun through the seasons, or of the Moon and Venus (Hively and Horn 1982). Romain (2000) summarizes the evidence for Ohio Hopewell, and concludes that many earthworks were aligned with significant solar and lunar azimuths. However, because of the poor condition of the remains and the differential growth factor, there is little consensus about this topic.

Settlement Patterns

Settlement patterns varied greatly during the Middle Woodland period depending upon latitude and the significance of domesticated plants. In the mid-continent, it appears that dispersed sedentism predominated in the major population centers and even in the hinterlands. Few nucleated communities have been documented, and in many areas most households apparently lived in modest homesteads within walking distance of a burial mound-earthwork complex. Nevertheless, in southern Appalachia and most of the Deep South, it is not unusual to find nucleated settlements directly associated with burial mounds and platform mounds.

These wide differences in settlement pattern nevertheless are cross-cut by the mortuary ceremonialism and pan-regional exchange of prestige goods and materials. In all areas, settlements appear largely to consist of the members of a household, composed of a family unit (e.g., Anderson and Mainfort 2002; Dancey and Pacheco 1997b). They normally contain the same kinds of artifacts, structures, and site facilities, and usually create small dumps adjacent to the occupied area. In Ohio, these dispersed sedentary households appear to have been part of a community centered on a sacred place occupied by the community's ancestors buried under earthen mounds and surrounded by earthen walls and ditches (Figure 5.9a).

In western Illinois, settlements were clustered at the mouths of major tributaries along the lower Illinois River with burial mounds on the valley floor and the overlooking bluffs (Figure 5.9b; see Struever and Houart 1972). On the lower Ohio River upstream from the mouth of the Wabash River, hamlet-sized settlements were distributed continuously for at least 15 km from the Crab Orchard tradition Mann site to the GE Mound, and beyond (Ruby 1997). Middle Woodland settlements along the Duck River in south central Tennessee show a similar dispersed distribution (Figure 5.9c). In the Swift Creek area of Georgia and neighboring states, certain places along major trade routes became more elaborate and contained a platform mound, burial mounds, and a settlement (Stephenson et al. 2002). Outside the sustaining area of these nucleated communities, settlements were small and generally sedentary. Not all Middle Woodland communities participating, even if minimally, in the Hopewell Interaction Sphere were sedentary. Fortier and Ghosh (2000) document this for the American Bottom region of southwestern Illinois, where there is evidence for a fission-fusion seasonal movement by the people of non-agricultural communities.

As might be expected, Middle Woodland tool kits and architecture vary depending on the local environment, yet there are some common features. Ceramics, for example, where they are found, often include two traditions, one utilitarian and the other ritual (Griffin 1952; Struever and Houart 1972). The former include large,

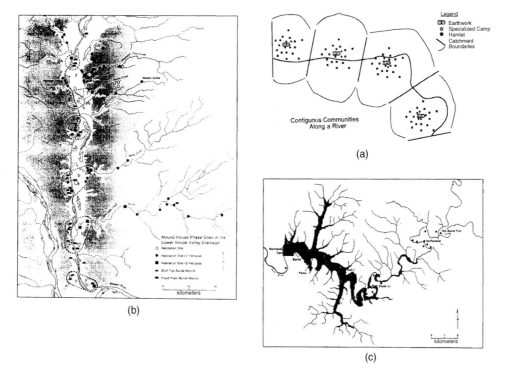

Figure 5.9 Examples of Middle Woodland period settlement pattern: (a) idealized pattern, southern Ohio (Dancey and Pacheco 1997b:fig. 1.2); (b) Mound House phase site distribution on the Lower Illinois River, western Illinois (Smith 1992:fig. 9.12); (c) site distribution on the Duck River, south central Tennessee (Smith 1992:fig. 9.21)

cord-marked and plain globular and sub-conoidal jars. The latter include small, highly decorated bowls along with tetrapodal oval and square jars and bilobed vessels. It is assumed that most utilitarian vessels were intended for cooking, yet the large sub-conoidal jars appear more suited for storage. The ground stone inventory includes grooveless axes (or celts) and adzes, and, in some places, hoes. Grinding instruments are not common, but pestles and pounders are present. Chipped stone tools are varied and were made by the bifacial and blade industry techniques. Hunting and butchering gear predominates in most cases. Perhaps because of their sedentary nature, most of the Middle Woodland domestic sites contain few intact tools. Broken and heavily recycled implements dominate the assemblages.

Several well-preserved Middle Woodland domestic sites in the Middle Ohio valley shed light on the perishable tools employed then. At the McGraw site (Prufer 1965), for example, a wide variety of bone and antler tools was recovered from a buried kitchen midden. Included are awls, needles, fishhooks, beamers, and spatulas. Turtle shells were apparently made into containers and freshwater shells into ladles and hoes. At the mouth of the Great Miami River, a similar suite of artifacts – including a wide variety of expedient flake tools for cutting, scraping, and incising – was recovered in buried middens at the Jennison Guard site (as at McGraw).

Both of these sites contained Hopewell Interaction Sphere artifacts. At McGraw were found Hopewell style ceramic design elements, human figurine parts, bladelets, and mica, while Jennison Guard (Blosser 1996) contained bladelets, copper nuggets, and mica cutouts in the shape of Ross Barbed projectile points, a ceremonial artifact found in abundance at the Hopewell Works. The assemblage from the Irving site in Illinois provides another example of the presence of symbolic and utilitarian artifacts in habitation debris. This is proof that Hopewell is not just a mortuary phenomenon.

Domestic settlements consisted of bent pole structures (square and round), drying racks, wind breaks, cooking pits, basins, dumps, and probably also activity yards where gear was repaired, games were played, stories told, and meals prepared. Most documented sites suggest that only one major dwelling was in use at any one time, although there might be another family in a nearby dwelling 200–300 m away. Many pit features served as earth ovens, and others as clay slacking basins for ceramic manufacture. Few are unmistakably constructed for storage; ceramic jars may have served this function. Most likely these places were the home base, the homestead, or the farmstead which provided sleeping places, a food preparation and serving facility, a space for primary socializing, reproducing, playing, rehearsing for upcoming ceremonies, and making dance costumes and objects for exchange. This pattern is represented in the lower Illinois valley at the Smiling Dan (Stafford and Sant 1985) and Massey-Archie (Farnsworth and Koski 1985) sites and in Ohio at the Murphy Tract (Pacheco 1997).

The livelihood of these reproductive units probably rested upon foraging and food-producing in the surrounding terrain. It is unlikely that they were totally self-sufficient and, as regional-scale research intensifies, it will probably be found that there were strong relationships between the dispersed households. Fie's (2000) ceramic analysis of lower Illinois River valley suggests as much. At a higher level, it would not be surprising to find biological connections over wide areas since the communities of small populations would have trouble finding unrelated marriage partners in their own or neighboring communities, particularly females.

If Middle Woodland communities were residentially stable and the members practiced intensive harvesting of wild and domesticated foods, they must have had a profound impact on the landscape. For one thing, the permanent residences with their dumps, or kitchen middens, would have constituted an artificial ecotone. Furthermore, mounds and earthworks added monumental figures and architectural elements to the landscape. Undoubtedly, paths and trails linking settlements, special-purpose sites, and materials sources would have become etched into the landscape. Likewise, mineral extraction permanently scarred the surface in some areas (e.g., Flint Ridge, Ohio). Where their landscapes included caves, there is evidence of Middle Woodland presence underground as well (Simek et al. 2001). Rockshelters in the Appalachian Plateau show a significant but minor Middle Woodland presence (Seeman 1996). It is distinctly possible as well that forests were managed by controlled burning. Recently, tools, pollen, macro-botanical remains, and stratigraphy at Cliff Palace Pond in eastern Kentucky suggest that forest management was a common practice in many parts of the Midwest as early as the Late Archaic period (Delcourt et al. 1998).

Explaining Hopewell: Social Reconstruction

It is hard to escape the feeling, shared by generations of archaeologists, that mortuary ritual was limited to a select segment of each community or region. Yet where studies have been done, the burial population was found to make up a complete social group with all age groups and both sexes represented in correct typical proportions (Buikstra 1976; Konigsberg 1985). Within each burial population, however, are decided disparities in the distribution of grave goods that point to the existence of differential access to rights and privileges. In Illinois it was found that at the Klunk-Gibson Mound Group the most lavish treatment was given to large adult males. At the Mound House site, also on the lower Illinois River, Buikstra et al. (1998) have documented a complicated set of routine practices at this sacred place that they believe required specialized knowledge possessed only by select members of a community.

The high quality of the craftsmanship in all media and all techniques has made some archaeologists confident that craft specialization existed among at least some populations (Griffin 1952). Nevertheless, there are others who argue that all communities contained their own skilled, but not specialized, artisans. Supporting the latter view is the discovery in several centers of the remains of what have been said to be craft houses where Hopewell artifacts were made (Baby and Langlois 1979). It appears that, while it might be possible to make a case for specialized production, it is not credible to think that the craft producers were divorced from direct participation in food-getting or food-processing. The driving force behind the exchanges might be a demand for "prestige goods" or symbols, not a techno-economic need (Spielmann 2002).

Not long ago, Struever and Houart (1972) proposed that Hopewell prestige goods and rare raw materials traveled through a functionally graded hierarchy that funneled artifacts to primary transaction centers, then to secondary centers, and finally to settlements. Seeman (1979) demonstrated, however, that the distributions of Hopewellian artifacts do not reflect an organized, socioeconomic hierarchical pattern in reality. Seeman also showed that the greatest variety of Hopewell Interaction Sphere artifacts and materials was in Ohio and that the scale of public architecture in this region far surpasses that of any other region.

Recently, strong arguments have been made in favor of a fundamentally egalitarian society with intra-community social ranking based upon achievement and prestige. From this perspective Hopewell populations are seen as composed of small-scale, tribal societies whose inter-tribal or inter-community relationships exhibited a "sequential hierarchy" (aka heterarchy) rather than a genuine, vertical hierarchy (see Braun and Plog 1982; Johnson 1982). A Hopewellian heterarchy might have involved *ad hoc* social relationships between individual communities that arose in response to problems facing the entire local population. Imagine, for example, that Hopewell communities distributed along the central Scioto River and central and North Fork of Paint Creek in Ross County, Ohio, experienced unpredictable surpluses or shortfalls. Without forming institutional bonds, people might have engaged in pan-community ceremonies that included leveling differences in wealth and redistributing surplus.

As elusive as it is archaeologically, there are some clues in the mortuary data as to the nature of the social group and some of its activities. First, it is evident in all cases of mortuary ceremonialism that the activity required a group; these were corporate or communal activities. Given the widely differing scales of investment, from a single crypt to earthwork enclosures, the corporate groups must have differed greatly in size and composition. Second, mortuary ceremonial practices imply attachment to the dead, to memories of the past, and to the land. Third, there are almost as many varieties of burial treatments as there are documented cases, implying that the burial program was not institutionalized. Fourth, the interments reflect a wide variation in the amount of energy expended on the event(s). It is commonly assumed that the variation was related to economic-based status differences (Tainter 1977). Fifth, all the mound and earthwork sites grew in size and area over variable periods of time. Sixth, many of the artifacts were parts of costumes and clothing. How could this be anything but evidence of dancing and public ceremony? Seventh, most of the prestige goods required special skills and imply some degree of craft specialization (Spielmann 1998).

These clues suggest that social groups were stable, since it is unlikely that groups of constantly shifting membership could sustain the commitment reflected in the corporate burial mound/earthwork centers. They suggest also that households, lineages, and possibly entire communities could vary in degree of prosperity and in the practice of craft specialization. While concentrations of wealth may have led to social divisions, the absence of institutionalized burial practices argues against a rigid social hierarchy (Braun 1979). Middle Woodland peoples practicing Primary Forest Efficiency appear to have changed little over hundreds of years in some regions. Some older explanations saw this as a successful adaptation to climatic conditions favorable to agriculture (Griffin 1960).

The human remains point to local origin and inter-regional independence. While Illinois and Ohio populations were distinct biologically (Reichs 1984), Sciulli and Mahaney (1986) analyzed skeletal remains from Terminal Late Archaic, Early Woodland, and Middle Woodland sites in Ohio and found reason to believe that the Ohio people were derived from the same population. Likewise, Buikstra (1982) found evidence for population continuity through the Archaic and Woodland periods in western Illinois. Given the small population sizes involved in each case, it is probable that men would have sought mates outside their own community or clan (DeBoer 1997).

Doubtless, there were language and dialect differences between regions in the eastern Woodlands. Seeman (1995) reminds us that there were at least 27 major languages in eastern North America shortly after European appearance and expansion. He thinks that as population densities in some areas increased, neighboring communities vied for access to productive parts of the environment, thus increasing language diversity as communication decreased between communities. If this is true, at least part of the Hopewell story may have to do with the emergence of a trade language such as a pidgin, Creole, or jargon.

Thus, while Hopewellian artifacts and mortuary practices seem embedded in local traditions, the enormous environmental variety included within eastern North America does not favor the existence of a unitary social organization. For this reason, it appears that Willey and Phillips's (1958) preference for Hopewell as a cultural horizon has garnered more support than viewing Hopewell as a distinct Culture. This is because the horizon concept more accurately captures the diffusional feel of Hopewell. Over a period of 300–400 years, there were successive, episodic bursts of exchange activity scattered across the east in various places, at various times, and with different outcomes. This also helps explain why there is no consistent "Hopewell package" containing all elements of the list of diagnostics. If these artifacts were related to the overt display of wealth and power, and displays varied depending on the degree of competition in the social group, finding Hopewellian artifacts in hinterland locations as well as central areas of larger populations does not require the wholesale importation of a Culture. On the other hand, it does demonstrate that small communities in marginal areas could tap into the exchange networks if they wanted to, and apparently many did.

Hopewellian archaeological remains have always been interpreted as representing cyclical, successive, episodic bursts of human activity. Modern analysis with museum collections more or less confirms early claims. Greber and Ruhl (2000) and Cowan (1996), for example, point out that events represented in the Ohio Hopewell mortuary excavations are of several different scales. At the lowest is the individual, where personal meanings were created through the burial program (Figure 5.10). Since burial was extended to all members of a community, it would not be unusual in a group of 250–300 people to have at least one death a year. Thus, there would always be activity at the center, especially if the program lasted for months, or years. A second scale would be generational and pertain to the entire community. The death of a prestigious person, such as a hereditary leader, is an example. Associated artifacts and practices should be dominated by symbols with community wide meaning. Higher yet are events that reflect society-wide values. The celebrated 52-year cycle of the Aztecs is an example, as is the American Centennial tradition. Thus, any given ceremonial/sacred place might have archaeological remains from one or more of these differentially orbiting individual-community-society cycles.

It is at the highest scale that there might be something to the idea that mounds and earthen architecture were oriented to the trajectory of astronomical bodies. Many archaeologists characterize the mound-earthwork complexes as sacred places. Thus, Byers (1996) argues that the Ohio Hopewell burial mound earthwork clusters were designed to serve as the place to hold Earth Renewal ceremonies. Sacredness may also explain why most earthwork interiors are relatively barren of visible, portable-size artifacts and waste deposits.

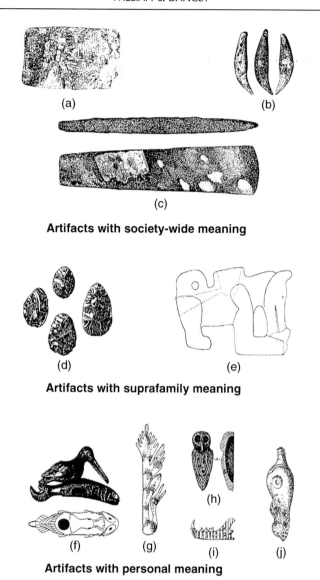

Artifacts with society-wide meaning

Artifacts with suprafamily meaning

Artifacts with personal meaning

Figure 5.10 An interpretation of the social significance of portable Hopewell artifacts (a) copper breastplate; (b) drilled bear canines; (c) copper celt; (d) oval bifaces from cache of >8,000 specimens; (e) dog effigy pipe; (f) effigy bird (roseate spoonbill) on fish pipe; (g) trumpeter swan effigy cut out of turtle carapace; (h) owl effigy "boatstone"; (i) cut and painted animal jaw; (j) duck head effigy plummet carved in shell. Specimens from the Hopewell Works ((a)–(d), (f)) and Seip Works ((e), (g)–(j)), Ross County, Ohio (Greber and Ruhl 2000; Shetrone and Greenman 1931); (g)–(j) are reproduced with permission of the Ohio Historical Society

The End of Hopewell

The demise of Hopewell is known in many circles as the Hopewell Collapse (Tainter 1988), in others as progressive evolution (Braun and Plog 1982). Here again, as with origins, it is difficult to know when and where Hopewellian attributes began to disappear from people's cultural repertoires. The Havana Hopewell people had apparently lost it by A.D. 200, two centuries earlier than Ohio Hopewell folks. The different timing of the so-called collapse also suggests that it may not be productive to think of it that way. Hopewell seems more to have dissolved than collapsed.

The probable cause of the eclipse of Middle Woodland mortuary ceremonialism is the emergence of full-scale agriculture, leading to the archaeological demarcation of the Late Woodland period (Johannessen 1993; Seeman and Dancey 2000; Wymer 1992). In the middle Ohio valley, for example, this process apparently began in hinterland areas as early as A.D. 200 (Dancey 1992). In any case, the descendants of the Hopewellians became nucleated and apparently were primary food producers whose staples included maygrass and chenopodia. Their mortuary program was much less elaborate and time-consuming, and their artifact inventory included mostly things made from local materials. Ceramic decoration became minimal to absent. Late Woodland settlements resemble those of agriculturalists in other parts of the world, lending further support to the idea that, while Middle Woodland people were heavily engaged with domesticated plants, they had not yet made cultigens the focal point of their economy.

The idea of collapse implies a breakdown in the organization of society – nothing works. While some archaeologists (Byers 1996) see evidence for intra- and inter-community conflict, and others for population displacement (Prufer 1964), it is hard to see the disappearance of Hopewell as a breakdown. The shift comes from within the area inhabited by Hopewellians, and the last Hopewellian sites do not show evidence of destruction. Older explanations treated the loss of the art and monuments as a social devolution. More recently it has been argued that Hopewell evolved into a more efficient risk-management system in which the elaborate mortuary displays became counterproductive (Braun and Plog 1982). Dunnell and Greenlee (1999) call the elaborate practices "waste behavior." They argue that energy was diverted from biological reproduction during a period when climate irregularities favored small families. As climate became predictable from year to year energy was turned from "waste behavior" to food production. It is fair to say that, like the concept of Hopewell itself, there is much yet to be known about how it came to an end.

Conclusion

For better or worse, the prehistoric earthen architecture of eastern North America defined Americanist archaeology. On the one hand, its discovery captured the minds of the early Euroamericans and focused 19th-century research on identifying the creators of the mounds and earthworks. On the other hand, a single-minded obsession with the monuments led to a dearth of information on non-mortuary remains, a condition that is only now being rectified. In spite of deficiencies in the data, it is apparent today that Hopewell most likely reflects the culmination, or climax, of a deep-rooted pattern of prestige-building that involved trade and exchange of exotic materials and artifacts. Simultaneously, human investment in plants with domestication potential increased gradually through the normal workings of society (consider Rindos's [1980] use of "mutualism" and "co-evolution"). As the contribution of domesticates to the diet increased, settlement stability increased, and population growth was on the positive side. In the context of such population pressure, Hopewell is believed to have blossomed, raising suspicions that the lavish Middle Woodland practices (i.e., "waste behavior") might have been related to the management of inter-community relationships and regulation of access to resources. As the risks abated, the elaborate practices ceased, and the energy of communities turned toward full-scale agriculture.

As this chapter describes, archaeological discoveries in eastern North America in the last decade or two have raised many questions about the very nature and meaning of the Hopewell, yet it is clear even today that there was a Middle Woodland period cultural climax that affected communities throughout the east. Furthermore, despite all of the controversy about the role of "sacred places" in the lives of these past peoples, few would dispute the proposition that the primary functions of such places are to maintain social order, reinforce cultural values, and facilitate intergroup relationships.

Despite parallels in other parts of the world today among people who live in dispersed sedentary settlement patterns with annual gatherings at sacred places, there are no cases of non-tropical cultigen food producers living in a temperate forest environment that have not been significantly altered by colonialism. We are left, then, with an enduring enigma, and a renewed challenge to a new generation of scholars and fieldworkers.

ACKNOWLEDGMENTS

I would like to thank the editors for the opportunity to contribute to this volume, and for their skillful help in fine-tuning the manuscript. Mark Seeman, Paul Pacheco, and Brian Fagan read earlier drafts and helped sharpen the prose, correct inaccuracies, and lead me in new directions. In the end, of course, the final responsibility for the content and thrust of the chapter rests on my shoulders.

REFERENCES

Anderson, David G., and Robert C. Mainfort, Jr., eds., 2002 *The Woodland Southeast*. Tuscaloosa: University of Alabama Press.

Asch, David, 1976 *The Middle Woodland Population of the Lower Illinois Valley.* Scientific Papers 1. Evanston, IL: Northwestern University Archeological Program.

Atwater, Caleb, 1820 *Description of the Antiquities Discovered in the State of Ohio and other Western States.* Worcester, MA: American Antiquarian Society.

Baby, Raymond S., and Suzanne M. Langlois, 1979 Seip Mound state memorial: Nonmortuary aspects of Hopewell. In *Hopewell Archaeology: The Chillicothe Conference.* David Brose and N'omi Greber, eds. Pp. 16–18. Kent, OH: Kent State University Press.

Blosser, Jack K., 1996 The 1984 excavation at 12D29S: A Middle Woodland village in southeastern Indiana. In *View from the Core: A Synthesis of Ohio Hopewell Archaeology.* Paul J. Pacheco, ed. Pp. 54–69. Columbus, OH: Ohio Archaeological Council.

Braun, David P., 1979 Illinois Hopewell burial practices and social organization: A reexamination of the Klunk-Gibson mound group. In *Hopewell Archaeology: The Chillicothe Conference.* David Brose and N'omi Greber, eds. Pp. 66–79. Kent, OH: Kent State University Press.

——1986 Midwestern Hopewellian exchange and supralocal interaction. In *Peer Polity Interaction and Socio-Political Change.* Colin Renfrew and John Cherry, eds. Pp. 117–126. Cambridge: Cambridge University Press.

Braun, David P., and Stephen Plog, 1982 Evolution of "tribal" social networks: Theory and prehistoric North American evidence. *American Antiquity* 47, 504–525.

Brose, David S., 1985 The Woodland period. In *Ancient Art of the American Woodland Indians.* David S. Brose, James A. Brown, and David W. Penney, eds. Pp. 43–91. New York: Harry N. Abrams.

Brown, James A., 1979 Charnel houses and mortuary crypts: Disposal of the dead in the Middle Woodland period. In *Hopewell Archaeology: The Chillicothe Conference.* David Brose and N'omi Greber, eds. Pp. 211–219. Kent, OH: Kent State University Press.

——1997 The archaeology of ancient religion in the Eastern Woodlands. *Annual Review of Anthropology* 26, 465–485.

Buikstra, Jane E., 1976 *Hopewell in the Lower Illinois Valley: A Regional Study of Human Biological Variability and Prehistoric Mortuary Behavior.* Scientific Papers 1. Evanston, IL: Northwestern University Archeological Program.

——1982 The Lower Illinois River region: A prehistoric context for the study of ancient diet and health. In *Paleopathology and the Origins of Agriculture.* Mark N. Cohen and George J. Armelagos, eds. Pp. 217–236. Orlando: Academic Press.

Buikstra, Jane E., Douglas K. Charles, and Gordon F. M. Rakita, eds., 1998 *Staging Ritual: Hopewell Ceremonialism at the Mound House Site, Greene County, Illinois.* Kampsville Studies in Archeology and History 1. Kampsville, IL: Center for American Archeology.

Byers, A. Martin, 1996 Social structure and the pragmatic meaning of material culture: Ohio Hopewell as ecclesiastic-communal cult. In *View from the Core: A Synthesis of Ohio Hopewell Archaeology.* Paul J. Pacheco, ed. Pp. 174–193. Columbus, OH: Ohio Archaeological Council.

Caldwell, Joseph R., 1962 Eastern North America. In *Courses Toward Urban Life: Archaeological Considerations of Some Cultural Alternates.* Robert J. Braidwood and Gordon R. Willey, eds. Pp. 288–308. Chicago: Aldine.

——1964 Interaction spheres in prehistory. In *Hopewellian Studies.* Scientific Papers, vol. 12, no. 2. Joseph R. Caldwell and Robert L. Hall, eds. Pp. 133–143. Springfield: Illinois State Museum.

Connolly, Robert P., 1998 Architectural grammar rules at the Fort Ancient hilltop enclosure. In *Ancient Earthen Enclosures of the Eastern Woodlands.* Robert C. Mainfort, Jr. and Lynn P. Sullivan, eds. Pp. 85–113. Gainesville: University Press of Florida.

Cowan, C. Wesley, 1996 Social implications of Ohio Hopewell art. In *View from the Core: A Synthesis of Ohio Hopewell Archaeology*. Paul J. Pacheco, ed. Pp. 128–149. Columbus, OH: Ohio Archaeological Council.

Dancey, William S., 1992 Village origins in central Ohio: The results and implications of recent Middle and Late Woodland research. In *Cultural Variability in Context; Woodland Settlements of the Mid-Ohio Valley*. Mark Seeman, ed. Pp. 24–29. MCJA Special Paper 7. Kent, OH: Kent State University Press.

Dancey, William S., and Paul J. Pacheco, eds., 1997a *Ohio Hopewell Community Organization*. Kent, OH: Kent State University Press.

Dancey, William S., and Paul J. Pacheco, 1997b A community model of Ohio Hopewell settlement. In *Ohio Hopewell Community Organization*. William S. Dancey and Paul J. Pacheco, eds. Pp. 3–40. Kent, OH: Kent State University Press.

DeBoer, Warren, 1997 Ceremonial centers from the Cayapas (Esmeraldas, Ecuador) to Chillicothe (Ohio, USA). *Cambridge Archaeological Journal* 7, 1–15.

Delcourt, Paul A., Hazel R. Delcourt, Cecil R. Ison, William E. Sharp, and Kristen Gremillion, 1998 Prehistoric human use of fire, the Eastern Agricultural Complex, and Appalachian oak-chestnut forests: Paleoecology of Cliff Palace Pond, Kentucky. *American Antiquity* 63, 263–278.

Dunnell, Robert C., and Diana M. Greenlee, 1999 Late woodland period "waste" reduction in the Ohio River valley. *Journal of Anthropological Archaeology* 18, 376–395.

Farnsworth, Kenneth B., and Ann L. Koski, 1985 *Massey and Archie: A Study of Two Hopewellian Homesteads in the Western Illinois Uplands*. Kampsville Archeological Center, Research Series, vol. 3. Kampsville: Center for American Archeology.

Fie, Shannon M., 2000 An integrative study of ceramic exchange during the Illinois Valley Middle Woodland period. Ph.D. dissertation, State University of New York at Buffalo.

Fortier, Andrew C., and Swastika Ghosh, 2000 The Bosque Medio site: A Hopewellian campsite in the American Bottom uplands. *Illinois Archaeology* 12, 1–57.

Greber, N'omi B., 1997 Two geometric enclosures in the Paint Creek valley: An estimate of possible changes in community patterns through time. In *Ohio Hopewell Community Organization*. William S. Dancey and Paul J. Pacheco, eds. Pp. 207–230. Kent, OH: Kent State University Press.

Greber, N'omi B., James B. Griffin, Tristine L. Smart, Richard I. Ford, Orrin C. Shane, III, Raymond S. Baby, Suzanne M. Langlois, Stephanie J. Belovich, David R. Morse, and Kent D. Vickery, 1983 *Recent Excavations at the Edwin Harness Mound, Liberty Works, Ross County, Ohio*. MCJA Special Paper 5. Kent, OH: Kent State University Press.

Greber, N'omi B., and Katherine C. Ruhl, 2000 *The Hopewell Site: A Contemporary Analysis Based on the Work of Charles C. Willoughby*, revised edition. Ft. Washington, PA: Eastern National.

Gremillion, Kristen J., 2002 The development and dispersal of agricultural systems in the Woodland period Southeast. In *The Woodland Southeast*. David G. Anderson and Robert C. Mainfort, Jr., eds. Pp. 483–501. Tuscaloosa: University of Alabama Press.

Griffin, James B., 1952 Some Early and Middle Woodland pottery types in Illinois. In *Hopewellian Communities in Illinois*. Thorne Deuel, ed. Pp. 93–130. Scientific Papers, vol. 5. Springfield: Illinois State Museum.

—— 1960 Climatic change: A contributory cause of the growth and decline of northern Hopewellian culture. *Wisconsin Archaeologist* 42(2), 21–33.

—— 1967 Eastern North American archaeology: A summary. *Science* 156, 175–191.

Hall, Robert L., 1980 An interpretation of the two-climax model of Illinois prehistory. In *Early Native Americans*. David L. Broman, ed. Pp. 401–462. The Hague: Mouton.

Hively, Ray, and Robert Horn, 1982 Geometry and astronomy in prehistoric Ohio. *Archaeoastronomy* 4, S1–S20.

Hughes, Richard E., 1992 Another look at Hopewell obsidian studies. *American Antiquity* 57, 515–523.

Hughes, Richard E., Thomas E. Berres, D. M. Moore, and Kenneth B. Farnsworth, 1998 Revision of Hopewellian trading patterns in midwestern North America based on mineralogical sourcing. *Geoarchaeology* 13, 709–729.

Johannessen, Sissel, 1993 Farmers of the Late Woodland. In *Farming and Foraging in the Eastern Woodlands*. C. Margaret Scarry, ed. Pp. 57–77. Gainesville: University of Florida Press.

Johnson, Gregory A., 1982 Organizational structure and scalar stress. In *Theory and Explanation in Archaeology*. Colin Renfrew, Michael J. Rowlands, and Barbara A. Segraves, eds. Pp. 389–422. New York: Academic Press.

Kellar, James H., 1979 The Mann site and "Hopewell" in the lower Wabash-Ohio valley. In *Hopewell Archaeology: The Chillicothe Conference*. David S. Brose and N'omi Greber, eds. Pp. 100–107. Kent, OH: Kent State University Press.

Knight, Vernon James, Jr., 2001 Feasting and the emergence of platform mound ceremonialism in eastern North America. In *Feasts: Archaeological and Ethnographic Perspectives on Food, Politics, and Power*. Michael Dietler and Bryan Hayden, eds. Pp. 311–333. Washington, DC: Smithsonian Institution Press.

Konigsberg, Lyle W., 1985 Demography and mortuary practice at Seip Mound One. *Midcontinental Journal of Archaeology* 10, 123–148.

Mainfort, Robert C., Jr., 1988 Middle Woodland ceremonialism at Pinson Mounds, Tennessee. *American Antiquity* 53, 158–173.

McGimsey, Chip, 2003 The rings of Marksville. *Southeastern Archaeology* 22(1), 47–62.

Moorehead, Warren King, 1922 *The Hopewell Mound Group of Ohio*. Publication 211, Anthropological Series, vol. 6, no. 5. Chicago: Field Museum of Natural History.

Morgan, William N., 1999 *Precolumbian Architecture in Eastern North America*. Gainesville: University Press of Florida.

Otto, Martha P., 1984 Masterworks in pipestone: Treasure from the Tremper Mound. *Timeline* 1(1), 18–33.

Pacheco, Paul J., ed., 1997 Ohio Middle Woodland intracommunity settlement variability: A case study from the Licking Valley. In Ohio *Hopewell Community Organization*. William S. Dancey and Paul J. Pacheco, eds. Pp. 41–84. Kent, OH: Kent State University Press.

Pacheco, Paul J., and William S. Dancey, n.d. Integrating mortuary and settlement data on Ohio Hopewell society. In *Recreating Hopewell*. Douglas K. Charles and Jane E. Buikstra, eds. (in preparation).

Penney, David, 1989 Hopewell art. Ph.D. dissertation, Columbia University.

Perino, Gregory F., 1968 The Pete Klunk Mound group, Calhoun County, Illinois: The Archaic and Hopewell occupations (with an appendix on the Gibson Mound group). In *Hopewell and Woodland Site Archaeology in Illinois*. James A. Brown, ed. Pp. 9–124. Bulletin 6. Urbana: Illinois Archaeological Survey.

Pickard, William H., 1996 1990 Excavations at Captiolium Mound (33WN13), Washington County, Ohio: A working evaluation. In *View from the Core: A Synthesis of Ohio Hopewell Archaeology*. Paul J. Pacheco, ed. Pp. 274–285. Columbus, OH: Ohio Archaeological Council.

Prufer, Olaf H., 1964 The Hopewell complex of Ohio. In *Hopewellian Studies*. Joseph R. Caldwell and Robert L. Hall, eds. Pp. 35–83. Scientific Papers, vol. 12, no. 2. Springfield: Illinois State Museum.

—— 1965 *The McGraw Site: A Study in Hopewellian Dynamics*. Scientific Publications, vol. 3, no. 1. Cleveland: Cleveland Museum of Natural History.

—— 1997 Fort Hill 1964: New data and reflections on Hopewell hilltop enclosures in southern Ohio. In *Ohio Hopewell Community Organization*. William S. Dancey and Paul J. Pacheco, eds. Pp. 311–330. Kent, OH: Kent State University Press.

Rafferty, Janet, 2002 Woodland period settlement patterning in the northern Gulf Coastal Plain of Alabama, Mississippi, and Tennessee. In *The Woodland Southeast*. D. G. Anderson and R. C. Mainfort, Jr., eds. Pp. 204–227. Tuscaloosa: University of Alabama Press.

Reichs, Kathleen J., 1984 Pearls or people: A biometric analysis of interregional exchange during Hopewell times. *Central Issues in Anthropology* 5(2), 47–65.

Rindos, David, 1980 Symbiosis, instability, and the origins and spread of agriculture: A new model. *Current Anthropology* 21, 751–772.

Riordan, Robert V., 1998 Boundaries, resistance, and control: Enclosing the hilltops in Middle Woodland Ohio. In *Ancient Earthen Enclosures of the Eastern Woodlands*. Robert C. Mainfort, Jr. and Lynn P. Sullivan, eds. Pp. 68–84. Gainesville: University Press of Florida.

Romain, William F., 2000 *Mysteries of the Hopewell: Astronomers, Geometers, and Magicians of the Eastern Woodlands*. Akron, OH: University of Akron Press.

Ruby, Bret J., 1997 The Mann phase: Hopewellian subsistence and settlement adaptations in the Wabash Lowlands of Southwestern Indiana. Ph.D. dissertation, Indiana University.

Russo, Michael, 1994 A brief introduction to the study of Archaic mounds in the Southeast. *Southeastern Archaeology* 13, 89–93.

Sciulli, Paul W., and Michael C. Mahaney, 1986 Evidence of local biological continuity for an Ohio Hopewell complex population. *Midcontinental Journal of Archaeology* 11, 181–199.

Seeman, Mark F., 1979 *The Hopewell Interaction Sphere: The Evidence for Interregional Trade and Structural Complexity*. Prehistory Research Series 5(2). Indianapolis: Indiana Historical Society.

—— 1992 Woodland traditions in the midcontinent: A comparison of three regional sequences. In *Long-Term Subsistence Change in Prehistoric North America*. Dale E. Croes, Rebecca A. Hawkins, and Barry L. Isaac, eds. Pp. 3–46. Research in Economic Anthropology, Supplement 6. Greenwich, CT: JAI Press.

—— 1995 When words are not enough: Hopewell interregionalism and the use of material symbols at the GE Mound. In *Native America Interactions*. Michael S. Nassaney and Kenneth E. Sassaman, eds. Pp. 122–143. Knoxville: University of Tennessee Press.

—— 1996 The Ohio Hopewell core and its many margins: Deconstructing upland and hinterland relations. In *View from the Core: A Synthesis of Ohio Hopewell Archaeology*. Paul J. Pacheco, ed. Pp. 304–315. Columbus, OH: Ohio Archaeological Council.

Seeman, Mark S., and William S. Dancey, 2000 The Late Woodland period in southern Ohio: Basic issues and prospects. In *Late Woodland Societies: Tradition and Transformation Across the Midcontinent*. Thomas E. Emerson, Dale L. McElrath, and Andrew C. Fortier, eds. Pp. 583–611. Lincoln: University of Nebraska Press.

Shetrone, Henry Clyde, and Emerson F. Greenman 1931 Explorations of the Seip group of prehistoric earthworks. *Ohio Archaeological and Historical Quarterly* 40, 343–509.

Simek, Jan F., Susan R. Frankenberg, and Charles H. Faulkner, 2001 Toward an understanding of prehistoric cave art in southern Appalachia. In *Archaeology of the Appalachian Highlands*. Lynn P. Sullivan and Susan C. Prezzano, eds. Pp. 49–64. Knoxville: University of Tennessee Press.

Smith, Bruce D., 1989 Origins of agriculture in eastern North America. *Science* 246, 1566–1571.

—— 1992 *Rivers of Change: Essays on Early Agriculture in Eastern North America*. Washington, DC: Smithsonian Institution Press.

Spielmann, Katherine A., 1998 Ritual craft specialists in middle range societies. In *Craft and Social Identity*. Cathy L. Costin and Rita P. Wright, eds. Pp. 153–160. Archeological Papers of the American Anthropological Association 8. Arlington, VA: American Anthropological Association.

—— 2002 Feasting, craft specialization, and the ritual mode of production in small-scale societies. *American Anthropologist* 104, 195–207.

Squier, Ephraim, and Edwin Davis, 1848 *Ancient Monuments of the Mississippi Valley: Comprising the Results of Extensive Original Surveys and Explorations*. Smithsonian Contributions to Knowledge 1. Washington, DC: Smithsonian Institution Press.

Stafford, Barbara D., and Mark B. Sant, eds., 1985 *Smiling Dan: Structure and Function at a Middle Woodland Settlement in the Illinois Valley*. Kampsville Archeological Center, Research Series, vol. 2. Kampsville, IL: Center for American Archeology.

Stephenson, Keith, Judith A. Bense, and Frankie Snow, 2002 Aspects of Deptford and Swift Creek of the south Atlantic and Gulf Coastal plains. In *The Woodland Southeast*. David G. Anderson and Robert C. Mainfort, Jr., eds. Tuscaloosa: University of Alabama Press.

Struever, Stuart, and Gail L. Houart, 1972 *An Analysis of the Hopewell Interaction Sphere*. In *Social Exchange and Interaction*. Edwin Wilmsen, ed. Pp. 47–79. Anthropological Papers 46. Ann Arbor: University of Michigan Museum of Anthropology.

Tainter, Joseph A., 1977 Woodland social change in west-central Illinois. *Midcontinental Journal of Archaeology* 2, 67–98.

—— 1988 *The Collapse of Complex Societies*. New York: Cambridge University Press.

Willey, Gordon R., 1966 *An Introduction to American Archaeology*, vol. 1: *North and Middle America*. Englewood Cliffs, NJ: Prentice-Hall.

Willey, Gordon R., and Philip Phillips, 1958 *Method and Theory in American Archaeology*. Chicago: University of Chicago Press.

Willey, Gordon R., and Jeremy Sabloff, 1993 *A History of American Archaeology*, 3rd edn. San Francisco: Freeman.

Wymer, Dee Anne, 1992 Trends and disparities: The Woodland paleoethnobotanical record of the mid-Ohio valley. In *Cultural Variability in Context: Woodland Settlements of the Mid-Ohio Valley*. Mark Seeman, ed. Pp. 65–76. MCJA Special Paper 7. Kent, OH: Kent State University.

6

Farming and Social Complexity in the Northeast

Elizabeth Chilton

Several of the chapters in this volume focus on issues of social complexity and its relationship to subsistence. In the northeastern United States the relationship between subsistence and social complexity is a topic that is at once poorly understood and hotly debated. There are several reasons for this: first, there was an enormous amount of diversity among the native groups of the Northeast both prior to and after European contact, and archaeologists have yet to come to terms with that diversity (cf. Hart and Rieth 2002). Second, there is no general agreement among archaeologists on the theoretical relationship between subsistence choices and sociopolitical organization. While some archaeologists believe there is a dependent relationship among farming, sedentism, and social complexity, others emphasize more diverse and varied trajectories of human history. Finally, there is a lack of consensus on definitions of "social complexity," making discussions of the matter all the more difficult.

In this chapter I explore the relationship among subsistence, settlement, and social choices during the Late Woodland period (A.D. 1000–1600) through a comparison between Algonquian-speaking peoples of New England and Iroquoian-speaking peoples of upstate New York (Figure 6.1). I review the archaeological and ethnohistorical evidence for these choices and suggest that they have had a significant bearing on contemporary native issues, particularly the federal recognition process and the implementation of NAGPRA (see Watkins, this volume). One of the most important goals of this chapter is to examine the pivotal role that New England archaeology has to play in our quest to understand the nature of social complexity.

New England as "Cultural Backwater"

The Northeast – and particularly New England – is often considered by archaeologists working outside the region to be a kind of cultural backwater. As Dena

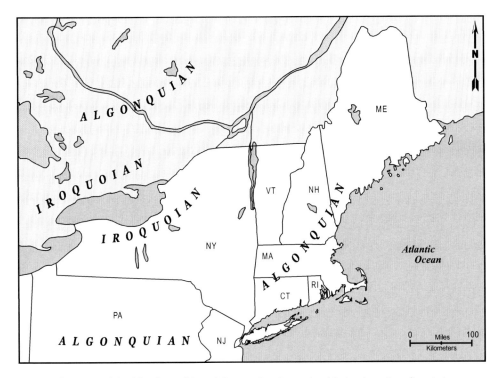

Figure 6.1 Map of the Northeast United States, showing major Native American linguistic groups around A.D. 1700

Dincauze (1980:29) put it more than 20 years ago, "the Northeast has tradition-ally been considered a marginal, culturally retarded outlier of the eastern United States." In James Fitting's *Development of North American Archaeology* (1973), David Brose's map of the Northeastern United States ends at New York's eastern border, completely excluding archaeological sites in Connecticut, Maine, Massachusetts, New Hampshire, Rhode Island, and Vermont. Because the intellectual traditions of Northeast archaeology began in upstate New York (Dincauze 1993), New England has historically been viewed as a periphery to an already marginal area. My 15 years of experience as a New England archaeologist have exposed me to many jeering comments by archaeologists working in other regions about the quality or quantity of material culture one is likely to find in the region. Members of the general public express surprise that anyone could even practice professional archaeology in New England.

So why is New England perceived as a cultural backwater? First, the archaeo-logical remains found in New England are less plentiful and perhaps less glamorous than those found elsewhere in North America. This is because, as you will see, there is no evidence for sedentism, craft specialization, or permanent architecture. Second, and as a result, the region has attracted the interest of relatively fewer archaeologists. Because there is a relatively small number of archaeologists, the region has not been well studied and, therefore, it is difficult to get major grant monies to study the archaeology of the region – overall a vicious cycle of marginalization.

This notion of New England as a cultural backwater takes on particular clarity when one considers archaeological interpretations of the Late Woodland period. In the greater Northeast, especially for the New York Iroquois, there has been quite a bit of archaeological research on the Late Woodland period. It is thought to have been a dynamic period: maize horticulture became important for subsistence, population increased and became more clustered, communities became more sedentary, and the incidence of intercommunity conflict increased (see Fenton 1978).

In contrast, there is relatively little published information for New England for this period, especially for the interior. Instead of large, sedentary farming villages, archaeologists encounter small and inconspicuous settlements that do not fit their expectations for this period (see Luedtke 1988; Thorbahn 1988). This absence of large horticultural villages has, on the surface, strengthened the case for New England as a "cultural backwater." Rather than accept this Iroquois-centric (or Irocentric: Bruchac and Chilton 2003) view of the Late Woodland Northeast, in my research I examine the different historical processes at work in the region as a means to understand cultural difference. In this regard I follow the lead of Dena Dincauze (1993), who suggests that we "center" New England, that we explore native societies in New England in their own right, on their own terms.

In the rest of this chapter I survey what is known – and unknown – about subsistence, settlement, and social complexity in the northeastern United States. Since the Iroquois are often held up as exemplars of the stereotypical Late Woodland lifestyle in the Northeast (hence, Irocentrism), I start by evaluating what we know about differences and similarities between them and the Algonquians of New England in terms of subsistence and settlement. I have written about Late Woodland subsistence and settlement extensively elsewhere, especially with respect to ceramic traditions and technologies (Chilton 1998, 1999a, 2002), so I will only summarize these briefly here. In the following summary, I use the term Iroquois to refer to the pre-contact five nations of upstate New York: the Cayuga, Mohawk, Oneida, Onondaga, and Seneca (Figure 6.2). These tribes formed the League of the Iroquois in the early 16th century (Snow 1994). I use the term Algonquian to refer to the Algonquian-speaking peoples of New England. New England, here, is defined as the modern New England states (Connecticut, Maine, Massachusetts, New Hampshire, Rhode Island, and Vermont), as well as eastern and coastal New York (Figure 6.3). It is important to note that Algonquian and Iroquoian language families are distinct enough from one another to be mutually unintelligible.

Subsistence

Archaeologists spend a lot of time, energy, and resources trying to determine what people ate in the past. This is not because archaeologists are obsessed with food, but because a society's foodways can tell us a lot about the larger environmental

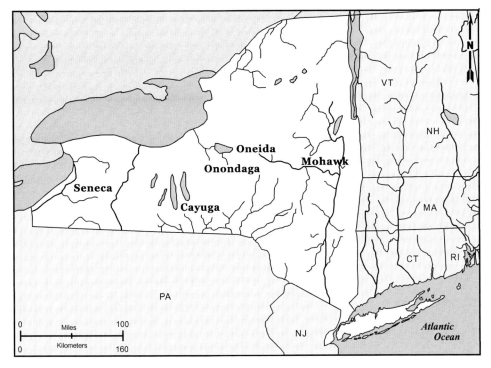

Figure 6.2 Map of New York State, showing the locations of the Five Nations of the Iroquoian Confederacy during the 17th century

context and social choices, including the division of labor, settlement, and political organization.

On the basis of both archaeological and ethnohistorical evidence, the Iroquois of the Late Woodland period were very much dependent on domesticated plants – maize, beans and squash – for subsistence, although they supplemented their diet by hunting and gathering. The earliest confirmed dates for maize – which was originally a tropical cultigen – in the Northeast are between A.D. 800 and 900 (Hart and Means 2002), coincident with the beginning of the Medieval Warm period (see Fagan 2000). This is also just prior to the time that the Iroquois are thought to have migrated into the region and either intermingled with, or wedged themselves in between, Algonquian groups in the Mohawk valley (see Crawford and Smith 1996; Snow 1996a).

A lot is known about the Iroquois of upstate New York from both the archaeological and ethnohistorical record. In terms of subsistence, the Iroquois practiced shifting horticulture where large tracks of forest were cut and burned before planting (Niemczycki 1984; see also Morgan 1962[1851]). Horticultural fields were very large, and much time was devoted to the cultivation, harvest, storage, and preparation of maize. It is important to note that the type of maize used in the Northeast – Northern Flint or closely related varieties (Fenton 1978) – was unlike modern

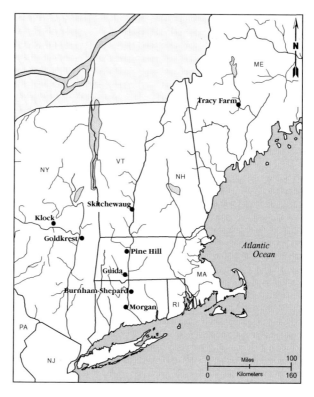

Figure 6.3 Map of the New England states, showing the location of key sites discussed in the text

sweetcorn in that it needed to be cooked for a long period of time over a hot fire. A lot of time was spent in the planting, cultivation, harvesting, drying, storage, and preparation of maize (see Fenton 1978; Morgan 1962[1851]).

In New England, while domesticated plants, particularly maize, were clearly present by A.D. 800, there is no archaeological evidence for intensive horticulture until after the arrival of Europeans (Chilton 1999a, 2002, contra Bendremer 1999; Peterson and Cowie 2002). There have been fairly large quantities of maize found at some Late Woodland period archaeological sites in the region. For example, Bendremer and Dewar (1994) report the recovery of 1,500 maize kernels at the Burnham Shepard site along the Connecticut River in Connecticut. Likewise, Lavin (1988) reports the presence of "numerous maize kernels" at the nearby Morgan Site. Heckenberger et al. (1992) identified 485 maize kernels and kernel fragments across seven storage pits at the Skitchewaug site in Vermont (although 4,288 nut-shells were recovered from the same features). Through our excavations at the Pine Hill site in Deerfield, Massachusetts, we recovered over 200 maize kernels and kernel fragments from one pit feature (Chilton et al. 2000). However, since there are approximately 200 kernels of maize on each cob of Northern Flint corn, all of these numbers must be kept in perspective. Also, since maize only preserves under very particular – and rare – circumstances (e.g., charring), we cannot assume that there is a one-to-one correlation between the number of kernels of maize found at a site and the importance of maize to the people who lived there during the Late Woodland period (Chilton 1999a, 2002). Instead, in order to gain a more complete picture of subsistence we need to examine the archaeobotanical record in its entirety and put it into the context of settlement patterns (see the next section).

If we examine the use of maize in New England within the larger context of plant exploitation, it is clear that maize was part of a much larger subsistence base. In both New England and New York, maize (and, later, beans) was a tropical cultigen that was adopted into what was likely an already complex system of indigenous horticulture or at least some kind of environmental management. While the domestication of floodplain weeds such as chenopod (*Chenopodium berlandieri*), marshelder (*Iva annua*), and sunflower (*Helianthus annuus*) has been well documented in the Midwest and Southeast (see Smith 1992), the same conclusive evidence has not been identified in the Northeast. Nevertheless, archaeobotanical analyses of plant remains in the region have revealed tantalizing evidence for the possible genetic alteration of certain indigenous plants, particularly chenopodium (see George and Dewar 1999; Sidell 2002). A wide variety of plant species have been recovered from New England sites, primarily through the method of soil flotation: chenopodium and a variety of other weed seeds, grass seeds, berries and other fleshy fruits, tubers, and many different kinds of nuts (see Bernstein 1999; Heckenberger et al. 1992; Largy et al. 1999; Sidell 1999). Native peoples also exploited a wide variety of land, air, and aquatic animals, large and small (see Chilton et al. 2000; Chilton and Doucette 2002; Largy et al. 2002). The archaeobotanical and faunal evidence thus supports the interpretation of a diverse foraging base for New England peoples.

Evidence for controlled use of fire as a means of forest and environmental management also suggests that native peoples were actively manipulating and experimenting with their natural environment (Johnson 1996; Patterson and Sassaman 1988). The effect of burning was the creation of habitats that attracted a wide variety of plants and animals, including berries, grasses, birds, and land mammals (Cronon 1983).

While New England Algonquians used maize by A.D. 800, it was apparently only a dietary supplement to an otherwise diverse diet. Ethnohistorical accounts and archaeological evidence reveal a diverse foraging base for New England Algonquians. This diet included hundreds of species of plants and animals: fish, fowl, clams, nuts, berries, tubers, and land mammals. For example, Wood (1977[1634]: 86) wrote concerning the peoples of Massachusetts Bay: "In the wintertime they have all manner of fowls of the water and of the land, and the beasts of the land and water . . . with catharres and other roots, Indian beans and clams. In the summer they have all manner of shellfish, with all sort of berries." For the interior, Isaack Rasieres (in Jameson 1909), writing in the 17th century, observed that people "support[ed] themselves with hunting and fishing, and the sowing of maize and beans."

While we know that the New England peoples practiced maize horticulture, it may not have consumed much of their time or energy. After the planting of maize, peoples would apparently disperse for two to three months as the maize ripened, to plant, hunt, and gather elsewhere (Cronon 1983:45). Thus, the Algonquians of the region were likely "mobile farmers" (Graham 1994) or "foraging horticulturalists" (Mulholland 1988), a cultural category of which we currently lack a sufficient understanding.

My analysis of Iroquoian and Algonquian ceramics from the Late Woodland period further supports my interpretation of subsistence differences between the two groups (Chilton 1996, 1998, 1999b). On the basis of certain technical differences, such as the type and density of materials added to the clay (temper), the vessel wall thickness and vessel size, and the types of pre-firing surface treatments, it is likely that Iroquoian vessels would have made better cooking vessels (Chilton 1998). Iroquoian pots were built to be resistant to thermal stress, but were more sensitive to mechanical stress, while the reverse was true for Algonquian pots. In other words, Iroquoian pots were better for cooking maize and were more specialized than Algonquian pots. Algonquian pots, on the other hand, could have served a variety of uses and were sturdier. The implications of this trade-off will be discussed in the next section.

Settlement

Settlement patterns, that is, the patterning of structures and features within an archaeological site and the distribution of sites across the landscape, are perhaps the most important body of archaeological evidence we have for interpreting ancient economies and social organization. For the Iroquois, settlement patterns have been intensively studied by archaeologists (e.g., Ritchie 1969; Ritchie and Funk 1973; Snow 1994). Archaeological evidence for Iroquoian settlement indicates that they resided in villages of up to a hundred multi-roomed longhouses (Figure 6.4; Fenton

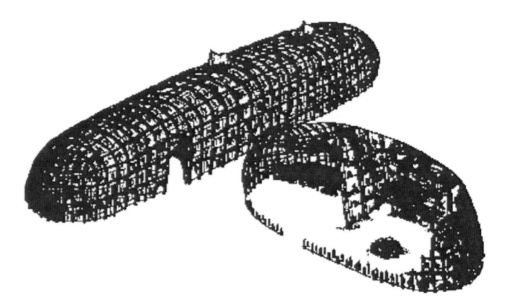

Figure 6.4 Cut-away of a longhouse (adapted from Snow 1980:87)

1978). The support posts from these longhouses decayed in place, leaving a dark, circular soil stain, called a postmold. Archaeologists can then trace the size and pattern of these postmolds to estimate the shape, size, and layout of houses and other structures. From these postmold patterns we know that longhouses could be more than 300 feet long (although these figures vary by site and time period: Snow 1994). Morgan (1962[1851]:64) states that the longhouses would have accommodated up to 20 families, each in its own compartment. So important is longhouse residence to self-identity that the League members still refer to themselves as Hodenosaunee or "people of the long house" (Morgan 1962[1851]; Snow 1994). Woodland villages were virtually permanent, being occupied for 25–50 years at a time, until firewood and/or prime agricultural fields became depleted (Tuck 1978).

The Iroquois population was relatively large during the Late Woodland period. Population estimates for 16th-century Mohawk villages (the easternmost tribe of the New York Iroquois) range between 600 and 1,300 people (Snow 1996b). Many Iroquoian villages after A.D. 1200 were palisaded for defense, and there is ample evidence during the Late Woodland period for inter-tribal warfare (Snow 1994). Evidence for warfare is not surprising given the evidence for sedentism and intensive horticulture: when one examines the big picture of human history and cultural evolution, it is only when people become dependent on few resources that they are willing – even forced – to compete, sometimes violently, for access to the resources and the land that produces these resources. Also, as societies become sedentary and grow in size, they require a restructuring of social relations that often leads to inter- and intra-group tensions.

In contrast to upstate New York, settlement pattern data are not plentiful for New England. This is in part due to historic disturbance, amateur digging, the scarcity of regional surveys, and geomorphological processes (Chilton 1999a). Hasenstab (1999) underscores this last point, arguing that Late Woodland villages sites are simply "hard to find," at least in the Connecticut valley, because of their presumed location deep beneath stratified riverine flood deposits.

However, if we examine the extant data, there is little evidence for Late Woodland structures of any kind – much less villages – in New England. There does seem to be evidence for year-round or nearly year-round habitation in some protected harbors on the coast (Bernstein 1993, 1999; Bernstein et al. 1997; Gwynne 1982), but this coastal sedentism is a process that does not seem to be associated with the adoption of maize horticulture (Ceci 1990). Instead, it is likely that the year-round availability of both marine and terrestrial resources in these areas was the impetus for increasing sedentism. This sedentism then likely paved the way for the adoption of horticulture (maize, as well as indigenous plants), rather than the other way around.

For the interior, identifying postmolds on Late Woodland sites is a cause to celebrate. But rarely do these postmolds form a pattern that would help us to identify structure size or shape. For the most part, postmold patterns appear to represent short-term wigwam-type structures (Figure 6.5). The overlapping pattern of these structures and other features, as well as a lack of well-defined middens, indicates repeated seasonal use of site locations over time (e.g., Chilton et al. 2000).

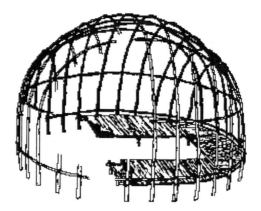

Figure 6.5 Cut-away of a wigwam (adapted from Salwen 1968:183)

Certainly, there is evidence for fairly large – though not necessarily year-round – Late Woodland sites in the lower Connecticut valley. As previously discussed, a fairly large amount of maize has been identified at the Morgan and Burnham-Shepard sites, but there are no published settlement pattern data for these sites (see Bendremer and Dewar 1994; Lavin 1988). In a few cases there is evidence for a single large structure or "longhouse" on New England sites, but these are rare and do not at all mirror the clustered longhouse patterns of Iroquoian sites from the same period. For example, the Goldkrest site, in eastern New York, apparently represents a multi-season fishing and foraging hamlet whose inhabitants exploited floodplain resources, supplemented by some local horticulture (Lavin et al. 1996). But the "longhouse" identified at Goldkrest was not occupied year-round or for multiple years. Instead, on the basis of the botanical remains it was interpreted as having been occupied in late summer and early fall (Lavin et al. 1996). At the Tracy Farm site in Maine, the dating of the "longhouse" structure is unclear (Cowie 2000). From the 587 postmolds recorded for the site two isolated structures were identified, a longhouse and a small circular "wigwam" (the latter is thought to date to the Middle Woodland period: Cowie 2000). Of the 19 storage pit features identified, all but five contained contact period artifacts; the excavators suggest that this longhouse represents a ceremonial lodge or a multi-family residence that was occupied after the rest of the group moved to the east side of the river when the mission was established there in the 1690s (Cowie 2000). Thus, the longhouse was most likely built after European contact, a process that had enormous effects on native demography, settlement, and social organization.

The ethnohistorical literature supports an interpretation of diversity and flexibility in New England settlements. In 1674 Josselyn (1833[1674]) reported on the impermanence of New England communities: "Towns they have none, being always removing from one place to another for conveniency of food . . . I have seen half a hundred of their Wigwams together in a piece of ground and within a day or two, or a week they have all been dispersed." In the second quarter of the seventeenth century, Johan de Laet (in Jameson 1909) said of Algonquian people living in the Hudson valley that "some of them lead a wandering life in the open aire without settled habitation . . . Others have fixed places of abode."

Williams (1963[1643]:135) also comments on the Algonquians' seasonal movements and the flexibility of their habitations: "In the middle of summer . . . they will flie and remove on a sudden from one part of their field to a fresh place . . . Sometimes they remove to a hunting house in the end of the year . . . but their great remove is from their Summer fields to warme and thicke woodie bottoms where they winter: They are quicke; in a halfe a day, yea, sometimes a few houres warning to be gone and the house up elsewhere . . ." Similarly, Gookin (1792:149) and Higgeson (1968 [1629]:123) report that the New England Indians were inclined to frequently move their dwellings from place to place. Cronon (1983:38) notes that, for some groups, the size and shape of dwellings would change, depending on population density and the time of year (e.g., small wigwams in the summer, multi-family longhouses in the winter).

Ceramic data, likewise, support the interpretation of a high degree of mobility and flexibility for New England peoples. Based on my analysis of native ceramics from western Massachusetts, I suggested that native peoples were making decisions about pottery manufacture that selected for resistance to mechanical stress over thermal stress (Chilton 1996, 1998). That is, by making pots with relatively thicker walls and dense temper, pots were better able to withstand the stresses of a mobile lifestyle, but they were not ideal maize-cooking pots on the whole. They were likely used for cooking maize and other plants at various times, but they were not primarily used for this purpose. Instead, it appears that they were used for the transport, storage, and cooking of a wide variety of foods and other materials.

Algonquian pots also showed greater diversity in virtually all attributes analyzed, including temper type and density, vessel size and shape, type of surface treatment, and decorative motif (Figure 6.6; Chilton 1996, 1998; see also Pretola 2000). This most likely reflects the relatively greater mobility and fluidity of social boundaries for Algonquian people. If, as I have proposed, groups were fissioning and fusing throughout the year in tandem with seasonal movements, pottery would have been produced in variable environmental and social contexts. This would explain the great heterogeneity in Algonquian ceramic attributes. For the Iroquois, living in year-round semi-permanent villages meant that pottery was produced in the same or similar ecological and social contexts over time. Accordingly, Iroquoian ceramics show a great deal of homogeneity in both decorative and technical attributes (Figure 6.7; Chilton 1998). Despite the distinctions between the pottery of these two culturally and linguistically disparate groups, similarities in stylistic motifs suggest that "Algonquians and Iroquoians interacted in an open and fluid system that allowed association and mixture of people and ideas" (Pretola 2000:114).

Another topic related to the issue of settlement patterns is the occurrence of large pit features on Late Woodland sites. Bendremer and Dewar (1994) and Petersen and Cowie (2002) believe that the presence of "storage pit" features

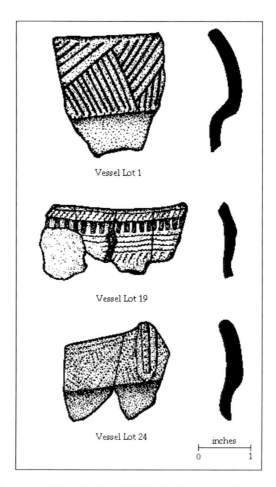

Vessel Lot 1

Vessel Lot 19

Vessel Lot 24

inches

0   1

Figure 6.6 Sherds from vessel lots 1, 19, and 24, Guida Farm site, Massachusetts

provides evidence for the importance of maize horticulture. However, there are several problems with such an interpretation. First, pit features were not an invention of the Late Woodland period. There are many pit features in New England that date to the Middle and Late Archaic periods (see Doucette 2003). Second, we simply do not fully understand the functional complexity of these features. At the Late Woodland period Pine Hill site in Deerfield, Massachusetts, only one of the 21 pit features identified contained maize (Chilton et al. 2000). Very little in the way of artifacts or food remains was recovered from these features. On the basis of feature contents and soil micromorphology, I have interpreted these features as short-term food-storage or food-processing features (Chilton et al. 2000; see also Moeller 1992). Of the five Late Woodland pit features excavated at the Lucy Vincent Beach site on Martha's Vineyard, thus far none has been found to contain maize, although the analysis of flotation samples is not yet complete (Chilton and Doucette 2002). Instead of assuming that all Late Woodland pit features are storage pits, what

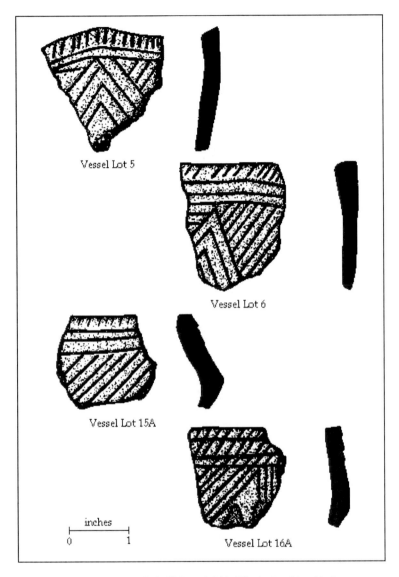

Vessel Lot 5

Vessel Lot 6

Vessel Lot 15A

inches

0   1

Vessel Lot 16A

Figure 6.7 Sherds from vessel lots 5, 6, 15A, and 16A, Klock site, New York

is needed is a comprehensive study of these features (e.g., Volmar 1998), which likely had a variety of functions.

In sum, instead of believing that we have simply had bad luck in locating Late Woodland villages, I now believe that archaeological sites are inconspicuous because of the relatively small size and high mobility of Algonquian communities during the Late Woodland period (for a parallel argument in western North America, see Ames, this volume). I should point out that this position is not shared by all New England archaeologists, many of whom believe that large farming villages, with multi-acre aggregations of longhouses surrounded by palisades must have existed, but that the evidence has yet to be recognized or found by archaeologists (Hasenstab 1999; see also Bendremer 1999; Petersen and Cowie 2002). Of course our interpretations are always subject to change in the light of new data, and I am hopeful that we will be able to test many of the extant hypotheses. But at present we have no evidence for formal villages, palisaded settlements, intensive horticulture, or warfare (that is, group-on-group, organized violence) in New England prior to European contact.

While I propose that the Algonquian communities of the interior were not sedentary, I am not suggesting that they were nomads. They were likely moving within well-defined and fairly large "homelands" (Handsman 1995) so that, while site locations were unstable, homelands likely showed great continuity of habitation and use over generations. Homelands would have included all of the individual and communal sites within a region, including hunting and foraging territories and seasonal settlements (Bruchac and Chilton 2003).

Mobility has important implications for understanding political organization. In contrast to the fairly structured, tribal political organization of the Iroquois, the Algonquians of New England apparently shared a loosely organized and flexible political organization. Instead of well-defined tribes, we know of a series of related communities with fluid social and political boundaries (Bruchac and Chilton 2003; Johnson 1999). Colonists and ethnohistorians mapped out what they thought were distinct native communities or tribes in western Massachusetts (Pocumtuck at Deerfield, Norwottuck at Northampton and Hadley, Agawam in the Springfield area, and Woronoco in Westfield). The fact that these are all Algonquian locative words rather than words describing people raises the question whether these are indeed separate "tribes" or one large related group (Bruchac and Chilton 2003). From ethnohistorical and archaeological research, we know that: (1) groups were congregating and dispersing in response to seasonal movements and for social gatherings, and (2) patterns of residence and the reckoning of kin were more flexible than those of the Iroquois (see Johnson 1999). The advantage to this social strategy is that, in the face of political disagreements, people could literally "vote with their feet." This would likely dispel tensions that might have otherwise led to violence. It is perhaps for this reason that there is no evidence for warfare prior to European colonization in New England.

It is clear that New England Algonquians had the knowledge and the technology to become sedentary farmers, and they had an adequate environment for intensive farming. The Connecticut valley is one of the most agriculturally rich areas in New England today, and would have been more than adequate for cultivating fairly large tracts of maize, beans, and squash. Ultimately, it is for cultural – not environmental – reasons that groups make decisions about investment in horticulture (Demeritt 1991). While incorporating maize into their diet for more than 800 years prior to contact, New England Algonquians did not become sedentary farmers. For that reason, New England offers us an opportunity to examine diversity strategies in the adoption of maize horticulture and, therefore, different trajectories of cultural evolution.

Social Complexity in a Global Context

Theoretical issues that have emerged in recent analyses of southern New England

> Native society makes this region one of intense interest, particularly to those concerned
> with the origins of, and relations between, agriculture, sedentism, and social inequal-
> ity, and their ideological and cosmological correlates. (Bragdon 1996:32)

For more than a hundred years, anthropologists and archaeologists have attempted
to classify both past and present human societies (e.g., Fried 1960, 1967; Morgan
1995 [1877]; Service 1962, 1975). These classifications are sometimes based on
subsistence or some other technological "achievement," but they most often deal
either implicitly or explicitly with presumed level of social complexity. In the 19th
century, Lewis Henry Morgan (1995 [1877]) assigned human societies to three
levels of social evolution (savagery, barbarism, or civilization) on the basis of a series
of technological achievements (such as pottery, agriculture, writing, etc.). The
model developed by Service (1962) focused on the institutionalization of leadership and integration of political economy in defining three different types of societies: bands, tribes, and chiefdoms. Service (1962) saw the shift between bands and
tribes as essentially correlated with the shift from foraging to agriculture and the
need for a shift in social structure that would allow for greater integration of groups.
Chiefdoms were seen as being more complex and organized than tribes, with the
presence of primary centers that coordinated economic, social, and religious
activities (Service 1962:143). Fried (1967) distinguished between societies in terms
of increasing social asymmetry – egalitarian, ranked, and stratified societies – and
emphasized the role of power and authority in these distinctions. In all of these
schemes, the level of social complexity or evolution is implicitly or explicitly correlated with subsistence, since it is assumed by many that farming is more reliable
than hunting and gathering for producing surplus, which is thought to have been
key in the formation of stratified, "complex" societies or civilizations.

Despite years of attempts to try to refine these typologies, very little consensus
has been reached (Feinman and Neitzel 1984). While these models can be useful
heuristic devices in coming to terms with the immense diversity of human societies,
they often prove to be intellectual straitjackets (see Yoffee 1993). Certainly, cultural
classifications – by definition – mask the complexity of social relations. In the case
of New England, because Algonquian peoples were clearly farming maize – a crop
that is thought to have had transformative significance for other North American
cultures – many archaeologists assume that there must have been significant social
correlates in this case. While most archaeologists in the region (and elsewhere)
implicitly make this assumption, others are more explicit. For example, Petersen
and Cowie (2002:265–266) "believe that the adoption of maize-beans-squash horticulture was a significant event . . . and that it brought some of the largest changes
ever to affect indigenous societies before the arrival of Europeans." Likewise,
Benison (1997:10) argues that the adoption of maize led to a "basic restructuring

of social relations." At present we lack archaeological data to support either of these perspectives.

John Hart (1999) attributes assumptions about the adoption of maize horticulture to "natural state models" in which all members of a particular type of society are expected to reflect the natural state. The assumption is that, once maize is adopted, "its natural state can be defined as effective and highly productive" (Hart 1999:139), that is, it becomes the center of a focal economy. However, as Hart (1999) points out, maize agriculture does not have a natural state because it is formed on the basis of the dynamic relationship between plants and human populations. Thus, the degree of reliance on maize – and the degree to which the incorporation of maize transformed ancient societies – cannot be determined simply on the basis of its presence in archaeological contexts. Arguing for maize horticulture as the impetus for presumed sedentism and extreme cultural transformation without concrete archaeological data minimizes the importance of indigenous, pre-maize horticulture in the region and the economic, ideological, and social transformations associated with these earlier developments.

I believe that the reason many New England archaeologists argue for intensive horticulture is that they want to be able to argue for the social complexity of the region's peoples. Many of New England's archaeologists want to elevate the region's archaeology – to "center" New England (Dincauze 1993). In doing so, many archaeologists strive to demonstrate that New England peoples were not backward and were not passive reactors to the Iroquois or to Europeans and that, in fact, they were evolutionarily "complex" prior to European contact (e.g., Bragdon 1996). Certainly – and wrongly – New England's native peoples have historically been relegated to the cultural backwaters of evolution, being classified as neither bands, tribes, or states, and denied "evolutionary complexity" (Bragdon 1996:xvi). But do societies require horticulture to be sedentary? Does sedentism in and of itself indicate social complexity? And does complexity require social hierarchy, that is, vertical social relations? When one reviews the archaeological literature it is clear that the answer to all of these questions is a resounding no (see also Ames, Lekson, Pauketat, and Sassaman, this volume).

Over the past decade or so, anthropologists have begun to outline models of so-called "transegalitarian societies," or "intermediate societies" which are neither egalitarian nor politically stratified (see Arnold 1996; Clark and Blake 1994; Hayden 1995). Models of increasing social complexity should, therefore, include the potential for horizontal complexity or heterarchy (see Coupland 1996; Creamer 1996; Crumley 1987; Feinman and Neitzel 1984). There are numerous archaeological examples of societies that are at once essentially egalitarian, yet quite large and complex (e.g., see Creamer [1996] for a discussion of the Rio Grande valley) or cases where there are alternating episodes of horizontal expansion and vertical reorganization in the formation of what we might call chiefdoms (e.g., Coupland 1996). Like these other examples, the Northeast allows us to examine the different historical trajectories of the Iroquois and New England Algonquians, even given relatively similar natural environments and access to technologies. In this case we need to look to historical explanations and the contexts of social choices made by each group.

Contemporary Native Issues

A strategy of mobile farming with fluid social boundaries is not simply an academically interesting topic – it has had important implications for how New England peoples have lived since European contact. Certainly, the more sedentary, tribal, Iroquoian peoples of upstate New York have fared better in the face of contact, at least if one measures success in terms of federal recognition, reservations, and historical continuity. The Iroquois were more formally recognized by Europeans during the initial contact period, in part because Europeans understood (relatively speaking) their use of land (intensive farming) and political organization (a form of representational government). In contrast, the English clearly did not understand the type of horticulture that was being practiced by New England peoples. Many of the New England planting fields would have seemed quite disorderly to Europeans, who at the time of contact were more accustomed to monocrop farming. In fact Europeans believed that New England's native peoples were not "improving" the land (Locke 1986 [1690]) and used this as an implicit justification for the taking of land. Europeans also did not understand or appreciate the more flexible and egalitarian social organization of New England native peoples. This in turn affected the ways that European colonists interpreted usufruct rights recorded in deeds during the contact period, and led to their near invisibility in historical writings after the end of the 17th century (Bruchac and Chilton 2003).

Mobile farming has important implications for the federal recognition process. For example, only one native group in the state of Massachusetts has received federal recognition from the US government to date – the Wampanoag Tribe at Gayhead (Aquinnah) on Martha's Vineyard. The Nipmuc in central Massachusetts have been seeking federal recognition for over 20 years; they received recognition in 2001 under President Clinton, only to have it revoked under President Bush later that year (Adams 2001a, 2001b). Likewise, the Mashpee on Cape Cod are still fighting a long, hard battle to win federal recognition (see Campisi 1991).

One reason that so few groups in New England have received federal recognition is that the federal recognition process requires that native groups document their identity as a distinct "tribe," with fixed social and territorial boundaries, and clear political influence over all of their members. Given the pre-contact lifeways of mobile farming, seasonal use of coastal sites, and frequent movements within a regional homeland, it is no wonder that the only group granted federal recognition thus far (the Wampanoag Tribe of Gayhead/Aquinnah) resides on a relatively small island. Unless or until New England archaeologists are able to demonstrate the importance and legitimacy of the homelands model for pre-contact New England, native peoples will not be able to rely on archaeological evidence to assist them in their petitions for federal recognition.

Federal recognition has important implications for tribal sovereignty and for land claims. The lack of federal recognition for native groups in New England today also has serious implications for the repatriation of human remains and other objects under NAGPRA, the Native American Graves Protection and Repatriation Act, which was passed in 1990 (Public Law 101–601). Under NAGPRA, tribes with federal recognition are currently in the best position to make claims for the repatriation of human remains, funerary objects, sacred objects, or objects of cultural patrimony from institutions receiving federal monies (Watkins 2000:55, this volume). When objects or human remains are affiliated with a tribe that does not have federal recognition, these items are said to be "culturally unidentifiable" under NAGPRA. These items can be requested by the tribe for repatriation, but the request must generally include letters of support from all of the surrounding federally recognized tribes who might conceivably make a claim, and must be approved by the NAGPRA Review Committee. In some cases, geographically or culturally related federally recognized tribes have been allowed to claim materials on behalf of their unrecognized neighbors (Nafziger and Dobkins 1999:89). Even so, if any federally recognized tribe decides to claim material rightfully belonging to an unrecognized tribe, the unrecognized tribe has no legal standing under NAGPRA to contest the claim.

Being excluded from the NAGPRA process because of a lack of federal recognition not only deprives groups of the opportunity to repatriate objects and the remains of their ancestors. It also deprives them, in some cases, of the opportunity to work with archaeologists on other aspects of their ancient past. While NAGPRA itself has been controversial, and has been problematic and difficult to implement (see Fine-Dare 2002; Mihesuah 2000; Thomas 2000; Watkins 2000), it has – sometimes forcibly – led to the formation of new relationships among native peoples and archaeologists. My own work with the Aquinnah on the excavation of a threatened archaeological site and the subsequent repatriation of burials unearthed there (Chilton and Doucette 2002) has had a profound effect on the way I practice archaeology. Collaborating with the Aquinnah not only affected what happened to the remains after the excavation was over. It affected every decision we made concerning that site: where to dig, how to dig, when to dig, what to sample, how to educate our students, how to analyze artifacts and samples, where the collections should be housed, how to backfill, how to report on our findings – how to do archaeology. Had the Aquinnah not had state or federal recognition, I might not have automatically or so completely collaborated with them: not because I wouldn't have wanted to do so, but when bureaucratic channels are opened – whether due to NAGPRA, state burial law, or cultural resource management legislation – relationships are formed (for better or for worse) that would not have formed otherwise. I am hopeful that if more archaeologists become aware of some of the stumbling-blocks to recognition that many native groups face, that they will assist in petitions for recognition and repatriation by applying the models discussed above – particularly the model of mobile farming and the homelands model – in their evaluation of continuity as expressed in the archaeological record.

Conclusions

So where do we go from here? It is clear that in order to understand the great diversity, complexity, and vitality of native peoples in North America, and in order to make our interpretations of the archaeological record more relevant to people living in the present, we need to be able to question our assumptions about the relationship between subsistence and social complexity. It is clear that people do not blindly make social changes on the basis of new technologies, such as maize horticulture. Instead, human choices must be viewed in their multilayered contexts of power relations, social organization, cultural traditions, environment, and history. Instead of automatically using traditional complexity models or cultural classifications, we need to explore new models of transegalitarian societies. In this way the study of New England Algonquians will potentially offer models for archaeologists who are trying to understand mobile farmers – or even sedentary foragers – in other parts of the world. Finally, in applying the results of our research, we need to keep our minds open to new models of cultural continuity, such as the homelands model, even in the face of what at first appears to be historical erasure.

ACKNOWLEDGMENTS

First and foremost, I would like to thank Tim Pauketat and Diana Loren for inviting me to contribute to this volume. Writing this chapter has been an unusually enjoyable experience. I wish to thank Siobhan Hart for the inspiration that her Masters project gave me for writing the section on contemporary native issues. I would like to express my deepest gratitude to my colleagues (past and present) at UMass for countless stimulating conversations and debates over the years that have profoundly affected my perspectives on New England peoples and archaeology in general. In particular, I wish to thank the follow people: Marge Bruchac, Claire Carlson, Dena Dincauze, Eric Johnson, Arthur Keene, Robert Paynter, and Martin Wobst. Marge Bruchac provided very helpful comments on drafts of this chapter. All pottery-sherd drawings are by Maureen Manning. Special thanks to Michael Sugerman for his editorial assistance and for many fruitful conversations and debates about cultural evolution at all hours of the day and night.

REFERENCES

Adams, Jim, 2001a Nipmuc recognition victim of Bush Hold: Connecticut AG enters the fray as well. In *Indian Country Today* (Lakota Times), p. A1. Rapid City, SD.
——2001b Nipmuc regroup, locals applaud as McCaleb denies recognition. In *Indian Country Today* (Lakota Times), p. A2. Rapid City, SD.
Arnold, Jeanne E., ed., 1996 *Emergent Complexity: The Evolution of Intermediate Societies*. Ann Arbor, MI: International Monographs in Prehistory.
Bendremer, Jeffrey C., 1999 Changing strategies in the pre- and post-contact subsistence systems of southern New England: Archaeological and ethnohistorical evidence. In *Current Northeast Ethnobotany*. J. P. Hart, ed. Pp. 133–156. New York State Museum Bulletin 494. Albany, NY.

Bendremer, Jeffrey C., and Robert E. Dewar, 1994 The advent of maize horticulture in New England. In *Corn and Culture in the Prehistoric New World*. S. Johannessen and C. Hastorf, eds. Pp. 369–393. Boulder, CO: Westview Press.

Benison, Chris, 1997 Horticulture and the maintenance of social complexity in Late Woodland southeastern New England. *North American Archaeologist* 18(1), 1–17.

Bernstein, David J., 1993 *Prehistoric Subsistence on the Southern New England Coast*. San Diego: Academic Press.

—— 1999 Prehistoric use of plant foods on Long Island and Block Island Sounds. In *Current Northeast Paleoethnobotany*. J. P. Hart, ed. New York State Museum Bulletin 494. Albany, NY.

Bernstein, D. J., et al., 1997 *Archaeological Investigation on the Solomon Property, Mount Sinai, Town of Brookhaven, Suffolk County, New York*. Institute for Long Island Archaeology, Department of Anthropology, State University of New York, Stony Brook.

Bragdon, Kathleen J., 1996 *Native Peoples of Southern New England*. Norman: University of Oklahoma Press.

Bruchac, Margaret M., and Elizabeth S. Chilton, 2003 *From Beaver Hill to Bark Wigwams: Reconsidering Archaeology and Historical Memory in the Connecticut River Valley*. Providence, RI: Society for Historical Archaeology.

Campisi, Jack, 1991 *The Mashpee Indians: Tribe on Trial*. Syracuse, NY: Syracuse University Press.

Ceci, Lynn, 1990 Radiocarbon dating "village" sites in coastal New York: Settlement pattern change in the Middle to Late Woodland. *Man in the Northeast* 39, 1–28.

Chilton, Elizabeth S., 1996 Embodiments of choice: Native American ceramic diversity in the New England interior. Ph.D. dissertation, University of Massachusetts, Amherst.

—— 1998 The cultural origins of technical choice: Unraveling Algonquian and Iroquoian ceramic traditions in the Northeast. In *The Archaeology of Social Boundaries*. M. Stark, ed. Pp. 132–160. Smithsonian Series in Archaeological Inquiry. Washington: Smithsonian Institution Press.

—— 1999a Mobile farmers of pre-contact southern New England: The archaeological and ethnohistorical evidence. In *Current Northeast Ethnobotany*. J. P. Hart, ed. Pp. 157–176. New York State Museum Bulletin 494. Albany, NY.

—— 1999b Ceramic research in New England: Breaking the typological mold. In *The Archaeological Northeast*. M. A. Levine, K. A. Sassaman, and M. S. Nassaney, eds. Pp. 97–114. Westport, CT: Bergin & Garvey.

—— 2002 "Towns they have none": Diverse subsistence and settlement strategies in native New England. In *Northeast Subsistence-Settlement Change: A.D. 700–1300*. J. P. Hart and C. B. Rieth, eds. Pp. 289–300. New York State Museum Bulletin 496. Albany, NY.

Chilton, Elizabeth S., and Dianna L. Doucette, 2002 Archaeological investigations at the Lucy Vincent Beach Site (19-DK-148): Preliminary results and interpretations. In *A Lasting Impression: Coastal, Lithic, and Ceramic Research in New England Archaeology*. J. E. Kerber, ed. Pp. 41–70. Westport, CT: Praeger.

Chilton, Elizabeth S., Tonya Baroody Largy, and Kathryn Curran, 2000 Evidence for prehistoric maize horticulture at the Pine Hill Site, Deerfield, Massachusetts. *Northeast Anthropology* 59, 23–46.

Clark, John E., and Michael Blake, 1994 The power of prestige: Competitive generosity and the emergence of ranked societies in Lowland Mesoamerica. In *Factional Competition and Political Development in the New World*. E. Brumfiel and J. Fox, eds. Pp. 17–30. Cambridge: Cambridge University Press.

Coupland, Gary, 1996 This old house: Cultural complexity and household stability on the northern Northwest Coast of North America. In *Emergent Complexity: The Evolution of Intermediate Societies*. J. E. Arnold, ed. Pp. 74–90. International Monographs in Prehistory, Archaeological Series 9. Ann Arbor, MI.

Cowie, Ellen. R., 2000 *Archaeological Investigations at the Tracy Farm Site (69.11 ME) in the Central Kennebec River Drainage, Somerset County, Maine* (Revised from 9/99), 2 vols. Farmington, ME: Archaeological Research Center, University of Maine at Farmington.

Crawford, Gary W., and David G. Smith, 1996 Migration in prehistory: Princess Point and the Northern Iroquoian case. *American Antiquity* 61(4), 782–790.

Creamer, Winifred, 1996 Developing complexity in the American Southwest: A case from the Pajarito Plateau, New Mexico. In *Emergent Complexity: The Evolution of Intermediate Societies*. J. E. Arnold, ed. Pp. 107–127. International Monographs in Prehistory, Archaeological Series 9. Ann Arbor, MI.

Cronon, William, 1983 *Changes in the Land: Indians, Colonists, and the Ecology of New England*. New York: Hill & Wang.

Crumley, Carole L., 1987 A dialectical critique of hierarchy. In *Power Relations and State Formation*. T. C. Patterson and C. W. Gailey, eds. Pp. 155–169. Washington, DC: American Anthropological Association.

Demeritt, David, 1991 Agriculture, climate, and cultural adaptation in the prehistoric Northeast. *Archaeology of Eastern North America* 19, 183–202.

Dincauze, Dena F., 1980 Research priorities in Northeast prehistory. In *Proceedings of the Conference on Northeastern Archaeology*, vol. 19. J. A. Moore, ed. Pp. 29–48. Amherst, MA: Department of Anthropology, University of Massachusetts.

——1993 Centering. *Northeast Anthropology* 46, 33–37.

Doucette, Dianna, 2003 Unraveling Middle Archaic expressions: A multidisciplinary approach towards feature and material culture recognition in southeastern New England. Ph.D. dissertation, Harvard University.

Fagan, Brian M., 2000 *The Little Ice Age: How Climate Made History 1300–1850*. New York: Basic Books.

Feinman, Gary M., and Jill Neitzel, 1984 Too many types: An overview of prestate societies in the Americas. In *Advances in Archaeological Method and Theory*, vol. 7. M. B. Schiffer, ed. Pp. 39–102. New York: Academic Press.

Fenton, William N., 1978 Northern Iroquoian culture patterns. In *Handbook of the North American Indians*, vol. 15. B. G. Trigger, ed. Pp. 296–321. Washington, DC: Smithsonian Institution Press.

Fine-Dare, Kathleen, 2002 *Grave Injustice: The American Indian Repatriation Movement and NAGPRA*. Lincoln: University of Nebraska of Press.

Fitting, James E., ed., 1973 *The Development of North American Archaeology: Essays in the History of Regional Traditions*. Garden City, NY: Anchor Books.

Fried, Morton H., 1960 On the evolution of social stratification and the state. In *Culture in History: Essays in Honor of Paul Radin*. S. Diamond, ed. Pp. 713–731. New York: Columbia University Press.

——1967 *The Evolution of Political Society*. New York: Random House.

George, David, and Robert E. Dewar, 1999 Chenopodium in Connecticut prehistory: Wild, weedy, cultivated, or domesticated? In *Current Northeast Ethnobotany*. Pp. 121–132. J. P. Hart, ed. New York State Museum Bulletin 494. Albany, NY.

Gookin, Daniel, 1792 Historical collections of the Indians in New England (1674). In *Massachusetts Historical Society Collections*, vol. 1. Pp. 141–225. Boston, MA: Monroe & Francis.

Graham, Martha, 1994 *Mobile Farmers: An Ethnoarchaeological Approach to Settlement Organization Among the Rarámuri of Northwestern Mexico.*

Gwynne, Margaret A., 1982 The Late Archaic archaeology of Mount Sinai Harbor, New York: Human ecology, economy and residence patterns on the southern New England coast. Ph.D. dissertation, State University of New York.

Handsman, Russell G., 1995 *A Homelands Model and Interior Sites: A Phase II Archaeological Study of Rhode Island Site 2050, Phoenix Avenue, Cranston, Rhode Island.* Report submitted to the Rhode Island Department of Transportation. Research Report 1, Public Archaeology Program, University of Rhode Island, Kingstown, RI.

Hart, John P., 1999 Maize agriculture evolution in the Eastern Woodlands of North America: A Darwinian perspective. *Journal of Archaeological Method and Theory* 6(2), 47–68.

Hart, John P., and Bernard K. Means, 2002 Maize and villages: A summary and critical assessment of current Northeast early Late Prehistoric evidence. In *Northeast Subsistence-Settlement Change: A.D. 700–1300.* J. P. Hart and C. B. Rieth, eds. Pp. 345–358. New York State Museum Bulletin 496. Albany, NY.

Hart, John P., and Christina B. Rieth, eds., 2002 *Northeast Subsistence-Settlement Change: A.D. 700–1300.* New York State Museum Bulletin 496. Albany, NY.

Hasenstab, Robert J., 1999 Fishing, farming, and finding the village sites: Centering Late Woodland New England Algonquians. In *The Archaeological Northeast.* Kenneth E. Sassaman, Mary Ann Levine, and Michael S. Nassaney, eds. Pp. 139–153. Westport, CT: Bergin & Garvey.

Hayden, Brian, 1995 Pathways to power: Principles for creating socioeconomic inequalities. In *Foundations of Social Inequality.* T. D. Price and G. M. Feinman, eds. Pp. 15–86. New York: Plenum Press.

Heckenberger, Michael J., James B. Petersen, and Nancy Asch Sidell, 1992 Early evidence of maize agriculture in the Connecticut River valley of Vermont. *Archaeology of Eastern North America* 20, 125–149.

Higgeson, Rev. J, 1968 [1629] New-England's plantation. In *Collections of the Massachusetts Historical Society for the Year 1792,* vol. 1. Pp. 117–124. New York: Johnson Reprint Corporation.

Jameson, J. F., 1909 *Narratives of New Netherlands, 1609–1664.* New York: Barnes & Noble.

Johnson, Eric S., 1996 *Discovering the Ancient Past at Kampoosa Bog, Stockbridge, Massachusetts.* Stockbridge, MA: University of Massachusetts Archaeological Services.

—— 1999 Community and Confederation: A Political Geography of Contact Period Southern New England. In *The Archaeological Northeast.* M. A. Levine, K. A. Sassaman, and M. S. Nassaney, eds. Pp. 155–168. Westport, CT: Bergin & Garvey.

Josselyn, J., 1833 (1674) *Two Voyages to New England,* vol. 3. Boston, MA: E. W. Metcalf.

Largy, Tonya B., et al., 1999 Corncobs and buttercups: Plant remains from the Goldkrest site. In *Current Northeast Paleoethnobotany.* J. P. Hart, ed. Pp. 69–84. New York State Museum Bulletin, vol. 494. Albany, NY: University of the State of New York.

Largy, Tonya B., et al., 2002 Lucy Vincent Beach: Another look at the prehistoric exploitation of piscine resources off the coast of Massachusetts, U.S.A. *Northeast Anthropology* 64, 67–73.

Lavin, Lucianne, 1988 The Morgan site: Rocky Hill, Connecticut. *Bulletin of the Archaeological Society of Connecticut* 51, 7–22.

Lavin, Lucianne, et al., 1996 The Goldkrest site: An undisturbed, multicomponent Woodland site in the heart of Mohikan territory. *Journal of Middle Atlantic Archaeology* 12, 113–129.

Locke, John, 1986 [1690] *An Essay Concerning the True, Original, Extent and End of Civil Government.* Buffalo: Prometheus Books.

Luedtke, Barbara E., 1988 Where are the Late Woodland villages in eastern Massachusetts? *Bulletin of the Massachusetts Archaeological Society* 49(2), 58–65.

Mihesuah, Devon A., ed., 2000 *Repatriation Reader: Who Owns American Indian Remains?* Lincoln: University of Nebraska Press.

Moeller, Roger W., 1992 *Analyzing and Interpreting Late Woodland Features.* Bethlehem: Archaeological Services.

Morgan, Lewis Henry, 1962 [1851] *League of the Iroquois.* New York: Corinth Books.

——1995 [1877] *Ancient Society.* Tucson: University of Arizona Press.

Mulholland, Mitchell T., 1988 Territoriality and horticulture: A perspective for prehistoric southern New England. In *Holocene Human Ecology in Northeastern North America.* G. P. Nicholas, ed. pp. 137–164. New York: Plenum Press.

Nafziger, James A. R., and Rebecca Dobkins, 1999 The Native American Graves Protection and Repatriation Act in its first decade. *International Journal of Cultural Property* 8(1), 77–107.

Niemczycki, Mary Ann Palmer, 1984 *The Origin and Development of the Seneca and Cayuga Tribes of New York State.* Rochester Museum and Science Center Research Records 17. Rochester, NY.

Patterson, William A., and Kenneth E. Sassaman, 1988 Indian fires in the prehistory of New England. In *Holocene Human Ecology in Northeastern North America.* G. P. Nicholas, ed. Pp. 107–135. New York: Plenum.

Petersen, James B., and Ellen R. Cowie, 2002 From hunter-gatherer camp to horticultural village: Late Prehistoric indigenous subsistence and settlement in New England. In *Northeast Subsistence-Settlement Change: A.D. 700–1300.* J. P. Hart and C. B. Rieth, eds. Pp. 265–288. New York State Museum Bulletin 496. Albany, NY.

Pretola, John P., 2000 Northeastern ceramic diversity: An optical mineralogy approach. Ph.D. dissertation, University of Massachusetts.

Ritchie, William A., 1969 *The Archaeology of New York State.* Garden City, NY: The Natural History Press.

Ritchie, William A., and Robert E. Funk, 1973 *Aboriginal Settlement Patterns in the Northeast.* Memoir 20. Albany, NY: New York State Museum and Science Service.

Salwen, Bert, 1968 Muskeeta Cove 2: A stratified Woodland site on Long Island. *American Antiquity* 33(3), 322–340.

Service, Elman R., 1962 *Primitive Social Organization: An Evolutionary Perspective.* New York: Random House.

——1975 *Origins of the State and Civilization.* New York: W. W. Norton.

Sidell, Nancy Asch, 1999 Prehistoric plant use in Maine: Paleoindian to Contact period. In *Current Northeast Ethnobotany.* J. P. Hart, ed. Pp. 191–223. New York State Museum Bulletin 494. Albany, NY.

——2002 Paleoethnobotanical indicators of subsistence and settlement change in the Northeast. In *Northeast Subsistence-Settlement Change: A.D. 700–1300.* J. P. Hart and C. B. Rieth, eds. Pp. 241–264. New York State Museum Bulletin 496. Albany, NY.

Smith, Bruce D., 1992 *Rivers of Change: Essays on Early Agriculture in Eastern North America.* Washington, DC: Smithsonian Institution Press.

Snow, Dean R., 1980 *The Archaeology of New England.* New York: Academic Press.

——1994 *The Iroquois.* Cambridge, MA: Blackwell.

—— 1996a More on migration in prehistory: accommodating new evidence in the North-ern Iroquoian case. *American Antiquity* 61(4), 791–796.

—— 1996b Mohawk demography and the effects of exogenous epidemics on American Indian populations. *Journal of Anthropological Archaeology* 15, 160–182.

Thomas, David Hurst, 2000 *Skull Wars: Kennewick Man, Archaeology, and the Battle for Native American Identity*. New York: Basic Books.

Thorbahn, Peter F., 1988 Where are all the Late Woodland villages in southern New England? *Bulletin of the Massachusetts Archaeological Society* 49(2), 46–57.

Tuck, James A., 1978 Northern Iroquoian prehistory. In *Handbook of North American Indians*, vol. 15, *Northeast*. B. G. Trigger, ed. Pp. 322–333. Washington, DC: Smithsonian Institu-tion Press.

Volmar, Michael A., 1998 The micromorphology of landscapes: An archaeological approach in southern New England. Doctoral dissertation, University of Massachusetts.

Watkins, Joe, 2000 *Indigenous Archaeology*. Walnut Creek, CA: AltaMira.

Williams, Roger, 1963 [1643] *The Complete Writings of Roger Williams*, vol. 1. New York: Russell & Russell.

Wood, William E., 1977 [1634] *New England's Prospect*. Amherst, MA: University of Massachusetts Press.

Yoffee, Norman, 1993 Too many chiefs? (or safe texts for the '90s). In *Archaeological Theory: Who Sets the Agenda?* N. Yoffee and A. Sherratt, eds. Pp. 60–78. Cambridge: Cambridge University Press.

7

The Evolution of the Plains Village Tradition

Dale R. Henning

Once considered uninhabitable, archaeologists now know that the Great Plains were occupied for over 12,000 years (Wood 1998). Near the end of this long period, there emerged what is generically known as the Plains Village tradition. This chapter explores the evolution of the Plains Village tradition by focusing on the Middle Missouri and Oneota traditions in the southern half of the northeastern Plains (Figure 7.1). The Plains Village tradition seems based upon three primary factors: (1) shifting climatic regimes, (2) technological changes, including adaptations to horticultural pursuits and the bow and arrow, and (3) bison herd expansion toward the east. These factors were apparently vital to development of the tradition and they permitted, even encouraged, Oneota people to migrate to the Plains periphery where they assumed many Plains Village characteristics (Figure 7.2).

Background

The *Plains* might best be defined as "that part of central North America that is comparatively level and treeless, and has a subhumid or semiarid climate in which the cultivation of domestic crops is precarious whether practiced by Native American gardeners or by modern farmers" (Wood 1998:10). To the east is the *Prairie Peninsula*, an area of mixed prairie and deciduous forest stretching as a wedge from the Plains to a point in northwest Indiana.

The natural border between the Plains and the Prairie Peninsula is often referred to as the Plains/Prairie *ecotone*, where plant and animal (including human) communities contend for dominance. Ecotones are often excellent locations for human settlement, where the plants and animals of both areas can be harvested, sometimes in relatively large numbers, without traveling long distances. Much of the following discussion relates to human activities along the ecotone between the northeastern periphery of the Plains and the Prairie Peninsula. The Prairie Peninsula, the USA's "corn belt," is sometimes referred to as the Midwest.

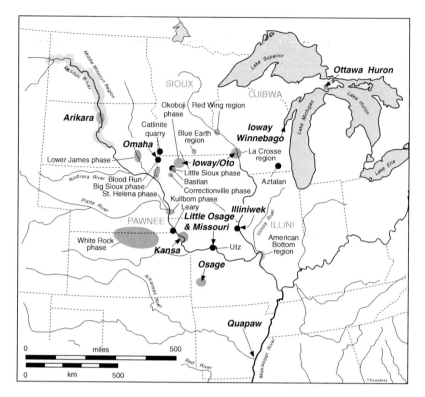

Figure 7.1 Map of regions and sites discussed in the text. *Full caps*: general locations of tribes with two or more subunits; *upper/lower-case bold*: arrows indicate locations of specific tribes at contact; *upper/lower-case plain*: select archaeological sites, regions, or phases

General dependence on horticulture was attained in the Prairie Peninsula by A.D. 800–900. By A.D. 1200 some cultivars were used even in the northernmost locales of the northeastern Plains (Schneider 2002). All groups discussed in any detail herein were horticulturalists who tended both indigenous species and some introduced cultigens, especially maize. While the relative importance of gardening activities appears to vary considerably, the overall effects were profound, amounting to dramatically greater populations and better quality of life. In addition, the bow and arrow replaced the dart- or spear-thrower on the northern Plains by A.D. 200, in the Prairie Peninsula by 600, and in the northeastern Plains by no later than 800 (Dyck and Morlan 2001:122–127; Pauketat and Loren, this volume). This equipment afforded far greater efficiency in hunting and warfare.

Plains Village evolution was hastened and enhanced by the increasing numbers and eastward movement of bison herds. Baerreis and Bryson (1965) hypothesized that a prolonged drought (ca. A.D. 1250–1450) induced deforestation and allowed plains-prairie grasses to expand eastward. That, in turn, supported more bison in the western Prairie Peninsula. Another important element is purposeful prairie-burning, which also enhanced and expanded the bison-grazing area (McClain 2000;

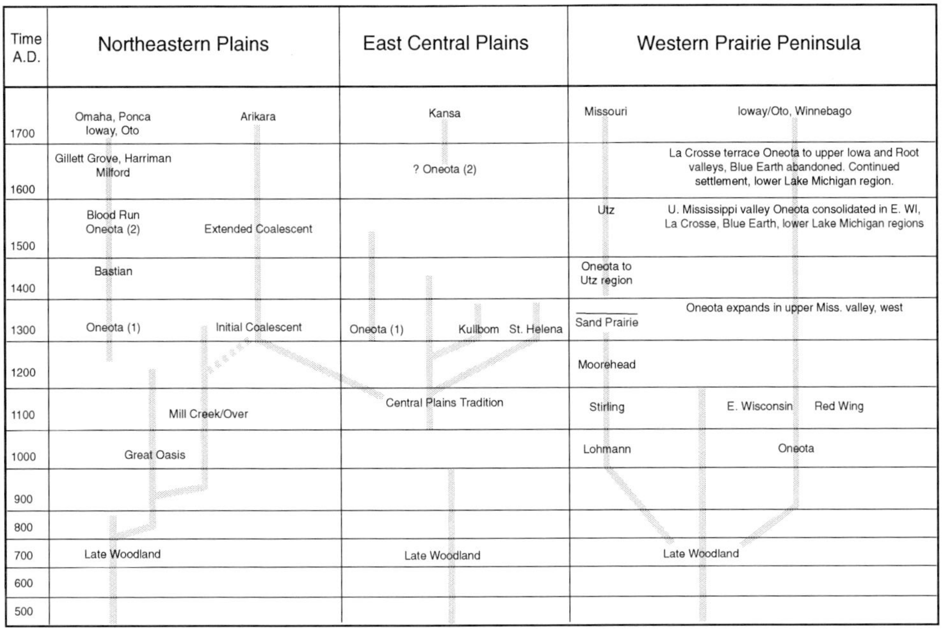

Time A.D.	Northeastern Plains	East Central Plains	Western Prairie Peninsula
1700	Omaha, Ponca Ioway, Oto Arikara	Kansa	Missouri Ioway/Oto, Winnebago
1600	Gillett Grove, Harriman Milford	? Oneota (2)	La Crosse terrace Oneota to upper Iowa and Root valleys, Blue Earth abandoned. Continued settlement, lower Lake Michigan region.
1500	Blood Run Oneota (2) Extended Coalescent		Utz U. Mississippi valley Oneota consolidated in E. WI, La Crosse, Blue Earth, lower Lake Michigan regions
1400	Bastian		Oneota to Utz region
1300	Oneota (1) Initial Coalescent	Oneota (1) Kullbom St. Helena	Sand Prairie Oneota expands in upper Miss. valley, west
1200			Moorehead
1100	Mill Creek/Over	Central Plains Tradition	Stirling E. Wisconsin Red Wing
1000	Great Oasis		Lohmann Oneota
900			
800			
700	Late Woodland	Late Woodland	Late Woodland
600			
500			

Figure 7.2 Timetable for archaeological complexes discussed and their hypothesized relationships

Risser 1990:136–137). Following the 16th-century wave of pandemic disease and subsequent decreased numbers of human predators, the herds were apparently allowed to increase and further extend their grazing range even to the Atlantic coast (Green 1993; Mann 2002).

The Initial Middle Missouri Tradition, Eastern Variant (IMMVe) (A.D. 850–1350)

The Initial Middle Missouri (IMM) tradition is one of several taxonomic units assigned to cultures that evolved in the Plains. Villagers grouped in the IMM shared a number of characteristics, including tightly organized, often fortified villages, rectangular semi-subterranean houses with long entrances, intensive gardening, hunting and gathering, use of the bow and arrow, and increasing reliance on bison hunting. The tradition flourished in the Middle Missouri region. The IMM encompasses western and eastern divisions or "variants," the IMMVw and IMMVe (Toom 1992). The eastern variant is defined within the northeastern Plains region, where it evolved. Specific focus will be upon the southern half of the northeastern Plains – wedged between the Middle Missouri region and the Red River down into south-central Minnesota – where the IMMVe flourished and where most early Oneota intrusions occurred.

Great Oasis and Mill Creek/Over are both subdivisions of the IMMVe. Great Oasis is generally believed to be the earlier and is credited with being ancestral to both the eastern and western variants of the IMM (Benn and Green 2000:477; Henning 1991; Henning and Toom 2003; E. Henning 1981; Tiffany and Alex 2001:90). Mill Creek/Over groups – once separately defined but discussed as one cultural tradition here – appear to have evolved directly out of Great Oasis, but their villages are characterized as tightly organized and often fortified, quite in contrast to the unfortified, non-stratified Great Oasis settlements. Mill Creek/Over middens are sometimes up to ca. 4 m deep, yielding evidence for multiple and successive occupations by the same people.

Prior to A.D. 850, the northeastern Plains was characterized by small Late Woodland villages, some horticultural pursuits, population growth, and extended interaction (Benn and Green 2000:431). These Late Woodland villagers are generally believed ancestral to the regional Great Oasis communities, who carried on many of their traditions, including trade. The presence of exotic stone and broad spatial similarities in pottery vessel form and decorative motifs attest to this social interchange that was promoted by Late Woodland people. Late Woodland Loseke ware is the most likely ceramic progenitor of Great Oasis High Rim ware (Benn and Green 2000:477). The two wares are functionally similar, but easily differentiated (Figure 7.3).

The Late Woodland tradition persisted to A.D. 1100 in the Midwest and eastern Plains. By then, the Plains Village tradition was well established throughout its primary range (Winham and Calabrese 1998:276–281). Great Oasis sites are recorded in the northwest quadrant of Iowa, southwest Minnesota, eastern South Dakota into the Middle Missouri region, and in central and eastern Nebraska (Alex and Tiffany 2000:340). Traditional Great Oasis groups retained their cultural identity well into the 13th century, interacting with Mill Creek/Over people at times (Henning 1996; cf. Alex 2000; Alex and Tiffany 2000; Tiffany and Alex 2001). The latest of several proposed Great Oasis phases is the Perry Creek, which offers undeniable evidence for close Great Oasis and Mill Creek/Over relationships ca. A.D. 1250 (Henning 1996).

Most Great Oasis site inventories suggest far more abundant and variable food resources than were utilized by their Late Woodland ancestors. In three houses excavated at Broken Kettle West, migratory birds, fish, mussels, and some deer and smaller mammals predominated while bison elements were rare (Baerreis et al. 1970). Yet, in Great Oasis components at the central Nebraska Packer and northwest Iowa Beals sites, bison bone was ubiquitous (Bozell and Rogers 1989; Henning 1967). Apparently, bison were not always readily available to Great Oasis hunters, but were exploited when they were. This inconsistent pattern of availability seems characteristic of life in an ecotone. Gardening was obviously important to Great Oasis people (Cutler and Blake 1973; Mead 1981). Maize, squash or pumpkin, domesticated sunflower, *Chenopodium*, and a host of edible wild seeds, nuts, and berries have been identified.

There is evidence for trade on most Great Oasis sites. Beads made of *Leptoxis*, freshwater snail shells that originated well to the south, are often recovered (Burch 1989:154–170). Marine shell objects are rare, but are found in Great Oasis contexts, despite strong assertions to the contrary (Tiffany and Alex 2001). Other

Figure 7.3 Late Woodland and Great Oasis rimsherds: (a) Great Oasis High Rim, Spring Brook site (13PM2); (b) Great Oasis Wedge Lip, Larson site (13PM61); (c) Late Woodland rimsherds, northwest of Chamberlain, SD (photographs courtesy David Benn)

exotica include Ogalalla orthoquartzite from the Bijou Hills in South Dakota, Nehawka chert from southeast Nebraska, and scoria (clinker) from the Missouri River valley. Pottery fragments perhaps similar to American Bottom Lohmann phase (A.D. 1050–1100) ceramics are reported from the West Broken Kettle Great Oasis site, further evidence for long-distance exchange among Great Oasis people (Tiffany and Alex 2001).

A.D. 850–1250 was a complex period of time in the Midwest and Plains. Late Woodland groups predominated in the American Bottom until ca. 1050, when Cahokia emerged (Pauketat, this volume). The Lohmann and Stirling phases (A.D.

1050–1200) appear to constitute Cahokia's pinnacle of development, with various effects on other cultural entities in the Midwest and Plains. Cahokians may have interacted with Great Oasis people, offering a source for exotic shell beads, but there is no recognized evidence for direct contact. There is also no evidence for Great Oasis interaction with either the contemporaneous Late Woodland or the early Plains Villager groups in the Central Plains region where some exotic shell is found (Johnson 2001; Steinacher and Carlson 1998; W. Wedel 2001). Some Great Oasis interaction may have taken place at the Cambria type-site and at some early components in the Red Wing region (Gibbon 1991; Gibbon and Dobbs 1991). Great Oasis people were contemporaries of the eastern Wisconsin Oneota (Overstreet 1998, 2001).

Mill Creek/Over evolution was once believed to be the result of Mississippian migrations. But, with much additional information available, an *in situ* development out of Great Oasis ancestry is now generally accepted. Three phases and localities have been defined (Figure 7.1). In Iowa, 35 sites are assigned to the Big Sioux and Little Sioux phases (Alex 2000:152–153). The Brandon site and an unanalyzed site nearby are tentatively assigned to the Big Sioux phase (Alex 1981a:139). Four villages and some related burial mounds found in the lower James River locality constitute the Lower James phase (Alex 1981a).

The time range I suggest for Mill Creek/Over (A.D. 950–1350) is comparable to dates for IMMVw components (Eighmy and LaBelle 1996; cf. Alex 2000:154). It is generally agreed that the IMMVe and IMMVw sites (the latter located in the middle Missouri River region and including the Swanson, Grand Detour, and Anderson phases) evolved simultaneously, shared many cultural characteristics, and disappeared from their respective locations at about the same time (Toom 1992). The Big and Little Sioux phase villages are small, rarely extending over half a hectare. Six sites, Kimball, Broken Kettle, and Joy Creek Major in the lower Big Sioux valley, and Phipps, Brewster, and Bultman in the Little Sioux drainage system, are deeply stratified – some over two meters – with superimposed living surfaces. It is notable that Great Oasis components are often found near Mill Creek/Over villages and some may be contemporaneous (E. Henning 1981).

Perhaps six of the Mill Creek/Over sites were fortified with ditches and/or stockades (Alex 2000:155). The excavated houses are usually substantial IMMV semisubterranean rectangular structures, sometimes set in rows (McKusick n.d.; Orr 1963). Those reported from Chan-ya-ta do not conform to that pattern (Tiffany 1982). In South Dakota, the Lower James phase sites are often larger, usually with only one identifiable component, and offer less evidence for midden development, probably because of the different topographies occupied (Alex 1981b:44). The deep middens, small spatial extent, and fortification common to Big and Little Sioux phase villages suggest that the occupants felt threatened and thus tightly enclosed their villages. Could this pattern have developed because of incursions by marauding Oneota groups based in the Mississippi valley?

Data from Mill Creek/Over sites suggest tightly knit communities that enjoyed considerable wealth and high status among their peers in the Midwest and Plains areas. Pottery wares and types are consistent throughout the middens, with the addi-

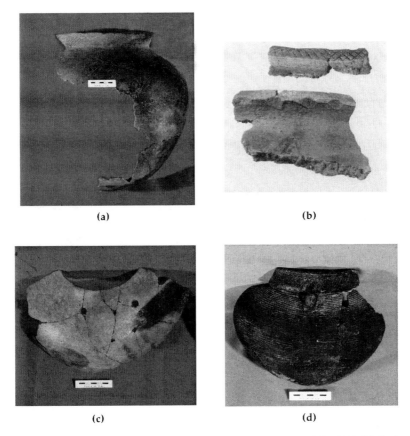

Figure 7.4 Mill Creek/Over rimsherds: (a) Chamberlain ware, Larson (13PM61); (b) Sanford ware (upper: Mitchell Modified Lip; lower: Kimball Modified Lip; same scale, length upper = 7 cm), 13PM61; (c) Seed Jar, Kimball (13PM4); (d) Foreman ware, Wittrock (13OB4)

tion of a few verified trade pieces and numerous copies of exotic forms (see Alex 2000 for summary). Mill Creek/Over potters appear to have followed their Great Oasis ancestors in the manufacture of Chamberlain and Sanford wares (Figure 7.4). The archeological remains suggest that food was plentiful. These people were "primarily farmers who also gathered substantial amounts of food from wild plants" (Dallman 1983:55). Cultigens include maize, bean, pumpkin, and a host of indigenous plants including sunflower, gourds, squash, goosefoot, little barley, knotweed, maygrass, and sumpweed or marshelder. Extensive raised garden beds were employed (Alex 2000:158–161). Domesticates were supplemented by nuts, fruits, bulbs, and other wild plants. At the Brewster site, plant materials may have satisfied over 90 percent of the inhabitant's dietary requirements (Dallman 1983:43).

Evidence for trade is found on many Mill Creek/Over sites (Anderson et al. 1979). *Leptoxis* beads and marine shell items are often recovered. These materials were once believed to have come directly from the American Bottom (Henning

1967, 1971; Tiffany 1991:334–336). Today, the evidence runs counter to this assumption, suggesting down-the-line, indirect movement of these exotica. Further, only a few Mill Creek/Over pottery fragments have been found in the American Bottom and most of the "Mississippian" vessel fragments from Mill Creek/Over sites are locally made copies. Food was plentiful in the American Bottom at this time, suggesting that "there might have been little reason . . . for the people of distant domains (more than 100 kilometers) to cooperate with or submit to Cahokia" (Pauketat and Emerson 1997:274). Nonetheless, Tiffany proposed and still adheres to the hypothesis that staples from Mill Creek/Over people were important to American Bottom villagers, who lavishly endowed them with exotica in exchange (Tiffany 1991, 2003:29–30; also see Alex 2000). My suggestion is that the few verifiable Mississippian trade materials found on IMMVe sites were luxury and ritual items given to persons of high status, not objects exchanged for staples (Pauketat, this volume). Routes for IMMV acquisition of marine shell and other exotica were probably indirect. We should look not just to the American Bottom, but to the upper Mississippi and Illinois valleys, the Ozark Highlands, the Caddoan region, and the Central Plains for sources of exotics found on many IMMV village sites. On the other hand, a few IMMV (both eastern and western variants) rimsherds have been reported in Late Woodland contexts in northeast Iowa, southeastern Wisconsin, and central Illinois (Benn and Green 2000:481; Finney and Stoltman 1991; Harn 1980:80; Orr 1963; Tiffany 1980). Pottery found in Big Sioux phase and some nearby Central Plains sites suggests interaction between those groups (Alex 2000:165; Henning 1969:279; Ives 1962:38–39).

Mill Creek/Over contemporaries and the departure of the IMMV

These were busy times. Mill Creek/Over contemporaries included traditional Great Oasis groups, related villagers in the IMMVw, Mississippians in the American Bottom, Caddoan groups in the southern Plains, Central Plains people, and Late Woodland groups from North Dakota into Wisconsin and south into the Ozarks. The IMMVe Cambria occupations are at least partially contemporaneous. Oneota people were in eastern Wisconsin, the Red Wing region, and the central Des Moines River valley before Mill Creek/Over groups vacated the northeastern Plains. There is also evidence for contemporaneous Oneota influence or presence, perhaps emanating out of the Red Wing region, among Sandy Lake groups in north-central Minnesota and in the Red River valley as early as A.D. 1100 (Michlovic and Schneider 1993).

The available data suggest that Mill Creek/Over groups interacted frequently with their IMMVw counterparts and with traditional Great Oasis people, occasionally with Cambria, Central Plains, Mississippi valley Late Woodland and Late Woodland Mississippian groups, and with Central Illinois valley Mississippian groups. There is very little evidence, if any, of interaction with Oneota people, who were probably hunting into the eastern Plains prior to the IMMV diaspora.

IMMV groups began moving out of the northeastern Plains region ca. A.D. 1300, apparently up the Missouri River to the mouths of the Bad and Cheyenne rivers, where they encountered "Extended variant" groups moving downstream (Wood 2001). Shortly after 1300, IMMV people disappeared from the archaeological record, probably joining and blending with Extended variant groups. While tribal identity is hidden by cultural complexity and change through several centuries, it seems plausible that the IMMV terminal variant was the pre-Columbian cultural antecedent of the Mandan Indians. As for the nearby and closely related Hidatsa, their antecedents appear to be more complicated (Winham and Calabrese 1998:299).

Climatic change was once believed to have been a major factor in these IMMV movements (Baerreis and Bryson 1965; Bryson et al. 1970; Bryson and Wendland 1967; Lehmer 1971). But, it is now generally agreed that, while recognizable climatic shifts did occur, there was little effect on the subsistence activities of IMMV populations and their successors in the eastern Plains beyond a shift toward greater reliance on bison. Bison herds increased in numbers and moved eastward, perhaps in part because of escalated droughtiness, but periodic firing of the prairie grasses by the inhabitants and other factors may have been equally important.

Cultural factors may have played the most significant role in the departure of IMMV groups from northwest Iowa, eastern South Dakota, and the middle Missouri River region. Oneota groups probably began exploiting this broad region before A.D. 1300. Oneota villages were established in the lower Little Sioux valley in Iowa, at the Leary site in southeast Nebraska, and in south-central Nebraska and north-central Kansas, probably before 1350. At about the same time, "Initial Coalescent" tradition people from the Central Plains were moving into the Middle Missouri region (Johnson 1998). They are generally believed to have been the ancestral Caddoan-speaking Arikara.

The cause for the Oneota entradas probably lies with the burgeoning availability of bison in the Plains/Prairie ecotone, but the Initial Coalescent move into the Middle Missouri region seems less explainable. It is possible that the IMMV villagers had abandoned the region prior to the arrival of these newcomers, but considering the permanence of their villages, the apparent need to fortify, and the quality of life they maintained up to the time of their departure, it seems most likely that they were forced to vacate. It is interesting that, while most IMMV and Initial Coalescent villages are fortified, the early Oneota villages apparently were not, suggesting that there was no lasting opposition to their presence.

The Oneota Tradition

Oneota traditional elements, with antecedents in regional Woodland groups, may be traced back to A.D. 900 (Benn 1995). Some ancient religious and social traditions may be extant in legends of tribes tied to the Oneota tradition as it evolved out of the Late Woodland in Wisconsin (Hall 1993; Salzer and Rajnovich 2000).

Reliable data and a series of radiocarbon assays clearly suggest that an Oneota tradition was established in eastern Wisconsin prior to Cahokia's florescence at A.D. 1050 (Overstreet 1998; Salzer and Rajnovich 2000). Not all Oneota people were directly influenced by the Cahokia phenomenon.

In fact, as American Bottom influence expanded (A.D. 1050–1150), a Late Woodland–Mississippian "confederation" developed in southern Wisconsin, temporarily displacing the emergent Oneota population around Aztalan (Overstreet 2000; Pauketat, this volume). During this time, most Oneota populations appear to have been restricted to the Red Wing region and to northern Wisconsin. Then, after ca. A.D. 1150, the Oneota returned to establish large villages in southern and eastern Wisconsin (Overstreet 1998:260).

The Red Wing region is vital to our understanding of Oneota evolution and the probabilities for interaction with Mississippian groups, but its history is variously interpreted. At one time, the Red Wing "focus" was identified as a fusion of Mississippian elements with older Woodland elements (Wilford 1955). More recent interpretations suggest that by A.D. 1000 there was a "pure" Oneota complex, the Bartron phase, found at the Bartron, Adams, and Double sites (Gibbon and Dobbs 1991). The Bartron phase was followed by an amalgamation of local Oneota characteristics with some diffused Mississippian artifact and settlement-subsistence patterns, the Silvernale phase of A.D. 1050 to 1250–1275.

Oneota's defining characteristics are summarized elsewhere (Henning 1998a, 2001). The pottery, often characterized as shell-tempered jars ranging from teacup size (often funerary offerings) to nearly a bushel in capacity, is diagnostic but variable depending on time and location (Figures 7.5 and 7.6). Projectile points are bifacially flaked and triangular. The bone and stone tool complexes are in great measure Plains-derived, with bison scapula digging tools, shaft straighteners, unifacial flake end scrapers, manos, and grinding slabs commonly found, except in the eastern Wisconsin Oneota manifestations. Villages are comparatively large, often exceeding 10 ha. Stockades are seldom reported, but some late groups built protective redoubts of heaped-up earth, either as part of the village or nearby (Henning 1998a:383; Wood 1973).

By the time Cahokian influences had receded, the Red Wing region was abandoned and a few Oneota groups had developed villages west of the Mississippi River, but not along the mainstem. Oneota villagers once again occupied eastern Wisconsin. Contemporaneous Oneota villages occupied the central Des Moines valley (Moffat 1998). The few scapula tools found on 13th- and 14th-century Oneota sites in the Mississippi drainage network are rarely accompanied by other bison elements, suggesting either that Oneota hunters were traveling west to kill the large mammals or that bison scapulae were an important trade item.

During the early 14th century we see explosive Oneota expansion, with settlements on the upper Mississippi valley, the central Missouri valley and along the eastern Plains. By 1350, permanent villages were established in the Blue Earth region of south-central Minnesota, in the La Crosse region, on the Mississippi Alluvial Plain in Iowa and Illinois, in the Chariton River region in central Missouri, along the lower Little Sioux River in western Iowa, at the Leary site in

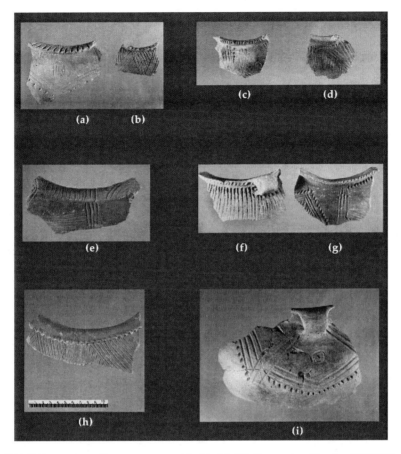

Figure 7.5 Early western Oneota pottery: (a), (b), (e), (h) Correctionville site (13WD6); (c), (d), (f), (g) Dixon site (13WD8); (i) typical Oneota rimsherd from Kullbom phase (Central Plains) house

southeastern Nebraska, on some White Rock phase sites of central Kansas and Nebraska, and on several Bold Counselor components in the central Illinois valley. No single region of origin has been established for the early western migrants to the Plains (Ritterbush 2000a, 2000b). Oneota villages in eastern Wisconsin continued to be intensively occupied during the 14th century (Overstreet 2000).

The data suggest two periods – referred to here as "stages" for lack of a better term – of intensive Oneota settlement. The first, those settlements listed above, took place ca. A.D. 1300–1450. The people were probably attracted by the "bison pull effect" and perhaps the prior successes of the IMMV and Central Plains villagers (Boszhardt 2000; Ritterbush 2000a, 2000b). Later (ca. A.D. 1500), another wave of Oneota migrants, both Dhegihan and Chiwere-speakers, probably moved westward to avoid both pandemic disease and attacks by powerful eastern tribes. Certainly, they too were drawn to the west by the benefits of bison availability and comparatively attractive environmental and social conditions.

(a)

(b)

(c)

(d)

Figure 7.6 Allamakee Trailed pottery: (a) Flynn cemetery (13AM51) (ca.15cm max. diam.); (b) New Albin burial (ca. 20cm max. diam.); (c) Flatiron terrace (13AM1)(orifice diam ca. 35cm); (d) rim-sherds, 13AM1, same scale (*lower*: ca.12cm long)

Oneota Stage One: the first settlers move west (A.D. 1300–1450)

Among the earliest western Oneota villages established were those of the Correctionville phase in the lower Little Sioux valley, the Leary village site located near the mouth of the Big Nemaha River, and some White Rock phase sites situated in central Kansas/Nebraska (Fishel 1999; Harvey 1979; Henning 1961, 1970, 1998a, 1998b; Logan 1998; Ritterbush 2000a, 2002b; Ritterbush and Logan 2000). At Dixon, the most intensively studied Correctionville phase site, three partial houses have been excavated (Fishel 1999; Harvey 1979). Human bone, some cut and polished, is found in pit features, and one storage pit produced a human femur and a fully articulated torso (Harvey 1979:75; Lillie 1999). There are no known cemeteries or mound burials identified with the Dixon site. The suite of radiocarbon dates suggests generations of intermittent occupations (Boszhardt et al. 1995).

Dixon faunal analyses suggest intensive bison hunting, the use of deer, dog, elk, and smaller mammals, and exploitation of riverine resources, including fish and shellfish (Jans-Langel 1999). Floral analyses suggest an exhaustive array of utilized plants (Schroeder 1999). Maize, cucurbits, beans, sunflower, chenopodium, amaranth, and marshelder were probably cultivated. Locally available seeds, including little barley, wild rye, barnyard grass, American lotus, burweed, marshelder, and fruits and nuts such as black nightshade, ground cherry, sumac, rose, blackberry or raspberry, grape, walnut, and hazelnut were collected.

Artifacts of the Correctionville phase offer some unique variations on the generalized Oneota theme. The pottery suggests a very generalized regional pattern, probably diffused by intermittent site occupations over several generations (Figure 7.5). Exceptional here are large numbers of grooved mauls, especially at the Correctionville site (one collector visited by the author in the late 1950s had over 50 picked up during gravel stripping). Much of the chipped stone from Dixon is derived from sources in Kansas and Nebraska (Fishel 1999:132). A few small pieces of worked catlinite, probably derived from glacial gravels and streambeds, are found on Correctionville phase sites.

The Leary site, located near the confluence of the Big Nemaha and the Missouri rivers, is situated on a series of low terraces (Hill and Wedel 1936; Ritterbush 2002a). As currently defined, the site covers at least 49 ha and may include mounds on a nearby ridge. Two rectangular Central Plains earth lodges and a confusing mixture of Central Plains and Oneota pottery indicate long-term or multiple Oneota occupations and apparent cross-cultural interaction. The remains also suggest a lively exchange in exotic materials.

Other sites that clearly suggest late Central Plains–Oneota interaction have since been found in the Kullbom phase Central Plains tradition sites just south of Council Bluffs, Iowa (Billeck 1993). Further, Oneota and Middle Missouri tradition objects are found in the Saint Helena phase dating from ca. A.D. 1200 (Blakeslee 1978:142). These sites offer evidence of very early Oneota entradas and suggest a brief period of positive interaction with established Central Plains groups.

The White Rock phase of south-central Nebraska and north-central Kansas represents a migration of Oneota people from the east ca. A.D. 1300–1450 (Logan 1998; Ritterbush and Logan 2000). The settlement and subsistence patterns, ceramics, and bone and stone tool complexes are similar to other western Oneota assemblages. Oneota people began to settle fairly permanently here about the time that Central Plains tradition groups were departing for the middle Missouri River region (Logan 1998; Ritterbush and Logan 2000). Regular contact with groups to the north and east is suggested, and trade apparently extended into southwestern Kansas, the southern Plains, and the American Southwest (Ritterbush 2002b).

Bastian, located just north of Cherokee, Iowa, extends discontinuously across about 30 ha on a high terrace above the Little Sioux River (Tiffany 1979). Unique site materials, location and radiocarbon assays combine to suggest a Bastian phase, ca. A.D. 1450, that bridges my hypothetical early and late stages of western Oneota settlements (Harvey 1979; Henning 1998b). Bastian is notable for the number of catlinite tablets and tablet fragments recovered from its surface (Hollinger 2000). Cut and broken pieces of red pipestone are ubiquitous to the site, suggesting that many objects were fabricated here when intensive quarrying began at Pipestone National Monument quarries.

The Chariton River region, located around the confluence of the Chariton and Missouri rivers, was settled as the western Oneota sites were established. While at some distance from our focal area, this setting was obviously a very important locus of Oneota interactions. Utz, at ca. 120 ha the largest site in this region, was very important from ca. A.D. 1450 (Bray 1991; Chapman et al. 1985; Henning 1970). Utz was the traditional home of the Chiwere-speaking Missouri tribe, who remained there until ca. A.D. 1727. Regional occupations began ca. A.D. 1300 on the Guthrey village and terminated in the 1770s when the Missouri left Gumbo Point and the Little Osage abandoned the Plattner site (Chapman et al. 1985; Henning 1970; Yelton 1998).

Oneota Stage Two: Dhegihan and Chiwere movements to the west (A.D. 1500–1700)

While the truth is veiled in centuries of archaeological deposits, I suspect that many ancestral Oneota who settled in the eastern Plains during Stage One spoke a Chiwere dialect. Nonetheless, Stage Two can be characterized by settlement in these western regions by identifiable Chiwere and Dhegihan groups and the beginnings of Oneota evacuation of the Mississippi River valley beginning ca. A.D. 1500. Blood Run, probably settled by Dhegihan-speaking ancestral Omaha, was established at about this time.

Precontact depopulation and shifting patterns of interaction in the eastern upper Midwest from ca. A.D. 1500 may have been stimulated primarily by warfare and pandemic disease (Green 1993). All resident tribes were apparently affected, but the Winnebago, or Ho-Chunk, were particularly hard hit and were characterized in early 17th-century French accounts as "formerly a populous and redoubtable nation" (Hall 1993; Overstreet 1993). The Missouri at the Utz site in central Missouri were also characterized as much reduced in numbers by both warfare and disease when first encountered by whites in the early 1700s (Chapman et al. 1985).

The earliest historic documentation of the upper Midwest suggests that inter-tribal warfare was a given, a pattern of some antiquity that probably increased in ferocity after Europeans began settling in North America (Hollinger 2001). In the 17th century, indigenous groups located east of the Mississippi were harassed by well-armed bands of Sauk and Fox, Ojibwa, Illiniwek, and other tribes moving in from the east, with effects felt well out onto the Plains (Wedel 1986).

The combination of pandemic disease and attacks by eastern groups with far superior weapons altered the upper Mississippi valley settlement patterns quickly and significantly. By 1600, prominent Oneota villages on the La Crosse terrace and in the Mississippi Alluvial Plain had been abandoned. Late in the 17th century, the Chiwere-speaking Ioway and Oto began to vacate the west side of the Mississippi valley, establishing villages around Iowa's lakes (Wedel 1981, 1986). In this early contact period, the Ioway and Oto were often closely linked, and are best referred to as Ioway/Oto.

The Dhegihan-speaking Siouan tribes – Omaha, Ponca, Osage, and Kansa – were all apparently late arrivals to the eastern Plains, originating somewhere east of the Mississippi valley (Dorsey 1886; Dorsey and Thomas 1907; Henning 1993, 1998a, 1998b, 2001). Radiocarbon assays from Blood Run indicate that Oneota, probably Omaha, occupations there began in the 16th century (Boszhardt et al. 1995; Henning 1998a, 2001; Wedel 1981). These dates suggest that the Omaha and Ponca (then one tribe) were the first Dhegihan-speakers to move to this Plains-Prairie ecotone.

The Blood Run site is the largest recorded Oneota site and is documented as the principal Omaha village from the 1690s to 1714 (Harvey 1979; Henning 1970, 1982, 1993, 1998a; Wedel 1981). Ethnohistoric accounts suggest that the Ioway, Oto, Arikara, and, possibly, the Cheyenne were periodic residents or regular visitors at Blood Run (Fletcher and La Flesche 1911; Wedel 1981, 1986). The archaeology of Blood Run reflects these varied cultural traditions.

Blood Run has a "core area" of 240 ha with concentrated occupations on both sides of the Big Sioux River. When the outlying related camp and village sites are included, the site encompasses as much as 320 ha extending for 5.6 km along the river on the Iowa side, with an additional 160 ha on the South Dakota side. Within the core area, early written descriptions record 275 large conical mounds, from 150 to 800 stone circles and ovals that are probably house outlines, a possible effigy mound, an earthen enclosure covering ca. 6 ha, an earthen serpent effigy over 90 m long, and at least seven large pitted Sioux Quartzite boulders (Henning 1982, 1998a; Keyes 1926). A map of a small uncultivated area south of Blood Run Creek prepared by F. W. Pettigrew in the late 1800s records mounds and the boulder outlines of over 75 circular structures ranging from 6 to 43 ft. in diameter and no fewer than six oval structures ranging from 30 × 60 ft. to 40 × 123 ft. (map on file, Siouxland Heritage Museum, Sioux Falls, SD). Most of the mounds were constructed for burial, some with several separate interments. Glass beads, brass and small iron objects, horse bones, even a dog skeleton (wrapped in hide) are recorded as inclusions along with traditional Oneota objects (Harvey 1979; Pettigrew 1891, 1901; Starr 1887, 1889).

The Blood Run villagers appear to have eaten well. Animal bone is commonplace and well preserved; articulated elements of bison, elk, and a broad range of smaller mammal bones are encountered. Butchered dog bone, second only to bison in animals represented, is often found, while deer elements are rare. Fish and shellfish were obviously taken from Blood Run Creek and the Big Sioux River. There is consistent evidence for broadly based horticultural pursuits (Tolmie and Green 1992). Among these remains are traditional Oneota bone and stone tools. Catlinite pipes, pipe blanks, preforms, beads, tablets, large chipped stone bifaces, and grooved mauls also characterize the site. Pottery from Blood Run suggests an amalgam of Arikara, Ioway/Oto, and Omaha pottery-making traditions, illustrating the eclectic character of the site (Figures 7.6 and 7.7).

Blood Run was undoubtedly an exchange center of considerable importance from A.D. 1500 until shortly after 1700. Copper and brass tubular beads, tinklers, ser-

Figure 7.7 Restored pottery vessels, Blood Run (13LO2): *upper* Oneota morphology, limestone-tempered, simple-stamped body suggests Arikara influence; *lower* typical Allamakee Trailed vessel (photographs courtesy Illinois State Museum)

pents and bracelets, glass beads, brass kettle fragments, small iron items, *Marginella* beads, conch columella beads, and other trade items, including a runtee, have been recovered. Runtees are flat disks made from the broadest portion of the outer whorl of a large marine gastropod (whelk or conch), characterized by paired longitudinal holes produced with a fine metal drill (Holmes 1883; Schoolcraft 1846). They are part of a complex of decorative objects produced ca. A.D. 1640–70 by Dutch artisans for the Indian trade, specifically with the Iroquois Five Nations (Sempowski 1989:92). Runtees are very rare west of Michigan's Straits of Mackinac, where some are recorded in Ottawa and Huron cemeteries (Cleland 1971; Nern and Cleland 1974). Available historic, ethnohistoric, and archaeological data suggest that the western runtees (one at Blood Run and 25 from pre-contact Arikara sites on the Missouri mainstem), the other shell and small European-derived items arrived down-the-line through Ioway/Oto traders prior to 1700 well before white men penetrated the area (Bass and Rucker 1976; Henning 2003).

The late 17th-century arrival of the Ioway/Oto in the northeastern Plains region seems clearly documented at three Okoboji phase villages (Henning 1998a). Also clear is their point of origin: the La Crosse region (Mott 1938; M. Wedel 1981, 1986). Here, in the Upper Iowa and Root River valleys, they probably maintained discontinuous residence into the late 1600s while intermittently occupying the Okoboji phase villages. Those sites, Gillett Grove, Harriman, and Milford, are located in the upper Little Sioux River valley near Lake Okoboji. Trade was obviously important to the occupants. Items found on Milford suggest direct contact with European traders while the trade materials on both Gillett Grove and Harriman suggest earlier indirect, down-the-line trade with Native American intermediaries. Gillett Grove once boasted 12 low mounds and an earthen enclosure about 100 yds in diameter (Henning 1961:32–33; Keyes 1926). The site is small, estimated at 0.8 ha. The Harriman village is located on a high terrace above the Little Sioux River. Twelve low mounds are mentioned in Keyes's notes (1926). As at Gillett Grove, pottery fragments are similar to Allamakee Trailed (Henning 1961:32, 1970:159). The Milford site is located a few miles southwest of West Okoboji Lake (Tiffany and Anderson 1993). Keyes's notes include discussion of mounds once visible on the Milford site (Michael Perry, personal communication, 2004). The pottery compares with Allamakee Trailed, suggesting occupation by the Ioway/Oto. Milford was the latest Okoboji phase village, judging from the gun equipage and heavy iron items found there. In addition to the Okoboji phase villages, the Ioway/Oto were frequent visitors/residents at Blood Run and with the Winnebago near Green Bay, Wisconsin, in the late 1600s (Henning 2003).

Stage Two patterns of interaction: evidence for trade

I once contended that Oneota groups interacted primarily with other Oneota (Henning 1970). But today there is increasing evidence for extended trade and contact with those outside that tradition, especially after A.D. 1500. Beginning at that time, we see generally comparable ceramic horizon styles on site complexes north, south, and west of the La Crosse region, suggesting social and religious exchange between far-flung village complexes. Red pipestone (probably southwest Minnesota catlinite) pipes, and incised tablets are found on some La Crosse region sites from ca. 1500 into the early contact period. Pipestone items found on most Oneota sites of that time period suggest intensive exchange of that commodity (Bray 1991; Henning 2003; Nolan and Conrad 1998). Very likely, much of the catlinite passed through Ioway/Oto traders' hands. And, considering the variety and numbers of exotics found at Blood Run and Utz, the occupants of those sites were premier traders enjoying relationships with non-Oneota partners as well. At Blood Run there is solid evidence for exchange with the ancestral Arikara and at least indirect interaction with groups well to the west and northwest. Utz remains suggest exchange with groups in the American Southwest and post-Cahokia Mississippian groups in the Bootheel of Missouri, a pattern that probably prevailed at least through the 16th century. The large catlinite disk-bowl pipes and other items found in Late Mississippian cemeteries in northeastern Arkansas and in Missouri's Bootheel were probably obtained through exchange with Missouri Indians located at Utz (O'Brien 1994:xxxiii, 302).

During the early contact period, ca. A.D. 1600–1700, Utz and Blood Run apparently gained importance while the La Crosse region and the Mississippi Alluvial Plain components, including the Lima Lakes locality occupations, were either truncated significantly or terminated (Boszhardt 1994; Nolan and Conrad 1998). The La Crosse terrace was vacant by ca. 1600, some of the population moving across the Mississippi into the Upper Iowa and Root River valleys. Perhaps the Osage and Kansa established their western villages at this time. There is solid archaeological evidence suggesting Pawnee–Oneota (probably Kansa) interaction at around 1700 (Grange 1968; Henning 1998a; W. Wedel 1959). Historic accounts of shortly after 1700 suggest Osage–Missouri and, at times, Osage–Kansa interactions, the Osage always dominating (Chapman et al. 1985).

For a time at least, the Ioway/Oto appear to have played a significant role as middlemen, providing a link between Blood Run and eastern Wisconsin. Briefly blessed by peaceful relationships with the Sioux, the "Algonquians," and the Omaha, the Ioway/Oto were allowed to move freely along an established east–west route (Wedel 1981, 1986). This allowed them to exchange red pipestone items and hides for glass beads, small objects of brass and iron, marine shell beads, disks, mask gorgets, and runtees, most of which came through down-the-line networks emanating from the east (Henning 2003). A single Dutch-made runtee from Blood Run and ca. 25 others from Arikara sites on the Missouri mainstem offer mute testimony to the extent and importance of this network (Bass and Rucker 1976; Bill Billeck, personal communication, 2002).

The Omaha are always located along the Big Sioux in the earliest historic documents. No documentation of their presence east of Blood Run has yet been forthcoming. For access to items from the east they were apparently dependent on Ioway/Oto ability to travel there (Henning 2003). This special position was short-lived, however. By 1702, the Sioux peace had disintegrated and the Algonquian-speakers had turned against them, stripping away their regional status as middlemen.

Summary and Conclusions

With the acquisition of the bow and arrow and incipient adaptation to horticultural pursuits, resident pre-IMMV Late Woodland groups became well adapted to the

Plains-Prairie ecotone. Climatic events were especially favorable to dependence on gardening during the period A.D. 800–1200 when their IMMV descendants evolved and prospered. Horticultural pursuits became increasingly important, providing a high percentage of the caloric intake of the regional inhabitants. Hunting and gathering were also important, with variable emphasis on specific animals and plants, probably depending on relative availability. The archaeological data suggest very successful IMMV environmental exploitation, producing abundant food with sufficient surpluses for storage and trade.

Cultural events outside the northeastern Plains also played important roles. The meteoric rise and fall of the Cahokia polity was a vital constituent in the cultural history of the Plains village people and the source for some of the exotic materials that seem ubiquitous to IMMV village sites. The IMMV people enjoyed high status among their Midwest and Plains peers, gaining ready access to these exotica and maintaining sufficient wealth to retain them.

Drying conditions apparently prevailed from A.D. 1200 to 1450–1550, but with little negative effect on regional horticultural pursuits. There were dramatic increases in bison availability, perhaps due to the extension of their preferred browse to the east. Several factors may have influenced herd proliferation and expansion into the Prairie Peninsula. The advantages of bison hunting were recognized not only by the indigenous groups, but also by others situated well to the east, especially Oneota people. Oneota hunters probably made hunting forays into the northeastern Plains region in the 13th century.

By A.D. 1350, the indigenous IMMV populations had left Iowa and South Dakota, moving northward in the Missouri River valley where their archaeologically defined material culture disappeared (Wood 2001). Actually, they probably integrated with groups of the Extended Middle Missouri tradition and assumed much of their material culture. The IMMV groups were probably pressured to move northward by Oneota people and Central Plains groups. Whatever coercive factors were at play, IMMV villagers were immediately replaced in the Middle Missouri region by both Oneota and Central Plains groups. Oneota bands moved into western Iowa, southeast Nebraska, south-central Nebraska and north-central Kansas while, almost simultaneously, Central Plains groups moved from Kansas and Nebraska into the Middle Missouri trench. The Central Plains and Oneota tradition people quickly established themselves as successful gardeners, hunters, and gatherers in their respective new homes.

By A.D. 1500, the effects of European presence on the continent were felt well into the North American interior, long before the indigenes saw a white man. Pandemic disease and incursions by displaced eastern tribes quickly affected the villagers located in the upper Mississippi drainage system, and their diaspora began. The Omaha/Ponca were apparently the first Dhegihan-speakers to arrive in the eastern Plains, settling on the extensive Blood Run village and remaining there for about two centuries. They maintained good relationships with the Arikara, then located in the Middle Missouri River region, and with the Ioway/Oto, who, by the mid-1600s, had established villages around Iowa's lakes about 80 miles to the east. The Ioway/Oto continued to maintain some villages in the Upper Iowa and Root River valleys and were, by virtue of peaceful relationships with the Sioux and some

Algonquian-speaking groups, able to travel freely between the Big Sioux and Mississippi rivers and beyond into the Green Bay area until about 1700. During this peaceful period, the Ioway/Oto were able to obtain down-the-line trade items, including some small European items. Their ability to move these objects appears to have benefited the Omaha/Ponca and the Arikara. The latter also acted as trader-middlemen, and continued to occupy multiple villages along the Missouri River for another century.

After the Kansa, the Osage may have been the last Dhegihan-speakers to move west. Their village sites, located on the upper Osage drainage in western Missouri and (the Little Osage) near the Utz site in central Missouri, offer very few traditional items, but large numbers of European objects, including guns. The Osage example is characteristic: across the grasslands, traditional items were quickly replaced by European trade items, bringing the archaeologists' Plains Village tradition to an end.

REFERENCES

Alex, Lynn M., 2000 *Iowa's Archaeological Past*. Iowa City: University of Iowa Press.

Alex, Lynn M., and Joseph A. Tiffany, 2000 A summary of the DeCamp and West Des Moines Burial sites in central Iowa. *Midcontinental Journal of Archaeology* 25(2), 313–351.

Alex, Robert A., 1981a The village cultures of the lower James River valley, South Dakota. Ph.D. dissertation, Department of Anthropology, University of Wisconsin, Madison. University Microfilms, Ann Arbor, MI.

——1981b Village sites off the Missouri river. In *The Future of South Dakota's Past*. Special Publication of the South Dakota Archaeological Society 2, 39–45.

Anderson, Duane C., Joseph A. Tiffany, Michael Fokken, and Patricia M. Williams, 1979 The Siouxland Sand and Gravel site (13WD402): New data and the application of Iowa's new state law protecting ancient cemeteries. *Journal of the Iowa Archeological Society* 26, 119–145.

Baerreis, David A., and Reid A. Bryson, 1965 Climatic episodes and the dating of the Mississippian cultures. *The Wisconsin Archeologist* 46(4), 203–220.

Baerreis, David A., Margie L. Staab, Robert A. Alex, Donna H. Scott, Lynn M. Betzler, Andrew Fortier, John E. Dallman, Raymond Treat, John Kelly, Larry A. Conrad, Ericka Thrash, and Edward Lugenbeal, 1970 Environmental archaeology in western Iowa. *Northwest Chapter of the Iowa Archeological Society Newsletter* 18(5), 3–15.

Bass, William M. III, and Marc D. Rucker, 1976 Preliminary investigation of artifact association in an Arikara cemetery (Larson Site), Walworth County, South Dakota. *National Geographic Society: Research Reports*, 1968 Projects, 33–48.

Benn, David W., 1995 Woodland people and the roots of the Oneota. In *Oneota Archaeology: Past, Present, and Future*. William Green, ed. Pp. 91–140. Office of the State Archaeologist Report 20. Iowa City: University of Iowa.

Benn, David W., and William Green, 2000 Late Woodland cultures in Iowa. In *Late Woodland Societies: Tradition and Transformation Across the Midcontinent*. Thomas E. Emerson, Dale L. McElrath, and Andrew C. Fortier, eds. Pp. 429–496. Lincoln: University of Nebraska Press.

Billeck, William, 1993 Time and space in the Glenwood locality: The Nebraska phase in western Iowa. Ph.D. dissertation, Department of Anthropology, University of Missouri-Columbia.

Blakeslee, Donald J., 1978 Assessing the Central Plains tradition in eastern Nebraska: Content and outcome. In *The Central Plains Tradition: Internal Development and External Relationships*. Office of the State Archaeologist Report 11. Iowa City: University of Iowa.

Boszhardt, Robert F., 1994 Oneota group continuity at La Crosse: The Brice Prairie, Pammel Creek, and Valley View phases. *The Wisconsin Archeologist* 75(3–4), 173–276.

—— 2000 Turquoise, rasps, and heartlines: The Oneota Bison Pull. In *Mounds, Modoc, and Mesoamerica: Papers in Honor of Melvin L. Fowler*. Steven R. Ahler, ed. Pp. 361–404. Scientific Papers, vol. XXVIII. Springfield: Illinois State Museum.

Boszhardt, Robert F., Wendy Holtz, and Jeremy Nienow, 1995 A compilation of Oneota radiocarbon dates as of 1995. In *Oneota Archaeology Past Present, and Future*. William Green, ed. Pp. 203–227. Office of the State Archaeologist Report 20. Iowa City: University of Iowa.

Bozell, J. R., and M. K. Rogers, 1989 A Great Oasis fauna from central Nebraska. *Central Plains Archaeology* 1, 3–36.

Bray, Robert T. 1991 *The Utz Site: An Oneota Village in Central Missouri*. The Missouri Archaeologist 52 (whole volume).

Bryson, Reid A., David A. Baerreis, and Wayne M. Wendland, 1970 The character of Late-Glacial and Post-Glacial climatic changes. In *Pleistocene and Recent Environments of the Central Great Plains*. W. Dort, Jr. and J. K. Jones, Jr., eds. Pp. 53–74. Lawrence: University Press of Kansas.

Bryson, Reid A., and Wayne Wendland, 1967 Tentative climatic patterns for some Late Glacial and Post-Glacial episodes in central North America. In *Life, Land and Water*. Proceedings of the 1966 Conference on Environmental Studies of the Glacial Lake Region. William J. Mayer-Oakes, ed. Pp. 271–298. Winnipeg: University of Manitoba Press.

Burch, J. B., 1989 *North American Freshwater Snails*. Hamburg, MI: Malacological Publications.

Carlson, Gayle F., 1997 A preliminary survey of marine shell artifacts from prehistoric archeological sites in Nebraska. *Central Plains Archeology*, 5(1), 11–48.

Chapman, Carl H. Leonard W. Blake, Robert T. Bray, T. M. Hamilton, Andrea A. Hunter, Deborah M. Pearsall, James H. Purdue, Eric E. Voigt, Robert P. Wiegers, and Jeffrey K. Yelton, 1985 *Osage and Missouri Indian Life Cultural Change: 1675–1825*. Final Performance Report on National Endowment for the Humanities Research Grant RS-20296. On file, Division of American Archaeology, University of Missouri-Columbia.

Cleland, Charles E., ed., 1971 The Lasanen site: An early historic burial locality in Mackinac County, Michigan. *Publications of the Museum, Anthropological Series* 1(1). East Lansing: Michigan State University.

Cutler, Hugh C., and Leonard W. Blake, 1973 *Plants from Archaeological Sites East of the Rockies*. St. Louis: Missouri Botanical Garden.

Dallman, John E., 1983 *A Choice of Diet: Response to Climatic Change*. Office of the State Archaeologist Report 16, Iowa City: University of Iowa.

Dorsey, James Owen, 1886 Migrations of Siouan tribes. *The American Naturalist* 20(3), 211–222.

Dorsey, James Owen, and Cyrus Thomas, 1907 *Handbook of American Indians North of Mexico*. Frederick W. Hodge, ed. Bureau of American Ethnology Bulletin 30, pt. 1. Pp. 612–614. Washington, DC: Government Printing Office.

Dyck, Ian, and Richard E. Morlan, 2001 Hunting and gathering tradition: Canadian Plains. In *Handbook of North American Indians*, vol. 13: *Plains*. William C. Sturtevant, ed. Pp. 115–130. Washington, DC: Smithsonian Institution.

Eighmy, J. L. and J. M. LaBelle, 1996 Radiocarbon dating of twenty-seven Plains complexes and phases. *Plains Anthropologist* 41, 29–52.

Finney, Fred A., and James B. Stoltman, 1991 The Fred Edwards site: A case of Stirling phase culture contact in southwestern Wisconsin. In *New Perspectives in Cahokia: Views from the Periphery*. James B. Stoltman, ed. Pp. 229–252. Madison, WI: Prehistory Press.

Fishel, Richard L., 1999 *Bison Hunters of the Western Prairies: Archaeological Investigations at the Dixon Site (13WD8), Woodbury County, Iowa*. Office of the State Archaeologist Report 21. Iowa City: University of Iowa.

Fletcher, Alice C., and Francis La Flesche, 1911 *The Omaha Tribe*. Annual Report, Bureau of American Ethnology 27. Pp. 17–654. Washington, DC.

Gibbon, Guy E., 1991 The Middle Mississippian presence in Minnesota. In *Cahokia and the Hinterlands: Middle Mississippian Cultures of the Midwest*. T. E. Emerson and R. B. Lewis, eds. Pp. 207–222. Urbana: University of Illinois Press.

Gibbon, Guy E., and Clark A. Dobbs, 1991 The Mississippian presence in the Red Wing area, Minnesota. In *New Perspectives on Cahokia, Views from the Periphery*. J. B. Stoltman, ed. Pp. 307–317. Monographs in World Archaeology 2. Madison, WI: Prehistory Press.

Grange, Roger T., Jr., 1968 Pawnee and Lower Loup pottery. *Nebraska State Historical Society Publications in Anthropology* 3. Lincoln: Nebraska State Historical Society.

Green, William, 1993 Examining Protohistoric depopulation in the upper Midwest. *The Wisconsin Archeologist* 74(1–4), 290–323.

Hall, Robert L., 1993 Red Banks, Oneota, and the Winnebago: Views from a distant rock. *The Wisconsin Archeologist* 74(1–4), 10–79.

Harn, Alan D., 1980 *The Prehistory of Dickson Mounds: The Dickson Excavation*. Illinois State Museum Reports of Investigations 35. Springfield: Illinois State Museum.

Harvey, Amy E., 1979 *Oneota Culture in Northwestern Iowa*. Office of the State Archaeologist Report 12. Iowa City: University of Iowa.

Henning, Dale R., 1961 Oneota ceramics in Iowa. *Journal of the Iowa Archeological Society* 11(2).

—— 1967 Mississippian influences on the eastern Plains border: An evaluation. *Plains Anthropologist* 12(36), 184–194.

—— 1969 Ceramics from Mill Creek sites. *Journal of the Iowa Archeological Society* 16, 192–280.

—— 1970 Development and interrelationships of Oneota culture in the lower Missouri River valley. *The Missouri Archaeologist* 32.

—— 1971 Origins of Mill Creek. *Journal of the Iowa Archeological Society* 18, 6–13.

—— 1982 *Evaluative Investigations of Three Landmark Sites in Northwest Iowa*. Decorah, Iowa: Luther College Archaeological Research Center.

—— 1991 Great Oasis and Emergent Mississippian: The question of trade. *Journal of the Iowa Archeological Society* 38, 1–4.

—— 1993 The adaptive patterning of the Dhegiha Sioux. *Plains Anthropologist* 38(146), 253–264.

—— 1996 The archeology of two Great Oasis sites in the Perry Creek valley, northwest Iowa. *Journal of the Iowa Archeological Society* 43, 7–118.

—— 1998a The Oneota tradition. In *Archaeology on the Great Plains*. W. Raymond Wood, ed. Pp. 345–414. Lawrence: University Press of Kansas.

—— 1998b Managing Oneota: A reiteration and testing of contemporary archeological taxonomy. *The Wisconsin Archeologist* 79(2), 9–28.

——2001 Plains Village tradition: Eastern periphery and Oneota tradition. In *Handbook of North American Indians*, vol. 13: *Plains*. William C. Sturtevant, ed. Pp. 222–233. Washington, DC: Smithsonian Institution.

——2003 The archeology and history of Ioway/Oto exchange patterns 1650–1700. *Journal of the Iowa Archeological Society* 50, 199–221.

Henning, Dale R., and Dennis L. Toom, 2003 Cambria and the Initial Middle Missouri Variant: An evaluation. *The Wisconsin Archeologist* 84(1–2).

Henning, Elizabeth R., 1981 Great Oasis and the Middle Missouri tradition. In *The Future of South Dakota's Past*. South Dakota Archaeological Society Special Publication 2. Vermillion.

Hill, Amos T., and Waldo R. Wedel, 1936 Excavations at the Leary Indian village and burial site, Richardson County, Nebraska. *Nebraska History Magazine* 17, 2–73.

Hollinger, R. Eric, 2000 Images of power: Meaning and social function of portable art. Paper presented at the Joint Midwest Archaeological/Plains Anthropological Conference. St. Paul, MN.

——2001 Oneota population movements: Aggressive territorial expansions and contractions. Paper presented to the 66th Annual Meeting of the Society for American Archaeology. New Orleans.

Holmes, William H., 1883 *Art in Shell of the Ancient Americans*. Second Annual Report of the Bureau of Ethnology, 1880–81. Pp. 179–305. Washington, DC.

Ives, John C., 1962 Mill Creek pottery. *Journal of the Iowa Archeological Society* 11(3), 1–57.

Jans-Langel, Carmen, 1999 Animal resource utilization. In *Bison Hunters of the Western Prairies*. R. L. Fishel, ed. Pp. 79–96. Office of the State Archaeologist Report 21. Iowa City: University of Iowa.

Johnson, Alfred E., 2001 Plains Woodland tradition. In *Handbook of North American Indians*, vol. 13: *Plains*. W. C. Sturtevant, ed. Pp. 159–172. Washington, DC: Smithsonian Institution.

Johnson, Craig M., 1998 The Coalescent tradition. In *Archaeology on the Great Plains*. W. Raymond Wood, ed. Pp. 308–344. Lawrence: University Press of Kansas.

Keyes, Charles R., 1926 Keyes notes, Blood Run site, dated July 7–14, 1926. On file, Office of the State Archaeologist, Iowa City.

Lehmer, D. J., 1971 *Introduction to Middle Missouri Archaeology*. Anthropological Papers, no. 1. Washington, DC: National Park Service.

Lillie, Robin, 1999 Human remains. In *Bison Hunters of the Western Prairies*. R. L. Fishel, ed. Pp. 109–116. Office of the State Archaeologist Report 21. Iowa City: University of Iowa.

Logan, Brad, 1998 Oneota far west: The White Rock phase. *The Wisconsin Archeologist* 79(2), 248–267.

Mann, Charles C., 2002 1491. *The Atlantic Monthly* 289(3), 41–53.

McClain, William, 2000 The hunts of Indian summer. *The Illinois Steward* 8(4), 19–22.

McKusick, Marshall B., n.d. Maps of the Wittrock site. On file, Office of the State Archaeologist. Iowa City: University of Iowa.

Mead, Barbara, 1981 Seed analysis of the Meehan-Schell site (13BN110), a Great Oasis site in central Iowa. *Journal of the Iowa Archeological Society* 28, 15–90.

Michlovic, Michael G., and Frederick E. Schneider, 1993 The Shea site: A prehistoric fortified village on the northeastern Plains. *Plains Anthropologist* 38(143), 117–138.

Moffat, Charles R., 1998 Oneota in the central Des Moines valley. *The Wisconsin Archeologist* 79(2), 165–226.

Mott, Mildred, 1938 The relation of historic Indian tribes to archaeological manifestations in Iowa. *Iowa Journal of History and Politics* 36, 227–314.

Nern, Craig F., and Charles E. Cleland, 1974 The Gros Cap cemetery site, St. Ignace, Michigan: A reconsideration of the Greenlees collection. *The Michigan Archaeologist* 20(1), 1–58.

Nolan, David J., and Lawrence A. Conrad, 1998 Characterizing Lima Lake Oneota. *The Wisconsin Archeologist* 79(2), 117–164.

O'Brien, Michael J., 1994 *Cat Monsters and Head Pots: The Archaeology of Missouri's Pemiscot Bayou*. Columbia: University of Missouri Press.

Orr, Ellison, 1963 Iowa Archeological Reports 1934–1939. *Archives of Archaeology Microcard Series* 20. Society for American Archaeology. Madison: University of Wisconsin Press.

Overstreet, David F., 1993 McCauley, Astor, and Hanson: Candidates for the provisional Dandy phase. *The Wisconsin Archeologist* 74(1–4), 120–196.

——1998 East and west expressions of the Emergent Oneota Horizon: Perceptual problems and empirical realities. *The Wisconsin Archeologist* 79(2), 29–37.

——2000 Late prehistoric cultural dynamics in southern Wisconsin. In *Mounds, Modoc, and Mesoamerica: Papers in Honor of Melvin L. Fowler*. S. R. Ahler, ed. Pp. 405–438. Scientific Papers vol. XXVIII. Springfield: Illinois State Museum.

——2001 Dreaded dolostone and old smudge stories: A response to critiques of Emergent Horizon Oneota ^{14}C dates from eastern Wisconsin. *The Wisconsin Archeologist* 82(1–2), 33–85.

Pauketat, Timothy R., and Thomas E. Emerson, 1997 Introduction: Domination and ideology in the Mississippian world. In *Cahokia: Domination and Ideology in the Mississippian World*, T. R. Pauketat and T. E. Emerson, eds. Pp. 1–29. Lincoln: University of Nebraska Press.

Pettigrew, Frederick W., 1891 The silent city. *Sioux Falls Press*, January 4, p. 1.

——1901 A prehistoric Indian village. *Bulletin of the Minnesota Academy of Natural Science*, 348–355.

Risser, Paul G., 1990 Landscape processes and the vegetation of the North American grassland. In *Fire in North American Tallgrass Prairies*. Scott L. Collins and Linda L. Wallace, eds. Pp. 133–169. Norman: University of Oklahoma Press.

Ritterbush, Lauren W., 2000a Analyzing western Oneota migration. *Current Archaeology in Kansas* 1, 13–17.

——2000b Western Oneota contact across the Plains. Paper presented at the 60th Annual Plains Anthropological Conference, Oklahoma City.

——2002a Leary site revisited: Oneota and Central Plains tradition occupation along the lower Missouri. *Plains Anthropologist* 47(182), 251–264.

——2002b Drawn by the bison: Late prehistoric native migration into the Central Plains. *Great Plains Quarterly* 22(4), 259–270.

Ritterbush, Lauren W., and Brad Logan, 2000 Late prehistoric Oneota population movement into the Central Plains. *Plains Anthropologist* 45(173), 257–272.

Salzer, Robert J., and Grace Rajnovich, 2000 *The Gottschall Rockshelter: An Archaeological Mystery*. Prairie Smoke Press, St. Paul.

Schneider, Fred, 2002 Prehistoric horticulture in the northeastern Plains. *Plains Anthropologist* 47(180), 33–50.

Schoolcraft, H. R., 1846 *Notes on the Iroquois*. New York: Bartlett & Welford.

Schroeder, Marjorie, 1999 Plant resource utilization. In *Bison Hunters of the Western Prairies*. R. L. Fishel, ed. Pp. 97–107. Office of the State Archaeologist Report 21. Iowa City: University of Iowa.

Sempowski, Martha L., 1989 Fluctuations through time in the use of marine shell at Seneca Iroquois sites. In *Proceedings of the 1986 Shell Bead Conference: Selected Papers*. Pp. 81–96. Research Records 20. Rochester, NY: Rochester Museum and Science Center.

Starr, Frederick, 1887 Mounds and lodge circles in Iowa. *American Antiquarian* 9, 361–363.

——1889 *Mound Explorations in Northwestern Iowa.* Proceedings of the Davenport Academy of Natural Sciences, no. 6.

Steinacher, Terry L., and Gayle F. Carlson, 1998 The Central Plains tradition. In *Archaeology on the Great Plains.* W. Raymond Wood, ed. Pp. 235–268. Lawrence: University Press of Kansas.

Tiffany, Joseph A., 1979 *An Archaeological Survey of the Bastian Oneota Site (13CK28), Cherokee County, Iowa.* Office of the State Archaeologist Research Papers. Iowa City: University of Iowa.

——1980 Late Woodland pottery in northeastern Iowa as seen from the Hartley Fort. Paper presented at the 38th Annual Plains Anthropological Conference, Iowa City.

——1982 Hartley Fort Ceramics. *Proceedings of the Iowa Academy of Science* 89:133–150.

——1991 Modeling Mill Creek–Mississippian interaction. In *New Perspectives on Cahokia: Views from the Periphery.* J. B. Stoltman, ed. Pp. 319–348. Monographs in World Archaeology 2. Madison, WI: Prehistory Press.

——2003 Mississippian connections with Mill Creek and Cambria. *Plains Anthropologist* 48(184), 21–34.

Tiffany, Joseph A., and Lynn M. Alex, 2001 *Great Oasis Archaeology: New Perspectives From the Decamp and West Des Moines Burial Sites in Central Iowa.* Plains Anthropologist Memoir 33.

Tiffany, Joseph A., and Duane Anderson, 1993 The Milford Site (13DK1): A postcontact village in northwest Iowa. In *Prehistory and Human Ecology of the Western Prairies and Northern Plains.* J. A. Tiffany, ed. Pp. 283–306. Plains Anthropologist Memoir 27.

Tolmie, Clare, and William Green, 1992 *Protohistoric Plant Use in Northwestern Iowa.* Paper presented at the 50th annual Plains Anthropological Conference, Lincoln, NE.

Toom, Dennis L., 1992 Early village formation in the Middle Missouri subarea of the Plains. In *Long-Term Subsistence Change in Prehistoric North America.* D. R. Cross, R. A. Hawkins, and B. L. Isaac, eds. Pp. 131–191. Research in Economic Anthropology Supplement 6. Greenwich, CT: JAI Press.

Wedel, Mildred Mott, 1981 The Ioway, Oto, and Omaha Indians in 1700. *Journal of the Iowa Archeological Society* 28, 1–13.

——1986 Peering at the Ioway Indians through the mist of time: 1650–circa 1700. *Journal of the Iowa Archeological Society* 23, 1–44.

——2001 Iowa. In *Handbook of North American Indians,* vol. 13: *Plains.* William C. Sturtevant, ed. Pp. 432–446. Washington, DC: Smithsonian Institution.

Wedel, Waldo R., 1959 *An Introduction to Kansas Archeology.* Bureau of American Ethnology Bulletin 174. Washington, DC: Smithsonian Institution.

——2001 Plains Village tradition: Central. In *Handbook of North American Indians,* vol. 13: *Plains.* William C. Sturtevant, ed. Pp. 173–185. Washington, DC: Smithsonian Institution.

Wilford, Lloyd A., 1955 A revised classification of the prehistoric cultures of Minnesota. *American Antiquity* 11, 32–40.

Winham, R. Peter, and Frances A. Calabrese, 1998 The Middle Missouri tradition. In *Archaeology on the Great Plains.* W. R. Wood, ed. Pp. 269–307. Lawrence: University Press of Kansas.

Wood, W. Raymond, 1973 Culture sequence at the Old Fort, Saline county, Missouri. *American Antiquity* 38, 101–111.

——1998 Introduction. In *Archaeology on the Great Plains.* W. R. Wood, ed. Pp. 1–15. Lawrence: University Press of Kansas.

——2001 Plains Village Tradition: Middle Missouri. In *Handbook of North American Indians*, vol. 13: *Plains*. William C. Sturtevant, ed. Pp. 186–195. Washington, DC: Smithsonian Institution.

Yelton, Jeffrey K., 1998 A different view of Oneota taxonomy and origins in the lower Missouri valley. *The Wisconsin Archeologist* 79(2), 268–283.

8

The Forgotten History of the Mississippians

Timothy R. Pauketat

The first Europeans in southeastern North America were Spaniards seeking cities of gold and fountains of youth. From Florida north and west across the coastal plain, conquistadors, colonists, and missionaries encountered American Indian towns populated by hundreds of farmers living in pole-and-thatch houses. These surrounded open plazas at the base of one or more four-sided earthen pyramids surmounted by large temples, special-purpose buildings, and elite domiciles. Maize fields were stretched out a day's walk away from the central town of each so-called chiefdom.

Archaeologists in the early 20th century gave the name Mississippian to many of these Indians, implying that they were historically related. Then came the 1960s, when archaeologists began to treat Mississippian societies as "systems" that adapted to farming maize in riverine environments (Smith 1978). This systems approach made the study of historical relationships moot. Accordingly, archaeologists have been content since then to argue over whether or not Mississippians were "complex" (read, hierarchical), governed by hereditary leaders who directed production, resolved disputes, and hosted religious ceremonies at central towns (Cobb 2003).

Unfortunately, the archaeological fixation on systems thinking and complexity implies that one Mississippian polity was pretty much like the next, that only the actions of the hereditary elite mattered (if actions mattered at all), and that knowing the degree of complexity somehow explains the Mississippians. All of these implications are misleading. For starters, not all complex, agricultural peoples in the eastern Woodlands of North America were Mississippian. Moreover, there is no good reason to assume that all Mississippians were equally complex. In fact, there was considerable cultural and linguistic diversity within and between some Mississippian populations. There were marked differences in people's reliance on maize as a staple crop (Fritz 1990). And there was a wide range of population densities and degrees of political-economic centralization.

So, what had happened, on the one hand, to make people Mississippian and, on the other, to make Mississippians different from each other? In this chapter, I will point in the direction of the answers to those questions, a direction that involves developing new theories of "culture-making" that highlight *how people made themselves Mississippian*, a simultaneously cultural and historical process.

The idea of culture-making suggests that cultural landscapes, traditions, identities, and memories were constructed, built, imagined, and created continuously by people in various social contexts (see Pauketat and Loren, this volume; Thomas 2001; Van Dyke and Alcock 2003). The most important point for archaeologists is that culture-making possessed a physicality: it resided in the movements of human bodies, in the making, wearing, or distributing of material things, and in the sensuous experiencing of spaces. In other words, archaeologists (and only archaeologists) can find, measure, and explain the "genealogies," "biographies," and "histories" of the corporeality, materiality, and spatiality of culture-making (e.g., Joyce 2000; Loren, this volume). Understanding the relationships between politics, religion, identity, migration, gender, and the like rests on understanding the contingent histories of people, places, and things.

Now, we must admit at the outset that, in studying culture-making, archaeologists are not wholly independent of the process that they study. In reality, archaeologists, in doing what they do, are also constructing memories and interpreting the meanings of the past through their experience with that past. For this reason, a little reflexivity is called for, at least enough to appreciate the experiences from which archaeologists get their ideas and through which they make their interpretations. These experiences include some outstanding finds and some fortuitous circumstances that have led archaeologists, and should lead us, to continuously rethink how cultures are made. I present some of these here, embedding my theoretical arguments about culture-making within the observations of each case. The combination of theory and data in this way will, I hope, point you, the reader, toward the inevitable conclusion: the past is constructed or interpreted by archaeologists today and was similarly constructed by people in past. As we shall see, the forgotten history of the Mississippians is both a present-day phenomenon and an ancient one.

We will begin at the western edge of the Mississippian world, in two locations where dramatic discoveries urge us to know more about the contingencies of Mississippi valley cultures and history (Figure 8.1). Next, we travel to the northern edge of that valley in order to get a sense of the scale and dimensions of Mississippianization, a process with some abrupt and long-lasting consequences. Afterwards, we turn south, seeking both the common processes and the divergent histories of the Mississippians. We then triangulate backwards in time to the Mississippian heartland and the great founding city of Cahokia. By the end, our journey will have given us a sense of how the experiencing of specific places, the manipulating of cultural things, and the living and dying of real people in the past constituted the history of peoples formally known as the "pre-historic" Mississippians.

A "King Tut" Tomb in the Arkansas Valley, A.D. 1400

American archaeology was still a nascent science in the 1920s when news of the discovery of King Tutankhamun's tomb in Egypt stirred the imaginations of trea-

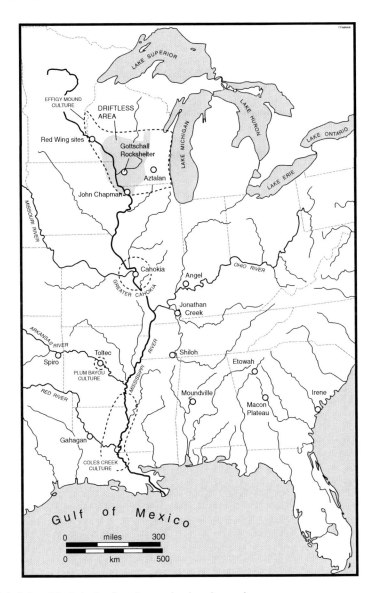

Figure 8.1 Select Mississippi valley sites and cultural complexes

sure-hunters worldwide. Economic hard times in the United States beginning in 1929 further inspired eight Arkansas and Oklahoma men to plan the massive looting of the earthen mounds at the Spiro site along the Arkansas River in eastern Oklahoma. Calling themselves the "Pocola Mining Company," these men opened up the largest mounds at the site in 1933–35, encountering in one of them the Great Mortuary, then dubbed by one newspaper reporter "A 'King Tut' Tomb in the Arkansas Valley" (Brown 1996:43).

The Spiro site had deep roots, founded in the public ceremonies of marginal eastern Woodlands people at A.D. 950. Those ceremonies celebrated community and memorialized the dead, burying them in accretional mounds of earth. By A.D. 1000, the first flat-topped mounds were built as stages for public ceremonial performances similar to those at earlier pre-Mississippian sites across the South (Knight 2001). Unlike later Mississippi valley peoples, Spiroans farmed little maize before A.D. 1200. Yet, their town emerged as a force in the Arkansas River valley, manifest in the cultural objects that the Spiroans accumulated from distant places (Brown 1996:199–200). Quite possibly, Spiroans ever so slightly altered the histories of peoples all along the ancient trade routes that traversed the region, the main route paved today as Interstates 40 and 44 between St. Louis, Missouri, and Albuquerque, New Mexico (Brown 1996). The histories of Caddoan-speaking peoples on the Plains to the north – the Pawnees and Arikara – might have been linked to Spiro and other Caddoan towns (e.g., Holder 1970).

Yet the Great Mortuary, rather than a demonstration of Spiroan power, is an impressive hoard of cultural objects, garments, and paraphernalia that dates late in the region's history, to about A.D. 1400 (Brown 1996:197). Along with the skeletal remains of the Caddoan elite of the day, there were hundreds of the finest weapons, tools, pots, capes, trade goods, bodily ornaments, and religious icons from distant corners of the known world: the southern Plains, the lower Mississippi valley, the Deep South, Cahokia, and even a smattering of Puebloan objects from the Southwest. Some were clearly made decades, even centuries, before being buried in the Great Mortuary, indicating that they had been obtained earlier and then warehoused or heirloomed up to that point (Brown 1996).

Thus, these were not merely trade goods or exchanged commodities. No, they were meaningful things with powerful histories that could not be easily forgotten. They were, in this sense, "inalienable" objects, each one imbued with stories telling of past owners, events, or places (Weiner 1994). Given their diverse points of origin, the material goods represent a kind of cultural-historical convergence, the construction of memories, if not the attempted consolidation of political power, by the living Spiroans through the disposition of the powerful pieces of their real or imagined history. It is doubtless significant that the biographies associated with each object or garment could not be easily removed from the realm of the living except perhaps through burial. Elimination of that which conducts history may be the simplest way to control the telling of history.

The Incident at Crow Creek, A.D. 1325

History was not at the forefront of the minds of local citizens looting the banks of a well-known "Initial Coalescent" village site overlooking Crow Creek near where it enters the Missouri River in 1978. The looters had arrived before archaeologist Thomas Emerson could begin excavations that would soon uncover hundreds of human bones eroding out of the bank into the water. Back from the Vietnam War several years earlier, Emerson was "unprepared for the scale of the bone deposits" and did not anticipate that excavations would become "a political and emotional issue between various tribal factions and governmental groups with the archaeologists as pawns" (Willey and Emerson 1993:232). They did. "Threats were made to take the remains, burn the camp, and beat up the crew, and finally, against the lives of the crew."

As uneasy as the project was in these pre-NAGPRA days, the emotional politics of the 1970s paled beside the discoveries at Crow Creek. It seems that, in the early 1300s, Caddoan-speaking ancestral Arikara had occupied the fertile middle Missouri River in present-day South Dakota. But events in the Mississippi valley and borderlands to the east may have led to an uneasy ethnic mix of eastern Siouan, Algonquian, and Caddoan peoples all along the eastern Plains in the 1300s (Henning, this volume; Krause 1998:68–69). Violence erupted in more than one location. At the Crow Creek site, a 7 ha village atop steep loess bluffs with some 50 lodges, the people were in the process of building a new defensive palisade wall and digging a 300 m long and 3 m deep ditch to fend off the attack they might have known was coming. But they did not build the fortifications fast enough.

In an overwhelming strike, attackers burned the village and massacred its inhabitants. Archaeologists found the remains of at least 486 bodies heaped in a segment of the incomplete fortification ditch. More burned body parts were found inside the burned lodges. Men, women, and children had been arrowshot, clubbed, hacked, and burned to death. Many of the victims were scalped and their bodies mutilated: tongues cut out, teeth broken, heads cut off, and bodies dismembered (Willey and Emerson 1993:259). Apparently, many young women had been captured or had escaped, as there were fewer than expected among the dead. A high incidence of carnivore gnawing marks on the human bones indicated that the bodies of the victims had lain dead on the ground for sometime before escapees returned or sympathizers arrived to heap the corpses and scattered arms, legs, and heads into the still open ditch.

This particularly violent episode, a kind of village-level ethnic cleansing, exemplifies through corpses the principle of historical change seen also at Spiro in the burial of cultural objects: elimination of that which conducts history may be the simplest (albeit Machiavellian) way to control the telling of history. The Crow Creek incident seems to have had its genesis in the ethnic strife associated with migrations. This, in turn, might have been related to the redefinition of the rules of warfare that had earlier been defined by what I will call *pax Cahokiana* (see below). Then again, *pax Cahokiana* had not arisen without major disruptions to social life of midwestern peoples three centuries before Crow Creek.

The Northern Disruption, ca. A.D. 1050

"Hidden in the upper reaches of a small valley" in southwestern Wisconsin is the Gottschall Rockshelter (Salzer and Rajnovich 2000). Since 1984, Robert Salzer, a white-haired veteran of Midwestern archaeology, has led excavation and preservation efforts at Gottschall. Today, one reaches the site by climbing down a rocky escarpment, keeping hold of a rope. At this site, about 10 m deep and just spacious enough for a short person to stand up, Salzer and associates are carefully excavating the finely stratified layers of Gottschall. Inside they have found a possible small earthen mound in the shape of a bird, a cache of arrowheads, painted and rolled up animal hides, a sculpted and painted stone representation of a human head, layers of ritually manufactured and colored soil, and the pictographs – painted representations of people, animals, and supernatural beings. There are some 40 pictographs arranged in six different rock panels (Salzer and Rajnovich 2000):

> One group of paintings is called the "Red Horn panel" and consists of a remarkable group of blue-grey images . . . including three highly detailed and carefully wrought human forms . . . drawn in a style [that] shares many similarities with Mississippian art to the south. . . . The three humans, [a] turtle and [a] big bird found on the panel are most likely part of a planned composition . . . placed on a deliberately sanded surface. (Salzer and Rajnovich 2000:23)

One of the human figures, in fact, is interpreted to be a representation of the legendary hero of the Ho-Chunk Indians of Wisconsin: Red Horn. Shown wearing a breechcloth, tattooed above the waist, and sporting a long braid of hair dyed red, Red Horn is said to have engaged in a high-stakes game or battle with a race of giants in the underworld, ultimately emerging victorious with the aid of his friends "Turtle and a thunderbird known as Storms-As-He-Walks" (Salzer and Rajnovich 2000:23). As it turns out, the other two human forms are larger than the Red Horn figure. Salzer thinks the two represent giants.

He also wonders if the Red Horn panel, radiocarbon-dated to the 10th or possibly very early 11th century A.D., represents actual historical figures, or perhaps a generalized account of actual events related to the beginning of the Mississippian period in southern Wisconsin (Salzer and Rajnovich 2000:65–67). Up until about A.D. 1050, the local Woodland peoples who occupied southern Wisconsin were known to build animal-shaped mounds at special ceremonial locations. However, these Effigy Mound peoples may have found themselves at the frontier of a rapidly expanding Mississippian shockwave, the expansion itself forcing localized migrations or accommodations of radical ideas, if not migrants, from the south. The shockwave is evident in the material and spatial contrasts between local Woodland and Mississippian settlements. Effigy Mound constructions ceased at about A.D. 1050 (Theler and Boszhardt 2000).

At this time, northerners acquired various Cahokia-made objects. These included the discoidal stones used to play a competitive, high-stakes, and inclusive team sport called "chunkey" that recapitulated fundamental cosmological principles: the rolling stone of this game perhaps signified the movement of the sun across the sky or the flight of a legendary arrow (see below). They also included Cahokia-style arrowheads, marine-shell bead necklaces, decorated "Ramey Incised" pots, carved redstone figures and smoking pipes, and a distinctive ear ornament that looks like a human head with an elongated nose made from marine shell or copper.

In addition to objects, there are some oddly out of place or intrusive Mississippian settlements, possible outposts or villages of displaced southern peoples scattered through the wooded hills of Wisconsin, eastern Iowa, northern Illinois, and southern Minnesota. In the north, most intrusive settlements were positioned along the Mississippi River in the Driftless Area, an unusually rugged and rocky landscape bypassed by Ice Age glaciers. But the best known and most telling site-unit intrusion is Aztalan, just to the east in south-central Wisconsin.

Aztalan was an Effigy Mound culture site up to the 11th century. But, sometime shortly after A.D. 1050, local people appear to have "invited" southern Mississippians up for an extended stay (Goldstein and Richards 1991). These migrants brought their world with them, creating some profound changes in the north. There are southern-style pots alongside northern Woodland types, distinctive Mississippian houses, and two modest flat-topped pyramids overlooking the sloping site's walled plaza, all enclosed by a large palisade wall complete with defensive bastions. Excavations in the early 1920s located a series of burned human body parts thrown out with the trash of the settlement. There were pieces of cracked human crania, an articulated hand, a variety of isolated mandibles, articulated human legs, and an arm. Besides this direct evidence of a most unusual method of dealing with the dead (enemies?), there are reasons to believe that some local people were frightened away from Aztalan once the southern Mississippian reinforcements moved in (Overstreet 2000).

Given the scale and character of this particular northern disruption, it may come as no surprise that Aztalan ultimately was burned to the ground some time during the 12th century. Actually, houses at a number of other 11th- and 12th-century sites in the Driftless Area to the west also burned, perhaps indicative of the severity of the cultural disruptions associated with Mississippianization in the north (Pauketat 2004). Perhaps realizing the potential threat, some of these northern people tried to stay out of harm's way, settling in more inaccessible places or hiding their settlements in out of the way secondary drainages. But even this was not sufficient to protect some of them (e.g., Benn and Powell 2002). Along with the occasional conflagration, there are indications of a considerable east–west cultural exchange and the occasional contact with Cahokians far to the south (see Henning, this volume).

We do not know whether all such southern contacts were friendly. We do know that some places, such as the John Chapman site at the southern end of the Driftless Area, look to have been multi-ethnic settlements, judging from the diversity of pottery technologies found during our 2003 excavations. Cahokian pots and copies of Cahokian pots are found side by side with northern Woodland wares. Apparently, if you can't beat them, join them.

Southern Chiefdoms, ca. A.D. 1100–1375

Cahokian pots, among other things, are also found south of the Mason-Dixon line. However, the significance of their presence there is uncertain, but not because of a lack of archaeological investigation. Archaeological resources were poured into the sunny South during the Great Depression with whole earthen pyramids and, less often, residential areas opened up at town sites: Macon Plateau, Spiro, Hiwassee Island, Moundville, Irene, Shiloh, Angel, and more.

These were unusual times for archaeology, with large crews of initially untrained, out-of-work locals run by the few professional archaeologists. All sorts of men and women were thrown together in the effort and massive amounts of raw data were accumulated, some still awaiting analysis. But the unusual times led to major conceptual advances. So, for instance, Antonio Waring, a physician in Savannah, Georgia, met the unconventional Preston Holder during excavations outside Savannah at the Irene site in 1938. Together, they made sense of the accumulating morass of Mississippian iconographic and artifactual data, defining the "Southeastern Ceremonial Complex" (Knight et al. 2001; Waring and Holder 1945). The bohemian, persnickety Holder, who grew up in a circus, would reappear later – after jumping bail in New Orleans and negotiating with headhunters in the Pacific during the Second World War – to conduct two of the most significant mound excavations ever at Cahokia (he subsequently assumed the role of elderly hippy professor at the University of Nebraska in the 1970s).

Less iconoclastic archaeologists carried out the largest Works Progress Administration excavations at the Macon Plateau site on the Ocmulgee River in central Georgia (Walker 1994). There, at the same time that looters were pillaging Spiro, federal crews uncovered what was thought to be an intrusive early Mississippian complex of large pyramidal mounds and public buildings (Figure 8.2). Larger than Aztalan, Macon Plateau might have been built by (or for) immigrant Tennesseans in the midst of an apparent local Woodland population (Williams 1994).

The presumed newcomers probably dressed and acted differently than local Georgians. Their heritage, traditions, and legends were doubtless also different, perhaps embodied by the costume of one person interred in the site's Funeral Mound that included a copper gorget and an unusual two-piece headdress: opposing fur-covered puma jaw segments matched with a pair of embossed oval copper plates decorated with radiating lines (wings?). This person may have personified a

Figure 8.2 Pyramids at the Macon Plateau site, Georgia

supernatural feline-bird figure associated with the immigrants rather than the locals (cf. Fairbanks 2003 [1956]). Certainly, their hooded ceramic bottles and angled-shoulder cooking jars (the latter with a particular bifurcate-style loop handle) are typical of Mississippians from eastern Tennessee at A.D. 1100 ± 50.[1] What historical implications might have attended the displacement of natives by foreigners, or the intrusion of a foreign cosmology and non-local cultural practices into a locality at about this time?

Whatever the consequences, Macon Plateau might not have been alone. Less dramatic population movements occurred within regions as a matter of course. Such movements have been said to be consequences of the fission and fusion of Mississippian organizations or the rise and fall of chiefly polities (Blitz 1999). For instance, the largest and best-known Mississippian center in Georgia, Etowah, was initially a modest place of three small platform mounds before it was briefly abandoned and then reoccupied after A.D. 1250. Like Macon Plateau, the early phases are tentatively dated.[2] During the next century and a quarter, the mounds were considerably enlarged, as Etowah served as the capital of a "complex chiefdom" (King 2003a).

Little is known about the earliest Mississippian "Etowah phase," while the later "Savannah phase" is more easily characterized owing to the discoveries made in Mound C. Here were buried hereditary leaders who imagined themselves the heirs to a superhuman leader similar to the Ho-Chunk hero Red Horn, painted in Gottschall Rockshelter (King 2003a, 2003b). Their depictions of themselves and the trappings of their political culture were the basis for Waring and Holder's Southeastern Ceremonial Complex. As seen here at Etowah, at Spiro, and elsewhere, Mississippian warrior-chiefs were often depicted as "Falcon Impersonators" or as reincarnations of Red Horn, and are shown rolling chunkey stones (see below), wielding scepters, and holding severed human heads with falconoid features (Phillips and Brown 1978). Thus, some variant of the Red Horn story seems to have legitimized Etowah's rulers and, according to King (2003b), served as charters for the establishment of chiefships and chiefly alliances in outlying areas, creating lesser officeholders who would have been beholden to Etowah if only in the reckoning of their genealogies. But this occurred only during the period ca. A.D. 1250–1375, an apparent result of the spread of the Southeastern Ceremonial Complex (Knight et al. 2001). The legend was apparently forgotten thereafter, evaporating from the iconographic repertoire of southeastern artisans.

The Making of a Heartland, ca. A.D. 900–1050

A legend might be considered a difficult if not largely irrelevant thing to trace archaeologically. Perhaps it was only transmitted by word of mouth. Perhaps it changed with each generation, or each retelling. And perhaps it was a fictitious narrative created long after the fact by descendants who had, at best, a vague understanding of the earlier events and characters. Thus, given these potentialities, aspects of a new theory of Mississippian origins might seem like a bolt out of the blue.

Archaeologists are coming to realize that science and legend are not necessarily so far apart. After all, as noted at this chapter's outset, histories are constructed by all people of the past via the manufacturing of craft objects, the weaving of cloth, the mounding of earth, the playing of games, etc. So, can archaeologists see a legend in the making among the remains of the Mississippians? Yes, perhaps.

The story begins in the Arkansas and lower Mississippi alluvial valleys. Between A.D. 700 and 1000, a large ceremonial site sat at the center of the "Plum Bayou culture" (Nassaney 2001; Rolingson 2002). Like those of their Spiroan neighbors upriver to the west and "Coles Creek" neighbors to the south, the mounds of Toltec were not substructural platforms for buildings, but were stages for public displays and feasting. Indeed, according to Michael Nassaney (2001), Toltec's platforms embodied an inclusive sort of centralized corporate authority, with a support population of Plum-Bayou people not quite ready for hierarchy. Sometime after A.D. 1000, Toltec was abandoned, opening up a population vacuum in the central Arkansas River valley. Where did the people go? Non-local pot styles made locally at 11th-century Cahokia indicate that unknown numbers of foreigners from southern Missouri, northeast Arkansas, and southeastern Illinois went there (Pauketat 2003). But wherever Toltecans ended up, their departure was the harbinger of an even more dramatic development happening at about the same time in a wide patch of floodplain near present-day St. Louis, Missouri, locally called the "American Bottom."

The period leading up to A.D. 1000 in the American Bottom was typified by the growth of villages and the intensification of horticultural practices, textile production, feasting, and a new sociality. People added maize to their gardens of native starchy-seed plants, squash, gourds, and sunflowers. They began spinning threads using spindle whorls, suggesting intensified cloth production (Alt 1999). They added red clay slips or films to pots that might have been used in public. And pots from one place were frequently left behind at other places.

In addition, archaeologists find round disks with concave sides at sites that date as early as A.D. 600 in southwestern Illinois and eastern Missouri. These appear to have been the ancient counterpart to the chunkey stones traded north after A.D. 1050 and depicted in Southeastern Ceremonial Complex art even later. The chunkey game typically involved two teams who would throw special sticks after the rolling stone, hurled by one player. As the northern evidence attests, the game was not widely played outside pre-Mississippian villages in the American Bottom region until *after* A.D. 1050. However, by the 18th and 19th centuries, the game was such a high-stakes contest that all of one's worldly possessions, if not one's spouse and children, could be forfeited if a bet was lost, making some so despondent as to commit suicide.

In sum, not only had the public domain in the central Mississippi valley been enlarged and politicized between A.D. 900 and 1050, but there is every reason to suspect the emergence of a new sociality embodied in cloth production, red pots, and an early version of the chunkey game. But this was just the beginning of the story. Around A.D. 1050, the large pre-Mississippian village of Cahokia was rebuilt into a veritable city as part of a unique moment in pre-Columbian history: Cahokia's "Big Bang" (Pauketat 2004).

A tale of one city, ca. A.D. 1050

The new city of Cahokia was planned, sprawling, and monumental. By some measures, it covered 13 km^2 (Fowler 1997). But all measures are somewhat arbitrary, and in reality it is difficult to delineate where Cahokia ended and the rural landscape began (Dalan et al. 2003:87). In part, this is because Cahokia was actually just one of three monumental precincts within a "central political-administrative complex" under construction by the late 11th century (Pauketat 2004). Cahokia was the largest concentration of people and public spaces, its 120 earthen pyramids and spacious central plazas centrally situated in the northern American Bottom. However, East St. Louis's 50 rectangular and circular platform mounds (the second largest Mississippian site anywhere) sat just 6 km to the southwest, connected to Cahokia by a succession of small pyramids and occupation areas strung out along an abandoned riverbank like beads on a necklace. Moreover, just 2 km away and across the Mississippi River were the 26 pyramids and single plaza of the St. Louis site. There were other outlier centers, too, up to 20 km away to the north, east, and south featuring from one to a dozen modest earthen pyramids up to 6 m in height (Figure 8.3).

Accumulated survey and excavation evidence reveals the Cahokia site proper to include clusters of pyramids and plazas surrounded by aggregations of as many as 1,000 or 2,000 houses per km^2 (Pauketat and Lopinot 1997). While population estimates have varied widely, the initial Mississippian Lohmann phase (A.D. 1050–1100) estimates, based on extrapolations of architectural density, range from 10,000 to 15,000 people for the Cahokia site alone. Estimates place the 12th-century population of the American Bottom proper, exclusive of adjacent upland localities, at 40,000 to 50,000 people (Milner 1998; Pauketat 2003). Given the known occupations of the uplands in the 1,000 km^2 area around Cahokia, a regional population in excess of 50,000 is not beyond the realm of possibility.

Evidence from the coring of mounds, geophysical surveys, and large-scale excavations of public and private spaces points toward a founding moment, sometime around A.D. 1050, when many of the earthen pyramids were built, the Grand Plaza was leveled, and hundreds of new hipped-roof houses and public buildings were rigidly sited at orthogonal angles according to Cahokia's master plan (see Fowler 1997; Young and Fowler 2000). That plan likely involved principal north–south and east–west axes that met in the central pyramid, Monks Mound, and the Grand Plaza which it fronted (Dalan et al. 2003: fig. 43). The numerous large, upright cypress posts found at Cahokia and at outlier towns were likely reference points for Cahokia's *axis mundi*. Cahokian surveyors demarcated the master plan in highly visible and redundant ways, making the experience of its spaces simultaneously an inculcation of a Cahokian sense of cosmological order.

Even centrally produced pots coupled routine practices – namely cooking or serving food – with Cahokians' idea of the cosmos. The so-called Ramey Incised jar, a smartly made, shiny black cookpot with a decorated inturned rim, took some skill to produce (Figure 8.4). The vessel was decorated with evocative motifs: eyes, wings, and tail feathers of sky-realm Thunderer deities. These were arranged in

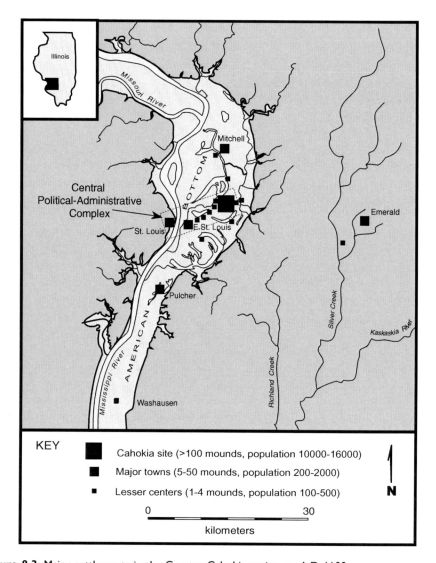

Figure 8.3 Major settlements in the Greater Cahokia region ca. A.D. 1100

quadrants, sometimes with the vessel lip oxidized red, giving the pot's design field a cross-in-circle configuration. For farmers – to whom many were given – the sensuous experience of using a Ramey Incised pot was to reaffirm cosmological order and Cahokia's place within it. As one reached into the earthenware pot's dark interior, one passed metaphorically from or through cosmological order into the earth where crops derived (Pauketat 2004). Thus, through the bodily movements associated with ordinary culinary practices, Cahokia mediated the forces of the universe.

Many of the same people using Ramey Incised pots could look up at any time of the day and view the giant thatched-roof buildings atop Monks Mound, which

Figure 8.4 Ramey Incised vessel rim, Mound 34, Cahokia (in the collections of the University of Michigan, Museum of Anthropology)

itself loomed over the floodplain at 30 m in height by the late 12th century (Figure 8.5). It would have been visible for many kilometers and, not inconsequentially, the people would have been under the watchful gaze of whoever was on top of it. Especially subject to this top-down gaze were those in the expansive plazas located on each of the four sides of Monks Mound, aligned to the cardinal directions. From that vantage point, one could see almost all of the other pyramids at the site *and* those of East St. Louis and St. Louis, including, to the south and west, nine of the ridge-top mortuary mounds famed for their mass burials and elite interments (Figures 8.6 and 8.7).

Unlike most Mississippian capitals, Cahokia's plan consists of a contiguous series of pyramid-and-plaza complexes, giving the place a uniquely agglomerative appearance, as if it grew through the attachment of specific corporate groups, communities, or enclaves. Cahokia looks to have been not one but several Mississippian towns combined into a single composite and "heterarchical" city. The East St. Louis and St. Louis sites, in this light, are simply flanking precincts of the whole. That whole may have consisted of separate cultural entities, status groups, or ritual areas, each associated with one or more of the ridge-top mounds.

Figure 8.5 Aerial view of Cahokia's principal pyramid, Monks Mound

That certain sectors of the site were home to residents who specialized in specific crafts might fit with the agglomerative mode of Cahokia's settlement history (see also Dalan et al. 2003:103). The best documented of these sectors was the so-called Kunnemann tract, located at the northern edge of downtown Cahokia. This tract has produced thousands – possibly tens of thousands – of microlithic drill bits and scraps of mollusk shell and broken beads indicative of intensive bead-and-pendant necklace manufacture (Mason and Perino 1961). Other residential areas have also produced high densities of the microtools, or statistically significant concentrations of spindle whorls, flint chippage, or igneous rock axhead-manufacturing debitage. There are also localized concentrations of broken pottery finewares, weaponry, ritual debris, or feasting detritus apparently associated with the events held in the public and sacred spaces (e.g., Pauketat et al. 2002).

The sociality of mounds

What had happened at A.D. 1050 to lead to all of this? The answer lies in part in the pyramids themselves. Excavations have shown that the earthen fills and surmounting buildings were built, enlarged, and rebuilt annually (Pauketat 2000b). Even if only some of the 200 mounds of the central administrative complex were under construction at A.D. 1050, the rate and scale of pyramid-building would have required builders to exhibit high levels of coordination not previously seen in the region. Would the workers have understood the deeper meanings of pyramids – ideas possibly imported from the Plum Bayou and Coles Creek regions? Or was

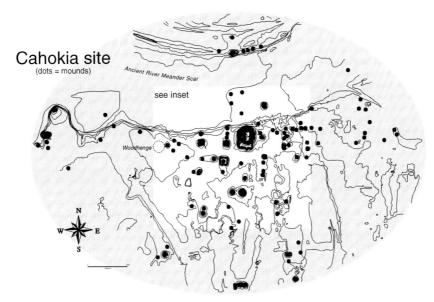

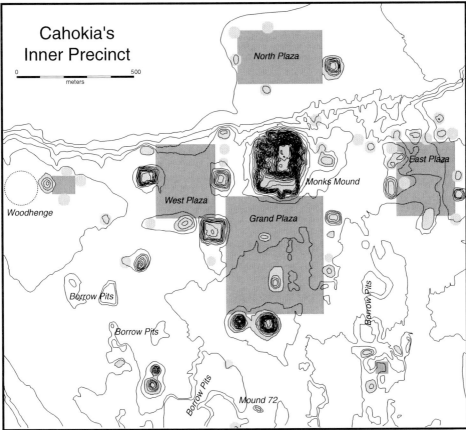

Figure 8.6 Plan view of the Cahokia site (*above*), and inner precinct (*below*) (original base map used by permission of Melvin L. Fowler)

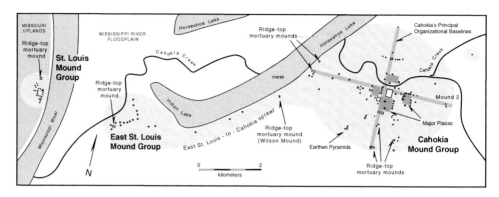

Figure 8.7 Distribution of earthen pyramids in the central political-administrative complex

the coordinated construction of Cahokia's mounds the means whereby disparate local sensibilities were homogenized? Cahokia's mound constructions, in a sense, could have created a new Cahokian memory, society, and ideology even if the idea had been borrowed (by somebody) from the Mid-South (Pauketat and Alt 2003).

Cahokia's new sociality as it involved mound construction is most clear in the unusual ridge-top mound mortuaries built only at and around the central political-administrative complex during the Lohmann and Stirling phases (A.D. 1050–1200). As it turns out, although the largest and most spectacular ridge-tops had been destroyed between 1869 and 1930, Preston Holder was the first professional archaeologist to excavate one of these most important of tombs, albeit under stressful "salvage archaeology" conditions in 1954. Holder excavated what remained of a mass burial of 175 individuals covered with shell beads, whole conch shells, and a chunkey stone after a bulldozer had nearly leveled the Wilson Mound (Young and Fowler 2000:59). Most of these were "secondary bundle burials" except for two women who had been executed and laid alongside the mass interment. One of the women had been decapitated and was missing her hands, while the other – wearing copper-covered earspools – had apparently died at the moment of childbirth, with the fetus trapped in the birth canal (Joyce Wike, personal communication, 2000).

Holder's discovery harkened back to old accounts made during the destruction of other ridge-top mortuaries in the greater Cahokia region, where multiple skeletons were found in two groups or two rows. It also presaged the even more remarkable find of Melvin Fowler in Mound 72 just 13 years later. Fowler, digging a kilometer due south of Monks Mound, happened upon the remains of another central mortuary (Fowler et al. 1999). When all was said and done four years later, he had documented an intricate mortuary program dating late in the Lohmann phase and involving a series of closely spaced events and over 260 bodies, the burials often referencing in some way the famous "beaded burial."

The beaded burial consisted of two men in association with a falcon-shaped cape of 20,000 mollusk-shell beads. One man was atop the cape, and the other was beneath it. Alongside them were a dozen bodies of adults, laid out in two groups, one individual in the first group having been "thrown down or not completely dead when positioned" (Rose 1999:64). Over the second group participants had piled a dozen chunkey stones, copper-covered chunkey sticks, strands of large mollusk-shell beads, a 7-liter heap of mica crystals (imported from the Appalachian mountains), and two piles of bundled arrows of which only the chipped-stone tips survived. Additional heaps of arrowheads, copper sheets, and 36,000 shell beads may have been deposited at this same time at the opposite end of the mortuary area (soon to be mounded over with earth). Not long after the beaded burial, "another pit just a few meters away was filled with the bodies of 53 women, laid out in two rows and in two layers. Associated with this burial of the 53 women were four beheaded and behanded men" (Fowler et al. 1999, cited in Pauketat 2004).

There were other elaborate mortuary rites that followed: more pits filled with women's bodies, more bundled burials, wrapped corpses on litters, and a particularly grisly execution of 39 men and women lined up and arrowshot or clubbed over the head, sometimes with sufficient force to decapitate the victim (Rose 1999). Most of these other group burials betray the same duality evident in the beaded burial; most also were probably public if not highly theatrical affairs (see Emerson and Pauketat 2002). After all, Mound 72 is only 500m south of the very public Grand Plaza where, among other things, huge community feasts were held in the late summer or autumn (Pauketat et al. 2002). Public executions seem an odd inversion of Thanksgiving-style feasts.

The physicality of a legend in the making

Analysts have recognized the parallels between the Mound 72 burials and general themes that run through the folklore of eastern Woodlands Indians. Native people frequently told stories of an Earth or Corn Mother and a male hero or pair of twin-brother heros (Hall 1997). Earth Mother, sometimes associated with the Evening Star, gave people maize, her body issuing forth the sacred crop in some manner. She lorded over the other evening stars, while the Morning Star was the sovereign of the early morning sky. Various Plains and Mississippi valley people believed that the Morning Star had had intercourse with the Evening Star, a union signified by arrow iconography (or perhaps the chunkey game's sticks and stones gendered male and female, respectively). The Pawnee even relived this sacred sex act by shooting an arrow into the heart of a female sacrificial victim (Weltfish 1977[1965]). Meanwhile, the Morning Star, or his cognate a great falconoid Thunderbird who resided in the sky realm, also assumed a human form. In the legends of Siouan-speaking peoples of the upper Midwest and eastern Plains, he was called "Red Horn," a heroic man with a long braid painted red and wearing "human-heads-as-earrings," sometimes able to change himself into an arrow in games against his brothers or against giants who lived under the earth. Two twin boys were born to Red Horn, at least one of these from his union with an underworld giantess, if not Earth Mother herself, before Red Horn was subsequently killed in the underworld. One of the sons – also associated with shell beads, long red hair, and "human heads attached to his nipples rather than to his ears" – resurrected his father and, in a sense, represents the reincarnation of Red Horn (Hall 1997).

Is it not interesting that these legends also seem to be embodied by some of the sculpted Cahokia-style redstone figures and figural smoking pipes that we now know were made sometime just after A.D. 1100 from raw materials available only near Cahokia (Emerson et al. 2003)? There are several depictions of Earth Mother among the Cahokia redstone carvings, as well as male warriors, chunkey players, shamans, and a culture hero who looks very much like Red Horn (Figure 8.8). The latter depiction, carried away to Spiro sometime after it was carved, shows a seated man with a long, forward-hanging braid, a feathered cape, shell bead necklace, human-head earrings, and a diamond-shaped motif on a head plate that constitutes a "locative," denoting action between worlds – this world and the underworld (*sensu* Reilly 2002).

The effect of this carving presumably was to embody the sacred Red Horn narrative in certain contexts where the object was unveiled and smoked by ritual

Figure 8.8 Sculpted Cahokia-style redstone figure from the Spiro site, Oklahoma (redrawn from Pauketat 2004:fig. 5.9)

participants. The various other representations would have done likewise. And, perhaps like these, we can understand the beaded burial complex in Mound 72 to have retold and recast the legend, if not also the related story of Earth Mother, this time embodied by corpses and cultural objects. The cast were all assembled there: twin falconoid men, chunkey players (friends and enemy giants?), an executed four-some (enemy giants?), and possible Earth Mother sacrifices. With them were other pieces of the story: bundles of distinctively Cahokian and foreign-style arrows, a cache of chunkey stones, copper-covered chunkey sticks, and mica crystals (a loca-tive denoting that the people participating in the mortuary theater were translo-cated between this world and the next).

This was quite a powerful rite: people and objects sacrificed in the name of a legend (or a person who would soon become legendary)! Cahokians, it seems, were *physically* constructing their own legendary history. It is not a coincidence, I suspect, that the other objects known from the various destroyed or partially excavated ridge-top mounds include the same array of things thought meaningful in the Red Horn legend and in Mound 72's beaded burial performance: chunkey stones, bead neck-laces, another bead-studded cape, a copper turtle rattle, and at least one pair of copper long-nosed god earpieces like those depicted on the Cahokia-style redstone sculpture of He-who-wears-human-heads-as-earrings (i.e., Red Horn).

In addition, Cahokia-made carved redstone figures, arrowheads, mollusk-shell beads, chunkey stones, Ramey Incised pots laden with the imagery of Thunderers, and a number of pairs of human-head ear ornaments were among those things dis-tributed by Cahokians to distant would-be leaders. The earpieces had long-noses and, according to Robert Hall (1991, 1997), were the insignia of a widespread ritual adoption ceremony not unlike the historically known Calumet (peace pipe) prac-tice, except in that the early Mississippian ceremony created "fictions of kinship between the powerful leader of a large polity [Cahokia] and his political clients in outlying areas" (Hall 1991:33, citing Gibbon 1974). To put it another way, the earpieces were "pieces" of a specific "place" – Cahokia (*sensu* Bradley 2000). They were inalienable things; wearing them evoked Cahokia. There are some 20 instances of long-nosed god ear-ornament finds in the eastern United States, from Red Wing, Minnesota, to Gahagan, Louisiana, and Spiro, Oklahoma. Presumably, there were at least as many instances of Cahokia's ritual adoptions. Legend and archaeology seem to be in agreement.

Chunkey, Culture-Making, and *Pax Cahokiana*, A.D. 1050–1200

To understand the pan-regional historical significance of the dispersal of Cahokian things in terms of a theory of culture making, we should consider the archaeology of the chunkey game. As noted earlier, an ancient version of chunkey was known from the greater Cahokia region as early as A.D. 600. However, chunkey was appar-ently *not* played outside the greater Cahokia region prior to the 10th or 11th century, at which time it was centralized within the Cahokia locality as part of the Big Bang (Pauketat 2004). The earliest region-wide chunkey games there probably took place in the newly leveled plazas where people gathered during semi-annual events that minimally involved feasting, temple renewal, and pyramid construction.

The spacious 19 ha Grand Plaza gives some sense of the potential scale of these games. Thousands of people could have gathered here for impressive festivals including those evidenced in a huge feasting refuse pit (Pauketat et al. 2002). A chunkey game at such times might have drawn on a substantial number of the participants, momentarily uniting Cahokians, local farmers in attendance, recent immigrants, and visitors as members of two opposing teams. Perhaps the team spirit of the game engendered the formation of coalitions whose shared experience of the game might have transcended old pre-Mississippian allegiances, leading to the pervasive community-wide order so evident in Cahokia's public spaces and mortuaries.

Potentially more important than this were the cultural implications of the game. Associated with Falcon Impersonators later in time and with Cahokia's central mortuaries, chunkey may well have been key to the creation of the legendary narratives of Cahokians (for a parallel Mesoamerican argument, see Hill and Clark 2001). Red Horn, it will be remembered, played a game against the underworld giants, and the mica crystals with the beaded burial or the head plate depicted on the red-stone sculpture seem to locate the story between worlds, in cosmological space. Importantly, the chunkey game was probably not an exclusive elite event, but a participatory communal game. At Cahokia, people presumably would have come together to play it under the gaze of those atop the pyramids. In so playing it, people may have been, in an important sense, participating in the construction of a new "political community" complete with its own group memory (Pauketat 2000a). This new order would have located the center of the cosmos in Cahokian space by retelling the story of a legendary hero through the movements of human bodies in the plazas and through the Cahokia-style gaming stones and sticks. If so, the Red Horn legend was not a mere political ideology promulgated by rulers, it was a common sense created by all of those who experienced Cahokia's chunkey games.

Perhaps the appearance of Cahokia-style chunkey stones across the Midwest and Mid-South (alongside local copies) was, then, a pan-regional extension of the same historical process evident at Cahokia proper. That is, the corporeality of Mound 72 and the Cahokian chunkey games is matched by the materiality of Cahokia's pan-regional retelling of the Red Horn saga, seen in the distribution of long-nosed god earrings, sculpted redstone figures and smoking pipes, Cahokia-style arrowheads, Ramey Incised pots featuring the iconography of Thunderers and Earth Mother symbolism, shell beads, and Cahokia-style chunkey stones. Cahokians, it appears, retold the central stories of the ages with their own inalienable cultural objects.

These objects would have been laden with Cahokian narratives telling of previous owners, places, and events, forever linking the recipients to the genealogy of Cahokians. Once again we see control over that which conducts history as a means of controlling history. To put it another way, the chunkey game gave pre-Columbian Mississippi valley history a decidedly Cahokian spin. That spin constituted a common pan-regional identity, or at least a set of memories that may well have located, for a time, the center of the cosmos at Cahokia. The long-term historical effects were profound. This founding city would have assumed the role of cosmo-logical capital that engendered a *pax Cahokiana* in the Mississippi valley.

After a time, of course, the memories of *pax Cahokiana* would have faded, retold through the generations in places and by people with experiences and concerns unlike those of the early Cahokian forebears. At Cahokia, households and corpo-rate groups began to ignore the rules of order at about the same time that the site's impressive 20,000-log palisade wall was built; all of this was happening just a century after Cahokia's explosive beginnings. Ultimately, it seems that factions of would-be ruling families split the Cahokian edifice asunder, and people left the region, some perhaps moving north into the Illinois River valley and others south into Missouri's Bootheel region, where several new (albeit more diminutive) Mis-sissippian polities emerged after A.D. 1150.

Later, these likely Siouan-speaking peoples moved west into the Great Plains, possibly ushering in ethnic strife of a sort that reared its horrific head at Crow Creek. By A.D. 1400, nothing remained of greater Cahokia besides the earthen pyramids to be viewed and reinterpreted by passers by and, finally, archaeologists. But the cultural shockwaves of the Cahokians and their descendants yet rippled in the stories of distant peoples, in their chunkey games, in the iconography of Falcon Impersonators, and in the migrations of those who had experienced Mississippi-anization in positive and negative ways. The upshot? Historically related and yet locally diverse populations.

Conclusion

Mississippianization was a two-way negotiation of memories, legends, and political relationships via human bodies, material culture, and space. It transcended soci-eties and was contingent on local histories of appropriation, accommodation, or resistance. While Cahokian culture contacts politicized and ethnicized many north-erners, their impacts on southerners could have been less dramatic, filtered through extant ceremonial centers and local cultural practices. Each southern locality had its own historical effects. The people of Macon Plateau, for instance, probably ushered in profound historical changes in the Deep South, personified by a dead feline-bird man and embodied in the scale of mound construction.

But it did not last. Etowah's monumentality and mortuary pomp were insuffi-cient to stave off collapse, and the middle-Mississippian Red Horn narrative – foreign to the Deep South – seems to have been forgotten during the various local-ized migrations that followed A.D. 1375. Soon thereafter, the people of Spiro buried a phenomenal hoard of things to memorialize a Southeastern Ceremonial Complex that, in reality, never existed as a homogeneous pan-regional phenomenon (Knight et al. 2001). Even Cahokia's political theater, monumentality, and appropriations of the cosmos did not forestall its abandonment by its support population.

Indeed, given the ritualized violence of the Mound 72 mortuary, we might suspect that Cahokia's hegemony had always been tenuous. When the oppor-tunities arose, the farmers left just several generations after their great-great-grandparents had helped build the first and only pre-Columbian city in the eastern Woodlands. With complete abandonment a century or more later, the idea of Cahokia was lost, perhaps even officially rejected and deconstructed. References to it were nearly erased from the narratives of its likely descendants (DeBoer and Kehoe 1999). What was left was buried among the objects in Spiro's Great Mortuary or retold as the disembedded legends of later peoples.

Mississippian history was forgotten, prompting us to ask questions. To what extent or how did Spiroans, Cahokians, Toltecans, or other early central people ever really control the local populace, homogenize local cultures, or completely convince local farmers to contribute without thought or question the funds and labor needed to build their earthen and wooden monuments? Might the fact that thousands of people vacated the greater Cahokia region over several generations (and possibly tens of thousands depending on birth/death rates) be telling us that social conditions there were intolerable? Did the experience of emigration lead expatriates to forget their heritage? Or did later Dhegiha-Siouan and Caddoan-speaking descendants of Mississippi valley and Arkansas valley peoples stop building mounds in order to knowingly eliminate Mississippian memories?

These questions are just a few that await future archaeologists who have yet to experience and reinterpret the history of the Mississippians. Remembering their history is no insignificant matter. The answers to the questions above are also the answers to questions of how the rise and fall of all past civilizations were matters of culture-making that, in turn, were related to religion, politics, warring, peacemaking, and ethnogenesis. Perhaps understanding such relationships in the past will also help us to understand similar relationships in today's globalizing world.

We have begun to figure out what happened to make people Mississippian and what happened to make them different from one another. The answers, I have argued, lie not in arguments over complexity but in the dimensions of culture-making. The answers will not be easy or uncontroversial. That is as expected. Archaeology is complicated and contentious. History itself is at stake. The experiences of archaeologists who have gone before testify that, when done right, the rewards are rich, the discoveries surprising, and the goals noble. Ask the archaeologists who dug at Aztalan, Crow Creek, Macon Plateau, Spiro, or Toltec. Ask those digging today at Cahokia, Etowah, or Gottschall. They will all answer that we must not forget the history of the Mississippians. Their history is also ours.

NOTES

1   Although guesstimated to date to A.D. 950–1100 (Williams 1994), these horizon markers, and new radiocarbon dates from the Jonathan Creek site in Tennessee, warrant the hypothesis that Macon Plateau was founded early in the 12th century (see Pauketat 2004; Schroeder 2003).

2   Although King (2003a) dates the Early Etowah phase to A.D. 1000–1100, four of the seven radiocarbon dates from four Early Etowah phase features have intercepts of A.D.

1160 to 1238. The one-sigma range of all seven dates falls between A.D. 899 and 1275 (King 2003a:table 8). Given the small excavated sample and limited structural evidence, the 100-year "Late Etowah" phase (A.D. 1100–1200) may in reality encompass the entire early Mississippian component.

REFERENCES

Alt, Susan M., 1999 Spindle whorls and fiber production at early Cahokian settlements. *Southeastern Archaeology* 18, 124–133.

Benn, David W., and Gina Powell, 2002 *Data Recovery Excavations at the Terminal Late Woodland Period Union Bench Site (13DB497), Dubuque County, Iowa*. Report prepared for the Iowa Department of Transportation, Bear Creek Archaeology, Inc., Cresco, Iowa.

Blitz, John H., 1999 Mississippian chiefdoms and the fission-fusion process. *American Antiquity* 64, 577–592.

Bradley, Richard, 2000 *An Archaeology of Natural Places*. London: Routledge.

Brown, James A., 1996 *The Spiro Ceremonial Center: The Archaeology of Arkansas Valley Caddoan Culture in Eastern Oklahoma*. Museum of Anthropology, Memoirs 29. Ann Arbor: University of Michigan.

Cobb, Charles, 2003 Mississippian chiefdoms: How complex? *Annual Review of Anthropology* 32, 63–84.

Dalan, Rinita A., George R. Holley, William I. Woods, Harold W. Watters, Jr., and John A. Koepke, 2003 *Envisioning Cahokia: A Landscape Perspective*. DeKalb: Northern Illinois University Press.

DeBoer, Warren R., and Alice B. Kehoe, 1999 Cahokia and the archaeology of ambiguity. *Cambridge Archaeological Review* 9, 261–267.

Emerson, Thomas E., and Randall E. Hughes, 2000 Figurines, flint clay sourcing, the Ozark Highlands, and Cahokian acquisition. *American Antiquity* 65, 79–101.

Emerson, Thomas E., Randall E. Hughes, Mary R. Hynes, and Sarah U. Wisseman, 2003 The sourcing and interpretation of Cahokia-style figurines in the trans-Mississippi South and Southeast. *American Antiquity* 68, 287–313.

Emerson, Thomas E., and Timothy R. Pauketat, 2002 Embodying power and resistance at Cahokia. In *The Dynamics of Power*. M. O'Donovan, ed. Pp. 105–125. Center for Archaeological Investigations, Occasional Paper 30. Carbondale: Southern Illinois University.

Fairbanks, Charles H., 2003[1956] *Archaeology of the Funeral Mound: Ocmulgee National Monument, Georgia*. Tuscaloosa: University of Alabama Press.

Fowler, Melvin L., 1997 *The Cahokia Atlas: A Historical Atlas of Cahokia Archaeology*, rev. edn. Studies in Archaeology 2. Illinois Transportation Archaeological Research Program. Urbana: University of Illinois.

Fowler, Melvin L., Jerome Rose, Barbara Vander Leest, and Steven A. Ahler, 1999 *The Mound 72 Area: Dedicated and Sacred Space in Early Cahokia*. Reports of Investigations 54. Springfield: Illinois State Museum.

Fritz, Gayle J., 1990 Multiple pathways to farming in precontact eastern North America. *Journal of World Prehistory* 4, 387–435.

Gibbon, Guy E., 1974 A model of Mississippian development and its implications for the Red Wing area. In *Aspects of Upper Great Lakes Anthropology*. E. Johnson, ed. Pp. 129–137. Minnesota Prehistoric Archaeology Series 11. St. Paul: Minnesota Historical Society.

Goldstein, Lynne G., and John D. Richards, 1991 Ancient Aztalan: The cultural and ecological context of a late prehistoric site in the Midwest. In *Cahokia and the Hinterlands:
Middle Mississippian Cultures of the Midwest.* T. E. Emerson and R. B. Lewis, eds. Pp.
193–206. Urbana: University of Illinois Press.

Hall, Robert L., 1991 Cahokia identity and interaction models of Cahokia Mississippian. In
Cahokia and the Hinterlands: Middle Mississippian Cultures of the Midwest. T. E. Emerson
and R. B. Lewis, eds. Pp. 3–34. Urbana: University of Illinois Press.

——1997 *An Archaeology of the Soul: North American Indian Belief and Ritual.* Urbana:
University of Illinois Press.

Hill, Warren D., and John E. Clark, 2001 Sports, gambling, and government: America's first
social compact? *American Anthropologist* 103, 1–15.

Holder, Preston, 1970 *The Hoe and the Horse on the Plains.* Lincoln: University of Nebraska
Press.

Joyce, Rosemary A., 2000 Heirlooms and houses: Materiality and social memory. In *Beyond
Kinship: Social and Material Reproduction in House Societies.* R. A. Joyce and S. D. Gillespie,
eds. Pp. 189–212. Philadelphia: University of Pennsylvania Press.

King, Adam 2003a, *Etowah: The Political History of a Chiefdom Capital.* Tuscaloosa: University of Alabama Press.

——2003b, Etowah–Lake Jackson connections: Ritual adoption, prestige goods exchange,
and status charters. Paper presented at the 60th Annual Meeting of the Southeastern
Archaeological Conference, Charlotte, NC.

Knight, Vernon James, Jr., 2001 Feasting and the emergence of platform mound ceremoni-
alism in eastern North America. In *Feasts: Archaeological and Ethnographic Perspectives on
Food, Politics, and Power.* M. Dietler and B. Hayden, eds. Pp. 311–333. Washington, DC:
Smithsonian Institution Press.

Knight, Vernon James, Jr., James A. Brown, and George E. Lankford, 2001 On the subject
matter of Southeastern Ceremonial Complex art. *Southeastern Archaeology* 20, 129–153.

Krause, Richard A., 1998 A history of Great Plains prehistory. In *Archaeology on the Great
Plains.* W. R. Wood, ed. Pp. 48–86. Lawrence: University of Kansas Press.

Mason, Ronald J., and Gregory Perino, 1961 Microblades at Cahokia, Illinois. *American
Antiquity* 26, 553–557.

Milner, George R., 1998 *The Cahokia Chiefdom: The Archaeology of a Mississippian Society.*
Washington, DC: Smithsonian Institution Press.

Nassaney, Michael S., 2001 The historical-processual development of Late Woodland societies. In *The Archaeology of Traditions: Agency and History Before and After Columbus.* T. R.
Pauketat, ed. Pp. 157–173. Gainesville: University Press of Florida.

Overstreet, David F., 2000 Cultural dynamics of the late prehistoric period in southern
Wisconsin. In *Mounds, Modoc, and Mesoamerica: Papers in Honor of Melvin L. Fowler.* S. R.
Ahler, ed. Pp. 405–438. Scientific Papers Series, vol. 28. Springfield: Illinois State
Museum.

Pauketat, Timothy R., 2000a Politicization and community in the pre-Columbian Mississippi valley. In *The Archaeology of Communities: A New World Perspective.* M. A. Canuto and
J. Yaeger, eds. Pp. 16–43. London: Routledge.

——2000b The tragedy of the commoners. In *Agency in Archaeology.* M.-A. Dobres and J.
Robb, eds. Pp. 113–129. London: Routledge.

——2001 A new tradition in archaeology. In *The Archaeology of Traditions: Agency and History
Before and After Columbus.* T. R. Pauketat, ed. Pp. 1–16. Gainesville: University Press of
Florida.

——2003 Resettled farmers and the making of a Mississippian polity. *American Antiquity* 68,
39–66.

——2004 *Ancient Cahokia and the Mississippians*. Cambridge: Cambridge University Press.

Pauketat, Timothy R., and Susan M. Alt, 2003 Mounds, memory, and contested Mississippian history. In *Archaeologies of Memory*. R. Van Dyke and S. Alcock, eds. Pp. 151–179. Oxford: Blackwell.

Pauketat, Timothy R., Lucretia S. Kelly, Gayle J. Fritz, Neal H. Lopinot, Scott Elias, and Eve Hargrave, 2002 The residues of feasting and public ritual at early Cahokia. *American Antiquity* 67, 257–279.

Pauketat, Timothy R., and Neal H. Lopinot, 1997 Cahokian population dynamics. In *Cahokia: Domination and Ideology in the Mississippian World*. T. R. Pauketat and T. E. Emerson, eds. Pp. 103–123. Lincoln: University of Nebraska Press.

Phillips, Phillip, and James A. Brown, 1978 *Pre-Columbian Shell Engravings from the Craig Mound at Spiro, Oklahoma, Part I*. Cambridge, MA: Peabody Museum Press.

Reilly, Kent, 2002 Vistas of memory: Art and symbolism in the later Mississippian period. Paper presented at the Ancient Cities of Power and Splendor: New Light on Cahokia and the Southeast symposium, the Pre-Columbian Society of Washington, DC.

Rolingson, Martha A., 2002 Plum Bayou culture of the Arkansas–White River basin. In *The Woodland Southeast*. D. G. Anderson and R. C. Mainfort, eds. Pp. 44–65. Tuscaloosa: University of Alabama Press.

Rose, Jerome C., 1999 Mortuary Data and Analysis. In *The Mound 72 Area: Dedicated and Sacred Space in Early Cahokia*. M. L. Fowler, J. Rose, B. Vander Leest, and S. A. Ahler. Pp. 63–82. Reports of Investigations 54. Springfield: Illinois State Museum.

Salzer, Robert J., and Grace Rajnovich, 2000 *The Gottschall Rockshelter: An Archaeological Mystery*. St. Paul, MN: Prairie Smoke Press.

Schroeder, Sissel, 2003 The significance of dating a conflagration at Jonathan Creek. Paper presented at the 60th Annual Meeting of the Southeastern Archaeological Conference, Charlotte, NC.

Smith, Bruce D., 1978 Variation in Mississippian settlement patterns. In *Mississippian Settlement Patterns*. B. D. Smith, ed. Pp. 479–503. New York: Academic Press.

Theler, James L., and Robert F. Boszhardt, 2000 The end of the Effigy Mound culture: The Late Woodland to Oneota transition in southwestern Wisconsin. *Midcontinental Journal of Archaeology* 25, 289–312.

Thomas, Julian, 2001 Archaeologies of place and landscape. In *Archaeological Theory Today*. I. Hodder, ed. Pp. 165–186. Cambridge: Polity.

Van Dyke, Ruth M., and Susan E. Alcock, eds., 2003 *Archaeologies of Memory*. Oxford: Blackwell.

Walker, John W., 1994 A brief history of Ocmulgee archaeology. In *Ocmulgee Archaeology, 1936–1986*. D. J. Hally, ed. Pp. 15–35. Athens: University of Georgia Press.

Waring, Antonio J., and Preston Holder, 1945 A prehistoric ceremonial complex in the southeastern United States. *American Anthropologist* 47, 1–34.

Weiner, Annette, 1994 *Inalienable Possessions: The Paradox of Keeping While Giving Away*. Berkeley: University of California Press.

Weltfish, Gene, 1977[1965] *The Lost Universe: Pawnee Life and Culture*. Lincoln: University of Nebraska Press.

Willey, P., and Thomas E. Emerson, 1993 The osteology and archaeology of the Crow Creek massacre. *Plains Anthropologist* 38, 227–269.

Williams, Mark, 1994 The origins of the Macon Plateau site. In *Ocmulgee Archaeology, 1936–1986*. D. J. Hally, ed. Pp. 130–137. Athens: University of Georgia Press.

Young, Bilone W., and Melvin L. Fowler, 2000 *Cahokia: The Great Native American Metropolis*. Urbana: University of Illinois Press.

9

Beyond the Mold: Questions of Inequality in Southwest Villages

Michelle Hegmon

For more than a century anthropologists have attempted to understand the organization and development of past and present indigenous cultures in the US Southwest, including work that produced some of the classic studies of social organization (e.g., Eggan 1950). However, despite this abundant research, Southwestern societies have remained beyond the mold of neoevolutionary typologies (e.g., Service 1971). On the one hand, this lack of fit has resulted in heated and sometimes unproductive debate, particularly about the presence or absence of "ranking" among the Pueblo peoples of the northern Southwest and their ancestors. On the other hand, lack of fit has prompted Southwestern researchers to also move beyond the mold and explore the diversity of social organizational forms in the Southwest. An understanding of the Southwest is critical for both social theorists and students who wish to grasp the tremendous variety of social processes in pre- and non-state societies.

One key issue is the relationship between social inequality and sociopolitical complexity. Recent research has decoupled these concepts in important ways, demonstrating that inequality is present even in relatively non-complex "egalitarian" societies (Flanagan 1989), and that relatively complex societies can have varying degrees and kinds of social inequality (Blanton et al. 1996). A different sort of decoupling has characterized recent work on the Southwest, as researchers have used or developed models of sociopolitical complexity that assume relatively little inequality between individuals.

This chapter focuses specifically on the existence and nature of social inequality in the prehispanic (pre-A.D. 1540) US Southwest (Figure 9.1), though of course inequality is linked to political and leadership strategies and the organization of complexity. I define inequality in the broadest sense as socially consequential unequal access to what Anthony Giddens (1984) calls authoritative and allocative resources, which include everything from material goods and productive capacity to knowledge and leadership roles. My primary focus is on inequality that

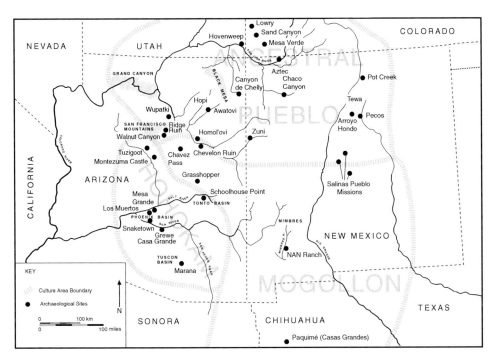

Figure 9.1 Map of the Southwest, showing principal culture areas and sites mentioned in text (after Plog 1997: fig. 149)

cross-cuts age and gender lines, though of course gender and other lines of social differentiation are interrelated.

Culture-Historical Background

The archaeological region known as the US Southwest encompasses most or all of New Mexico and Arizona as well as parts of Texas, Colorado, Utah, Nevada, Chihuahua, and Sonora. The region is broadly divided into three general culture areas: Hohokam/Salado in southern Arizona; Mogollon, across much of the southern and central Southwest; and Ancestral Pueblo (formerly called Anasazi) in the north. I focus here on the period after the development of the earliest villages (i.e., around A.D. 800 in the north, earlier in the Hohokam region). The three largest and most elaborate political developments in the Southwest were Casas Grandes (usually classified as Mogollon), Chaco (Ancestral Pueblo), and Hohokam (both the pre-Classic regional system and the Classic in the Phoenix and Tucson Basins). However, since the first two (Casas Grandes and Chaco) are covered by Lekson (this volume), I do not discuss them in detail. As a result, my discussion of complexity and clear-cut inequality is somewhat biased toward the Hohokam.

Across much of the Southwest, the centuries prior to A.D. 1150 were times of growth and expansion, including the development of the Chaco and pre-Classic

Hohokam regional systems and the Classic Mimbres florescence. The end of the Hohokam regional system (which spread across much of southern Arizona) was followed by more localized intensification, known as the Hohokam Classic (A.D. 1150–1450) focused in the Phoenix and Tucson basins. Ballcourts, the primary form of public architecture in the Hohokam pre-Classic, were replaced by platform mounds in the Classic. In the northern Southwest, although the Chaco regional system ended by the mid-1100s, settlement continued in many areas. Then, just prior to A.D. 1300, large parts of the northern Southwest were depopulated or even abandoned completely. This is the beginning of the Pueblo IV (A.D. 1300–1540) period, and it represents a marked change in settlement, ritual organization, and site structure. Many of the people who left the northern Southwest moved to the eastern part of the Southwest, along the Rio Grande. Also by A.D. 1300 distinctions between Mogollon and Ancestral Pueblo had mostly disappeared.

Ethnography has provided great insights for Southwest archaeologists. Perhaps obviously, there are fairly direct lines between Ancestral Pueblo remains and contemporary Pueblo societies, which have been the subject of much ethnographic research. Contemporary pueblos also trace their roots to Mogollon and Salado remains, although these lines are less straightforward. There are certainly links between Hohokam remains and contemporary O'odham speakers (including the Pima and Tohono O'odham) in southern Arizona, although again the line is less than straightforward because of major changes and depopulations at the end of the Hohokam sequence.

Historical Perspectives

Early anthropological research in the Southwest generally assumed that some kind of powerful leaders or chiefs were part of Southwestern society, past and present. But as archaeologists began to focus on details of past social organization, especially as part of the New Archaeology in the 1960s, many worked with the assumption that Pueblo (or sometimes all Southwestern) societies, which generally lack overt displays of wealth, were egalitarian. This perspective may harken back to Ruth Benedict's (1934) characterization of the Zuni as Apollonian, and it has also been bolstered by ethnographic literature that emphasizes integration and especially kinship, since kin-based organization is traditionally contrasted with the political organization/government of complex societies. Ethnographers have certainly described non-egalitarian aspects of Pueblo society – Dozier (1970:154) discusses "despotic rule by the religious-political hierarchy" – though political processes and inequality tend to be underplayed.

In the 1970s a number of archaeological studies concluded that there had been considerable sociopolitical complexity in the Southwest (Upham 1982:2). Although the multidimensional nature of social complexity was recognized, by the 1980s focus was primarily on the question of whether the pueblos were or were not ranked/egalitarian (summaries are provided by Feinman 2000; McGuire and Saitta 1996). Those arguing for the presence of ranking pointed to multi-tiered settlement patterns, labor-intensive monumental architecture, and uneven distributions of elaborate artifacts; advocates of egalitarianism focused on the dearth of rich burials or elite residences. Debate was often vituperative, with researchers seemingly talking past each other. One possible reason for the divergent conclusions may have been that advocates of ranking focused on evidence for overall complexity, whereas advocates of egalitarianism focused on the lack of evidence for personal aggrandizement.

One of the most detailed (and strongly criticized) arguments was made by Upham, who argued that the 14th-century "regional system contained sets of competing centers that were controlled by relatively centralized decision-making hierarchies and linked by commodity exchange" (1982:164). Pueblo population levels certainly have declined substantially since European contact. Upham argues that prehispanic population levels were very high and declined precipitously as a result of epidemics, though others (e.g., Reff 1987) do not see much evidence for epidemics or massive population reductions. Upham argued that prehispanic societies were likely much more complex than those described by ethnographers. Among other things, Upham viewed an uneven distribution of polychrome pottery (found primarily at the largest sites) as evidence for "status hierarchies [that] controlled the distribution of and restricted the access to these commodities" (1982:133). He also found evidence of hierarchy in the mortuary remains at Chavez Pass (the focus of his research) and at the contemporary site of Grasshopper.

Others strongly disagreed with Upham, for at least two reasons. First, he had cited (1982:133) early studies based on small samples of burials at Grasshopper. Later analyses based on larger collections (e.g., see summary in Whittlesey and Reid 2001) found little evidence of social hierarchy. Second, it became clear that the uneven ceramic distribution resulted from temporal differences; that is, the smaller sites which lacked polychrome ceramics were earlier (Cordell 1999:90; Henderson 1979). Today there seems to be little dispute regarding the ceramic distribution, but interpretation of the mortuary evidence at both sites is far from resolved, and apparently contradictory evidence has recently been interpreted as a dialectic of equality and hierarchy (McGuire and Saitta 1996).

Several lines of thinking and research helped move archaeology beyond the either/or (egalitarian *or* ranked) debate. First, Upham's work directed focus toward more nuanced readings of ethnographies. He drew in part on work by ethnographer Elizabeth Brandt, who later (1994) summarized ethnographic evidence that pueblos fit a textbook definition of stratified societies:

> Using standard criteria for stratification, the Pueblos as a type must be seen as stratified and hierarchical, with varying degrees of centralized coercive political authority and power, and unequal access and control over resources. They have elites and well-developed systems of social ranking that are recognized in terminological and behavioral differences. (Brandt 1994:20)

Among other things, Brandt and Upham emphasized that, although there were relatively few marked differences in material wealth, there were substantial hereditary differences in access to ritual knowledge, knowledge that could lead to political and economic power, including control of land. Even in the clan-based western Pueblos, certain clans (or lineages) dominated ritually (and possibly in terms of access to land), and within those clans certain individuals inherited access to important leadership roles. Second, general theoretical statements (Flanagan 1989; Paynter 1989) argued that some kinds of social inequality were pervasive even in what were generally considered to be egalitarian societies. And in the same year Johnson (1989) argued that, although Southwestern societies were not complex in the same way as the Near Eastern civilizations he studied, there are other ways of thinking about social hierarchies. By the 1990s, many Southwest archaeologists had begun to focus on issues such as leadership strategies, alternative forms of organization, or dimensions of complexity. My discussion in the remainder of this chapter focuses on this literature.

Political Organization

Neo-evolutionary schemes had assumed a fairly neat correspondence between scale, political organization, and degree of social inequality. Populations of more than 1,000–2,500 at some Southwestern settlements suggest that some kind of complex political organization was present (Kosse 1996). Although concepts of political organization and hierarchy have been decoupled in recent research, some discussion of political forms and leadership strategies is necessary for understanding social inequality.

The distinction between *corporate* and *network* leadership strategies put forth by Blanton et al. (1996) has been influential in the Southwest. The corporate–network and egalitarian–hierarchical continua are different dimensions, and while corporate strategies may be associated with very large political formations (such as Teotihuacan), they are characterized by a de-emphasis of individual leaders. Masking, which is common in Pueblo societies, is one means of de-emphasizing individuals (Mills 2000a:8–9, citing Steiner 1990). Feinman et al. (2000; see also Feinman 2000) argue that corporate strategies became increasingly important in the Southwest after the pithouse-to-pueblo transition (ca. A.D. 800), in part because architectural and other evidence indicates that the scale of organization and political action increased at this time. Bayman (2002) similarly sees the beginning of the Hohokam Classic as involving a shift to more corporate strategies. His argument is based on the distribution of artifacts associated with leadership (e.g., shell trumpets, copper bells, turquoise mosaics); these were associated primarily with individual males (burials) in the pre-Classic, but mostly on or near platform mounds in Classic.

Another dimension of organization emphasized by Saitta (1994; see also McGuire and Saitta 1996) concerns the production and distribution of surplus labor, that is, labor beyond what is needed to meet subsistence needs. Uneven distribution of surplus labor is the basis of social inequality, but marked individual inequalities result only when surplus labor is appropriated by specific individuals (subsumed labor flow). In contrast, *communalism*, or the collective appropriation of surplus labor and its products, can be the basis of large-scale organization and mobilization, in the absence of individual elites. Developments in Chaco Canyon and in post-Chacoan villages in the central Southwest are interpreted as evidence for communalism, though in all cases there is also evidence of tension, as well as relatively hierarchical formations.

Political forms that involve large-scale organization but relatively little inequality include *confederacies* (alliances among relatively equal tribes or villages) and *heterarchies* (in which different leaders predominate in different realms [Crumley 1995; Rautman 1998]). Spielmann (1994) originally proposed that clusters of villages in the post-1300 Rio Grande region were organized as confederacies, though later research revealed that villages within a cluster tended to dominate in different realms (Graves and Spielmann 2000). In a similar vein, Rice (1998, 2000) argues that Hohokam and Salado irrigation systems were not managed through a centralized political authority but rather that the organization was a product of segmentary competition, often leading to warfare. While Rice does not suggest that the Hohokam/Salado were egalitarian, he does argue against the presence of a centralized decision-making hierarchy.

Two key trends characterize recent research on political organization in the prehispanic Southwest, as summarized above. First, there are few overt disagreements with Brandt's (1994) ethnography-based argument that the Pueblos are/were stratified; indeed, her chapter is (positively) cited very widely. Second, there is considerable emphasis on models of complex political organizations that involve either minimal individual social differentiation or non-material differentiation. The potentially contradictory elements of these trends have received little attention, and I suggest that (despite the citations of Brandt) there has been some reluctance to discard the egalitarian assumption. A better understanding of social inequality – the focus of this chapter – is needed to address and possibly resolve this apparent contradiction.

The Basis of Inequality

A general definition of inequality as socially consequential unequal access to resources links aspects of the social and material realms in ways that are theoretically interesting but methodologically potentially problematic. In this section, I attempt to maintain some level of distinction between the distribution of resources (authoritative and allocative) and social relations, in order to understand their interrelations. Specifically, drawing on ethnographic and archaeological accounts from across the Southwest, I consider what, if anything, is distributed unequally and what the distribution means regarding the nature of social inequality. In general, I use the term "unequal" with regard to the distribution of resources, and "inequality" with regard to social relations. I consider an uneven distribution to be evidence for social inequality if (1) there is evidence that access was deliberately/socially restricted; or (2) there is evidence that the unevenness had real social or material consequences.

Ritual

Ethnographic accounts of Pueblo society describe considerable inequality with regard to ritual, in several respects. Rituals and sacred knowledge (as well as ritual paraphernalia) are generally controlled (or even owned) by a restricted segment of society, and intellectual property is protected through elaborate secrecy mechanisms in some eastern pueblos. The Tewa (an eastern Pueblo group) divide human society into three hereditary categories, including the most auspicious "Made People," who comprise eight priesthoods that coordinate the religious as well as political and economic life of the Pueblo (Ortiz 1969). Among the western Pueblos, certain powerful clans or kinship groups control both the knowledge and the paraphernalia associated with necessary rituals. In some cases individuals or restricted groups even own or control ritual spaces (kivas and shrines). In many respects control of ritual can be considered an authoritative or power resource (see Potter and Perry 2000), and it can also have direct material consequences: for example, calendrical knowledge regarding agriculture would create an avenue for leaders to have access to more crops.

While ritual-based inequality may not involve major differences in material wealth, and thus can be difficult to detect archaeologically, it is not invisible. Architecture provides important archaeological evidence of restrictions on access to ritual. Some sites have more, or more elaborate, public architecture than others, and access to these sites or to the public architecture was often restricted by surrounding walls or other construction techniques. Whether or not these patterns should be interpreted as evidence of social inequality depends on the overall context, in terms of both time and space. In general, evidence for restrictions on access is best interpreted in comparison with occupations where such restrictions appear to be minimal. Thus I structure this discussion not chronologically but in order to facilitate comparisons.

Probably the most clear-cut evidence of social inequality in ritual access is seen in Classic Hohokam/Salado remains: platform mounds, surrounded by substantial compound walls, were clearly important loci for rituals, and their elevated position would have provided a broad "view-shed" for leaders to look down on surrounding compounds and monitor activities (Figure 9.2). A few people lived on the mounds (at least in the later Classic), some lived within the compounds, and many lived outside of the compounds, an arrangement interpreted as "exclusionary" (Gregory 1987; Harry and Bayman 2000; Wilcox 1991). Pre-Classic ritual architecture (i.e., ballcourts) provides an important point of contrast that bolsters this interpretation. Although ballcourts are generally found only at larger sites, they are typically interpreted as loci for community gatherings. Ballcourts are not surrounded by walls and they seem to have been constructed (surrounded by gradually sloping berms) so as to accommodate many spectators/participants (Figure 9.3). Wilcox and Sternberg (1983) estimated that the entire village of Snaketown could have attended games/events in the local ballcourt. The construction of steep-sided mounds and surrounding walls in the subsequent period would

Figure 9.2 Platform mounds inside compound walls at the Casa Grande site

have represented a stark and socially significant break with this tradition. The distribution of ritual artifacts, which are more common in association with the
mounds, supports this interpretation of exclusionary tactics in the Classic. For
example, *Conus* shell tinklers (interpreted as part of ritual costumes) were mostly
found at platform mound communities, suggesting that "fewer people participated
directly in the ritual dimensions of Sonoran Desert social life in the Classic period"
(Bayman 2002:83).

In the Puebloan Southwest there is evidence of uneven access to ritual, though
the nature of the unevenness, the extent to which it resulted from deliberate restrictions, and the relationship to social inequality vary across time and space. Again,
patterns of change provide some of the clearest insights. Some of the earliest
Puebloan villages (in the late Basketmaker III and Pueblo I periods, ca. A.D.
700–900) typically have great kivas – interpreted as community gathering-places –
on the periphery of residential areas. However, at a time of in-migration in the 800s,
people in the Dolores River valley (southwest Colorado) began building smaller
but elaborate ritual structures, and in almost all instances these were built in
walled-off areas surrounded by relatively large pueblos. This new form lasted only
a few decades, and when people left the area they apparently returned to the earlier,
more communal form of ritual architecture. Schachner (2001) suggests that these

Figure 9.3 Ballcourt at the Casa Grande site

developments represented a (failed) attempt by burgeoning leaders/elites to institute a new kind of ritual control by restricting access to ritual.

The same general forms of Puebloan ritual architecture continue until around
A.D. 1300, though ritual architecture is increasingly incorporated into sites, and
larger sites consistently have more special ritual spaces (such as great kivas) and a
higher ratio of kivas to habitation rooms (Feinman 2000). These larger sites are
generally interpreted as community centers (Varien 1999), with the implication that
people who lived in surrounding smaller sites shared access to the ritual structures.
While this interpretation is not unreasonable, only some people lived in sites with
important ritual structures and thus would have had more direct access to ritual
than others. The same could be said of (roughly contemporaneous) Hohokam
ballcourts, also found on larger sites. However, in contrast to ballcourts, which seem
to have been designed so as to maximize open access, the boundaries of some
Pueblo sites were marked with various kinds of architectural features, including low
walls, suggestive of social restrictions. Also, the placement of some habitation rooms
in the late Pueblo III site of Sand Canyon Pueblo suggests that leaders may have
maintained special control over ritual facilities (Lipe 2002).

In the subsequent (post A.D. 1300) Pueblo IV period, different patterns emerge.
On the one hand, architectural boundaries are quite clear-cut, in that Pueblo IV

villages enclose and restrict access to formal plazas. Uneven distributions of ritually important fauna and artifacts – at the intra and inter-site level and in mortuary remains – all also suggest that access to Pueblo IV ritual was uneven (Graves and Spielmann 2000; Howell 2001; Potter and Perry 2000). This arrangement is not unlike that seen in the Hohokam Classic, though with at least one major difference. Among the Classic Hohokam it appears that some people – those who lived on or near the mounds – had much more direct access to ritual than others. In contrast, in Pueblo IV times most people lived in villages with plazas; thus plaza-based rituals would have been internally inclusive (Crown and Kohler 1994; Potter 2000; Potter and Perry 2000).

In summary, in the Hohokam region by the Classic period there is strong evidence that a limited group of people had special access to or control over ritual and others were excluded. In contrast, although various lines of evidence suggest various ways that ritual was somehow restricted in the Pueblo area, there is no time and place in which it appears that certain groups/classes of people were prevented from participating in public rituals. Although we know from ethnographic accounts that ritual knowledge was often tightly controlled in Pueblo society, access to the rituals themselves does not seem to have become exclusionary.

Productive resources

Ethnographic accounts make clear that productive resources were distributed unequally among Southwestern peoples. At Hopi, Levy (1992) documents that access to prime land was unequal and recent migrants were often forced to farm the poorest areas. Brandt (1994:16) reports that leaders may control more than half of a community's land. And Parsons (1939) found that leaders' fields were frequently worked by others. Similarly, leaders may have had more access to large game, both by controlling the distribution of hunted meat and by having special hunting privileges (Potter and Perry 2000:71). Simulation studies (Pauketat 1996) demonstrate that even minor differences in access to productive resources can develop into significant differences in accumulation and debt.

Unequal access to productive resources raises two interrelated interpretive issues. First, scarcity may have been at least as important as surplus, and Levy (1992) argues that inequality is a means of manipulating scarcity. Thus, in stressful times "hierarchy becomes the means to expel some portion of the population" (McGuire and Saitta 1996:209). Simulation studies (Hegmon 1991) also indicate that restrictions on access are an important means of managing irregular yields. Obviously, the relative importance of surplus vs. scarcity would have been different in different times and places. Johnson (1989) argues that the possibilities for surplus production in and around Chaco Canyon were minimal (in contrast to Mesopotamia) and thus that inequalities were unlikely to be based on surpluses. However, Plog (1995) notes that at least two cases (Casas Grandes and Hohokam) with relatively clear-cut inequality are also associated with surplus production. Second, the relative importance of surplus vs. scarcity also affects the nature of leadership. If surplus production was possible, then elite status may have been linked to wealth or elites' ability to control surpluses. In these cases, it is reasonable to ask how inequality was financed (Plog 1995:196). In contrast, if scarcity was the major issue, then although elites may have managed production, it is unlikely that such control was the basis of their status. Most Southwestern ethnographies concern areas where scarcity is more likely than surplus, but in other areas of the world such as the New Guinea Highlands, it is clear that individual leaders (i.e., big men) or elite lineages emerge in part because of their control of wealth.

Archaeological evidence for unequal distributions of larger game and unequal access to food storage areas is widespread (e.g., Graves and Spielmann 2000; Potter 2000; Potter and Perry 2000). In most cases there are few data regarding whether these uneven distributions had a real effect on diet and nutrition. One exception is Chaco Canyon, where Akins (1986) found that residents of Chacoan Great Houses were better off nutritionally than those in the small sites.

The relationship between productive resources and social inequality depends heavily on whether land or labor is a primary limiting factor. In the case Levy (1992) describes at Hopi, highly productive land was in short supply, thus lower-status latecomers had limited access to this prime land. Several archaeological studies of population movements suggest similar dynamics were present in the past. Specifically, Shafer – drawing on construction dates and paleoclimatic reconstructions – argues that immigrants joined the Classic Mimbres NAN Ranch Village community in times of drought (1999). Mimbres mortuary remains, which include multiple sub-floor burials in what appear to be core habitation rooms, are interpreted as a means of asserting long-established claims to land. Similarly, migrants into Classic Hohokam sites may have had limited access to prime fields or irrigation systems (Elson and Abbott 2000:132). Harry and Bayman (2000) suggest that immigrants to the Classic Hohokam Marana community were excluded from established trade networks. In the Tonto Basin, although there was probably no shortage of land, immigrant settlements were on the edge of local systems and may have been forced/expected to be a defensive outpost (Elson et al. 2000).

In contrast, if labor, rather than land, were in short supply, newcomers would have been welcome. With the possible exception of the horrific La Plata case (discussed in the next paragraph) I know of no archaeological evidence of elite control of others' labor in the Southwest, though such evidence would be difficult to come by except in extreme cases where laborers were abused. However, several studies do suggest that labor was in demand and social units at various scales may have competed to attract migrants and young people. In one pre-Classic Hohokam case, surpluses derived from canal irrigation may have been the goal (McGuire 1992); in two others the environment probably precluded surplus production (Herr 1999; Stone and Downum 1999). These interpretations have complicated implications regarding social inequality. On the one hand, if labor was valued, then inequalities within units might have been minimized, an interpretation supported by McGuire's (1992, 2001) mortuary analysis, which shows that young people (i.e., prime laborers) were treated particularly well at death. On the other hand, success in labor recruitment might have been the basis for growing inequalities between social units.

Finally, there is at least one case in the prehispanic Southwest in which it appears that a group of people was systematically denied access to the basic necessities of life. La Plata River valley (northern New Mexico) was a relatively lush productive environment. Yet in remains from this area dating from approximately 1000–1300, there is a set of female burials that reveal stark evidence of overwork and maltreatment, including bodily violence that resulted in broken bones. This is different from the violence of warfare (of which there is increasing evidence in the Southwest). Rather, Martin and Akins (2001:244) suggest that these women represent a subclass, possibly of recent migrants, treated like indentured servants, and controlled by elites or an owning class "who had the power to enforce domination of this subgroup."

Material goods

One reason that issues of inequality are so complex in the Southwest is that there is, or at least seems to be, relatively little material differentiation, even when there are ethnographic reports of elites. Archaeologically, there is a *general* correlation between relatively complex political developments, settlement size, and material elaboration, including elaborate construction as well as the circulation of exotics and preciosities, such as turquoise, cotton, and polychrome (Plog 1995:200). The issue, however, is whether access to these special materials was restricted, a question that involves at least two dimensions. First, did some people/elites have more (quantity or quality) than others, were they materially richer? Second, did some people have special control over goods desired or needed by others?

Ethnographically and archaeologically, evidence for the first kind of differentiation is minimal. One possible exception is O'odham oral traditions that describe oppression by elites who lived in Hohokam Great Houses (Teague 1993). But otherwise, even in cases, as described above, where there is unequal access to means of production (land or labor) this does not seem to result in marked differences in material goods or residences. In almost all archaeological cases, detailed analyses of the distribution of material at the intra-site or intra-community level reveal little marked differentiation, suggesting that access to these materials was not limited to one class of people. Specific studies include Seymour's (1988) analysis of marine shell bracelets at the Hohokam pre-Classic site of Snaketown and multiple studies of iconographic (and perhaps symbolically charged) Pueblo IV pottery styles (e.g., Crown [1994] regarding Salado Polychrome; Hays [1989] regarding Katsina motifs; and van Keuren [2000] on Fourmile Polychrome). Even in the Hohokam Classic, evidence for unequal distributions is subtle. Detailed studies of Marana, a non-core early Classic platform mound, revealed little evidence of uneven distribution within the compound. Furthermore, although there were robust differences across the community, no artifact classes were exclusively associated with the platform mound (Bayman 2002; Fish and Fish 2000; Harry and Bayman 2000).

Architectural differentiation is similarly minimal. In the Pueblo areas, most residences were relatively similar to one another in terms of room size and

Figure 9.4 Multi-story adobe Great House at the Casa Grande site

construction; there are exceptions (e.g., NAN Ranch village) but the level of differentiation is fairly minimal. As mentioned above, some Pueblo III habitation
rooms are associated with ritual structures and are thought to have been occupied
by leaders who controlled the rituals, but these rooms are do not stand out in terms
of their construction or size (Lipe 2002). Of course there are extraordinarily elaborate structures (e.g., Chacoan Great Houses), but these do not appear to be primarily residential, and the possible habitation areas within them are internally not
much different than residential areas in contemporary small sites. In the later part
of the Hohokam Classic what appear to be residential structures were built on top
of platform mounds (Figure 9.4). While most researchers (see Elson and Abbott
2000; Gregory 1987; Wilcox 1991.) interpret these as elite residences, they are
special primarily in terms of location, rather than construction style.

In contrast, there is myriad evidence in the Southwest of uneven control over
the production and distribution of what Spielmann (2002) terms "socially valued
goods." Once again many Southwestern cases are not a good fit for the classic
molds, in part because the value and control involve ritual and knowledge as well
as material. I discuss several issues with regard to production, distribution, and
exchange networks.

Specialized craft production has been documented in many instances in the
prehispanic Southwest. Cross-culturally, specialization is sometimes the purview
of relatively impoverished communities with limited potential for agriculture (what

Brumfiel and Earle [1987] call *productive specialization*). Conversely, in other instances elite households manufacture valuable crafts, an organizational form known as *embedded specialization*. Specialized large-scale manufacture of shell ornaments in non-riverine parts of the Hohokam area (Howard 1993; McGuire and Howard 1987) may be an example of productive specialization (although Hohokam specialized production is not always associated with agricultural poverty [Harry 2000]). Also in the Hohokam area there are some indications of embedded specialization (see summary in Mills 2000b). Specifically, communities associated with platform mounds produced more special goods, including shell as well as agave (Fish and Fish 2000), and the intra-site distribution of shell-working debris indicates that production was concentrated in certain households (Seymour and Schiffer 1987). Neitzel (1991) argued that shell jewelry was a Hohokam status item beginning in the later pre-Classic.

Other studies of craft production and specialization in the Southwest do not fit either the embedded or productive specialization models. In a number of cases the goods and materials from certain places seem to have become particularly sought after, in ways that would have contributed to social inequalities, despite the fact that apparently similar goods would have been widely available. Spielmann (2002), drawing on Richard Bradley's "pieces of place" concept, suggests that the places with which those goods were associated, and perhaps the people from those places, gained some special cultural significance (see also Pauketat, this volume). One example involves Fourmile Polychrome ceramics, which appeared ca. A.D. 1325 and are characterized by asymmetrical representational motifs with possible ritual significance. In contrast to earlier geometric types, Fourmile Polychrome was produced only in a restricted area of eastern Arizona. Van Keuren's (2000) detailed analysis of the design execution suggests that people outside of this area attempted to copy/emulate the designs but were not familiar with the principles of Fourmile design execution. Another example concerns 15th-century glaze-painted pottery from the eastern Pueblo area. The pottery was made in a number of locations (using similar techniques and recipes), and potters could have obtained lead (necessary for the glaze paint) from various sources. However, lead isotope analyses (Habicht-Mauche et al. 2000) show most potters obtained their lead from one source and thus that communities near this source may have controlled its distribution. These findings suggest that many wanted what few controlled or could produce (e.g., "real" Fourmile designs, lead from the "right" source), although it is not clear if the materials were desired because they were produced or controlled by special people or if some people were special because of their special relation to the material, or (most likely) if the causality between special status and special goods was complex and recursive.

One much-discussed model for understanding linkages between material goods and social inequality involves the prestige goods economy, which posits that powerful people controlled access to goods that were necessary for social reproduction (e.g., goods needed to legitimate marriage). Unfortunately, archaeological signatures of prestige goods economies are likely to be subtle, since the valuables are necessary for most people and thus would be found in most contexts, although there might be more in association with powerful people. One very large-scale analysis of the pan-Southwest distribution of marine shell found little support for a prestige goods model in the Hohokam area (Bradley 2000). However, evidence from a more detailed study of Hohokam shell (Bayman 2002) could be interpreted in terms of a prestige goods model (although this is my conclusion, not necessarily Bayman's). Bayman argues that widely distributed *Glycymeris* shell bracelets were important "symbols of membership" in Hohokam society, and in the Classic period, the importation and production of these was concentrated at platform mounds. This distribution *could* result from politically powerful people controlling access to goods that were necessary for social reproduction, although other interpretations are possible as well.

Finally, in earlier literature there is much discussion of the elite control of exchange, including managerial models (e.g., Neitzel 1991; Teague 1985) and alliances that controlled the distribution of valuable goods such as polychrome ceramics (e.g., Cordell and Plog 1979; Upham 1982). However, recent analyses have refuted these suggestions in a number of cases. For example, Adams et al. (1993) found that, although Jeddito Yellow Ware was made by a limited number of people (community specialization), it was widely distributed in many contexts and not controlled by elites. Salado Polychrome also does not fit the mold, although for different reasons: This distinctive, widespread type was actually locally made in numerous locations (Crown 1994). Considering pottery as well as other materials, Rice (2000) found no support for the argument that elites at Salado platform mounds managed or controlled access to long-distance exchange. Cordell (1999) recently made clear that she no longer accepts the earlier arguments, to which she contributed, for elite alliances.

Treatment at death

An enormous amount of theoretical and empirical work in recent decades makes clear that treatment at death is by no means a direct reflection of treatment during life. Accepting this general premise, here I will consider evidence for variable treatment at death and how this variability has been interpreted regarding issues of inequality in the Southwest. Goldstein (2001:250) summarizes the situation for the Southwest as a whole as indicative of relatively little inequality: "I am more struck by the variability and *lack* of differentiation in mortuary practices than I am by strong evidence of ranking or stratification." However, in a number of contexts there are indications of various kinds of inequality in the mortuary record, and these can be divided into three general categories.

First, in only a few cases in the prehistoric Southwest are there elaborate and expensive burials, clearly different from other contemporary graves, that can reasonably be interpreted as evidence of hereditary elites. Specifically, among the Classic Hohokam there are burials (inhumations) that stand out because they were placed in specially prepared graves (adobe-lined pits and even sarcophagi), often located in special places (on or near platform mounds), and because they have more goods (especially more whole and exotic goods) than others (Mitchell and Brunson-Hadley 2001). A similar situation may be present in the late Gila phase (A.D. 1320–1450) Salado area, where an elaborate log-cribbed multiple interment was found in association with the Schoolhouse Point platform mound (Loendorf [2001] describes the pattering, though the conclusion regarding evidence for an elite class is mine, not necessarily his; see also Fish and Fish [2000]). Hohmann (2001) makes a similar argument for the Late Elden phase in northern Arizona, although the graves he identifies (statistically) as elites are not especially distinct or rich.

A cluster of burials in the northern part of Pueblo Bonito, Chaco Canyon, may also fit this category, although the patterning is somewhat enigmatic (see Lekson, this volume). The burials' placement in this enormous Great House was unusual, they were interred with enormous numbers of ornaments, and their stature was greater and health during life better than that of their contemporaries (Akins 2001). However, the labor involved in their interment was not extraordinary, and at least one seems to have been killed in battle. Thus it may be that the special burial had to do more with an extraordinary death than with social inequality during life. Also, it may be noteworthy that these burials are relatively early in the Chaco sequence and predate the height of Great House construction.

Second, in many times and places in the Southwest there are a few graves that are somewhat different and more elaborate than others within a given cemetery or local context. Also, there are a few individual graves that are exceptionally rich, though they do not appear to be part of an overall burial tradition (and thus are different from the first category, discussed in the preceding paragraphs). Both kinds of cases can be interpreted as evidence of leaders (religious or otherwise), though not necessarily as elites. Examples of the first case (sets of slightly more elaborate graves) are numerous. They are seen among the Hohokam Classic (Mitchell and Brunson-Hadley 2001) and pre-Classic (Neitzel's [1991] analysis of Snaketown and Grew, as cited by Bayman [2002:77]), the Salado (Loendorf 2001), and Classic Mimbres (Gilman 1990), and the late prehistoric and early historic Zuni (Howell 2001; Howell and Kintigh 1996). Examples of the second type of case (exceptional individuals) include Burial number 140 at Grasshopper, interpreted as a sodality leader by Whittlesey and Reid (2001); and the "Magician" buried at Ridge Ruin (near Flagstaff) with an enormous quantity of artifacts and generally interpreted as a priest.

Third, there are a several cases in which there is some limited degree of differentiation between groups of graves, although the magnitude of difference is not nearly that discussed in the first category. For example, the South Roomblock at the Classic Mimbres site NAN Ranch Ruin stood out from the rest of the site in that its architecture was slightly more substantial and elaborate. Graves in this roomblock were also slightly richer; they generally had more and more different kinds of artifacts. These lines of evidence are suggestive of some degree of inequality between the residents of the South Roomblock and the rest of the site, though probably not the existence of a separate elite category. A similar interpretation is suggested by Loendorf (2001) for the Roosevelt phase Salado.

Conclusions: The Nature of Inequality and Leadership

The US Southwest has mostly been excluded from anthropological discussions of complex societies, probably because many Southwestern societies defy the complexity mold. However, recent work has demonstrated that there are many ways of being complex (Nelson 1995), many paths to complexity (Feinman 1995), many evolutionary trajectories (Yoffee et al. 1999), and many ways of organizing leadership (Blanton et al. 1996; Godelier 1991), and the Southwest has increasingly been part of these discussions. Focus here has been on one dimension of complexity – social inequality – and on the many forms inequality can take. Although some researchers working in the Southwest have shied away from issues of inequality, the area provides important examples of cases in which inequality is present but not materially grounded. There is much Southwestern cases have to offer to a general understanding of this complex dimension of complexity.

The distinction between corporate and network modes of leadership – originally developed with reference to Mesoamerica (Blanton et al. 1996) – is today widely used for interpreting political processes in the Southwest (Feinman 2000; Feinman et al. 2000; chapters in Mills 2000c). In corporate strategies, leadership is not personalized, ostentatious displays are discouraged, and tendencies toward network strategies are dampened. Other models of decentralized organization and leadership such as heterarchy, confederacy, and alternating moieties similarly emphasize processes in which the role of individual leaders is downplayed and opportunities to accumulate economic inequalities are minimized. Generally, such interpretations of leadership also emphasize its religious or ritual basis: leaders do not necessarily have more wealth, but they have more information or more control over ritual.

I do not dispute the broad applicability of these alternative models of leadership to the Southwest. At the same time, I emphasize that "alternative" strategies should not be assumed to be egalitarian. An archetype of corporate leadership is classic Teotihuacan (Blanton et al. 1996), and even if the leaders of that great city were "faceless," no one is suggesting that they were not powerful or that inequality was minimal. The Southwest is not Teotihuacan, but we also should not forget Teotihuacan. More specifically, ritual can be a powerful basis for leadership and differentiation, and resulting inequalities should not be assumed to be minor or materially insignificant. In a similar vein, Plog and Solometo (1997) have shown that religion and religious developments (specifically the origins of the Katsina religion around A.D. 1300) were not necessarily peaceful but may actually have been linked to violence and warfare. These kinds of conclusions challenge earlier interpretations that viewed ritual as an alternative to political hierarchies (Rappaport 1971). Ethnographically, and probably in the past as well, leaders have/had real (perhaps even despotic) control over others' lives, in ways that affect people's physical as well as spiritual well-being, and ritual. Although the inequality does not often appear to be *based on* differences in wealth, in some cases it does seem to result in differences in access to material goods, including sustenance and shelter. The dearth of ostentatious differentiation may even serve to mask important differences in other kinds of wealth (McGuire 2001; Potter 2000: 301–302).

In at least some theoretical perspectives on power and leadership, there is a link between, on the one hand, relatively open paths toward leadership (i.e., achieved status) and leadership based on the control/accumulation of wealth, and, on the other hand, more closed paths and leadership based on criteria other than wealth (i.e., ascribed status); this contrast is part of the distinction Godelier (1991) draws between big and great men). The Southwest fits this general model, in that access to positions of leadership or high status does not appear to have been open to all. Ethnographic accounts make clear that leaders were drawn from only certain hereditary groups (clans, moieties, the Tewa Made People), and mortuary analyses confirm that this was the case archaeologically as well (Howell and Kintigh 1996). Thus, although Southwestern leaders were not "chiefs" in the sense of classic chiefdoms, their status was certainly ascribed.

Finally, earlier neoevolutionary models tended to interpret the development of complex organizations as a kind of social adaptation, working with the assumption that administrative organizations and leaders/elites somehow benefited or even were necessary for the good of society as a whole. Recent theoretical statements have moved away from this perspective, and, as the chapters in this volume demonstrate, social inequality rarely contributes to the greater good. The Southwest offers a stark example to support this conclusion. Although, as I have discussed above, there is various evidence of various kinds of social inequality across time and space in the Southwest, there is one case – the Classic Hohokam – in which materially apparent inequality, including the presence of elites, is clear-cut. Late Classic Hohokam elites lived in special kinds of houses on or near platform mounds, had special access to status goods, and received elaborate burials. But an understanding of this social inequality is not complete unless we also understand that these elites presided over a time of great misery (Abbott 2003). The people who lived at that time had by far the worst health problems of any known prehistoric Southwestern population. Specifically, burials from Pueblo Grande display osteological evidence (including enamel hypoplasia and lesions) indicative of severe anemia, malnutrition, and infectious diseases in close to 100 percent of the burial population (Sheridan 2001). It is difficult to know whether the elites took advantage of a difficult situation to enhance their own status and possibly contributed to this misery, or, conversely, whether elites emerged because they were able to help manage the problems. It is almost certain that the causality was complex. Regardless, it is clear that – at least in the Southwest – the emergence of elites should not be viewed as social evolutionary progress.

ACKNOWLEDGMENTS

I am grateful to the volume editors as well as to Jim Bayman and Kate Spielmann for providing valuable comments and helping with references. Tim Pauketat also provided the photographs and drafted the map.

REFERENCES

Abbott, D. R., 2003 *Centuries of Decline during the Hohokam Classic Period at Pueblo Grande.* Tucson: University of Arizona Press.

Adams, E. C., M. T. Stark, and D. S. Dosh, 1993 Ceramic distribution and exchange: Jeddito Yellow Ware and implications for social complexity. *Journal of Field Archaeology* 20, 3–21.

Akins, N. J., 1986 *A Biocultural Approach to Human Burials from Chaco Canyon, New Mexico.* Reports of the Chaco Center 9, Branch of Cultural Research. Santa Fe: National Park Service.

——2001 Chaco Canyon mortuary practices: Archaeological correlates of complexity. In *Ancient Burial Practices in the American Southwest.* D. R. Mitchell and J. L. Brunson-Hadley, eds. Pp. 167–190. Albuquerque: University of New Mexico Press.

Bayman, J. M., 2002 Hohokam craft economies and the materialization of power. *Journal of Archaeological Method and Theory* 9, 69–95.

Benedict, R., 1934 *Patterns of Culture.* New York: Houghton Mifflin.

Blanton, R. E., G. M. Feinman, S. A. Kowaleski, and P. N. Peregrine, 1996 A dual-processual theory for the evolution of Mesoamerican civilization. *Current Anthropology* 37, 1–14.

Bradley, R. J., 2000 Networks of shell ornament exchange: a critical assessment of prestige economies in the North American Southwest. In *The Archaeology of Regional Interaction: Religion, Warfare, and Exchange Across the American Southwest and Beyond.* M. Hegmon, ed. Pp. 167–187. Boulder: University Press of Colorado.

Brandt, E. A., 1994 Egalitarianism, hierarchy, and centralization in the Pueblos. In *The Ancient Southwestern Community: Models and Methods for the Study of Prehistoric Social Organization.* W. H. Wills and R. D. Leonard, eds. Pp. 9–23. Albuquerque: University of New Mexico Press.

Brumfiel, E. M. and T. K. Earle, 1987 Specialization, exchange, and complex societies: an introduction. In *Specialization, Exchange, and Complex Societies.* E. M. Brumfiel and T. K. Earle, eds. Pp. 1–9. Cambridge: Cambridge University Press.

Cordell, L., 1999 How were Precolumbian Southwestern polities organized? In *Great Towns and Regional Polities in the Prehistoric American Southwest and Southeast.* J. E. Neitzel, ed. Pp. 81–94. Dragoon: Amerind Foundation, and Albuquerque: University of New Mexico Press.

Cordell, L. S., and F. Plog, 1979 Escaping the confines of normative thought: a reevaluation of Puebloan prehistory. *American Antiquity* 44, 405–429.

Crown, P. L., 1994 *Ceramics and Ideology: Salado Polychrome Pottery.* Albuquerque: University of New Mexico Press.

Crown, P. L., and T. A. Kohler, 1994 Community dynamics, site structure, and aggregation in the northern Río Grande. In *The Ancient Southwestern Community: Models and Methods for the Study of Prehistoric Social Organization.* W. H. Wills and R. D. Leonard, eds. Pp. 103–117. Albuquerque: University of New Mexico Press.

Crumley, C. L., 1995 Heterarchy and the analysis of complex societies. In *Heterarchy and the Analysis of Complex Societies.* R. M. Ehrenreich, C. L. Crumley, and J. E. Levy, eds. Pp. 1–5. Archeological Papers 6. Washington, DC: American Anthropological Association.

Dozier, E. P., 1970 *The Pueblo Indians of North America.* New York: Holt.

Eggan, F., 1950 *Social Organization of the Western Pueblos.* Chicago: University of Chicago Press.

Elson, M. D., and D. R. Abbott, 2000 Organizational variability in platform mound-building groups of the American Southwest. In *Alternative Leadership Strategies in the Prehispanic Southwest.* B. J. Mills, ed. Pp. 117–135. Tucson: University of Arizona Press.

Elson, M. D., M. T. Stark, and D. A. Gregory, 2000 Tonto Basin local systems: Implications for cultural affiliation and migration. In *Salado.* J. S. Dean, ed. Pp. 167–192. Dragoon: Amerind Foundation, and Albuquerque: University of New Mexico Press.

Feinman, G. M., 1995 The emergence of inequality: A focus on strategies and processes. In *Foundations of Inequality.* T. D. Price and G. M. Feinman, eds. Pp. 255–279. New York: Plenum.

—— 2000 Corporate/network: A new perspective on leadership in the American Southwest. In *Hierarchies in Action: Cui Bueno.* M. W. Diehl, ed. Pp. 152–180. Occasional Paper 27, Center for Archaeological Investigations. Carbondale: Southern Illinois University.

Feinman, G. M., K. G. Lightfoot, and S. Upham, 2000 Political hierarchies and organizational strategies in the Puebloan Southwest. *American Antiquity* 65, 449–470.

Fish, P. R., and S. K. Fish, 2000 The Marana mound site: patterns of social differentiation in the early Classic period. In *The Hohokam Village Revisited.* D. E. Doyel, S. K. Fish, and P. R. Fish, eds. Pp. 244–275. Southwestern and Rocky Mountain Division of the American Association for the Advancement of Science.

Flanagan, J. G., 1989 Hierarchy in simple egalitarian societies. *Annual Review of Anthropology* 18, 245–266.

Giddens, A., 1984 *The Constitution of Society.* Berkeley: University of California Press.

Gilman, P. A., 1990 Social organization and Classic Mimbres period burials in the S.W. United States. *Journal of Field Archaeology* 17, 457–469.

Godelier, M., 1991 *Big Men and Great Men: Personifications of Power in Melanesia.* Cambridge: Cambridge University Press.

Goldstein, L., 2001 Ancient Southwest mortuary practices: Perspectives from outside the Southwest. In *Ancient Burial Practices in the American Southwest.* D. R. Mitchell and J. L. Brunson-Hadley, eds. Pp. 249–253. Albuquerque: University of New Mexico Press.

Graves, W. M., and K. A. Spielmann, 2000 Leadership, long-distance exchange, and feasting in the Protohistoric Rio Grande. In *Alternative Leadership Strategies in the Prehispanic Southwest.* B. J. Mills. ed. Pp. 45–59. Tucson: University of Arizona Press.

Gregory, D. A., 1987 The morphology of platform mounds and the structure of Classic period Hohokam sites. In *The Hohokam Village: Site Structure and Organization.* D. E. Doyel, ed. Pp. 183–210. Southwestern and Rocky Mountain Division of the American Association for the Advancement of Science.

Habicht-Mauche, J. A., S. T. Glenn, H. Milford, and A. R. Flegal, 2000 Isotopic tracing of prehistoric Rio Grande glaze-paint production and trade. *Journal of Archaeological Science* 27, 709–713.

Harry, K. G., 2000 Community-based craft specialization: The West Branch site. In *The Hohokam Village Revisited.* D. E. Doyel, S. K. Fish, and P. R. Fish, eds. Pp. 197–220. Southwestern and Rocky Mountain Division of the American Association for the Advancement of Science.

Harry, K. G., and J. M. Bayman, 2000 Leadership strategies among the Classic period Hohokam: A case study. In *Alternative Leadership Strategies in the Prehispanic Southwest.* B. J. Mills, ed. Pp. 136–153. Tucson: University of Arizona Press.

Hays, K. A., 1989 Katsina depictions on Homol'ovi ceramics: Toward a fourteenth-century Pueblo iconography. *Kiva* 54, 297–311.

Hegmon, M., 1991 The risks of sharing and sharing as risk reduction: Interhousehold food sharing in egalitarian societies. In *Between Bands and States*. S. A. Gregg ed. Pp. 309–329. Carbondale: Southern Illinois University Press.

Henderson, K., 1979 *Archaeological Survey at Chavez Pass Ruin, Coconino National Forest, Arizona: The 1978 Field Season*. Tempe: Report submitted to the Department of Anthropology, Arizona State University, and Flagstaff: USDA Forest Service, Coconino National Forest.

Herr, S. A., 1999 The organization of migrant communities on a Pueblo frontier. Ph.D. dissertation, Department of Anthropology, University of Arizona, Tucson.

Hohmann, J. W., 2001 A study of Sinagua mortuary practices and their implications. In *Ancient Burial Practices in the American Southwest*. D. R. Mitchell and J. L. Brunson-Hadley, eds. Pp. 97–122. Albuquerque: University of New Mexico Press.

Howard, A. V., 1993 Marine shell artifacts and production processes at Shelltown and the Hind site. In *Shelltown and the Hind Site: A Study of Two Hohokam Craftsman Communities in Southwestern Arizona*. W. S. Marmaduke and R. J. Martynec, eds. Pp. 321–423. Flagstaff: Northland Research.

Howell, T. L., 2001 Foundations of political power in ancestral Zuni society. In *Ancient Burial Practices in the American Southwest*. D. R. Mitchell and J. L. Brunson-Hadley, eds. Pp. 149–166. Albuquerque: University of New Mexico Press.

Howell, T. L., and K. W. Kintigh, 1996 Archaeological identification of kin groups using mortuary biological data: An example from the American Southwest. *American Antiquity* 61, 537–554.

Johnson, G. A., 1989 Dynamics of Southwestern prehistory: Far outside, looking in. In *Dynamics of Southwestern Prehistory*. L. S. Cordell and G. J. Gumerman, eds. Pp. 371–389. Washington, DC: Smithsonian Institution Press.

Kosse, K., 1996 Middle-range societies from a scalar perspective. In *Interpreting Southwestern Diversity: Underlying Principles and Overarching Patterns*. P. R. Fish and J. J. Reid, eds. Pp. 87–96. Anthropological Research Papers 48. Tempe: Arizona State University.

Levy, J. E., 1992 *Orayvi Revisited: Social Stratification in an "Egalitarian" Society*. Santa Fe: School of American Research Press.

Lipe, W. D., 2002 Social power in the central Mesa Verde region, A.D. 1150–1290. In *Seeking the Center Place: Archaeology and Ancient Communities in the Mesa Verde Region*. M. D. Varien and R. H. Wilshusen, eds. Pp. 203–232. Salt Lake City: University of Utah Press.

Loendorf, C., 2001 Salado burial practices. In *Ancient Burial Practices in the American Southwest*. D. R. Mitchell and J. L. Brunson-Hadley, eds. Pp. 123–148. Albuquerque: University of New Mexico Press.

Martin, D. L., and N. J. Akins, 2001 Unequal treatment in life as in death: Trauma and mortuary behavior at La Plata (A.D. 1000–1300). In *Ancient Burial Practices in the American Southwest*. D. R. Mitchell and J. L. Brunson-Hadley, eds. Pp. 223–248. Albuquerque: University of New Mexico Press.

McGuire, R. H., 1992 *Death, Society, and Ideology in a Hohokam Community*. Boulder: Westview Press.

——2001 Ideologies of death and power in the Hohokam community of La Ciudad. In *Ancient Burial Practices in the American Southwest*. D. R. Mitchell and J. L. Brunson-Hadley, eds. Pp. 27–44. Albuquerque: University of New Mexico Press.

McGuire, R. H., and A. V. Howard, 1987 The structure and organization of Hohokam shell exchange. *Kiva* 52, 113–146.

McGuire, R. H., and D. Saitta, 1996 Although they have petty captains, they obey them badly: The dialectics of prehispanic Western Pueblo social organization. *American Antiquity* 61, 197–216.

Mills, B. J., 2000a Alternative models, alternative strategies: leadership in the Prehispanic Southwest. In *Alternative Leadership Strategies in the Prehispanic Southwest*. B. J. Mills, ed. Pp. 3–18. Tucson: University of Arizona Press.

—— 2000b Gender, craft production, and inequality. In *Women and Men in the Prehispanic Southwest: Labor, Power, and Prestige*. P. L. Crown, ed. Pp. 301–344. Santa Fe: School of American Research Press.

Mills, B. J., ed., 2000c *Alternative Leadership Strategies in the Prehispanic Southwest*. Tucson: University of Arizona Press.

Mitchell, D. R., and J. L. Brunson-Hadley, 2001 An evaluation of Classic period Hohokam burials and society: Chiefs, priests, or acephalous complexity? In *Ancient Burial Practices in the American Southwest*. D. R. Mitchell and J. L. Brunson-Hadley, eds. Pp. 45–67. Albuquerque: University of New Mexico Press.

Neitzel, J., 1991 Hohokam material culture and behavior: The dimensions of organizational change. In *Exploring the Hohokam: Prehistoric Desert Peoples of the American Southwest*. G. J. Gumerman, ed. Pp. 177–230. Albuquerque: University of New Mexico Press.

Nelson, B. A., 1995 Complexity, hierarchy, and scale: A controlled comparison between Chaco Canyon, New Mexico, and La Quemada, Zacatecas. *American Antiquity* 60, 597–618.

Ortiz, A., 1969 *The Tewa World: Space, Time, Being and Becoming in a Pueblo Society*. Chicago: University of Chicago Press.

Parsons, E. C., 1939 *Pueblo Indian Religion*. Chicago: University of Chicago Press.

Pauketat, T. R., 1996 The foundations of inequality within a simulated Shan community. *Journal of Anthropological Archaeology* 15, 219–236.

Paynter, R., 1989 The archaeology of equality and inequality. *Annual Review of Anthropology* 18, 369–399.

Plog, S., 1995 Equality and hierarchy: Holistic approaches to understanding social dynamics in the Pueblo Southwest. In *Foundations of Social Inequality*. T. D. Price and G. M. Feinman, eds. Pp. 189–206. New York: Plenum Press.

—— 1997 *Ancient Peoples of the American Southwest*. New York: Thames & Hudson.

Plog, S. and J. Solometo, 1997 The never-changing and the ever-changing: The evolution of Western Pueblo ritual. *Cambridge Archaeological Journal* 7, 161–182.

Potter, J. M., 2000 Ritual, power, and social differentiation in small-scale societies. In *Hierarchies in Action: Cui Bueno*. M. W. Diehl, ed. Pp. 295–316. Occasional Paper 27, Center for Archaeological Investigations. Carbondale: Southern Illinois University.

Potter, J. M., and E. M. Perry, 2000a Ritual as power resource in the American Southwest. In *Alternative Leadership Strategies in the Prehispanic Southwest*. B. J. Mills ed. Pp. 60–78. Tucson: University of Arizona Press.

Rappaport, R. A., 1971 Ritual, sanctity, and cybernetics. *American Anthropologist* 73, 59–76.

Rautman, A. E., 1998 Hierarchy and heterarchy in the American Southwest: A comment on McGuire and Saitta. *American Antiquity* 63, 325–333.

Reff, D. T., 1987 The introduction of smallpox in the Greater Southwest. *American Anthropologist* 89, 704–708.

Rice, G. E., 1998 War and water: An ecological perspective on Hohokam irrigation. *Kiva* 63, 263–301.

—— 2000 Hohokam and Salado segmentary organization: The evidence from the Roosevelt platform mound study. In *Salado*. J. S. Dean, ed. Pp. 143–166. Dragoon: Amerind Foundation, and Albuquerque: University of New Mexico Press.

Saitta, D. J., 1994 Class and community in the prehistoric Southwest. In *The Ancient Southwestern Community: Models and Methods for the Study of Prehistoric Social Organization*. W. H. Wills and R. D. Leonard, eds. Pp. 25–43. Albuquerque: University of New Mexico Press.

Schachner, G., 2001 Ritual control and transformation in middle-range societies: An example from the American Southwest. *Journal of Anthropological Archaeology* 20, 168–194.

Service, E. R., 1971 *Primitive Social Organization: An Evolutionary Perspective*, 2nd edn. New York: Random House.

Seymour, D. J., 1988 An alternative view of Sedentary period Hohokam shell-ornament production. *American Antiquity* 53, 812–829.

Seymour, D. J., and M. B. Schiffer, 1987 A preliminary analysis of pithouse assemblages from Snaketown, Arizona. In *Method and Theory for Activity Area Research: An Ethnoarchaeological Approach*. S. Kent, ed. Pp. 549–602. New York: Plenum Press.

Shafer, H. J., 1999 The Classic Mimbres phenomenon and some new interpretations. In *Sixty Years of Mogollon Archaeology: Papers from the Ninth Mogollon Conference, Silver City, New Mexico, 1996*. S. M. Whittlesey, ed. Pp. 95–105. Tucson: SRI Press.

Sheridan, S. G., 2001 Morbidity and mortality in a Classic-period Hohokam community. In *Ancient Burial Practices in the American Southwest*. D. R. Mitchell and J. L. Brunson-Hadley, eds. Pp. 191–222. Albuquerque: University of New Mexico Press.

Spielmann, K. A., 1994 Clustered confederacies: Sociopolitical organization in the Protohistoric Río Grande. In *The Ancient Southwestern Community: Models and Methods for the Study of Prehistoric Social Organization*. W. H. Wills and R. D. Leonard, eds. Pp. 45–54. Albuquerque: University of New Mexico Press.

——2002 Feasting, craft specialization, and the ritual mode of production in small-scale societies. *American Anthropologist* 104, 195–207.

Stone, G. D., and C. E. Downum, 1999 Non-Bosrupian ecology and agricultural risk: Ethnic politics and land control in the arid Southwest. *American Anthropologist* 101, 113–128.

Teague, L. S., 1985 The organization of Hohokam exchange. In *Proceedings of the 1983 Hohokam Symposium*. A. E. Dittert, Jr. and D. E. Dove, eds. Pp. 397–419. Occasional Paper 2. Phoenix: Arizona Archaeological Society.

——1993 Prehistory and the Traditions of the O'Odham and Hopi. *Kiva* 58, 435–455.

Upham, S., 1982 *Polities and Power: An Economic and Political History of the Western Pueblo*. New York: Academic Press.

Van Keuren, S., 2000 Ceramic decoration as power: Late prehistoric design change in east-central Arizona. In *Alternative Leadership Strategies in the Prehispanic Southwest*. B. J. Mills, ed. Pp. 79–94. Tucson: University of Arizona Press.

Varien, M. D., 1999 *Sedentism and Mobility in a Social Landscape: Mesa Verde and Beyond*. Tucson: University of Arizona Press.

Whittlesey, S. M., and J. J. Reid, 2001 Mortuary ritual and organizational inferences at Grasshopper pueblo, Arizona. In *Ancient Burial Practices in the American Southwest*. D. R. Mitchell and J. L. Brunson-Hadley, ed. Pp. 68–96. Albuquerque: University of New Mexico Press.

Wilcox, D. R., 1991 Hohokam Social Complexity. In *Chaco and Hohokam: Prehistoric Regional Systems in the American Southwest*. P. L. Crown and W. J. Judge, eds. Pp. 253–276. Santa Fe: School of American Research Press.

Wilcox, D. R., and Charles Sternberg, 1983 *Hohokam Ballcourts and their Interpretation*. Archaeological Series 160. Tucson: Arizona State Museum.

Yoffee, N., S. K. Fish, and G. R. Milner, 1999 Comunidades, ritualities, chiefdoms: Social evolution in the American Southwest and Southeast. In *Great Towns and Regional Polities in the Prehistoric American Southwest and Southeast*. J. E. Neitzel, ed. Pp. 261–271. Dragoon: Amerind Foundation, and Albuquerque: University of New Mexico Press.

10

Chaco and Paquimé: Complexity, History, Landscape

Stephen H. Lekson

In Puebloan archaeology, Chaco and Paquimé represent the most likely candidates for sociopolitical complexity (Figure 10.1). Note that "Puebloan archaeology" is taken here to include both Anasazi and Mogollon regions. Elsewhere in the Southwest, the Hohokam region offers a third very convincing candidate (see Hegmon, this volume).

"Complexity" here means hierarchical, centralized political structures: one or a few making decisions for the many. The one or the few might be elected, appointed, anointed. Their decisions may have met resistance; they may have been ignored. But the roles were real, and the institutionalization of centralized decision-making marks an interesting turning-point in human history and evolution. "Complexity" here does not mean scientific complexity (of the Santa Fe Institute variety), which certainly has a role to play in the study of political complexity (Kantner 2002). Nor is "complexity" here the more diffuse, post-modernly complicated complexity which leads to questions like "Ask not if they were complex; ask rather how they were complex?" (paraphrasing Mills 2000). Both are excellent questions; but in the Southwest, nagging uncertainties about the first question "if" remain to be resolved before we can usefully grapple with the second question "how." Reconstructions (for example) of the development of Pueblo social structure or ceremonial systems that ignore ancient complexity risk missing likely causes for that development – an argument to which we will return at the end of this chapter.

Complexity is a particular (and particularly virulent) form of social inequality, which existed in many forms in the ancient Southwest (Hegmon, this volume). We focus on complexity because it has special significance: it's how we, ourselves, do business. Complexity is of more than anthropological interest.

Claims for Southwestern complexity – hierarchical, centralized political structures – seem improper, even vulgar, in a region best known for pueblos. Pueblos are egalitarian, communal, peaceful farming villages, steadfast in their ancient traditions. Or so goes our stereotype; today's pueblos are rather more complex than

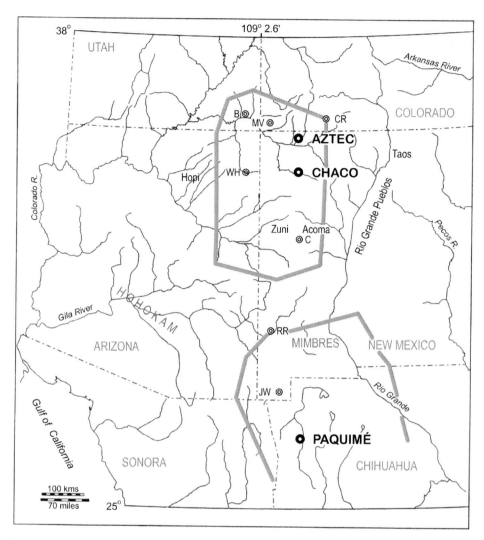

Figure 10.1 Chaco and Casas Grandes regions. B: Bluff; C: Candelaria; CR: Chimney Rock; JW: Joyce Wells; MV: Mesa Verde; RR: Redrock; WH: White House

that utopian image suggests. The same was almost certainly true for their ancient ancestors. Pueblos today do, indeed, have remarkable facilities to discourage aggrandizing leadership, and thus to avoid the burdensome baggage we recognize as hierarchical, centralized government. But some ancient Southwestern societies apparently did not; they were socially and politically complex.

Southwestern archaeology sometimes appears obsessed with complexity, for and against. Heated (and sometimes hyperbolic) rhetoric surrounding complexity reflects the difficulties of removing the past from the procrustean framework of the Pueblo present: escaping the confines of the tyranny of the ethnographic – to mix two famous Southwestern metaphors. We recognize as coffee-table-book bromide the formula: "happy peaceful people living in harmony with their environment and with each other;" but, that image remains a strange attractor, a black hole into which evidence (which elsewhere might signal complexity) vanishes without a trace. Elite housing, high-status burials, conspicuous accumulation of wealth, socially sanctioned violence, primate centers with vast regions – all these aspects of Southwestern prehistory can be and often are explained with alternative leadership strategies rigorously excluding chiefs, kings, or rulers; that is, without complexity. Ritual and rule are not exclusive, of course; kings are often divine. But there is a tendency to assume an ancient separation of church and state, and to favor the former over the latter.

Hierarchical, centralized government in the Southwest was never very elaborate or very successful. Its modest remains can, in consequence, support alternate scenarios in which ritual replaces royalty, ceremony supersedes scepter, prayerful consultation precludes political coercion. Why do those alternate explanations, elaborate sometimes to the point of strain, seem preferable to the simpler notions of political complexity? North America was awash in complexity, a continent of chiefs and kings: the Great Sun in the east, *tlatoani* to the south, headman in the west. The vast majority of North American native peoples lived under (or around) various forms of political leadership. Complexity would seem the default option, the obvious interpretation of sites like Chaco and Paquimé; yet we seek alternatives. We propose unusual, even unique, social and political formations for Southwestern ruins. Gregory Johnson (1989:386) noted: "we have garden variety 'chiefdoms' and 'early states' stacked ten deep under the lab table, but elaborate sequential hierarchies [his alternative to complexity at Chaco Canyon] may have been a rare phenomenon." Rare, too, are the "primitive communes," "anti-structures," and "ritualities" proposed for Chaco and other ancient Southwestern societies that look, to the under-nuanced and un-deconstructed eye, complex. Rare and therefore unlikely; but not, of course, impossible. Still, rarity should elicit caution.

The Southwest has long been a rare bird in political philosophy: it is the first home and last refuge of primitive communism, fueling utopian dreams. Lewis Henry Morgan saw Chaco as the ur-commune, the source of New World primitive communism. Chaco got things done – great art, great architecture – without kings or classes. Engels read Morgan, Marx shot pool with Engels, and the rest is history – the history, in fact, of most of the 20th century. Morgan's other New World communes, from Aztec to Iroquois, vanished before the press of evidence; only the Southwest remains. Southwestern archaeology's influence on modern political philosophy was and remains real, but that tale is too long to tell here. Sufficient, here, should be the suggestion that Southwest archaeology's curious obsession with complexity might actually matter.

Chaco

Chaco Canyon is part of a well-established cultural history of the Anasazi or Ancestral Pueblo region, which includes sites such as Mesa Verde and Hovenweep.

A variety of phase or stage sequences have been proposed to describe that history, with the "Pecos System" being most widely used. The term specific to Chaco Canyon at its height is the Bonito phase, subdivided into three sub-phases: Early Bonito phase (A.D. 900–1040), Classic Bonito phase (A.D. 1040–1100) and Late Bonito phase (A.D. 1100–1140). The Bonito phase is roughly equivalent to the "Pueblo II" period of the Pecos System, and "Pueblo I" is often used to describe the archaeology of Chaco Canyon prior to the Bonito phase.

Chaco Canyon is at approximately latitude 36° N, 108° W in the northwestern quarter of the state of New Mexico, USA. At Pueblo Bonito, the elevation is 1,608 m above mean sea level (AMSL). The canyon is near the center of the "San Juan Basin," a term borrowed from geology and applied by archaeology to a region about 200 km in diameter, comprising the Chaco River drainage and related portions of the San Juan River (into which the Chaco River flows). The San Juan Basin is in the southern half of the Colorado Plateau, a vast region of canyons and mesas around the "Four Corners" of the states of New Mexico, Arizona, Utah, and Colorado.

The Chaco River, or Chaco Wash, is today a deeply entrenched *arroyo* which flows only after heavy rains. Chaco Canyon receives less than 20 cm of annual precipitation. Annual average temperature is 49.8°F with a range from lows of −38°F to highs of 102°F. The span of frost-free days (the growing season) is short, always less than 150 days and often less than 100 days. By these measures, Chaco is not productive place for maize agriculture (Vivian 1990:22). Local vegetation is desert grassland, with sparse pygmy forests of pinyon and juniper. Wood resources are scarce.

At Pueblo Bonito, the canyon is approximately 0.8 km wide, with sheer sandstone cliffs rising over 30 m from the flat valley floor (Figure 10.2). The cliffs terrace

Figure 10.2 Pueblo Bonito, Chaco Canyon, looking southeast

back to mesa tops over 150 m above the canyon floor. Those dimensions are typical of the length of canyon within the National Park, which runs 17 km in a fairly straight line from southeast to northwest. The sandstone of the cliffs provides excellent materials for masonry construction.

Climate in the ninth through 12th centuries was not notably different from modern conditions; annual precipitation varied generally varied between 20 and 25 cm, with alternating periods of drought and increased moisture (which correlates reasonably well with construction of sites). Extensive systems to collect rainfall have been documented, particularly on the north side of the canyon; this water was used for agricultural (Vivian 1990) and, probably, for domestic consumption. The Chaco Wash had cycles of *arroyo* cutting and filling, with a notable episode of filling (that is, raising the level of the wash) from A.D. 1025 to 1090 (again, correlating well with construction). Filling was caused by a dune that crossed and closed the downstream end of the canyon, ponding water behind it; this natural dam was maintained by the addition of a constructed masonry dam (Force et al. 2002).

The biotic environment during the ninth to 12th centuries was much the same as it is today (with the exception of species introduced after colonization). Wood resources were never abundant, and the few local stands of larger trees were soon depleted. Most of the tens of thousands of large beams required for construction came from mountain forests up to 60 km distant from the canyon.

Archaeology has plumbed Chaco's depths for over a century (Lister and Lister 1981). Richard Wetherill, the cowboy-archaeologist who discovered Mesa Verde, initiated the first excavations at Pueblo Bonito in 1896; the last major field work of the National Park Service's Chaco Project ended in 1988. Research at recognized Great Houses in the larger Chacoan region began in the 1920s at sites like Lowry, Chimney Rock, and Village of the Great Kivas, and continues today at sites throughout the Chacoan region (Kantner and Mahoney 2000).

Several major institutions have sponsored excavations at Bonito phase sites (Figure 10.3): the American Museum of Natural History at Pueblo Bonito (1896–1900), the Smithsonian Institution and National Geographic Society at Pueblo Bonito and Pueblo del Arroyo (1921–27), the Museum of New Mexico and the University of New Mexico at Chetro Ketl (1920–34), and the National Park Service at Kin Kletso (1950–51) and Pueblo Alto (1976–78). Particularly in the early excavations, institutional rivalries affected interpretations of the Bonito phase. To some degree, Chacoan archaeology suffers an embarrassment of riches: too much data, with site publications often long delayed or never completed.

The earliest archaeologists, such as Neil Judd (who excavated Pueblo Bonito in the 1920s) and Edgar Hewett (Chetro Ketl in the 1930s), assumed that Bonito phase structures were analogous to modern pueblos such as Zuni or Acoma. They looked to modern pueblos for models of Chaco Canyon's social and political structures. They considered each Great House to be a separate town or pueblo, ordered by the communal associations evident today at Hopi, Zuni, Acoma, and the other pueblos. This view of Chaco prevailed until the 1970s, when new evidence and the reanalysis of old data suggested that Chaco was perhaps more complex than modern pueblos.

Figure 10.3 Chetro Ketl, Chaco Canyon, looking east-southeast

Tree-ring dating, developed in the 1920s, revealed that Bonito phase structures were remarkably large for their Pecos system stage, Pueblo II, more comparable in scale to the very large pueblos of Pueblo III and Pueblo IV. Moreover, tree-ring dating demonstrated that the Bonito phase "Great Houses" were contemporary with much smaller Pueblo II-style sites in Chaco Canyon; that is, there were at least two styles of architecture in Chaco Canyon during the Bonito phase: anomalously monumental Great Houses and smaller, less formal sites which more closely resemble Pueblo II-style architecture elsewhere in the Anasazi region.

Some interpreted these data as a multi-ethnic community, much like the Hopi pueblos (Vivian 1990; Vivian and Mathews 1964). The apparent anomaly of Bonito phase "Great Houses" prompted other archaeologists in the 1950s and 1960s to question the Bonito phase's place in the Anasazi (Ancestral Pueblo) sequence: was the Bonito phase the result of influence or import from the high civilizations of Mexico? The interpretation of Bonito phase as the result of Mesoamerican influences was widely (but not universally) held by Chaco archaeologists in the early 1970s (Lister 1978). The "New Archaeology" of the 1970s and 1980s favored local adaptation to extra-regional influences; Mesoamerican explanations were rejected in favor of the evolution of the Bonito phase as a "complex cultural ecosystem" (Judge 1979). New Archaeology in the Southwest also explored complex political structures, not previously suggested for Anasazi sites: managerial elites, chiefs, and other political structures that went far beyond egalitarian Pueblo models. In the

1990s and early 2000s, debate has seemed to center on the nature of Bonito phase political structure, with opinions ranging from communal (Saitta 1997; Wills 2000) to centralized hierarchy (Lekson 1999a; Wilcox 1993).

Chacoan landscape, architecture, and artifacts

The archaeology of Chaco Canyon centers on a dozen remarkable buildings called "Great Houses" (Figure 10.4). Great Houses began in the early 10th century (and perhaps as early as the late ninth century) as monumentally up-scaled versions of regular domestic structures – the small, single family "unit pueblos" of the Pueblo I and II periods – but Great Houses took a canonical turn in form and function that distinguished them from regular residences. An entire "unit pueblo" would fit into a single large room at a Chaco Great House. The largest Great Houses were concentrated in 2 km diameter "downtown" zone at the center of Chaco Canyon, around Pueblo Bonito (Judd 1954, 1964); these Great Houses include Pueblo Alto (Windes 1987), Chetro Ketl (Lekson 1983), Pueblo del Arroyo (Judd 1959), and Kin Kletson (Vivian and Mathews 1964) along with scores of smaller structures

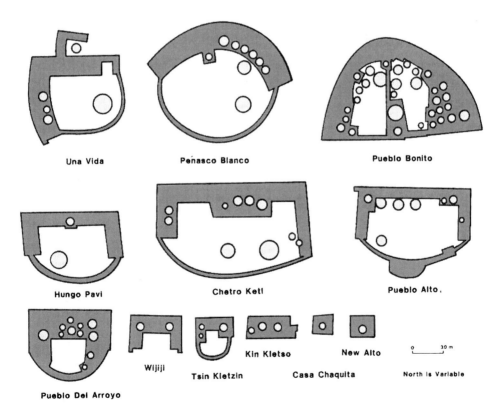

Figure 10.4 Chaco Great Houses

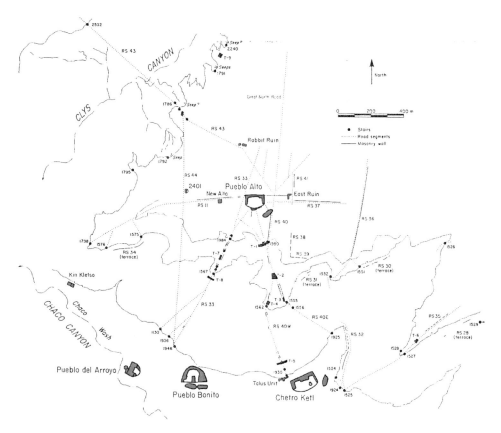

Figure 10.5 "Downtown" Chaco, north half. Site numbers indicate stairways marked by circles, RS numbers indicate road segments, and T numbers mark ceramic transects. Heavy black lines outline road curbing or the masonry retaining walls of terraces (courtesy Thomas C. Windes, *Investigations at the Pueblo Alto Complex*, Publications in Archaeology 18F, National Park Service, Santa Fe:fig. 5.2)

(Figure 10.5). The "cityscape" extends beyond this central zone; an oval area with a maximum radius from Pueblo Bonito of about 8.5 km has been proposed for the Chaco core area and some archaeologists would extend the core area to encompass Great Houses up to 15 km away.

Each Great House has a unique construction history; as noted above, Great House construction was concentrated in the span from A.D. 1020 to about 1140. Pueblo Bonito will be offered as typical (or perhaps arch-typical) of Chaco Canyon Great Houses. It took almost three centuries (A.D. 850 to 1125) to complete Pueblo Bonito. The "roads" of ancient Chaco (of which more below) led viewers to the edge of Chaco's sheer sandstone cliffs, where the "D"-shaped groundplan of Pueblo Bonito was spectacularly evident. The building began as a huge version of Pueblo I "unit pueblo," built three stories tall ("unit pueblos" were one short story).

Figure 10.6 Doorways, Pueblo Bonito, Chaco Canyon

Beginning about A.D. 1020, the architects of Pueblo Bonito began a series of a half-dozen major additions, each of which was enormously larger than anything previously built in the Pueblo world. The culmination, when building ceased about A.D. 1125, was almost 700 rooms, stacked four and perhaps five stories tall, covering an area of almost 0.8 ha. Only the outmost of Pueblo Bonito's rooms had sunlight; the vast majority of interior rooms were dark and limited of access, suited only for storage (Figure 10.6). We now believe that only a score of families lived in this huge building. They were very important families, and they had control of (or at least access to) enormous numbers of storage rooms.

Pueblo Bonito, like other Great Houses, was expensively built. That is, the labor per unit measure of floor area or roofed volume was much larger than comparable costs for "unit pueblos." Pueblo Bonito and the other Great Houses were distinguished by their site preparation (leveling and terracing); extensive foundations; massive, artfully coursed masonry walls; overtimbered roofs and ceilings (hundreds of thousands of large pine beams brought from distant forests); carpentry, that can only be appreciated today from masonry remnants of elaborate wooden stairways, balconies, and porticos; and features and furniture unique to these remarkable buildings (Figure 10.7). Among these last were colonnades (an import from

Figure 10.7 Banded masonry at Penasco Blanco, Chaco Canyon

Mexico), unique raised platforms (for storage or sleeping?) built within rooms, and the use of large sandstone disks (approximately 1 m in diameter and 30 cm thick), stacked like pancakes as foundations or dedicatory monuments beneath major posts (Figure 10.8).

The organization of labor demonstrated in Great House architecture was unlike the family economy of unit pueblos: at Great Houses, whole rooms were devoted to batteries of corn-grinding *metates* fixed in bins, where meal was prepared by gangs of grinders for larger groups; and huge ovens were found in the plazas where, presumably, cooking for larger groups took place. The few families who actually lived in Pueblo Bonito could not have built it themselves. It seems likely that others built the huge building, and that much of the domestic work (grinding corn, cooking, etc) was done by others as well.

The Great Houses were major elements of a complex, planned city that mirrored the Chacoan world order (Sofaer 1997). Space was an important aspect of design: the spaces between Great Houses were landscaped and designed, so Chaco Canyon was not a dense architectural aggregation. That cityscape had many other elements: roads, mounds, Great Kivas, small sites.

"Roads" appear much as that name implies: long, straight, wide (typically 10 m) engineered constructions which link sites to sites and sites to places, not unlike the causeways of La Quemada and the *sacbe* of the Maya (Figure 10.9). Human traffic certainly walked on Chacoan roads. Where roads meet cliff, elaborate ramps were constructed and wide stairways were carved out of the living rock. It appears, however, that the symbolic or monumental properties of roads were as important

Figure 10.8 Colonnade, Chetro Ketl, Chaco Canyon

as transportation. The dense network of roads in "downtown" Chaco created redundant, parallel routes clearly unnecessary for pedestrian functions (Figure 10.5).

"Mounds" encompass a range of earthen structures with (presumably) a variety of purposes, but a limited variety of shapes. Most mounds are oval, unfaced accumulations of earth, trash, and construction debris. A few mounds have more formal geometric shapes. Attached to Pueblo Bonito were two huge, low, rectangular, masonry-walled, flat platforms. Stairs led up to their heavily plastered surfaces, each larger in area than a basketball court. We do not know what structures, if any, stood on these platforms. Other earthworks include large berms running along road, and huge "trash mounds" at some (but, importantly, not all) Great Houses (Windes 1987; Wills 2001).

Great Kivas were large, round, subterranean chambers up to 20 m in diameter; each was a single large room with an encircling bench, presumably to seat audiences for ritual or other performances. Great Kivas had a long history in Anasazi building, both before and after Chaco, but, at Chaco Canyon and at related Chacoan sites, they were built with the monumental technologies and scales of Great Houses.

Finally, small sites ("unit pueblos" and aggregates of several "units") were a major element of Chaco Canyon. Hundreds of small sites, clearly residential, line the canyon, particularly along the south cliffs.

Figure 10.9 Chaco road (*lower left to upper right*) running from Chaco Canyon to Pueblo Pintado (*center top*); modern truck track (*lower right to upper left*)

The artifacts of Chaco Canyon, with some notable exceptions, were very much like other, contemporary Anasazi pottery and lithic industries (Figure 10.10). Indeed, some major classes of artifacts were manufactured in other Anasazi districts: the majority of the pottery found at some Great Houses was made not in Chaco but at Chaco-related communities up to 60 km distant. Conversely, one intriguing class of ceramic vessel was found almost exclusively at Chaco: all but 20 of almost 200 cylinder vases (resembling Mesoamerican forms) came from two rooms in Pueblo Bonito. Chaco Canyon is notable for long-distance imports: about 35 copper bells and about 35 scarlet macaws, all presumably from west Mexico, were found at Chaco, notably concentrated at Pueblo Bonito. These are larger numbers than at any other 11th-century Pueblo II site and, indeed, more than all other excavated 11th-century Pueblo II sites combined. Turquoise, too, is conspicuous at Chaco Canyon. Some estimates place the number of recovered pieces at over 100,000, mostly in the form of small discoidal beads. Workshops for the manufacture of turquoise beads were found at many small and large sites at Chaco Canyon, but the source(s) of the stone were not local. The huge Cerrillos turquoise mines, just south of Santa Fe, New Mexico are clearly implicated in Chacoan production of turquoise (Mathien 1997). Cerrillos is located almost 200 km east of Chaco.

Figure 10.10 Chaco Black-on-White jar (left), Gallup Black-on-White bowl (right) (vessels in the collections of the University of Colorado Museum)

Chaco Canyon Great Houses produced remarkably few burials for buildings of their size. From a century of excavations at the Canyon, only about 660 burials are documented (however, it is suspected that many more burials were removed in illicit digging) (Akins 2001). Fewer than 70 burials were found in extensive excavations at Pueblo Bonito; Swarts Ruin (a contemporary pueblo in the Mogollon region), with one quarter the number of rooms of Pueblo Bonito, produced over 1,000 burials. However, several of the burials of Pueblo Bonito were notable for their richness. Two, in particular, represent the best Anasazi candidates for elite burials: two adult males, placed in a wooden crypt in the oldest part of Pueblo Bonito, accompanied by remarkable quantities of grave goods. In the chamber above this burial crypt were 15 disarticulated individuals; they would be consistent with retainers, but other interpretations have been offered (Akins 2001). Notably, also in the rooms above the burial crypt were almost all of the known cylinder vases.

The Chacoan region

Chaco Canyon appears to have been the center of a large "regional system," marked by between 150 and 200 small Great Houses and roads (Figure 10.1). These "outlier" Great Houses were built with much of the same technology and design principles of the Chaco Canyon Great Houses, but are typically about one-twentieth the size of Pueblo Bonito. These smaller Great Houses are usually surrounded by scattered communities of unit pueblos.

A good example of an outlier Great House is provided by Chimney Rock, near Pagosa Springs, Colorado. The architecture of the Chimney Rock Great House very closely resembles that of Pueblo Bonito and other Chaco Canyon Great Houses, and contrasts very sharply with well-documented local traditions. These contrasts are so marked that Chimney Rock's excavator proposed that the site was built by a group directly from Chaco Canyon (Eddy 1977). Archaeologists are almost unanimous in accepting the site as a "Chaco outlier." Chimney Rock is about 140 km northeast of Chaco, which suggests a generally acceptable distance for a Chacoan region.

At many outlier Great Houses, there are clear indications of roads, often oriented toward other Great Houses or to Chaco Canyon. Some roads lead out from Chaco for up to 60 km; however, it is not clear that all road segments at outlier Great Houses actually continue the many kilometers to Chaco Canyon (or other destinations).

It seems likely that roads are formally constructed only at their ends, and are either less formal or absent in the stretches between termini. Paralleling the roads was a remarkable network of fire-signal or mirror-signal stations, typically represented by large, formal masonry fireboxes places on pinnacles or high spots (Hayes and Windes 1975). This line-of-sight signaling network is under-studied, but probably extends (with one or two "repeater" stations) to the outermost distribution of Great Houses. The geographic distribution of Great Houses, Great House communities, and road segments covers over 150,000 km^2; however, many archaeologists believe that Chaco Canyon's direct influence extended only over the much smaller San Juan Basin (30,000 km^2; Vivian 1990).

The region suggested by Great Houses and roads extends at least as far as 140 km northeast from Chaco (the distance from Chaco Canyon to Chimney Rock pueblo); that same radius touches or encompasses generally accepted Great Houses at Mesa Verde to the northwest (Far View House), Canyon de Chelly to the west (White House), Zuni to the southwest (Village of the Great Kivas, and others), and Acoma to the southeast (Candelaria site, and others). Beyond that 140 km radius, more distant (but still convincing) Great House outliers are known from Utah over 240 km northwest of Chaco, such as the Bluff Great House near Bluff, Utah (Cameron 2002). Other possible Great Houses can be cited at comparable distances to the west, southwest, and south.

Interpreting the Chaco phenomenon

The "Chaco phenomenon" is defined by Great Houses, which are enormous, expensive, monumental versions of contemporary small houses. Construction of Great Houses required a high degree of organization of large amounts of labor and materials. Excavations indicate that only small numbers of people lived in the Great Houses (Windes 1987), far too few to build them.

What were the "extra" rooms? Various suggestions have been offered, but most of these rooms appear to be designed for short- or long-term storage, based on the ubiquitous occurrence of very small, sealable entries (commonly seen on store rooms and granaries throughout the Four Corners region). Many Great House residences lack corn-grinding facilities (ubiquitous in smaller houses) and there is a dearth of large firepits (presumably for cooking). These features are indeed present at Great Houses, but in special rooms or spaces dedicated to large-scale production: rooms with batteries of multiple mealing bins and isolated structures containing huge ovens. Food preparation was architecturally segregated, and it seems reasonable to think of "kitchens" serving Great House families. Great Houses combine "expensive" housing, unusual organization of domestic spaces and activities, and remarkable amounts of storage space. This appears to be a remarkably clear incidence of stratified housing, with a small fraction of the population living in palace-like structures and most people living in serviceable but otherwise undistinguished homes.

Great Houses were only one (albeit spectacular) component of Chacoan architecture. The cityscape itself was formal and canonical in ways not seen among contemporary settlements, however large. Mounds, roads, ramps, large cleared "plazas," garden systems, and other sizeable structures were major components of a settlement plan unique in its contemporary region. The "built environment" of Chaco Canyon may have required as much or more labor than the Great Houses themselves. And the design of that built environment strongly suggests centralized planning and authority spanning decades, or even centuries.

Based on the burials of Pueblo Bonito, the Great House residents were larger and perhaps healthier than their small house contemporaries (Akins 2001, personal communication 2002). Recent research indicates that men were more robust, and women far less prone to "squatting facets" seen on many contemporary women (from hours of work, grinding corn on metates) (Nancy Akins, personal communication, 2002). The men of Pueblo Bonito were stronger and the women did not work. The spectacular burials at Pueblo Bonito (described above) are the clearest examples of high-status burials in the Pueblo Southwest. In particular, the two males buried in the wooden "crypt" seem very likely candidates for hierarchical leaders.

Based on excavations at Pueblo Alto, much (and, at times, most) of the pottery used at that Great House was not made at Chaco, but rather from distant villages. This situation probably holds true at most or all Chaco Canyon Great Houses. High proportions of imported pottery have been interpreted as evidence of periodic feasting (Toll 2001) and other explanations have been offered; but it seems safe to suggest that the residents of Chaco Great Houses may not have manufactured the utensils found at those sites. Lithics were dominated by local, low-quality stones, but significant quantities of exotic cherts and obsidians are found throughout Chaco Canyon (Cameron 2001). Quotidian artifacts at Chaco Great Houses were not dissimilar from those at contemporary small houses and in the surrounding region, but the geographic origin of many of those artifacts was remarkable.

The concentration of rare and exotic materials in Pueblo Bonito (such as cylinder vases, macaws, and copper bells) is notable, and unmatched by Chetro Ketl and other excavated Great House sites. Chaco Canyon had more macaws and copper bells than all contemporary excavated sites outside the canyon combined, and most of these were found at Pueblo Bonito. The concentration of prestige items along with high-status burials suggest that Pueblo Bonito was first among its elevated equals, and perhaps the most important of the Great Houses.

All sites at Chaco Canyon, however, seem implicated in turquoise production: workshops and production debris were found at many small and Great Houses in Chaco Canyon (Mathien 1997). Such evidence is rare at contemporary sites outside the Chaco core. As discussed above, turquoise came from the Cerrillos mines near Santa Fe, and perhaps other mines even more distant. The discovery of an anomalous, Chaco-related settlement (not a Great House) adjacent to the Cerrillos mines suggest a degree of control over this resource (Wiseman and Darling 1986). There is little question that sizeable quantities of turquoise moved from the Southwest to the high civilizations of Mesoamerica, and it seems likely that Chaco Canyon played a key role in that trade.

The presence of Chaco-like "outlier" Great Houses demonstrates a material connection between the center and its region, more dramatic than pottery styles or exchange ever could. Chacoan roads, originally assumed to be a continuous network of transportation corridors leading back to Chaco Canyon, have been shown to be at least as much symbolic monuments as transportation connections. This is not to say that people did not walk on roads (they did), but road segments pointing back to Chaco, to other Great Houses, or to prominent natural features, may have "connected" distant Great Houses to those places without complete physical linkage.

Thus, it seems safe to conclude that the Chaco region was much larger than the Chaco core, the 10–15 km radius around Pueblo Bonito; that is, far beyond the area of daily, personal interactions. The region had a strongly hierarchical settlement structure (Chaco Canyon, secondary Great Houses, and small houses). Van Dyke (2002) notes an interesting pattern of Great Kivas within the Chacoan region: the Chaco Core has many Great Kivas, "outlier" communities near Chaco have few or none, while more distant communities have Great Kivas. There is a suggestion of socially sanctioned use of force during the time of Chaco Canyon and Aztec Ruins (LeBlanc 1999; Lekson 2002b). Prior to Chaco's rise, the pueblo area was marked by small-scale, but escalating, raiding and feuding. About A.D. 900, an era of unprecedented peace began – about the same time as the initial Great House construction at Chaco Canyon. Peace continued throughout the 10th, 11th, and 12th centuries.

Toward the end of this peaceful span, several score isolated incidents of what appears to have been socially sanctioned violence occurred: small and large groups of men, women, and children were executed (Turner and Turner 1999). These executions have been interpreted as punishments for witchcraft or as political terror, directed presumably from Chaco. Whatever their cause, they evidently did not represent a return to raiding or warfare, as settlement patterns did not change to reflect defense.

Small house communities previously had been loosely structured, with individual houses scattered at some distance from neighbors, and that pattern continued through the mid-13th century. If the executions had not been socially sanctioned (that is, accepted as a part of social and political life), it seems likely that the small sites would have aggregated into large towns, or moved to defensive locations – which is precisely what happened in the mid-13th century in big towns such as Sand Canyon and cliff dwellings such as Cliff Palace.

By the mid-13th century, social order had deteriorated, and raiding and warfare returned, at an elevated level. The executions may have constituted an extreme form of social control; their contemporaneity with Chaco Canyon and Aztec Ruins suggests that social controls emanated from those regional centers. Other explanations are possible (Darling 1999; Dongoske et al. 2000), but taken in combination with other evidence, it seems likely that Chaco Canyon had use of force – an important aspect of many complex societies.

Finally, Chaco Canyon appealed, conspicuously, to the power of distant lands. The import of copper bells and macaws from western Mexico, the use of Mesoamerican architecture symbols such as roads and colonnades, and the likely export of turquoise to Mesoamerica all linked Chaco Canyon to great civilizations to the south. The existence of those civilizations would likely have been known to all Southwestern peoples, but Chaco Canyon appears to have made efforts to link itself physically and perhaps politically to those sources of power. Distant contacts and alliances are common tactics of emerging elites on the edges of larger civilizations, often solidified by actual travel by local leaders to the great but distant centers of power (Helms 1988).

Chaco Canyon seems a fairly obvious example of complexity, particularly if viewed as a fledgling, emergent elite on the margins of Mesoamerica. Situations like that suggested for Chaco Canyon are commonplace in history and archaeology. There are strong counter-interpretations that emphasize egalitarian, communal models of Chaco Canyon and its region (e.g., Saitta 1997; Wills 2000). These are thoughtful, well-reasoned readings of the evidence, and they will be discussed in the conclusions of this chapter.

Between Chaco and Paquimé

Great House construction at Chaco Canyon ends about A.D. 1125. Most archaeologists agree that the canyon was largely abandoned, but some argue for substantial occupation through the 13th century (Wilcox 1993). It appears, however, that the organizing principles which created Great Houses and the Chaco cityscape shifted, physically, 85 km to the north to the Totah District of the San Juan River drainage (near Farmington and Aztec, New Mexico). The Totah District is the eastern portion of the "Four Corners" region, famous for Mesa Verde cliff dwellings. In the Totah District, huge Great Houses, indistinguishable from the largest Chaco Canyon structures, were built between approximately 1090 and 1280, in part contemporary with Mesa Verde (Figure 10.1).

The Totah sites were almost due north of Chaco Canyon; they were connected to the canyon by a very elaborate road (the "Great North Road"), which may have been a monument linking the first center at Chaco Canyon and the second center at Aztec Ruins. (Aztec Ruins is misnamed; it was not associated with the Aztecs of ancient Mexico). While the purpose of the Great North Road is debatable, there is general agreement that several large Great Houses and many smaller structures at and around Aztec Ruins constituted a center comparable to Chaco in architectural technology, scale, formality, and design (Judge 1989). The shift from Chaco to Aztec may have begun as early as the late 1080s. It was clearly evident by 1110–1125, when large-scale construction ceased at Chaco and commenced at Aztec Ruins.

There is disagreement about Aztec's subsequent history. There is also debate on Aztec's role in the larger Four Corners region; some archaeologists believe Aztec was the center of a region encompassing most of the Four Corners (Lekson 1999a), while others believe that Aztec's sphere of influence was smaller, and more local. In any event, Aztec's era was marked by increasing violence and warfare throughout the Four Corners (LeBlanc 1999; Lekson 2002b), and by droughts in the mid-12th and late 13th centuries. It was an uneven, eventful time.

The 13th century was the era of Mesa Verde cliff dwellings in the Four Corners (northern San Juan) region. Cliff dwellings, such as Cliff Palace, were not the largest Mesa Verde sites; scores of larger towns (built in open plains or on mesa-tops) were scattered over southwestern Colorado and southeastern Utah. Some of these towns were four or five times larger than the largest cliff dwellings. Population in the Four Corners area (including the Mesa Verde, Totah, and other districts) reached as many as 30,000 people by about 1250. By 1300, the region was almost entirely empty.

Most of the Four Corners population migrated to the areas of today's pueblos in Arizona and New Mexico. The influx of thousands of new people in the 13th century undoubtedly played a role in the development of modern pueblo social and ceremonial structures (Adams 1991). In these areas, history after 1300 led ultimately to the modern pueblos, from Hopi and Zuni on the west to the Rio Grande pueblos on the east.

To the south, events and developments were no less dramatic, if less widely known today. In a domino effect, the massive population movements of the 13th century propelled Puebloan peoples into the Sonoran deserts (creating the "Salado" culture; Dean 2000) and into the Chihuahuan deserts (Lekson 2002a; Lekson et al. 2002). Groups were "pushed" from the north, but there were also remarkable developments in the south that served as significant "pulls" or attractions. Around Phoenix, Arizona, the long-lived Hohokam tradition culminated in a complex society surpassing in many respects that of Chaco (see Hegmon, this volume). Hohokam civilization was supported by elaborate canal irrigation systems on the Salt and Gila rivers; huge floods in the late 14th century crippled the canals, and Hohokam society diminished thereafter, and was effectively gone by 1450. Intriguingly, Hohokam and the contemporary Pueblo civilizations at Chaco and Aztec interacted little, if at all (Crown and Judge 1991). There is better evidence for significant interaction between the late Hohokam "Salado" and Paquimé (Di Peso 1974; Lekson 2002a).

In northwestern Chihuahua, just south of New Mexico, an even more spectacular development arose in the Casas Grandes region, centered on the city of Paquimé. Paquimé began sometime after 1200 and (like Hohokam) ended about

1450. It was probably the most complex and cosmopolitan city ever created in the Puebloan Southwest.

Paquimé

Paquimé is part of the Chihuahuan or Casas Grandes tradition, and often considered to be part of the Mogollon culture area (which included other cultural traditions such as Mimbres and Jornada). Di Peso (1974), who excavated Paquimé, proposed a series of six periods for the Casas Grandes area. In chronological order, these are: Preceramic, Plainware, Viejo, Medio, Tardio, and Españoles. As discussed below, issues of continuity and discontinuity in this sequence are central to the differing interpretations of Paquimé. The Viejo and Medio periods are most relevant to Paquimé: the Viejo period immediately precedes the site, while the Medio period was the era of Paquimé. The archaeology of the Viejo period, which is assumed to begin about A.D. 700, is poorly known. The Medio period is now dated from A.D. 1200 to 1450 (Dean and Ravesloot 1993; Whalen and Minnis 2001). The Tardio and Españoles periods span time from the fall of Paquimé (about A.D. 1450) through Spanish colonization.

Paquimé is located at approximately 30° 30' N, 108° W in the northwestern quarter of the state of Chihuahua, Mexico, at an elevation of 1475 m AMSL (Figure 10.1). The site is located in the Casas Grandes valley, in the northwestern reaches of the vast Chihuahua desert. The Rio Casas Grandes is a closed basin; that is, it runs from its headwaters in the Sierra Madre Occidental, to the west of Paquimé, through the Casas Grandes valley and into the desert, where the river empties into a large ephemeral lake or *playa*, about 120 km north of Paquimé. Its waters do not reach the Rio Grande, or the Gulf of Mexico. The entire drainage area is 16,600 km^2; the length of the Casas Grandes valley currently under intensive agriculture is about 20 km long. Much of the geology of the Casas Grandes valley is volcanic, with rhyolites, andesites, and other volcanic rocks outcropping in the Sierra Madre and its foothills, and more varied geology in the small basin-and-range mountains of the lower Casas Grandes valley. These stones are hard to shape for masonry construction, and good building stone is not easily available near the site of Paquimé.

The Rio Casas Grandes is a permanent river. Its waters support large-scale agriculture in the Casas Grandes valley today through an extensive system of irrigation canals, which probably parallel ancient systems (Doolittle 1993). Irrigation is necessary because the valley receives about 30 cm of rainfall, and severe droughts are not uncommon. The average frost-free span for the region is about 225 days. The combination of permanent flow in the Rio Casas Grandes with a long growing season make the Casas Grandes valley an excellent place for agriculture, and historically it was known as one of the most productive regions of northern Chihuahua (Whalen and Minnis 2001:75). Local vegetation is desert and semi-desert grasslands; gallery forests along the river constitute the main wood resources. The sources of pine beams used for construction have not been determined, but they likely came from distant forests in uplands and mountains to the west.

Paquimé was built on low terraces above the Casas Grandes valley floor, just below a point where the Rio Casas Grandes emerges from a narrows in the foothills. Most of the site is on a high terrace, with more limited construction "spilling over" onto low terraces and alluvial ridges just above the valley floor. The Casas Grandes valley is broad, with low bordering terraces. At the town of Nuevo Casas Grandes, the valley is about 3 km wide.

The Casas Grandes region does not have the detailed reconstructions of climate and environment available for Chaco Canyon. We have no reason to believe that environment in the 13th through 15th centuries was dramatically different than today's. The river undoubtedly provided ample water for floodplain farming, presumably accomplished through canal systems roughly paralleling those currently in use. Valley bottom farming was augmented by extensive upland systems of terraces and other soil- and water-control constructions (known generally as *trincheras*) (Whalen and Minnis 2001). Individual trincheras systems covered areas as large as 100,000 m². Although most of these systems were smaller, there were hundreds and probably thousands of these upland farming zones. Domestic water for Paquimé came from a very large spring 3.6 km northwest of the site. Water from this spring was channeled through Paquimé by an elaborate system of canals and settling ponds: Paquimé had running water.

Archaeology was aware of Paquimé from at least the year 1884, when the site was visited and mapped by Adolph Bandelier (1892). No major work was undertaken until 1958–61, when Charles Di Peso of the Amerind Foundation excavated about one-third of the site. His monumental report – eight oversize volumes – was published in 1974 (Di Peso 1974; Di Peso et al. 1974). This work established Paquimé as a major center in Southwestern prehistory, but 15 years were to pass before renewed fieldwork, in a major survey of the Casas Grandes region by Michael Whalen and Paul Minnis that began in 1989 (Whalen and Minnis 2001). The 1990s witnessed a welcome increase in field projects by the Instituto Nacional de Antropología y Historia, the Universities of New Mexico, Oklahoma, and Tulsa, the Museum of New Mexico, and the University of Calgary, and extensive reinterpretation of Di Peso's Paquimé (e.g., Bradley 2000).

Di Peso presented Paquimé as an outpost of Mesoamerica, established by state-sponsored explorer-merchants, similar to later Aztec *puchteca*. This interpretation was based on the abundance of Mesoamerican architectural forms and artifacts at Paquimé, and Di Peso's opinion that Viejo period populations were too small and underdeveloped to account for Paquimé. According to Di Peso, *puchteca* organized and directed the construction of Paquimé, and led its subsequent florescence in the Medio period. He extended this model to Chaco Canyon, suggesting that Chaco was an outpost of Paquimé. Subsequent redating of Paquimé demonstrated that Chaco Canyon ended at least a century before Paquimé began, but Di Peso's arguments for strong connections between Paquimé and Mexico remain unaffected by this correction.

Di Peso's interpretation was strongly historical, an extreme version of the culture history of American archaeology in the 1940s through 1960s. His report was published in 1974, in the early days of "New Archaeology," inimical to Di Peso's historicity. The thorough presentation of data in Di Peso's report led to a spate of "New Archaeology" papers reinterpreting Paquimé's ontogeny. Chronology was critical: Di Peso dated the Medio period from A.D. 1060 to 1340; subsequent reanalysis established that this dating was wrong, and a dating of A.D. 1200 to 1450 is now generally accepted (Dean and Ravesloot 1993; Whalen and Minnis 2001; see also Lekson 1999a).

Many (but not all) recent researchers now reject Mesoamerican origins for Paquimé, favoring a local evolutionary development (Whalen and Minnis 2000, 2001, 2003); however, an absence of data from the late Viejo and early Medio periods impedes the full development of these models. A modest population in the Viejo and early Medio periods makes the rise of Paquimé difficult to explain without some sort of "outside" involvement. Is the absence of evidence, in this case, evidence of absence? It must be noted that very little research has been undertaken in the Casas Grandes region, compared to the Anasazi area and Chaco Canyon. Whalen and Minnis (2003) argue that early Medio period components are obscured by later settlements contemporary with Paquimé, and offer the example of the Tinaja site, about 20 km west of Paquimé. Architecturally, the Tinaja site closely resembles Paquimé, and it had an associated "I"-shaped ballcourt. A suite of ^{14}C dates on charred wood mostly predate 1300 (the upper value on two-sigma spans for ten dates they accept range from 1270 to 1300). Whalen and Minnis interpret this site as an earlier version of Paquimé (and thus evidence for substantial populations prior to Paquimé). However, most archaeologists believe that Paquimé began about 1250 (contra Lekson 1999a, who argues for a later beginning), so the Tinaja site could be contemporary and not precedent to Paquimé.

Paquimé's landscape, architecture, and artifacts

Until the 1970s very little was known about the archaeology of northwestern Chihuahua, and today the level of research lags far behind that on the Anasazi area of Chaco Canyon (Whalen and Minnis 2001:ch. 2). There are hundreds (and probably thousands) of Medio period ruins in Chihuahua; Paquimé appears to be by far the largest, perhaps by a factor of six (Whalen and Minnis 2001:140). It has been suggested that a concentration of sites immediately surrounding Paquimé constitute a "core area" with a radius of about 15 km around the center (Whalen and Minnis 2001:174, 182ff).

Di Peso describes "roads" from Paquimé throughout the Casas Grandes area, but these are under-studied. Roads visible in aerial images appear to be broad and formally constructed. Only slightly better known is the network of fire-signaling stations, with a central hub on Cerro de Moctezuma near Paquimé (Di Peso 1974; Swanson 2003). Apparently, a signaling system of stations on high points interconnected much of the Paquimé area. In the absence of detailed survey and architectural data, the criteria for definition of Paquimé's region are largely ceramic; however, excavation of several adobe-walled sites in extreme southwestern New Mexico demonstrated the presence of several architectural features characteristic of

Paquimé, among them "I" -shaped ballcourts and the unique, raised adobe fireboxes seen throughout Paquimé. The largest of these sites is Joyce Well, "on the frontier of the Casas Grandes world" (Skibo et al. 2002), at a distance of approximately 140 km north of Paquimé.

There are, unfortunately, few data on contemporary domestic architecture in the Casas Grandes area away from Paquimé. Medio period "small site" architecture shared Paquimé's technology but with thinner walls forming smaller rooms in modest, single-story buildings (Whalen and Minnis 2001:110–111). (Note that these "small sites" are significantly larger than the unit pueblos of the Chacoan era.) Average room size at Paquimé is twice that of the rooms measured at small sites in neighboring drainages and at more distant sites such as Joyce Wells in southwestern New Mexico. Several large sites, intermediate in size between Paquimé and "small sites," appear to share some or all of Paquimé's architectural traits (with important exceptions, discussed below). These may represent secondary centers, perhaps analogous to outlying Great Houses.

Paquimé itself covers an area of 357,000 m². This area includes a dense concentration of ritual/ceremonial monuments, open plazas, single-story and "high-rise" (Di Peso's term) multi-story adobe structures (often built around smaller, enclosed plazas), reservoirs, and canals, and other features (Figure 10.11). According to Di Peso (1974:vol. 2), Paquimé began as a dozen or more independent, widely spaced,

Figure 10.11 Rooms and plazas at Paquimé, Casas Grandes, Chihuahua, looking west. Note the line of turkey-breeding pens, middle foreground

single-story adobe compounds. These were followed by an explosive "urban renewal" (again, Di Peso's term) creating the dense, massive structure seen today. A period of decline was marked by strife and finally abandonment. Given that the Medio period is now dated from A.D. 1200 to 1450 (some archaeologists argue that Paquimé itself began after 1250: see Lekson 1999a), Paquimé was probably built and occupied over a span of as long as two and a half centuries or as short a time as a century. Paquimé's walls were massive, "puddled" or poured adobe (thick mud, with or without binder inclusions). There is disagreement about the exact technique employed; Di Peso thought Paquimé's walls were poured into forms, while many archaeologists believe that the walls were "puddled" by hand in low courses. Puddled adobe walls were not unknown in the southern Southwest prior to Paquimé (Cameron 1998), but the use of massive walls (however constructed) to achieve multiple stories appears to be a Medio phase innovation.

The rooms were large, tall, and mostly rectangular, with heavily timbered upper-story floors and roofs. Many rooms were more complex in shape, with "L"-shapes and even more complicated forms (one room resembles an abstract butter-fly in plan). These shapes created small nooks and re-entrants which accommodated shelf-like "sleeping platforms," but which may also have served to strengthen and buttress multi-storied walls by "folding" long walls into vertically "corrugated" forms. These unusual forms (and the massive width of walls) may have been necessary because puddled or poured adobe is not an ideal technology for multi-storied building. Other internal features includes small, raised adobe fireboxes, sometimes carved into geometric or effigy forms. These distinctive features occur at the base of walls, often at mid-wall, and appear to be characteristic of Paquimé.

The building appears to be composed of smaller units Di Peso (1974:vol. 2) defined as subunits by doorway interconnections (see also Wilcox 1999); these appear to be rectangular compounds of rooms around small, interior, closed plazas. In the excavated portions of the site, perhaps a dozen such units together make up the "high-rise," with free-standing compounds scattered around its margins.

There is some disagreement over the final city plan of Paquimé. The excavated portions of the site run approximately north–south along the edge of a low terrace above the Rio Casas Grandes valley. Ruins of undetermined size extend down into the valley bottom, particularly along an alluvial ridge that parallels the terrace edge. Di Peso (1974) suggested that the dense "high-rise" formed a huge inverted "U"-shaped building (open to the south), including both terrace-edge and alluvial-ridge areas; this "U" surrounded a large central plaza. Other archaeologists question the existence of the lower, valley-bottom arm of the "U," suggesting instead that Paquimé was essentially an "L"- or "I"-shaped architectural mass (cf. Lekson 1999b). Di Peso conducted extensive excavations in an external plaza area (that is, west and outside the "U"- or "L"-shaped "high-rise"), and that area was dense with monuments and service features. These included at least five masonry-faced platform mounds ("pyramids" in Di Peso's terms) and effigy mounds (in the forms of a plumed serpent, a decapitated bird, and a cross); two or three ballcourts in the "I"-shape form typical of Mesoamerica (Figure 10.12); two large reservoir/settling ponds for water channeled to Paquimé from distant springs; courtyards with multiple pens for raising and keeping turkeys and macaws (Figure 10.13); areas dedicated to huge ovens for processing large quantities of agave (a local succulent); and other esoteric structures. Notably, all of the known monumental architecture is to the west of the "high-rise" – that is, on the terrace above the "high-rise," away from the river valley.

There are no precedents in the Southwest for this concentration of monumental structures, or for clearly Mesoamerican forms such as "I"-shaped ballcourts. Other architectural details, such as the extensive use of colonnades, also influenced Di Peso's conclusions that Paquimé was a Mesoamerican outpost (Figure 10.14). Significantly, there is only one possible kiva (a distinctly Puebloan feature) at Paquimé (Lekson 1999b) and many archaeologists question that identification. We know very little about the other sites in the Casas Grandes region. Research is ongoing, but it appears that some of the architectural features and many of the technologies seen at Paquimé also appear at other smaller (but still large!) Medio period sites in the region (Whalen and Minnis 2001).

Many aspects of ceramic and lithic industries continued or paralleled local traditions (insofar as these might be known from Mimbres sites, one to two centuries earlier than Paquimé and 250 km to the north; for an excellent summary see Hegmon 2002). Pottery was remarkably varied in form and decoration, but within the canons of Southwestern ceramic traditions (Figure 10.15). Notable examples of unusual forms are "hand drums": open-ended, waisted tubes which Di Peso

Figure 10.12 Ballcourt and mound, Paquimé, Casas Grandes, Chihuahua

Figure 10.13 Macaw-breeding pens, Paquimé, Casas Grandes, Chihuahua

Figure 10.14 Remnants of colonnade, Paquimé, Casas Grandes, Chihuahua

Figure 10.15 Ramos Polychrome jar (vessel in the collections of the University of Colorado Museum)

interpreted as percussion instruments. This form is not known from other regions of the Southwest. There is some evidence that pottery was produced off-site, at kilns closer to fuel sources in the Sierra Madre, but sourcing studies have only just begun (Woosley and Olinger 1993). Lithics included pieces of stunning workmanship made from exotic materials, but again the majority of Paquimé lithic materials and tool types were not out of place in other Southwestern industries.

Several important artifact classes at Paquimé, however, were spectacular and unprecedented in the region. Indeed, the organization of production at Paquimé may have been unique in the Southwest, with remarkably large-scale operations for breeding macaws and turkeys, processing agave, and manufacturing shell orna-ments, serpentine sculptures, and very well made, unusually formal metates (Minnis 1988; Van Pool and Leonard 2002). Quantities of exotic or imported materials far exceed those at other Southwestern sites: two tons of sea shell (from as far away as Maztalan, Mexico); over 100 kg of serpentine from Redrock, New Mexico, 275 km to the north (Lekson 2002a); 300 finished copper artifacts from west Mexico (Vargas 1995); and almost 500 macaws (some of which came from coastal west Mexico, and some of which were bred at Paquimé). Turquoise was not a major import (only about 2 kg was found), although major prehistoric mines are known at Old Hachita, New Mexico, about 180 km north of Paquimé.

From excavations of about one-third of the site, Paquimé produced the remains of 576 individuals, of whom 447 were formal burials (Ravesloot 1988:21). Burials at Paquimé have been interpreted as indicating several tiers of social or political ranking (Ravesloot 1988). At the apex were secondary burials of defleshed bones in huge jars, deposited in a crypt-like space in a major platform mound or pyramid. The second tier includes two adult males placed in wooden crypts in an otherwise unremarkable area of Paquimé, accompanied by remarkable quantities of grave goods. In the crypts and in the chambers above them were scores of disarticulated individuals; they would be consistent with retainers, but other interpretations have been offered (Ravesloot 1988; Whalen and Minnis 2001). Notably, also almost all of the known hand drums were found in the rooms above the burial crypts. The secondary jar burials and the crypt burials represent the pinnacle of Paquimé society. Recent reanalyses support Ravesloot's conclusions, but suggest that "this pinnacle does not appear to be an extremely lofty one" compared to more complex systems (Whalen and Minnis 2001:180–181).

Interpreting Casas Grandes

Di Peso considered Paquimé to be the political and commercial hub of a very large region, extending into southern New Mexico and southeastern Arizona. Other archaeologists extend that area even farther (Schaafsma and Riley 1999:fig. 1), while others have argued that Paquimé's region of political control was, in fact, much smaller (Whalen and Minnis 2001). Paquimé was emphatically interpreted as a complex political system by its excavator, Charles Di Peso. Paquimé's complexity, according to Di Peso, was imported: "The socio-cultural ethos which marked this center and its sister communities did not come into being by spontaneous generation, but rather by direct economic relationship with some older southern city" through the vehicle of *puchteca*, who were commissioned by Mesoamerican kings to find and exploit distant, simpler societies (Di Peso 1974:328). Di Peso compared *puchteca* to the Hudson Bay Company or the Dutch East India Company of more recent colonial times. Complexity was imposed upon Paquimé; or, rather, Paquimé was created as a satellite of distant, hyper-complex Mesoamerican states.

Di Peso based his interpretation on the conspicuous (indeed, spectacular) presence of artifacts from western and central Mexico and architectural forms closely resembling Mesoamerican forms. Like Chaco, the evidence for complexity itself included architecture, burials, material imports, prestige goods, regional structure, social use of force, and extra-regional contacts.

The multi-storied, terraced compounds of Paquimé far more closely resembled Pueblo architecture than the domestic architecture of northern Mexico and Mesoamerica (Lekson 1983, 1999b), but colonnades, "I"-shaped ballcourts, "pyramids," and other monumental structures at Paquimé strongly suggest Mexican prototypes. Paquimé is particularly notable for its Mexican contacts. The evidence can support Di Peso's contention that Paquimé was a Mesoamerican outpost; it can also support arguments that Paquimé was local, with very close connections to the south. Undeniable is the fact that Paquimé demonstrates much stronger connections to Mexico than any other Pueblo site. The Southwest met Mesoamerica at Paquimé. (For an alternate view, see Whalen and Minnis 2003.)

Paquimé was remarkable for its import of materials: tons of shell from the Gulf of California, and serpentine, copper artifacts, and tropical birds (macaws) in quantities unknown elsewhere in the Southwest. The meaning of these imported and prestige goods is a matter of question. Di Peso considered them indicative a mercantile economy; Whalen and Minnis (2000, 2001) suggest that they indicate elite hoarding. Several important categories of materials were produced (rather than simply accumulated) at Paquimé. Minnis (1988) notes several examples of specialized production: turkey- and macaw-breeding, shell jewelry manufacture, and agave-processing. Production in every case was on an impressively large scale, and it is difficult to reconcile these industries with hoarding. In either case – commerce or hoarding – a complex sociopolitical structure is indicated.

Di Peso suggested that Paquimé was the political center of a "sovereignty" in excess of 200,000 km^2 (Di Peso 1974:328). Whalen and Minnis (2001:194) suggest a region one-third to one-half that size, with an interpreted maximum radius of about 140–160 km (the distance to Joyce Wells and nearby ballcourts in southwestern New Mexico). A southern boundary for the Medio phase has been identified at a comparable distance of about 160 km south of Paquimé.

Whalen and Minnis divide this region into three zones: a core of about 15–20 km ("a day's walk") around Paquimé, a middle zone, and an outer periphery (Whalen and Minnis 2001:194). Insofar as is known from admittedly spotty survey, "I"-shaped ballcourts are concentrated in the core, largely absent from the middle zone, and reappear in the outer periphery (at sites like Joyce Wells). Other features and artifacts conspicuous at Paquimé follow similar distributions: "the near-complete absence there [in the middle zone] of almost all of the core features and facilities, from ballcourts to birdcages to agricultural terrace systems" (Whalen and Minnis 2001:191). Some features, such as ballcourts and platform hearths, appear in the outer periphery, but others, such as bird pens, are absent. Di Peso believed that Paquimé held political power over this entire region; Whalen and Minnis (2001) suggest that Paquimé directly controlled only the innermost core area.

The role of violence and socially sanctioned force at Paquimé is a matter of considerable debate, currently in the absence of significant evidence from beyond the site itself. Di Peso (1974) noted the presence of numerous trophy or display skulls and long bones at Paquimé. It is even possible that the putative apex of Paquimé burials – multiple defleshed individuals in large urns, placed in a chamber of a large platform mound – may instead represent trophy or display bones. We lack, however, excavations and evidence of socially sanctioned violence away from Paquimé. It is noteworthy that Medio period sites are seldom located in defensive settings, although late Medio period cliff dwellings are well known from the Sierra Madre, west of Paquimé. The city itself may have fallen to warfare, even massacre (Di Peso 1974; Le Blanc 1999:252; Ravesloot 1988), but the identity of its assailants is far from clear. Taken together, these aspects of Paquimé suggest a complex political structure. To Di Peso, Paquimé was a highly centralized, hierarchical center; for Whalen and Minnis, Paquimé was more local, with less regional centralization and perhaps less autocratic rule than is implied by Di Peso. In either case, Paquimé was complex; the argument is one of degree.

Complexity, History, and Landscape

Chaco (in the 11th and early 12th centuries) and Paquimé (in the late 13th through early 15th centuries) are the most likely candidates for complexity in the Pueblo world. (Hohokam, a non-Puebloan tradition in southern Arizona, was probably politically complex, also; see Hegmon, this volume.) Today, Paquimé is generally accepted as politically complex, but Chaco's complexity is a matter of debate.

Histories of interpretations of Chaco constitute a sizeable sub-literature (e.g., Judge 1989; Lister and Lister 1981; Mills 2002; Sebastian 1992; Vivian 1990). For at least the first five decades at Chaco, researchers such as Lewis H. Morgan, A. V. Kidder, Neil M. Judd, and Edgar L. Hewett generally accepted that its sites represented societies much like modern pueblos, which were thought to be essentially egalitarian and communal. That is, Chaco was not complex (as the term is used here). While pueblos are not leaderless, they do indeed have social structures and leveling mechanisms that discourage the development of political hierarchies, chiefs, and kings. Pueblos are a textbook example of non-hierarchical, non-centralized, town-dwelling agriculturalists. The interpretation of Chaco as a Pueblo society, in more sophisticated variations, continues to be held by many Southwestern archaeologists (e.g., Vivian 1990).

By the 1950s, tree-ring dating made it clear that Chaco was chronologically precocious: its huge buildings appeared in the Pueblo II stage rather than the expected Pueblo III stage. Archaeologists sought causes for this anomaly. The presence of copper bells, macaws, colonnades, and platform mounds suggested a Mexican source for Chaco's developments. The culture-history paradigm of American archaeology in the 1940s through 1960s allowed and encouraged extra-regional interactions and influences in interpretation.

By the late 1960s, a significant minority argued for Mexican inspiration or derivation of Chaco; the majority continued to see Chaco as a troubling local development. Proponents continue to argue for a Mexican derivation of Chaco (Turner and Turner 1999), but in general culture-history approaches (such as Mexican interventions) were swept away by the local adaptive models favored by New Archaeology in the 1970s.

In the New Archaeology, Southwestern valleys were seen as natural laboratories for local evolutionary adaptations. Smaller scales could not make Chaco go away; it remained unusual, perhaps even unique in Pueblo prehistory. Claims for locally evolved political complexity at Chaco crystallized in the 1970s as part of a larger debate about political differences between ancient sites and modern pueblos. Researchers such as Judge (1979), Sebastian (1992), and Wilcox (1993), among many others, argued for variably centralized and hierarchical political structures at Chaco. The term "state" was heard, briefly.

The pendulum, Foucault-like, swung back to the simple side in the 1980s and 1990s, with a series of interpretations of Chaco as a ceremonial center (vacant or sparsely populated). While almost all analysts agree that "ceremonial center" does not negate the presence of leaders, at issue is the nature and scope of leadership. As Mills (2002:79) notes, "within this general model are those who view leaders as obtaining followers through competitive actions . . . and those who see hierarchically organized ritual leaders who cooperatively manage the labor of others." That is, within the ceremonial-center school, there are those who see the seeds of complexity (as the term is used here) and those who do not.

With ripples of British post-processual archaeology reaching the Southwest, the intellectual climate favors "alternative leadership" (Mills 2000) models for Chaco, disarticulating old definitions of complexity and positing un-hierarchical and non-centralized models. It is possible to for scholars to speak of Chaco as an anti-structure (Wills 2000, 2001), a commune (Saitta 1997), a locus of high devotional expression (Renfrew 2001), or as a corporate chiefdom (aka "intermediate society") with "relatively faceless leaders" (Earle 2001:27). It is rather more difficult, these days, to speak of Chaco as a centralized hierarchy.

Paquimé has not suffered swings of interpretation like Chaco, from simple to complex to post-modernly complicated simplicity. Paquimé is generally and uncontroversially considered complex, although there are arguments (of course) about the degree and form of that complexity (Di Peso 1974; Schaafsma and Riley 1999; Whalen and Minnis 2001). Paquimé's simpler path to complexity results, in part, because research at Paquimé began very late (Di Peso 1974); in part, because far fewer archaeologists have professional "stakes" in Paquimé (there is less need to argue); and, in part, because the archaeology of Paquimé is indeed remarkable, with its ballcourts and "pyramid" mounds and treasure troves of exotica. To paraphrase Gregory Johnson (1989): Paquimé *looks* complex.

Di Peso (1974) suggested a powerful central authority, imported from the south and based on *puchteca* economics, with sovereignty over a vast domain. Schaafsma and Riley (1999) suggest that ritual, not economy, was the motor, but retain the southern source through the vehicle of *cacique* – a Mesoamerican religious leader, "with the essential religious objects that declared his right to rule and his accompanying priests and other retainers moved into the Casas Grandes valley and precipitated the development of Paquimé" (Schaafsma and Riley 1999:248). Whalen and Minnis (2001, 2003) attribute complexity at Paquimé to local adaptive and historical dynamics, and set its limits far lower than Di Peso. They emphasize the role of ritual, severely limit the geographic span of control, but retain structures of hierarchy and centralization. Even in a volume on "alternative leadership" in the ancient Southwest, Paquimé remains modestly complex (Whalen and Minnis 2000).

There are far more questions about complexity at Chaco than at Paquimé. As suggested here, the reasons for that situation may be, in part, historical – the differing histories of research at Chaco and Paquimé. As presented above, Chaco and

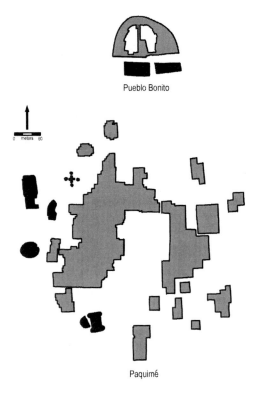

Pueblo Bonito

Paquimé

Figure 10.16 Pueblo Bonito and Paquimé

Paquimé seem comparable in many aspects of architecture, burials, material imports, prestige goods, regional structure, social use of force, and extra-regional contacts, although Paquimé has more of everything than Chaco.

The architecture of both Chaco and Paquimé was notably monumental and (in terms of labor) costly (Figure 10.16). While there is some argument over the actual size and shape of Paquimé, Di Peso's estimates of its total roofed area (about 138,000 m^2) is remarkably close to the total roofed area of Chaco Canyon Great Houses (about 114,000 m^2). (A minimal estimate of Paquimé reduces its total to about 50,000 sq m.) Both centers had considerable investment in non-roofed, non-residential structures: platform mounds (at both), roads, ramps and related structures at Chaco, and ballcourts at Paquimé. Both had strong burial evidence for elite individuals or strata.

At both Chaco (Pueblo Bonito) and Paquimé, two adult males were buried in wooden sub-floor crypts with remarkable quantities of grave goods; over each, many additional individuals in skeletal disarray were placed, piled, or stacked; and in each case, a cache of unique ceramic vessels was stored or deposited in the room above the crypt (cylinder vases at Chaco, hand drums at Paquimé). The burial evidence for elites is strong, and startlingly similar.

At Chaco, there is excellent evidence for bulk import of ceramics and substantial import of lithics. At Paquimé, sourcing studies are underdeveloped, but on typological grounds a great deal of pottery appears to have arrived from afar. While both sites were rich (fabulously so, by impoverished Southwestern standards), Paquimé produced many more prestige goods than Chaco. Chaco manufactured and kept large quantities of turquoise jewelry, and accumulated a sizeable number of macaws and copper objects. Paquimé itself produced macaws by the hundreds and made fancy metates and serpentine stools; it acquired astonishing quantities of shell from the Gulf of California (which were then manufactured into jewelry) and accumulated hundreds of copper objects from western Mexico.

The parallels in regional organization are intriguing. Both Paquimé and Chaco were by far the largest sites in their respective regions, and both (with justification) have been called "primate" centers. The structures and scales of their regions were comparable: a primate center/city, a core area of 15–20 km radius, a zone of clear connections to sites up to 140–160 km (e.g., Chimney Rock and Joyce Well), and arguable associations with sites up to 240–270 km distance (e.g. Bluff Great House and Redrock).

Intriguingly, important public or ceremonial architecture was concentrated (appropriated?) within each center to the exclusion of settlement in the inner zone of its regions: Great Kivas at Chaco (Van Dyke 2002) and ballcourts at Paquimé (Whalen and Minnis 2001) were found in unusually high numbers at the primate center, but were absent or in low frequencies in the inner region. These features reappear in more distant peripheries. Both Paquimé and Chaco appear to have been nodes (and presumably centers) of extensive, elaborate line-of-sight signaling networks. Chaco had elaborate "roads"; we are not sure of the nature and extent of road-like features at Paquimé and in the Casas Grandes region.

Violence played conspicuous, but varying roles in both polities. While display or "trophy" skulls and bones were not uncommon at Paquimé, Chaco had more (and more convincing) evidence for the use of force: the executions at outlying settlements. (Of course, very few outlying settlements have been excavated in the Casas Grandes region.)

Both Chaco and Paquimé conspicuously employed artifacts, architectural forms, and symbolism borrowed from or shared with contemporary civilizations of Mexico; Paquimé on a far more lavish scale than Chaco. Paquimé was far more "Mexican" than Chaco; but Chaco was the most "Mexican" site of its time.

There are differences, to be sure: Chaco was perhaps more violent, Paquimé perhaps more cosmopolitan. The city plans differed: Chaco used space between buildings, Paquimé concentrated its architectural mass in a compact block. These differences may reflect, in part, larger changes in Puebloan architectonics: Pueblo II settlements of Chaco's time were almost always dispersed, while Pueblo IV sites of Paquimé's time were famously compact and dense. Chaco had scores of kivas; Paquimé had, at most, one. These numbers may also reflect more general trends in Pueblo II and Pueblo IV architecture throughout the Pueblo region; numbers of kivas per site plummet from the earlier period to the later.

Along similar lines, differences in artifact classes (such as pottery) at Chaco and Paquimé reflect pan-Southwestern or pan-Pueblo trends in these two periods, a century or more apart. As noted above, the numbers and classes of exotic artifacts and prestige goods differ: perhaps more import of quotidian artifacts at Chaco (although this remains to be seen), and almost certainly more import and production of prestige items at Paquimé.

But, in many important ways, Chaco and Casas Grandes *looked alike*. Indeed, Di Peso (1974) devoted considerable space to a point-by-point comparison of the two sites, in support of his argument (ultimately disproved on chronological grounds) that Chaco was an outpost of Paquimé. Material and organizational similarities between Chaco and Paquimé were real, and have been noted by many other archaeologists (e.g., Le Blanc 1989; Lekson 1999a). Indeed, important aspects of Chaco and Paquimé are so similar that Whalen and Minnis (2001) use Sebastian's (1992) model of complexity at Chaco for their reconstruction of complexity at Paquimé.

It has been suggested that Chaco and Paquimé were connected, historically and symbolically, first by Di Peso (1974) and more recently by Lekson (1999a; cf. Whalen and Minnis 2003). Evidence, far more detailed than the general similarities summarized above, links the two; space precludes discussion here. Paquimé may have followed directly after Chaco, or there may have been an intermediate center at Aztec Ruins, in northern New Mexico (Lekson 1999a). Was Paquimé heir to Chaco (with rulers from Chaco relocating to Paquimé), or was Paquimé a later center appealing to forms and symbolism of the earlier center? Or did both Chaco and Paquimé employ, independently, the forms and symbolism from a Mexican model? It is, of course, possible that the two had no meaningful commerce or connection; but then we have equifinality that requires a return to simple evolutionary faith for patterned emergence of complexity. It seems more likely that history and geography played roles. I conclude with remarks on geography and thoughts on history.

One of the perceived obstacles to complexity at Chaco Canyon and Paquimé, and to their historical connection, is geographic scale. Their regions seem excessive; the distance between the two is daunting (over 600 km). Distance is seen as an insurmountable barrier: "transaction costs" constrained the engagement of center and peripheries (Whalen and Minnis 2001:195). Was political power a bulk commodity, with transportation costs? Southwestern systems were probably not "staple-financed" (Earle 2001); it seems far more likely that they operated with prestige goods, so markedly abundant at Chaco and Paquimé. Concentration of preciosities at archaeological sites may represent hoarding; extensive production of turquoise jewelry at Chaco and large-scale breeding of macaws at Paquimé suggest otherwise.

Perhaps distance was less a barrier than an opportunity: Mary Helms (1988) wrote persuasively about the power of distance for chiefdoms, petty kingdoms, and other fledgling complex societies on the edge of great civilizations. Local rulers appealed to (and often traveled to) larger polities, and used those distant experiences, contacts, and exotica to buttress and justify their rule. So, too, for

Chaco Canyon and Paquimé; and, perhaps, for local leaders at their outliers, trips to the great Southwestern centers constituted, symbolically, far longer journeys to Tollan – real or imaginary.

How could Chaco Canyon usefully interact with, much less politically influence, outliers as far away as Chimney Rock or the Bluff Great House? How could Paquimé project its power to distant Joyce Well? Again, distance – and the Southwest itself – may have shaped polities into larger but looser formations than in other parts of the world. Chaco's and Paquimé's regions were big, but not dense. Space separated center from periphery and periphery from periphery. That space was, perhaps, no barrier. Southwestern skies are wonderfully clear; Southwestern land is nothing if not vistas. Mesas and canyons, basins and ranges, offer vast fields of view: the *genius loci* of the desert. Recall the elaborate networks of line-of-site signaling stations at both Chaco Canyon and Paquimé. Chimney Rock was built at a unique site that allowed a clear view of distant Huerfano Peak. Huerfano Peak, covered with fireboxes and shrines, looks directly out to distant Pueblo Alto, at Chaco Canyon. From Chaco to Chimney rock, 140 km, in a single "repeat." If Southwestern polities were built on feathers and fripperies, they may have been administered by smoke and mirrors. Power may have been demonstrated, not inhibited, by action over distance.

If the Southwest supported modestly complex entities, they should be remembered. They are, in Pueblo traditional histories (Lekson 1999a:143–150). Today's Pueblo people remember a "people who had enormous amounts of power: spiritual power and power over people . . . [who] lived in Chaco" (Paul Pino, in Sofaer 1999). Chaco Canyon is remembered as a place where things happened that were improper for Pueblo people: things like political complexity.

Historically, it is interesting to consider what caused the leveling mechanisms and communal structures for which modern pueblos are uniquely known. Did the ancient Southwest evolve, inexorably, to that remarkable condition? Or did Pueblo people create and institute those social structures inimical to hierarchy, *in reaction* to episodes of complexity in their past? Chaco Canyon was, perhaps, not a happy place: "some people who come here [to Chaco] feel there was an aspect of this place that was, perhaps, darker" (Phil Tuwalstiwa, in Sofaer 1999). (Recall that Chaco either employed or degenerated into frightful violence.) Chaco represents an episode of complexity, the memory of which shapes Pueblo worldviews today.

How long was the Pueblo world complex? Chaco may have been as short-lived as 70 years: A.D. 1020 marked the beginning of intense construction at Chaco (Lekson 1984) and by A.D. 1090 the focus shifted north to Aztec Ruins (Judge 1989). Or Chaco may have lasted as long as four centuries: A.D. 850 marks the starting date for Great House construction and A.D. 1250 the approximate end-date of occupation. And then there's more. Many archaeologists believe that something like Chaco continued at Aztec Ruins until at least A.D. 1140 and perhaps through A.D. 1280 (Judge 1989; Lekson 1999a). And a few archaeologists argue that the principles (and perhaps principals) of Chaco Canyon actively structured Paquimé, which dates from about A.D. 1250 to 1450 (Lekson 1999a). So, how long? At minimum, Chaco lasted perhaps little over six decades; at maximum, the sequence of Chaco, Aztec, and Paquimé lasted six centuries.

Sixty or seventy years is not a bad run: three generations, and perhaps two life-spans – the two adult males buried in the crypt of Pueblo Bonito? If these were rulers, did their roles continued at Aztec or Paquimé? We do not know enough about Aztec Ruins to answer that question, but recall the two very similar burials at Paquimé. Even at seventy years, Chaco Canyon was not a brief episode; and it seems possible that complexity at Chaco Canyon was not a passing anomaly. It may have been the beginning of a much longer history – a tradition, an institution – of centralized hierarchy, played out over centuries at Aztec Ruins and Paquimé. In either event, short or long, when complexity left the Colorado Plateau and the homelands of the modern Pueblos, the people who stayed behind created new cultural controls – social structures, ceremonial systems – to make sure it would never happen again.

REFERENCES

Adams, E. Charles, 1991 *The Origin and Development of the Pueblo Katsina Cult*. Tucson: University of Arizona Press.

Akins, Nancy J., 2001 Chaco Canyon mortuary practices: Archaeological correlates of complexity. In *Ancient Burial Practices in the American Southwest*. Douglas R. Mitchell and Judy L. Brunson-Hadley, eds. Pp. 167–190. Albuquerque: University of New Mexico Press.

Bandelier, Adolph F. A., 1892 *Final Report of Investigations Among the Indians of the Southwestern United State*, vol. 2. Papers of the Archaeological Institute of America, American Series 4. Cambridge, MA.

Bradley, Ronna Jane, 2000 Recent advances in Chihuahuan archaeology. In *Greater Mesoamerica: The Archaeology of West and Northwest Mexico*, Michael S. Foster and Shirley Gorenstein, eds. Pp. 221–239. Salt Lake City: University of Utah Press.

Cameron, Catherine M., 1998 Coursed adobe architecture, style, and social boundaries in the American Southwest. In *The Archaeology of Social Boundaries*. Miriam Stark, ed. Pp. 193–217. Washington, DC: Smithsonian Institution Press.

——2001 Pink chert, projectile points, and the Chacoan regional system. *American Antiquity* 66(1), 79–102.

——2002 Sacred earthen architecture in the Northern Southwest: The Bluff Great House Berm. *American Antiquity* 67(4), 677–695.

Crown, Patricia L., and W. James Judge, eds., 1991 *Chaco and Hohokam: Prehistoric Regional Systems in the American Southwest*. Santa Fe: School of American Research Press.

Darling, J. Andrew, 1999 Mass inhumation and the execution of witches in the American Southwest. *American Anthropologist* 100, 732–752.

Dean, Jeffrey S., ed., 2000 *Salado*. Tucson: University of Arizona Press.

Dean, Jeffrey S., and John C. Ravesloot, 1993 The chronology of cultural interaction in the Gran Chichimeca. In *Culture and Contact: Charles C. Di Peso's Gran Chichimeca*. Anne I. Woosely, and John C. Ravesloot, eds. Pp. 83–103. Albuquerque: University of New Mexico Press.

Di Peso, Charles C., 1974 *Casas Grandes: A Fallen Trading Center of the Gran Chichimeca*, vols 1–3. Dragoon: Amerind Foundation.

Di Peso, Charles C., John B. Rinaldo, and Gloria J. Fenner, 1974 *Casas Grandes: A Fallen Trading Center of the Gran Chichimeca*, vols 4–8. Dragoon: Amerind Foundation.

Dongoske, Kurt E., Deborah L. Martin, and T. J. Ferguson, 2000 Critique of the claim of cannibalism at Cowboy Wash. *American Antiquity* 65, 179–190.

Doolittle, William E., 1993 Canal irrigation at Casas Grandes: A technological and developmental assessment of its origins. In *Culture and Contact: Charles C. Di Peso's Gran Chichimeca*. Anne I. Woosely, and John C. Ravesloot, eds. Pp. 133–151. Albuquerque: University of New Mexico Press.

Earle, Timothy, 2001 Economic support of Chaco Canyon society. *American Antiquity* 66(1), 26–35.

Eddy, Frank W., 1977 *Archaeological investigations at Chimney Rock Mesa, 1970–1972*. Memoirs of the Colorado Archaeological Society 1. Boulder, CO.

Force, Eric R., R. Gwinn Vivian, Thomas C. Windes, and Jeffrey S. Dean, 2002 *Relation of the "Bonito" Paleo-Channels and Base-Level Variations to Anasazi Occupation, Chaco Cayon, New Mexico*. Archaeological Series 194. Tucson: Arizona State Museum.

Hayes, Alden C., and Thomas C. Windes, 1975 An Anasazi shrine in Chaco Canyon. In *Collected Papers in Honor of Florence Hawley Ellis*. Theodore R. Frisbie, ed. Pp. 143–156. Papers of the Archaeological Society of New Mexico 2. Santa Fe.

Hegmon, Michelle, 2002 Recent Issues in the archaeology of the Mimbres region of the North American Southwest. *Journal of Archaeological Research* 10(4), 307–357.

Helms, Mary W., 1988 *Ulysses' Sail: An Ethnographic Odyssey of Power, Knowledge, and Geographical Distance*. Princeton: Princeton University Press.

Johnson, Gregory A., 1989 Dynamics of southwestern prehistory: Far outside – looking in. In *Dynamics of Southwest Prehistory*. Linda S. Cordell and George J. Gumerman, eds. Pp. 371–389. Washington, DC: Smithsonian Institution Press.

Judd, Neil N., 1954 *The Material Culture of Pueblo Bonito*. Smithsonian Miscellaneous Collections 124. Washington, DC: Smithsonian Institution Press.

——1959 *Pueblo del Arroyo, Chaco Canyon, New Mexico*. Smithsonian Miscellaneous Collections 138(1). Washington, DC: Smithsonian Institution Press.

——1964 *The Architecture of Pueblo Bonito*. Smithsonian Miscellaneous Collections 147(1). Washington, DC: Smithsonian Institution Press.

Judge, W. James, 1979 The development of a complex cultural ecosystem in the Chaco Basin, New Mexico. In *Proceedings of the First Conference on Scientific Research in the National Parks*, pt. 3. R. M. Linn, ed. Pp. 901–906. Washington, DC: National Park Service.

——1989 Chaco Canyon–San Juan Basin. In *Dynamics of Southwest Prehistory*. Linda S. Cordell and George J. Gumerman, eds. Pp. 209–261. Washington, DC: Smithsonian Institution Press.

Kantner, John, 2002 Complexity. In *Darwin and Archaeology: A Handbook of Key Concepts*. John P. Hart and John Edward Terrell, eds. Pp. 89–106. Westport, CT: Bergin & Garvey.

Kantner, John, and Nancy M. Mahoney, eds., 2000 *Great House Communities Across the Chacoan Landscape*. Anthropological Papers of the University of Arizona 64. Tucson: University of Arizona Press.

LeBlanc, Steven A., 1999 *Prehistoric Warfare in the American Southwest*. Salt Lake City: University of Utah Press.

Lekson, Stephen H., 1983 Chaco architecture in continental context. In *Proceedings of the Anasazi Symposium 1981*. Jack E. Smith, ed. Pp. 183–194. Mesa Verde, CO: Mesa Verde Museum Association.

——1984 *Great Pueblo Architecture of Chaco Canyon*. Publications in Archaeology 18B. Albuquerque: National Park Service.

——1999a *Chaco Meridian: Centers of Political Power in the Ancient Southwest*. Walnut Creek, CA: AltaMira Press.

——1999b Was Casas a pueblo? In *The Casas Grandes World*. Curtis F. Schaafsma and Carroll L. Riley, eds. Pp. 84–92. Salt Lake City: University of Utah Press.

——2002a *Salado Archaeology of the Upper Gila*. Anthropological Papers of the University of Arizona 67. Tucson: University of Arizona Press.

——2002b War in the Southwest, war in the world. *American Antiquity* 67(4), 607–624.

Lekson, Stephen H., ed., 1983 *The Architecture and Dendrochronology of Chetro Ketl, Chaco Canyon, New Mexico*. Reports of the Chaco Center 6. Albuquerque: National Park Service.

Lekson, Stephen H., Curtis P. Nepstad-Thornberry, Brian E. Yunker, Toni S. Laumbach, David P. Cain, and Karl W. Laumbach, 2002 Migrations in the Southwest: Pinnacle Ruin, southwestern New Mexico. *Kiva* 68(2), 73–101.

Lister, Robert H., 1978 Mesoamerican influences at Chaco Canyon, New Mexico. In *Across the Chichimec Sea*. Carroll L. Riley and Basil C. Hedrick, eds. Pp. 233–241. Carbondale: Southern Illinois University Press.

Lister, Robert H., and Florence C. Lister, 1981 *Chaco Canyon: Archaeology and Archaeologists*. Albuquerque: University of New Mexico Press.

Mathien, Frances Joan, 1997 Ornaments of the Chaco Anasazi. In *Ceramics, Lithics, and Ornaments of Chaco Canyon*, vol. 3. Frances Joan Mathien, ed. Pp. 1119–1219. Santa Fe, NM: National Park Service, US Department of the Interior.

Mills, Barbara J., 2000 Alternative models, alternative strategies: leadership in the Prehispanic Southwest. In *Alternative Leadership Strategies in the Prehispanic Southwest*. B. J. Mills, ed. Pp. 3–18. Tucson: University of Arizona Press.

Mills, Barbara J., 2002 Recent research on Chaco: Changing views on economy, ritual and society. *Journal of Archaeological Research* 10(1), 65–117.

Minnis, Paul E., 1988 Four examples of specialized production at Casas Grandes, northwestern Chihuahua. *Kiva* 53(2), 181–194.

Ravesloot, John C., 1988 *Mortuary Practices and Social Differentiation at Casas Grandes, Chihuahua, Mexico*. Anthropological Papers of the University of Arizona 49. Tucson: University of Arizona Press.

Renfrew, Colin, 2001 Production and consumption in a sacred economy: The material correlates of high devotional expression at Chaco Canyon. *American Antiquity* 66(1), 14–25.

Saitta, Dean J., 1997 Power, labor, and the dynamics of change in Chacoan political economy. *American Antiquity* 62(1), 7–26.

Schaafsma, Curtis F., and Carroll L. Riley, 1999 Introduction. In *The Casas Grandes World*. Curtis F. Schaafsma and Carroll L. Riley, eds. Pp. 3–11. Salt Lake City: University of Utah Press.

Sebastian, Lynne, 1992 *The Chaco Anasazi: Sociopolitical Evolution in the Prehistoric Southwest*. Cambridge: Cambridge University Press.

Skibo, James M., Eugene B. McCluney, and William H. Walker, 2002 *The Joyce Well Site: On the Frontier of the Casas Grandes World*. Salt Lake City: University of Utah Press.

Sofaer, Anna, 1997 The Primary Architecture of the Chacoan Culture: A Cosmological Expression. In *Anasazi Architecture and American Design*. Baker H. Morrow and V. B. Price, eds. Pp. 88–132. Albuquerque: University of New Mexico Press.

Sofaer, Anna (producer), 1999 *The Mystery of Chaco Canyon* (video). Oley, PA: Bullfrog Films.

Swanson, Steve, 2003 Documenting prehistoric community networks: A case study in the Paquimé valley. *American Antiquity* 68(4), 753–767.

Toll, H. Wolcott III, 2001 Making and breaking pots in the Chaco world. *American Antiquity* 66(1), 56–78.

Turner, Christy G. II, and Jacqueline A. Turner, 1999 *Man Corn*. Salt Lake City: University of Utah Press.

Van Dyke, Ruth M., 2002 The Chacoan Great Kiva in outlier communities. *Kiva* 67(3), 231–247.

Van Pool, Todd L., and Robert D. Leonard, 2002 Specialized ground stone production in the Casas Grandes region of northern Chihuahua, Mexico. *American Antiquity* 67(4), 710–730.

Vargas, Victoria D., 1995 *Copper Bell Trade Patterns in the Prehispanic U.S. Southwest and Northwest Mexico*. Archaeological Series 187. Tucson: Arizona State Museum.

Vivian, Gordon, and Tom W. Mathews, 1964 *Kin Kletso: A Pueblo III Community in Chaco Canyon, New Mexico*. Technical Series 6, pt. 1. Globe: Southwest Parks and Monuments Association.

Vivian, R. Gwinn, 1990 *The Chaco Prehistory of the San Juan Basin*. San Diego: Academic Press.

Whalen, Michael E., and Paul E. Minnis, 2000 Leadership at Casas Grandes, Chihuahua, Mexico. In *Alternative Leadership Strategies in the Prehispanic Southwest*. Barbara J. Mills, ed. Pp. 168–179. Tucson: University of Arizona Press.

——2001 *Casas Grandes and its Hinterlands: Prehistoric Regional Organization in Northwest Mexico*. Tucson: University of Arizona Press.

——2003 The local and the distant in the origins of Casas Grandes, Chihuahua, Mexico. *American Antiquity* 68(2), 314–332.

Wilcox, David R., 1993 The evolution of the Chacoan polity. In *The Chimney Rock Archaeological Symposium*. J. McKim Malville and Gary Matlock, eds. Pp. 76–90. USDA Forest Service General Technical Report RM-227. Rocky Mountain Forest and Range Experiment Station, Fort Collins, CO.

——1999 A preliminary graph-theoretic analysis of access relationships at Casas Grandes. In *The Casas Grandes World*. Curtis F. Schaafsma and Carroll L. Riley, eds. Pp. 93–104. Salt Lake City: University of Utah Press.

Wills, W. H., 2000 Political leadership and construction of Chacoan Great Houses, A.D. 1020–1140. In *Alternative Leadership Strategies in the Prehispanic Southwest*. Barbara J. Mills, ed. Pp. 19–44. Tucson: University of Arizona Press.

——2001 Ritual and mound formation during the Bonito phase in Chaco Canyon. *American Antiquity* 66, 433–452.

Windes, Thomas C., 1987 *Investigations at the Pueblo Alto Complex, Chaco Canyon, New Mexico, 1975–1979*. Publications in Archaeology 18F, vols 1–3. Santa Fe: National Park Service.

Wiseman, Reggie N., and J. Andrew Darling, 1986 The Bronze Trail Group: More evidence for a Cerrillos–Chaco turquoise connection. In *By Hands Unknown*. Anne Poore, ed. Pp. 115–143. Papers of the Archaeological Society of New Mexico 12. Santa Fe: Ancient City Press.

Woosley, Anne I., and Bart Olinger, 1993 The Casas Grandes ceramic tradition. In *Culture and Contact: Charles C. Di Peso's Gran Chichimeca*. Anne I. Woosley and John C. Ravesloot, eds. Pp. 105–131. Albuquerque: University of New Mexico Press.

11

Social and Physical Landscapes of Contact

Stephen W. Silliman

The study of culture contact and colonialism holds a unique place in North American archaeology. History and prehistory collide in this realm. I do not mean the crashing of Western history onto imaginary pristine shores of ahistorical, homogeneous, indigenous cultures. As other chapters in this volume attest, precontact societies and lifeways on the North American continent were as varied and full of history as any; they just did not record their histories in written words. By collision, I mean the presumed incompatible intersections of "prehistorians" and "historical archaeologists." The former tend to see their realm of study, Native American cultures, not extending beyond the arrival of European colonists with any resemblance to their "traditional" forms. The latter tend to restrict their studies to North American contexts with documentary evidence, meaning that they frequently focus on European colonial places and institutions. As a result, Native American people struggling and surviving in colonial worlds of North America after 1492 can slip through these artificial research cracks (Lightfoot 1995). Fortunately, many archaeologists have been working on the elusive interface between precontact and postcontact history, and this chapter summarizes a few highlights and revelations of the past few decades.

The archaeology of culture contact is unique for yet another reason: it is one of the few research domains in North American archaeology that can take a comparative, continental approach. The topic of culture contact and colonialism, terms that I hesitantly interchange throughout the chapter, can be broadly construed since diverse Native American peoples encountered assorted versions of Western expansion, colonialism, capitalism, and worldviews in many places across North America. Certainly, the colonial fronts varied greatly, as did the numerous and distinct Native American groups that they encountered. However, only in the context of colonialism can one discuss some of the real commonalties of experience between Native societies in New England and California or the Southwest and Florida. Otherwise, precontact North American indigenous cultural practices were highly diverse despite regional connections, and individuals did not consider themselves "Native American" but rather, for example, Kashaya Pomo (northern California), Apalachee (northern Florida), or Wampanoag (eastern Massachusetts). Moreover, in the context of colonial contact, Native American people across the continent began combating the shared experience of weighty politics of assimilation, acculturation, and proclaimed disappearance.

Because of the links forged in the context of colonialism, I organize this chapter by issue rather than region. I engage with aspects of social theory, but I refrain from referencing that literature to keep the chapter manageable and focused on North American contexts. The notion of "landscape" is a useful metaphor to organize the issues because it combines the physical and social, local and global, setting and outcome, and spatiality and materiality. I recognize that one cannot begin to fathom the intricacies of culture contact experiences without a detailed understanding of the local histories that anchored Native American groups. Similarly, one cannot track the complex effects of colonialism without acknowledging the depth and difference of its multiple fronts – for example, Spanish Catholic missions, Dutch settlements, Russian fur-trade outposts, or British forts. Yet, I must collapse the subtleties of both precontact and colonial variability to make my points. My focus on archaeological issues provides a guide to traversing the multifaceted landscapes of colonialism and culture contact, and I select cases from well-researched regions like the Southeast, Northeast, and West Coast to illustrate. To provide any semblance of the richness of contact archaeology in a chapter of this length requires that I minimize some regions in place of more detail in others. My choices partly reflect personal research interests and partly mirror the publication visibility of certain regions, but they never mean to deny the variety of approaches and regions participating in the broad project of North American post-contact archaeology.

Physical and Biological Landscapes

Students of North American culture contact agree that the arrival of Europeans marked the beginning of significant changes in physical and biological landscapes. From the expansion of European plants and animals into North American habitats to European over-harvesting of indigenous species, and from the deadly spread of pathogens and epidemics to the substantial impacts of colonialism on the health and diet of the indigenous population, issues involving the physical and biological landscape have taken a leading role in contact-period studies.

Archaeologists have become major players in the debates surrounding environmental change, disease, health, diet, and their impacts on Native American bodies and cultures during this tumultuous period. To organize these topics, I divide physical and biological landscapes into environmental change, disease and demography, and health and diet. All three topics interrelate since they concern changes in the plant, animal, and disease environment during the settlement of North America by Europeans, but they differ in scale. Environmental change is a regional phenomenon, disease and demography often operate on populations, and health and diet relate very much to individuals. Of course, individuals experience disease and make up larger demographic patterns, but this analytical distinction serves to clarify the archaeological studies.

Environmental change

Any discussion of environmental change in the contact period engages with the conclusions put forward in the landmark book, *Ecological Imperialism* (Crosby 1986). Crosby argues that North America transformed into a physical landscape of remarkable similarity to Europe by the intentional and accidental introduction of European crops and weeds, livestock and commensal species, and diseases into the New World. Significantly, this ecological expansion often occurred well in advance of the colonists themselves. The importance of this ecological transformation was not that this was the first time Native Americans had witnessed or had a hand in the alteration of the physical environment. One must recall the precontact changes wrought by agricultural fields of the eastern Woodlands, irrigation systems of the Southwest, and fire-management tactics by West Coast hunter-gatherers. The problem was that this post-Columbian transformation was rapid, immense, and pan-regional.

Although environmental change was widespread, it did not immediately usher in radical changes in North American ecological settings. For instance, many expected that the Spanish colonization of *La Florida* would have resulted in livestock overrunning indigenous species, but zooarchaeological work in mission, town, and Native village sites has demonstrated that local animal species found their way into Native American and Spanish kitchens (Reitz 1990, 1993). This suggests that cattle may not have been as abundant as an overextended "ecological imperialism" might predict. On the other hand, introduced plants made rapid time across the continent. Plant specialists have found European species in great abundance in the earliest bricks of 18th-century Spanish California missions.

Disease and demography

In addition to tackling evidence for environmental change, students of the contact period face the daunting task of evaluating the impacts of European diseases on Native Americans. Contrary to some scholars' notions of North Americans as "disease-free," Native America had its share of infectious diseases and maladies. However, these did not prepare the biological population for a host of novel pathogens to which they had no immunity. Questions of what Old World diseases affected which people, how much, how often, and when are essential ones for this time period for two reasons. First, historical documents, oral histories, and skeletal evidence tell of the horrendous casualties suffered by Native American people exposed to European diseases such as smallpox, influenza, measles, and diphtheria (Crosby 1986; Dobyns 1983). Many of these diseases took on epidemic if not pandemic proportions, spreading rapidly and destructively into many regions. Some have argued that the disease toll was so severe and ubiquitous that all Native American groups experienced a demographic collapse.

The second reason is a related one. If the disease toll was a great as projected by some scholars, such as Dobyns's (1983) estimates approaching 90–95 percent mortality across North America in the early 1500s, then anthropologists must entertain the possibility that historical observations made about Native Americans in the two or three centuries after these pandemics are about people greatly changed from precontact periods (Dunnell 1991). As such, ethnohistorical or ethnographic documents may not serve as appropriate analogs for interpreting the "prehistory" of Native America. The extreme position has been characterized as the "new demographic paradigm," epitomized by Dobyns's assertion that "aboriginal lifeways for the native peoples of North America clearly terminated with the large-scale depopulation caused by the initial smallpox epidemic in 1520–25" (Dobyns 1983:25).

Controversy has mobilized numerous archaeologists to critically evaluate the notion of a widespread demographic collapse of Native American populations (Kealhofer and Baker 1996; Larsen 1994; Larsen et al. 2001; Ramenofsky 1987). Their findings suggest that a more nuanced view is required, one that takes into account the timing of contact and disease, type of society (e.g., mobile versus sedentary, hierarchical versus egalitarian) involved, amount of European–Native interaction, and susceptibility of Native American populations as a result of malnutrition, parasites, crowding, labor exploitation, and pre-existing diseases. A call for contextual studies does not deny the possibility that protohistoric demographic collapse may have occurred in some regions. However, growing evidence suggests that demographic decline may have been more a consequence of sustained, rather than first, contact with Europeans (Kealhofer and Baker 1996) and that historic rather than protohistoric epidemics were often the more deadly (Walker and Johnson 1992).

A continental and uniform demographic collapse simply seems unwarranted in the face of recent research, as does the position held by Dunnell that Native Americans in the post-Columbian era were effectively shut off from their heritage and cultural practices. A more reasonable stance is that the colonial period was just one point on the trajectory linking precontact and contemporary Native communities (Lightfoot 1995) and that the impact of disease was highly variable and regionally specific (Kealhofer and Baker 1996; Ramenofsky 1987; Verano and Ubelaker 1992). Certainly, anthropologists recognize that a massive, disease-induced decline in Native American populations occurred and that such a demographic diminution resulted in considerable loss of cultural knowledge and practices, but historic, and by extension contemporary, Native American groups were not completely severed from their past social, political, economic, and religious practices.

Archaeologists approach the topic of North American disease and demography in a number of ways. A primary entry relies on ethnohistorians' use of archival sources that document population sizes or particular cases of diseases. These are excellent sources of information, but they do little to clarify the impact of diseases on groups outside the purview of European writers. This fingers a serious problem with Dobyns's model of demographic collapse: how can we extrapolate the waves of deadly epidemics in areas undocumented by Europeans without the careful use of archaeological data? Doing otherwise simply assumes rather than tests what we propose to explain. Archaeologists have taken their cue and entered the debate with interesting and diverse data.

One such dataset involves comparing demography and settlement patterns before and after European contact. Archaeologists have demonstrated that some regions, such as the Southeast, show a major shift in settlement pattern before contact, one that may have helped buffer later European intrusions (Johnson and Lehmann 1996). However, not all areas survived early disease in the Southeast, such as riverine but not rural Caddoan populations who succumbed to 16th-century epidemics as evidenced by changes in mound construction, cemeteries, and settlement patterns (Perttula 1991). Some groups, such as the eastern Pueblo of the Southwest, had pre-existing strategies of "demographic and organizational flexibility" for dealing with environmental fluctuations that may have adapted them to better handle disruptions caused by epidemic disease (Palkovich 1996:192). Other areas, such as the Midwest, showed abandonment during late precontact times, perhaps as chiefdoms established buffer zones between competing polities (Milner 1992). Still other studies seem to indicate a rise in protohistoric populations following initial contact until actual European colonization, such as in California (Kealhofer 1996).

The best method for evaluating demographic collapse involves examining sites that span the precontact, protohistoric, and historic periods with tight chronologies. Ramenofsky (1987) offers one of the most detailed studies for the Southeast, New York, and the middle Missouri River areas. Using sophisticated seriation and population computation techniques, Ramenofsky tracked the "disease centuries" for the three regions and offered critical evaluations of Dobyns's pandemics. She found parts of the Southeast ravaged by disease in the 16th century following de Soto's *entrada*, but she concluded that middle Missouri and central New York populations avoided decimation until the 17th century (Ramenofsky 1987; see also Chilton, Henning, this volume). Additional research has revealed that Iroquois survival had much to do with migration, group absorption, and the political power of the Five Nations Confederacy (Snow 1992). Ramenofsky (1987:170–171) concluded that Dobyns's initial smallpox pandemic seemed likely, but that his projected waves of other pathogens require serious reconsideration.

A seemingly clearer assessment of demographic collapse is the analysis of human skeletal remains, but these offer ambiguous data. Skeletal remains reveal what individuals suffered and often how they died, but in and of themselves, they do not tell anything about demographic collapse. Only with large sample sizes and relatively complete demographic life tables does this become possible. Moreover, while multiple burials may be the result of post-epidemic mass interment, the ability to distinguish these from pre-existing cultural practices of multiple interment, accretional burials, or other factors remains elusive. The many historical observations of greater numbers of dead than living Native Americans could bury suggest that cemeteries may not offer the final resolution to this issue. Finally, the largest problem in contact-period bioarchaeology is one that plagues all studies: "The epidemics so frequently documented in narrative accounts are almost never identifiable in skeletal series" (Larsen 1994:113). Conditions that do leave skeletal signatures are (1) bouts of anemia or growth disruption that frequently result from malnutrition, diarrhea, parasites, or infection, or (2) skeletal lesions that result from trauma or infection. As such, the skeletal features can serve as a proxy measure of disease loads and overall health despite their non-specificity. Since the skeletal pathologies record events primarily during childhood, they attest more to the biological state of *survivors* than to particular conditions as clear agents of death (Larsen 1994; Larsen et al. 2001).

Health and diet

Native American health and diet intimately connect to the parameters of ecological change, disease, and demography. Health and diet are the on-the-ground, microscale, and almost biographical level where the regional and macroscale factors have their impact and often their very origin. Stated differently, amidst the alterations in the plant, animal, and disease environments are individuals living and dying, making choices, struggling for biological and cultural survival, and adapting to novel circumstances. Physical bodies and food refuse frequently record these actions, and archaeologists have made noteworthy advances using these lines of evidence. Bioarchaeological studies have provided rich evidence of Native American health and diet during contact and colonial periods, as have zooarchaeological and paleoethnobotanical analyses.

Native American health during colonial periods has received considerable attention in the context of studying Old World diseases in North America. As they have in other archaeological contexts, bioarchaeological studies have focused on the identification of disease, physiological deficiency, trauma, and repetitive activity in human skeletons. To make sense of osteological data requires careful comparisons between skeletons from before and those from after European contact; only with the "baseline" of precontact patterns can archaeologists assess the *relative* changes in health. Currently, the most thorough bioarchaeological projects have focused on the Spanish borderlands in the Southeast region during the 16th through 18th centuries.

In the colonial-period Southeast, Larsen and his colleagues have isolated a number of biological consequences of contact for Native American health. Their studies of coastal Georgia and coastal/inland Florida have shown a number of patterns, which they recently synthesized and expanded (Larsen et al. 2001). First, the frequency of microscopic (Retzius lines) and macroscopic (hypoplasia) tooth defects, which indicate metabolic stress in childhood, increased between the precontact and mission periods. Second, similar studies of the mission period revealed an increase in infectious disease through periosteal lesions on bones and an increase in iron deficiency through lesions on the cranium (porotic hyperostosis) and in the eye orbits (cribra orbitalia). Third, they discovered an increase in skeletal robusticity and an elevation in osteoarthritis, particularly in the late mission period, indicating that individuals did more repetitive, heavy, physical work as part of Spanish labor requirements. Males showed a more marked increase in osteoarthritis over women from precontact to colonial periods as a likely consequence of enforced work activities, but all showed an earlier onset of osteoarthritis (Larsen et al. 1996:115–117). Fourth, studies of bone biomechanical properties reveal reduced overall mobility, despite a few males demonstrating remarkably high mobility as a result of hauling heavy loads over long distances. Fifth, very little evidence of trauma appears on the contact-period skeletons from the Southeast (Larsen 1994:130), suggesting that general living conditions in the colonial world, rather than outright physical conflict, took a greater biological toll on Native Americans. In sum, these patterns suggest a decline in Native American health in and around the Spanish missions because of increased infections, poor living conditions, alterations in diet, and strenuous colonial labor. Many of these patterns of declining health occurred in other regions, such as Texas (Miller 1996), the Southwest (Stodder and Martin 1992), and California (Walker et al. 1989; Walker and Johnson 1994), but with significant variability.

The issue of Native American health ties directly to diet. How did the colonial period affect Native American diets and what impacts did this have on nutrition and cultural practices? The previous discussions regarding anemia and growth arrest due to malnutrition offer some insights into the quality of Native diet and its general decline in colonial contexts, but I turn here to specific assessments of the composition of contact-period diets. Bioarchaeology provides one entry through the analysis of skeletal isotopes and the frequency of dental caries. Zooarchaeological and paleoethnobotanical research provides a more common way, one that can detail the diversity of plants and animals in past diets while respecting Native American preferences for leaving skeletal remains undisturbed and unstudied. Sitting at the forefront of studies of diet are questions about which introduced plants and animals entered the Native American menu. The answers are far from simple since they vary from region to region, group to group, and colonial front to colonial front.

To sample the diversity, it is worthwhile to discuss again the Spanish borderlands region of the Southeast, Southwest, and California. A combination of biological and environmental studies indicate that Native groups in the Southeast shifted their precontact subsistence balanced between marine foods, maize agriculture, and terrestrial plants and animals strongly toward a focus on maize and a regional homogenization of diet during Spanish colonization. The conclusion relies on skeletal isotope data from precontact and mission burials (Larsen et al. 2001); increased frequencies of mission-period dental caries, meaning the consumption of starchier foods (Larsen et al. 2001); and the prevalence of maize and decline of marine foods in the faunal and floral records (Reitz 1990; Ruhl 1993). The particular mixture varied somewhat by environmental region, and often the early Spanish diets differed little from the Native American ones (Reitz 1993; Scarry 1993). These indicate an adaptation of Spanish residents to local food resources, undoubtedly provided in part by Native peoples through colonial tribute requirements.

In California, archaeologists have investigated a variety of contact-period and colonial sites for information on Native American diet. The 19th-century Russian colony of Ross on the northern California coast reveals an intriguing mixture of foods that combined the maritime focus of the Native Alaskans transported there as workers, the terrestrial focus of the local Native American groups, and the live-stock and crop emphasis of the resident Russians (Wake 1997). The combination appears to comprise part of the negotiation of gender and identity between Native Americans and Native Alaskans in the shadow of the Russian stockade (Lightfoot et al. 1998). In addition, the Spanish California mission contexts dating between 1769 and 1834 look remarkably similar to those in the Southeast: a strong focus on cattle as the main source of animal food accompanying a noticeable reliance on wild fauna. The same pattern held in the plant foods, with introduced wheat and barley taking a primary role in Native diets (Walker and Johnson 1992), but only with continued use of locally gathered plants (Allen 1998). On Mexican-Californian ranchos that followed the 1834 dissolution of the Spanish missions, Native American laborers, at least in northern California, appear to have followed a similar pattern of relying heavily on the cattle, sheep, wheat, and barley provisioned by the rancho owner while also drawing on numerous wild resources such as fish, waterfowl, acorns, and grass seeds (Silliman 2004).

Social Landscapes

Archaeologists cannot begin to interpret contact and colonial periods, even in the realm of environmental change and diet, without attention to the social landscapes of colonial North America. These landscapes include the relationships between people that structured the use of the biological environment, the ways that disease spread, the biocultural context for health, and the choices surrounding diet. They are also the realms for considering questions of exchange, identity, labor, and gender that frequently form the anthropological center of colonial studies. Because the social landscape varied highly depending on the Native Americans and Europeans involved and the colonial context of the interaction or exchange, I opt again to focus on broad issues that drive archaeological research and that illuminate Native American responses to colonialism.

Many would agree that the hallmark of North American studies of culture contact and colonialism is the attention to cultural change and persistence. Terminology has shifted considerably over the past six decades, as have the related theoretical frameworks, but the goal has always been to make the combination of material culture and historical documents speak to cultural and social issues. The persistent quest is to ascertain whether Native Americans held tightly to their own cultural traditions, adopted Europeans customs and material culture, or created something new. Regardless of one's stated position, this has *never* been a neutral question because politics – national, local, ethnic, historical, disciplinary, and personal – are wrapped up tightly with issues of cultural change and persistence. To explore the issues of the social landscape of colonialism, I focus on two primary topics: choices and traditions. These are non-traditional ways to group the following studies, and I take a few liberties in revisiting archaeological works to chase down the lines that connect distant and disparate Native American communities in the throes of colonialism.

Choices

Studying culture contact and colonialism in North America means studying Native American choices. Choice is a deceptively simple word, and I want to clarify my use of the term. By choice, I mean the ability of an individual to act in the face of alternatives and in ways congruent with past practices and future expectations. In simplest of terms, individuals as social agents make choices that are both intentional and thought out and those that are routine and comfortable. By emphasizing choice, I do not imply that everyone has the ability to choose based on autonomous free will or volition. This is not a theoretically viable position given the variety of constraints and opportunities that surround social action. Besides, to make that claim for Native Americans embroiled in the oppressive regimes of colonialism denies historical reality. As Milliken (1995) put it, many Native Americans were in "a time of little choice" during the colonial period, but this does not deny the possibilities of *some* choice and the necessity of looking at decisions, strategies, or even habits deployed by indigenous people as they encountered Europeans (see Silliman 2001a). The recognition of Native choice goes a long way toward undercutting arguments that privilege European motivations, goals, or desires as fully determining the course of colonialism and history.

Trade and exchange

From intermittent first encounters to the extensive fur and hide trade, exchange formed the basis of many Native American and European relationships. Trade relationships served to introduce European material culture into Native American communities and into pre-existing trade networks across vast regions. Since introductions do not happen passively, these can reveal key embodiments of Native American choice – what to trade for and with, whom to interact with, and when to invest in trading alliances.

Whether De Soto's *entrada* into the Southeast in 1539–43 or Sir Francis Drake's landing on the coast of California in 1575, the nature of "first encounters" across North America hinged on exchange relationships. For better or worse, many archaeologists view the appearance of trade goods, particularly 16th-century items, at sites as a marker for the protohistoric period – the time before full-fledged, sustained, or in some regions even actual contact between Indians and Europeans. Early exchanges resulted in the transfer of more than material goods; they just as frequently meant unintentional trafficking in genes and germs. Early exchange relationships laid the groundwork for the colonial fur trade. Spanning the continent from New England across the Great Lakes and Canada to the shores of the West Coast, the fur trade involved a complex field with many players. Wolf offered one of the most detailed treatments of this phenomenon in *Europe and the People without History* (Wolf 1982), and this work has greatly influenced the ways that archaeologists think about episodes of contact. Wolf made it clear that the fur trade resulted in over-harvesting, economic reorientation, inter-tribal conflict, and resettlement, and that local processes relate, in part, to the broader European economic system.

The fur trade certainly served as a stage for international colonial politics, such as the tensions between France and England over America's fur harvest. One might characterize it as a manifestation of Immanuel Wallerstein's "World Economy," where Native people served as periphery suppliers of raw materials, goods, and labor that translated into wealth in core European nations. Yet, however global the reach of its supply and demand, the fur trade is important for studies of contact because of the on-the-ground relationships forged between Europeans and Native people, men and women, and traders and trappers. Careful analyses have shown that Native Americans were active players in the fur trade and not pawns in an otherwise global economy (Kardulias 1990; Turnbaugh 1993). Native men and women often forged fictive kin ties with European trappers to bring them into *indigenous* social relations, and groups like the Dakota sought to participate in the enterprise on their own terms, which frequently did not conform to the profit motive of the fur company (Whelan 1993). That is, Native choices partially directed the flow of goods.

The politics of Native choices in European trade relations are similarly visible in the Southeast deerskin trade. Primarily involving British traders in Charlestown, South Carolina and interior Native groups, the 18th-century deerskin trade provided a context in which some Native Americans opted to reorient their social and economic worlds. The competing geopolitics of English settlers on the eastern side of the greater Southeast, and French settlers on the southern and western perimeters, served as colonial parameters for Native American social action. They provided points of contention and opportunity, but they cannot be considered sole *causes* of cultural change. For instance, research has shown that the Chickasaw, centered in northern Mississippi, altered their stone tool production and quarrying activities to emphasize thumbnail scrapers, which they sought for efficient deerskin-processing (Johnson 1997, 2000). The intensification of stone tool production may reflect their trading relations with the English, who seem to have undersupplied them with metal and firearms.

Material culture
Successfully tracking the role of Native choice in trade and exchange hinges, in part, on identifying the range of *possible* choices. Archaeologists must ascertain what items were available to Native Americans through exchange, barter, provisioning, or payment-in-kind and what material objects individuals actually selected from that range. This is easier said than done, especially when one has very few colonial inventory lists or orders specifically designed to secure items for Native American consumption. Yet, archaeologists are uniquely blessed with access to the material culture chosen and used by Native Americans. This empirical information helps counteract the tendency to assume the parameters of Native choices. We have all heard the well-worn, and frequently incorrect, presumption that Native Americans dropped stone tool technology as soon as they could get their hands on metal. This should be an empirical, historical, and contextual question rather than an *a priori*,

uniform assumption. Archaeologists have recently documented not only the context-dependent strategies involving stone tool use, but also the possibility of continued use of stone tools well into the colonial period (Cobb 2003). In addition, archaeologists must continue striving to see beyond just the material things themselves to the activities or meanings that they supported to see if cultural practices or simply the implements for doing them changed (see Rogers 1993 for an example).

At a general level, archaeologists can assess material culture choices through broad categories of recovered artifacts. Archaeologists can address whether Native Americans sought "practical" or "functional" items or ones devoted to bodily decoration and ritual. For instance, did Native consumers prefer utilitarian items such as iron knives or hoes, or did they focus their efforts on securing less "functional" items like beads, bells, or other decorative items? Waselkov and Smith (2000) found that the Creek sought ornamental objects first. For the Creek, the adoption of European goods had much less to do with technological superiority than with social necessity as these commodities contributed to the breakdown of once restricted prestige goods (Wesson 2001). These studies, and many more like them, contradict the notion that Native Americans made their material culture choices based solely on Western notions of technology and economy.

At a specific level, one can compare particular artifact patterns to assemblage-wide patterns to see how Native choices played out. It is frequently possible to determine if individuals adopted European items for particular purposes or if they actually refused otherwise available European goods in favor of indigenous ones. In southern California, the Chumash in the late 18th century selectively adopted metal tools from the nearby Spanish mission colonies (Bamforth 1993). Native individuals selected metal implements for labor-intensive tasks such as drilling shell for beads or woodworking, but they retained lithic raw material for fishing and for projectile points, even though both might have been "better" served with metal tools. These patterns, Bamforth (1993) argues, undermine any attempt to offer explanations based on technological superiority or efficiency (cf. Ames, this volume). In a rather different case in northern California, Native Americans working on Rancho Petaluma in the mid-1800s opted to make and use stone tools for many, although not all, of their tasks, despite the availability of metal tools and the distance to lithic raw material sources (Figure 11.1; Silliman 2003). This continuity was an active choice in the face of alternatives and not a vestigial pastime. Stone tool production and acquisition may have served to connect rancho workers to the broader indigenous social landscape and may have become an active identity marker.

Traditions

Cultural traditions are not passed down blindly or passively from the past but are active negotiations by people in the present (Pauketat 2001). They are made and remade each time an individual enacts them, uses them for their own benefit, or questions their efficacy and appropriateness. This process involves elements of

Figure 11.1 View of Petaluma Adobe, Petaluma Adobe State Historic Park, California

choice, both conscious and habitual. In the realm of colonial North America, a focus on traditions tends to mean an emphasis on identities and the ways that Native Americans held to a past identity or forged a new one. Some have seen cultural traditions as passive entities passed down through individuals and reflected in material culture, whereas others have underscored the vigor with which individuals revisit their traditions and recast them in novel situations and the active role of material culture in constituting those traditions. I chart the terrain between these two poles, where most North American archaeologists work, in three subsections: (1) acculturation, (2) accommodation, resistance, and identity, and (3) difference.

Acculturation
The earliest unified approach to traditions in North American culture contact was the acculturation approach of the 1930s. This program adhered to an implicit version of tradition, one that stressed bounded cultural groups adopting or rejecting cultural traits of other groups, as epitomized in Redfield et al. (1936). Far from being a politically neutral academic quest, early acculturation studies evaluated the amount of culture change that had taken place in Native American groups to explain why Indian peoples had not completely assimilated to mainstream United States culture, or melted into the pot, so to speak. In theory, acculturation meant any exchange of cultural traits between groups that resulted in their adoption by a

"recipient" culture. Contrary to recent opinion, the acculturation approach could accommodate active social agents, resisting or adopting cultural traits for a variety of political, religious, or personal reasons. In practice, however, acculturation came to mean primarily the shift in Native American groups toward Euroamerican lifestyles and material culture (Cusick 1998; Rubertone 2000). Acculturation became a shopping-list way of measuring cultural change where Native Americans could only passively screen but not actively resist cultural change. Unfortunately and unexpectedly, archaeology had a minimal role to play in these early acculturation studies.

Archaeology, or at least material culture studies, joined the acculturation program in the 1950s. The now classic study by Quimby and Spoehr (1951) took the lead by developing a classification scheme to handle the variety of traditional, introduced, novel, and modified items found in Native American sites and museum collections dating to the postcontact period. Their goal was to categorize form, material, use, and technology; they saw no clear way to address meaning or, for that matter, cultural tradition. Archaeologists in the 1960s and 1970s picked up this classification scheme and began to modify and apply it to archaeological contexts. The acculturation approach experienced a revival in the 1980s with the innovative work of Farnsworth (1989, 1992) in California at Mission Nuestra Señora de la Soledad, and his comparisons to other missions. In his approach, Farnsworth added a number of artifact categories to try to capture more subtlety in Native American use and adoption of European items, and he devised mathematical ratios to measure the rates and effects of acculturation in the Spanish mission environment. These he applied to different excavated contexts in the mission quadrangle of Mission Soledad, hoping to link the acculturation process to the broader world economy.

Farnsworth met with some success when deciphering trends in mission economy, but the methodology did not attract many followers. Currently, the method of utilizing quantifiable artifact ratios as an index of cultural change is regarded by many as ill-suited to handling the true subtleties and ambiguities of material culture made meaningful by its makers and users (Lightfoot 1995). The largest deficiency seems to be the passive role that it affords material culture. Artifacts are portrayed as reflecting cultural or social patterns presumed to be independent of, or ontologically prior to, them rather than as active elements in the construction of those cultural or social realms.

Accommodation, resistance, and identity
Instead of relying on artifact ratios as the method and acculturation as the theoretical framework, other archaeologists of colonial North America have leaned toward contextual methods of artifact analysis, models that incorporate the use of space, and theoretical approaches that deal more with accommodation, resistance, and cultural practices. In these approaches, cultural traditions take on more salience and more visibility. Some archaeologists approach identity – individual negotiations of tradition – through particular classes of artifacts, whereas others seek a broader picture of daily practices in cultural spaces (see Loren 2000, this volume).

For the Southeast specifically and North America generally, Deagan led the charge with her groundbreaking work on 16th- through 18th-century Spanish St. Augustine (Deagan 1983). As a colonial settlement founded by Spanish settlers, St. Augustine contained interethnic marriages between Spanish or *criollo* (New World-born) men and Native American women. Deagan interpreted artifact collections and spatial arrangements of known interethnic households to reveal male, Spanish expression in household organization and public appearance and female, Native American expression in the realm of private household ceramic use and food preparation. The dichotomy allowed Deagan to trace the role of Native women in colonial households and their maintenance of identity (Deagan 1996). Rather than acculturation, with its often one-way flow of cultural change, this perspective led to models of transculturation with complex, multidirectional exchanges of cultural practices (Deagan 1998).

In addition to the secular settlement of St. Augustine, the Southeast offers other cases of Native American identity politics in the Spanish mission system. One of the best cases derives from the Apalachee mission of San Luis de Talimali in northwest Florida. Mission San Luis was founded in 1656 at the request of Apalachee leaders following years of conflict on the frontier of Spanish *La Florida*. Like many other Spanish mission sites, San Luis served both the Spanish purpose of Catholic conversion and the Native agenda of political alliance in a volatile colonial region. One of the most interesting discoveries is that, despite the consistent Spanish attempts to alter Native American cultural practices, the Apalachee at San Luis maintained many of their precontact traditions (McEwan 2000). For example, the San Luis settlement was laid out on a Spanish-style plaza with the church and friary on one side and a large Apalachee council house on the other (Figure 11.2). The Native council house occupied a prominent place at the site as a center for political and cultural activities (Scarry and McEwan 1995). At the same time, the Apalachee buried their dead, like other mission populations, with clear nods to Catholicism, a set of religious practices that they may have adopted for the purposes of indigenous power and political struggles (McEwan 2001). The Apalachee held on to many aspects of architecture, leadership, subsistence, and material culture that predated Spanish entry into the New World, not as a passive retention but as an active manipulation of tradition.

On the other side of the continent, the Russian settlement of Colony Ross in northern California offers a compelling case of the negotiation of tradition (Figure 11.3). Founded in 1812 as a fur trade outpost for the procurement of sea otter pelts, Colony Ross served an economic and administrative function. Unlike the Spanish missions not far from its doorstep, the Russian residents directed little effort to converting Native peoples to the Russian Orthodox faith or to altering their cultural practices. Until its 1841 abandonment, the colony was one of the earliest multiethnic communities in the region, with Russian managers and their families living in a redwood stockade, Creoles of Russian and Native descent residing outside the walls, Native Alaskan men and local Native Californian women co-residing on the ocean terrace near the Russian "fort," and California Indian people living nearby (Lightfoot et al. 1993). Native Alaskan men had left their Arctic

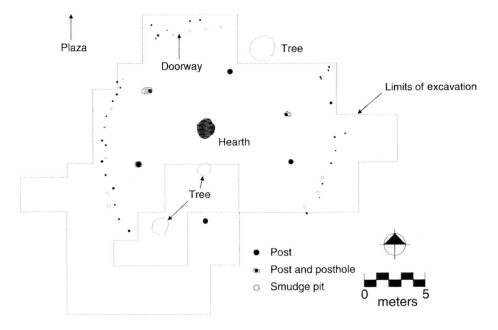

Elite Apalachee residential structure

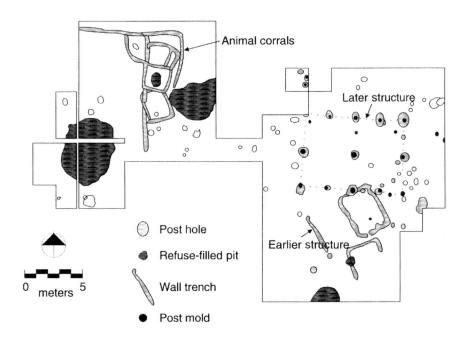

Spanish domestic structures

Figure 11.2 Plan view of elite Apalachee house and Spanish residences excavated at Mission San Luis de Talimali, Florida (reproduced by permission of the Society for American Archaeology from *American Antiquity* 60(3), Scarry and McEwan [1995:figs 4 and 5])

Figure 11.3 View of Native Alaskan Village Site outside the Russian stockade at Colony Ross, Fort Ross State Historic Park, California (reproduced by permission of the photographer, Daniel F. Murley)

homelands more than a thousand miles away, frequently under coercion and force, to work for the Russian enterprise.

Many seasons of fieldwork by Lightfoot and his colleagues have revealed poignant features of the material culture, foodways, and living spaces of the Native people associated with this community (Lightfoot et al. 1998; Martinez 1997; Wake 1997). Results indicate that interethnic unions between Native Alaskan men and California Indian women comprised key points of cultural negotiation and expression, an aspect not at all unlike that noted by Deagan for *La Florida*. The key difference here was that these marriages bound together different Native groups. Research at Colony Ross revealed that Native people living in the shadow of the Russian outpost had not created a creolized identity, despite their intimate and daily intercourse with Russians and other Native groups. Instead, Native Alaskan men and California Indian women expressed their identities differently yet simultaneously in daily practices, in the instantiation of cultural traditions. For example, the site layout and location on the windswept coastal terrace revealed a distinctly Alaskan character, while the cooking practices, material culture, except for marine mammal-hunting gear, and refuse patterns exhibited a markedly Californian flavor

(Lightfoot et al. 1998). Although adopting "Western" material culture such as ceramics, glass, and metal into their material repertoire, the Native groups showed no inclination toward a Russian or non-Native identity.

Shifting to yet another corner of North America, southern New England hosts different issues with regard to archaeological studies of cultural tradition. Colonialism in New England involved a complex interaction of trade, conversion attempts, military conflict, and slow dispossession of lands and resources by a growing colonial population. The study of tradition in these colonial contexts can be illustrated with a case example: the late 17th-century Narragansett cemetery in Rhode Island known as RI-1000. A rich site containing almost 50 graves of men, women, and children with a wide variety of Native- and European-derived mortuary goods, the RI-1000 locality has been the source of academic disputes about what the burials and material culture patterns meant for Native American traditions and struggles in the colonial world. Nassaney took the position that the burial data indicated Native Americans forging new identities, ones that merged aspects of traditional practices with introduced material and cultural features of colonial settlers (Nassaney 1989). In a sense, he envisioned individuals strategically positioning themselves in the novel material and political context of colonialism as a way to survive. Turnbaugh (1993) offered a corollary position that the variations in quantity and type of burial goods denoted individuals with different levels of access to material goods and an increase in sociopolitical ranking. He envisioned the graves as attempts to blend old traditions with new (Turnbaugh 1993:147).

On the other hand, Robinson and Rubertone saw the burials and associated material goods as an indication of Narragansett resistance to colonization, as maintenance of their traditions in the face of difficult times (Robinson et al. 1985; Rubertone 1989). The conclusion was that the RI-1000 cemetery revealed an intensification of burial ritualism. The one element on which all contending authors seem to agree is the prominent role played by the *mockatassuit*, or Narragansett mortician, in the layout and preparation of the large cemetery. Recently, Rubertone has expanded her perspective with a nuanced study of RI-1000, hovering close to the data to explore the intricacies and possibilities of every person buried in the cemetery (Rubertone 2001). Rubertone's approach garners remarkable insight into the cultural, gender, and even age-specific identities, to "reveal people in different dimensions than simply those of politics and entrepreneurship" as they maintained community identity and kinship (Rubertone 2001:164).

What the foregoing approaches offer to the study of postcontact Native American groups that the earlier approaches to acculturation did not is a portrayal of active indigenous social actors and their material culture. The Native players in this drama are more real, more vested in their experiences, and correspondingly more difficult to label in unequivocal terms. Although these studies have better illuminated the active role played by individuals and material culture, other archaeologists have taken such perspectives further to argue for individuals that are even more active. In addition to being tied to past practices, tradition in this formulation is more about situational and strategic use of material culture to express, if not also make, identity. This move tends to foreground identities that individuals forge in opposition to others, in the face of novel alternatives, or in a self-conscious attempt at group affiliation.

The Southeast again offers a key example of how such an approach to ethnogenesis has illuminated Native American lives in the colonial period. The Guale on the southern Atlantic coast had a deep cultural tradition prior to Spanish contact, but they did not appear to share anything that could be defined as an ethnic identity (Saunders 2001). On the other hand, by 1663 the Yamassee had formed as an ethnic group composed of refugees from the Georgia piedmont. Both groups have been interpreted through archaeological classifications and studies of Altamaha pottery, thought to be a "negotiated tradition" between the Guale and the Spanish that the Yamassee adopted to indicate colonial allegiance (Saunders 2001). At the same time, the Yamassee displayed diets much more like their precontact antecedents than their contemporaries in Spanish mission contexts (Larsen et al. 2001:107–108).

Native Americans negotiated cultural traditions whenever they incorporated particular European items to fashion an ethnic identity. Individuals may have made, used, traded, or displayed items as a way of materializing their identities, of making them visible. For the Seminole case in Florida, Weisman (2000) argued that ethnogenesis in the early 1800s was marked materially by the wearing of European military clothing and the explicit rejection of Western ceramics. The former served as a source of symbolic power when confronting Euroamerican troops; the latter denoted an explicit rejection of key symbols of the dominant society. The lack of non-Native ceramics is quite notable, given the prevalence of them in Southeastern Native communities at this time and the presence of glass and metal goods in Seminole site assemblages (Weisman 2000).

Difference

Most discussions of tradition relate to groups, cultures, or societies, but the archaeology of colonial North America has also investigated difference. By difference, I mean distinction within a Native group depending on one's gender, age, status, class, labor role, or political allegiance. These studies take up the recent challenge "to understand the different experiences of those who survived not only European contact but also proclamations about acculturation, assimilation, hybridization, and resistance" (Rubertone 2000:439, emphasis mine).

Gender research in colonial North America is very much about tradition and about difference. Gender relations have distinct and powerful histories in Native American groups, and gender expectations, roles, and identities underwent significant change and often attack in colonial periods. As a result, indigenous people crafted new traditions of intermarriage, new ways of coping with forced gendered divisions of labor, and new strategies for dealing with sexual violence and control. The studies of Spanish St. Augustine (Deagan 1983, 1996) and Russian Colony Ross (Lightfoot et al. 1998) described above epitomize the insight that a gender focus can offer to archaeology. They foreground the relations between men and women who came from different cultural traditions but retained their distinctiveness while combining their practices in new households. In this way, gender sits at the core of new and negotiated traditions that involve Native Americans in the post-Columbian era. In addition, Voss (2000) has tackled gender issues in the colonial period, but in a unique way. For Spanish colonial California, Voss revealed that sexual relations – particularly violence – partly account for the spatial arrangements of California Indian villages during the Spanish reign. Native individuals, particularly women, also struggled with restrictive and overbearing modes of sexual and gender control in the confines of Spanish mission dormitories (Voss 2000).

Another window into difference is labor and its corresponding relations and occupations. Many indigenous people in North America joined the economic world of colonialism as laborers – trappers, hunters, miners, ranch hands, agricultural workers, builders, whalers, and translators, for example. Although individuals may have made the choice in the context of diminished resources and opportunities, labor provides a way of looking at Native control over their engagement with colonialism. On the other hand, colonial labor also established contexts in which Native people had little choice over their participation in work tasks. Yet, archaeologists can still discern the outlines of Native American social agency in the midst of forced labor (Silliman 2001b, 2004). For example, my own work has shown that Native American residents at Mission San Antonio in central California may have affiliated with some labor tasks and not with others (Silliman 2001b). Affiliation means choosing to use and display tools of colonial labor activities in the household as a way to materially express and maintain novel identities. More clearly than the mission case, the archaeological study of Rancho Petaluma in 19th-century northern California reveals the role of colonial labor in Native American experiences (Silliman 2004). Native women introduced sewing items into their households, which stemmed in part from their daily required activities on the rancho. In contrast, Native men did *not* bring home tools associated with their required duties of livestock herding, cattle butchery, or farming (Silliman 2004). The discrepancy suggests the gendered nature of social and household strategies for coping with labor regimes and for materializing their identities.

An additional line of difference is political affiliation. Historically and realistically, archaeologists know that not everyone in Native groups agreed on trade alliances, political decisions, or even the everyday choices of contending with colonialism and Europeans. Despite the difficulties of recognizing intragroup differences, archaeologists of the colonial era have demonstrated the potential to address these divergences using material remains. For instance, Waselkov identified political factions in Alabama Creek groups with differing allegiances to English or French (Waselkov 1993). In the late 17th and early 18th centuries, the Creek incorporated refugees from outlying groups, formed a confederation for mutual protection, and tolerated internal factions. After 1715, those factions vied for trade with the French and English. Using grave goods from Creek burials, Waselkov determined that both factions could be seen in graves dating between 1720 and 1760 in the region, and, more importantly, that both factions were present at a single town (Waselkov 1993).

Final Thoughts

The studies reviewed in this chapter should underscore the ability of archaeological research to explore the specifics of colonialism and culture contact and to illuminate the finer details of Native Americans maneuvering the complex colonial world in North America. The examples presented herein are only a sampling, as I regretfully had to exclude work in regions such as the Arctic, Northwest Coast, Midwest, and Plains. Contrary to the recent statement by one of archaeology's preeminent spokespersons that "archaeology is an anonymous discipline, concerned with the generalities of human culture rather than the deeds of individuals, providing relatively little information on European contact" (Fagan 1997:34), this chapter has demonstrated that archaeology has much to offer the topic of Native American – and other indigenous – responses to European colonialism. I would go so far as to argue that archaeology frequently offers *more* information on contact and colonialism than the overprivileged historical record alone because it illuminates the Native American side of colonialism and culture contact and the material aspects of everyday life.

This chapter has traced the contours of what that illumination would look like as archaeology brings indigenous choices, traditions, bodies, and experiences out of the shadows cast by colonialism. Obviously, archaeology can be plagued with the ambiguities of whether or not particular artifacts or patterns represent worldviews, practices, identities, genders, adaptations, or political economies, but a similar ambiguity probably surrounded individuals' interaction with those same items of material culture when they were first used and discarded. Our confrontation of the ambiguity and, at the same time, the possibility is what makes this realm of North American archaeology so vital and invigorating. The archaeology of North American colonial encounters provides the vital link between the deep, rooted history of Native Americans on the continent and their contemporary cultures and struggles in today's world in the legacy of colonialism. While reclaiming Native American history in the aftermath of European contact, the archaeological study of colonialism also serves as the disciplinary hinge that keeps the door between "prehistory" and "history" always swinging so that archaeologists may move back and forth through it, drawing on each other's insights and methods and recognizing that, more times than not, they are studying the same kinds of issues.

REFERENCES

Allen, R., 1998 *Native Americans at Mission Santa Cruz, 1791–1834: Interpreting the Archaeological Record.* Los Angeles: Institute of Archaeology, University of California.

Bamforth, D. B., 1993 Stone tools, steel tools: Contact period household technology at Helo. In *Ethnohistory and Archaeology: Approaches to Postcontact Change in the New World.* J. D. Rogers and S. M. Wilson, eds. Pp. 49–72. New York: Plenum Press.

Cobb, C., ed. 2003 *Stone Tool Technology in the Contact Era.* Tuscaloosa: University of Alabama Press.

Crosby, A. W., 1986 *Ecological Imperialism: The Biological Expansion of Europe, 900–1900*. Cambridge: Cambridge University Press.

Cusick, J., 1998 Historiography of acculturation: An evaluation of concepts and their application in archaeology. In *Studies in Culture Contact: Interaction, Culture Change, and Archaeology*. J. G. Cusick ed. Pp. 126–145. Carbondale: Center for Archaeological Investigations, Southern Illinois University.

Deagan, K., 1983 *Spanish St. Augustine: The Archaeology of a Colonial Creole Community*. New York: Academic Press.

—— 1996 Colonial transformation: Euro-American cultural genesis in the early Spanish-American colonies, *Journal of Anthropological Research*, 52(2), 135–160.

—— 1998 Transculturation and Spanish American ethnogenesis: The archaeological legacy of the Quincentenary. In *Studies in Culture Contact: Interaction, Culture Change, and Archaeology*. J. G. Cusick, ed. Pp. 23–43. Carbondale: Center for Archaeological Investigations, Southern Illinois University.

Dobyns, H. F., 1983 *Their Numbers Become Thinned: Native American Population Dynamics in Eastern North America*. Knoxville: University of Tennessee Press.

Dunnell, R. C., 1991 Methodological impacts of catastrophic depopulation on American archaeology and ethnology. In *Columbian Consequences*, vol. 3: *The Spanish Borderlands in Pan-American Perspective*. D. H. Thomas ed. Pp. 561–580. Washington, DC: Smithsonian Institution Press.

Fagan, B. M., 1997 *Clash of Cultures*, 2nd edn. Walnut Creek, CA: AltaMira Press.

Farnsworth, P., 1989 The economics of acculturation in the Spanish missions of Alta California. *Research in Economic Anthropology*, vol. 11, B. Isaac, ed. Pp. 217–249. Greenwich, CT: JAI Press.

—— 1992 Missions, Indians, and cultural continuity. *Historical Archaeology* 26(1), 22–36.

Johnson, J. K., 1997 Stone tools, politics, and the eighteenth-century Chickasaw in northeast Mississippi. *American Antiquity* 62(2), 215–230.

—— 2000 *The Chickasaws*. In *Indians of the Greater Southeast: Historical Archaeology and Ethnohistory*. B. G. McEwan, ed. Pp. 85–121. Gainesville: University Press of Florida.

Johnson, J. K., and G. R. Lehmann, 1996 Sociopolitical devolution in northeast Mississippi and the timing of the de Soto Entrada. In *Bioarchaeology of Native American Adaptation in the Spanish Borderlands*. B. J. Baker and L. Kealhofer, eds. Pp. 38–55. Gainesville: University Press of Florida.

Kardulias, P. N., 1990 Fur production as a specialized activity in a World System: Indians in the North American fur trade. *American Indian Culture and Research Journal* 14(1), 25–60.

Kealhofer, L., 1996 The evidence for demographic collapse in California. In *Bioarchaeology of Native American Adaptation in the Spanish Borderlands*. B. J. Baker and L. Kealhofer, eds. Pp. 56–92. Gainesville: University Press of Florida.

Kealhofer, L., and B. J. Baker, 1996 Counterpoint to collapse: Depopulation and adaptation. In *Bioarchaeology of Native American Adaptation in the Spanish Borderlands*. B. J. Baker and L. Kealhofer, eds. Pp. 209–222. Gainesville: University Press of Florida.

Larsen, C. S., 1994 In the wake of Columbus: Native population biology in the postcontact Americas. *Yearbook of Physical Anthropology* 24, 471–492.

Larsen, C. S., M. C. Griffin, D. L. Hutchinson, V. E. Noble, L. Norr, R. F. Pastor, C. B. Ruff, K. F. Russell, M. J. Schoeninger, M. Schultz, S. W. Simpson, and M. F. Teaford, 2001 Frontiers of contact: Bioarchaeology of Spanish Florida. *Journal of World Prehistory* 15(1), 69–123.

Larsen, C. S., C. B. Ruff, and M. C. Griffin, 1996 Implications of changing biomechanical and nutritional environments for activity and lifeways in the Eastern Spanish Borderlands. In *Bioarchaeology of Native American Adaptation in the Spanish Borderlands*. B. J. Baker and L. Kealhofer, eds. Pp. 95–125. Gainesville: University Press of Florida.

Lightfoot, K. G., 1995 Culture contact studies: Redefining the relationship between prehistoric and historical archaeology. *American Antiquity* 60(2), 199–217.

Lightfoot, K. G., A. Martinez, and A. M. Schiff, 1998 Daily practice and material culture in pluralistic social settings: An archaeological study of culture change and persistence from Fort Ross, California. *American Antiquity* 63(2), 199–222.

Lightfoot, K. G., T. A. Wake, and A. M. Schiff, 1993 Native responses to the Russian mercantile colony of Fort Ross, northern California. *Journal of Field Archaeology* 20, 159–175.

Loren, D. D., 2000 The intersections of colonial policy and colonial practice: Creolization on the 18th-century Louisiana/Texas frontier. *Historical Archaeology* 34(3), 85–98.

Martinez, A., 1997 View from the ridge: The Kashaya Pomo in a Russian-American company context. In *The Archaeology of Russian Colonialism in the North and Tropical Pacific*. P. Mills and A. Martinez, eds. Pp. 141–156. Kroeber Anthropological Society. Berkeley: University of California.

McEwan, B., 2000 The Apalachee Indians of northwest Florida. In *Indians of the Greater Southeast: Historical Archaeology and Ethnohistory*. B. G. McEwan ed. Pp. 57–84. Gainesville: University Press of Florida.

—— 2001 The spiritual conquest of La Florida. *American Anthropologist* 103(3), 633–644.

Miller, E., 1996 The effect of European contact on the health of indigenous populations in Texas. In *Bioarchaeology of Native American Adaptation in the Spanish Borderlands*. B. J. Baker and L. Kealhofer, eds. Pp. 126–147. Gainesville: University Press of Florida.

Milliken, R. T., 1995 *A Time of Little Choice: The Disintegration of Tribal Culture in the San Francisco Bay Area 1769–1810*. Menlo Park, CA: Ballena Press.

Milner, G. R., 1992 Disease and sociopolitical systems in late prehistoric Illinois. In *Disease and Demography in the Americas*. J. W. Verano and D. H. Ubelaker, eds. Pp. 103–116. Washington, DC: Smithsonian Institution Press.

Nassaney, M. S., 1989 An epistemological enquiry into some archaeological and historical interpretations of 17th century Native American–European relations. In *Archaeological Approaches to Cultural Identity*. S. J. Shennan, ed. Pp. 76–93. London: Unwin Hyman.

Palkovich, A. M., 1996 Historic depopulation in the American Southwest: Issues of interpretation and context-embedded analyses. In *Bioarchaeology of Native American Adaptation in the Spanish Borderlands*. B. J. Baker and L. Kealhofer, eds. Pp. 179–197. Gainesville: University Press of Florida.

Pauketat, T., 2001 A new tradition in archaeology. In *The Archaeology of Traditions: Agency and History Before and After Columbus*. T. R. Pauketat, ed. Pp. 1–16. Gainesville: University Press of Florida.

Perttula, T. K., 1991 European contact and its effects on aboriginal Caddoan populations between A.D. 1520 and A.D. 1680. In *Columbian Consequences*, vol. 3: *The Spanish Borderlands in Pan-American Perspective*. D. H. Thomas, ed. Pp. 501–518. Washington, DC: Smithsonian Institution Press.

Quimby, G. L. and A. Spoehr, 1951 Acculturation and material culture. *Fieldiana: Anthropology* 36(6), 107–147.

Ramenofsky, A. M., 1987 *Vectors of Death: The Archaeology of European Contact*. Albuquerque: University of New Mexico Press.

Redfield, R., R. Linton, and M. J. Herskovits, 1936 Memorandum for the study of acculturation. *American Anthropologist* 38, 149–152.

Reitz, E. J. 1990 Zooarchaeological evidence for subsistence at La Florida missions. In *Columbian Consequences*, vol. 2: *Archaeological and Historical Perspectives on the Spanish Borderlands East*. D. H. Thomas, ed. Pp. 543–554. Washington, DC: Smithsonian Institution Press.

—— 1993 Evidence for animal use at the missions of La Florida. In *The Spanish Missions of La Florida*. B. McEwan, ed. Pp. 376–398. Gainesville: University Press of Florida.

Robinson, P. A., M. A. Kelley, and P. E. Rubertone, 1985 Preliminary biocultural interpretations from a seventeenth-century Narragansett Indian cemetery in Rhode Island. In *Cultures in Contact: The European Impact on Native Cultural Institutions in Eastern North America, A.D. 1000–1800*. W. W. Fitzhugh, ed. Pp. 107–130. Washington, DC: Smithsonian Institution Press.

Rogers, D., 1993 The social and material implications of culture contact on the Northern Plains. In *Ethnohistory and Archaeology: Approaches to Postcontact Change in the Americas*. D. Rogers and S. M. Wilson, eds. Pp. 73–88. New York: Plenum Press.

Rubertone, P., 1989 Archaeology, colonialism, and 17th-century Native America: Towards an alternative interpretation. In *Conflict in the Archaeology of Living Traditions*. R. Layton, ed. Pp. 32–45. London: Unwin Hyman.

—— 2000 The historical archaeology of Native Americans. *Annual Review of Anthropology* 29, 452–446.

—— 2001 *Grave Undertakings: An Archaeology of Roger Williams and the Narragansett Indians*. Washington, DC: Smithsonian Institution Press.

Ruhl, D. L., 1993 Old customs and traditions in new terrain: Sixteenth- and seventeenth-century archaeobotanical data from La Florida. In *Foraging and Farming in the Eastern Woodlands*. C. M. Scarry, ed. Pp. 255–283. Gainesville: University Press of Florida.

Saunders, R., 2001 Negotiated tradition? Native American pottery in the Mission Period in La Florida. In *The Archaeology of Traditions: Agency and History Before and After Columbus*. T. R. Pauketat, ed. Pp. 77–93. Gainesville: University Press of Florida.

Scarry, C. M., 1993 Plant production and procurement in Apalachee Province. In *The Spanish Missions of La Florida*. B. McEwan, ed. Pp. 322–375. Gainesville: University Press of Florida.

Scarry, J. F., and B. G. McEwan, 1995 Domestic architecture in Apalachee Province: Apalachee and Spanish residential styles in the late prehistoric and early historic period Southeast, *American Antiquity* 60(3), 482–495.

Silliman, S. W., 2001a Agency, practical politics, and the archaeology of culture contact. *Journal of Social Archaeology* 1(2), 184–204.

—— 2001b Theoretical perspectives on labor and colonialism: Reconsidering the California missions. *Journal of Anthropological Archaeology* 20(4), 379–407.

—— 2003 Using a rock in a hard place: Native American lithic practices in colonial California. In *Stone Tool Technology in the Contact Era*. C. Cobb, ed. Pp. 127–150. Tuscaloosa: University of Alabama Press.

—— 2004 *Lost Laborers in Colonial California: Native Americans and the Archaeology of Rancho Petaluma*. Tucson: University of Arizona Press (in press).

Snow, D. R., 1992 Disease and population decline in the Northeast. In *Disease and Demography in the Americas*. J. W. Verano and D. H. Ubelaker, eds. Pp. 177–186. Washington, DC: Smithsonian Institution Press.

Stodder, A. L. W., and D. L. Martin, 1992 Health and disease in the Southwest before and after Spanish contact. In *Disease and Demography in the Americas*. J. W. Verano and D. H. Ubelaker, eds. Pp. 55–73. Washington, DC: Smithsonian Institution Press.

Turnbaugh, W. A., 1993 Assessing the significance of European goods in seventeenth century Narragansett society. In *Ethnohistory and Archaeology: Approaches to Postcontact Change in the Americas*. J. D. Rogers and S. M. Wilson, eds. Pp. 133–160. New York: Plenum Press.

Verano, J. W., and D. H. Ubelaker, eds. 1992 *Disease and Demography in the Americas*. Washington, DC: Smithsonian Institution Press.

Voss, B. L., 2000 Colonial sex: Archaeology, structured space, and sexuality in Alta California's Spanish-colonial missions. In *Archaeologies of Sexuality*. R. Schmidt and B. L. Voss eds. Pp. 35–61. London: Routledge.

Wake, T. A., 1997 Subsistence, ethnicity, and vertebrate exploitation at the Ross Colony. In *The Archaeology of Russian Colonialism in the North and Tropical Pacific*. P. Mills and A. Martinez, eds. Pp. 84–115. Berkeley: Kroeber Anthropological Society, University of California.

Walker, P. J. and J. R. Johnson, 1992 Effects of contact on the Chumash Indians. In *Disease and Demography in the Americas*. J. W. Verano and D. H. Ubelaker, eds. Pp. 127–139. Washington, DC: Smithsonian Institution Press.

——1994 The decline of the Chumash Indian population. In *In the Wake of Contact: Biological Responses to Conquest*. C. S. Larsen and G. J. Milner eds. Pp. 109–120. New York: Wiley-Liss.

Walker, P. L., P. Lambert, and M. J. DeNiro, 1989 The effects of European contact on the health of Alta California Indians. In *Columbian Consequences*, vol. 1: *Archaeological and Historical Perspectives on the Spanish Borderlands West*. D. H. Thomas, ed. Pp. 349–364. Washington, DC: Smithsonian Institution Press.

Waselkov, G. A., 1993 Historic Creek Indian responses to European trade and the rise of political factions. In *Ethnohistory and Archaeology: Approaches to Postcontact Change in the Americas*. J. D. Rogers and S. M. Wilson eds. Pp. 123–131. New York: Plenum Press.

Waselkov, G. A., and M. T. Smith, 2000 Upper Creek archaeology. In *Indians of the Greater Southeast: Historical Archaeology and Ethnohistory*. B. G. McEwan ed. Pp. 242–264. Gainesville: University Press of Florida.

Weisman, B. R., 2000 Archaeological perspectives on Florida Seminole ethnogenesis. In *Indians of the Greater Southeast: Historical Archaeology and Ethnohistory*. B. G. McEwan ed. Pp. 299–318. Gainesville: University Press of Florida.

Wesson, C. B., 2001 Creek and Pre-Creek revisited. *The Archaeology of Traditions: Agency and History Before and After Columbus*. T. R. Pauketat ed. Pp. 94–106. Gainesville: University Press of Florida.

Whelan, M. K., 1993 Dakota Indian economics and the nineteenth-century fur trade, *Ethnohistory* 40(2), 246–276.

Wolf, E. R., 1982 *Europe and the People without History*. Berkeley: University of California Press.

12

Creolization in the French and Spanish Colonies

Diana DiPaolo Loren

The Concept of Creolization

During the 17th and 18th centuries, the southeastern United States was colonized by the Spanish and French, who brought Africans to work for them in a region already occupied by a large indigenous population (some of whom have been discussed in previous chapters of this volume). These events set into motion new social practices, new definitions of self, other, and personhood, new hierarchies of class, ethnicity, race, and gender, and new official and unofficial histories as these diverse groups lived, worked, fought, intermarried, and died with one another. These processes that occurred in the colonial Southeast are best described as those of creolization.

From the outset, some archaeologists would argue that creolization is not the proper term to use when talking about the cultural transformations that occurred when people of different races and ethnicities became socially and culturally intertwined during the colonial period. Truthfully, there has been some confusion in the use of the terms "creole" and "creolization," resulting from their long history within anthropology and in other disciplines. For some scholars, the term would be quite specific, referring to its linguistic roots (see Dawdy 2000). As Trouillot (2002:192) notes, "creole language became the first product of the creolization process to attract the attention of scholars." But interest in creolization now extends beyond language. So, for other researchers, "creole" specifically refers to the emergence of a Spanish American or *criollo* society (Ewen 1991). Still others treat the term much more broadly, stating that it refers to hybridization or syncretization of culture resulting in a plural population (Ferguson 1992; Lyons and Papadopoulos 2000; Silliman 2001, this volume). Here I draw from this last definition and use the term "creolization" to refer to the process of identity formation in the colonial period in the Southeastern United States. While researchers of the Spanish colonial period tend to use the term *mestizaje* to refer to this process of racial intermixture, a broadly writ "creolization" can be used to discuss cultural changes, the creation of alternative histories, and the diverse lived experiences for all groups undergoing identity reconstruction in colonial regions of North America.

These arguments over proper terminology highlight the current focus on this issue within anthropology, and more recently within archaeology. In the 1980s, the focus of anthropological studies switched from examining the colonial center and its European population to investigating colonized peoples and their interactions with European colonizers (Callaway 1993; Comaroff and Comaroff 1992; Cusick 1998; Delle et al. 2000; Ruhl and Hoffman 1997). Moving beyond dichotomous discussions of colonized and colonizer has enabled anthropologists to highlight the ambiguous population that emerged in colonial centers – mixed-bloods or peoples of mixed racial and ethnic parentage such as *casta*, *mestizo*, creole, mulatto, and *métis*. As Ann Stoler and other researchers have noted, mixed-bloods lived in an uncertain space (neither European or Native American but almost always under colonial rule) and, like many of the colonized, silenced in historical accounts (Boyer 1997; Cooper and Stoler 1997; Cope 1994; Deagan 1996; Hill 1996; Stoler 1989; Trouillot 2002). But theories of creolization should not only draw out mixed-bloods, but all colonial peoples who underwent identity transformations in multi-ethnic contexts. Conceptualized broadly, creolization captures complex processes of identity formation and differential experiences of occupants of early America: Native American, European, African, and mixed-blood women and men from different social and economic groups (St. George 2000:4). Creolization brings to light the interrelations of individuals from diverse social, economic, ethnic, racial, and political backgrounds, accompanied by a concern with the relationships between colonized and colonizer (Boyer 1997; Cooper and Stoler 1997; Deagan 1996; Hall 1992, 2000; Lightfoot 1995; Lightfoot and Martinez 1995; Stoler 1989). At the same time, creolization cannot be understood outside of the contexts in which it occurred (Trouillot 2002:195).

Mixed-blood, African, Native American, and European men and women of a variety of social and economic backgrounds created plural communities throughout colonial America (St. George 2000; see also Delle et al. 2000). In the 18th-century Spanish colonies of Texas and Florida as well as the 18th-century French colony of Louisiana, Europeans and Africans lived and worked with Native Americans, creating multiethnic communities and households (Deagan 1996; Usner 1992). By the mid-18th century, there were large numbers of mixed-bloods in these colonies, the biological result of interethnic and interracial sexual relations between colony inhabitants, resulting in a population uniquely different than imagined by the French and Spanish Crowns. Colonial communities were not mirror images of their European counterparts, but rather new, hybrid creations that can best be examined and described under the rubric of creolization. It was in the context of these new social, sexual, political, and economic relations in plural communities and households that new cultural practices, ideals, traditions, and beliefs were formulated through the use of material culture (see Trouillot 2002:189). These new practices and beliefs were tied to existing beliefs and practices, but were creatively reformulated in new, difficult, and often dangerous contexts. Colonial leaders intended to limit the emergence of new practices and beliefs, perhaps in an attempt to recreate the familiar or to limit the unfamiliar. Laws and strictures drawn up by the French and Spanish Crowns and their officials were meant to limit quotidian practices, such as interracial marriage and sexual relations, religion, dress, diet, trade, household architecture, and household activities (Boyer 1997; Cope 1994; Loren 2001a, 2001b; Stoler 1989). Despite these efforts, creolization continued to occur.

Given that creolization occurred within the household and that new identities were constituted using the material culture of everyday life, this process can be studied archaeologically. This is not to say that creolization was a process that occurred everywhere in the same way. Rather we need to historicize and contextualize this process (Trouillot 2002). Here I outline some of the history regarding the use of creolization in anthropological literature, touching on its relationship to notions of acculturation. I highlight how other archaeologists have studied the process, using case studies from the French and Spanish colonies in the Southeastern United States. Finally, I discuss some emerging directions for the study of creolization within archaeology.

The Importance of Creolization

While there is a long history of studying the "other" within anthropology – in fact, this was one of the initial defining goals of the discipline – studies emerged in the 1980s that viewed colonial situations from the "bottom up," focusing on the "people without history" such as lower-status Europeans, women, Africans, and, more recently, mixed-bloods (Roseberry 1991; Wolf 1982). These studies argued that previous interpretations had overlooked large parts of colonial populations and, therefore, tended to simplify many colonial contexts. Latin American scholars, on the other hand, have long placed emphasis on the marginality of mixed-bloods (Gruzinski and Wachtel 1997). *Mestizaje* (the mixing of races) is a concept used to explain unequal power relations in the Spanish colonial past and the emergence of a national identity that denies colonial racial hierarchy in the present (Gruzinski and Wachtel 1997). *Mestizaje* in Latin American literature, however, has been overlooked as a central concept within much anthropological and archaeological research of colonial North America (cf. Deagan 1988, 1996). This silence within North American research may be for historical reasons; the result of the tenuous and ambiguous positioning of mixed-bloods within colonial society (Trouillot 1995). In response, anthropologists have tried to fill in these silences – in the Caribbean, Africa, India, and parts of colonial North America – noting that in colonial centers the majority of the population was mixed-race, so that colonial communities should now be conceptualized as pluralistic and more than just simply colonial state versus colonial subject (Boyer 1997; Callaway 1993; Cope 1994; Lightfoot 1995; Lightfoot and Martinez 1995; Silliman 2001; Stoler 1989; Trouillot 2002).

Ann Stoler (1989:135) cautions against the conceptualization of the colonizer as a singular group – a unified, conquering elite – because doing so overlooks the interplay between metropole and colony (see also Deagan 1996; Gruzinski and Wachtel 1997). Anthropologists researching both Old and New World contexts have pointed to this, noting that colonized and colonizer were impacted not only by the metropole, such as Mexico City or Quebec, but also by local social and political situations (Deagan 1996; Gruzinski and Wachtel 1997; Usner 1992). Despite the supposed impact of the metropole, each colonial region was subject to incongruities of rule and power that emanated from local interpersonal relations (Cope 1994).

While several ongoing archaeological projects focus on the nature of pluralism within colonial American communities – Fort Ross in California (Lightfoot 1995; Lightfoot and Martinez 1995), Puerto Real in the Caribbean (Deagan 1995), and Spanish Florida (Deagan 1983, 1988, 1996; Ewen 1991; McEwan 1991) – there remain regions in North America including the colonial Southeast where the history of creolization is marked by silence. Many of the areas in the Southeast, especially Louisiana, have a strong Creole heritage that had its roots in the colonial period. Before turning to this area, I first outline creolization's history within archaeology.

Creolization within archaeology

For many years, archaeological notions of culture change resulting from contact between groups during the colonial period dovetailed with the concept of acculturation. While acculturation studies have had lengthy critiques over the years, it still remains a key concept in many archaeological interpretations regarding processes of identity formation (see Silliman, this volume). Anthropological studies of acculturation emerged in the 1930s when Redfield, Linton, and Herskovits defined acculturation as "phenomena which result when groups of individuals having different cultures come into continuous first-hand contact, with subsequent changes in the original culture patterns of either or both groups" (Redfield et al. 1936:149). In the 1940s, Kroeber built on their definition to further define acculturation as "comprising those changes produced in a culture by the influence of another culture which result in increased similarity in the two" (Kroeber 1948:425). Kroeber (1948:434) noted that acculturation was an inevitable process for the minority, implying the passive acceptance of dominant traits – the end product was the melting-pot where the minority became part of the majority. While history was evoked in these definitions, little attention was given to historical processes (Trouillot 2002:193).

Based on early theories, Quimby and Spoehr (1951) designed a classification system for museum collections that analyzed changes in material culture as a result of European contact (see Silliman, this volume). In this system, distinctions were made between European items, on the one hand, and items that were produced by Native Americans on the other. According to Quimby and Spoehr, European-style objects produced by Native Americans (such as brass tinkling cones made from pieces of European kettles that were fashioned into cones and hung from clothing) signaled a higher degree of acculturation than simply the incorporation of European goods by Native Americans. This object-based theory of acculturation was based upon measuring the degree and rate of change by examining the transfer or acceptance of different traits and, in archaeology, through the percentage of different European or native materials. As such, the meaning objects acquired through use was disregarded, as was the use of Native American objects by Europeans.

Quimby and Spoehr's categorization system has had a long and enduring impact on the methodologies used to analyze colonial period material. In particular, the schema for categorizing archaeological collections as either "native" or "European" has remained almost unchanged since the 1950s. For example, glass and shell beads found in New World contexts are almost unfailingly classified as Native American objects in archaeological labs and museum collections (see Thomas 1991). This historical (mis)categorization impacts our interpretations of these objects and who would have used them in the past – 18th-century Spanish women didn't wear shell beads, did they? Certain assumptions about Europeans and Native Americans (rather than those people betwixt and between categories) emerge from these classificatory methods. And those assumptions have tended to remain, despite changes in anthropological theories of creolization that have occurred since the 1950s, a point I revisit later in this chapter.

During this period when notions of acculturation were developing within social anthropology and archaeology, creolization was developing as a topic within linguistic anthropology. While works on creole language (mostly centering on Caribbean communities) began in the mid-19th century, it was in the 1970s that linguistic scholarship on creolization had its greatest impact in anthropology, especially in the works of Sidney Mintz and Richard Price (Ferguson 2000:7; see also Trouillot 2002). Drawing from these influences James Deetz, a historical archaeologist, used the term "creolization" to make connections between creole language and the cultural hybridity he observed at the 18th-century site of Parting Ways, an African American community in the Northeast (Deetz 1977:149–150). In his discussion of Parting Ways, Deetz discussed how freed Africans in the community constructed an "African-American lifestyle through architecture, settlement patterns, and food ways using objects that were almost entirely Anglo-American but in ways that were West African" (Deetz 1977:148–149). He noted that this process of change at Parting Ways was not a simple one of acculturation, "but rather such a process is known as creolization, the interaction between two or more cultures to produce an integrated mix which is different than its antecedents" (Deetz 1996:213).

Other archaeologists, such as Leland Ferguson (1992) and Kathleen Deagan (1983), also utilized creolization to capture the emergence of new identities, again casting aside the passivity implied by acculturation. In *Uncommon Ground*, Ferguson (1992) examined the cultural and material transformations undergone by Africans who became African Americans. In this influential book, Ferguson attended to issues of power, domination, resistance, and inequality, noting that it was through material culture (particularly colonoware and diet) that new African American identities were constituted (Ferguson 1992). For those archaeologists

studying Spanish American communities, Kathleen Deagan's work on the archaeology of creolization at St. Augustine was truly groundbreaking.

Spanish St. Augustine

Kathleen Deagan was the first archaeologist to detail *mestizaje* in colonial Florida
(Deagan 1983). Prior to her research, the history of racial mixing that occurred in
Spanish St. Augustine remained an unwritten chapter in American history (Deagan
1983:56). Deagan stressed the importance of gender relations – especially the prevalence of sexual relations between European men and Native American women –
and drew out notions of status, noting how mixed-race offspring had to make their
own social space in colonial hierarchies. *Mestizaje* occurred at the household level
that was the nexus of cultural transformations; it was where mixed-blood identities
were formulated and new cultural traditions were crafted. Deagan outlined different forms of creolization by examining different households at St. Augustine: one
of a *criollo* family and one of a *mestizo* family. In the *criollo* household, creolization
was the translation of Spanish culture in the New World, while the *mestizo* household showed the material remnants of new traditions being formed from multiethnic interrelations. Labor by Native American wives and Spanish husbands indicated
how this took place in *mestizo* households: Native American women working in the
kitchen incorporated local elements while the public, male-centered portion of the
household maintained visibly Spanish elements: ornamentation, clothing, and table-
ware (Deagan 1983). Deagan stated that these processes of formulating new identities drawn from several cultural traditions were common in much of the New
World. I share with Deagan the conviction that creolization is a process that can be
understood archaeologically. In the rest of this chapter, I outline creolization in
other parts of the Southeast, drawing on case studies from Spanish Texas and
French Louisiana.

The Process of Forming Colonial Identities: From Static to Fluid

As Lightfoot (1995:201) notes, "colonial settlements were pluralistic entrepôts
where peoples of diverse backgrounds and nationalities, lived, worked, socialized,
and procreated." The people inhabiting French Louisiana, Spanish Florida, and
Spanish Texas in the 18th century included Native Americans (such as the Natchez,
Natchitoches, and Choctaw), Africans, French, Spaniards, and mixed-bloods (such
as *mestizas*, mulattos, and quadroons). The colonization of the southeastern United
States by the Spanish and French, and the arrival of Africans, put into place new
hierarchies of class, ethnicity, race, and gender on top of those already existing in
indigenous communities (Trouillot 2002). Sexual relations between and among
these groups brought further layers of complexity into colonial communities with
the emergence of racial labels such as *mestizo* and mulatto. Due to this diversity,
much colonial policy was about keeping people in line – that is, categorization of
its population. Along with a host of other laws regarding trade and political relationships, many French and Spanish policies were devoted to defining and main-

taining the boundaries of racial intermixing. The French Code Noir and the Spanish concept of *limpieza de sangre* (purity of blood) prohibited interracial marriage and sexual relations; despite these laws interracial marriages and sexual relations were common among French, Spanish, Native Americans, and Africans (Avery 1996:61–62; Usner 1992).

But changing social, political, and economic interactions between groups redefined the way colonial identity was constructed not only for Europeans but also for other groups, such as Native Americans and Africans. Colonial identity should, then, be conceptualized as malleable, shifting through time and within groups, and constructed at the intersections of gender, status, race, ethnicity, and power (Callaway 1993; Cooper and Stoler 1997; Cope 1997). Not all categories were fully realized or had an impact on colonial societies and social organizing principles because of differences with colonial discourses and the nature of different colonial communities; i.e., plantations, outposts, and cities (Trouillot 2002:195). For example, race may have been a more influential concept in the 18th-century Spanish presidio of Los Adaes than it was in 18th-century Philadelphia, given the former's relationship to the Spanish Crown (see Cannadine 2001).

Mindfulness of the *process* of creolization allows for an examination of how individuals negotiated social, racial, and political boundaries to construct new social identities (Comaroff 1996:169; Lightfoot and Martinez 1995:474; Loren 1999, 2001b). More than just reflecting on the pluralistic nature of communities and households, we can seek to draw out how people negotiated and articulated cultural practices to form new ones. Much of this focus on negotiation of colonial identities is tied to research that stresses the inconsistencies of colonial rule and the differential experiences of colonial individuals (see Loren 2001b; Stahl 2002; Upton 1996). Each individual's lived experience within these contexts further added to the complexities as many people strove to change and reshape existing boundaries.

The next two sections discuss these issues of categorization: how colonial subjects were categorized by the Crown and officials is outlined in "Categorization from above," while the recategorization that occurred as individuals moved through boundaries in processes of creolization is outlined in "Categorization from within".

Categorization from above: imperial definitions

Some anthropological examinations of colonial situations have detailed how colonizers took control of space and land – and by extension people – by defining and classifying space and those who occupied that space (Cohn 1996). Separations were made to classify those who controlled the land versus those who occupied and worked the land. In this way, the bounding and classification of the colonized became an inherent part of colonization. Under colonial domination, the categories such as *español* and *mestizo*, Christian and pagan, master and slave became important dividing tools for the process of ruling and controlling the actions of subjugated populations. Marking difference, especially in terms of skin color or race, served as a way to visually codify and categorize an individual and their actions. Colonial categories, however, went beyond mere skin color and included gender and status differences. Categories such as mulatto, quadroon, *Indio*, *casta*, and *gens de couleur libre* could simultaneously denote race, gender, and status (Callaway 1993; Cope 1994).

The Crown and local colonial officials defined social identities and status for children of mixed parentage, applying labels such as *mestizo* and quadroon. Racial boundaries were to be maintained by establishing rules of conduct for people of mixed heritage in order to establish and enforce essentialized group identities for colonial "others." Sanctions not only essentialized others, but also policed the boundaries of "us" (Comaroff 1997; Cooper and Stoler 1997; Stoler 1989). Mixed-race relations and the emergence of mixed-bloods threatened white prestige and was envisioned as the embodiment of European degeneration and moral decay, resulting in the contamination of pure blood and thereby leadership (Callaway 1993; Cope 1994). Creolization undermined European privilege to land and its occupants because now there was a population that stood between colonized and colonizer. If a mixed-blood was part European, shouldn't that individual be allowed the same rights and privileges as his/her father? Or should the mixed-blood be forced to live in slavery or poverty like his/her mother? As a result, boundaries were established to confirm the legitimacy of white rule and to put a growing mixed-blood population firmly in its place.

While French colonials devised relatively general racial categories for mixed-bloods, such as *métis* and quadroon, the Spanish *régimen de castas* was an elaborate categorical system that marked boundaries between *gente decente* (respectable people) and *gente baja* (lower classes). This system, established at the turn of the 18th century, was developed to hierarchically grade individuals by racial and ethnic criteria according to their phenotype (Boyer 1997:64). Native Americans held a slightly higher position than Africans in Spanish colonial society because the former had the potential to be civilized through conversion. Native American ancestry meant that one could be socially redeemable, while African ancestry held the taint of slavery, debasement, and possible Moorish descent. Thus, individuals with African ancestry were situated at the lowest echelon of Spanish society with little chance for social advancement (Cope 1994:24).

Individuals with mixed-race ancestry were graded between Spanish (the highest race) and African (the lowest race). Influenced by the ideology of *limpieza de sangre* (purity of blood), varieties of mixed-bloods, including *mestizos* and mulattos, were situated within the system according to their percentage of whiteness. The *régimen de castas* attempted to structure social, political, economic, and sexual interactions between groups in New Spain. Preserving racial purity and the wealth, power, and status (*calidad*) that accompanied *Español* was behind these categorizations (Boyer 1997). The *casta* system served to filter out undesirables, but at the same time, manipulating *casta* was often a way to gain power and status denied by official racial ideologies (Cope 1994:25).

Colonial discourse on racial ideologies and social hierarchy in French and Spanish colonial contexts created an imagined ordering of the daily lives of colonial subjects intimately tied to commonly understood notions of taste and social distinction, which outlined how colonial subjects should act, dress, and live. Thus, restrictions on diet, marriage, sexual relations, trade, religion, occupation, and dress for each colonial category became an important part of the colonial enterprise (Castelló Yturbide 1990; Cohn 1996; Gruzinski and Wachtel 1997; Shannon 1996; Stoler 1989). The importance of this discourse in the colonial enterprise has left an indelible mark, as is seen in the writings about and illustrations of imagined communities of "proper" settlers, soldiers, slaves, and officials that fill colonial archives. These archival residues have in turn served to inform official histories of the colonial period, while the unofficial histories of the people who chose not to live according to these laws still remain to be told.

Categories in theory: colonial images of others
Broadly speaking, text and images of colonies and colonial peoples were produced for an elite, educated, and noble audience. Funded and produced in the context of colonial expansion, colonial images were assertions of power and possession. For Europeans, print legitimated possession. Through the act of representation (in the form of narratives, maps, or illustration), European monarchies and their colonial officials took possession and asserted control over land and subjects (Greenblatt 1991; Hall 2000:47, 54; St. George 2000). Representation of difference lay at the heart of these acts of possession. In this way images serve as an archive of the quest for difference – rather than the depiction of difference – that emerges from colonial discourse. Thus, in colonial images, we are not seeing life as it was, but rather life as it was imagined (Pinney 1997:20), an important distinction to note when viewing colonial images from Spanish Texas and French Louisiana.

During the 18th century, over 500 *casta* paintings were produced in New Spain (García Saíz 1989). *Casta* paintings depicted multiethnic families and followed a specific pattern of illustrating social differences that resulted from the union of people of different races (Figure 12.1). In the paintings, the race of all family members was depicted, as was the family's place in colonial society. Race and status dictated appropriate diet, occupation, and dress for each group, while at the same time allowing one to visually discern another's place in colonial society.

Casta paintings illustrated particular markers of difference, visible signs that could be tabulated against group identities that emerged from a long history of defining difference (see Pinney 1997:29). *Casta* paintings reflected Spanish social classes and perceptions as well as racial concerns that existed both in the colony and the metropole (see Cannadine 2001). *Casta* paintings depicted examples of types and gave particular attention to identifying features of costume and material artifacts. For example, in his painting entitled *De Español, y de India Produce Mestiso,* Juan Rodríguez Juárez depicted an Indian wife, her Spanish husband, and their *mestizo* children (Figure 12.2). The husband is depicted in a frock coat and ruffled shirt while holding a three-cornered hat – clothing that befits his social identity. His wife, while wearing what looks to be hand-woven dress, also wears the pearl jewelry more commonly worn by women of the upper classes or married to men from the upper classes.

Another series of images emerged from French Louisiana. Alexander de Batz's well-known 18th-century illustrations of Native Americans and Africans in colonial

Figure 12.1 *Castas* of New Spain, from Joachin Antonio de Bafarás's manuscript, *Origen, costumbres, y estado presente de mexicanos y philipinos*, 1763 (courtesy of the Hispanic Society of America)

Louisiana provide examples of imperial discourse on difference of colonial subjects. Produced during his tenure as Royal Engineer in Louisiana from 1730 to 1760, de Batz's on-location images offered ethnographic detail about the particular manners and customs of Native Americans in Louisiana. In particular, de Batz distinguished among the different groups that inhabited the colony, from a Tunica family to chiefs,

Figure 12.2 *De Español, y de India Produce Mestiso*, ca. 1725, attributed to Juan Rodríguez Juárez (Sir Edward Hulse, Breamore House, Hampshire, England)

warriors, and Native American and African children (Figure 12.3). Native Americans and Africans drawn by de Batz were always depicted partially clothed or naked, even when wearing winter dress. At no point were Native Americans depicted with trade goods (such as glass beads or cloth), nor were Africans depicted in European-style clothing. Rather, de Batz depicted these colonial others in presumably authentic dress, clearly distinguishing different groups by dress style. For example, in his illustration entitled *Sauvages Tchaktas Matachez en Guerriers*, de Batz distinguished the Natchez chief (depicted on the right) from the Choctaw warriors (depicted on the left) by their clothing: their tattooing, the staffs they held, their headdresses, and their stature (Figure 12.4). An African boy (again, distinguished by his dress) is depicted in the foreground tending to a Native American child.

De Batz's depictions of dress in these illustrations were in line with how the French Crown and its officials imagined how people should dress according to race and status – not a conglomeration of styles but distinctly different styles. Conspicuously absent from such images are other residents of colonial Louisiana: individuals of mixed racial ancestry a growing population within the colony. So, the negotiation of colonial categories is not found in colonial images, such as *casta*

Figure 12.3 Alexander de Batz, *Desseins de Sauvages de Plusieurs Nations*, 1735 (Peabody Museum of Archaeology and Ethnology, Harvard University, Photo T2377)

Figure 12.4 Alexander de Batz, *Sauvages Tchaktas Matachez en Guerriers*, 1735 (Peabody Museum of Archaeology and Ethnology, Harvard University, Photo T2376)

paintings and the work of de Batz, which depicted only one view of colonial discourse. Yet these paintings and illustrations have fixed our vision of how colonial peoples should look, and left a lasting impression in official histories.

Categorization from within: colonial peoples define themselves

Colonial categories were not stable or unyielding. Ann Stoler (1989:136) defines colonial communities as "unique colonial configurations," highlighting how the process of identity formation played differentially in local communities as well as in multiethnic households: full of contradictions, competing agendas and categories, and concerns of bodily appropriateness (see also Hall 2000; Loren 1999, 2001a, 2001b). As Stoler (1997:202) notes, "in each colonial arena . . . gender distinctions, gender prescriptions, colonial knowledge and racial membership were simultaneously invoked and strategically filled with different meanings for varied projects." Therefore, the success of the colonial enterprise depended upon some degree of flexibility. The practice of creating categories was one of exclusion as it usually only included colonizing (Spanish or French) men as legitimate elites and rulers of colonial society. Labels for colonizing male elites usually remained consistent through colonization and were based on assumed homogenous ancestry. Colonial others, on the other hand, were given diverse labels through the colonial period. When a mixed-race population grew, so did colonial categories of difference. All categories restricted action and power in social and political scenarios for colonial actors, but the desire and need to cross these boundaries heightened.

Research by Cope (1994) and Boyer (1997) on racial categories in 17th-century Mexico illustrate how categories were purposefully negotiated by mixed-bloods to gain power and social status. Cope (1994:15) notes that some mixed-bloods were not considered *vecinos* (citizens) and held a marginal, anomalous place in Mexico, as some elites even refused to recognize their existence. While some mixed-bloods managed to gain power and economic status in colonial Mexico, these situations were rare. Therefore, mixed-bloods often "self-fashioned" social identity by acting, dressing, and talking like an individual from another group. Mixed-bloods, who were often familiar with the cultures of both parents, were particularly adept at this practice and some were able to obtain authority, authenticity, and power in situations where these rights were denied (Boyer 1997:67; see also Cooper and Stoler 1997; Shannon 1996). Thus, racial categories were "loose" and rarely were applied consistently to one individual over time.

The practice of self-fashioning was not limited to mixed-bloods, as such strategies were often employed by European, African, and Native American men and women wishing to enter other colonial situations not always open to them. Reconfiguring one's identity through fashion, posture, mannerisms, and language, however, often allowed entrance into other social and political worlds. These newly constructed identities provided a way to obtain the authority, authenticity, and power that were typically denied (Loren 2001a; Stoler 1989; see also Meskell 1999). Thus, as discussed below, new identities were consciously created or masked, as subjects manipulated official mandated identities to distinguish themselves from others.

The art of self-categorization: a Tunica chief and a French official
The ethnohistorical record redounds with accounts of elite French men who refashioned themselves to move into other political worlds. An example is Father Morfi's mid-18th-century description of Anthanase DeMézières, commandant of the French post of Natchitoches:

> Many Frenchmen . . . can scarcely be distinguished from the Indians. For they imitate them not only in their nakedness, but even in painting their faces. In testimony of this truth . . . Such was Lieutenant-Captain Don Anthanase DeMézières called Captain Pinto, because he painted his face . . . Referring to the woodsmen and Canadians scattered about Louisiana, and to the uniform which they should be obliged to wear . . . they should be obliged to wear them, because their greatest pleasure is to appear naked except for a breech-clout. Let us now see who abandon all decorum and go about unclothed. I surmise that only those of the lower class do this habitually, but it appears that some of the higher rank likewise do so. (Hackett 1934, 1:249)

Morfi was concerned by lower-status practices of dressing in a native fashion, even if an official did so for political reasons. But these practices, even when they occurred in political realms, are evidence of creolization, the need to reconstruct identities in a multiethnic context. Despite Morfi's disgust at these practices by French elites, Native American leaders were permitted to dress like the French, as is evidenced in the following account.

Father Pierre François-Xavier de Charlevoix, a Jesuit who traveled through Louisiana between 1720 and 1722, described his visit to the Tunica chief in 1720 and stated that "The chief received us very politely; he was dressed in the French fashion, and seemed to be not at all uneasy in that habit . . . He has long left off the dress of a savage, and he takes pride appearing always well-dressed, according to our fashion" (Swanton 1911:312–313). This suggests the French believed that the Tunica dressed properly and acted appropriately in their interactions with them. While the latter of the two accounts can be interpreted to suggest that the Tunica subscribed to French ideologies (at least regarding dress), this account also implies that the Tunica recognized that effective and productive dealings with the French meant wearing their clothing in certain political contexts.

These accounts suggest an important contradiction. Native American leaders would shrug off conventional dress in political contexts, while elite and lower-status Europeans were vilified by the Crown and colonial officials for their actions. So while Native Americans could presumably creolize to become more European, there was an anxiety associated with Europeans doing so to become less European. Colonial peoples, so carefully defined and so closely watched, were blurring categorical lines through their bodies to subvert colonial order (at least in the minds of officials) by merely dressing like someone else. The archaeological record provides some insights into how this took place.

Understanding Creolization Processes in the Archaeological Record

Through creolization, "new" colonial peoples could define themselves as different not only by calling themselves by a new name but also through new social practices. Material culture was purposefully used in these transactions – dress, the architectural form of one's home, food preferences – and actively constituted social identities. For example, individuals used material culture to change their identity by refashioning themselves after another group or in a unique combination of dress. This concept has been explored for those who took on the role of cultural broker (Shannon 1996), but not for other colonial individuals who wished to manipulate their identity for reasons other than trade. Because archaeological data embody the materiality of daily life that contributes to the formation of identity, material culture data can be used to investigate this process.

Earlier in this chapter, I discussed how archaeologists have recently begun to construct theoretical approaches to interpreting colonial sites as multiethnic while at the same time holding to the traditional methodologies. The residue of Quimby and Spoehr's "European" and "Native American" classes has remained, as archaeologists continue to use these categories in their methodologies that assume a one-to-one relationship between material culture and ethnicity. Typically, material culture is placed into either of these categories with the assumption of assimilation when combinations of "European" and "Native American" objects occur in the same context. Yet this classification dismisses the kinds of interactions that occurred between groups on the colonial frontier, as it separates people and their activities into discreet units. Another drawback of this kind of interpretation is that a *cate-*

gory of material culture is supposed to indicate ethnicity (Upton 1996). Categories of "native" and "European" material culture alone relate almost no information on the ways in which individuals used material culture in processes of identity formation. Artifacts acquire symbolic meaning and value through use and activities, rather than being assigned categories based on where they were produced (Jones 1997; Lightfoot 1995; Lightfoot and Martinez 1995; Upton 1996).

An emphasis on identifying particular identities in the archaeological record often leads, as Ann Stahl (2002:33) notes, to the essentializing trap of linking artifacts to particular groups (see also Upton 1996). For example, colonoware is often equated with emerging African American identities, while sewing objects are often equated with women, following the assumption that all women (and perhaps only women) sew (see Beaudry 2002). What is missing from these analyses is the recognition that objects often have multiple meanings in identity constructions (see Beaudry 2002; see also Hall 2000; Meskell 1999). Here, I focus on one aspect of creolization – dressing the body – and discuss the material culture combinations associated with this process.

Clothing and adornment: dressing the bodies of creolized peoples

Creolization involved the purposeful manipulation of material culture to (mis)represent oneself in a particular fashion for personal, sexual, economic, or political reasons. Architecture, dress, and ceramics were just some of the ways in which one could draw on the universe of colonial expressions to identify oneself in the world. However, not all categories of material culture are appropriate to investigating nuanced processes such as bodily experiences and identity negotiations. As Deagan (2002:4) notes, artifacts associated with clothing and personal adornment – buckles, bracelets, beads, and thimbles – are often imbued with "a great deal more information about gender, beliefs, value systems, social opportunities and social identities."

How one dressed was a physical manifestation of what group one belonged to, and prohibitions regarding how one should dress (and whom one should not dress like) went hand in hand with racial terminology. Throughout the colonial Southeast, laws and regulations were enacted to restrict dressing practices: Europeans as well as Africans were to don European-style clothing appropriate to their status and gender while Native Americans dressed in buckskin, not in European-style clothes. Notions of what was proper play into how material culture related to clothing and adornment found in the archaeological record is interpreted.

Objects related to dress (usually falling under the category of "small finds") can include clothing artifacts, such as buttons and buckles, as well as items worn over clothing, such as necklace beads, guns, knives, and religious medals (see Beaudry 2002). Knives and guns can also be included in the universe of artifacts related to dress, as these items were also worn on the body to visually constitute identity. On multiethnic French and Spanish colonial sites, archaeologists have tended to view small finds relating to dress as either "Indian" (such as glass beads or brass tinkling cones) or "European" (such as religious medals and brass buttons) (e.g., Walthall and Emerson 1992; Waselkov 1999). Following from this, artifacts associated with clothing (such as buttons, buckles, bracelets, etc.) are then fit into static interpretive categories. For example, it is often (and perhaps incorrectly) assumed that Native Americans wore glass beads sewn on their clothing and European men wore brass buttons on their coats, European women wore jewelry while African men had none. In such interpretations, little attention is given to how dress was related to active processes of identity construction. Rather than simply dressing one's body, presentation of the body through dress and adornment is one of the most visual manifestations of one's identity and self. Artifacts associated with dressing, then, can provide information on processes of creolization, especially when combinations of seemingly disparate "Native American" and "European" objects suggest that colonial people fashioned themselves in unique ways.

Dressing on the Texas frontier: Los Adaes
Situated along the eastern border of 18th-century Spanish Texas (just miles from French Louisiana), Los Adaes was inhabited by Spanish and mixed-blood military personnel and their families as well as civilian settlers from New Spain, French refugees, Native Americans, and some escaped African slaves from French Louisiana (Avery 1995; Gregory 1983; Loren 1999). Artifacts associated with dress at the site include glass beads, buttons and buckles, gun parts, religious medals, and finger rings. All of these objects seem to suggest the dress of both upper and lower classes as well as European and native dress styles. It is tempting to say that these different artifact types would correspond with the different people who occupied the site – for example, that belt buckles were from the dress of Spanish men while seed beads were from the beaded buckskin clothing of Caddo men or women. Yet, this kind of interpretation overlooks the ways in which colonial individuals continually and creatively refashioned themselves using different kinds of material culture. That is, they drew on the different kinds of clothing available to them to fashion their dress. So, colonial individuals could have easily worn objects together on their body that could simultaneously be considered European and native, upper- and lower-class. The practice of combining different kinds of dress is certainly discussed at some length in the ethnohistorical record. So, then, perhaps we should look at the combinations of different kinds of artifacts in the archaeological record with new eyes. Maybe everyone was not dressing as they should, but perhaps some of the population were mixing different dress styles in daily practice.

Each of the four households excavated at Los Adaes contained a variety of items in unique combinations: glass beads (commonly associated with Native American clothing) were found with brass military belt buckles (worn on the trousers of men), elaborate shoe buckles (from fancy shoes of men or women) were found with shell beads (again commonly associated with Native American clothing), and brass military buttons (commonly associated with male uniforms) were found with brass tinkling cones and earrings (commonly associated with the dress of Native American women) (Avery 1996; Gregory 1973, 1983, 1984). These combinations suggest that many of the individuals at the site had access to a variety of objects, thus enabling them to creatively configure dress styles by wearing items commonly associated with different ethnic and gender identities together in daily life but in different patterns than usually anticipated. These new mixtures of objects worn suggest the processes of creolization at play – that individuals were struggling with existing identities and forming new ones using material culture to showcase themselves in a different light.

Dressing in French Louisiana: Haynes Bluff and Bloodhound

Similar combinations of dress artifacts have been found at French colonial sites in the Southeast. Located in present-day western Mississippi, the site of Haynes Bluff was a multiethnic community occupied in the first third of the 18th century by Tunica, Yazoo, Karoa, and Ofo peoples and perhaps some French (see Brain 1988; Usner 1992:48–49). The Lower Mississippi Survey run out of Harvard University's Peabody Museum excavated the site in 1974. During the course of their excavations, some burials were recovered that again suggest processes of creolization at work. For example, an adult male was buried wearing French guns, glass beads (perhaps the remnants of beaded clothing), and glass bead necklaces and bracelets (Brain 1988:209–211). These combinations seem somewhat straightforwardly Native American, but the inclusion of a French gun in the burial does suggest that this item was related to this person's social identity (perhaps as part of his relations with French people). Another adult male was buried wearing French guns and glass beads (from a beaded garment), and also triangular glass bead pendants (made from European glass beads melted into triangular shapes) were strung from the hair, along with iron coils and an elaborate leather headdress (Brain 1988: 211–213). In this burial, European objects were worn along with Native American ones but in seemingly unusual combinations that perhaps pushed against existing European perceptions of gender identities, signaling the process of creolization.

These processes are found at other colonial Louisiana sites. Excavations in 1977 at the Bloodhound site by the Lower Mississippi Survey revealed several burials from the first half of the 18th century (Brain 1988:166–177). The Bloodhound site is also located in western Mississippi and was likely occupied by the Tunica, but again some French may have lived in or near the site (Usner 1990:48–49). Like those individuals buried at Haynes Bluff, burials at Bloodhound contained a variety of "French" and "Native American" objects. Of particular interest are burial 4, an adult woman buried wearing a frock coat and trousers (dress commonly associated with French men), and burial 6, an adolescent child buried wearing bracelets of large glass beads and copper wire bracelets, as well as a shirt embroidered with hundreds of turquoise beads, brass bells tied around his knees, and an ornate shell bead necklace that included a copper crucifix (Brain 1988:171–173). These combinations are notable not only because of their uniqueness, but because the combinations of artifacts found with these individuals goes against popular notions and official histories and images of the dress of colonial peoples. What we have here is a glimpse at the unofficial histories and images of the lived, colonial experience.

Dress artifacts found at these colonial sites in French Louisiana and Spanish Texas were found in seemingly incongruous but new combinations that were worn by different people in life and death. Here again, the dress conventions of these individuals at death may have signaled how material culture was used in new and interesting combinations in the reformulation of identity through dress and processes of creolization in the making.

Conclusions: Further Steps in Creolization Studies

Creolization, understood here as the process of reformulating identities, was a fixture of life in the colonial Southeast. It occurred in households and communities, where distinct cultural traditions were met and reshaped through new social, sexual, and political interactions. Throughout the colonial period, different identities were asserted and reasserted, whether they were pre-existing identities or newly formulated ones (see Pauketat 2001:7–8). The push and pull of reshaping identities in the processes of creolization occurred largely through material culture (what people wore, what they ate, what their houses looked like, etc.) and was ongoing through the colonial period. The differential experiences of colonial subjects shaped how they used material culture to construct and reconstruct their identities, allowing individuals to recreate themselves on social landscapes, to experience and live alternative histories.

Our utilization of different sources in the study of creolization is imperative, as some stories have been hidden in official histories. Thus, the comparison of categories found in archives, colonial images, and official histories with the residues of daily practices found in the archaeological record help us understand how colonial individuals embodied new social traditions (Trouillot 1995). These emerging identities, practices, and traditions were multi-layered in local contexts, as deeply textured and complex as the colonial population itself. Although seemingly disorganized, the combinations of artifacts found in French and Spanish colonial sites suggest how creolization took place – how individuals from different backgrounds embodied social traditions that existed in tension with official distinctions, personal tastes, local concerns, and the desire to move beyond rigid social hierarchies.

Trouillot (2002) calls our attention to the importance of the social contexts in which creolization occurred. While creolization did occur in many colonial areas (the Caribbean, Southeast US, Oceania, etc.), the ways in which people constructed their identities were unique to their communities. Creolization studies of yore took this process as inevitable, occurring similarly at different areas around the globe. Yet to understand its nuances and in order to grasp how peoples restructured their lives, we must understand processes of creolization at the intersections of local contexts, larger colonial discourses, and global traditions.

REFERENCES

Avery, George, 1996 *Annual Report for the Los Adaes Station Archaeology Program*. Natchitoches, LA: Department of Social Sciences, Northwestern State University.

Beaudry, Mary C., 2002 "Re-vision": Filling gaps and silences in how we think and write about small finds. Paper presented at the Annual Meeting of the Society for Historical Archaeology, Mobile, AL, January 10.

Boyer, Richard, 1997 Negotiating *Calidad*: The Everyday Struggle for Status in Mexico. *Historical Archaeology* 31(1), 64–73.

Brain, Jeffrey P., 1988 *Tunica Archaeology*. Papers of the Peabody Museum of Archaeology and Ethnology, 78. Cambridge, MA: Harvard University.

Callaway, Helen, 1993 Purity and Exotica in Legitimating the Empire: Cultural Construction of Gender, Sexuality, and Race. In *Legitimacy and State in Twentieth-Century Africa: Essays in Honour of A. H. M. Kirk-Greene*. Terence Ranger and Olufemi Vaughan, eds. Pp. 31–61. Oxford: St. Antony's College.

Cannadine, David, 2001 *Ornamentalism: How the British Saw their Empire*. Oxford: Oxford University Press.

Castelló Yturbide, Teresa, 1990 La indumentaria de las Castas del Mestizaje. *La Pintura de Castas, Artes de Mexico* 8, 74–78.

Cohn, Bernard S., 1996 *Colonialism and its Forms of Knowledge*. Princeton: Princeton University Press.

Comaroff, Jean, 1996 The empire's old clothes: Fashioning the colonial subject. In *Cross-Cultural Consumption: Global Markets, Local Realities*. David Howes, ed. Pp. 31–61. New York: Routledge.

Comaroff, John, and Jean Comaroff, 1992 *Ethnography and the Historical Imagination*. Boulder, CO: Westview Press.

Cooper, Frederick, and Laura Ann Stoler, eds., 1997 *Tensions of Empire: Colonial Cultures in a Bourgeois World*. Berkeley: University of California Press.

Cope, R. Douglas, 1994 *The Limits of Racial Domination: Plebian Society in Colonial Mexico City, 1660–1720*. Madison: University of Wisconsin Press.

Cusick, James, ed., 1998 *Culture Contact: Interaction, Culture Change and Archaeology*. Carbondale: Southern Illinois University Press.

Dawdy, Shannon Lee, 2000 Preface. *In* Creolization. Shannon Lee Dawdy, ed. *Historical Archaeology* 34(3), 1–4.

Deagan, Kathleen A., 1983 *Spanish St. Augustine: The Archaeology of a Colonial Creole Community*. New York: Academic Press.

—— 1988 Neither History nor Prehistory: The Questions that Count in Historical Archaeology. *Historical Archaeology* 22(1), 7–12.

—— 1996 Colonial Transformations: Euro-American Cultural Genesis in the Earliest Spanish Colonies. *Journal of Anthropological Research* 52(2), 135–160.

—— 2002 *Artifacts of the Spanish Colonies of Florida and the Caribbean 1500–1800*, vol. 2; *Personal Portable Possessions*. Washington, DC: Smithsonian Institution Press.

Deagan, Kathleen A., ed., 1995 *Puerto Real: The Archaeology of a Sixteenth-Century Spanish Town in Hispaniola*. Gainesville: University Press of Florida.

Deetz, James, 1977 *In Small Things Forgotten: The Archaeology of Early American Life*. New York: Anchor Books.

—— 1996 *In Small Things Forgotten: The Archaeology of Early American Life*, expanded and revised edn. New York: Doubleday.

Delle, James A., Stephen A. Mrozowski, and Robert Paynter, eds., 2000 *Lines That Divide: Historical Archaeologies of Race, Class, and Gender*. Knoxville: University of Tennessee Press.

Ewen, Charles R., 1991 *From Spaniard to Creole: The Archaeology of Hispanic American Cultural Transformations at Puerto Real, Haiti*. Tuscaloosa: University of Alabama Press.

Ferguson, Leland, 1992 *Uncommon Ground: Archaeology and Early African America, 1650–1800.* Washington, DC: Smithsonian Institution Press.

——Introduction. In Creolization. Shannon Lee Dawdy, ed. *Historical Archaeology* 34(3), 5–9.

García Saíz, María Concepcíon, 1989 *Las Castas Mexicanas: Un Género Pictórico Americano.* Mexico City: Olivetti.

Greenblatt, Stephen, 1991 *Marvelous Possessions: The Wonders of the New World.* Chicago: University of Chicago Press.

Gregory, Hiram F., 1973 Eighteenth-century Caddoan archaeology: A study in models and interpretations. Ph.D. dissertation, Southern Methodist University.

——1983 Los Adaes: The archaeology of an ethnic enclave. *Geoscience and Man* 23, 53–57.

——1984 *Excavations 1982: Presidio de Nuestra Señora del Pilar de Los Adaes.* Natchitoches, LA: Northwestern State University.

Gruzinski, Serge, and Nathan Wachtel, 1997 Cultural interbreedings: Constituting the majority as a minority. *Comparative Studies in Society and History* 39(2), 231–250.

Hackett, Charles Wilson, 1934 *Pichardo's Treatise on the Limits of Louisiana and Texas,* 5 vols. Austin: University of Texas Press.

Hall, Martin, 1992 Small things and the mobile, conflictual fusion of power, fear, and desire. In *The Art and Mystery of Historical Archaeology: Essays in Honor of James Deetz.* Ann Yentsch and Mary Beaudry, eds. Pp. 373–399. Boca Raton: CRC Press.

——2000 *Archaeology and the Modern World: Colonial Transcripts in South Africa and the Chesapeake.* London: Routledge.

Hill, J. D., 1996 Introduction: Ethnogenesis in the Americas, 1492–1992. In *History, Power and Identity: Ethnogenesis in the Americas, 1492–1992.* J. D. Hill, ed. Pp. 1–19. Iowa: University of Iowa Press.

Jackson, Jack, 1995 *Imaginary Kingdom: Texas as Seen by the Rivera and Rubí Military Expeditions, 1727 and 1767.* Austin: Texas State Historical Association.

Jones, Sîan, 1997 *The Archaeology of Ethnicity: Constructing Identities in the Past and the Present.* London: Routledge.

Katzew, Ilona, 1996 Casta painting: Identity and social stratification in colonial Mexico. In *New World Orders: Casta Painting and Colonial Latin America.* Ilona Katzew, ed. Pp. 8–29. New York: Americas Society Art Gallery.

Kroeber, A. L., 1948 *Anthropology.* New York: Harcourt, Brace & World.

Lightfoot, Kent, 1995 Culture contact studies: Redefining the relationship between prehistoric and historical archaeology. *American Antiquity* 60(2), 199–217.

Lightfoot, Kent G., and Antoinette Martinez, 1995 Frontiers and boundaries in archaeological perspective. *Annual Review of Anthropology* 24, 471–492.

Loren, Diana DiPaolo, 1999 Creating social distinction: Articulating colonial policies and practices along the 18th-century Louisiana/Texas frontier. Ph.D. dissertation, State University of New York at Binghamton.

——2001a Manipulating bodies and emerging traditions at the Los Adaes Presidio. In *The Archaeology of Traditions: Agency and History Before and After Columbus,* Timothy R. Pauketat, ed. Pp. 58–76. Gainesville: University of Florida Press.

——2001b Social skins: Orthodoxies and practices of dressing in the Early Colonial lower Mississippi valley. *Journal of Social Archaeology* 1(2), 172–189.

Lyons, Claire L., and John K. Papadopoulos, eds., 2002 *The Archaeology of Colonialism.* Los Angeles: Getty Research Institute.

McEwan, Bonnie, 1991 The archaeology of women in the Spanish New World. *Historical Archaeology* 25(4), 33–41.

Meskell, Lynn, 1999 *Archaeologies of Social Life: Age, Sex, Class et cetera in Ancient Egypt.* Oxford: Blackwell.

Pauketat, Timothy R., 2001 A new tradition in archaeology. In *The Archaeology of Traditions: Agency and History Before and After Columbus.* Timothy R. Pauketat, ed. Pp. 1–16. Gainesville: University of Florida Press.

Pinney, Christopher, 1997 *Camera Indica: The Social Life of Indian Photographs.* Chicago: University of Chicago Press.

Quimby, George I., and Alexander Spoehr, 1951 Acculturation and Material Culture. Fieldiana: *Anthropology* 3(6), 107–147.

Redfield, R., R. Linton, and M. J. Herskovits, 1936 Outline for the Study of Acculturation. *American Anthropology* 38, 149–152.

Roseberry, W., 1991 *Anthropologies and Histories.* New Brunswick, NJ: Rutgers University Press.

Ruhl, Donna L., and Kathleen Hoffman, eds., 1997 Diversity and social identity in Colonial Spanish America: Native American, African, and Hispanic communities during the Middle period. *Historical Archaeology* 31 (1) (whole volume).

St. George, Robert Blair, 2000 Introduction. In *Possible Pasts: Becoming Colonial in Early America.* Robert Blair St. George, ed. Pp. 1–32. Ithaca, NY: Cornell University Press.

Shannon, T. J., 1996 Dressing for success on the Mohawk frontier: Hendrick, William Johnson, and the Indian fashion. *William and Mary Quarterly* 53, 13–42.

Silliman, S. W., 2001 Agency, practical politics, and the archaeology of culture contact. *Journal of Social Archaeology* 1(2), 184–204.

Stahl, Ann B., 2002 Colonial entanglements and the practices of taste: An alternative to logocentric approaches. *American Anthropologist* 104(3), 827–845.

Stoler, Ann L., 1989 Rethinking colonial categories: European communities and the boundaries of rule. *Comparative Studies in Society and History* 31(3), 134–161.

Swanton, John Reed, 1911 *Indian Tribes of the Lower Mississippi Valley and Adjacent Coast of the Gulf of Mexico.* Bureau of American Ethnology, Bulletin 43. Washington, DC: Smithsonian Institution.

Thomas, Nicholas, 1991 *Entangled Objects: Exchange, Material Culture, and Colonialism in the Pacific.* Cambridge, MA: Harvard University Press.

——1994 *Colonialism's Culture: Anthropology, Travel and Government.* Princeton: Princeton University Press.

Trouillot, Michel-Rolph, 1995 *Silencing the Past: Power and the Production of History.* Boston: Beacon Press.

——2002 Culture on the edges: Caribbean creolization in historical context. In *From the Margins: Historical Anthropology and its Futures.* Brain Keith Axel, ed. Pp. 189–210. Durham: Duke University Press.

Upton, Dell, 1996 Ethnicity, authenticity and invented traditions. *Historical Archaeology* 30(2), 1–7.

Usner, Daniel H., 1992 *Indians, Settlers and Slaves in a Frontier Exchange Economy: The Lower Mississippi Valley before 1783.* Chapel Hill: University of North Carolina Press.

Walthall, John A., and Thomas E. Emerson, eds., 1992 *Calumet and Fleur-de-lys: Archaeology of Indian and French Contact in the Midcontinent.* Washington, DC: Smithsonian Institution Press.

Waselkov, Gregory A., 1999 *Old Mobile Archaeology.* Mobile: University of South Alabama, Center for Archaeological Studies.

Wolf, Eric, 1982 *Europe and the People Without History.* Berkeley: University of California Press.

13

Before the Revolution: Archaeology and the African Diaspora on the Atlantic Seaboard

Theresa A. Singleton

The Atlantic seaboard of North America was not only the site of the first permanent English settlement in North America; it was also where the first African American communities arose. Therefore, any study that seeks to understand the initial period of African American culture in North America must begin there. The Atlantic seaboard is a diverse area with numerous sub-regions, all with complex settlement and social histories. Consequently, scholars generally subdivide the African American experience along the Atlantic seaboard into smaller regions. This discussion follows the subdivision of Ira Berlin (1998) into three major regions: the Chesapeake (Virginia, Maryland, and Delaware); the coastal Southeast or Lowcountry (South Carolina, Georgia, and northern Florida); and the Northeast (New England, and New York, New Jersey, and Pennsylvania). Within each region, distinctive African American societies developed. The purpose of this chapter is to examine how archaeology has contributed to our understanding of African American life in each of the three regions.

The focus is on the genesis or birth of African American communities in the period prior to the American Revolutionary War as seen primarily from the interpretation of 18th-century archaeological resources. During the 18th century, the black population along the Atlantic seaboard significantly increased due to both massive African importations through the slave trade and natural increase. More significantly, blacks, both African-born and American-born, began forming communities and creating distinctive African American cultures. Following the American Revolution, a host of changes – ideological, agricultural, technological, and territorial – had a profound impact in shaping the African American experience for the 19th century: the abolition of slavery in the northern states, the westward spread of slavery into former Indian lands, and the invention of the cotton gin and subsequent cotton boom. Consequently, many aspects of African American life in the 18th century were abandoned and lost to more recent historical consciousness. Archaeology has played a vital role in restoring the memory of cultural practices that were lost or abandoned.

This discussion is not intended to be a comprehensive look at the archaeology of African American life in these areas. Rather, it is an effort to compare and contrast the archaeological record of African American life within the three areas focusing on two interrelated themes. Certainly a recurrent theme, not only along the Atlantic seaboard but also within the archaeological study of the African diaspora as a whole, is the examination of archaeological and written evidence that provides insights into and understanding of identity formation and transformation among African American communities.

Some archaeologists look toward African influences in the material culture of people of African descent produced and used as indicators of identity. The 18th century is the best time period to examine such influences in North America because it was the period with the greatest numbers of African-born residents. Societal structures (racism, inequality, etc.) also impacted the construction of identity. As a subordinated group in North America, African Americans struggled to obtain some control of their lives. Thus, analyzing agency, defined here as direct or indirect action, provides a second theme central to understanding the strategies African Americans used in their attempt to undermine those who wielded power over them. Elizabeth Brumfiel has suggested that identity is closely tied to agency because actors' sense about who they are and how they should act influences their action (2000:252). Identity formation is viewed here as a dynamic process shaped by the interrelationship of human action and social structures.

Archaeological work in each of the three regions is uneven, and varies quite a bit within each region. Eighteenth-century African American life on plantations is best understood from archaeological research undertaken in Virginia for the Chesapeake and South Carolina for Lowcountry. The discussion of the Northeast considers only two sites from two different states: New York and Massachusetts.

The Chesapeake Region

Slavery was introduced to the Chesapeake incidentally. The first documented Africans to come to Virginia, and to the English colonies of North America as a whole, arrived aboard a Dutch ship in 1619 that anchored where the James River empties into the Chesapeake Bay. In exchange for provisions, the captain of the ship paid the colonial officials for the "twenty and odd Negroes" on board the ship (Boles 1984:9). Fifteen of the twenty ended up at Flowerdew Hundred, a plantation founded in 1619 by George Yeardley, Virginia's first governor, and excavated by the late James Deetz (1993:3) during the 1980s. At Flowerdew and other early 17th-century settlements, Africans lived and worked alongside white indentured servants, raising livestock and producing crops such as tobacco. Both Africans and white indentures most likely lived under the same roof as landowners; therefore no discrete archaeological deposits associated with African laborers have been identified during the formative years of English settlement.

Mathew Emerson (1999) has posited that this early African presence is represented in the decorative motifs embellished on locally made, terracotta pipes found throughout the Chesapeake during the 17th century. This decorative style consists of the patterned use of lines and stamps in geometric and zoomorphic shapes highlighted in white inlay. He believes the designs to be an African aesthetic because of their widespread use in West Africa before the mass shipment of Africans to the Chesapeake. Emerson's interpretation of Chesapeake pipes has been highly contested by those who have attributed the making of these pipes to Native Americans (Mouer et al. 1999). Emerson's interpretation of Chesapeake pipes argues an African presence in the archaeological record of the 17th century, but it fails to provide information about the lives of African people during that time.

Scholars have debated whether Africans living in Virginia during the first 50–60 years after the arrival of first Africans occupied a social position similar to that of white indentured laborers or whether, like their successors in the 18th century, they were enslaved for life. Indentured servants worked for a specified period of time for a person with whom they had entered into a contractual agreement. Despite the fact that landowners often found ways to extend the length of such contracts, indentured workers would eventually be freed (Morgan 1975:308–311), whereas enslavement was a lifelong and inheritable social position: children born to slaves were also enslaved. Africans, only 5 to 7 percent of the population at this time, may have taken advantage of their undefined legal status by acquiring their freedom after a period of bound labor (Berlin 1998:29). Some of these Africans settled along the eastern shores of Virginia and Maryland, and formed the first enclaves of legally free blacks in English North America (Breen and Innes 1980; Davidson 1984; Deal 1993). Preliminary archaeological work has begun at these early settlements. In Maryland, Davidson identified the general location of some of these settlements using plats and other archival sources. In Virginia, Mathew Emerson has begun the exploratory survey and testing of sites presumably related to these early free black communities (personal communication, 2003).

Beginning in the 1670s, the racial basis for slavery was made explicit when laws distinguishing between slaves and indentured servants appeared. From then on, people of African descent were slaves, not servants, and indentured servants were people of European descent. Shortly after the time when racial slavery was institutionalized, many Virginian slaveholders began housing white and black bound laborers in separate quarters. This practice was even commented upon by Durand de Dauphine, a visitor to Tidewater Virginia in 1686–87, who observed: "They [Virginia landowners] build . . . a separate house for the Christian slaves, one for the Negro slaves" (quoted in Epperson 2001:55). Terrence Epperson has suggested that Rick Neck and Utopia, two early plantations in Tidewater Virginia, offer the prospect for studying the transition from indenture to slave labor, because they have archaeological remains of late 17th- and 18th-century quarters presumably used for bound labor (Epperson 2001:66–67).

Excavations at Rich Neck yielded two late 17th-century earthfast houses and a burial. At Utopia four discrete temporal and spatial housing phases were unearthed dating from approximately 1670 to 1750. Analysis and additional research at these sites are ongoing, but when completed should yield information on the extent to which the material lives of enslaved and indentured laborers differed, if at all.

As the importation of African laborers increased, enslaved Africans supplanted white indentured labor in the early 1700s. During the first three decades of the 18th century African-born slave laborers dominated the slave population, but by mid-century the number of African laborers had declined and Virginian-born laborers increased. The slave population began to reproduce itself through natural increase, the only slave community of the three considered herein to do so. The shift from white indenture to enslaved black labor increased crop productivity, as was the case on English plantations elsewhere in the Americas (Eltis 2000:220–221), but at a huge cost to slave workers. Rights and privileges that many blacks once shared with white indentured laborers in the 17th century completely vanished. Slave laborers were now subjected to brutal work regimes, corporal punishment, crowded living conditions, and meager food rations.

The predominance of Africans, and, by 1740, African Virginians, on 18th-century plantations influenced the cultural landscape – the ways those who live on a landscape define it – in subtle ways. Slave housing was built utilizing Anglo-Virginian carpentry techniques, but the placement of houses in a square formation surrounding an open courtyard, as was the case at Utopia plantation, may be related to African usage of domestic space: the courtyard could serve as a central place for cooking and socializing (Walsh 1997:103). Another and more ubiquitous way in which Afro-Virginians modified the built environment imposed upon them was through digging sub-floor pits within the interior living spaces of slave houses. These rectangular or square pits of various sizes and depths were not part of the original construction of the buildings. Enslaved people dug the pits to the clay sub-soil underneath the house while still occupying it. The pits have straight sides and flat bottoms, and some were lined with wood or partitioned into sections (Samford 1999:77–79). Inside the house, floorboards were most likely used to cover the opening of the pits. Over 150 of these pits have been excavated, and they are typically found in 18th-century slave quarters. Some quarters have numerous pits (Kelso 1984:119–123; Franklin 2001:41). Only one has been identified from a 17th-century dwelling (Samford 1999:78; Mouer 1993:150).

These pits could obviously serve many purposes, and archaeologists debate what these purposes were. Most believe they were used primarily for the storage of food and personal possessions, possibly to hide pilfered items. Patricia Samford challenges such functional interpretations for some pits; instead she offers an interpretation suggesting that some pits contained ritual objects, and, therefore, are the remains of household shrines. She bases this interpretation on ethnographical accounts describing religious practices of the Igbo and Yoruba, African cultural groups who buried protective charms or poured libations into holes cut into earthen floors. Many objects contained in one pit are similar to ones associated with African religions and are curiously white – fossilized shell, white kaolin pipes, white ceramics, and stones. The color white, she suggests, is sacred and an important symbol in many West African religions. Pollen analysis from this pit indicated high levels of grape pollen, supporting the possibility that libations of wine were poured into the pit (Samford 1999:81–83).

Samford's interpretation of storage pits offers a tantalizing possibility that adds to the growing body of literature on the archaeological study of African American religion (e.g., Fennell 2000, 2003; Orser 1994; Wilkie 1997). The storage pits she interprets as religious offerings are quite different from the caches of presumed religious artifacts recovered from urban sites in Annapolis, Maryland. The features from Annapolis, dating primarily from the 19th and 20th centuries (with one dating to the 1790s), have been interpreted as Hoodoo (Leone and Fry 2001:143). Hoodoo, a southern folk term, refers to African American conjuring practices, one of the suite of remedies and therapies used in African American doctoring which, in turn, formed an integral part of slave religion (Fett 2002:36, 85).

Numerous descriptions of conjuring are found in oral histories and folklore dating to the same time period as the Annapolis archaeological contexts. No similar body of oral testimony, however, exists for the 18th century, making it difficult to demonstrate that the storage pits Sanford studied were of a religious nature. Moreover, the materials found within the pits are often secondary deposits – debris thrown in the pit that had been used or discarded elsewhere. This situation makes identifying a storage pit as a religious context problematical because some of the materials within it may have come from another location on the site. Only pits with primary refuse would be good candidates for interpretation as altars or other religious offerings, and only a small number have apparently satisfied this requirement.

For whatever reasons enslaved people dug the pits, it does appear that pits were, on occasion, a source of conflict between slaveholders and slave laborers. A few scattered written accounts indicate that slaveholders were suspicious that enslaved people were using them to hide stolen goods (e.g., Kelso 1984:201). Yet, the fact that they were so prolific in Virginia slave houses suggests slaveholders and overseers more typically accommodated, rather than opposed, slaves' desire to dig and use these pits. In this sense, the action of digging pits is, perhaps, more significant than how they were used. The digging of pits illustrates slave agency, and slaves' efforts to challenge slaveholder control over their living spaces.

Enslaved laborers of the Chesapeake sought to shape their material world in other realms of material culture as well. Slaveholders provided enslaved laborers with minimal amounts of food, clothing, or other supplies throughout the Americas. Enslaved people supplemented meager rations through independent economic activities of their own, such as producing food for themselves as well as for sale to others, raising livestock, hunting and fishing, producing finished goods (e.g. baskets, furniture, or pottery), marketing their own products, and consuming or saving the proceeds obtained from these activities. These activities are referred to as the internal slave economy (Berlin and Morgan 1991:1). The extent to which enslaved people participated in the internal economy varied from place to place and through time.

In the Chesapeake, enslaved laborers were not dependent upon the slave economy for survival because slaveholders supplied most of their provisions. The slave economy, however, did permit them to enrich their diet and acquire a few personal and household objects. During the first part of the 18th century, when the slave population was largely African-born and slaveholders were trying to extract every bit of labor they could to increase crop productivity, enslaved laborers tended gardens, hunted, and fished, but there was little surplus to trade beyond their owners' estates. After mid-century, when declining productivity of tobacco gave way to mixed cultivation that combined tobacco with grains, enslaved laborers expanded their gardens and flocks and became more engaged in trade beyond the plantation (Berlin 1998:119, 136).

This shift in the slave economy is also suggested in the archaeological record, particularly in foodways. Maria Franklin compared and contrasted the faunal assemblages from two periods: an early (1740–65) context, and a late (1765–78) context at the slave village at Rich Neck plantation. She observed that domestic species, particularly cattle and pig, increased while non-domestic species decreased from the early to late periods, though the collection of wild food resources was still important (2001:99–102). Franklin suggests that the shift may have resulted from a number factors, including the increase of slaveholder rations or independent raising of livestock by enslaved people (2001:99–102). The historiography supports the latter possibility.

Material goods also increased in frequency during the second half of the 18th century, not only at slave sites, but at the sites of Anglo-Virginians as well. The increased amount of consumer goods corresponds with an unprecedented flow of inexpensive goods in the Chesapeake. How or why these goods show up in slave quarters is unclear (Walsh 1998:149), but, like the increased amounts of domestic animal foods, may be related to more opportunities to engage in trade or barter. Lorena Walsh has suggested that the increase in consumer goods at slave sites in the Chesapeake occurred when enslaved people at the plantations she studied were devising ways to survive as comfortably as possible within the institution of slavery. They opted for this strategy, she believes, because hopes for freedom either through running away or manumission had become increasingly unlikely (Walsh 1998:150). Additionally, these second-and third-generation, American-born enslaved people had grown up accustomed to European standards and tastes in clothing and personal possessions, and sought to acquire items of their own choosing and self-expression rather than merely accepting items supplied to them.

During and after the American Revolution, the economy of the Chesapeake became more diversified. The shift from tobacco to more mixed farming increased, resulting in excess labor and slaveholders' need to reduce the number of enslaved laborers. Slave labor was put to use in a variety of non-agricultural industries for the first time, including the textile production, iron manufacturing, and maritime trades. Other enslaved laborers were relocated to the newly opened lands in Kentucky, Tennessee, and Alabama, sometimes with their previous owners, or sold in the internal slave trade. The relocation of enslaved laborers from the Chesapeake may partially explain the presence of storage pits within slave quarters found in Tennessee and Kentucky at 19th-century sites (Singleton and Bograd 1995:19). Still, a large number of enslaved laborers were manumitted, usually through wills after the owner's death. On the eve of the revolution the number of free blacks was very small as manumissions dwindled to very low levels. After the revolution this situation changed, in large part because of the excess labor, but also some slave-holders were affected by the ideals of liberty emanating out of the revolution.

The Lowcountry of South Carolina

Permanent English settlement of South Carolina began in 1670, over 60 years after the founding of Virginia, but by 1700 South Carolina contained a larger propor-tion of enslaved laborers and was more dependent upon slave labor than the Chesa-peake. Slavery developed more rapidly in the Lowcountry than in the Chesapeake because South Carolina, unlike Virginia, was viewed as a slave society from the very beginning (Morgan 1998:2–3). The founders of the colony specifically targeted Bar-badians, who were experienced colonists and familiar with slavery. Enslaved blacks comprised from one-quarter to one-third of the earliest settlers of Carolina (Wood 1974:25). The Chesapeake tobacco economy, on the other hand, was established on white indentured labor that supplied the bulk of labor needs during most of the 17th century.

The early period of Lowcountry slavery resembled Chesapeake slavery in that slave workers labored alongside white indentured servants and enslaved Native Americans. Once rice became the staple crop for developing a plantation economy, however, importation of African labor greatly accelerated. By the 1720s, enslaved Africans outnumbered whites in the Lowcountry by two to one, and in some plantation districts the ratio of blacks to whites was considerably higher (Berlin 1998:143–144). Slaveholder complacency with a black majority was tested when a small group of slave workers waged the Stono rebellion, killing over 20 whites in 1739 (Wood 1974:314–326). Other Africans overtly defied their enslavement by running away to Spanish Florida, where they received refuge from slavery. The Spaniards granted them a town and a fort of their own, named Gracia Real de Santa Teresa de Mosé just 2 miles north of St. Augustine (Deagan and Landers 1999).

The black-to-white ratio, along with other characteristics, provided the context for developing a slave society in the Lowcountry that was quite different from that of Chesapeake, and, in some ways, more similar to the British West Indies. The Lowcountry, like the West Indies, had a predominance of African rather than American-born laborers in the slave population. Rice required lots of labor and was cultivated on large estates with large numbers of enslaved laborers. It was not uncommon for rice plantations to have 100 or more slave laborers.

These labor demands, combined with little natural increase in the slave popula-tion during the 18th century, were met by importing Africans on a large scale. Enslaved Africans lived on rice plantations relatively isolated from white planters, who fled from disease-ridden, swampy rice lands during part or all of the year. Slaveholder absenteeism from the plantation was another characteristic Lowcoun-try slave society had in common with those of West Indies. Unlike many slaveholders in Jamaica and Barbados, who resided in England for long periods of time, Low-country slaveholders went to their residences in coastal towns or cities, or other areas that were a few days' journey from their plantations (Berlin 1998:152). Absenteeism limited interaction between master and slave, which in turn may have restricted slaveholder interference in certain aspects of slave life. This situation undoubtedly facilitated the development of a slave culture with a strong African character.

The vibrant culture that enslaved Africans and their descendants created and remade in the Lowcountry of South Carolina and Georgia is well documented, and has received considerable scholarly attention. These studies demonstrate that the language, music, foodways, folktales, crafts, and religion combined African, European, and Native American elements to form a creole culture, often referred to as Gullah, which is also the name of the creole language still spoken in the area today (Crook 2001). Archaeological studies of Lowcountry slave communities also provide insights into this process of creolization (Ferguson 1992), primarily in the areas of housing, foodways, and craft production.

Lowcountry slave housing exhibited more African-like characteristics than Chesapeake housing. This was possibly due to the large numbers of Africans in the Lowcountry slave population, and the abundant building materials similar to those used in tropical climates (Morgan 1998:118). Mud construction is of particular importance as it has been recovered archaeologically as well as referenced in written sources. Excavations at two 18th-century plantations, Yaughan and Curriboo in South Carolina, yielded remains of mud-wall structures (Wheaton and Garrow 1985:243–248).

The construction technique utilized to build the structures has been debated – the excavators believed that the mud was laid in courses reinforced with upright posts, while others have suggested that the mud was plastered over a woven wooden lattice, a technique known as wattle-and-daub (Ferguson 1992:64). Both building techniques were widespread in sub-Saharan Africa, but were also known in European and Native American building traditions. The mud-wall houses most likely derived from an amalgam of building traditions rather than being solely a transplanted African practice. Similar clay-wall construction utilizing the wattle-and-daub technique was prevalent throughout the Caribbean and often used for slave housing (Chapman 1991). References to "mud huts," both in the recorded oral interviews with former enslaved people and in contemporary traveler accounts, always refer to people of African descent as either the builders and/or the inhabitants of such structures. John Davis, a traveler to South Carolina, observed a free black couple living in a mud dwelling: "I reached a mud-hut which stood adjoining a chimney . . . I peeped through a chink in the wall of this lonely hut. I soon discovered it was the habitation of Old Billy and Billy's old wife. I could distinguish an old negro-man and negro-woman, huddled together" (Davis 1909[1803]:140). Because people of African descent are most often associated with either building or inhabiting mud dwellings in both the Caribbean and South Carolina, they most likely played a significant role in adapting mud construction for use on plantations.

Enslaved workers also exerted their influence in the production of locally made pottery, referred to as colonoware. Colonoware is a general term used to refer to low-fired, hand-built, locally produced earthenware used for preparing, serving, and storing food. It is recovered in large quantities on 18th-century Lowcountry sites, particularly at slave settlements. Some varieties of this pottery were apparently made on plantations, as is evidenced from pots with spall fractures – breaks in the pot resulting from poor firing. Other varieties point to Native American manufacture because they are identical to ones associated with Native Americans of the historic period such as the Catawba. Enslaved people most likely acquired Native American-made colonoware through trading relationships. Colonoware is also found at slave sites in the Chesapeake, but in smaller quantities than on the South Carolina sites, and evidence that colonoware was made on plantations has not been forthcoming.

Colonoware has received a great deal of attention from archaeologists because it is the most prolific handcrafted artifact found on African American sites, some of which African Americans presumably made. Before archaeological investigations were undertaken at slave sites, archaeologists assumed Native Americans were the sole makers of these wares (Noël Hume 1962). Whether or not African Americans produced colonoware, or simply used Indian-made vessels, is also significant. These wares were presumably used to prepare slow-cooking dishes such as okra soup, gumbo, and rice, and bean dishes such as "hoppin John" that black South Carolinians are believed to have introduced to Lowcountry cuisine (Singleton and Bogard 2000). Colonoware production and usage is another characteristic of Lowcountry slave life that was similar to slave life in the Caribbean. Afro-Caribbean potters made comparable earthenwares on several islands, most notably in Jamaica, where pottery apparently was produced at regional centers and traded through a variety of venues, including slave markets held on Sundays (Hauser 2001).

Virtually nothing is known about production sites for colonoware because the vessels were fired on open hearths that leave little evidence of pottery firing (Ferguson 1992:27). Carl Steen has tentatively identified the core area for colonoware production as extending northward from Charleston to Myrtle Beach, South Carolina, and inland from the coast for about 30 miles. He bases his observation on the distributions of colonoware pottery recovered from plantation sites (1999:101). It is often assumed that the productive unit for colonoware pottery is the plantation, though it is doubtful that every plantation produced colonoware. It is also unclear how and where the pottery was traded.

The task labor system utilized in the production of Lowcountry plantation staples enabled enslaved laborers to have time to tend gardens, to hunt and fish, and to produce basketry and woodwork (Crook 2001; Morgan 1982:587–591, 1998:179–187). It may have also facilitated the making of colonoware pottery. The task labor system was the organizational structure for slave labor. Under the task system, enslaved laborers were assigned a certain amount of work by the day. When the task was completed, the enslaved person was free for the rest of the day. Most regular plantation work was defined by task units, including clearing, draining, plowing, hoeing, weeding, laying fence, and so forth.

Additionally slave workers were classified into full, three-quarter, half, and one-quarter hands according to their physical ability to perform tasks. Most tasks began at sunrise and were completed between 1 and 4 o'clock in the afternoon (Crook

2001:25). But some tasks could last considerably longer, particularly if the over-seer or driver misjudged the length of time needed to complete them (Morgan 1998:180). Despite some onerous tasks, the task system permitted workers to divide their time between activities that served the plantation economy and those that served the internal slave economy. Surplus items produced during free time were sold or traded to other enslaved laborers, or sold to the plantation owner. Pottery could have been one of the goods produced, as could basketry or woodworking, and then traded through exchange networks.

Task labor may partially account for the latitude that enslaved people had in making elements of their material world such as the mud-wall houses and colonoware pottery. Ray Crook sees the labor system as having played a major role in shaping Gullah culture as a whole. He criticizes scholars, particularly archaeol-ogists, for their failure to view the "task system as the material force underlying the construction of Gullah as a coherent cultural form" (2001:26). Crook's strong materialist stance, however, does not consider enslaved people as actors who created creole cultures throughout the Americas, which they accomplished despite the odds against them and, for the most part, in the absence of task labor.

Moreover, the task system had its downside. Slaveholders manipulated task labor to work to their advantage, as those in power do with any mode of production. Because task labor provided enslaved people with the incentive to produce goods for themselves and for sale, slaveholders simply reduced the amount they con-tributed toward slave sustenance. This was particularly the case with regards to meat provisions that were, as Philip Morgan (1998:137) observes, "much stingier in the Lowcountry than in the Chesapeake." Food remains at Lowcountry sites support this interpretation. At the sites of Yaughan and Curriboo, very small amounts of animal bone were recovered and non-domestic species were present, but rare. These findings prompted the excavators to conclude that the slave diet of the 18th century was primarily vegetal, and hunting of relatively minor importance to the overall sub-sistence (Wheaton and Garrow 1985:256). This interpretation, however, is in con-trast with post-revolutionary sites on the Georgia Coast, where non-domestic food resources contributed a substantial portion to making the slave diet adequate and nutritious. By the 19th century, the Lowcountry slave diet included more animal protein, but primarily though the efforts of enslaved people.

Task labor continued to be utilized in the coastal Southeast until the abolition of slavery in 1865, but the African character of slave material culture, as seen in colonoware production and use and in mud-wall slave houses, declines near the end of the 18th century, and eventually disappears during the 19th century. The reasons for these changes are unclear. The increased availability of mass-produced household utensils, perhaps, made pottery production unnecessary except for vessels having specialized uses. For example, foods containing okra were often pre-pared in clay vessels to prevent the okra, which is green, from turning black (Yentsch 1994:203). On the other hand, the disappearance of mud-wall housing may be related to efforts on the part of some slaveholders to build slave housing out of what they perceived as more permanent construction materials than wattle-and-daub, such brick, stone, or wooden clapboards.

The American Revolution disrupted the Lowcountry's plantation order, but the aftermath of the war did not incite an emancipationist sentiment toward enslaved laborers as it had done in the Chesapeake or in the North. Rice cultivation was eventually restored, and a new crop – long-staple cotton, also known as sea-island cotton – was introduced to the area. Sea-island cotton differed from the short-staple variety grown throughout the southern United States after the successful development of the cotton gin in that it was a finer quality of cotton used in the manufacture of lace and delicate fabrics. Many Lowcountry planters acquired several plantations, some engaged in rice culture and others for sea-island cotton. Rice, however, remained the primary staple for the area, which had expanded to as far north as Cape Fear, North Carolina, and as far south as the St. Johns River in Florida (Berlin 1998:143). For the most part, the Lowcountry slave population was not forced to relocate over long distances like many enslaved people of the Chesapeake. As the rice coast expanded, some enslaved people were sent to new locations along the coast, but not to new regions that produced different kinds of crops. Despite the disappearance of colonoware production and mud-wall slave houses, the relative stability of the Lowcountry's slave population and its limited contact with whites contributed to the continuity of many other cultural practices established during the 18th century to later times.

The North

As in the Chesapeake and the Lowcountry, slavery was introduced to the northern English colonies in the 17th century. Each northern colony utilized slavery to some degree, but the Northeast did not develop slave societies wherein slave labor was central to the production of staple crops or used exclusively in other economic activities. Even when demands for slave labor grew increasingly in the 18th century, it was most often used alongside white indentured or wage labor.

Slavery developed unevenly in the Northeast. In most of New England, it was marginal to the economy, whereas in some parts of New York, New Jersey, and Pennsylvania it was a major component of the labor force. The availability of white labor determined the demand for slave labor. White immigration to the North decreased and African importation increased during times of economic opportunity in Europe. The reverse was true during times of economic hardship in Europe – white immigration increased and African importation halted. Still, in some portions of the Northeast, particularly in cities, and later in the most fertile agricultural areas, slave labor sometimes comprised a third or more of the workforce (Berlin 1998:178–179).

A myth emerged during the time of slavery and persists to the present that northern slavery was somehow milder than southern slavery. This myth stems from characteristics of northern slavery that were often assumed to indicate that it was benign. These characteristics include: first, northern slavery was not centered on the production of plantation staples; second, enslaved workers worked alongside white workers, sometimes their owners; third, enslaved workers either lived close to their masters or in their masters' houses (White 1991:80). Many historians have pointed out, however, that close proximity of slave workers to slaveholders was not necessarily an advantage for enslaved workers, whose labor and private lives were subjected to closer scrutiny from slaveholders than were those of laborers living and working some physical distance away from owners. Additionally, both written and archaeological sources on the living conditions and health status of enslaved laborers in New York City, for example, refute the notion that northern slavery was mild.

Slave labor figured prominently in New York City from the very beginning. The Dutch began to import enslaved Africans in 1626, a year after the settlement, then called New Amsterdam, was founded. When the English conquered the colony in 1664 and renamed it New York, the English continued the importation of African labor (Cantwell and Wall 2001) For most of the 18th century, New York was second only to Charleston, South Carolina, in the number of enslaved persons owned by its inhabitants (White 1991:3). The average slaveholding was small, only one or two enslaved workers who usually lived in the homes or worksites of their owners. Most slave laborers worked as domestics, particularly females who greatly outnumbered males. Slave men worked as coachmen, cooks, and servants and in rope-making, tanning, and maritime trades (White 1999:10–12). Some artisans trained their enslaved laborers to work in highly skilled crafts, but chronic complaints from non-slaveholding white artisans about slave competition may have restricted the number of enslaved persons entering these highly specialized trades (Berlin 1998:180). Slave laborers fulfilled a variety of labor needs, most of which were unskilled and semi-skilled jobs.

Regardless of their occupations, analyses of skeletal remains recovered from the African Burial Ground, an 18th-century cemetery in lower Manhattan, indicate New York's slave population endured a great deal of physical hardship carrying out their jobs. Most adult men and women in the studied population had enlarged muscle attachments and muscle tears indicative of excessive muscular strain. Fractures of the spine and skull base resulted from carrying loads on the head that were too heavy for the neck and spine to support (Blakey 2001:412; Cantell and Wall 2001:292). Children were put to work at an early age and, like the adults, their bodies were compromised for their bones show signs of work-related stresses. One juvenile suffered from severe arthritis, possibly from spending long hours in a kneeling or similar position (Susan Good-Null, personal communication, 2000).

Skeletal analyses also confirm that slavery in New York was far from mild. Malnutrition was prevalent, particularly among the children and those adults who were probably born in the Americas. About a third of the population is presumed to have been born in Africa based on preliminary DNA studies and the presence of dental modifications (filed teeth), a cultural practice conducted during childhood in many African societies, identified on 26 adults (Blakey 2001:412). More than half of the population suffered from infectious diseases such as yaws, pinta, and meningitis. Severe anemia, either sickle-cell anemia or resulting from deficient diets and infectious disease, affected about half of the population. Mortality was high, particularly infant mortality estimated at 50 percent of slave infants. This rate was considerably higher than the infant mortality of the slaveholding class inferred from the study of church records. Data from these records also indicate New York residents of English descent, both men and women, lived much longer than African men and women (Blakey 2001:412). At least one individual died violently: a female, found with lead gunshot in her chest. Her bones indicate that she received repeated blows to her face and a twisting fracture to her arm (Cantwell and Wahl 2001:293). Her injuries and death are consistent with the ways in which enslaved people were sometimes punished for overt acts of resistance such as running away. Although murder was an extreme means of punishment, as it meant the loss of property, it did occur in all slave societies when slaveholders perceived a particular individual to be recalcitrant and unlikely to accept his or her slave status.

Mortuary practices at the African Burial Ground provide glimpses into the ways in which African burial customs were combined with European American material culture. The deceased were placed in hexagonal coffins typically used in early American graves of the 17th and 18th centuries. A variety of grave goods, including coral, shells, pipes, pottery, quartz crystals, and personal objects, were placed inside or on top of coffins. A heart-shaped design was formed using heads of iron nails on the coffin lid of a grave belonging to a male in his early thirties. The heart-shaped design has been interpreted as the Sankofa symbol used by the Akan people of present-day Ghana and the Ivory Coast which means to turn one's head to the past in order to build the future (Ofori-Ansa 1996:30). This symbol, along with others, is found on an Akan ritual cloth used at very special ceremonies honoring the ancestors. In another grave, a middle-aged female was buried with a string of beads around her hips. The beads are believed to have been brought from Africa. Both the male found in the coffin with the Sankofa symbol and the female were probably African natives as they both had filed teeth. Some of the project team archaeologists believe that both of them occupied a special status within the slave community, possibly as ritual healers or leaders, because of the special attention given to their burials.

Burial grounds, however, were more than final resting-places for loved ones. They were important gathering-places for slave communities in pre-revolutionary northern cities, and possibly the first African American institutions in North America (Berlin 1998:62). White observers described black men and women dressed in their finest clothes, accompanied by music, marching to the burial ground, where they left food and drink at the graves of friends. On Sundays and other special days, enslaved people "could be seen dividing into numerous little squads dancing after the manner of their several nations in Africa, and speaking and singing in their native dialects" (Nash 1988:13). The burial ground played a central role in the formation of 18th-century African American communities in urban settings. It was the center of black cultural life that was later replaced by black churches, benevolent societies, and fraternal organizations in the 19th century.

Slavery was gradually abolished in the North during the years following the American Revolutionary War and first three decades of the 19th century. Ira Berlin has referred to this process as the "slow death of slavery in North" (1998:228–255). The death of slavery was particularly slow in New York State, where slavery lingered on until it officially ended in 1827. Even after abolition, the line between slavery and freedom was blurred for many former slave men and women who were forced to work and live with former masters under a new form of bound labor that closely resembled slavery (Berlin 1998:238–239). Conditions were particularly harsh in rural areas where former enslaved people became part of the northern landless, and had to eke out a living as best as they could. Many newly freed black men and women migrated to cities seeking more secure employment. Those who remained in the countryside attempted to establish villages with their own schools and churches, but they usually needed some form of public or private assistance (Berlin 1998:241). This was certainly the case for the residents who founded the settlement of New Guinea in Plymouth, Massachusetts, known today as the Parting Ways site (Deetz 1996:187–211).

Four black revolutionary veterans – Cato Howe, Prince Goodwin, Plato Turner, and Quamany – founded the settlement of New Guinea on 94 acres of land which the town of Plymouth provisionally granted Cato Howe in 1792. The four men cleared the land, built their houses, and lived at the settlement with their families until 1824, but the land continued to be the property of the town. The four men were also buried there, and a historical marker identifies their graves today. While information on their backgrounds is sketchy, it appears that they were all enslaved prior to the American Revolution and all, except Prince Goodwin, were manumitted in return for their military service in 1778. Prince Goodwin returned to his previous owners and apparently continued working for them after slavery was abolished. Life was difficult for the four black households. They owned few possessions and received small pensions from the government because of their poor circumstances (Deetz 1996:189–192).

Archaeological investigations were undertaken at the site in the mid-1970s. The archaeology revealed that architectural patterns, food remains, and ceramics differed from Anglo-American counterparts of the time. The most striking difference is in the architectural features. The floor plans of the houses at Parting Ways were consistently $3.6\,m^2$ ($12\,ft.^2$), whereas Anglo-American houses of the same time period were usually $4.8\,m^2$ ($16\,ft.^2$). Deetz (1998:203) suggested that the difference in floor plans reflected different usages of space, stating that "the twelve-foot unit is more broadly characteristic of African-American building" based upon studies conducted on southern vernacular housing such as the shot-gun and West African house types. Traces of mud walling associated with postholes were found on a dirt floor from a Parting Ways structure similar to the mud wall and post construction, discussed earlier, in South Carolina.

The overall settlement pattern and placement of the houses was also found to be different from that of Anglo-American ones. The four men placed their houses in the center of the property close to each other. This is curious given the fact that the town map shows discrete portions of the 94 acres designated to each of the four men (Deetz 1996:204). Why they chose to place their houses next to each other is unclear. Some scholars have suggested this spatial plan is similar to those of African compounds (e.g. Jones 1985:198). Unlike enslaved workers in the Chesapeake and Lowcountry, the Parting Ways residents could more fully execute a cultural landscape of their choosing because they were removed from the imposed spatial constraints of slavery. Perhaps the Parting Ways layout reinforced their common identity and fostered mutual support and sharing with each other.

Differences from contemporary Anglo-American patterns were also seen in foodways and, to a lesser extent, in the ceramics. At 18th-century Anglo-American sites in New England the sawing of bone is common. No sawn bone was found at Parting Ways, and the majority of the bone found was cattle feet. Whether the selection of cattle feet represents the residents' preference or their improvised circumstances is unknown. Zooarchaeologist Joanne Bowen (1996) warns archaeologists not to judge food selection in the past based upon present-day standards of what is considered poor-quality meat. Even elite households in the 17th and 18th centuries regularly consumed foods considered poor people's food today. Thus, the cattle feet may have been intentionally selected both for their price and for their suitability in making nutritious soups and stews from bony cuts.

Ceramics were found to be different in two ways. Red, unglazed earthenware jars made in the Caribbean and used to ship sugar or tamarind, an African fruit grown in the West Indies, were recovered that had not been found on Anglo-American sites at the time of the excavations. The tamarind jars still present an unresolved curiosity. Did the occupants acquire the jars because of their contents – tamarind or sugar? Or, were the jars recycled to them and used for the storage of food or liquid? Similar jars were later recovered at a site in Portsmouth, New Hampshire, where blacks were a part of the household, and from a trash pit in Salem, Massachusetts, an important 19th-century port town dealing in West Indian commodities. Unfortunately, the answer to these questions may always be unknown. Deetz suggested the tamarind jars may represent one of the distinctive ways in which African Americans chose to fashion their material world. The other ceramic difference was the recovery of high-quality ceramics such as hand-painted creamware rarely recovered at sites occupied by people of modest means. The dates of manufacture for the ceramics, however, indicate they were out of fashion by the time the Parting Ways people acquired and used them. Deetz (1996:199) reasoned that wealthier townspeople of Plymouth or their former masters gave the ceramics to them. The presence of out-of-date, high-quality ceramics is a typical characteristic of sites once occupied by African Americans and other people of limited means.

The Parting Ways site, though excavated over 25 years ago, when the archaeological study of African American life was just beginning, remains highly significant. It is one of the few sites dating to the revolutionary era that provides insights into the ways in which a community of African Americans shaped their lives after their manumission from slavery. Although we will probably never know whether or not certain aspects of the archaeological record represented the residents' cultural preferences, their poverty, or a combination of both, without the archaeology we would know very little about their lives.

Conclusion

Most laypersons, when they think about slavery in North America, tend to think about the 19th century, when slavery was limited to the southern United States and the vast majority of enslaved workers labored on cotton plantations. This chapter has focused on the century preceding the spread of cotton plantations, when slavery was used to some degree throughout what was then British North America. An effort has been made to piece together the archaeological findings from a variety of sites (slave villages, a cemetery, a free black settlement) and to integrate them within the historiography of 18th-century African American life rather than treating them as isolated vignettes disconnected from historical analysis of the places and times under consideration.

In other words, the archaeological findings can be used in conjunction with written sources to develop historiographies of African American life. The archaeological data do not just fill in gaps, though they often lend tangible evidence to support or to refute written statements. The archaeology actually exposes how lives were lived in different places when larger historical events and processes were taking place. Without archaeology, the digging of storage pits, the making of pottery, the placing of houses in African compound-like arrangements, and the physical effects of slave labor on the bodies of the enslaved could not be inferred from written sources alone. These archaeological observations were not only lost until the present time, but the cultural practices from which they were derived were also lost to the generations of African Americans who were born, who lived, and who died after the start of the 18th century. In this way, archaeology provides a means to re-claim the past – long forgotten, misremembered, or silenced.

REFERENCES

Berlin, Ira, 1998 *Many Thousands Gone: The First Two Centuries of Slavery in North America.* Cambridge, MA: Harvard University Press.

Berlin, Ira, and Philip Morgan, eds., 1991 *The Slaves' Economy: Independent Production By Slaves in the Americas.* London: Frank Cass.

Blakey, Michael L., 2001 Bioarchaeology of the African diaspora in the Americas. *Annual Review in Anthropology* 30, 387–422.

Boles, John B., 1984 *Black Southerners, 1619–1869.* Lexington: University Press of Kentucky.

Bowen, JoAnne, 1996 Foodways in the 18th-century Chesapeake. In *The Archaeology of 18th-Century Virginia.* T. R. Reinhart, ed. Pp. 87–130. Richmond, VA: Spectrum Press.

Brumfiel, Elizabeth M., 2000 On the archaeology of choice: Agency studies as research stratagem. In *Agency and Archaeology.* M.-A. Dobres and J. Robb, eds. Pp. 246–255. London: Routledge.

Cantwell, Anne-Marie, and Diana diZerega Wall, 2001 *Unearthing Gotham: The Archaeology of New York City.* New Haven: Yale University Press.

Chapman, William, 1991 Slave villages in the Danish West Indies. In *Perspectives in Vernacular Architecture, IV.* T. Carter and B. L. Herman, eds. Pp. 108–120. Columbia: University of Missouri Press for the Vernacular Architecture Forum.

Crook, Ray, 2001 Gullah and the task system. *Anthropology of Work Review* 22(2), 24–28.

Davidson, Thomas E., 1983 *Free Blacks on the Lower Eastern Shore of Maryland, the Colonial Period: 1662 to 1775.* Maryland Historical Trust Series 42. Annapolis, Maryland.

Davis, John, 1909[1803] *Travels of Four Years and a Half in the United States of America; During 1798, 1799, 1800, and 1802.* Reprint with introduction and notes by A. J. Morrison. New York: Henry Holt.

Deagan, Kathleen A., and Jane Landers, 1999 Fort Mosé: Earliest free African-American town in the United States. In *"I, too, am America": Archaeological Studies of African-American Life.* T. A. Singleton, ed. Pp. 261–282. Charlottesville: University Press of Virginia.

Deal, Douglas J., 1993 *Race and Class in Colonial Virginia: Indians, Englishmen, and Africans on the Eastern Shore during the 17th Century.* New York: Garland Press.

Deetz, James, 1993 *Flowerdew Hundred: The Archaeology of a Virginia Plantation, 1619–1864.* Charlottesville: University Press of Virginia.

——1996 *In Small Things Forgotten: An Archaeology of Early American Life,* expanded and revised edn. New York: Anchor Books.

Eltis, David, 2000 *The Rise of African Slavery in the Americas.* Cambridge: Cambridge University Press.

Emerson, Mathew, 1999 African inspirations in a new world art and artifact: Decorated pipes from the Chesapeake. In *"I, Too, Am America": Archaeological Studies of African-American Life.* T A. Singleton, ed. Pp. 47–82. Charlottesville: University Press of Virginia.

Epperson, Terrence, 2001 "A separate house for the Christian slaves, one for the Negro slaves": The archaeology of race and identity in late 17th-century Virginia. In *Race and the Archaeology of Identity,* C. E. Orser, Jr., ed. Pp. 71–87. Salt Lake City: University of Utah Press.

Fennell, Christopher C., 2000 Conjuring boundaries: Inferring past identities from religious artifacts. *International Journal of Historical Archaeology* 4(4), 281–313.

——2003 Group identity, individual creativity, and symbolic generation in a BaKongo diaspora. *International Journal of Historical Archaeology* 7(1), 1–31.

Ferguson, Leland G., 1992 *Uncommon Ground: Archaeology and Early African America, 1650–1800.* Washington, DC: Smithsonian Institution Press.

Fett, Sharla, 2002 *Working Cures: Healing, Health, and Power on Southern Slave Plantations.* Chapel Hill: University of North Carolina Press.

Franklin, Maria, 2001 The archaeological dimensions of soul food: Interpreting race, culture, and Afro-Virginian identity. In *Race and the Archaeology of Identity.* Charles E. Orser, Jr., ed. Pp. 88–107. Salt Lake City: University of Utah Press.

Hauser, Mark W., 2001 Determining the extent of market exchange in 18th-century Jamaica through the analysis of local coarse earthenware. Ph.D. dissertation, Syracuse University, Syracuse, New York.

Jones, Steven L., 1985 African-American tradition in vernacular architecture. In *The Archaeology of Slavery and Plantation Life.* T. A. Singleton, ed. Pp. 195–213. Orlando: Academic Press.

Kelso, William Kelso, 1984 *Kingsmill Plantations, 1619–1800: Archaeology of Country Life in Colonial Virginia.* Orlando, FL: Academic Press.

Leone, Mark, and Gladys Marie-Fry, 2001 Spirit management among Americans of African descent. In *Race and the Archaeology of Identity.* C. E. Orser, Jr., ed. Pp. 143–157. Salt Lake City: University of Utah Press.

Morgan, Edmund S., 1975 *American Slavery, American Freedom: The Ordeal of Colonial Virginia.* New York: W. W. Norton.

Morgan, Philip D., 1998 *Slave Counterpoint: Black Culture in the 18th Century Chesapeake and Lowcountry.* Chapel Hill: North Carolina Press.

Mouer, L. Daniel, 1993 Chesapeake creoles: The creation of folk culture in colonial Virginia. In *The Archaeology of 17th-Century Virginia*. T. R. Reinhart and D. J. Pogue, eds. Pp. 105–166. Richmond: Archeological Society of Virginia.

Mouer, L. Daniel, Mary Ellen N. Hodges, Stephen R. Potter, Susan L. Henry Renaud, Ivor Noël Hume, Dennis J. Pogue, Martha W. McCartney, and Thomas E. Davidson, 1999 Colonoware pottery, Chesapeake pipes, and "uncritical assumptions." In *"I, Too, Am America": Archaeological Studies of African-American Life*. T. A. Singleton, ed. Pp. 83–115. Charlottesville: University Press of Virginia.

Nash, Gary B., 1988 *Forging Freedom: The Formation of Philadelphia's Black Community, 1720–1840*. Cambridge, MA: Harvard University Press.

Noël Hume, I., 1962 An Indian ware of the colonial period. *Quarterly Bulletin of the Archaeological Society of Virginia* 17(1), 2–12.

Ofori-Ansa, Kweku, 1995 Identification and validation of the Sankofa symbol. *Update: Newsletter of the African Burial Ground and Five Point Archaeological Projects* 1(8), 30.

Orser, Charles E. Jr., 1994 The archaeology of slave religion in the Antebellum South. *Cambridge Archaeological Journal* 1, 33–45.

Samford, Patricia, 1999 "Strong is the bond of kinship": West African style ancestor shrines and sub-floor pits in African-American quarters. In *Historical Archaeology, Identity Formation, and the Incorporation of Ethnicity*. M. Franklin and G. Fesler, eds. Pp. 71–91. Williamsburg, VA: Colonial Williamsburg Research Publication.

Singleton, Theresa, 2000 Breaking typological barriers: Looking for the colono in colonoware pottery. In *Lines that Divide: Historical Archaeologies of Race, Class, and Gender*. J. A. Delle, S. A. Mrozowski, and R. Paynter, eds. Pp. 3–21. Knoxville: University of Tennessee Press.

Singleton, Theresa, and Mark Bograd, 1995 *The Archaeology of the African Diaspora in the Americas*. Guides to the Archaeological Literature of the Immigrant Experience 2. Tuscon, AZ: Society for Historical Archaeology.

Steen, Carl, 1999, Stirring the ethnic stew in the South Carolina backcountry: John de la Howe and Lethe Farm. In *Historical Archaeology, Identity Formation, and the Incorporation of Ethnicity*. M. Franklin and G. Fesler, eds. Pp. 93–120. Colonial Williamsburg Research Publications, Williamsburg, VA.

Walsh, Lorena, 1997 *From Calabar to Carter's Grove: The History of a Virginia Slave Community*. Charlottesville: University Press of Virginia.

Wheaton, Thomas R., and Patrick H. Garrow, 1985 Acculturation and the archaeological record in Carolina Lowcountry. In *The Archaeology of Slavery and Plantation Life*. T. A. Singleton, ed. Pp. 239–259. Orlando: Academic Press.

White, Shane, 1991 *Somewhat More Independent: The End of Slavery in New York City, 1770–1810*. Athens: University of Georgia Press.

Wood, Peter, 1974 *Black Majority: Negroes in Colonial South Carolina from 1670 through the Stono Rebellion*. New York: W. W. Norton.

Yentsch, A. E., 1994 *A Chesapeake Family and their Slaves: A Study in Historical Archaeology*. Cambridge: Cambridge University Press.

14

Representing and Repatriating the Past

Joe Watkins

> For every skeleton that has reached the security – if not dignity – of an anthropological storage room, easily ten thousand have been ground under bulldozers, floated away under reservoirs, or ended up with their skulls grinning on mantelpieces as candle-holders or bookends. (King 1972:31)

In a 1972 article, Thomas King discussed ways American Indians could deal with the loss of their cultural heritage and provided model policies for their protection. King's suggestions made sense if the tribes wanted to "protect" their cultural material from destruction by vandals or heavy equipment, but it also played on the fears of American Indians by graphically reinforcing the idea that there were people who would go so far as to use skulls as decorator items. And, by noting the "security – if not dignity – of an anthropological storage room," King reinforced the archaeologists' belief that we were "saving" these materials. But were we saving them for American Indians or for ourselves, and, for that matter, did American Indians *really* want us to be "saving" them in an "anthropological storage room"?

The conflict between American Indians and anthropologists regarding the scientific collection and repatriation of American Indian human remains and items of cultural significance has often been a contentious one. But the conflicts that have led to the repatriation acts of 1989 and 1990 did not begin in the 1980s, but perhaps more than three centuries ago.

Relationships and Representations

On November 19, 1620, Pilgrim explorers in search of the inhabitants of their new land happened across "a place like a grave." They dug into it, and found "the bones and skull of a man [and] . . . the bones and head of a little child," along with cultural material placed with the bodies. Not content to leave the material alone, they "brought sundry of the prettiest things away with us, and covered the corpse up again" (Heath 1963:27–28). Only eight days after the Pilgrims had anchored off Cape Cod, American Indian graves had already been plundered for their contents.

Throughout the remainder of American history, American Indian human remains and items of cultural significance have been lost as a result of the drive to obtain "pretty things" or to obtain information to satisfy scientific curiosity. But anthropologists were not the only, or even the original, culprits. Jack Trope and Walter EchoHawk (2000:126–128) offer a history of the use and abuse of American Indian bodies from the founding of colonies through the 18th and 19th centuries, including the collection of American Indian crania by Dr. Samuel Morton in the 1840s to "scientifically prove, through skull measurements, that the American Indian was a racially inferior 'savage' who was naturally doomed to extinction" (Trope and EchoHawk 2000:126). The skulls needed for the comparative "cranial library" were gathered by Indian agents, physicians, grave robbers, and military personnel from old and recent graves, defeated tribes, and battlefields (Bieder 2000:24). Additionally, with the Surgeon General's Order of 1868, army personnel were directed to procure American Indian crania and other body parts for the Army Medical Museum. But the passage of the Antiquities Act of 1906 defined precontact ("prehistoric") human skeletal remains as "archaeological resources" and gave control of them to archaeologists and other scientists.

Historian Robert Bieder notes that the representation of the American Indian body in 19th-century American anthropology changed from one of "classification of racial groups based primarily on external physical characteristics" to "internal characteristics linked to heredity" (Bieder 2000:32). This change allowed the American scientific public to shift its focus on causative factors for the state of the American Indian from looking at the environment to looking at the individual: any deficiencies exhibited by Indians were their fault; their destiny lay entirely within their own hands and did not depend on environmental factors.

On a more specific line of inquiry, a number of anthropologists (cf. Bettinger 1991; Downer 1997; Ferguson 1996; Kehoe 1998; Lurie 1988; McGuire 1992a, 1992b; 1997; Meltzer 1983; Trigger 1980, 1986, 1989) have traced the history of anthropology and its relationships with American Indians. Anthropologists have come to understand that science does not operate in a vacuum from the social structure in which it occurs, and that attitudes have influenced not only the manner in which the government has treated the American Indians but also the way that anthropologists have studied and portrayed them. Trigger (1980:662) writes: "problems social scientists choose to research and (hopefully less often) the conclusions that they reach are influenced in various ways . . . (among them) . . . the attitudes and opinions that are prevalent in the societies in which they live." He goes on to argue that, during the first half of America's existence (1770s through the 1870s), American Indians were held to be inferior to civilized men in order to rationalize the seizure of Indian lands, and that, eventually, racial myths grew to supplant any other myths about the Indians as a justification for waging war on the Indians and violating their treaty rights.

One example of the scientific treatment of the American Indian has been labeled the "Moundbuilder controversy" (see King et al. 1977; McGuire 1992a; Meltzer 1985; Willey and Sabloff 1993; see also Adovasio and Pedler, this volume). The Moundbuilders were believed to have been a non-Indian race (perhaps related to the Danes, Vikings, Hindus, or prehistoric Mexicans) who either had withdrawn from eastern North America or had been exterminated by the "newly arrived" Indians. Most writers of the period felt that these Moundbuilders had constructed the enormous mounds encountered by travelers in America because American Indians were not thought to be capable of such feats of engineering. Two notable exceptions to this school of thought were Samuel F. Haven (1856) and Henry R. Schoolcraft (1854), contemporary "archaeologists" who opposed the "Mound-builder as separate race" hypothesis.

But the controversy was not only a scholarly debate. As Don Fowler (1987:230) noted: "The Myth of the Moundbuilders was never official government policy, but it did bolster arguments for moving the 'savage' Indians out of the way of white 'civilization'." The extermination of American Indians by westward-moving settlements of the United States was made morally easier by the apparent primitiveness of the natives, and the controversy served well as a justification for exterminating the Indian groups that had destroyed North America's only "civilized" culture (Trigger 1980:665).

McGuire (1992a:820) argues that the Moundbuilder myth also worked to remove the Indians' ancestors from the history of the United States: "By routing the red savages, the new, civilized, White American race inherited the mantle, the heritage, of the old civilization. . . ." Lawrence Kuznar (1997:83) feels that archaeologists helped American Indians by proving scientifically that they were more accomplished than thought during a time when the American government was "carrying out genocidal wars against Native Americans and when the stereotype of the savage, intractable, almost sub-human Indian was decidedly useful to many," but David Meltzer (1983) argues that the archaeologists who finally finished off the Moundbuilder myth (such as Cyrus Thomas of the Bureau of Ethnology and Fredrick Ward Putnam of the Peabody Museum) were not necessarily pro-Indian as much as pro-scientific, preferring to emphasize scientific views rather than cataclysmic theories that relied on intrusive or extinct races as a means of explanation. Regardless of the reasons behind the archaeologists' actions, by the time archaeologists finally proved the mounds were products of the ancestors of the American Indians, the Indians mostly had been dispossessed of their land.

While archaeologists were not the only culprits to have used American Indian human remains as study objects – "Human remains were obtained by soldiers, government agents, pothunters, private citizens, museum collecting crews, and scientists in the name of profit, entertainment, science, or development" (Trope and EchoHawk 2000:125) – they were perhaps the most visible. As James Riding In (1992:12) wrote:

Individuals who violate the sanctity of the grave outside of the law are viewed as criminals, Satan worshippers, or imbalanced. When caught, tried, and convicted, the guilty are usually incarcerated, fined, or placed in mental institutions. Yet public opinion and legal loopholes have until recently enabled white society to loot and pillage with impunity American Indian cemeteries. Archaeology, a branch of anthropology that still attempts to sanctify this tradition of exploiting dead Indians, arose as an honorable profession from this sacrilege.

Although a distinction between "grave-robbing" and "archaeological excavation" has often been made, to many American Indian tribal groups it makes no difference whether the disturbance is caused by grave looters or by qualified archaeologists. "To them, the only difference between an illegal ransacking of a burial ground and a scientific one is the time element, sun screen, little whisk brooms, and the neatness of the area when finished" (Mihesuah 1996:233).

Repatriation History

In 1968, archaeologist Roderick Sprague and physical anthropologist Walter Birkby conducted a program that, although it impacted human remains, failed to follow the standard procedure of excavating and storing the remains. Under the terms of an agreement between the Nez Perce tribe and the excavators, information on the skeletal material was obtained in the field and the material then reburied in a tribal cemetery with appropriate ceremony (Sprague and Birkby 1970). But such a program was definitely the exception rather than the rule, and, with the publication of Vine Deloria's book *Custer Died For Your Sins* in 1969, the relationship between archaeologists and American Indians took a decided turn. Prior to the book's publication, there was little indication of American Indian distrust and discontent with the discipline of archaeology, but following its publication, American Indians became openly critical of archaeology and the actions of archaeologists.

American Indian protests for the period 1969–79 (Watkins 1994:appendix B) showed that their distrust of archaeology and archaeologists revolved primarily around the perceived threat to their ancestors and human remains. The general attitudes of the more radical Indians in the 1970s were easily recognized by articles such as "Indian skeleton" (Anon. 1970:12); "Don't exploit our dead or our ceremonies or our dances" (Anon. 1971:1); and "Archaeologists and the Indians" (Hall 1971:10). The American Indian movement's disruption of excavations at Welch, Minnesota, in 1971 exemplifies the physical actions taken to confront the issue, as were organized protests aimed at getting American Indian human remains and sensitive material out of public displays, such as the occupation of the Southwest Museum in Los Angeles in 1971. Additionally, tribal groups began addressing the desire for the repatriation of human remains and artifacts with the fight for the return of the Onondaga wampum belts in 1969 from the State Museum of New York. Such actions, while viewed by some as only the rumblings of malcontents, spurred the discipline to examine the relationships between American Indians and anthropologists and the underlying structures upon which they were constructed.

Archaeology, Physical Anthropology, and Museums Approach the Subject

Among the first archaeologists to confront the conflict between American Indians and archaeologists publicly was Elden Johnson: "These protesters say, in effect, that the responsibility acknowledged, but not always met, by the ethnographer toward the people studied is a responsibility that the professional archaeologist must also meet, and to meet it, the archaeologist must first recognize it" (Johnson 1973:129). Joseph Winter's (1980:124) view of the American Indian and archaeologist controversy seems more to the point: "This confrontation is basically a conflict of values in which the representatives of competing cultures hold radically differing views of resource definition, ownership, significance, and use." In 1984, he continued, "our cultural resource laws and policies regarding preservation and excavation, our other forms of management of scientifically significant resources, and our perceptions of Indian cultures and sites as objects of study all reflect definite cultural biases" (Winter 1984:40).

Even though archaeologists as individuals were seemingly unaware of American Indian concerns with the discipline, some programs were examining relationships at the national level. In 1974, the National Park Service awarded a grant to the Society for American Archaeology to fund a series of "Six Seminars on the Future Direction of Archaeology" (McGimsey and Davis 1977). One of these seminars, "Archaeology and Native Americans," reviewed the relationship between archaeologists and American Indians in an attempt to "alleviate misunderstanding, to increase communication, to sensitize archaeologists to Native American concerns, and to sensitize Native Americans to the capability of archaeology to contribute to an understanding of the heritage we have all gained from Native American cultures" (McGimsey and Davis 1977:90). This was one of the first attempts to "institutionalize" the approach of archaeologists to the conflict between them and American Indians, and it is interesting to note that the framers of the seminars considered American Indian concerns to be one of the six major issues facing the discipline at that time.

During the late 1970s, various federal agencies had "in-house" policies concerning human remains. Within the Department of the Interior, the Heritage Conservation and Recreation Services (HCRS) maintained a "Policy on Disposition of Human Remains" which served as a model for most other federal agencies involved with the excavation of human skeletal material from archaeological sites. The policy called for reburial of skeletal materials recovered from marked or identified deliberate interments when direct kinship to individuals could be demonstrated and also where a "demonstrable ethnic affinity to specific living groups of Native Americans or others" could be established, but only after "appropriate documentation and study are completed" (HCRS 1978). Those human remains that could not be identified to a specific contemporary ethnic group were to be maintained within collections.

In 1985, a conference on reburial issues held in Chicago at the Newberry Library's Darcy McNickle Center for the History of the American Indian brought together 23 participants representing a range of interest groups, including academic and administrative archaeologists; American Indian spiritual, tribal, and political leaders; physical and cultural anthropologists; lawyers; museum administrators; and historians. Discussions centered around five major topics: (1) reasons for insisting upon reburial; (2) reasons for objecting to reburial; (3) reasons for scientific study of human skeletal populations; (4) exploration of possible resolutions; and (5) the next step (Dincauze 1985:1).

A report of the meeting provided a "Consensus of the Reburial Conference" (Quick 1985:175): the necessity for respect for human remains (no. 1), the need for public education (no. 4), the need to protect materials from vandalism, looting, and desecration (no. 5), and the need for cooperation between anthropologists and American Indians (nos. 2, 4, and 6). Statement no. 7 called for materials such as "a statement on the ethics pertaining to excavation and reburial; possible changes to ARPA, NHPA, appropriate federal laws and regulations, model state level legislation (nonprescriptive); and . . . the matter of deaccession" (Quick 1985: 175).

In April 1986, the Society for American Archaeology held a plenary session on "The Treatment of Human Remains" at its 51st annual meeting. The goal was to "refine a series of principles for ethical and socially responsible actions in situations involving the excavation, analysis, curation and ultimate disposition of human remains by archaeologists" (Watson 1986:1). This session resulted in the issuance of a "Statement concerning the treatment of human remains" in May 1986 (SAA 1986) that called for the concerns of different cultures to be channeled through "designated representatives and leaders"; stated that all human remains should receive appropriate scientific study; opposed universal or indiscriminate reburial of human remains; and opposed any federal legislation seeking to impose a uniform standard for determining the disposition of all human remains. Such a statement is understandable, given the fact that it is the Society *for* American Archaeology, but in response to this statement, the National Congress of American Indians adopted two resolutions that dealt with the treatment of human remains exhumed by archaeologists. The first resolution condemned the United States Department of the Interior's policy regarding the disposition of human remains and recommended litigation to invalidate the policy. The second resolution supported "the efforts of Indian and Native governments and organizations to reclaim and protect their national treasures and cultural patrimony" (SOPA 1986:3).

In April 1987, the Society of Professional Archaeologists (SOPA) introduced a proposed reburial policy that dealt with ethical and legal considerations in the treatment of human remains (Niquette 1987:1). The proposed policy would have affected those remains with at least 50 years of elapsed time following their interment, and called for: exhumation when relocation or protection was not feasible; no exhumation of human remains for research or training purposes if they were not in danger; balancing cultural and religious importance with their significance in contemporary and predictable future research; consultation with biological or culturally related groups of the deceased, including tribes currently or previously occupying the land in which the deceased lay; non-reinterment of human remains and related artifacts until their research significance had been exhausted (including for perpetuity and subjection of the materials to analyses that partially destroyed or modified them); reinterment of human remains of lesser significance in accordance with state or local law and/or the wishes of biological or cultural descendants (or tribal groups who occupy or previously occupied the lands in which the deceased lay); and, finally, reinterment of human remains and grave-associated artifacts "having demonstrated cultural or religious significance of such magnitude that their analysis would impose an unconstitutional burden on the free exercise of religion by their descendants" (Niquette 1987:2).

In October 1987, the editor of the SOPA newsletter presented responses to this proposed policy (Gummerman 1987:12). Various suggestions were made for addition to the proposed policy ("curation in the ground – reburial after initial study has been exhausted") and deletion from the policy ("reburial . . . only where there is a clear and demonstrable familial connection between living people and the bones they claim. Mere claims for spiritual affinity with bones thousands of years old are meaningless and nothing but an anti-intellectual ploy").

In 1990, Lynne Goldstein and Keith Kintigh, representatives of the Society for American Archaeology's Reburial Committee, approached the problem of reburial, stating that the issue of reburial "cannot be solved strictly as a matter of ethics" (1990:587) and argued for a change in the way archaeologists deal with Native Americans: "We must change the way we do business without abrogating our responsibilities to the archaeological record or the living descendants of the people we study" (Goldstein and Kintigh 1990:590).

But archaeologists were not the only group studying the issue of reburial and repatriation. The American Anthropological Association's Reburial Commission was an outgrowth of an *ad hoc* committee set up to study, report on, and offer guidelines in regard to American Indian requests to rebury ancestral remains and associated grave goods held in museums, universities, and other depositories for research purposes. Its report in March 1991 (AAA 1991) provided an overview of the development of American anthropology and offered suggestions to "guide activities at the local and national levels" (AAA 1991:28). Among these were involvement of Indian people in the processes of decision-making; more networking between the Indian and anthropological communities; better education about the historical usefulness of archaeology and biological anthropology; encouragement of social science training for Native Americans; development of tribal and intertribal museums and cultural centers; and the production of timely reports and films on archaeological work that is of interest to non-specialists. In closing they state "[T]he issue of human remains is not a simple issue of human rights or respect for the dead" (AAA 1991:28).

Ultimately, the quest for understanding and the development of informal policies regarding the repatriation of human remains ended in the passage of the National Museum of the American Indian Act (NMAIA) in 1989 and the Native American Graves Protection and Repatriation Act (NAGPRA) in 1990. These acts changed the underlying structures upon which the relationships between archaeologists and American Indians were based, and their passage gave American Indians some of the tools necessary to implement the changes they had protested for in the 1970s. Many authors (Hutt 1992; Hutt et al. 1992; Tsosie 1997; Welsh 1992), believe that NAGPRA is human rights legislation aimed at providing equal treatment to all human remains under the law, without consideration of "race" or cultural background.

Although American Indian groups attempted to recover items of cultural importance (i.e. the Zuni War Gods from the Millicent Rogers Museum, the Denver Art

Museum, and the Smithsonian Institution; wampum belts from the State Museum of New York), most issues have dealt with those items associated with human remains (funerary objects or "grave goods"). Questions have been raised about the ownership of these objects, and about whether the objects associated with human remains should be returned with those human remains. Arguments about the scientific importance of the material, the insecure nature of many American Indian-owned museums, the difficulties of determining ownership (individual v. tribal, tribal v. tribal, and so forth), and the legal status of museum ownership were first analyzed by Blair (1979), who ultimately stated that the best way to protect Indian artifacts was to prevent their removal from tribal lands by preventing excavation or protecting against looting (similar to King's argument in 1972).

Museum professionals were concerned with the passage of legislation that allowed tribal groups to regain their important artifacts, but others took a wider perspective on the issue. In "A philosophical perspective on the ethics and resolution of cultural properties issues," Karen Warren (1989:25), suggested that those involved with the study and preservation of the past should turn their views toward an integrated perspective on cultural issues to encourage all of us to "rethink the dispute as one of preservation (not, or not simply, one of ownership) of the past" (Warren 1989:22). In this sense, the importance rests more on the preservation of an object for the sake of cultural heritage rather than on which individual (or institution) retains (or regains) the physical object in question.

With the passage of the NMAIA in 1989 and NAGPRA in 1990, Congress established procedures that allowed American Indians to request certain classes of artifacts and cultural material held in museums and federal agencies.

Repatriation Legislation

Since so much has been written about the two major repatriation acts they will be presented in very brief summary. The reader is referred to the numerous websites associated with the National Park Service's NAGPRA Program or any of the many NAGPRA-related sites on the internet. Since the NMAIA was the first of the repatriation acts, it will be discussed first, but since NAGPRA has had perhaps the most widespread impact on museums and anthropologists, it will be discussed in more detail.

The National Museum of the American Indian Act and its amendment

With the passage of the NMAIA (Public Law 101-185) in 1989 Congress established the new National Museum of the American Indian and, at the same time, it also required the Smithsonian to inventory, document, and, if requested, repatriate culturally affiliated human remains and funerary objects to federally recognized Native groups. In 1996 the NMAIA was amended to add new categories of objects subject to repatriation and to establish deadlines for the distribution of object summaries and inventories of the Smithsonian's collections to tribes. Definitions of the object categories subject to repatriation generally follow the language of NAGPRA.

Categories of materials that are eligible for return under the NMAIA include: (1) human remains of individuals whose identity is known; (2) culturally affiliated human remains; (3) associated and unassociated funerary objects; (4) sacred objects; and (5) objects of cultural patrimony. In addition, under long-standing museum policy, tribes may request the return of objects transferred to or acquired by the National Museum of the American Indian illegally or under circumstances that render the museum's claim to them invalid.

Culturally affiliated human remains are defined in the legislation as human remains that share a relationship with a present-day American Indian tribe that can be demonstrated based on a preponderance of available evidence. Associated and unassociated funerary objects are items that, as part of the death rites of a culture, are believed to have been intentionally placed with an individual of known affiliation at the time of death or later. The only distinction between whether a funerary object is considered unassociated or associated is whether or not the museum has the human remains with which it was originally interred. Sacred objects are specific ceremonial objects that are needed by traditional Native American religious leaders in order for present-day adherents to continue practicing their traditional Native American religions. Objects of cultural patrimony are more difficult to define, and vary among tribes. In general, they are cultural objects that were originally owned by the entire tribe rather than a single individual, and which have an ongoing historical, traditional, or cultural importance to the Native group. Because the objects were tribally rather than individually owned, they cannot have been alienated, appropriated, or conveyed by any individual at the time they were acquired. An example of an item of cultural patrimony for American citizens would be the original Bill of Rights.

Repatriation of Native American human remains and certain cultural objects may be made by lineal descendants of named individuals, federally recognized Native American tribes, federally recognized Native Alaskan villages, and Native Hawaiian organizations named in the Act. Requests from state-recognized Native American tribes are reviewed by the museum on a case-by-case basis.

The NMAIA also required the Smithsonian to establish a special committee to monitor and review the process of inventory, identification, and repatriation. This external review committee consists of seven individuals, four of whom must be Native Americans. The review committee may, upon the request of any affected party, review any findings relating to the origin or the return of human remains and cultural objects. It also assists the Secretary of the Smithsonian in resolving disputes between groups, or between a group and the Institution, with regard to the disposition of collections that may arise.

The Native American Graves Protection and Repatriation Act

NAGPRA (Public Law 101-601) affirms the rights of lineal descendants, Indian tribes, and Native Hawaiian organizations to custody of Native American human remains, funerary objects, sacred objects, and objects of cultural patrimony held in federal museums or agencies, or in museums that receive federal funds.

Signed into law by President George Bush in November 1990, NAGPRA places the responsibility for compliance upon federal agencies and museums that receive federal funds. It requires all federal departments, agencies, or instrumentalities of the United States (except for the Smithsonian Institution) to complete summaries and inventories of Native American materials in their control (including those held by non-governmental repositories) and to ensure compliance regarding inadvertent discoveries and intentional excavations of human remains conducted as part of activities on federal or tribal lands.

Museums as defined in NAGPRA are more than just places which house artifacts and collections. The definition includes any institution or state or local government agency (including any institution of higher learning) that has possession of, or control over, items covered under the Act and which receives federal funds. The two important terms – "possession," meaning the physical custody of objects with sufficient legal interest to lawfully treat them as part of the museum's collection, and "control," having a legal interest in objects sufficient to lawfully permit the museum to treat the objects as part of its collection, whether or not the objects are in the physical custody of the museum – were also defined. Generally, a museum that has loaned objects to any entity (individual, museum, or federal agency) is considered to retain control of those objects, although the objects may not be in the physical custody of the museum. Objects in the museum's collection that have been received on loan from another individual, museum, or federal agency are considered to be in the control of the loaning museum.

The Act also provided an expanded definition of the phrase "receives federal funds." As defined in the Act, a museum that receives funds from a federal agency through any grant, loan, contract (other than a procurement contract), or arrangement by which a federal agency makes or made available funds to a museum is included. If a larger entity of which the museum is a part receives federal funds (i.e., a university museum where the university receives federal funds), then the museum must comply with NAGPRA regulations. NAGPRA also applies to certified local governments and tribal museums if they receive federal funds through any grant, loan, or contract. The Act does not apply to private individuals and museums that do not receive federal funds and which are not part of a larger entity that does receive federal funds.

The statute lays out a mechanism for federal land managers, museums, and agency officials to consult with lineal descendants and tribal groups and reach a determination regarding the proper disposition of objects covered under Act that might be excavated or discovered on federal or tribal lands. The processes for dealing with excavations or discoveries on federal or tribal lands are different than those for dealing with the disposition of objects within museum or federal agency collections.

The system outlined by the statute provides a framework for resolving issues surrounding the disposition of Native American human remains, funerary objects, sacred objects, and objects of cultural patrimony excavated or discovered on federal or tribal lands or held in federal or museum collections.

Native American groups hailed the passage of NAGPRA as an opportunity to right centuries-old wrongs perpetrated against American Indian graves. In a symposium sponsored by the *Arizona State Law Journal*, many authors discussed the "new" law as it impacted various institutions that dealt with Native American human remains and cultural material. In discussing the legislative history of the law, Trope and EchoHawk (2000:139) note, "NAGPRA is, first and foremost, human rights legislation . . . designed to address the flagrant violation of the 'civil rights of American's first citizens'." Additionally, Maricopa County Superior Court judge Sherry Hutt sees NAGPRA as a law that will "strengthen federal prosecutors' ability to protect Native American graves and cultural treasures by hampering the profit incentive" (Hutt 1992:135), the same thing federal and local archaeologists had attempted to do regularly through education and legislation.

A more complete discussion of the scientific response to the repatriation legislation is provided in Watkins (2000), but, needless to say, it ranged from complete support to total opposition. Zimmerman (1997:92–112) provides a good summary of the repatriation issues as they have impacted the discipline of archaeology. His article discusses the four stages that archaeology went through in dealing with repatriation: denial, dialogue, analysis, and compromise.

In the "denial" phase, Zimmerman argues, the discipline challenged Indian claims, rationalizing that "academic freedom has precedence and that the remains are the heritage of all cultures" (1997:93). This stance, that the goals of science as a worldwide, humanist pursuit are somehow more important than the wishes of individual cultures, is still heard as an excuse for the unfettered practice of archaeological excavations in societies throughout the world (cf. Gough 1996; Meighan 1992; Mulvaney 1991). During the "dialogue" phase, Zimmerman notes that, while not all archaeologists agreed that problems existed, the discipline began a series of dialogues to gain an understanding of American Indian perceptions of the problems. It is interesting to note that archaeologists continue to court "dialogues" (cf. Mihesuah 1996).

Zimmerman's third phase, "analysis," came about as "some anthropologists became curious about why the controversy arose and why it continued. The issue itself became a matter of intellectual investigation" (Zimmerman 1997:101). Anthropologists began to study the processes that evolved along with the changing relationships between anthropologists and indigenous populations. Zimmerman's last phase, "compromise," provides a brief listing of some "historical" (if the late 1960s might be considered historical) compromises made between American Indians and archaeologists. It also provides a glimpse of the reasoning behind American Indian attempts at getting national repatriation laws passed rather than state or local laws (1997:105).

NAGPRA falls heavily on those individuals who analyze and interpret human remains subject to repatriation as well as on those who initially encounter those remains. In articles such as "Human skeletal remains: preservation or reburial?" (Ubelaker and Grant 1989), "Why anthropologists study human remains" (Landau and Steele 1996), and "NAGPRA is forever: The future of osteology and the repatriation of skeletons" (Rose et al. 1996), biological anthropologists and osteologists outline the types of information that result from the study of human remains. Although these might be construed to be nothing more than a justification for the continued study of human remains, they nonetheless offer an attempt to educate not only American Indians but also other anthropologists about the uses of osteo-logical information concerning lifestyles of human beings.

While the passage of NAGPRA gave American Indians some of the tools necessary to implement the changes they had protested for in the 1970s, some American Indians complained that scientists were using the inventories and summaries required of museums as a means of obtaining additional scientific data under the guise of complying with NAGPRA. While the law does not authorize the initiation of new scientific studies, it does not preclude it when the museum deems it necessary for determining the cultural affiliation of a set of human remains (section 5(b)(2)), or when the materials are " indispensable for completion of a specific scientific study, the outcome of which would be of major benefit to the United States" (section 7(b)).

In the 1995 oversight hearing on the implementation of NAGPRA, Jesse Taken Alive, chairman of the Standing Rock Sioux Tribe, noted:

> It was only when Native people . . . rose to stop the racist practice of the robbery and study of our graves was the "loss" to science loudly and arrogantly lamented. Amid great gnashing of teeth, *the rush was on* to study, document, analyze, and further desecrate our relatives before the precious "scientific and cultural materials" could be "destroyed" through reburial.
>
> *In our view, the science and museum industries have only themselves to blame that they did not correctly catalog and store our dead relatives while they had them, and should not now be allowed to gather one more iota of data from our relatives under the cloak of NAGPRA* . . . (Taken Alive 1996:231; emphasis in original)

Additionally, many American Indian groups cannot understand why the graves protection portion of NAGPRA was not applied to all lands within the United States, rather than just to federal or tribal lands, since the entire continent was at one time Indian land. The National Congress of American Indians, the oldest and largest national organization representing American Indians, called for "amendatory language to the NAGPRA to extend protection of funerary remains and objects on all lands within the exterior boundaries of the U.S. wherever they may be situated" (NCAI Resolution no. NV93170). NAGPRA Review Committee chairwoman Tessie Naranjo of Santa Clara Pueblo noted that the Review Committee itself experienced frustration over this issue (Naranjo 1996:149).

Why is such extension of NAGPRA important? According to Melinda Zeder's survey of American archaeologists (1997:47), approximately 49 percent of archaeologists worked either within the government (23 percent), the private sector (18 percent), or within a museum setting (8 percent). Although these figures might vary from the true proportions of archaeologists employed in these areas, Zeder feels they are a good fit to the actual makeup of American archaeology (1997:48).

If one assumes that private sector and museum archaeologists are as closely tied to federal regulations as their government counterparts, only about one-half of American archaeologists are bound by NAGPRA or the NMAIA. Academic archaeologists, those more often participating in "pure research," are less confined by federal regulations and made up 35 percent of the survey population. When these archaeologists conduct research on federal or tribal lands, their research is covered by NAGPRA, as are the artifacts that they collect. However, if their research is conducted on private land, they are less restrained. While the artifacts might eventually come under control of NAGPRA (if the museums where the artifacts are curated receive federal funds), their initial excavations may not be as stringently controlled.

The ascription of property rights to archaeological resources is, as Ruthann Knudson (1995:4) notes, "a complicated legal, as well as social, issue." While human remains may be protected under various state laws, federal intervention on private land is sometimes seen as a violation of the "takings clause" of the Constitution if the landowner is somehow denied access or free use of his property without adequate compensation.

Another point of concern to American Indians is in relation to Native American human remains and funerary objects whose cultural affiliation has not been established. At the 1995 oversight hearing on the implementation of NAGPRA, Cecil Antone, Lieutenant Governor of the Gila River Indian Community at Sacaton, Arizona, noted that, "Even though they are not identified [as to culture], they are human beings. They were human beings" (Antone 1996:37). Jesse Taken Alive of the Standing Rock Sioux Tribe said the tribe believes "those remains dating back 500 years or more are American Indians. . . . Give them back to the people and let us decide how that should be done, because, after all, as American Indians, as indigenous people, those are our ancestors" (Taken Alive 1996:42).

Even the NAGPRA Review Committee felt this issue was a point of frustration. Dan Monroe, a member of the committee in 1996, noted in testimony at the oversight hearing that:

> [T]he controversy is hottest in respect to disposition of ancient Native American remains . . . [which] can seldom be affiliated with a specific tribe. . . . Native Americans almost unanimously argue that they are culturally and otherwise affiliated with these remains and that their religious and cultural beliefs dictate that the remains be returned and reburied. (Monroe 1996:125; emphasis in original)

In 1999, the NAGPRA Review Committee issued a set of Draft Principles of Agreement Regarding the Disposition of Culturally Unidentifiable Human Remains (NAGPRA Review Committee 1999). These principles presented guidelines for the ultimate disposition of these types of remains. While no specific remedies are defined for every case, they do offer suggestions for disposition in cases where the human remains are associated with a non-federally recognized tribe, suggest regional consultations where such approaches would prove beneficial, and for situations where the human remains represent a population for which there are no present-day cultural survivors.

While all tribes agree that human remains of unrecognized American Indian groups are, have been, and always will be American Indian, many are concerned about extending rights to all groups under NAGPRA. In a statement prepared for the March 1997 Review Committee meeting in Oklahoma, seven tribes from southwestern Oklahoma – the Apache Tribe of Oklahoma, the Caddo Tribe, the Comanche Tribe, the Delaware Tribe of Western Oklahoma, the Fort Sill Apache, the Kiowa, and the Wichita and Affiliated Tribes – felt repatriation should apply only to federally recognized groups. While they felt that human remains, regardless of affiliation, should not be left in museums, they expressed a concern that to repatriate human remains to non-federally recognized tribes could potentially assign rights and authority to groups that have come into existence without a legitimate claim of continuity. The working group felt that culturally unidentifiable human remains should be repatriated to federally recognized tribes on whose aboriginal lands the remains were found, with the Review Committee making decisions in cases where multiple tribes claimed the same ancestral lands.

The passage of the National Museum of the American Indian Act and the Native American Graves Protection and Repatriation Act forced the discipline of archaeology to react more strongly than was necessary. While the importance of human remains in the study of past diets, lifeways, and cultures has been recognized by various authors, archaeology nonetheless failed to make clear the objectives of wishing to retain control over human remains and cultural objects encountered within excavations.

The impact of the law's requirements was immediately felt by those museums which were required to prepare inventories of the human remains and associated grave goods, sacred items, and items of cultural patrimony within their collections. The inventories were then forwarded to American Indian groups, which were often forced to wade through computer-generated listings in an effort to discover those items for which they had an interest. The sudden influx of such lists strained tribal programs, many of which were already under-funded, and forced some to either curtail aspects of their cultural resource activities or to try to come to grips with the mountain of data they didn't know what to do with.

Archaeologists and organizations were quick to recognize the problems involved in consultation and repatriation of material recovered or donated before the current legislative controls, but legal analyses of NAGPRA pointed out that archaeologists were not entitled to "own" the materials which the tribes were requesting, and that the control of such objects covered under the law was vested in the tribes or in members of the tribes.

While museum officials and curators might have been concerned with the loss of items within their collections, archaeologists appeared to be more concerned with the freedom to pursue "science" and the academic quest for answers to questions which most American Indians might not care about. Additionally, as is the case in the Kennewick situation, anthropologists soon entered into the legal arena in a fight to retain the right to attempt to answer questions that influence the worldwide knowledge base.

Kennewick

A long-drawn-out, detailed discussion of the situation related to Kennewick Man is not warranted here. For specific information, the reader is referred to the website maintained by the *Tri-City Herald* (http://www.kennewick-man.com); to books written by Roger Downey (2000) and David Hurst Thomas (2000), and to articles published in such popular publications as *The New Yorker* (Preston 1997), the *U.S. News and World Report* (Petit 1998), *Discover* (Wright 1999), and *Newsweek* (Begley and Murr 1999), to name but a few.

The human remains discovered on the shore of the Columbia River in 1996 by a couple of college students set NAGPRA on its ear. The remains were originally treated as a crime scene by Dr. James Chatters, the excavator, because the skull appeared "Caucasoid" and because that is the way most discoveries of human remains are treated. Once a projectile point was discovered embedded in the pelvis of the skeleton, things got even more interesting. Chatters sent off a portion of bone and, when the dates came back indicating the remains were approximately 9,200 years old, NAGPRA went into action (see also Ames, Adovasio and Pedler, this volume).

The human remains were treated as an "inadvertent discovery" under NAGPRA. After consultation with tribes in the area, the Corps of Engineers (who controlled the federal land upon which the remains were found) determined to repatriate the remains to the Umatilla. But, shortly before the remains were to be returned, eight anthropologists filed suit in district court to block the repatriation.

From the beginning, the remains intrigued scientists, but American Indians were not amenable to further study. To representatives of the Umatilla, it didn't matter how old the remains were. "If this individual is truly over 9,000 years old, that only substantiates our belief he is Native American," Armand Minthorn was quoted as saying (Minthorn 10/27/96). He went on:

> Some scientists say that if this individual is not studied further, we, as Indians, will be destroying evidence of our own history. We already know our history. It is passed on to us through our elders and through our religious practices.
>
> Scientists have dug up and studied American Indians for decades. We view this practice as desecration of the body and a violation of our most deeply held religious beliefs. Our beliefs and policies also tell us this individual must be reburied as soon as possible.

Thus, the question at the outset was not a question of science versus religion, as some of the popular press reported, but a conflict between American Indian philosophy and that of American science. And the scientists were not of a single mind in relation to their philosophy. Articles and letters in the American Anthropological Association's *Anthropology News* discussed the political and academic implications of Kennewick, especially in relation to the scientific and social definitions of "race."

But with the publication of the results of the analyses of the skeletal material (Powell and Rose 1999), it became obvious that science was facing the possibility of losing one of the "founder populations" of North America. The fact that the skeleton was not related to *any* recent human groups, especially any American Indian groups, made it more difficult to justify repatriating it to any particular Indian group and easier to justify continued study. The fact that the Archaic populations of the United States which temporally follow show some resemblance to the Kennewick material hints that the Archaic groups *may* have derived some of their morphological characteristics from the population of which the Kennewick individual was a member. Equally intriguing is the distinctiveness of the Archaic population of the southeastern United States from the western Archaic populations (Powell and Rose 1999).

While there were certainly conflicts between the scientific possibilities raised by the discovery of a nearly complete skeleton such as "The Ancient One," the principal issue tested throughout the conflict has been the legal question of whether NAGPRA should apply to materials of such antiquity. Many individuals were quick to see the legal ramifications of the situation, and attorneys more often focused on the case law relating to human remains. In 1997, Amanda Horn examined the legal issues surrounding NAGPRA and its application to the ancient human remains and the battle between archaeologists "for the right to control the disposition of human remains discovered on federal land in Washington" (Horn 1997:503). Horn's examination focused on Congress's failure to recognize the religious relationship between cultural items (including human remains) and the tribes, on the differences in application of certain state statutes regarding Native American human remains, and on a history of the Kennewick discovery.

In conclusion, Horn realizes that "Kennewick man will probably be subjected to a complete scientific examination before he is released to a tribe for reburial" (1997:516), that the disposition of the remains will "significantly impact decisions regarding the control of remains discovered in the future" (1997:517), and also that "the discovery and the long journey that the Kennewick man will inevitably travel before being put to rest, solidifies a foundation for discussion between the Native Americans and archaeologists" (1997:517).

Horn's analysis was an accurate assessment of the situation regarding Kennewick. At present, the future of the remains is uncertain. The scientific analyses that were permitted have failed to provide any additional scientific or physiological information that would help the Department of the Interior in its decision concerning the disposition of the remains, even though the Department of the Interior has ruled they should be repatriated to the Umatilla Tribe based on the preponderance of the evidence (Babbitt 2000).

If truly ancient remains such as those exemplified by the Kennewick material are excluded from protection or disposition under NAGPRA, the court will need to provide guidance on how old human remains must be in order to be considered "ancient," as well as whether "science" or "tribal oral history" should be used to define that threshold. The NAGPRA Review Committee has partially addressed this issue but it has yet to be resolved. Additionally, the court decision might also affect the scientific exception clause of NAGPRA which allows for the scientific study of materials when the results of such are deemed to be of major benefit to the United States government. The study of human remains of such antiquity will likely be deemed to be "of benefit to the United States," especially in relation to the information present regarding early peoples of the New World, but, since NAGPRA is silent on this issue in relation to inadvertent discoveries, the court decision might set precedent regarding legislative intent.

The testing of some of the major inadequacies and ambiguities of NAGPRA has just begun, and both the scientific and Native American communities are awaiting the results.

Summary

The excavation of the burials of individuals of American Indian descent has been a primary point of concern between both American Indians and archaeologists, as noted by Anderson (1985), Buikstra (1981), Rosen (1980), Talmage (1982), and others. Available published American Indian opinions tend to view this as a conflict between Indian and non-Indian spiritual or religious values (Deloria 1969; Quick 1985), while most archaeologists (Buikstra 1981; Meighan 1984; Talmage 1982) tend to view the problem as a conflict between scientific and non-scientific values.

As is readily apparent, American Indian concerns also have focused on the inconsistent application of various federal and state laws regarding the protection of human remains. In the past, unmarked American Indian graves have not been afforded the same protection as unmarked non-Indian graves, but, in some instances, state and local laws may be more restrictive than federal laws. In North Dakota, for example, it is a class B felony to disturb a burial, as well as a misdemeanor if an individual knows of a burial location but does not report it (Del Bene and Banks:1990).

Even prior to the passage of NAGPRA, the idea of repatriation led many archaeologists to believe that all excavations would be controlled by radical Indians claiming religious infringement (Meighan 1984); physical anthropologists decried the potential loss of a large and necessary (in their view) database (Buikstra 1981); and ethnologists and museologists were afraid of losing a large body of cultural material from museum collections. In short, the scientific community, beginning with the discussion of the repatriation of the Iroquois wampum belts in 1970, rose against the perceived threat to its databases – material culture and human remains alike – from those whose ancestors were the subjects of those databases.

In 1995 Ruthann Knudson wrote: "We all have a right to our past, and our past is the worldwide record of the human experience" (1995:3). But Alice Kehoe (1998:215), in discussing the "collective past" archaeologists expound, notes that archaeologists might have again presupposed that American Indians want to "share" their past. According to Larry Zimmerman (1995:66), archaeologists talk about sharing history when in reality they want a convenient means of maintaining an upper hand. He writes: "The problem is control. I sense that . . . most archaeologists would be reluctant to relinquish control." In 1980 Winter asked: "Should we [archaeologists] always respond positively to Native Americans, just because they are 'Indians'?" (1980:126). American Indians might also have asked: "Should the federal government always respond positively to scientists just because they are scientists?"

REFERENCES

AAA (American Anthropological Association), 1991 Reburial Commission report. *Anthropology Newsletter* 32(3; March).

Anderson, Duane, 1985 Reburial: Is it reasonable? *Archaeology* 38(5), 48–51.

Anon., 1970 Indian skeleton. *Akwesasne Notes* (Rooseveltown, NY) 2(6), 12.

Anon., 1971 Don't exploit our dead or our ceremonies or our dances. *Akwesasne Notes* (Rooseveltown, NY) 3(6), 1.

Antone, C., 1996 Statement to the Committee. Native American Graves Protection and Repatriation Act: Hearing before the Committee on Indian Affairs, United States Senate, One Hundred Fourth Congress, first session, an oversight hearing on Public Law 101-601, to provide the authority and mechanism for the repatriation of Native American human remains, funerary objects, sacred objects, and objects of cultural patrimony. December 6, 1995. Washington, DC: Superintendent of Documents.

Babbitt, Bruce, 2000 Letter from the Secretary of the Interior to the Secretary of the Army dated September 11. Electronic version at <http://www.cr.nps.gov/aad/kennewick/babb_letter.htm> (last accessed April 9, 2001).

Begley, Sharon, and Andrew Murr, 1999 The first Americans. *Newsweek* 26(April), 50–57.

Bettinger, Robert, 1991 *Hunter/Gatherers: Archaeological and Evolutionary Theory*. New York: Plenum Press.

Bieder, Robert E., 2000 The representations of Indian bodies in nineteenth-century American anthropology. In *Repatriation Reader: Who Owns American Indian Remains?* Devon A. Mihesuah, ed. Pp. 19–36. Lincoln: University of Nebraska Press.

Blair, Bowen, 1979 Indian Rights: Native Americans versus American museums – a battle for artifacts. *American Indian Law Review* 7(1), 125–154.

Buikstra, Jane, 1981 A specialist in cemetery studies looks at the reburial issue. *Early Man* 3, 26–27.

Del Bene, Terry, and Kimball Banks, 1990 Skeletons in the closet: An assessment of North Dakota's procedures for protecting human remains. Paper presented at the 48th Annual Meeting of the Plains Anthropological Society, Oklahoma City.

Deloria, Vine, Jr., 1969 *Custer Died For Your Sins: An Indian Manifesto*. London: Macmillan.

Dincauze, Dena, 1985 Report on the conference on reburial issues. *Bulletin of the Society for American Archeology* 3(5), 1–3.

Downer, Alan, 1997 Archaeologist–Native American relations. In *Native Americans and Archaeologists: Stepping Stones to Common Ground*. N. Swidler, K. Dongoske, R. Anyon, and A. Downer, eds. Pp. 23–34. Walnut Creek, CA: AltaMira Press.

Downey, Roger, 2000 *Riddle of the Bones: Politics, Science, Race, and the Story of Kennewick Man*. New York: Copernicus Books.

Ferguson, T. J., 1996 Native Americans and the practice of archaeology. *Annual Review of Anthropology* 25, 63–79.

Fowler, Donald D., 1987 Uses of the past: Archaeology in the service of the state. *American Antiquity* 52(2), 229–248.

Goldstein, Lynne, and Keith Kintigh, 1990 Ethics and the reburial controversy. *American Antiquity* 55(3), 585–591.

Gough, Austin, 1996 The new official religion and the retreat of Western science. *Archeology in New Zealand* 39, 131–138.

Gummerman, George, 1987 The struggle toward a SOPA reburial policy. *SOPA Newsletter* 11(8), 1–2.

Hall, Louis, 1971 Archaeologists and the Indians. *Akwesasne Notes* (Rooseveltown, New York) 3(6), 10.

HCRS (Heritage Conservation and Recreation Services), 1978 Policy on disposition of human remains. Manuscript in possession of the author.

Heath, Dwight B., ed., 1963 *Mourt's Relation: A Relation or Journal of the English Plantation Settled at Pilgrims at Plymouth in New England, by Certain English Adventurers both Merchants and Others.* New York: Corinth Books.

Horn, Amanda L., 1997 The Kennewick man loses sleep over NAGPRA: Native Americans and scientists wrestle over cultural remains. In *Sovereignty Symposium X.* Pp. 501–524. Oklahoma City: Oklahoma Bar Association.

Hutt, Sherry, 1992 Illegal trafficking in Native American human remains and cultural items: A new protection tool. *Arizona State Law Journal* (24)1, 135–150.

Hutt, Sherry, Elwood W. Jones, and Martin E. McAllister, 1992 *Archeological Resource Protection.* Washington, DC: National Trust for Historic Preservation/Preservation Press.

Johnson, Elden, 1973 Professional responsibilities and the American Indian. *American Antiquity* 38(2), 129–130.

Kehoe, Alice Beck, 1998 *The Land of Prehistory: A Critical History of American Archaeology.* New York: Routledge.

King, Thomas F., 1972 Archeological law and the American Indian. *The Indian Historian* 5(3), 31–35.

King, Thomas F., Patricia Parker Hickman, and Gary Berg, 1977 *Anthropology in Historic Preservation: Caring for Culture's Clutter.* New York: Academic Press.

Knudson, Ruthann, 1995 The archaeological public trust in context. In *Protecting the Past.* George S. Smith and John E. Ehrenhard, eds. Pp. 3–8. Boca Raton: CRC Press.

Kuznar, Lawrence A., 1997 *Reclaiming a Scientific Anthropology.* Walnut Creek, CA: AltaMira Press.

Landau, Patricia M., and D. Gentry Steele, 1996 Why anthropologists study human remains. *American Indian Quarterly* 20(2), 209–228.

Lurie, Nancy Oestreich, 1988 Relations between Indians and anthropologists. In *Handbook of North American Indians*, vol. 4: *History of Indian–White Relations.* W. Washburn, ed. Pp. 548–556. Washington, DC: Smithsonian Institution Press.

McGimsey, Charles R., and Hester A. Davis, eds., 1977 *The Management of Archeological Resources: The Airlie House Report.* Special Publication of the Society for American Archeology. Washington, DC.

McGuire, Randall, 1992a Archeology and the first Americans. *American Anthropologist* 94(4), 816–836.

—— 1992b *A Marxist Archaeology.* Orlando: Academic Press.

—— 1997 Why have archaeologists thought real Indians were dead and what can we do about it? In *Indians and Anthropologists: Vine Deloria, Jr. and the Critique of Anthropology*. Thomas Biolsi and Larry J. Zimmerman, eds. Pp. 63–91. Tucson: University of Arizona Press.

Meighan, Clement, 1984 Archeology: Science or sacrilege? In *Ethics and Values in Archeology*. E. Green, ed. Pp. 208–223. London: The Free Press.

—— 1992 Some scholars' views on reburial. *American Antiquity* 57, 704–710.

Meltzer, David, 1983 The antiquity of man and the development of American archaeology. In *Advances in Archaeological Method and Theory*, vol. 8. M. Schiffer, ed. Pp. 1–51. New York: Academic Press.

—— 1985 North American archaeology and archaeologists, 1879–1934. *American Antiquity* 50, 249–260.

Mihesuah, Devon A., 1996 American Indians, anthropologists, pothunters, and repatriation: Ethical, religious, and political differences. *American Indian Quarterly* 20(2), 229–250.

Minthorn, Armand, 1996 Human remains should be reburied. Electronic version at <http://www.umatilla.nsn.us/kennman.html>.

Monroe, Dan, 1996 Statement to the Committee. Native American Graves Protection and Repatriation Act: Hearing before the Committee on Indian Affairs, United States Senate, One Hundred Fourth Congress, first session, an oversight hearing on Public Law 101-601, to provide the authority and mechanism for the repatriation of Native American human remains, funerary objects, sacred objects, and objects of cultural patrimony. December 6, 1995. Washington, DC: Superintendent of Documents.

Mulvaney, John, 1991 Past regained, future lost: The Kow Swamp Pleistocene burials. *Antiquity* 65, 12–21.

NAGPRA Review Committee, 1999 *Draft Principles of Agreement Regarding the Disposition of Culturally Unidentifiable Human Remains*. Electronic version at <http://www.cast.uark.edu/other/nps/nagpra/DOCS/rcrec003.html> (consulted February 2003).

Naranjo, Tessie, 1996 Statement to the Committee. Native American Graves Protection and Repatriation Act: Hearing before the Committee on Indian Affairs, United States Senate, One Hundred Fourth Congress, first session, an oversight hearing on Public Law 101-601, to provide the authority and mechanism for the repatriation of Native American human remains, funerary objects, sacred objects, and objects of cultural patrimony. December 6, 1995. Washington, DC: Superintendent of Documents.

Niquette, Charles M., 1987 A proposed SOPA policy on the treatment of human remains. *SOPA Newsletter* 11(4), 1–2.

Petit, Charles, 1998 Rediscovering America. *U.S. News and World Report*, October 12, 56–64.

Powell, Joseph, and Jerome Rose, 1999 Chapter 2: Report on the osteological assessment of the "Kennewick Man" skeleton (CENWW.97.Kennewick). *Report on the Non-Destructive Examination, Description, and Analysis of the Human Remains from Columbia Park, Kennewick, Washington*. Washington, DC: US Department of the Interior. Electronic version at <http://www.cr.nps.gov/aad/Kennewick/powell_rose.htm> (consulted May 2003).

Preston, Douglas, 1997 The lost man. *The New Yorker*, June 16, 70–81.

Quick, Polly, ed., 1985 *Proceedings of the Reburial Conference*. Washington, DC: Society for American Archaeology.

Riding In, James, 1992 Without ethics and morality: A historical overview of imperial archaeology and American Indians. *Arizona State Law Journal* (24)1, 11–34.

Rose, Jerome C., Thomas J. Green, and Victoria D. Green, 1996 NAGPRA is forever: The future of osteology and the repatriation of skeletons. *Annual Review of Anthropology* 25, 81–103.

Rosen, Lawrence, 1980 The excavation of American Indian burial sites: A problem in law and professional responsibility. *American Anthropologist* 82(1), 5–27.

SAA (Society for American Archaeology), 1986 Statement concerning the treatment of human remains. *Bulletin of the Society for American Archaeology* 4(3), 78.

SOPA (Society of Professional Archaeologists), 1986 NCAI Speaks to reburial issues. *SOPA Newsletter* 11(1), 3.

Sprague, Roderick, and Walter W. Birkby, 1970 Miscellaneous Columbia Plateau burials. *Tebiwa* 13(1), 132.

Taken Alive, Jesse, 1996 Statement to the Committee. Native American Graves Protection and Repatriation Act: Hearing before the Committee on Indian Affairs, United States Senate, One Hundred Fourth Congress, first session, an oversight hearing on Public Law 101-601, to provide the authority and mechanism for the repatriation of Native American human remains, funerary objects, sacred objects, and objects of cultural patrimony. December 6, 1995. Washington, DC: Superintendent of Documents.

Talmage, Valerie, 1982 The violation of sepulture: Is it legal to excavate human burials? *Archeology* 35(6), 44–49.

Thomas, David Hurst, 2000 *Skull Wars: Kennewick Man, Archaeology, and the Battle for Native American Identity*. New York: Basic Books.

Trigger, Bruce, 1980 Archeology and the image of the American Indian. *American Antiquity* 45(4), 662–676.

——1986 Prehistoric archaeology and American society: An historical perspective. In *American Archaeology Past and Future*. D. J. Meltzer, D. D. Fowler, and J. A. Sabloff, eds. Pp. 187–215. Washington, DC: Smithsonian Institution Press.

——1989 *A History of Archaeological Thought*. Cambridge: Cambridge University Press.

Trope, Jack F., and Walter EchoHawk, 2000 The Native American Graves Protection and Repatriation Act: Background and legislative history. In *Repatriation Reader: Who Owns American Indian Remains?* Devon A. Mihesuah, ed. Pp. 123–168. Lincoln: University of Nebraska Press.

Tsosie, Rebecca, 1997 Indigenous rights and archaeology. In *Native Americans and Archaeologists: Stepping Stones to Common Ground*. Nina Swidler, Kurt Dongoske, Roger Anyon, and Alan Downer, eds. Pp. 64–76. Walnut Canyon, CA: AltaMira Press.

Ubelaker, Douglas, and Lauryn Guttenplan Grant, 1989 Human skeletal remains: Preservation or reburial? *Yearbook of Physical Anthropology* 32, 249–287. New York: Alan R. Liss.

Warren, Karen J., 1989 A philosophical perspective on the ethics and resolution of cultural properties issues. In *The Ethics of Collecting Cultural Property: Whose Culture? Whose Property?* P. Messenger, ed. Pp. 1–25. Albuquerque: University of New Mexico Press.

Watkins, Joe, 1994 Ethics and value conflicts: Analysis of archeologists' responses to questionnaire scenarios concerning the relationship between American Indians and archeologists. Unpublished Ph.D. dissertation, Southern Methodist University.

——2000 *Indigenous Archaeology: American Indian Values and Scientific Practice*. Walnut Creek, CA: AltaMira Press.

Watson, Patty Jo, ed., 1986 Announcement of plenary session. SAA Annual Meeting, New Orleans, April 24, 1986. *Bulletin of the Society for American Archeology* 4(1), 1.

Welsh, Peter H., 1992 Repatriation and cultural preservation: Potent objects, potent pasts. *University of Michigan Journal of Law Reform* 25 (3–4), 837–865.

Willey, Gordon R., And Jeremy A. Sabloff, 1993 *A History of American Archaeology*, 3rd edn. San Francisco: W. H. Freeman.

Winter, Joseph C., 1980 Indian heritage preservation and archaeologists. *American Antiquity* 45(1), 121–131.

——1984 The way to somewhere: Ethics in American archaeology. In *Ethics and Values in Archeology*. E. Green, ed. Pp. 36–47. London: The Free Press.

Wright, Karen, 1999 First Americans. *Discover*, February, 53–63.

Zeder, Melinda, 1997 *The American Archaeologist: A Profile*. Walnut Creek, CA: AltaMira Press.

Zimmerman, Larry, 1995 Regaining our nerve: Ethics, values, and the transformation of archaeology. In *Ethics in American Archaeology: Challenges for the 1990s*. Mark J. Lynott and Alison Wylie, eds. Pp. 64–67. Washington, DC: Society for American Archaeology.

——1997 Anthropology and responses to the reburial issue. In *Indians and Anthropologists: Vine Deloria, Jr. and the Critique of Anthropology*. T. Biolsi and L. Zimmerman, eds. Pp. 92–112. Tucson: University of Arizona Press.

15

Labor and Class in the American West

Dean J. Saitta

Historical archaeology has become increasingly identified with study of the structures and rhythms of global capitalism (Delle et al. 2000; Leone 1995; contributors to Leone and Potter 1999; Little 1994; Matthews et al. 2002; Orser 1996; Paynter 1988). This approach foregrounds social divisions and conflicts – around class, power, ethnicity, gender – and their embodiment in material culture. It has balanced inquiry and produced more complete accounts of the past. Just as importantly, it has encouraged self-consciousness about the social value and political utility of archaeology (Leone 1995). This orientation offers new possibilities for connecting archaeology to contemporary life and for diversifying archaeology's public audience. This is to the good for a discipline that must be ever vigilant about its public image.

Historical archaeology in the American West has been caught up in this wave of redefinition and self-reflection. Ten years ago historical archaeologists began to shift their focus from classic, "Wild West" sites like forts, stagecoach stops, and battlegrounds to "counterclassic" studies of "wage earners, women, minorities, urbanization, and industrialization" (Hardesty 1991:4; see also Wylie 1993). Parallel development of a similarly reflexive New Western History (Limerick 1991) encouraged this shift. The ensuing years have witnessed a maturation of such studies, with archaeologists accomplishing what the New Western Historians did not: namely, integration of historical and archaeological records into more comprehensive understandings of the past (Wylie 1993). Today, Western historical archaeology is bringing together a variety of concerns around class, ethnicity, conflict, social transformation, and the local and global processes that shape them (e.g., Van Bueren 2002; Wurst and Fitts 1999).

Since 1997, I have been helping to extend this project with my colleagues Philip Duke, Randy McGuire, and a dedicated group of students from around the United States and the world. We have been working on mining camps and striker tent colonies associated with the 1913–14 Colorado coal field strike. Our central focus

Figure 15.1 Ludlow Tent Colony, 1913 (Denver Public Library, Western History Collection, Z-193)

is the Ludlow Tent Colony, a National Historic Register site located just north of Trinidad, Colorado. From September 1913 to December 1914 the site was home to striking coal miners and their families (Figure 15.1). They were striking the Colorado Fuel and Iron Company, one small part of the John D. Rockefeller Jr. industrial empire.

The Colorado coal field strike was one of the most violent in United States history. It resulted in an estimated 66 deaths and an unknown number of wounded. The defining events were the Ludlow massacre of April 20, 1914, in which 25 people, including two women and 11 children, lost their lives during a Colorado state militia assault on Ludlow, and the subsequent Ten Days' War in which armed strikers seized control of the mining district. Although the strike was eventually broken in December of that year, the events of the strike and, especially, the deaths of women and children, outraged the American public. The resulting Congressional inquiry forced some key reforms in management–labor relations and was a turning-point in worker struggles for union recognition. Indeed, Ludlow was crucial for delivering many of the workplace rights that we enjoy today.

Although the events in southern Colorado were not unusual for the time, they represent a particularly dramatic convergence of industrial-era tensions and strug-gles around class and power. Indeed, the Colorado coal field strike has been described as the best example of open class warfare in United States history. While well known in union and labor history circles as an archetypal example of indus-trial struggle, the Colorado strike is not well known outside of these circles. This was forcefully demonstrated by our 1997 survey of visitors to the Ludlow Massacre

Memorial. Nearly 70 percent arrive at Ludlow expecting to find a monument to an *Indian* massacre or some other episode of the Indian Wars. They rarely expect a monument to American Labor Wars. This is powerful testimony to public ignorance of the cultural and historical processes that shaped the American West. Ludlow is surely an important part of the "hidden history" of the West, and the United States generally (Walker 2000).

In this chapter I discuss how archaeology is helping to draw out, fill in, and establish the relevance of this hidden history. In first part of the chapter I present a background history of the coal field strike. I do this in some detail precisely because the events in Colorado are so widely unknown. Indeed, they never fail to elicit audible gasps when described to professional and public audiences. Next, I situate Ludlow in a wider global context. I then consider its place in a typology of historical narratives for making sense of the past. These narratives can be described as official, vernacular, and critical. They are shaped and reshaped through time to fit the interests and demands of contemporary society (Foote 1997; Trouillot 1995). In the fourth part I summarize what archaeology is contributing to a critical history of the Colorado coal field strike. Finally, I consider why this research matters against a backdrop of issues in contemporary American industrial life. A key point is that the issues struggled over at Ludlow are still in play today. Thus, archaeology in this context is well positioned to educate the public in ways that have contemporary relevance and that can help to perpetuate the discipline.

Southern Colorado Coal Field History

Prelude to a strike

The southern Colorado coal field is on the east side of the Rocky Mountains. It lies in two southeastern counties, Las Animas and Huerfano. The coal seams occur in the foothills of the Sangre de Cristo Range. Coal mines were located up canyons where the coal seams were exposed by erosion. These fields were a major source of high-grade bituminous coal that was used to produce coking coal, or coke. Coking coal fueled the new industrial capitalism, especially the steel industry that supplied rails for the expanding United States transportation network.

In 1913 Colorado was the eighth largest coal-producing state in the United States (McGovern and Guttridge 1972). Because of the railroads' need for a steady supply of coking coal, the southern field was heavily industrialized. It was also dominated by a few large-scale corporate operations. The largest of these operations was the Colorado Fuel and Iron Company, or C.F.&I., based in Pueblo. Founded in 1880, C.F.&I. produced 75 percent of Colorado's coal by 1892. It became the largest coal-mining, iron ore-mining, and steel-manufacturing enterprise in the West, earning the moniker "Pittsburgh of the West." In 1903 C.F.&I. was acquired by the Rockefeller corporate empire. In 1906, the *Engineering and Mining Journal* estimated that 10 percent of Colorado's population depended on C.F.&I. for their livelihood (Whiteside 1990:8–9).

In the early 20th century C.F.&I. and the other large southern field operators had nearly total control over the economic and political life of Las Animas and Huerfano counties. Most of the miners lived in company towns. They rented company houses, bought food and equipment at company stores, and bought alcohol at company saloons. Many of these expenses were automatically deducted from a miner's wages. Although it was illegal by 1913, scrip, a form of currency redeemable only at the company store, was still in use in the southern Colorado coal towns. Company store prices could be as much as 30 percent higher than those at independent stores outside the coal towns (Long 1985). Doctors, priests, school-teachers, and law enforcement officers were all company employees. The company selected the contents of town libraries and censored movies, books, and magazines. Entries to the towns were gated and patrolled by armed mine guards (Beshoar 1957:2; McGovern and Guttridge 1972:23). Contemporary accounts described the situation as feudal (Seligman 1914a, 1914b).

The Colorado mines themselves were notoriously unsafe. They operated in fla-grant violation of several state laws that regulated safety and the fair compensation of miners. Miners died in Colorado at over twice the national average (McGovern and Guttridge 1972:66; Whiteside 1990:74–75). Hand-picked coroner's juries absolved the coal companies of responsibility for these deaths almost without excep-tion. For example, in the years from 1904 to 1914, the juries picked by the sheriff of Huerfano County, Jeff Farr, found the coal operators to blame in only one case out of 95 (Whiteside 1990:22). Instead, victims were accused of "negligence" or "carelessness" (Yellen 1936). One of the great ironies of the 1913–14 strike is that workers were probably safer during the period when state militiamen were shooting at them than they would have been had they still been toiling in the mines.

The mine workforce itself was largely "third-wave" immigrant labor from southern and eastern Europe, including Sicilians, Tyroleans, Tuscans, Cretans, Macedonians, and others. In America these ethnic groups came to be lumped as "Italians" and "Greeks." Mexicans and African Americans also contributed to the ethnic mix. These workers had been brought into Colorado as strikebreakers in 1903, replacing an earlier, second wave of immigrant miners from Ireland and Wales (Beshoar 1957:1; McGovern and Guttridge 1972:50). In 1912, 61 percent of Colorado's coal miners were of "non-Western European origin" (Whiteside 1990:48). Before the 1913 strike the United Mine Workers of America, which sought to unionize these workers, counted 24 distinct languages in the southern field coal camps.

This mix of ethnicities obviously had consequences for organizing the miners and maintaining unity during the strike. It is well documented in the papers of Lamont Bowers, C.F.&I. board chairman and CEO, that the company would pur-posely mix nationalities in the shafts so as to discourage worker communication and solidarity (Clyne 1999; Long 1989b). The ethnic mix also resulted in the strike and its violence being seen – at least in the context of some official histories – as the result of a belligerent Greek and Balkan culture, rather than the working con-ditions that existed in the southern Colorado coal fields.

The United Mine Workers of America was founded in 1890 and made its first appearance in the Western states in 1900 with a strike in Gallup, New Mexico. In 1903, the UMWA led a strike in the southern Colorado coal field. This strike failed as operators successfully employed replacement labor and strikebreaking agencies (Vallejo 1998). This defeat did not extinguish the union spirit, however, and organizing continued in a variety of covert ways. In fact, Long (1989a) provides a strong basis for disputing the recent argument of Clyne (1999:8–13) that the union in southern Colorado was "like a comet," streaking through and then flaming out with every episode of labor unrest. Union organizing, like tactics of resistance generally, often "covers its tracks" (Paynter and McGuire 1991; Scott 1985). It is thus likely that union activity had a more sustained history in the southern coal field than Clyne allows. Clyne does, however, raise the interesting issue of the relationship between union organizing and the activities of the various Old World fraternal and ethnic organizations or "lodges" that organized workers in the company towns (Clyne 1999:75–76). These organizations may have collaborated with the union to foster worker solidarity during times of labor unrest.

In 1912 the coal companies fired 1,200 southern miners on suspicion of union activities. In the summer of 1913 the UMWA, spearheaded by national organizers such as Frank Hayes and John Lawson, opened its biggest push yet in the south. In September of that year the UMWA announced a strike when the operators would not meet a list of seven demands:

1   Recognition of the United Mine Workers union.
2   A 10 percent increase in wages on the tonnage rates. Each miner was paid by the ton of coal he mined, not by the hour.
3   An eight-hour working day.
4   Payment for "dead work." Since miners were only paid for the coal they mined, work such as shoring, timbering, and laying track was not paid work.
5   The right to elect their own checkweighmen. Miners suspected, generally with good reason, that they were being cheated at the scales that weighed their coal. They wanted a miner to check the scales.
6   The right to trade in any store, to choose their own boarding places, and choose their own doctors.
7   Enforcement of Colorado mining laws, some of which already addressed a few of these demands.

Approximately 90 percent of the workforce struck, numbering around 10,000 miners and their families.

Those who lived in the company towns were evicted, and on September 23, 1913 they hauled their possessions out of the canyons through freezing rain and snow to about a dozen tent sites rented in advance by the UMWA. The tent colonies were placed at strategic locations at the entrances to canyons in order to intercept strikebreakers. Ludlow, with about 150 tents holding 1,200 people, was the largest of the colonies and also served as strike headquarters for Las Animas County. The UMWA supplied tents and ovens, and provided the strikers with food, medical attention, and weekly strike relief. This amounted to $3 per week for each miner, $1 for each wife, and $0.50 for each child. Many important personages in American labor history became involved in the strike on the side of labor, including Mary "Mother" Jones, Upton Sinclair, and John Reed.

Confrontation and conflict

The coal operators reacted quickly to the strike. Replacement miners were imported from across the country and abroad. Baldwin-Felts detectives – specialists in breaking coal strikes – were brought in from West Virginia. Violence characterized the strike from the very beginning, with both sides committing shootings and murders (Beshoar 1957; McGovern and Guttridge 1972; Papanikolas 1982). The first casualty actually occurred in advance of the strike on August 13, when a young Italian American union organizer named Gerald Lippiatt was shot dead on the streets of Trinidad by a Baldwin-Felts detective (Long 1989b).

The coal companies soon mounted a campaign of systematic harassment against the strikers. This harassment took the form of high-powered searchlights that played on the tent colonies at night, surveillance from strategically placed machine-gun nests, and use of the "Death Special," an improvised armored car that periodically sprayed the colonies with machine-gun fire. The first exchange of gunfire occurred at Ludlow on October 7 (Long 1989a). On October 17 the armored car fired into the Forbes tent colony, about 5 miles south of Ludlow, killing and wounding several people. On October 24 mine guards fired into a group of strikers in Walsenberg, killing four of them (Foner 1980; Vallejo 1998). The purpose of this harassment may have been to goad the strikers into violent action, which would provide a pretext for the Colorado Governor to call out the state militia. This would shift the financial burden for breaking the strike from the coal companies to the state. With violence escalating and the operators pressing him, Governor Elias Ammons called out the militia on October 28, 1913.

In November Governor Ammons issued an order allowing militiamen to escort strikebreakers into the coal towns. This indicated to the strikers that state power had joined the side of the operators (Long 1985). During the strike, C.F.& I. billeted militiamen on company property, furnished them with supplies from the company store, and advanced them pay (Adams 1966). On a visit to the strike zone, Colorado state senator Helen Ring Robinson observed militiamen entering the offices of C.F.&I. to receive paychecks (Long 1989a:290).

The sympathies of the militia leadership exacerbated the tensions. The militia commander, a Denver ophthalmologist named John Chase, had been involved in suppressing a 1904 miners' strike at Cripple Creek (Jameson 1998). Following the pattern set at Cripple Creek, Chase essentially declared martial law in the strike zone. This period of unofficial and illegal martial law included mass jailing of strikers, the suspension of habeas corpus, the torture and beating of prisoners and, on January 22, 1914, a cavalry charge on a demonstration of miners' wives and children in downtown Trinidad. Women and children were important contributors to the miner's cause throughout the strike, specializing in picketing of mine entrances and verbal abuse of militiamen (Long 1989a). In this instance they were marching to demand the release of Mother Jones, who had been jailed earlier in the month for her organizing activities.

On March 11 the militia tore down tents at the Forbes colony. To one UMWA official this indicated the beginning of a reign of terror designed to drive the miners back to work (Long 1989b). By spring 1914, as the cost of supporting a force of 695 enlisted men and 397 officers in the field gradually bankrupted the state, all but two of the militia companies were withdrawn. The mining companies replaced the militiamen with mine guards and private detectives under the command of militia officers. With this move the neutrality of the militia was completely destroyed and it now became little more than a strikebreaking force (Sunsieri 1972).

Massacre

The exact sequence of events on April 20, 1914 is uncertain. As McGovern and Guttridge (1972:344) point out, little has been written of the events that led to the Ludlow massacre that is not emotional and distorted. The principals – coal operators, union leaders, militiamen, miners – have been cast in both noble and sinister lights. Much depends on preconceived attitudes about management and workers, and the way that one constructs, filters, and relates historical facts.

Rumors of an impending militia attack on the Ludlow tent colony had circulated for some days prior to April 20th. The earlier militia attacks on Forbes and at Walsenburg provided a justification for striker paranoia (Vallejo 1998:96; Yellen 1936:234). At 9 a.m. on April 20th militia activity increased around a machine-gun nest located on Water Tank Hill, approximately 1.5 km to the south of the Ludlow colony. Those miners who were armed took protected positions in a railway cut and prepared foxholes to draw machine-gun fire away from the colony. Our archaeological excavations at Ludlow indicate that strikers were armed with a variety of weapons, including Winchester rifles and shotguns. The militia detonated two bombs, perhaps as a signal to troops in other positions. Within minutes militiamen and miners were exchanging gunfire.

After a few hours of firing one of the survivors noted that the Ludlow tents were so full of holes that they looked like lace (O'Neal 1971). In the colony there was pandemonium. Some colonists sought refuge in a large walk-in well where they stood knee-deep in freezing water for the rest of the day. Others took refuge behind a steel railroad bridge at the northwest corner of the colony. Many people huddled in the cellars they had dug under their tents. The camp's leaders worked all day to get people to a dry creek bed north of the camp, and from there to the home of a sympathetic rancher. Many colonists ultimately bivouacked in the Black Hills to the east of Ludlow.

In the early afternoon a 12-year-old boy named Frank Snyder came up out of his family's cellar and was shot dead. As the day wore on the force facing the miners grew to almost 200 militiamen and two machine guns. At dusk a train stopped in front of the militia's machine guns and blocked their line of fire. The train crew restarted the train in response to militia threats, but by then most of the people in the colony had fled. By 7 p.m. tents were in flames and militiamen were looting the colony.

Toward evening Louis Tikas, the Greek leader of Ludlow Tent Colony, and two other miners were taken prisoner by the militia. They were summarily executed. Implicated in the murders was a militia lieutenant named Karl Linderfelt. Linderfelt was a professional soldier, Spanish American War veteran, and former head of mine guards for C.F.&I. He had also been present at Cripple Creek as a company guard. Linderfelt commanded Company B, which consisted entirely of mine guards and was the most despised of all militia units stationed in the southern coal field (Papanikolas 1982).

During the battle four women and ten children took refuge in a cellar dug beneath a tent. All but two, Mary Petrucci and Alcarita Pedregone, suffocated when the tent above them was burned. The dead included Mary Petrucci's three children and Alcarita Pedregone's two children. This cellar became infamous as the "Death Pit," and is now preserved in concrete at the Ludlow Massacre Memorial. The known fatalities at the end of the day were 25 people, including three militiamen, one uninvolved passerby, and 11 children (Figure 15.2).

When news of Ludlow got out, striking miners at the other tent colonies went to war. For ten days they fought pitched battles with mine guards and militiamen

Figure 15.2 Ludlow Tent Colony after the Colorado state militia assault, April 20, 1914 (Denver Public Library, Western History Collection, Z-199)

along a 40-mile front between Trinidad and Walsenburg (Figure 15.3). In largely uncoordinated guerrilla attacks, the strikers destroyed several company towns and killed company employees.

The fighting ended when a desperate Governor Ammons asked for federal intervention. President Woodrow Wilson complied, and on April 30th sent federal troops to Trinidad to restore order. The army confiscated guns from both sides, and gun shops and saloons were closed. The army also had orders not to escort out-of-state strikebreakers into the coal towns. However, C.F.&I. president Jesse Welborn later testified that strikebreakers came freely to Colorado from other states and were protected by the army as they took jobs in the coal towns (Long 1989a:299).

After order was restored the Ludlow Tent Colony was rebuilt and the strike dragged on for another seven months. During this time President Wilson sought to broker a settlement between the coal companies and strikers (Yellen 1936). His efforts were unsuccessful. The strike was eventually terminated by the UMWA on December 10, 1914. With strike funds depleted and new strikes called in other parts of the country the UMWA could no longer support the Colorado action. Some strikers with families remained on UMWA strike relief until February 1915. Others with families were rehired by C.F.&I. (Scamehorn 1992:51). Many drifted out-of-state, and still others joined the ranks of the unemployed.

Aftermath

The Ludlow massacre electrified the nation. Demonstrations and rallies protesting the killing of women and children erupted in cities all across the country (Long 1989a:296). Nearly every newspaper and magazine in the country covered the story, with pro- and anti-company editorials appearing side by side (Figure 15.4; see Long 1989a:308). John D. Rockefeller Jr. was excoriated in the national press and demonized in the eyes of the American public by such prominent progressives as Upton Sinclair and John Reed. In early 1915 a spectacular series of Congressional hearings exposed Rockefeller's role as a leading strategist in dealing with the Colorado strike (Foner 1980; Yellen 1936:220).

The widespread national reaction to Ludlow focused attention on living conditions in the Colorado coal towns and on workplace conditions throughout the United States (Adams 1966; Gitelman 1988). Rockefeller engaged labor relations expert W. L. Mackenzie King, who later became prime minister of Canada, to develop a plan for a series of reforms in the mines and company towns of southern Colorado. Known as the Colorado Industrial Plan, these reforms called for a worker grievance procedure, infrastructural improvements to company towns (e.g., construction of paved roads and recreational facilities such as YMCAs), enforcement of Colorado mining laws, and the election of worker representatives to serve with management on four standing committees concerned with working conditions, safety, sanitation, and recreation (Adams 1966; Gitelman 1988). The plan also forbade discrimination against workers suspected of having been union members in the past. However, it did not provide for recognition of the UMWA or agree to the principle of collective bargaining (Adams 1966).

The Setting of the Coal Field War 1913-1914

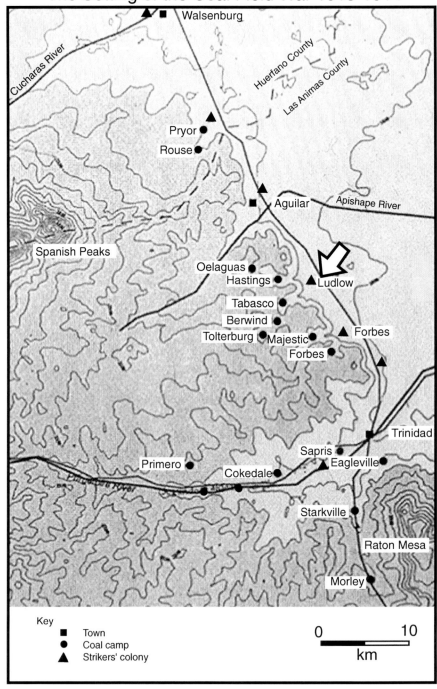

Figure 15.3 Map of the 40-mile front between Trinidad and Walsenburg

Figure 15.4 Cover of the periodical *Masses* (Denver Public Library, Western History Collection)

The Colorado Industrial Plan effectively established a company union. Feeling that there was little alternative, Colorado miners accepted the plan. It became effective on January 1, 1916 (Scamehorn 1992). But critics such as UMWA vice-president Frank Hayes condemned the plan as "pure paternalism" and "benevolent feudalism" (Adams 1966). Mother Jones declared the plan a "fraud" and a "hypocritical and dishonest pretense" (Adams 1966). Still, it served as the model for many other company unions, which spread across the country and by 1920 covered 1.5 million workers, about 8 percent of the workforce.

It is not clear what direct, practical impacts the Colorado Industrial Plan had on the lives of miners and their families. Some scholars see such industrial-era reforms as little more than corporate welfare, or an attempt to control immigrant workers by "Americanizing" them. The conventional wisdom is that the plan produced some real material gains for workers in the company towns (Crawford 1995; Roth 1992).

However, more research is required to settle this issue, especially archaeological research, since many of the claims for improvement originate with the coal companies themselves. Certainly the reforms were limited, as is indicated by the fact that throughout the 1920s the southern coal fields continued to be embroiled in strikes. Widespread union recognition in southern Colorado only came with New Deal legislation of the 1930s.

The Coal Field Strike in National and Global Context

Although especially dramatic, the hostilities at Ludlow were not unique for the times. They typified a period of industrial violence that defined the first couple of decades of the 20th century. This period is generally – and paradoxically – known as the Progressive Era. During the Progressive Era industrialization was established as the driving economic force in American society. Resources, human labor, and machine technology were brought together in largely urban contexts of factory production. Industrial production was accompanied by a deepening social class division between those who owned the technological means of producing wealth and those who contributed labor for its production. Progressive Era violence was thus sparked by two conflicting, class-based visions of workplace relations. Capital's vision privileged ownership as the most important party, on the assumption that business takes all the risks in producing national wealth. Labor's vision saw workers as central, given that worker effort directly creates national wealth.

Progressive Era clashes between capital and labor were as intense in the United States as in any nation faced with rapid economic and political change. Strikes, riots, and massacres punctuated the time period at regular intervals across the country (Foote 1997). On May 3, 1886 police killed four strikers and wounded many others during a violent confrontation between unionized workers and non-union strikebreakers at the McCormick Reaper Works in Chicago. This incident preceded by one day the bombing in Haymarket Square that killed and wounded several police and protestors. On July 6, 1892 Pinkerton security guards opened fire on striking Carnegie mill steelworkers in Homestead, Pennsylvania. Eleven strikers and spectators and seven guards were shot dead. On September 10, 1897 19 unarmed striking coal miners and mine workers were killed and 36 wounded by a sheriff's posse for refusing to disperse near Lattimer, Pennsylvania. On June 8, 1904 a battle between state militia and striking miners at Dunnville, Colorado ended with six union members dead and 15 taken prisoner. On December 25, 1909 a bomb destroyed a portion of the Llewellyn Ironworks in Los Angeles where a bitter strike was in progress. On February 24, 1912 police beat women and children during a textile strike in Lawrence, Massachusetts. Numerous other examples from across the nation could be cited. Ludlow's distinctiveness in this context of industrial violence stemmed from its relative geographical isolation on the Western frontier and the number of women and children who were casualties there (McGovern and Guttridge 1972).

Ludlow was also distinctive in terms of its especially high concentration of immigrant labor. Immigration combined with industrialization to form a volatile context for Progressive Era conflict. Many immigrants to America came to establish new lives, but others were looking for income that they could use to improve their lives back in their homelands. Whatever their motives, Progressive Era immigrant workers, like immigrants during earlier periods of American industrialization, largely came from rural, pre-industrial backgrounds. They were new to industrial production, and thus they brought work habits to the factory gate that could frustrate discipline- and cost-conscious manufacturers (Gutman 1977). American work rules and the idea of the "work week" also conflicted with a variety of other old-country cultural and religious practices. Gutman (1977) provides a number of examples. A Polish wedding in a Pennsylvania mining or mill town lasted three to five days. Eastern European Orthodox Jews held a festival eight days after the birth of a son without regard to what particular day that was (Gutman 1977:23). Greek and Roman Catholic workers shared the same jobs but observed different holy days, an annoyance to many employers. A chronic tension thus existed between native and immigrant men and women fresh to the factory and the demands imposed upon them by the regularities and disciplines of factory labor (Gutman 1977:13).

Industrialization and immigration opened the doors to intensified exploitation of working people by corporate interests all across the United States. There were no laws protecting workers' rights or union activity in 1913–14. Workers in many places were denied freedoms of speech and assembly. While labor's cause to redress these conditions has not always been a noble struggle for justice (Foote 1997), in almost every instance the fight between capital and labor was unequal. Capital was able to mobilize tremendous resources, from control of railroad and telegraph to control of local police and government, to further its agenda and suppress labor's cause (Harvey 1996). Progressive Era political and economic discourse came to be dominated by, as framed by Gitelman (1988), the Labor Question: "Can some way be found to accommodate the interests of Capital and Labor, or is their conflict – often violent and almost always incendiary in its emotional charge – bound to breach the existing order?"

The hostilities at Ludlow were also of a piece with processes and conflicts extending deeper into the history of the American West. As indicated earlier, the American West has long enjoyed romantic, mythic status as an open, empty region where rugged, bootstrapping individuals could make their fortunes unfettered by the constraints of class and ethnic background. The scholarly work of Frederick Jackson Turner, especially his 1893 essay *The Significance of the Frontier in American History*, did much to advance this classic, "triumphal" narrative of Western history (see also Turner 1920). While Turner's work was crucial for legitimizing the study of Western history, it left much out of the story. New Western Historians, among others, have challenged the romantic Turnerian image (Cronon et al. 1992; Limerick 1987, 1991; see also Nash 1991; Smith 1950). They have demonstrated the embeddedness of Western life and culture in larger, global historical processes of conquest, ethnic conflict, population migration, economic exploitation, and political domination. They have shown the effect of these processes on *all* sectors of society and on a variety of ethnic groups.

Indeed, even the West's great iconic symbol of economic free agency and self-sufficiency – the cowboy – is now known to have been shaped by capitalist class relationships emanating from the industrialized East and beyond. Many cowboys were wage laborers in the employ of ranches often organized as joint stock companies. Many didn't even own their own horses. As Papanikolas (1995:75) puts it, "Strip a cowboy of his horse . . . [and he was] but one more seasonal worker attached to the industrial world by railroads that led to Chicago stockyards and ranches owned as often as not by Eastern bankers or Scottish investors." The freedom of the cowboy was simply the freedom to choose his own master or to starve (McGuire and Reckner 2002:46). Most Americans have heard about the 1881 gunfight at the OK Corral; far fewer have heard about the 1883 Texas "Cowboy Strike" in which several hundred cowboys walked off their jobs at five major ranches (Curtin 1991:56–59), or the 1885 cowboy strike on Wyoming's Sweetwater (McGuire and Reckner 2002; Papanikolas 1995). Wallace Stegner, arguably our leading chronicler and writer about Western life, notes that "Cowboys didn't make the West; they only created the image by which it is mis-known. People like Louis Tikas made the West . . ." (Stegner 1982).

Class struggle of the sort that would explode with particular ferocity at Ludlow is thus deeply embedded in the history of the West and in a broader set of national and global processes. As noted earlier, Ludlow is generally regarded as the best example of open class warfare in American history. In the words of George West, a federal investigator of the coal field strike, "This rebellion constituted perhaps one of the nearest approaches to civil war and revolution ever known in this country in connection with an industrial conflict" (quoted in Long 1989a:170). This is an astonishing fact for many Americans. Astonishing, because we Americans need our myths, especially myths of simpler, timeless places that can serve as an antidote to the economic uncertainty and political insecurity of modern times. New Western Historians have connected belief in a West devoid of conflict and struggle to modern economic and political anxieties that require, for their containment, seamless, mythic, triumphal narratives (Cronon et al. 1992). These and other narratives are the subject of the next section.

Ludlow, Public Memory, and Official History

As noted previously, Ludlow and other sites of American industrial struggle are important to labor historians and unions but are generally erased from public memory. Public memory is a body of beliefs and ideas about the past that help a public or society understand its past, present, and future (Bodnar 1992:15). We can better understand the erasure of sites like Ludlow by drawing on Bodnar's distinction between *official* history and *vernacular* history. Official history is nationalistic and patriotic, emphasizing citizen duties over citizen rights. It emphasizes social unity and the continuity of the social order, and glosses over periods of contradiction, rupture, and transformation. Official history is progressive and triumphal. The ugly and violent events addressed by official history – like the Civil War – are usually presented as always having resulted in a better nation. Official history is publicly funded and professionally managed.

In contrast to official history, vernacular history is diverse and changing. Vernacular histories are local rather than national in orientation. They ultimately derive from the first-hand, everyday experience of those "ordinary people" who were directly involved with history's events. Vernacular histories are "passed around the kitchen table." In Bodnar's words, vernacular histories "convey what social reality feels like, rather than what it should be like" (Bodnar 1992:14). They thus threaten the sacred and timeless nature of official history. Vernacular histories of Ludlow are pro-union. They emphasize the militia's role in starting the shooting on April 20th and implicate the militia in many more atrocities against colonists on the day of the massacre. They also count many more casualties in the conflict, suggesting, for example, that additional bodies were removed from Ludlow during the three days that elapsed between the militia's closing of the burned camp and the arrival of Red Cross relief workers.

The distinction between official and vernacular history is, of course, ideal. How much vernacular history is expressed in public memory is a matter of negotiation between official and vernacular interests in communities. However, it is usually official history that wins in the end. Labor conflict and struggle, and vernacular histories generally, lack the onwards and upwards tendency of official history. As described by Foote (1997), labor's history is one of fits and starts, precedents and setbacks. It is a movement that has lurched from one crisis to another, trying to wrestle change out of diversity. It is a story that does not readily yield to grand, unified narratives. Labor conflict has little visibility in official history, and thus tangible evidence of this past – monuments and memorials marking labor's struggles – are few and far between. Labor's tangible memorials tend to be "homemade" and controversial in larger social circles. Memorials erected in crucibles of industrial conflict – like Harlan County, Kentucky and Windber, Pennsylvania – are often destroyed by civic authorities (Beik 1999; Scott 1995).

The silence of official history on the subject of labor struggle is not simply a case of powerful interests dominating the writing of history. Rather, it is often a case of the struggle being subconsciously ignored (McGuire and Walker 1999). In contemporary American ideology the United States is a classless society. Except for a few people who are very rich or very poor, Americans are all "middle-class." Cultural leaders in the United States, including those who produce and represent history, come from the ranks of middle-class professionals. They are purveyors of loyalty to larger political structures and existing institutions (Bodnar 1992:15). Thus, events that bear a resemblance to class warfare or even draw attention to the existence of classes are not easily squared with America's ideology of classlessness. Interestingly, this was not necessarily the case in the 19th century, when Americans commonly described their society in terms of class (Long 1989a). For example, in 1901 the Colorado Commissioner of Labor raised few eyebrows when he noted that "the absurdity of the old-time asininity that the interests of the laborer and the capitalist are identical is apparent to all intelligent people who understand the real cause of the conflict between the classes" (quoted in Long 1989a:53).

To see history as narrative and to recognize the existence of different kinds of histories is not to say that history is myth, or to take a relativist stance toward historical fact, or to bow to the gods of revisionism and political correctness. Such criticisms are fashionable today as researchers of hidden histories find more room to work within colleges, universities, and other institutions of cultural production like museums and heritage organizations. Rather, to see history as narrative is to say that facts and events are selectively filtered, screened, and interpreted in keeping with theoretical preconceptions and existing social realities. This is a central proposition of what we might call *critical* history. History, practiced well, is aware of this filtering process and the controlling biases of race, class, gender, and nationalism (Gorn 2000; see also Trigger 1984). Well-practiced history also recognizes conquest, conflict, exploitation, and domination. It looks squarely at the past, "warts and all" (Limerick 1998). Good history is "knowledge of painful things, painfully arrived at" (Gorn 2000).

At present, institutions of cultural production in southern Colorado privilege official history by emphasizing the area's place in romantic, mythic narratives of the "Old West." For example, Trinidad's civic leaders capitalize on their remarkably well-preserved late 19th-century downtown – the Corazon de Trinidad ("Heart of Trinidad") National Historic District – to celebrate its status as a rest stop on the Santa Fe Trail. Here, wagon trains could pause and recoup before heading over Raton Pass into New Mexico. Westward expansion and growth are the dominant themes of this official history. Histories of coal mining, company towns, and labor struggle – while not totally erased – are nonetheless marginal.

When coal mining history *is* addressed, it is through a soft-focus lens. That is, the history is sanitized, romanticized, and redefined as "heritage" (see also Brooke 1998; Lowenthal 1996; Poirier and Spude 1998). Such is the case at the town of Cokedale, a well-preserved company town located to the southwest of Ludlow. Here, the homey details of coal camp life are emphasized, along with the benevolent paternalism of the coal companies (but see Clyne 1999 for a demythologization, albeit indirect, of this homey image). Labor struggles, when mentioned, are attributed to outside agitators. This is in keeping with trends seen in other deindustrializing regions of the United States, such as the coal mining and steel towns of Pennsylvania (Abrams 1994; Brant 1996; Mondale 1994; Staub 1994; Stewart 1997). This trend is disturbing because it does not serve the cause of accurate history.

Colorado Coal Field Archaeology

The scholarly goal of the Colorado Coal Field War Archaeological Project is to produce a more complete, and thus more accurate, history of industrial process on the Western frontier. Official histories of Ludlow, when they address this episode in American industrial relations, focus on famous people and events, and the organizing activities of the UMWA. We have only anecdotal information about the everyday lives and relationships of the ethnically diverse population that comprised the labor force. Archaeology can flesh out their side of the story, address official history's blindspots, and help produce a fuller understanding of cultural and historical process.

Our approach is informed by a relational view of class (Wurst 1999). Class is understood as a fluid set of processes that govern the appropriation of surplus labor, and that articulate in complex ways with non-class processes governing flows of property, power, and meaning. Class relations are historically situated and over-determined by kinship, community, gender, and ethnicity. We are interested in the specific class and non-class strategies that workers used to resist exploitation, build solidarity across ethnic boundaries, make a living while out on strike, and inter-relate with wider communities.

Specific research questions include the following. To what extent did the shared domestic experience of women and children in the company towns reinforce the class solidarity built up among men in the mine shafts? Once on strike, how did families support themselves, especially given minimal strike relief? How was the considerable ethnic diversity of the tent colonies integrated so as to defuse tension and foster a collective class consciousness that could sustain the strike for 15 months? To what extent did coal camp life really improve following the strike?

To answer these questions we are taking a comparative perspective on coal camp and tent colony life. The Ludlow excavations provide the strike context, and we are excavating in pre- and post-strike contexts at the Berwind coal camp above Ludlow, from which many of the Ludlow colonists came. We are looking to test documentary and vernacular accounts of life in the coal camps and tent colonies as well as to investigate other ways – unrecorded by history – in which miners might have been coping with their circumstances.

The archaeological contexts have good integrity and abundant remains. The assemblages at Ludlow – clothing, jewelry, children's toys, bullets, cartridges – speak to a hurried, catastrophic abandonment. We have only begun to analyze the material, but a few observations provide a sense of how our findings compare to the historical record and the expected responses of labor to strike conditions.

From photos of burned and demolished tents we know that the tents were constructed over wooden joists laid directly on the ground to support a wooden platform and frame. Our excavations have uncovered one of these platforms, defined by stains in the earth and rows of nails that followed the joists (Figure 15.5). A wide variety of artifacts associated with the floor – men's and women's clothing, toys, diaper pins – indicates occupation by a family. The assemblage also includes a suspender part bearing an inscription in Italian of "Society of Tyrolean Alpinists," and several Catholic religious medallions. This suggests Italian Catholic ethnicity, and provides a reference point for reconstructing the spatial organization of the camp. Future study will attempt to determine the extent to which the spatial organization of ethnic groups in the tent colony duplicated or departed from the ethnic segregation of the company towns.

Historical photos also indicate that cellars were dug beneath the Ludlow tents. Historians suggest that these cellars were used as shelter from gunfire. Excavation

Figure 15.5 Excavated tent platform (courtesy Mark Walker)

of tent cellar locations reveals a variety of uses beyond protection, including storage and possibly habitation. Sub-floor features range in size from small pits to "full basements" measuring 2 × 2.5 × 2 m deep. They are very well prepared – hard-packed and/or fabric-lined – with wall niches for storage. Thus, the miners were clearly dug in for the long haul.

We are especially interested in what dietary remains at Ludlow can tell us about patterns of local interaction and support, specifically the extent to which strikers may have drawn on local merchants and other sources. Our trash pit and midden excavations reveal an enormous reliance on canned foods, much more than what we see in working-class contexts at Berwind (Figure 15.6). Some of this canned food is undoubtedly union-supplied. At the same time, some features contain lots of evidence for home canning, such as mason jars. This would certainly imply access to local farmers or gardens for fresh vegetables and fruit. Similarly, cow bones showing up in Ludlow deposits may suggest local supply from area ranchers. Further faunal analysis may disclose patterns of meat-sharing within the tent colony.

It is interesting to consider the strikers' use of national brands in canned food and milk as a possible *cover* for local support in the form of prepared foods and garden and ranch products. The tent colonies were subject to search, and thus any distinctive, locally produced goods could have been traced to particular merchants. In his work on marginalized households in Annapolis, Mullins (1999) shows that

Figure 15.6 Excavated trash pit with cans

African Americans purchased national name brand, price-controlled foods as a way to avoid exploitation by local merchants. Strikers at Ludlow may have done the same, but in this instance as a strategy to protect local, striker-friendly merchants from harassment by coal company operatives and state militiamen. This would make sense as part of labor's commitment to using *place* – understood as social ties of kin and community that link workers to family and friends employed in local business, health care, and law enforcement – as a way to offset capital's greater command of *space* through control of markets, telegraph, railroad, and other technologies (Harvey 1996).

Our most direct evidence of local connections lies in beer and whiskey bottles, whose embossing and labeling reflects Trinidad origins. The frequency of alcohol bottles is higher at Ludlow compared to what we see in the working-class precincts in Berwind. Social drinking is an important part of male working-class culture. Corporate control of the company towns meant control of leisure. Greater alcohol consumption at Ludlow reflects either the greater freedom of workers from company surveillance given their control of place or, alternatively, efforts to relieve boredom and stress under strike conditions. Companies certainly pushed prohibition after the strike, as reflected by the relative paucity of liquor bottles in excavated post-strike assemblages at Berwind.

Comparisons of pre- and post-strike coal camp deposits reveal some interesting changes in household strategy over time. Wood's (2002) study of the Berwind remains shows how working-class women in the company towns were able to raise families on miners' wages that would not even feed two people. Trash dating before the strike contains lots of tin cans, large cooking pots, and big serving vessels. Families took in single male miners as boarders to make the extra income and women used canned foods to make stews and soups to feed them. After the strike the companies discouraged boarders but the wages still remained very low. The tin cans and big pots disappear from the trash to be replaced by canning jars and lids, and the bones of rabbits and chickens. Women and children who could no longer earn money from boarders instead produced food at home to feed the family. As noted earlier, it remains to be seen whether post-strike contexts suggest an overall improvement in worker living conditions over time.

Analysis of coal field archaeological material is thus producing some potentially interesting leads for reconstructing labor's strategies in Western coal towns and striker tent colonies. In the next section, I take up the other, explicitly political, goal of the project: our use of these findings to engage contemporary working-class histories and interests.

Ludlow in Contemporary Political Context

The last coal mines in the southern Colorado coal field closed in 1996 when capital moved its focus to the northern fields in Wyoming. Trainloads of this northern coal now rumble daily past the ruined Ludlow depot and our archaeological excavations. Although the southern coal fields are quiet, many of the everyday realities that provided context for the Ludlow massacre – workplace danger, corporate greed, chronic tension between capital and labor, and official neglect of America's working people and their histories – are still with us.

Coal mining remains a dangerous occupation. Since 1910, when the Bureau of Mines began compiling statistics, 80,400 men have died in American coal mines, and 1.5 million others have suffered disabling injuries (McGovern and Guttridge 1972). On September 23, 2001 two explosions rocked the Blue Creek No. 5 underground mine in Brookwood, Alabama, the nation's deepest at 2,140 feet beneath the surface. Thirteen coal miners were killed in the explosions. According to the federal Mine Safety and Health Administration the coal company, Jim Walter Resources Inc., has a mixed safety record. In 2000 its count of serious injuries was nearly double the industry average. Subsequent investigation into the September

2001 disaster revealed that prior to the explosions MSHA inspectors had cited Walters Resources for 31 violations – including high levels of free-floating combustible coal dust – that they allegedly never followed up on (Roberts 2002).

The Quecreek mining incident in Pennsylvania that riveted the American public and much of the world for more than three days in July 2002 is also relevant. Although it ended with the joyful rescue of nine trapped miners, it raised additional questions about mine safety in contemporary America. The number of coal miner deaths in America has risen each of the past three years. Yet, the Bush Administration is currently lobbying to cut the Mine Safety and Health Administration's budget, primarily from the agency's coal enforcement division (Roberts 2002). In light of the Pennsylvania incident, enforcement would seem to be the one area that requires beefing up, not trimming down, lest we repeat the workplace tragedies that led to Ludlow.

Perhaps the most relevant current example of the chronic tension between labor and capital is directly linked to the events of 1913–14. It concerns the current strike in Colorado pitting Pueblo steelworkers against Rocky Mountain Steel – formerly C.F.&I. – a subsidiary of Oregon Steel. The steelworkers have been on strike since October 1997 to stop forced overtime and thus regain one of the basic rights for which the Ludlow strikers died: the eight-hour workday. The Pueblo strikers have used Ludlow as a powerful symbol in their struggle. They rally at the UMWA's annual Ludlow memorial service, and they have set up a symbolic "Camp Ludlow" at Oregon Steel headquarters in Portland. In fact, it is the power of Ludlow's symbolism that led Oregon Steel to change the name of its Pueblo subsidiary from C.F.&I. to Rocky Mountain Steel, as a way to distance itself from the events of 1914. But Oregon Steel is determined to break the steelworkers union and thus deprive workers of another of the basic rights for which the Ludlow strikers fought: the right to collective bargaining.

Thus, we should not be fooled into thinking that the concerns of the old industrial world have any less resonance in, or are any less relevant to, today's "post-industrial" one. On this point, Zinn (1970:100) considers three ways to read the Ludlow massacre. One reading is to view Ludlow narrowly, as an incident in the history of the trade union movement and the coal industry. On this reading, Ludlow is an "angry splotch" in the past, fading rapidly amidst new events. A second reading is to see Ludlow as a problem in personal responsibility. This reading focuses on who was to blame. Rockefeller and his corporate managers? Tikas and his unruly Greek compatriots? Linderfelt and his hired guns? A third reading sees Ludlow as a commentary on a larger set of questions concerning the structural relationship of government to corporate power, and the relationship of both to social protest movements.

It is this third reading that connects Ludlow to the present, and articulates with the concerns of a critical archaeology. Our project has embraced this reading, and in so doing has become a form of political action (Leone 1995; Ludlow Collective 2001). Our scholarship is fused with working-class interests and histories, and this anchors the various public outreach initiatives generated by our work. Our work has been featured in numerous local and regional newspaper articles and on

Colorado Public Radio. In these contexts we remind citizens that the workplace rights we enjoy and tend to take for granted today were won via struggle and paid for in blood. We share the speaker's platform with union leaders at the annual Ludlow memorial service and thereby contribute to that 85-year-old commemorative tradition – a tradition evidenced by one of the more evocative artifacts produced by our excavation, a bent, rusted wreath stand recovered from a trash-filled, still undated privy. Our Summer Teacher Institutes consider ways to incorporate Colorado's nationally and internationally significant labor history into high school curricula, and ways to fruitfully negotiate between competing official, vernacular, and critical histories. Our middle-school classroom history trunk seeks to enlighten an even younger generation about Colorado's labor history. These varied activities cultivate an audience for archaeological work and help to perpetuate our discipline while they promote critical thought about society and, at times, gently agitate for change.

Our project is also contributing in more tangible ways to public memorialization of labor history sites. We have produced an interpretive kiosk for Ludlow and a historical marker for Berwind that is modeled on Corazon de Trinidad markers celebrating Santa Fe Trail history. They remind tourists of the Colorado immigrant's role in building the West, and Ludlow's legacy for securing workplace rights. They add to an emerging commemorative landscape recognizing southeastern Colorado's mining history (e.g., Figure 15.7). In 1996 the homemade UMWA signs directing tourists to the Ludlow Massacre Memorial were replaced by official brown heritage signs. In May 1997 a memorial to coal miners who died in southern Colorado mines was erected by the Hispanic Chamber of Commerce in the middle of the Trinidad Historic District. All these efforts add a much-needed critical, counter-classic quality to the area's existing commemorative landscape.

Conclusion

In 1991 a United States House of Representatives report confessed that "the history of work and working people . . . is not adequately represented or preserved" in the United States (report cited in Foote 1997:303). The Colorado Coal Field War Archaeological Project is an attempt to redress this situation in the American West. Our work has produced some promising leads for fleshing out working-class agency and history in a region long dominated by seamless, mythic narratives of territorial expansion and progress. It has also connected with political issues around work in contemporary America. Ludlow is still a place to be reckoned with in this regard. By raising public awareness of the coal field strike we narrow the gulf between past and present and make archaeology relevant to contemporary life.

Our work is also helping to enrich an impoverished commemorative landscape. Foote (1997) predicts that we will see more recognition of "landscapes of violence and tragedy" – including landscapes of labor struggle – in the years ahead. He suggests that many sites will be commemorated as a way to thwart destruction by economic development, much as Civil War sites were saved. But we might also hope that such sites will be commemorated by civic *choice* as the blindspots of official

Figure 15.7 The Ludlow Massacre Memorial

history become too conspicuous and compelling to ignore. Archaeology can and should play an important role in this effort.

The events that took place in the southern Colorado coal field are not happy ones. By acknowledging their existence, fleshing them out via archaeological research, and analyzing them from a critical perspective we produce more complete, and better, histories. To the extent that this critical encounter with unhappy events also broadens the cast of characters involved in the making of America, we produce more democratic histories. Blind allegiance to "Fourth of July historiography" – one that celebrates heroic events and suppresses horrific ones – is not befitting a genuine democracy (Dower 1995). By struggling with the ambiguities in, and conflicts between, alternative histories of America's past we can better sharpen our skills of critical thought, evaluation, and debate. In so doing we stand to gain better histories, better students, and better citizens.

ACKNOWLEDGMENTS

This chapter draws on many ideas and insights that have been percolating over the last six years among students and professors associated with the Colorado Coal Field War Archaeological Project. Substantive contributions have been made by Mark Walker, Randy McGuire, Paul Reckner, Margaret Wood, and Phil Duke. The Colorado Coal Field War Archaeological Project has been generously supported by a broad spectrum of community institutions, including the Colorado Historical Society–State Historical Fund, Trinidad State Junior College, the Trinidad History Museum, the United Mine Workers of America, UMWA Trinidad Local #9856, the Colorado Endowment for the Humanities, and the Colorado Digitization Project. This chapter also draws on the work of colleagues who have contributed to Colorado Endowment of the Humanities Summer Teacher Institutes. These include participating scholars Joe Bonacquista, Silvio Caputo, Joanne Dodds, Sybil Downing, Philip Duke, Jay Fell, Julie Greene, Randall McGuire, Laurel Vartebedian, Mark Walker, Margaret Wood, and Zeese Papanikolas.

REFERENCES

Abrams, J., 1994 Lost frames of reference: Sightings of history and memory in Pennsylvania's documentary landscape. In *Conserving Culture: A New Discourse on Heritage*. M. Hufford, ed. Pp. 24–38. Urbana: University of Illinois Press.

Adams, G., 1966 *The Age of Industrial Violence, 1910–1915: The Activities and Findings of the U.S. Commission on Industrial Relations*. New York: Columbia University Press.

Beik, M., 1999 Commemoration and contestation: Remembering the unsung miners of Windber Pennsylvania. Paper presented at the North American Labor History Conference, Detroit, Michigan.

Beshoar, B., 1957 *Out of the Depths: The Story of John R. Lawson, a Labor Leader*. Denver: Colorado Historical Commission and Denver Trades & Labor Assembly.

Bodnar, J., 1992 *Remaking America: Public Memory, Commemoration, and Patriotism in the Twentieth Century*. Princeton, NJ: Princeton University Press.

Brant, J., 1996 Unemployment: The theme park. *New York Times Magazine*. January 28, 46–47.

Brooke, J., 1998 West celebrates mining's past, but not its future. *New York Times*, October 4.

Clyne, R., 1999 *Coal People: Life in Southern Colorado's Company Towns, 1890–1930* Denver: Colorado Historical Society.

Crawford, M., 1995 *Building the Workingman's Paradise: The Design of American Company Towns*. London: Verso.

Cronon, W., G. Miles, and J. Gitlin, 1992 Becoming West: Toward a new meaning for Western history, *Under an Open Sky: Rethinking America's Western Past*. W. Cronon, G. Miles, and J. Gitlin, eds. Pp. 3–27. New York: W. W. Norton.

Curtin, D., 1991 Structuring history: Perceptions of American cowboy culture. Master's thesis, Binghamton University, Binghamton, NY.

Delle, J., S. Mrozowski, and R. Paynter, eds., 2000 *Lines That Divide: Historical Archaeologies of Race, Class, and Gender.* Knoxville: University of Tennessee Press.

Dower, J., 1995 How a genuine democracy should celebrate its past. *The Chronicle of Higher Education,* June 16.

Foner, P., 1980 *History of the Labor Movement in the United States,* vol. 5: *The AFL in the Progressive Era, 1910–1915.* New York: International Publishers.

Foote, K., 1997 *Shadowed Ground: America's Landscapes of Violence and Tragedy.* Austin: University of Texas Press.

Gitelman, H., 1988 *Legacy of the Ludlow Massacre: A Chapter in American Industrial Relations.* Philadelphia: University of Pennsylvania Press.

Gorn, E., 2000 Professing history: Distinguishing between memory and the past. *The Chronicle of Higher Education,* April 28.

Gutman, H., 1977 *Work, Culture, and Society.* New York: Vintage Books.

Hardesty, D., 1991 Historical archaeology in the American West. *Historical Archaeology* 25, 3–6.

Harvey, D., 1996 *Justice, Nature and the Geography of Difference.* Oxford: Blackwell.

Jameson, E., 1998 *All That Glitters: Class, Conflict, and Community in Cripple Creek.* Urbana: University of Illinois Press.

Leone, M., 1995 A historical archaeology of capitalism. *American Anthropologist* 97, 251–268.

Leone, M., and P. Potter, eds., 1999 *Historical Archaeologies of Capitalism.* New York: Plenum Press.

Limerick, P., 1987 *The Legacy of Conquest.* New York: Norton.

—— 1991 What on earth is the New Western History? In *Trails: Toward a New Western History.* P. Limerick, C. Milner, and C. Rankin Lawrence, eds. Pp. 81–88. Lawrence: University of Kansas Press.

—— 1998 Hard look at heroes. *The Denver Post,* June 7, G-01.

Little, B., 1994 People with history: An update on historical archaeology in the United States. *Journal of Archaeological Method and Theory* 1, 5–40.

Long, P., 1985 The women of the Colorado fuel and iron strike. In *Women, Work and Protest: A Century of US Women's Labor History.* R. Milkman, ed. Pp. 62–85. London: Routledge & Kegan Paul.

—— 1989a *Where the Sun Never Shines: A History of America's Bloody Coal Industry.* New York: Paragon House.

—— 1989b The voice of the gun: Colorado's great coalfield war of 1913–1914. *Labor's Heritage* 1, 4–23.

Lowenthal, D., 1996 *Possessed by the Past: The Heritage Crusade and the Spoils of History.* New York: The Free Press.

Ludlow Collective, 2001 Archaeology of the Colorado Coal Field War, 1913–1914. In *Archaeologies of the Contemporary Past.* V. Buchli and G. Lucas, eds. Pp. 94–107. London: Routledge.

Matthews, C., M. Leone, and K. Jordan, 2002 The political economy of archaeological cultures. *Journal of Social Archaeology* 2, 109–134.

McGovern, G., and L. Guttridge, 1972 *The Great Coalfield War.* Boston: Houghton Mifflin.

McGuire, R., and M. Walker, 1999 Class confrontations in archaeology. *Historical Archaeology* 33, 159–183.

McGuire, R., and P. Reckner, 2002 The unromantic West: Labor, capital, and struggle. *Historical Archaeology* 36, 44–58.

Mondale, C., 1994 Conserving a problematic past. In *Conserving Culture: A New Discourse on Heritage.* M. Hufford, ed. Pp. 15–23. Urbana: University of Illinois Press.

Mullins, P., 1999 "A bold and gorgeous front": The contradictions of African-American consumer culture. In *Historical Archaeologies of Capitalism*. M. Leone and P. Potter, eds. Pp. 169–194. New York: Plenum Press.

Nash, G., 1991 *Creating the West: Historical Interpretations, 1890–1990*. Albuquerque: University of New Mexico Press.

O'Neal, M. T., 1971 *Those Damn Foreigners*. Minerva, CA: Hollywood Press.

Orser, C., 1996 *A Historical Archaeology of the Modern World*. New York: Plenum Press.

Papanikolas, Z., 1982 *Buried Unsung: Louis Tikas and the Ludlow Massacre*. Salt Lake City: University of Utah Press.

—— 1995 Cowboys, wobblies, and the myth of the West. In *Trickster in the Land of Dreams*. Z. Papanikolas, ed. Pp. 73–91. Lincoln: University of Nebraska Press.

Paynter, R., 1988 Steps to an archaeology of capitalism. In *The Recovery of Meaning: Historical Archaeology in the Eastern United States*. M. Leone and P. Potter, eds. Pp. 407–433. Washington, DC: Smithsonian Institution Press.

Paynter, R., and R. McGuire, 1991 The archaeology of inequality: Material culture, domination, and resistance. In *The Archaeology of Inequality*. R. McGuire and R. Paynter, eds. Pp. 1–27. Oxford: Blackwell.

Poirier, D., and R. Spude, eds., 1998 *America's Mining Heritage*. Washington, DC: National Park Service.

Roberts, C., 2002 Protecting the coal miner. *Pittsburgh Gazette*, July 30.

Roth, L., 1992 Company towns in the Western United States. In *The Company Town: Architecture and Society in the Early Industrial Age*. J. Garner, ed. Pp. 173–205. New York: Oxford University Press.

Scamehorn, H. L., 1992 *Mill and Mine: The CF&I in the Twentieth Century*. Lincoln: University of Nebraska Press.

Scott, J. 1985 *Weapons of the Weak: Everyday Forms of Peasant Resistance*. New Haven: Yale University Press.

Scott, S., 1995 *Two Sides To Everything: The Cultural Construction of Class Consciousness in Harlan County, Kentucky*. Albany: State University of New York Press.

Seligman, E., 1914a The crisis in Colorado. *The Annalist*, May 4.

—— 1914b Colorado's civil war and its lessons. *Leslie's Illustrated Weekly Newspaper*, November 5.

Smith, H. N., 1950 *Virgin Land: The American West as Symbol and Myth*. New York: Vintage Books.

Staub, S., 1994 Cultural conservation and economic recovery planning: The Pennsylvania Heritage Parks program. In *Conserving Culture: A New Discourse on Heritage*. M. Hufford, ed. Pp. 229–244. Urbana: University of Illinois Press.

Stegner, W., 1982 Foreword. In *Buried Unsung: Louis Tikas and the Ludlow Massacre*. Zeese Papanikolas. Pp. xiii–xix. Salt Lake City: University of Utah Press.

Stewart, D., 1997 Saving American Steel. *Smithsonian*, August, 86–93.

Sunsieri, A., 1972 *The Ludlow Massacre: A Study in the Mis-employment of the National Militia*. Waterloo, IA: Salvadore Books.

Trigger, B., 1984 Alternative archaeologies: Nationalist, colonialist, imperialist. *Man* 19, 355–370.

Trouillot, M., 1995 *Silencing the Past: Power and the Production of History*. Boston: Beacon Press.

Turner, F. J., 1920 *The Frontier in American History*. New York: Holt, Reinhart & Winston.

Vallejo, M. E., 1998 Recollections of the Colorado coal strike, 1913–1914. In *La Gente: Hispano History and Life in Colorado*. V. De Baca, ed. Pp. 85–104. Denver: Colorado Historical Society.

Van Bueren, T., ed., 2002 Communities Defined by Work: Life in Western Work Camps. *Historical Archaeology* 36 (whole volume).

Walker, M., 2000 Labor history at the ground level. *Labor's Heritage* 11, 60–75.

Whiteside, J., 1990 *Regulating Danger*. Lincoln: University of Nebraska Press.

Wood, M., 2002 Fighting for our homes: An archaeology of women's domestic labor and social change in a working class, coal mining community, 1900–1930. Ph.D. dissertation, Syracuse University.

Wurst, L., 1999 Internalizing class in historical archaeology. *Historical Archaeology* 33, 7–21.

Wurst, L., and R. Fitts, eds., 1999 Confronting Class. *Historical Archaeology* 33 (whole volume).

Wylie, A., 1993 Invented lands/discovered pasts: The westward expansion of myth and history. *Historical Archaeology* 27, 1–19.

Yellen, S., 1936 *American Labor Struggles*. New York: Harcourt, Brace.

Zinn, H., 1970 *The Politics of History*. Boston: Beacon Press.

Glossary

agency The active construction of social relations, *identities*, and *histories* by individuals in social contexts. Agency may involve conscious choices and strategies, spontaneous cultural actions, and traditional *practices*.

agriculture Intensive crop production involving fields rather than just gardens (as opposed to *horticulture*).

amaranth The starchy seeds from this annual plant were boiled or parched. With other starchy seeds (maygrass, goosefoot, little barley, and knotweed), a source of carbohydrates.

American Bottom A 120 km stretch of Mississippi River floodplain, 4–16 km wide, between the points where the Missouri and Kaskaskia rivers empty into the Mississippi.

AMS (Accelerator Mass Spectrometry) **dating** A specialized *radiocarbon dating* technique that requires less carbon than conventional carbon-14 techniques.

anaerobic Oxygen-poor depositional context that inhibits bacterial growth and preserves organic artifacts.

Archaic As originally defined, a cultural-historical period, stage, or tradition characterized by non-sedentary to semi-sedentary hunter-gatherer people of the early *Holocene* era.

artifact A portable, culturally modified object with observable or measurable *attributes*.

assemblage A set of artifacts from a cultural feature, site, region, or time period about which inferences are made by archaeologists.

atlatl Central Mexican (Nahuatl) word for a spearthrower stick used to propel a spear or *dart* with significantly enhanced thrust and killing power.

attribute The smallest observable unit of analysis of an *artifact*, *feature*, or human body.

axis mundi Literally "world axis," a term that refers to the idea held by many ancient peoples that there was a central point in the universe that linked this world with upper and lower worlds.

behaviorism Advocating behavior, rather than *culture*, as the basis for long-term changes in human populations. Behavior has its basis in universal cognitive, physiological, or neurological qualities of the human species rather than in the specificities of cultural histories.

B.P. Radiocarbon dates are usually expressed as "rcybp" (radiocarbon years before present) or simply "B.P." (before present) with "present" taken to be A.D. 1950, the date after which atomic testing led to elevated levels of radioactive carbon isotopes in the earth's atmosphere.

cache A deposit of cultural objects, stashed for later use or buried as part of a commemorative event. Pronounced "cash."

ceremonial center An place with sacred connotations or a long history of use where populations meet to practice community rituals.

charnel house Derived from "carnal," meaning literally a "flesh house." A sacred building where human remains of the ancestors were stored or buried, sometimes the same as a temple.

chenopodium, or **chenopods** Also called "goosefoot," the starchy seeds of this annual plant were either boiled or parched. With other starchy seeds (maygrass, amaranth, little barley, and knotweed), a source of carbohydrates.

chiefdom A territorial and hierarchical yet *communal* society with a centralized but kin-based elite who administered the food-producing populace.

chronometric Methods for the construction of archaeological chronologies including absolute and relative dating techniques.

city A populous center distinguished by the segregated administrative, religious, residential, and storage facilities of distinct social groups, craft producers, *specialists*, and administrators. Cities are usually large sites where otherwise unrelated social groups live together in such urban or proto-urban arrangements.

collectors Sometimes called *logistical hunter-gatherers*, characterized by large base camps occupied on a semi-permanent basis. Also refers to present-day people who obtain or excavate material culture from an archaeological site.

communal Based on the principles or practices of a *community*.

community Sometimes conflated with a *settlement*, a social *identity* that forms around collective experiences often but not exclusively in the context of particular settlements. Communities form as people "imagine" themselves attached to a particular place or *tradition*, comprised of or cross-cutting other social identities (lineages, clans, houses, families, etc.).

complex As in a ceremonial complex or agricultural complex, a term used to group together a series of *sites*, symbols, crops, or objects that share a historical relationship.

component The archaeological remains of a single *phase*, period, or time *horizon* at a single site, as in the "Late Period component of the Channel Islands." There may be several components at any given site.

conch or whelk shell The shell of a marine gastropod or snail widely used in the manufacture of bodily ornaments (such as pendants, gorgets, or beads).

corporate or corporate group A relationship among people within a *community* defined by a common *identity*, common purpose or interests, collective effort, and ancestry. Depending on context, these often include kin-based groups (lineages or extended families), but could also include age-based, gender-based, or status-based groups.

corporeality The bodily dimension of culture-making and lived experience.

cosmology A set of beliefs about the organizing principles of the universe, its creation, and the place of supernatural forces and people in it.

creole A term most often used to refer to someone of mixed racial ancestry in New World contexts. Also sometimes used by those studying the Spanish colonial contexts to refer to a first-generation individual of pure Spanish ancestry living in the New World.

creolization A term used to refer to processes of *identity* creation by peoples in multiethnic or *pluralistic* communities who combined new and more familiar cultural *traditions* and material culture to create new social, political, and cultural *practices* and traditions.

cucurbits A genetic grouping of plants that includes squash, pumpkins, and gourds. These were possibly cultivated in eastern North America as early as or earlier than in Mesoamerica. They comprise an important component of *horticultural* complexes.

cultigen A cultivated crop subject to the selective pressures that lead to *domestication*.

cultural evolution Processes that affect the long-term development of *societies* or human *behaviors*. Sometimes used as synonymous with long-term historical change, evolutionism may also be seen as antithetical to historical approaches to culture change, which include advocates of theories of human *agency*, *practice*, and embodiment.

culture The isolatable practices of a group of people, usually living in proximity, and their descendants over time. Typically conceived of as distinguishing a group of people from others.

culture history The lived experiences and cultural changes of a population in the aggregate. Also, a mode of archaeological investigation, common to the first half of the 20th century, concerned with the tracking of cultures through time and across space, where culture was assumed to be shared and normative.

dart point The chipped-stone, groundstone, or bone tip of a fletched spear or projectile propelled with the aid of an *atlatl*.

Direct Historical Approach Associated with William D. Strong and Walter Wedel in their work with Plains groups, this approach consists of the application of analogies derived from more recent peoples to the presumed ancestors of those peoples.

domestication The process whereby plants (*cultigens*) or animals become genetically altered through cultural practices (*horticulture*, *agriculture*, arboriculture, aquaculture) such that they evolve into a population (of domesticates) distinct from their wild progenitors.

down-the-line exchange The transfer of objects from hand to hand or between a string of trading partners or relatives such that the endpoint of an object is far removed from its origin point.

Eastern Agricultural Complex An array of cultigens and domesticates that came under cultivation during the Archaic and Woodland periods in the eastern United States: amaranth, chenopodium, cucurbits, knotweed, sunflower, maygrass, little barley, and more.

ecotone The unique transition zone between two ecological zones.

egalitarian A term for any society in which status differences are not significant and not inherited, but are the products of individual achievements during life and are subject to change in different settings.

equifinality The principle that different historical trajectories or alternate causes may lead to a common end result (i.e., social inequality, food production intensification, etc.).

essentialize The problematic treatment of a phenomenon as if it is a thing, a fact, or an "essence" that itself does not change and therefore requires no historical explanation. North American archaeologists have commonly essentialized such things as culture, ritual, households, kin groups, communities, gender, and power strategies.

ethnoarchaeology The study of present-day, living people to understand how certain types of human behavior left behind archaeological signatures, such that archaeologists can use them as analogs to interpret the past.

evolution In biology, descent with modification; in archaeology, the modification of a thing, population, or society without agency and thus outside the control of people. See *cultural evolution*.

experimental archaeology The replication of some past activity (say, pot-making or flintknapping) in order to understand the relationship between the physical properties of raw material, the mechanics of manufacture or use, and the array of technical choices open to a person in the past.

feature A non-portable element of the cultural landscape such as a hearth, a postmold, a pit, a house, or an activity area.

focus In the terms of the Midwestern Taxonomic System of William C. McKern, a grouping of components at a number of different sites with some social or cultural significance.

foragers Hunter-gatherers characterized by ephemeral camps occupied on a seasonal basis. Sometimes called *residential mobility*, entire band groups moved across the land to extract resources from known locations. Sometimes treated as if at the opposite end of the mobility spectrum from *collectors*.

formation processes The cultural or natural forces involved in the structuring of the archaeological record, including the deposition or accumulation of human residues and the weathering or deterioration of culturally modified things and landforms. Also called depositional processes and closely related to taphonomic processes.

gorgets Ornaments suspended from necklaces like pendants but typically with two suspension holes so that the ornament is prevented from freely rotating, thus exposing one side to view. Often made of shell or stone.

heterarchy Sometimes seen as an alternative to *hierarchy*, actually refers to the non-hierarchical relationship between social segments, groups, factions, etc. within a society or within a hierarchical tier such that multiple lines of authority are associated with different groups or practices (example: the coexistence of independent religious and political hierarchies).

hierarchy A formal and lasting relationship in which one party has greater power, control, or status than another.

history, official The construction of social *memory* sanctioned by authorities. Often known as popular histories.

history, vernacular or unofficial The unsanctioned construction of social *memories* through cultural *practices*, lived experiences, or everyday political actions. This accounting is often silenced in popular histories.

Holocene The geological epoch that describes the post-Pleistocene era, the warmer conditions present most everywhere by 10,000 B.P. that continues today.

horizon, horizon markers A cultural phenomenon that cross-cuts peoples and *regions* and is identifiable by a common material or *iconographic* marker or set of symbols.

horticulture The low-intensity *practices* of gardening.

hunter-gatherers People who make a living by collecting or foraging the natural bounty of the environment without organized labor investments that alter that environment.

hybridity The condition of multiple overlapping and interdigitated cultural differences in one place or region that cross-cut social *identities* and peoples and thus possess generative potential.

iconography A set of written symbols or motifs that form a body of meaning or a discourse.

identity A set of practices, meanings, or characteristics attributed to a bounded group of people.

ideology A politicized or projected set of cultural practices and dispositions that unify or cross-cut a people, a landscape, or larger body of cultural practices and dispositions. Individuals and populations can likewise be characterized by multiple ideologies.

landscape The terrain upon which people experience reality, recursively related to the cultural construction of that reality by people.

lineage A specialized form of kinship group based on descent through a line of people, often people of one sex (matrilineal, patrilineal), that joins people over time, binding ancestors and descendants.

locality Loosely used to designate a geographic area that includes a number of *settlements*, *communities*, or subpopulations. In contemporary anthropological terms, a historical divergent area within a macro-scale cultural pattern or global community.

logical positivist A person who adheres to the philosophical position that holds knowledge to be a deductive process, where specific conclusions are reached by starting with general law-like principles.

logistical mobility The movements of a group of *collectors* according to logistical planning that target resource extraction, retrieval by small task groups and return to the base camp.

maize Corn, *domesticated* in Mesoamerica from the wild teosinte plant and subsequently carried to North America, either through visitations or in a *down-the-line* fashion.

materiality The material dimension of culture-making, cultural *landscapes*, or *practices*. The principle of materiality underlies one contemporary sense of human *agency*, and holds that thought and action are not easily separable and occur through experience in the material dimension.

memory More than simply an individual neurological capability, refers to social memory, a collective construction that entails power relations, lived experiences, compromises, and the promotion of the recollections of some over others.

mica A rare, thin, flat, mirror-like and flaky crystalline mineral that forms in large platelets in black (biotite) or clear whitish (muscovite) varieties. Used for special cut-outs during Middle Woodland times and as portals into other dimensions.

Mississippian An archaeological culture variously used to describe a *horizon*, a time period, and a type of political organization or cultural adaptation.

moundbuilders Today, a colloquial description of the Native Americans who built the earthen tumuli between ca. 3500 B.C. and the present. Also a reference to the presumed lost race thought by 19th-century Euroamericans to have built the earthworks.

mounds A generic term that includes burial tumuli, truncated earthen pyramids, enclosures, a variety of platforms, and trash heaps.

NAGPRA The Native American Graves Protection and Repatriation Act, passed in 1990. NAGPRA outlines definitions of human remains or cultural objects that can be repatriated to present-day Native American tribes and the processes by which that *repatriation* can take place. Not all Native American human remains or cultural objects are subject to the law.

narrative A specific accounting, story, *ideology*, or constructed social *memory* that purports to situate people in history. A series of contingent narrative constructions constitutes what archaeologists consider as cultural history.

neoevolutionism A school of thought emerging in the 1950s that revived the theories of 19th-century cultural *evolutionists*, namely that culture is the adaptive, technological means whereby societies or populations change to fit the environmental exigencies in which they find themselves. Food production intensification was thought to result from increasing population density, leading *hunter-gatherer* bands and *horticultural tribes* to transform themselves into centralized *chiefdoms* and, ultimately, *states*.

normativism In anthropology, the understanding that *cultures* were learned and shared sets of "norms," or customs, beliefs, and ways of doing that allowed people to identify each other.

obsidian A black volcanic glass formed when lava was extruded and cooled very rapidly. Used in the production of chipped stone tools by western North Americans and by Middle *Woodland* people in the eastern United States.

Paleoindian Native Americans associated with widespread fluted point technologies (such as Clovis or Folsom types). They may have passed through an ice-free corridor at the end of the Pleistocene era, perhaps encountering low-level pre-Paleo populations in the process.

phase A short unit of time defined in the context of a cultural *region* or *locality*, sometimes also thought to correlate with a *society* at one point in time.

phenomenology The study of how reality emerges from people's experience, or the philosophical position that order derives from the phenomenon in question.

pithouse A semi-subterranean to subterranean house built in an excavated depression or pit, moderating the house temperature inside. Found across North America throughout history.

Pleistocene Also known as the Ice Age, this glacial epoch saw the first human colonization of North America. It preceded the present-day *Holocene* era and ended about 10,000 B.P.

pluralism The coexistence of different people, *identities*, or cultural *practices* in one *community* or *locality*.

political community An imagined *community* integrated around a political ideal or politically motivated person or subgroup. The scale of integration ranges from the individual settlement to the cultural region or *polity*.

political economy The distribution of economic and cultural capital in a *society*, especially with regard to the control of these resources.

polity A politically structured *society* or a population organized around or integrated by administrators with the power to effectively direct a significant portion of the population, such as a *chiefdom*.

post-processualism In the 1980s and 1990s, a loose aggregation of archaeologists who held non-*logical positivist* epistemologies or theories of how we know what we know. Named by Ian Hodder after the postmodern developments in literature and the arts, post-processualists did not abandon scientific knowledge, but many did jettison its *behaviorism*.

pottery Fired ceramic vessels or other objects where the ceramic body consists of clay and a crushed admixture, or temper, to improve the firing and performance qualities of the object.

power The socially situated ability of an individual's person or actions to alter those of others.

practice In anthropology, the embodiment or enactment of culture by individuals in social contexts. In some schools of thought, "praxis" is preferred, a term used since Aristotle.

prestige goods Portable objects thought to confer social standing, esteem, or honor to the person or group who, depending on the specificities of the cultural context, either retains them or gives them away. Importantly, value resides in the social or supernatural relationships embodied by the objects, not in the objects themselves.

processualism Initially synonymous with the "New Archaeology" movement in Anglo-American archaeology dating to the 1960s that linked *logical positivism* with *behaviorism* and *neoevolutionism*. More recently, associated with scientific methods in archaeology or with the commitment to the explanation of cultural processes.

pseudomorph A form that resembles another form.

pueblo Literally "town" in Spanish. Today, it typically connotes a multi-room southwestern settlement with adobe or masonry walls.

radiocarbon dating An absolute *chronometric* technique based on the principle that organisms absorb radioactive carbon isotope 14 when alive. Carbon 14 decays at a known rate, allowing organic tissues to be accurately dated.

rank, social ranking An inherited or institutionalized relationship between unequal *corporate groups* allowing more or less access to status positions or privileges. Common to bounded territorial *societies*, especially *chiefdoms*.

region Either a natural province defined on the basis of its physiography or biota, or a cultural province defined by the historical relationships and experiences of the human population.

repatriation The practice of returning cultural objects or human remains to the heirs or descendants who demonstrate a relationship of shared group *identity* to the original people. The process by which repatriation can or cannot take place is defined by *NAGPRA*.

residence patterns The varying results of cultural *practices* involving with whom a married couple and their children live. Patrilocality involves living with the husband's relatives, and matrilocality or uxorilocality with the wife's. Other variations mix some combination of the two or change through time.

residential mobility Refers to the established annual pattern of the movement of hunter-gatherer peoples where an entire band moves from place to place across a landscape.

seriation The construction of a temporal series of *artifact attributes, assemblages, features,* or *sites* using some time-sensitive formal characteristics of a class of material culture.

seriological A quality pertaining to the understanding of blood and blood groupings.

settlement A sedentary or semi-sedentary habitation site. Also refers to the process of colonizing or territorializing a portion of the continent.

site A discrete locus of aggregate human social activities in space. Typically reserved for loci larger than *features* or neighborhoods but smaller than localities or regions, that is, *settlements*, ritual places, camps, or extractive locations.

society An inferred organization at the scale of the *locality* or the *region*.

Sonoran Agricultural Complex An array of cultigens and domesticates that came under cultivation during the Archaic and Basketmaker periods in the southwestern United States that include squash, beans, pigweed, cotton, and maize.

spatiality The spatial dimension of culture-making or *practice* contingent on the principle that thought and action are not easily separable from spatial experience.

specialist A person who does or makes something not done or made by others in the service of the collective and at the expense of other domestic practices common to the populace.

spindle whorl A perforated weight used to generate rotational momentum centered on a spindle and used in the spinning of fibers into threads, twine, or rope.

state A highly centralized *society* governed by an administrative bureaucracy and typified by more urban, class-stratified social conditions.

stone-boiling A technique of cooking foods in liquids involving placing red-hot rocks into a leather bag or a pot in order to boil the contents.

structure, structuration The regular patterns or sets of practices (and the making of those patterns or practices) identifiable by people as the rules, norms, traditions, standards, or customs with which they associate themselves. Structuration is nearly synonymous with *practice*.

taphonomy In archaeology, the study of the human transformation of biological organisms, especially animal carcasses, into cultural residues (bone tools, animal-food waste, etc.)

temporality The temporal dimension of culture-making, cultural landscapes, or practices where thought and action are occur through experience.

Tollan In the Aztec language, Nahuatl, the name of the legendary source of civilized practices for the Aztecs and many other Postclassic people. Also called Tula.

Toltec In Mexico, a person from Tollan; in North America, a Late Woodland ceremonial center in the central Arkansas River valley.

tradition A *memory* of how things have happened in the past that defines practices in the present. For some archaeologists, this implies cultural continuity. For others, social memories are creations in the present and, thus, traditions are the media of culture change.

transculturation The multi-directional process of culture-making whereby people, dominant or subordinate, shape each other's cultural histories.

trans-egalitarian A term used by some to characterize people who are neither strictly *egalitarian* nor *hierarchical* but have attributes of both variously across space and through time. Typically associated with *hunter-gatherers* or *horticulturalists*.

tribal A term used by *neoevolutionists* to refer to people lacking a central government but characterized by complex *corporate structures* or *heterarchies*.

Woodland A period, stage, or way of life associated with the forested environments of eastern North America between about 500 B.C. or later to the beginnings of the *Mississippian* period or European contact.

worldview A *structured* way of interpreting one's surroundings and relationships. Unlike *ideology*, archaeologists tend to de-emphasize its political qualities.

Index

Page references in italics indicate maps and figures.

Printed in the USA/Agawam, MA
January 15, 2013

571916.042